Performing Images

Opera

in

Chinese

Visual

Culture

節

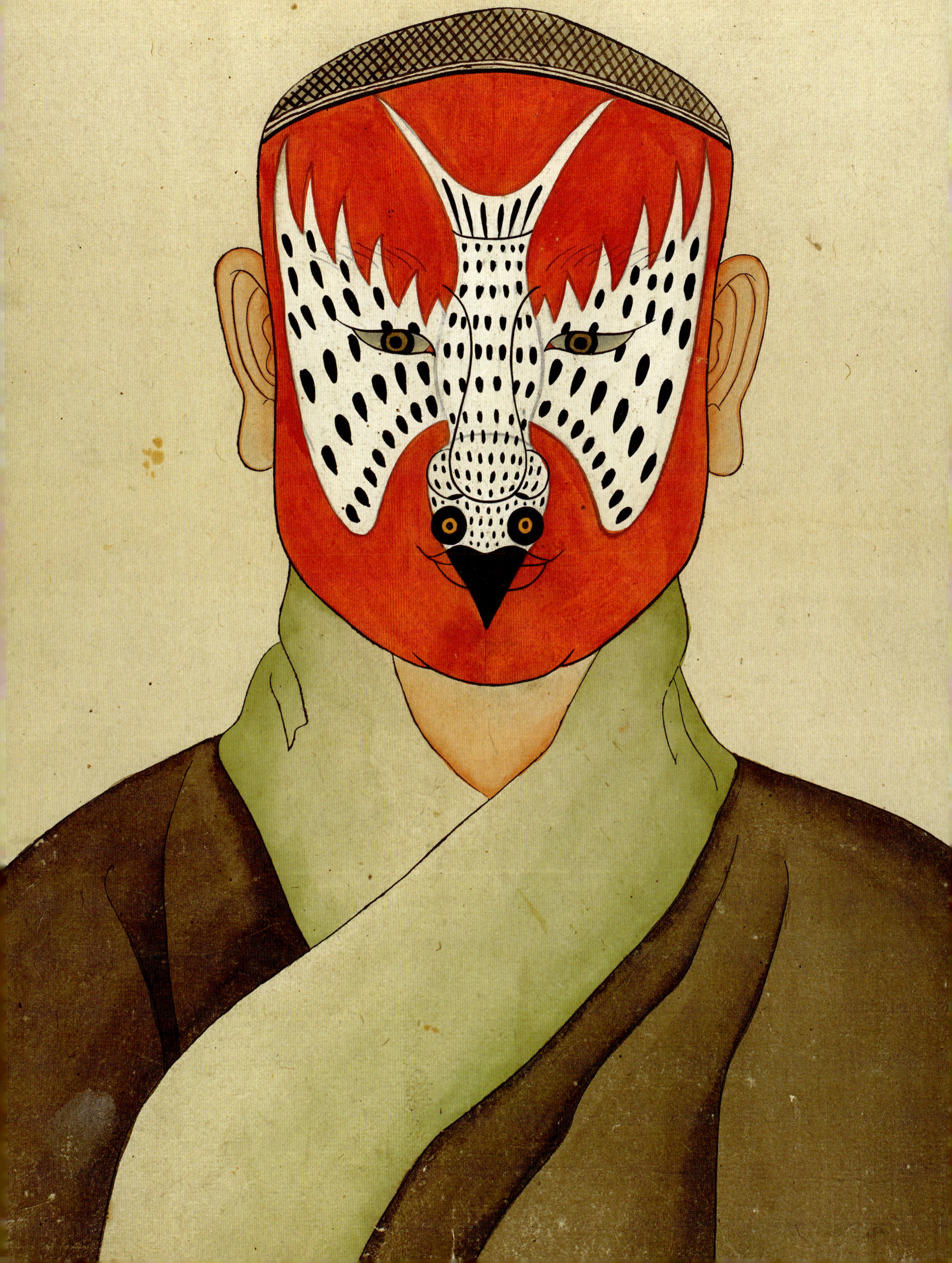

Performing Images

Opera in Chinese Visual Culture

Judith T. Zeitlin
Yuhang Li

With Contributions by
Bo Songnian
Jonathan Hay
David G. Johnson
Ni Yibin
Mei Mei Rado
Wu Hung

SMART MUSEUM OF ART
THE UNIVERSITY OF CHICAGO

Published on the occasion of the exhibition *Performing Images: Opera in Chinese Visual Culture*, co-curated by Judith T. Zeitlin and Yuhang Li and organized by the Smart Museum of Art, The University of Chicago
February 13–June 15, 2014

The exhibition and catalogue have been made possible by the Smart Museum's Pamela and R. Christopher Hoehn-Saric Exhibition Fund and its Andrew W. Mellon Foundation Endowment, Mary Smart and the Smart Family Foundation, Janis Kanter and Thomas McCormick and the Kanter Family Foundation, the Walter E. Heller Foundation, and Gay-Young Cho and Christopher Chiu. Support for related programming is provided by The Franke Institute for the Humanities and the Center for East Asian Studies at the University of Chicago. Additional funding for the catalogue is provided by the Confucius Institute at the University of Chicago and Furthermore—a program of the J. M. Kaplan Fund.

Distributed by the University of Chicago Press.

ISBN: 978-0-935573-55-8

Smart Museum of Art
The University of Chicago
5550 S. Greenwood Avenue
Chicago, Illinois 60637
773.702.0200
smartmuseum.uchicago.edu

Design and production: Glue + Paper Workshop LLC, Chicago

Editors: Judith T. Zeitlin, Yuhang Li, Richard A. Born

Copy Editor: Amy Teschner

Production Assistant: Jie Shi

Color Separations: Embassy Graphics, Winnipeg, Canada

Printing and binding: Asia Pacific Offset, China

Cover: detail, cat. 47.6

Reverse cover: detail, cat. 9b

Front flap: detail, cat. 27

Title page: detail, cat. 46.1

Pages 34–35: detail, cat. 7

Page 72: detail, fig. 3.6

Pages 120–21: detail, cat. 37.1

Page 201: detail, cat. 47.4

Library of Congress Cataloging-in-Publication Data

Performing images : opera in Chinese visual culture / by Judith Zeitlin and Yuhang Li ; with contributions by Bo Songnian, Jonathan Hay, David G. Johnson, Ni Yibin, Mei Mei Rado, and Wu Hung.

pages cm

Summary: "Writing in the early nineteenth century, the French traveler and cleric Abbe Huc exclaimed: 'There is, perhaps, not a people in the world who carry so far their taste and passion for theatrical entertainments as the Chinese.' Although the spectacle of this theater is well known, with its colorful costumes, props, and face painting, the extent to which opera was favored in Chinese pictorial and decorative motifs across the full spectrum of visual media-from courtly scroll paintings, popular New Year prints, illustrated woodblock books, and painted fans to carved utensils, ceramics, textiles, and dioramas-will surprise many. As the first comprehensive publication in English on the subject, *Performing Images* is not only a major interdisciplinary contribution to existing scholarship—featuring eight new essays by experts in the fields of traditional and modern Chinese literature, art, material culture, and history-but also a visual spectacle in its own right. A companion volume to the exhibition of the same name at the Smart Museum of Art, *Performing Images* contains more than one hundred color reproductions and fifty-four illustrated catalogue entries. Together, text and image offer new insight into traditional Chinese culture, visual arts, and theater, and reveal how Chinese visual and performing traditions were aesthetically, ritually, and commercially intertwined"—Provided by publisher.

"Published on the occasion of the exhibition Performing Images: Opera in Chinese Visual Culture, co-curated by Judith T. Zeitlin and Yuhang Li and organized by the Smart Museum of Art, University of Chicago." Includes bibliographical references. ISBN 978-0-935573-55-8 (pbk.)

1. Opera in art—Exhibitions. 2. Art, Chinese—Exhibitions. 3. Operas, Chinese—Exhibitions. 4. Art and society—China—Exhibitions. I. Zeitlin, Judith T., 1958- author. II. Li, Yuhang, author. III. Hay, Jonathan, 1956- World-making in performance and painting. IV. David and Alfred Smart Museum of Art.

N8234.O63P47 2014

704.9'4978210951—dc23

2013043319

Contents

Foreword and Acknowledgments

It is a privilege for the Smart Museum of Art to present *Performing Images: Opera in Chinese Visual Culture*. The first major exhibition of its kind in the West, it offers an extraordinary perspective on a remarkable tradition. During the Qing dynasty (1644–1911), the passion for opera and theater permeated the everyday visual and material world. Spanning all strata of Chinese society and manifested throughout Chinese visual culture, this preoccupation asserts itself in an astonishing range of products—from the artifacts of theatrical performance to everything from scroll paintings and popular prints to illustrated books, painted fans, ceramics, textiles, utensils, and dioramas. *Performing Images* brings together a sampling of some of the most compelling examples of these varied media, and in so doing sheds new light on not only the role of opera in China but also its pervasive influence.

The project's two curators, Judith T. Zeitlin, a scholar of Chinese literature in the University of Chicago's Department of East Asian Languages and Civilizations and Program in Theater and Performance Studies, and her former doctoral student Yuhang Li, now on the faculty of the Art History Department at the University of Wisconsin, Madison, originally planned for a small exhibition at Chicago's Field Museum of Natural History, which possesses a notable collection of objects related to Chinese opera. This was a natural outgrowth of Professor Zeitlin's research into the history of opera in China and its relationship to material culture. But the ambition for the project grew when the two scholars realized that there were many equally captivating objects depicting opera housed at other museums—works of art that had rarely been the subject of any exhibition or publication. It was at that point that they applied for and received a 2010 Smart Museum Faculty Initiatives grant, which enabled them to travel across the country to identify possible works for a considerably larger project. The success of the trip encouraged them to propose *Performing Images* to the Smart Museum shortly thereafter.

The exhibition and catalogue exemplify one of the important ways that the Smart Museum participates in the University of Chicago's commitment to collaborative, interdisciplinary discovery. By providing an accessible forum for significant faculty research, projects like *Performing Images* draw upon the extraordinary intellectual energy of the University and make it available to a broad public. The Museum also has frequently provided a forum for younger scholars to present their research through exhibitions and catalogues; this is certainly true here, where the students in Professor Zeitlin's fall 2012 graduate seminar on the history of Chinese opera and visual culture had the opportunity to research and write catalogue entries and compile the foundation for part of the bibliography and chronology among other supplemental texts included in this volume.

The current project provides a natural extension of the Smart Museum's pioneering presentations of Chinese contemporary and classical art, including more recently *Echoes of the Past: The Buddhist Cave Temples of Xiangtangshan* (2010) and *Displacement: The Three Gorges Dam and Contemporary Chinese Art* (2008). Thanks to the efforts of the Museum's consulting curator Wu Hung, Harrie A. Vanderstappen Distinguished Service Professor in Art History and East Asian Languages and Civilizations and Director of the Center for the Art of East Asia at the University (and the curator of *Displacement*), the Museum has also long sought to explore the vitality of contemporary East Asian art in relation to tradition, and thus we are delighted that Wu Hung has developed a smaller contemporary exhibition, *Inspired by the Opera: Contemporary Chinese Photography and Video*, to accompany *Performing Images*, which includes a tightly focused display of photographs by the contemporary Chinese master Liu Zheng and a selection of videos by Chen Qiuling, Liu Wei, and Cui Xiaowen. Their work is also the subject of Wu Hung's contribution to this publication.

Performing Images is a complex project, requiring the skills and talents of many tireless individuals. Above all, we are deeply grateful to Professors Zeitlin and Li for their extraordinary research and their interest in giving that research public expression at the Smart Museum through the present exhibition and publication. It has been a privilege to work with them. Professor Zeitlin has been a passionate and assiduous partner to the Museum throughout the project's gestation; there is no way to thank her adequately for the enormous effort she has invested.

At the Smart Museum, Richard A. Born, Senior Curator, took on the responsibility for oversight with his customary thoughtful dedication, determined to ensure the success of every element of the project. The superb quality of the results bears witness to his labor. Curatorial Intern Jie Shi has proven invaluable in his role as Curatorial Assistant on this project, and also assisted with production of the catalogue. Angela Steinmetz, Head Registrar, has managed complex loan negotiations with her customary aplomb. Sara Patrello, Assistant Registrar, has overseen the complexities of rights and reproduction for the catalogue and exhibition with unflagging determination. Michael Christiano, Director of Education and Interpretation, has led his team in developing a rich and wide-ranging array of programs including live performances, a film series, and a scholarly symposium. And, as always in the case of such demanding initiatives at the Smart Museum, nearly every member of the staff, from curatorial to registration, from art handlers to external relations, has contributed in fundamental ways to the successful realization of the project. Their consistently high professional standards and their remarkably harmonious collegiality have resulted, yet again, in outstanding achievements.

For their insightful essays, we are grateful to all of the contributors to this catalogue, including the two co-curators as well as Bo Songnian, Professor in Chinese Art History, Central Academy of Fine Arts, Beijing; Jonathan Hay, Ailsa Mellon Bruce Professor of Fine Arts, Institute of Fine Arts, New York University; David G. Johnson, Professor Emeritus in the Department of History, University of California, Berkeley; Ni Yibin, an independent scholar of Chinese art history in Shanghai; Mei Mei Rado, Bard Graduate Center: Decorative Arts, Design, History, Material Culture; and Wu Hung of the University of Chicago. Two long-time collaborators have again devoted their considerable professional talents to this catalogue: Amy Teschner is to be thanked for her graceful editing, just as Joan Sommers and Amanda Freymann are to be congratulated for a beautiful catalogue design and for their diligence and care throughout the book's production.

The broader landscape of the University of Chicago has proven no less supportive. It is standard practice at the Smart Museum to organize exhibition workshops well in advance of major projects' public presentation to ensure that the full range of the University's resources infuse and strengthen them. On this occasion, colleagues from several departments and others from elsewhere in Chicago participated, lending their perspective and expertise. The presentation of *Performing Images* has served as an occasion to organize a quite remarkable array of programs of Chinese arts and culture across the University as part of Envisioning China. We thank the Logan Center for the Arts, particularly Bill Michel and Leigh Fagin, Amy Iwano at the University of Chicago Presents, and Steven Albert and Charles Newell of the University's Court Theatre for their willingness to develop ambitious programming in concert with the Smart Museum's exhibition project. Among our programmatic partners across campus and in the city, we wish to acknowledge the advice and support of Xinyu Dong, Assistant Professor, Department of Cinema and Media Studies; Julia Gibbs, Assistant Director, Film Studies Center; and Ralph Gao Jingyi, Consul for Cultural Affairs, Chinese Consulate General in Chicago. In addition, Chicago's Goodman Theatre is participating through the presentation of *The White Snake* during the period *Performing Images* is on view. These varied activities testify to the vitality of the arts on the University of Chicago campus and indeed in the city; the Smart Museum is pleased to have had the opportunity to work with so many talented professionals.

The exhibition could not have been presented, of course, were it not for the generosity of the lenders. In many cases, they have been asked to part with works that are fragile and rarely travel. We are particularly grateful to Richard Lariviere, President, and all of his colleagues at the Field Museum of Natural History, as it is their holdings that inspired this project, and they have lent generously. In addition, we thank our colleagues at the American Museum of Natural History, the Brooklyn Museum, the Metropolitan Museum of Art, all in New York; the Museum of Fine Arts, Boston; the Philadelphia Museum of Art; the San Francisco Asian Art Museum; the Jordan Schnitzer Museum of Art at the University of Oregon in Eugene, the East Asian Collection of the University of Chicago's Regenstein Library, the C. V. Starr East Asian Library, University of California, Berkeley, and the Sir Michael Butler Collection and Butler Family Collection in Dorset, United Kingdom.

The fragility of many of the objects included in the exhibition makes it likely that a visit to the Smart Museum will offer the first and only time to see them on display together, making us all the more grateful to those who have generously provided the essential financial support. The exhibition and catalogue have been made possible by the Smart Museum's Pamela and R. Christopher Hoehn-Saric Exhibition Fund and its Andrew W. Mellon Foundation Endowment, Mary Smart and the Smart Family Foundation, Janis Kanter and Thomas McCormick and the Kanter Family Foundation, the Walter E. Heller Foundation, and Gay-Young Cho and Christopher Chiu. Support for related programming is provided by The Franke Institute for the Humanities and the Center for East Asian Studies at the University of Chicago. Additional funding for the catalogue is provided by the Confucius Institute at the University of Chicago and Furthermore—a program of the J. M. Kaplan Fund.

It is always deeply gratifying to be able to present an exhibition of such originality, beauty, and importance to the public. We hope that this publication will not only serve as a guide to the exhibition, but also make a lasting contribution to the study of the profound relationship between Chinese opera and material culture—and stimulate further research and dialogue on this fascinating subject. Finally, we want to express our gratitude to the remarkable storytellers and artists of imperial China whose work has proven a delight and an inspiration for generations, including all of us who had the privilege of being involved with this project.

Anthony G. Hirschel
Dana Feitler Director
Smart Museum of Art, The University of Chicago

Preface

The idea for *Performing Images: Opera in Chinese Visual Culture* germinated around 2008 when one of us, Yuhang Li, then a PhD student in the department of East Asian Languages and Civilizations at the University of Chicago, and formerly an independent researcher on the Chinese textile collection at the Field Museum in Chicago, arranged a visit for the other, Judith Zeitlin, then one of her professors, to the museum to show her the holdings in storage related to Chinese opera. The Field is particularly strong in this area because Berthold Laufer (1874–1934), the eminent sinologist and anthropologist who served as the main East Asian curator there from 1908 to 1934, loved the theater. The two expeditions that he led to China for the Field, the first in 1908–10, and the second in 1923, gave him an especially good opportunity to build their Chinese opera collection. Excited by the striking imagery and historical value of this trove of virtually unknown materials, Zeitlin suggested to Li on the spot that we co-curate an exhibition on the visual and material culture of Chinese opera, primarily from the Qing dynasty (1644–1911) when surviving materials are most abundant.

From the first, we agreed that our exhibition would focus on the representation of opera in the greatest possible variety of visual and material forms rather than on real artifacts used in performance. (This is one reason we decided not to include puppets.) In this respect, *Performing Images* differs radically from the way Chinese opera has often been shown in ethnographic museums, where manikins wearing costumes and holding theatrical props primarily showcase Chinese folkways and performance traditions. In this way, our exhibition goes beyond the mere display of operatic artifacts to give audiences insight into the role that operatic imagery played in multiple facets of everyday life and recurring celebrations. Our larger aim is to explore the interpenetration and influence of operatic images and ideas on Chinese art and culture (and vice versa).

Originally we simply planned to curate a small show based on the Field Museum materials at the Smart Museum, but with strong encouragement from Deputy Director and Chief Curator Stephanie Smith and Director Anthony G. Hirschel, our sights quickly became much more ambitious. Thanks to the Andrew W. Mellon Foundation, the Smart Museum was able to award us a 2010 Faculty Initiatives grant for research travel to various US museums to investigate their collections.

Our first stop was New York, where we followed the Laufer connection to the American Museum of Natural History (AMNH). Laufer had undertaken his first expedition to China for AMNH from 1900 to 1904 so there we found a cache of early opera-related materials, including a large collection of popular New Year woodblock prints (*nianhua)* that Laufer had purchased in Shanghai. Laurel Kendall, Division Chair and Curator of Asian Ethnology, was a crucial early supporter and we are greatly indebted to her published research on Laufer and unflagging enthusiasm for our project. At the Metropolitan Museum of Art, we want to express our deep appreciation to Maxwell K. Hearn, Douglas Dillon Curator in Charge of the Department of Asian Art for generously giving us complete access to their rich Chinese art collection, and to J. Kenneth Moore, Frederick P. Rose Curator in Charge, Department of Musical Instruments, for extending himself to the fullest. Mei Mei Rado, then Collections Management Assistant in Asian Art at the Metropolitan Museum, now a PhD student in art history at the Bard Graduate Center, was our invaluable guide there and became our most important collaborator, contributing an essay and many entries to the catalogue as well as important ideas to the exhibition.

At the Metropolitan Museum we also made our most exciting discovery when we requested to see something listed in their database simply as a "Chinese opera album." No one had any idea what was in it, so when we opened the book in the Met's study room, we gasped out loud: We had stumbled upon a real treasure. Here in perfect condition lay a painted album of 100 court-style portraits of opera characters that matched the famous (and much smaller) set in the National Library of China. No other discovery was quite as dramatic, but in almost every place we went we found something wonderful and unexpected. Few of the things we saw had been published; many had never even been publicly exhibited.

At each institution we visited, the curators, librarians, and collections managers offered us their expertise and went to great length to help us track down promising objects. We would like to thank Jamie Kelly, Collections Manager at the Field Museum, for his help on multiple visits, not only to us, but also for Judith Zeitlin's classes; Joan Cummings, the Lisa and Bernard Selz Curator of Asian Art at the Brooklyn Museum; Shi-yee Liu, Hwai-ling Yeh-Lewis, and Joseph Scheier-Dolberg, all Department of Asian Art, The Metropolitan Museum of Art; Katherine Skaggs from the American Museum of Natural History; Hiromi Kinoshita then at the Boston Museum of Fine Arts, now the Hannah L. and J. Welles Henderson Associate Curator of Chinese Art at the Philadelphia Museum of Art and Hyunsoo Woo, Associate Curator of Korean art at Philadelphia; Deborah Rudolph, Executive Manager of Administrative and Editorial Services at the C. V. Starr East Asian Library at the University of California, Berkeley; Shawn Eichman, Curator of Asian Art and Sara Oka, Curator of Textiles at the Honolulu Academy of Art; Ling-en Lu, Associate Curator of Early Chinese Art from the Nelson-Atkins Museum of Art; Nancy Berliner, then at the Peabody Essex Museum in Salem, Massachusetts, now the Wu Tung Curator of Chinese Art at the Museum of Fine Arts Boston. For invaluable assistance in our research we also gratefully extend our thanks to Jay Xu, Director, and Michael Knight, Senior Curator of Chinese Art, the Asian Art Museum of San Francisco; Anne Rose Kitagawa, Chief Curator of Collections and Asian Art and Director of Academic Programs at the Jordan Schnitzer Museum of Art, University of Oregon, Eugene; Elinor Pearlstein, Asian Art Curator at the Art Institute of Chicago; and Katherine Butler, the Butler Family Collection and Sir Michael Butler Collection, Dorset, United Kingdom.

While we were unable to include a selection of Min Qiji's color prints of *Romance of the Western Chamber (Xixiang ji)*, dated 1640, from the Museum für Ostasiatische Kunst der Stadt Köln (Museum of East Asian Art of Cologne) as originally planned, we express our sincere appreciation to Dr. Adele Schlombs, Director, and Dr. Petra Roesch, Curator, for their time and support.

In the fall of 2012, Judith Zeitlin offered a graduate seminar on the history of Chinese opera and visual culture at the University of Chicago where she worked out ideas for the exhibition. The seminar provided an opportunity for students working in several different departments to research and write catalogue entries for individual objects. We thank them—Alia Breitweiser, Naixi Feng, Ranting Jiang, and Yuqian Yuan—as well as graduate students Thomas Kelly and Katherine Alexander who also contributed catalogue entries and compiled sections of the back matter. Jie Shi, PhD student in art history and Curatorial Intern at the Smart Museum, deserves deep thanks for compiling sections of the back matter and for his help with many aspects of the catalogue and exhibition. We are also grateful to two University of Chicago alumnae with doctorates in art history who contributed entries: Catherine Stuer, Assistant Professor, Denison University, and Mia Yinxing Liu, a postdoctoral fellow at Yale University.

Professor Bo Songnian, Emeritus Professor from the Central Academy of Fine Arts in Beijing and author of one of the catalogue essays, deserves our special gratitude. He generously put his great erudition on Chinese opera and folk art at our disposal and helped us repeatedly to identify difficult operatic scenes and figures. We also thank Jonathan Hay, Ailsa Mellon Bruce Professor of Fine Arts at the Institute of Fine Arts at New York University, who invited us to present our ideas at a workshop at just the right time, and Susan Naquin, Professor Emeritus of Chinese History from Princeton University, who provided her usual trenchant advice as commentator. The Art History and Art faculty at Grinnell College and the Center for Chinese Studies at the University of California, Berkeley, also provided valuable early audiences for this project. We are indebted to Professors Catherine Swatek at the University of British Columbia, David Rolston at the University of Michigan, Ann Arbor, and Jeehee Hong at Syracuse University for contributing their expertise on Chinese drama at key moments and to Professors Grace Fong at McGill University and Wai-yee Li at Harvard University for advice on poetic translation. Dr. Zhou Yuan, Curator of the East Asian Collection of the Regenstein Library at the University of Chicago deserves our special thanks for encouraging us to exhibit rare books from the collection. We thank Ariel Zeitlin Cooke and Alia Breitweiser for expertly helping to edit essays and entries at very short notice. Wu Hung, Harrie A. Vanderstappen Distinguished Service Professor of Art History and Consulting Curator at the Smart Museum, has been a great resource, offering his acumen and experience whenever needed, and curating an exhibition on contemporary Chinese art in conjunction with *Performing Images*. Finally, we owe our greatest thanks to Senior Curator Richard A. Born for his indefatigable effort to bring this exhibition and catalogue to fruition.

Judith T. Zeitlin and Yuhang Li

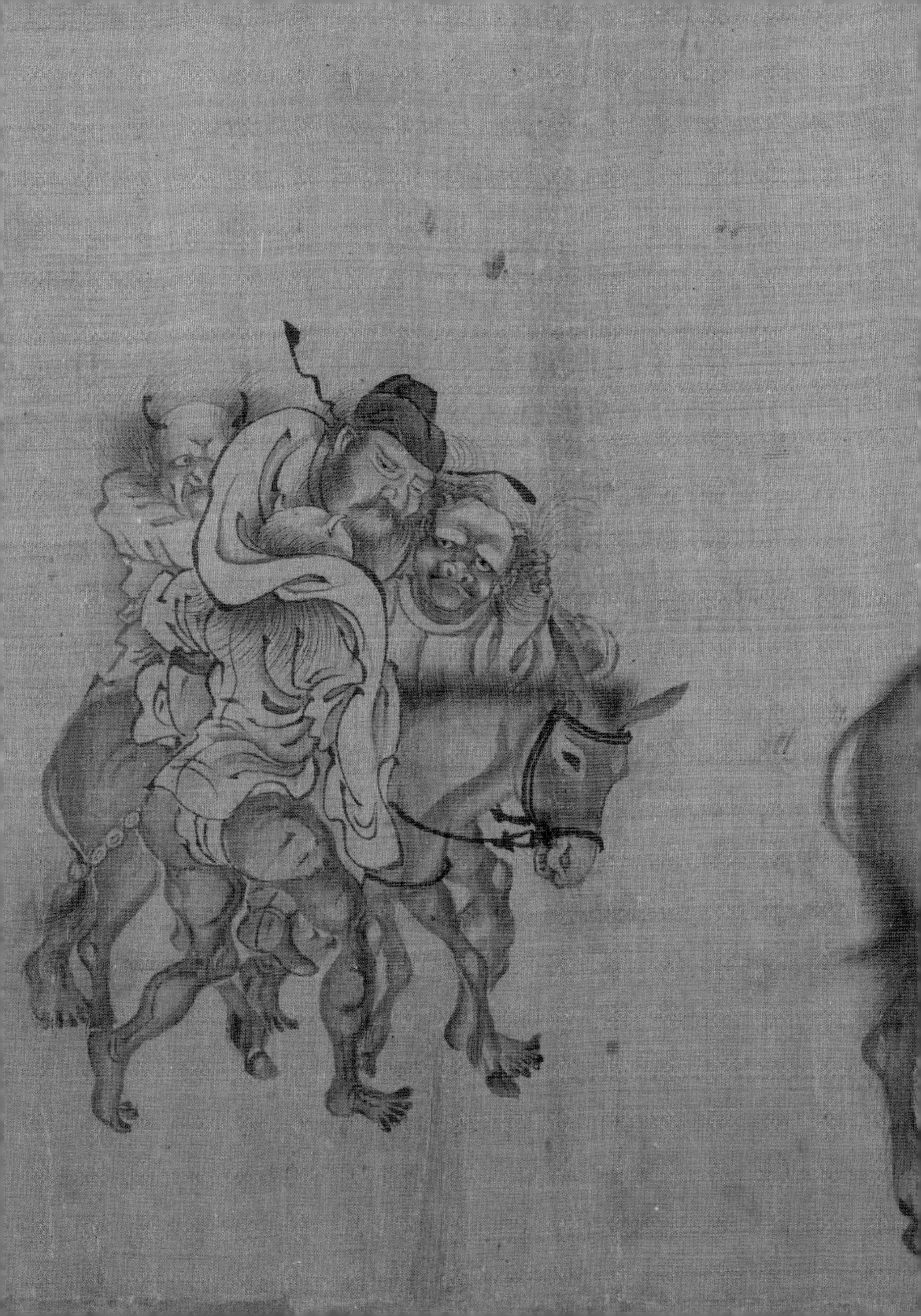

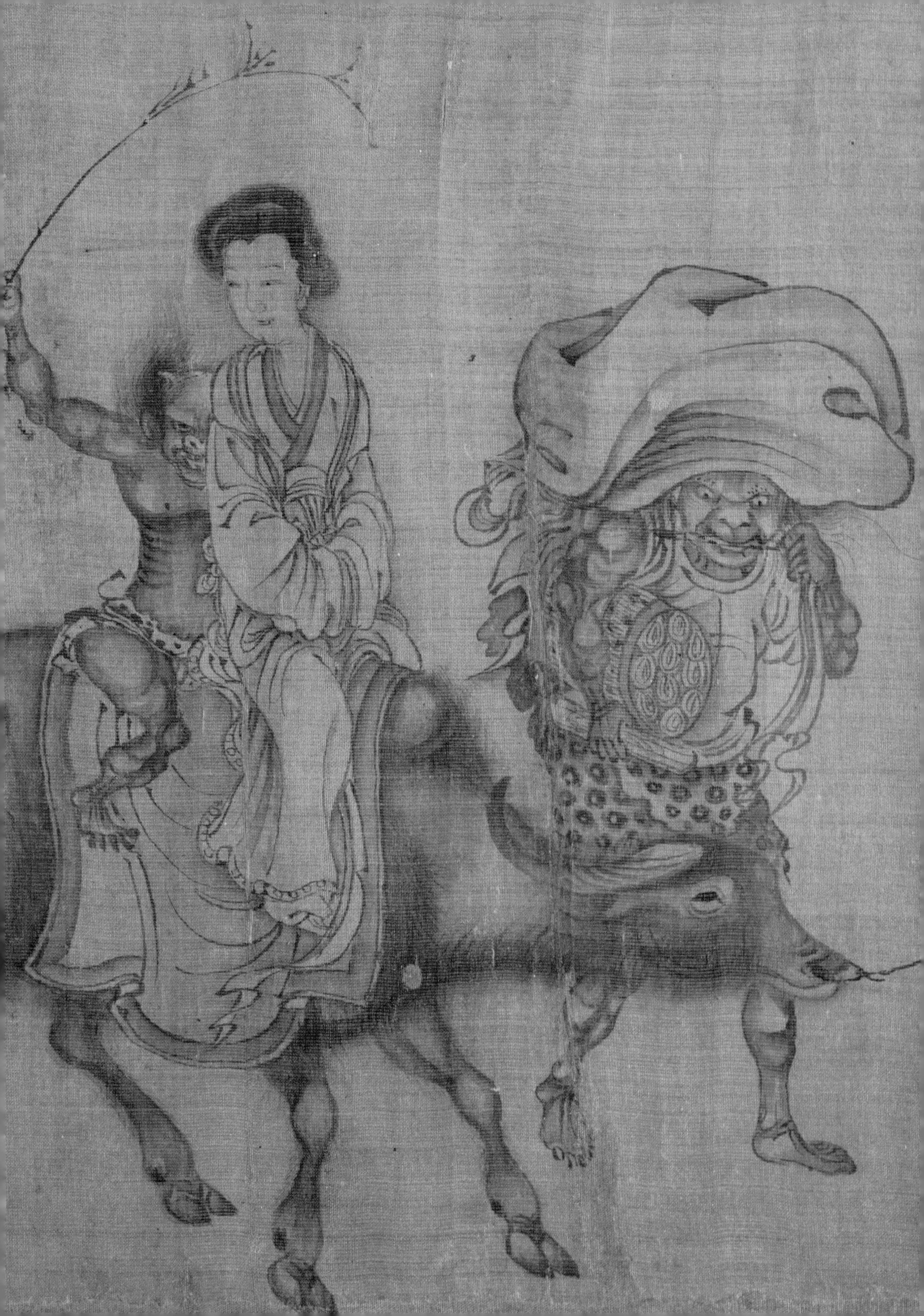

JUDITH T. ZEITLIN

Introduction

Toward a Visual Culture of Chinese Opera

Writing in the early nineteenth century, the French traveler and cleric Abbé Huc exclaimed, "There is, perhaps, not a people in the world who carry so far their taste and passion for the theatrical entertainments as the Chinese."[1] This taste and passion permeated the social and ritual world of late imperial China from the village to the city to the court. Chinese opera is world famous as spectacle with its colorful costumes, painted faces, and the stylized movements of its performers. But few know how frequently operatic characters and stories also appeared as pictorial images and decorative motifs on a wide spectrum of traditional media and objects, including scroll paintings, illustrated books and popular prints, painted fans, ceramics, textiles, musical instruments, carved bibelots and figurines, architectural ornaments, snuff bottles, miniature dioramas, playing cards, and eventually, photography, advertising, and film.

What links or distinguishes these different treatments of operatic motifs in design and function? How are the pictorial, literary, and performing traditions intertwined aesthetically, ritually, and commercially? What kinds of connections can be drawn between this striking visual heritage and the redeployment of Chinese opera elements in contemporary Chinese experimental art? In the exhibition *Performing Images: Opera in Chinese Visual Culture* and this accompanying catalogue, we attempt to answer such questions as we engage with concrete images and objects.

Theater came late to a civilization as ancient as China's, but even so, its emergence as the full-fledged art form we call Chinese opera can be traced back at least a millennium, to the eleventh and twelfth centuries. For this early period covering the Song (960–1279) and Jin (1115–1234) dynasties, no scripts—if indeed they were used—survive. Apart from some textual descriptions and titles, the extant evidence is mainly visual and material, including a few court-style paintings, temple stages, stele epigraphy, and most astonishingly, a wealth of tomb decoration depicting stages and costumed actors.[2] Theatrical entertainment flourished during the subsequent Yuan dynasty (1271–1368), and many more texts remain, including our earliest printed plays, but no visual or material trace survives of the great commercial urban theaters at this time. Extant stages, stele epigraphy, and murals from temples in rural China, however, continue to provide important evidence for the development of theater during the Yuan. Surviving visual and material evidence of this and other kinds is even more abundant and varied for the late imperial period, the Ming (1368–1644) and Qing (1644–1911) dynasties. Taken together, these sorts of material remains have given rise to a small but vibrant new field of scholarship in China called "the cultural relics of opera" (*xiqu wenwu*).

This field, however, has tended to focus on architecture, archaeology, and epigraphy and on the reconstruction of the history of Chinese opera, rather than on the impact of opera on visual culture, particularly in the form of decorative objects and pictures, as this exhibition aims to do. Most of the images and artifacts in *Performing Images* date from the Qing, China's last dynasty, in part because opera so flourished and proliferated in this era, in part because much more of the visual and material record survives from this comparatively recent period, and in part because opera costumes and colorful depictions of operatic motifs appealed to foreign tourists, collectors, and anthropologists who visited China from the nineteenth century on, and therefore abound in the North American and British collections that are the sources for this exhibition.

With the exception of two scroll paintings (cats. 7 and 44), none of the objects with entries in this catalogue belongs to the narrow province of what was traditionally considered fine arts in China. Representations principally related to the theater—regardless of the costliness of the materials and the degree of skill required to produce such images and artifacts—instead belonged to the much wider category of a popular, shared visual culture. This was true even of products like painted albums and printed books produced by imperial workshops and luxury goods fashioned by skilled craftsmen of expensive materials like ivory, rhinoceros horn, porcelain, lacquer, or slit silk tapestry (*kesi*). It was of course even more often the case with cheap, disposable prints available for sale everywhere and embroideries and papercuts made in the home. This multiplicity of forms attests to the power that opera wielded in shaping the visual imagination and material landscape of late imperial China.

The seven essays in this catalogue address these issues from a variety of approaches and angles. Three of the essays focus on one of the fundamental social contexts for traditional opera: the city, the village, and the court. Jonathan Hay's essay begins with the formative period of the Song and Jin dynasties to develop some bold parallels between the deployment of space and time in urban theater and painting, parallels that persist in an altered form in late Ming literati opera and art. David Johnson's text examines the prevalence of theatrical imagery to decorate buildings and objects in rural China as a sign of the deep penetration of opera into village life and the large role opera played in shaping the worldview of ordinary people during the late imperial period. Mei Mei Rado tackles opera in the Qing imperial court, specifically the relationships among palace institutions, theatrical performance, and visual modes of portraying stage characters in painted albums. Two of the other essays concentrate on a specific medium: Yuhang Li addresses textiles and clothing, not the ordinary costumes worn by actors playing a character on stage, but an extraordinary type of garment decorated with narrative scenes from specific operas or stringed ballad storytelling (*tanci,* a genre closely related to opera). Bo Songnian looks at different modes of depicting opera in the popular genre of woodblock prints known as New Year pictures (*nianhua*), so called because they were usually purchased right before the New Year to paste up at home, and then torn down and replaced the following year. By contrast, Ni Yibin offers an iconographic study of two scenes from a single play—the widely illustrated *Romance of the Western Chamber* (*Xixiang ji*)—to show how each scene evolved over time in different media. Finally, Wu Hung's essay, which accompanies a related exhibition of Chinese contemporary experimental art at the Smart Museum, explores how four different artists in the 1990s creatively reappropriated elements from the rich visual vocabulary of traditional Chinese opera in their photographs and videos.

In this introduction, I outline some basic characteristics of Chinese opera and its historical development for the general reader and then lay out three important conceptual areas within the exhibition: (1) space and event, (2) ritual and imagery, and (3) pattern and surface. I conclude with a thematic overview of *Romance of the Western Chamber* to illustrate the ways in which the literary, theatrical, and visual traditions continuously intersected and influenced one another.

What Is Chinese Opera?

All traditional style Chinese theater (*xiqu*) can be considered "opera" because Chinese plays always involve sung verse. Indeed, until reformist-minded Chinese intellectuals began experimenting with Western-style drama in the early twentieth century, which even today is differentiated as "the spoken play" (*huaju*), theater in China was virtually inconceivable without characters who sing most of the time.[3] As in its European counterpart, Chinese opera subsumes character and plot into a basic system of highly conventionalized role-types, which has historically required specialized training for the performer and been immediately recognized by its audience. Even more than in nineteenth-century Italian opera—where the part of the hero goes to the tenor, the baritone plays the villain or valet, the soprano takes the role of the virtuous heroine, and the mezzo her mother or rival—role-type is everything in Chinese opera. In Qing times, as in Peking opera today, the four most basic role-types were *sheng* (male lead), *dan* (female lead), *jing* (painted face), and *chou* (clown). Although certain role-types demanded that the performer use specific timbres and pitch levels, role-type was not, as in Western opera, chiefly aligned with vocal range, and members of either sex or eunuchs could, in principle, sing any role. (In practice, convention and regulation tended to favor single sex-troupes [all male or all female] in late imperial China.)[4] The names of the role-types, the number of role-types, and the fineness of the distinctions between them change over time and depend on the variety of opera, but the all-determining nature of role-type in structuring character and dramatic action in Chinese opera, even shaping the very conception of theater itself, cannot be overemphasized.

Like all comparisons across time and space, the analogy to European opera can only be taken so far. There are, of course, many differences, but we can single out three broad areas as exerting the most crucial influence on visual culture. First, Chinese opera is a composite art form in which physical movement is as fundamental as voice, and actors are trained to master an extensive repertory of stylized gestures, mimed actions, and dance steps to accompany their singing and speech.[5] In certain genres such as Peking opera and *Kun* opera (so called because the music originated in the Kunshan area near Suzhou), performers are renowned for their expressive manipulation of elegant "water sleeves" (*shui xiu*), long white silk sleeve extensions sewn onto the costume (fig. 3.12). The more physically demanding roles, such as warriors, clowns, and demons, also incorporate martial arts, slapstick, and acrobatics (cat. 1).

A second significant difference is that, at least until very recently, there was no composer, no one who wrote the musical score for a given play. Instead, new lyrics were written to the tunes of preexisting arias in strict prosodic forms like Yuan northern drama (*zaju*) or Kun opera, or for a system of commonly used tunes, as in the looser Peking opera and clapper opera (*bangzi*, a northern form of opera in which a sounding block struck with a stick dominates the musical accompaniment).[6] In every variety of opera, lyrics were intermixed with spoken dialogue and various forms of declamation and recited verse.[7] For much of its history (particularly from the thirteenth to eighteenth centuries), Chinese opera attracted talented writers, developing an important textual tradition as dramatic literature. In fact, these plays lie at the heart of literary tradition in China. Plays were widely published and reprinted in multiple sorts of editions and anthologies, many of them beautifully illustrated, for a large reading public. The most famous of these plays, such as *Romance of the Western Chamber* and *The Peony Pavilion* (*Mudan ting*), are still frequently performed today, and indeed rank among the masterpieces of Chinese literature. The woodblock printed illustrations created for these plays are likewise regarded as among the finest examples of Chinese graphic art and have served as important sources for designs on decorative objects.

The third major difference is sociological. In a recent history of Western opera, Carolyn Abbate and Roger Parker reassert that "opera for most of its history has seemed strange and exotic to most of its audience" and that "opera in its primary, theatrical form has typically been the province of elite groups."[8] The same cannot be said of Chinese opera, which has genuinely popular roots and appealed to all segments of society throughout most of its history. In part, this widespread public familiarity with opera can be attributed to the flexibility of performance venues. In no way limited to the palace or commercial playhouse, opera was performed

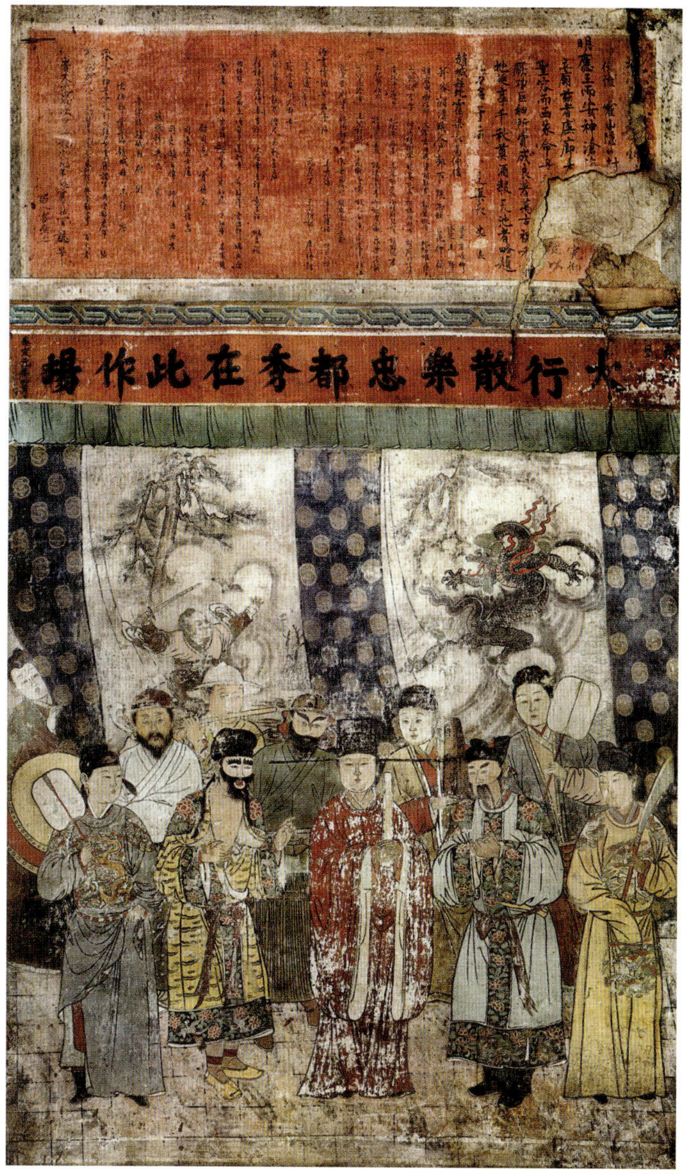

I.1
Chinese, Yuan Dynasty (1279–1368)
The Taihang Actress Zhongduxiu Standing Onstage, Costumed as an Official and Holding a Tablet of Office, Surrounded by Her Zaju *Troupe of Players and Musicians*, 1324
Wall painting, $153\frac{7}{16} \times 122\frac{13}{16}$ in. (390 × 312 cm)
Prince Mingying's Hall, Guangsheng Temple, Hongdong county, Shanxi province

almost everywhere: on temporary open-air stages or permanent ones, many attached to temples, in private salons and gardens, at restaurants and even brothels. As an indispensable feature of the ritual calendar and included in public and private celebrations, opera enjoyed the patronage of the court, temples, and officials; rich merchants and literati; petty urbanites and rural folk. Naturally there were major distinctions in the relative prestige of certain opera genres, styles, and plays. Likewise, productions varied widely in cost, scale, and opulence; performers occupied different niches along the spectrum of skill and professionalism, just as the audience varied greatly in their degree of education and connoisseurship. Regional and local differences in performing style, music, and dialect also provided some fundamental divisions. Nonetheless, by the late imperial period, a shared knowledge of opera (including familiarity with the basic performing conventions and with the broad repertory of operatic stories and characters) constituted a common culture across class, occupation, gender, and region in China.

Theatrical Space and Theatrical Event

When Europeans encountered the Chinese opera outside the court in the nineteenth and early twentieth centuries, they noted its empty stage, the absence of a built set and no attempt to represent realistic interior or exterior scenery. "Empty stage" is actually something of a misnomer because Chinese opera did deploy a modicum of stage furniture—desks, chairs, and screens—for a range of practical and symbolic purposes. Additionally, hangings, valences, lanterns, and calligraphic inscriptions decorated the stage, so it wasn't completely bare. Through much of Chinese history, however, the minimum required to constitute a stage was a rug to demarcate space and provide a proper surface for movement—indeed, in classical Chinese texts, "rug" (*qushu*) can even be used as a term for theater.[9] For operatic performances held at banquets in private homes or top courtesan houses—the favored venues for the Ming dynasty elite, which persisted, though to a lesser extent, into the Qing—a rug in the middle of a hall surrounded by tables and chairs for the guests was a sufficient makeshift theater. In the exhibition, the visual convention of representing the stage as a carpet can be seen on an early Qing blue and white porcelain vase from the Butler Family Collection, England (cat. 10), and on an embroidered apron in the American Museum of Natural History, New York (cat. 11).

Ordinarily, however, an operatic stage required not just a performing space marked by a small rug but a specially constructed raised platform. This stage could be placed inside a larger building or in open air as long as it had a concealed offstage space from which actors could enter and exit. A playful convention developed in pictorial representations of the theater to expose this invisible world to the viewer by depicting someone—an actor, a stagehand—pulling open a curtain to peek out from backstage.

I.2
Unidentified Court Artists
Chinese, Qing Dynasty (1644–1911)
Detail from Copy of the Kangxi Emperor's Sixtieth Birthday Celebration, Scroll II: *Old North Entrance of Daliang Village Stage*, late 18th century
Handscroll, ink and color on silk, 17 3/4 × 2,499 in. (45 × 6,347.5 cm)
The Palace Museum, Beijing

I.3
Chinese, Qing Dynasty (1644–1911)
Backstage View of the "West Fourth Bannermen Releasing Life Stage," 1718
Woodblock print book illustration from *Magnificent Record of the Emperor's Birthday (Wanshou shengdian)*, 1718 edition
The Palace Museum, Beijing

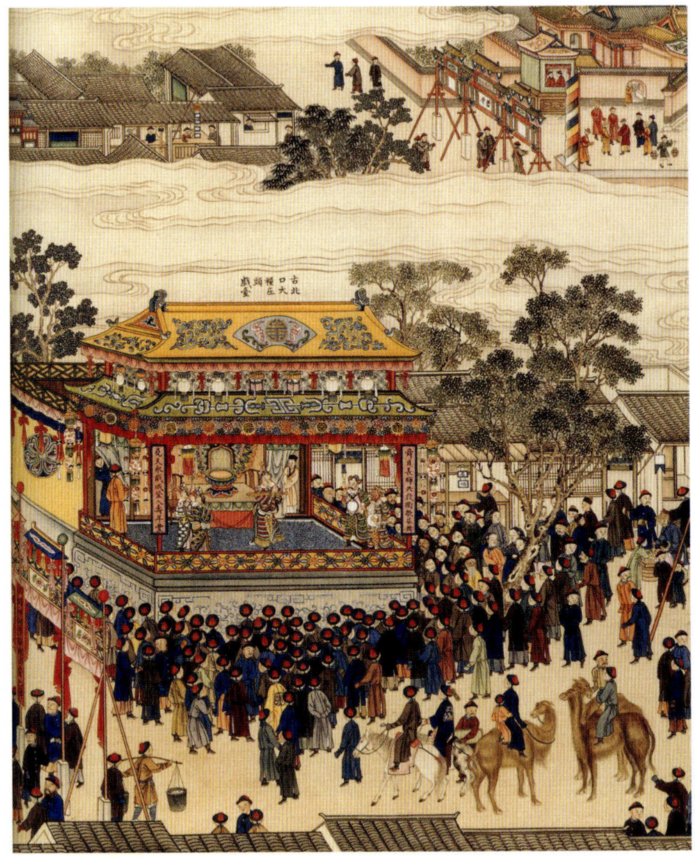

In the famous Yuan dynasty mural at the Guangsheng Monastery in Shanxi, which commemorates a performance held there by the actress Zhongduxiu and her troupe in 1324, the back stage curtain is being stealthily drawn to one side by a small, white-faced figure partially hidden behind it (figs. I.1 and 1.4).

Later Chinese stages came to be constructed with two stage doors, the left one (stage right) designated for entrances and the right one (stage left) for exits, as they are still made today. These were not actual doors, but openings covered by a curtain, which would be lifted as an actor entered and exited. In this detail of a temporary outdoor theater from an enormous two-part handscroll painting in the Palace Museum, Beijing, commemorating the public celebrations for the Kangxi Emperor's sixtieth birthday in 1713, two figures can be seen lifting the door curtains on either side of the stage to convey the pictorial illusion of backstage space (fig. I.2). This unusually elaborate temporary theater has a double roof adorned with auspicious symbols and colored imperial yellow, but the typical stage structure with its three-quarter thrust, open box frame, inscribed pillars on either side, and low balustrade separating actors from audience is quite typical. On the blue carpeted stage, a Buddhist-themed operatic scene is in full swing while a throng of spectators—mainly officials but also women, children, and peddlers—gathers below. Striking a theatrical pose on one foot and cradling his sword in his arms, the Bodhisattva Weituo is flanked by the Four Heavenly Kings in stage armor.[10]

The Kangxi birthday painting features a remarkable number of theaters (nearly fifty), with minutely detailed representations that are depicted from a variety of angles.[11] The basic composition of the picture unfolds along the emperor's homecoming route from the northwestern suburbs of Beijing to the Forbidden City, allowing the artists to represent front, back, and side views of the stages constructed on either side of the road for the occasion. The previous example presents a conventional full frontal view. In another example from a palace woodblock print based on this Kangxi birthday painting, however, we see the usual visual relationship between front stage and backstage completely reversed: here the front of the stage is mainly obstructed while the busy backstage is delightfully open to view (fig. I.3).[12] Three musicians peer through a lattice to watch what is happening onstage, but the rest of the figures on the platform—mainly actors, judging from their fake beards and costumes—are interacting with each other or others down below.

There are a number of possible explanations why this and other pictures expose the ordinarily concealed backstage, but the simplest is that the device downplays the fictive stage world of the characters and highlights the performance as a theatrical event. Of course, traditional Chinese understanding of the theater has always encompassed an awareness of the doubleness of theater, the sense that a dramatic performance constitutes something simultaneously real and unreal. But generally speaking, it is rare for the stage itself to be represented in Chinese images of opera *unless* a picture depicts a particular theatrical event, that is, one taking place at a specific site and occasion, with a certain cast and audience. Aside from illustrations of a "play within a play" in a dramatic text or of a play being performed in a novel, our richest Ming and Qing sources for visual depictions of opera stages are the detailed paintings and prints of festivals and imperial processions.[13] These

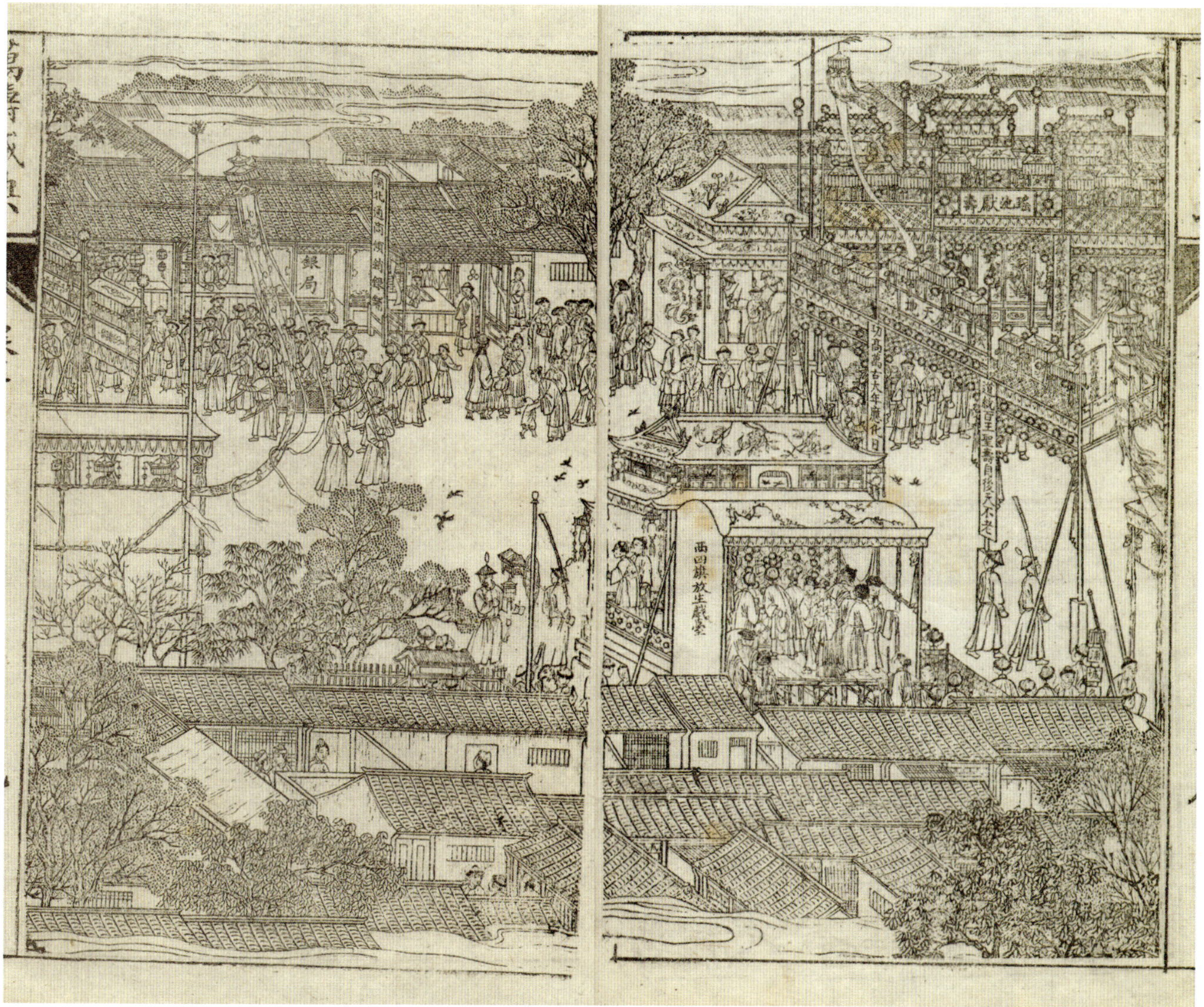

include the paintings and prints commemorating the eightieth-birthday celebration of the Qianlong emperor in 1790 (cat. 9) and a handscroll painting of the public festivities for Qianlong's mother's sixtieth birthday in 1751 as well as the Kangxi emperor's sixtieth birthday pictures discussed above (cat. 8).

The imperial birthday pictures are landmarks in the depiction of Chinese opera as public spectacle. In particular, the brightly colored scroll versions vividly locate opera performance within a larger festive street atmosphere of *renao*—the noise and excitement of crowds—effectively showing how opera was both an indispensible component of any special occasion *and* deeply integrated into the fabric of everyday life (fig. 3.1). These pictures represent the streets of the capital lined with all manner of temporary stages; they showcase opera most prominently, but also the related arts of storytelling, drumming, dancing, and acrobatics. The stages are in turn embedded in an extravagant display of other temporary pavilions, decorations, archways, and inscriptions. And all around them are not only streams of spectators but also the hustle and bustle of ordinary people going about their daily business. This idyllic vision is central to the political rhetoric of the pictures. The profusion of opera stages—each sponsored by a different province, prince, government agency, military unit, or neighborhood association—is a concrete sign of a peaceful, prosperous, and happy realm, which reconfirms the Qing dynastic mandate to rule.[14] As an inscription pasted on the right pillar of the Kangxi birthday theater in figure I.2 reads, "The lasting radiance of a latter-day sage-king causes singing and dancing in the streets."

At the other end of the spectrum we find the only New Year print in the exhibition to depict a stage and an audience (cat. 13). Printed on cheap paper and purchased by anthropologist Berthold Laufer on his first expedition to China in 1902, the print shows an opera scene being performed by an all-female "Pussycat Opera" (*Mao'er xi*) troupe in what is clearly a brothel. The stage is a recognizable variant of the Kangxi birthday painting model most typical of Qing commercial playhouses.[15] During the late Qing dynasty, theatrical images of opera scenes with costumed characters executing moves with props and furniture as though on stage were a popular subject for New Year pictures (see Bo Songnian's essay in this catalogue). The exhibition includes several of these, all part of a large collection purchased by Laufer on the same expedition (cats. 14–16).

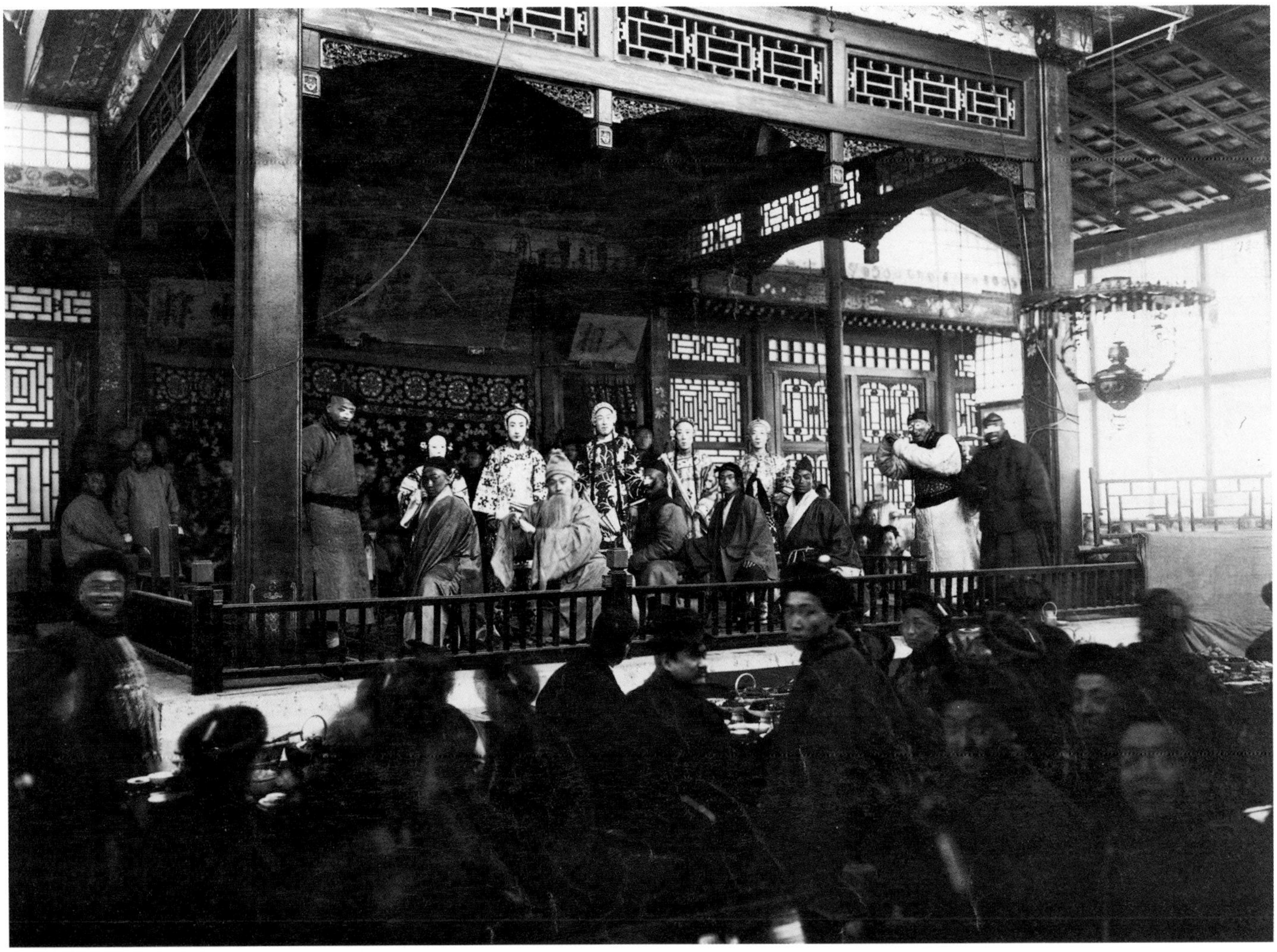

They all adopt the same outward orientation toward the viewer, but usually dispense with the theater architecture, and invariably omit the audience. In the Pussycat Opera print, by contrast, the point of showing the stage is once again to emphasize the theatrical event, in this case, what is going on in the audience during a performance within the social milieu of a high class brothel.

In another image probably purchased, or even commissioned, by Laufer on the same expedition a photograph of a playhouse in Beijng produces an oddly similar effect (fig. I.4). The stage itself, with its open wooden box design, columns, and low railing, is the familiar Qing type. The photograph provides a clear view of the lattice dividing front and backstage, as well as the stage entrance and exit doors on either side. [16] Strangely, no one in the audience seems in the slightest bit interested in the Peking opera cast members on stage, who are arranged in two rows as if for a curtain call. Instead, the spectators are craning their heads curiously in the opposite direction, while the actors seem to be looking over the audience to something beyond the space of the photograph. The absent object attracting so much attention must be the photographer and his camera. The theatrical event recorded in this photograph is in fact the reaction to the photographer's visit to the playhouse.

Shared Imagery and Ritual Function

The dictates of social and religious occasions had a striking influence on both opera performance and the decorative arts in late imperial China. Specific occasions such as weddings, funerals, birthdays, or festivals had ritual aspects that determined which plays were selected for performance, or pictorial motifs for display and gifts. Generally speaking, we may divide these ritual aspects into two broad categories: on the one hand, to protect from baleful influences and to exorcise evil spirits, and on the other, to ask for good fortune and express auspicious wishes. In service of these needs, opera and image were mutually reinforcing and even potentially interchangeable. A picture could be brought to life through performance, while performance could affect the iconography of a picture.

The demon-queller Zhong Kui provides the clearest example of the interrelated ritual uses of picture and performance. Two images of him appear in the exhibition, one on a magnificent handscroll by the Yuan dynasty painter Yan Geng (cat. 7) in the Metropolitan Museum of Art and the other on a blue-and-white nineteenth-century porcelain snuff bottle in the Asian Art Museum of San Francisco

I.4
Chinese, Late Qing Dyansty (1644–1911)
Peking Opera Performers and Audience inside a Beijing Commercial Playhouse, probably purchased 1902–04
Silver gelatin print
American Museum of Natural History Library
336390

I.5
Chinese, Ming Dynasty (1368–1644)
Detail from The Lantern Festival Celebration in the Court of the Ming Emperor Xianzong (Ming Xianzong yuanxiao xingle tu)*: Zhong Kui Parade*, 15th century
Handscroll, ink and color on silk
National Museum of China (former History Museum), Beijing

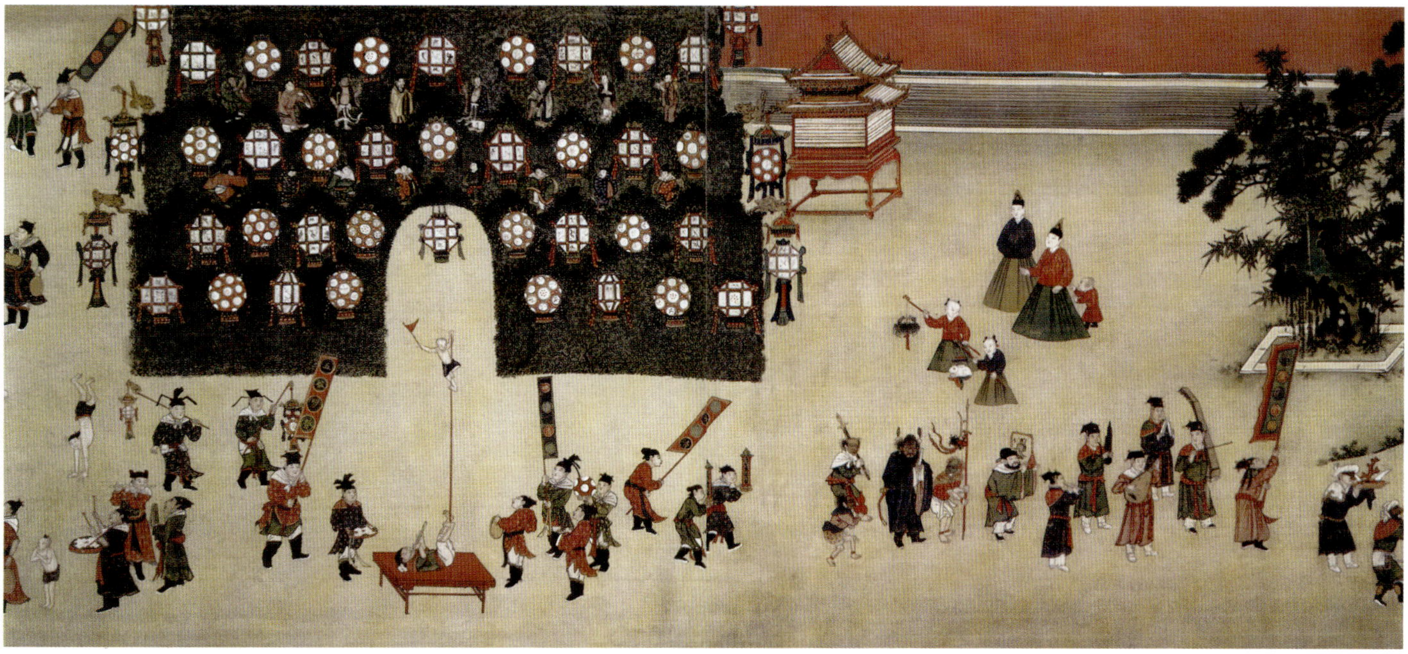

(cat. 49). The cult of Zhong Kui was associated with the rituals of exorcism and carnivalesque celebrations of the New Year's season, and later, with those of the Dragon Boat Festival (*Duanwu jie*) at the start of the pestilential summer season. It became customary at these times of the year to display Zhong Kui's image and to sponsor processions and plays featuring him.

Although a powerful protector deity, Zhong Kui started out as the ghost of a grotesquely ugly, impoverished scholar, and he is usually portrayed as a comic figure wearing a bobbling scholar's cap in both the theatrical and painting traditions. In Yan Geng's handscroll *The Demon Zhong Kui Giving His Sister Away in Marriage*, Zhong Kui looks disheveled and drunk, slumped over his donkey, while his sister rides serenely on her water buffalo. They are escorted by an entourage of little demons, some banging on drums or playing the flute, others ostentatiously lifting weights and twirling weapons. *Zhong Kui Marries Off His Sister* (*Zhong Kui jia mei*) is a New Year's play still in the operatic repertory with Zhong Kui as a painted-face role, his costume grotesquely padded to distort the body.[17] With the exception of the procession itself and the antics of the little demons, however, this painting does not directly represent a performance context, and Zhong Kui, his sister, and even the demons are portrayed as though they were "real" figures, rather than players dressed up as these characters.

The same is not true of a palace handscroll painting that dates from the fifteenth century and now in the National Museum of China, Beijing, which depicts the carnival of the Lantern Festival (on the fifteenth day of the first lunar month) in the court of the Ming emperor Xianzong (r. 1465–1487). One section of the scroll shows a Zhong Kui parade led by a small band of musicians in ordinary dress (fig. I.5). This time it is clear that the artist has painted an actor costumed as Zhong Kui and three masked players as his demon entourage. In the middle marches a man who is holding up a framed panel with a picture of an identically costumed Zhong Kui in miniature. The interchangeable relationship between a Zhong Kui performance and a Zhong Kui image could not be more apparent.

Opera and the visual arts shared a common code of images, facilitating the similarity in usage between the two for celebratory occasions. Auspicious wishes were expressed through a fixed vocabulary of symbolic images operating within a shared visual culture that stretched from village to palace across the expanse of China.[18] Some ubiquitous examples are the bat, whose name *fu*[a] is a homophone for good fortune (*fu*[b]); the peach, the mythological

I.6
Chinese, Late Qing Dynasty (1644–1911)
Peking Opera Performers, probably purchased 1902–04
Silver gelatin print
American Museum of Natural History Library
333625

fruit of immortality, which signifies long life; and the scepter, whose name *ruyi* means "as you desire," and whose finial can be formed in a cloud or fungus shape, both equally auspicious symbols. On decorative objects, illustrations of theatrical stories are frequently juxtaposed with auspicious symbols, either around a border to frame a single scene, as in a *famille rose* plate with a scene from *Romance of the Western Chamber* in the Philadelphia Museum of Art (cat. 39) or to fill the empty spaces between a sequence of scenes, as on the Daoist robe in the Field Museum of Natural History, which is woven with scenes from *The Pearl Pagoda (Zhenzhuta),* discussed in Yuhang Li's essay in this catalogue (cat. 27).

Both in the realm of material culture and in the realm of theatrical entertainment, offerings with shared imagery were exchanged as gifts and performed in conjunction with different kinds of religious holidays and private festivities. For example, paintings and objects festooned with symbols of longevity, such as peaches, Daoist immortals, cranes, and so on, were commonly given as birthday presents. In the exhibition, a late Ming pipa (pear-shaped lute) from the Metropolitan Museum of Art, is a veritable cornucopia of such images (cat. 5). The back of the instrument is honeycombed with ivory hexagons carved with auspicious pictorial motifs; its pegbox terminates in a carved wooden bat or butterfly, with yin-yang symbols on the wings. The pipa was one of the major instruments used to accompany sung arias, especially in southern opera; in recognition of this operatic connection, perhaps, the ivory string holder on the instrument's belly is decorated with a scene from *Romance of the Western Chamber.*[19]

Opera scenes with titles such as "Presenting Birthday Wishes" (*Qingshou* or *Shangshou*), which portray Daoist immortals or other religious or mythological figures holding peaches as props, were commonly performed at birthday celebrations both in private homes and at court.[20] This phenomenon is taken to extreme in the representations of the birthday processions of the Kangxi and Qianlong emperors. The Qianlong painting even features a performance of the "Three Heavenly Stars of Happiness, Wealth, and Longevity" (*Fu, Lu, Shou*) offering auspicious omens, including an outsized peach, on a fanciful peach-shaped stage. A woodblock palace print of this scene, now in the Regenstein Library at the University of Chicago, appears in the exhibition (cat. 9a).[21] The advantage of opera over the decorative arts is that through performance, good wishes could not only be conferred but also physically enacted, and in this sense, symbolically fulfilled.

Decorative Pattern and Surface

The claim that the actor's body makes the stage is a truism in writing on Chinese opera. In terms of material culture, we may say that the dazzling costumes worn by the actor and the decorated flags, whips, weapons, and other props make the stage. A beautiful silk embroidered robe in the Metropolitan Museum of Art from the mid- to late nineteenth century, which was designed for the role of a princess, is included in the current exhibition to provide a sense of the magnificence and workmanship of the finest opera costumes (cat. 6). Although no commoner troupe could rival the resources of the palace in its heyday, costumes and other textiles were by far the most important and greatest capital investment for any troupe.[22] For instance, in a rare inventory dating from 1922 of the stage trunks for the opera troupes maintained by the prominent Kong clan, the descendants of Confucius, in Qufu, Shandong province, we see a list of eighteen graded trunks of different kinds of costumes, four trunks of door hangings and valences, two trunks of weapons and other props, six round baskets for headgear, hair pieces, and beards, but only two large property trunks for stage desks and chairs.[23]

In Jonathan Hay's recent book on the decorative object in early modern China, he calls our attention to the importance of profuse surface decoration in Chinese visual and material culture. "A topography of sensuous surface—a surfacescape—is the principal feature shared by two-dimensional and three-dimensional objects," he asserts.[24] Although the live actor in performance lies outside of Hay's purview, his argument is in fact highly relevant to the three-dimensional costumed human body on the stage and the two-dimensional images of opera characters in paintings, popular prints, textiles, and photographs. The operatic alchemy of transforming a human being into a "surfacescape" is particularly pronounced in the case of the *jing,* the painted-face role (also called the "variegated-face role" [*hualian*] in Peking opera). In principle, the colors, patterns, and design of the makeup and outfit in Peking

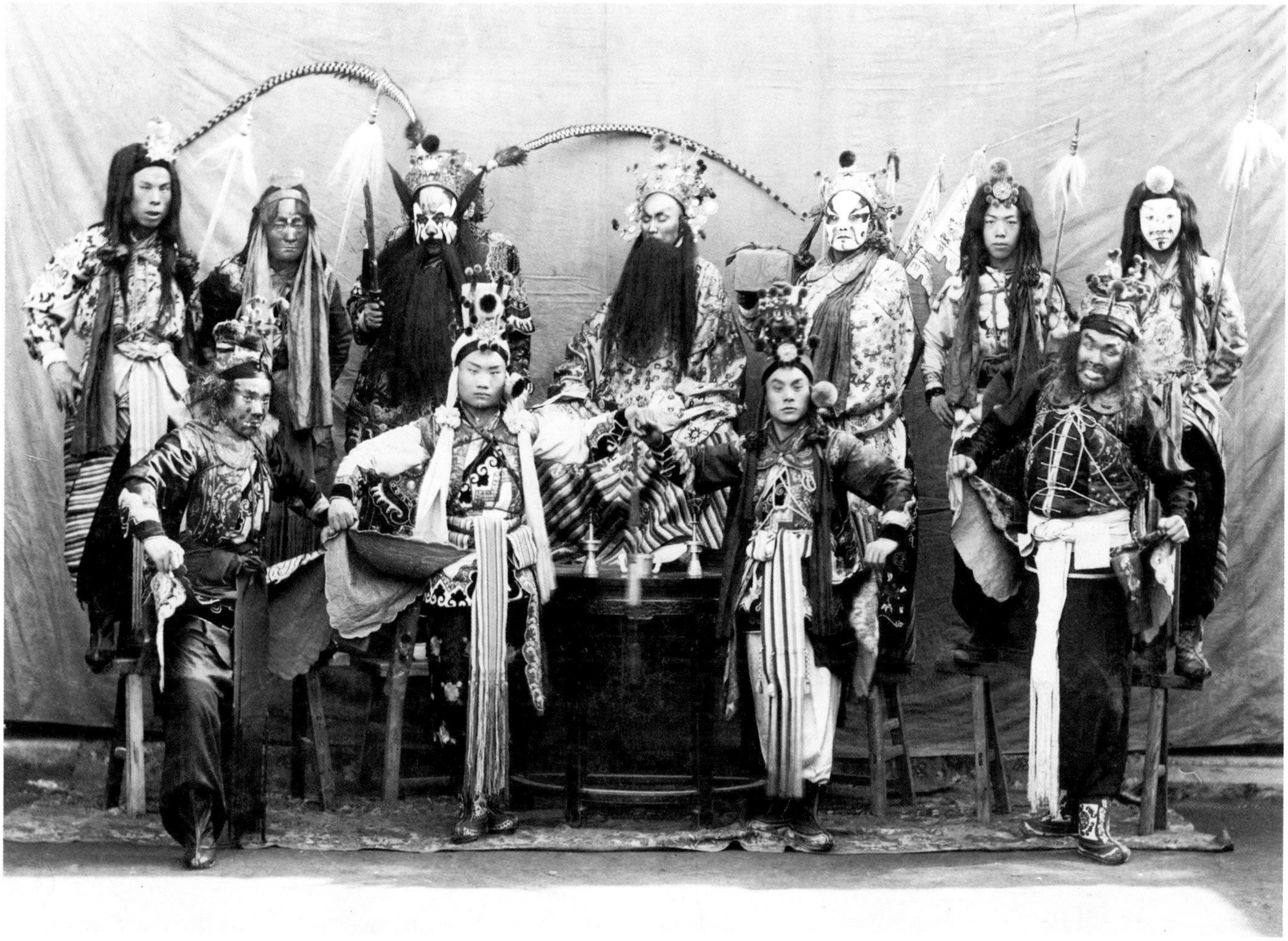

opera are symbolically coded to provide information about the character's social status, age, occupation, and moral disposition. Yet at times the makeup is so complicated that the human facial features completely dissolve into an abstract surface design that blends still further with the hyper-ornamented, and distorting patterns and shapes of the costume.

This kaleidoscopic effect is even more exaggerated in pictures of operatic characters. For example in the masklike images of painted faces from an album in the Field Museum, and included in the exhibition, the human features of the face—eyes, nose, mouth—are flattened and entirely obliterated to become a blank canvas for an ornately designed swallow, butterfly, or crab (cat. 46.1 and 46.5, see also Mei Mei Rado's essay in this catalogue). Or take a nineteenth-century album painting in imperial court style, now in the Metropolitan Museum of Art, of the villainous general of Wei, Xiahou Dun, a character from one of the innumerable operas on the civil war of the Three Kingdoms period (220–280 CE) (cat. 47.12). The four flags on his back signify the multiple battalions he commands; the animal face embroidered on his armor reinforces his high status as a general; and the predominance of matte white face paint and the asymmetrical swirls obscuring half his face signal his evil, treacherous nature. Much of the visual pleasure of the painting comes from the superabundance of formal abstract patterns, which to adapt Hay's perspective again, seems to transform "the decorative surface" of the human body and face "into a screen onto which signs and symbols are projected."[25]

The transformation of opera into a decorative surface of pattern and color is found just as often in the cheapest, most ephemeral pictures, such as New Year prints. One such print from the American Museum of Natural History in the exhibition depicts a Peking opera titled *The Great Upsurge of Mount Liang: Subduing Guan Sheng* (*Daxing Liangshan: Soufu Guan Sheng*), which is based on an episode from *The Water Margin* (cat. 51). The picture shows the captured government general Guan Sheng, a heroic, red painted-face role, lying prostrate on the ground. The complex patterns and colors of his armor, makeup, and headdress merge into the costumes of the outlaws from Mount Liang who surround him, and into the mountain and cloud designs on the screen next to them. (The outlaw chief Song Jiang, as he would on stage, is standing on a chair concealed behind this screen to indicate that he is surveying the action from their mountain headquarters.) Even without color, a black-and-white photograph from Laufer's first expedition to China effectively transforms a Peking opera troupe arrayed in full costume and face paint against a makeshift blank backdrop into a decorative surfacescape (fig. I.6).

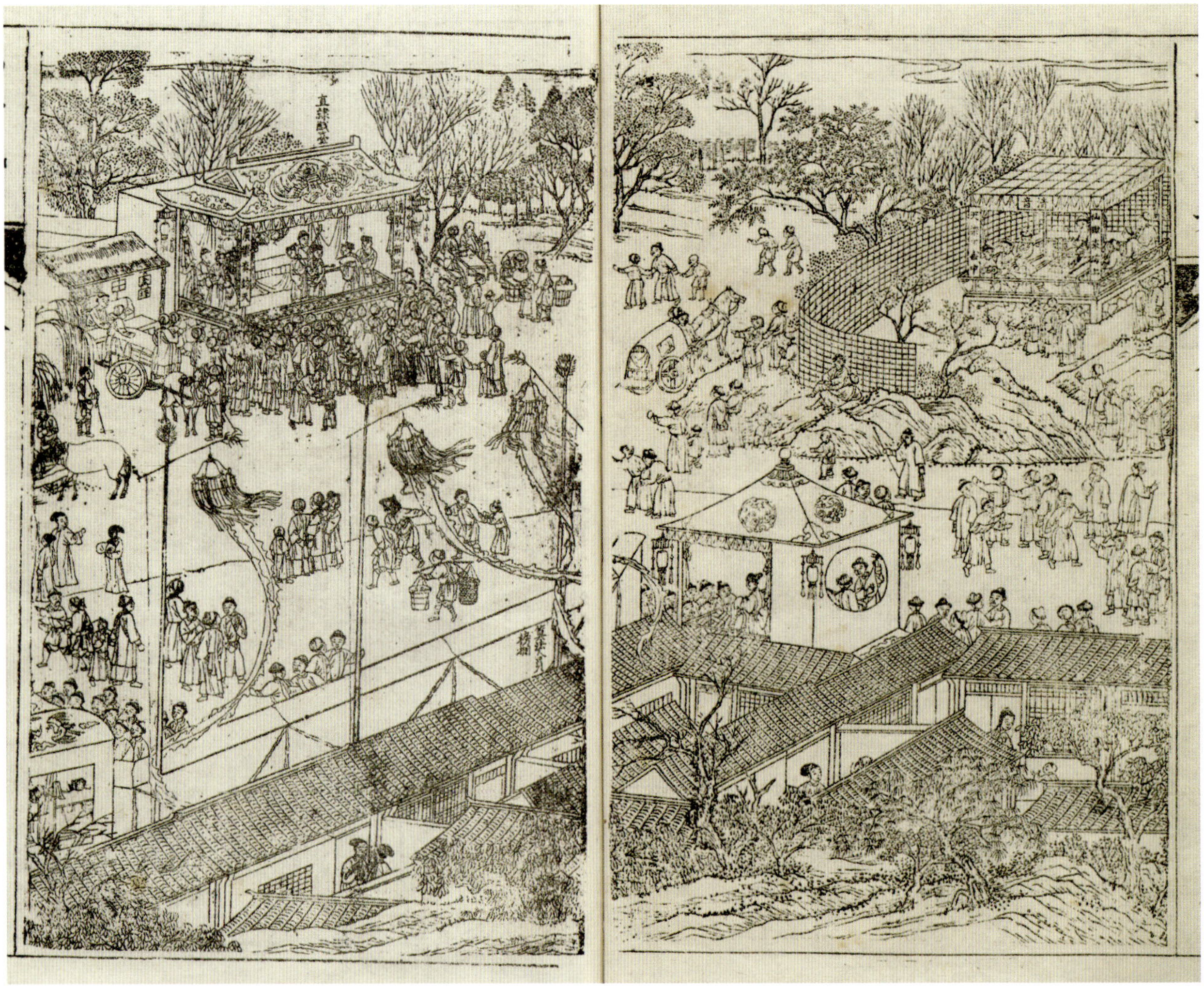

A Multiplicity of Forms: *Romance of the Western Chamber*

To understand the multiplicity of forms a single play could assume in the literary, performance, and visual traditions, there is no better example for study than *Romance of the Western Chamber*. In recognition of the play's protean influence, the exhibition devotes an entire section to its representations in different media. A brief review of the play's history therefore provides an appropriate ending to this introduction.

Romance of the Western Chamber originated as a tale by the Tang poet Yuan Zhen (779–831) about the brief unhappy love affair between a student surnamed Zhang and his cousin Oriole (Yingying). By no later than the early thirteenth century, the story was being performed as a *chantefable* and had acquired a happy ending.[26] The Yuan playwright Wang Shifu (circa 1250–1300) turned this new version into an unusually long five-part northern drama (*zaju*) of twenty acts to create the most beloved Chinese romance of all time.

The play begins with the arrival of Student Zhang at the Monastery of Universal Salvation (Pujiu Si) . There he falls in love with the beautiful and talented Oriole, who is coincidentally also staying there with her widowed mother to attend memorial services for Oriole's late father. When local bandits headed by Flying Tiger Sun suddenly menace the temple, Oriole's mother promises her daughter to any man who can protect them. Student Zhang saves the day by getting a message to his friend General Du, who defeats the bandits. But Oriole's mother unaccountably reneges on her promise. With the help of Oriole's pert maid Crimson (Hongniang), Zhang arranges a nighttime assignation with Oriole but when he jumps over the wall into her garden for the expected tryst, she instead berates him for his lack of morals. Dejected, he falls ill with longing; she eventually relents, and again with Crimson as go-between, the two spend the night together. After Oriole's mother detects the affair, she agrees that Student Zhang can indeed marry her daughter, but only if he first passes the civil service examinations. While Student Zhang is away in the capital at the examinations, Oriole's mother treacherously betroths her to another man, the boorish Zhang Heng. But of course all comes out right in the end. Student Zhang takes top place in the examinations, and after his triumphant return to the temple, with the intercession once again of his friend General Du, Oriole's mother relents and accepts him as her son-in-law. The play concludes with the joyful celebration of Zhang and Oriole's wedding. (For a detailed synopsis of the play by part and act, see page 217.)

I.7
Chinese, Late Qing Dynasty (1644–1911)
"Startled by Beauty" Scene from Romance of the Western Chamber (Xixiang ji) *performed on the "Zhili Province Stage,"* 1879
Photo-lithograph (after original 1718 woodblock album) book illustration from *Magnificent Record of the Emperor's Birthday, First Installment* (*Wanshou shengdian, chuji 1–4 juan*), 1879 edition
East Asian Collection, The Joseph Regenstein Library, The University of Chicago, 2789 3213

I.8a–b
Chinese, Ming Dynasty (1368–1644)
Student Zhang Spies on Oriole Burning Incense in the Garden and the Two of Them Match Poems by Moonlight, from Part 1, Act 3 of Romance of the Western Chamber (Xixiang ji), 1498
Woodblock print book illustrations from *Romance of the Western Chamber* (*Yuanben chuxiang Bei Xixiang ji*) by Wang Shifu (ca. 1250–1300), 1498 edition
East Asian Collection, The Joseph Regenstein Library, The University of Chicago

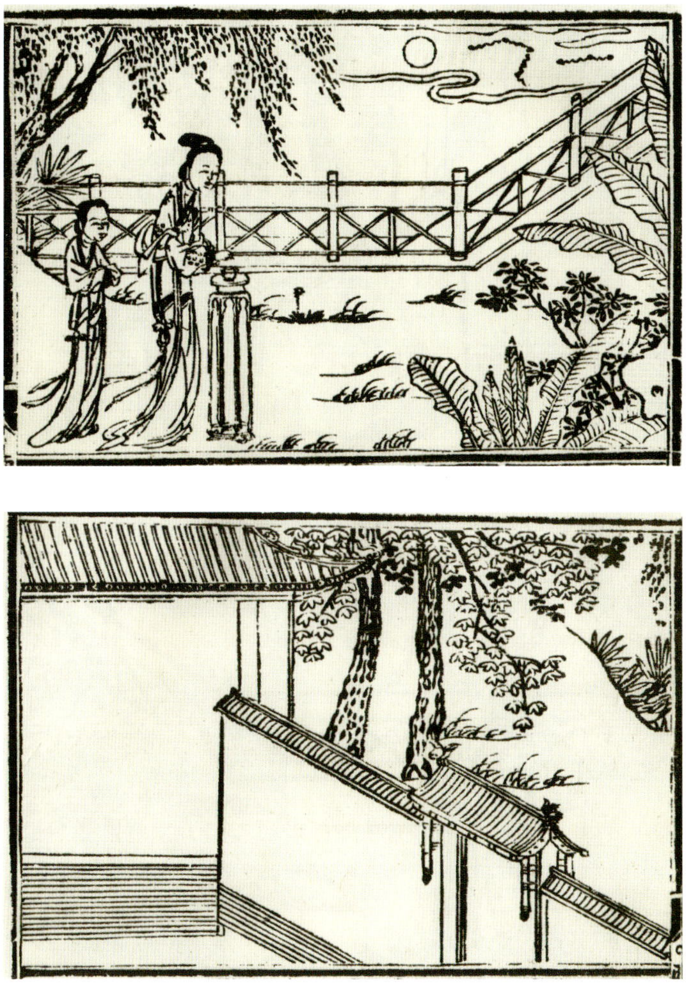

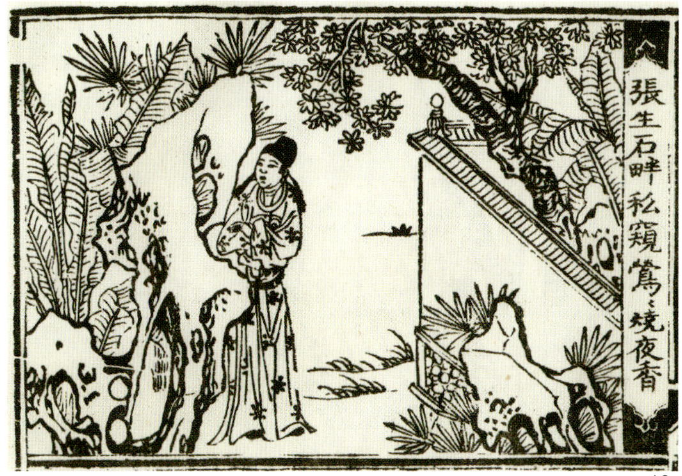

I.8a

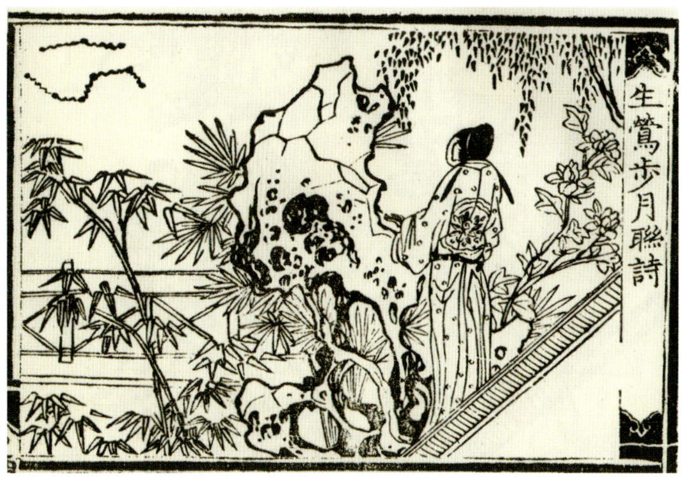

I.8b

During the Ming and Qing dynasties, versions of the play were published in over 100 different complete woodblock editions, many of them illustrated by different artists, dwarfing the popularity of any other play in Chinese print history.[27] The opera has remained continuously in the performance repertory, adapted as a southern romantic comedy (*chuanqi*) in the sixteenth century when the old northern music was disappearing, and then developed as single act excerpts (*zhezi xi*) when performing full-length plays went out of fashion and new operatic genres arose. We can recognize one such excerpt—the popular "Startled by Beauty" (part 1, act 2)—being rehearsed on the rug decorating the early Qing dynasty blue-and-white vase from the Butler Family Collection in the exhibition (cat. 10) and being performed on an outdoor stage in the Kangxi Emperor's birthday pictures (fig. I.7).[28]

The earliest extant imprint of the play, which dates from 1498, is noteworthy for its adaptation of the handscroll format for its illustrations, so that in the continuous space above the text, a complete pictorial narrative of the play unfolds over the pages (fig. I.8). A good example of this technique appears in the book's illustration of the episode in which Student Zhang spies on Oriole in the garden at night. On the right-side page of the illustration we see him peering from behind a garden rock at Oriole and Crimson, who are burning incense in the moonlight on the opposite left-side page. Turning the page, we find only a deserted garden wall on the right-side page, while Student Zhang appears on the left-side page, now with his back toward us as he chants a poem to Oriole from behind another garden rock.

I.9
Min Qiji, publisher, Chinese, active in Wucheng (Huzhou), Zhejiang Province, 1580–after 1661
Student Zhang Riding to the Monastery of Universal Salvation (Pujiu Si), from Romance of the Western Chamber (Xixiang ji), *Represented as a Handscroll*, 1640
Album leaf 1 from a loose folio of twenty-one leaves, polychrome woodblock print, sheet: 10 1/32 × 12 11/16 in. (25.5 × 32.2 cm)
Museum für Ostasiatische Kunst, Cologne, R 62,1

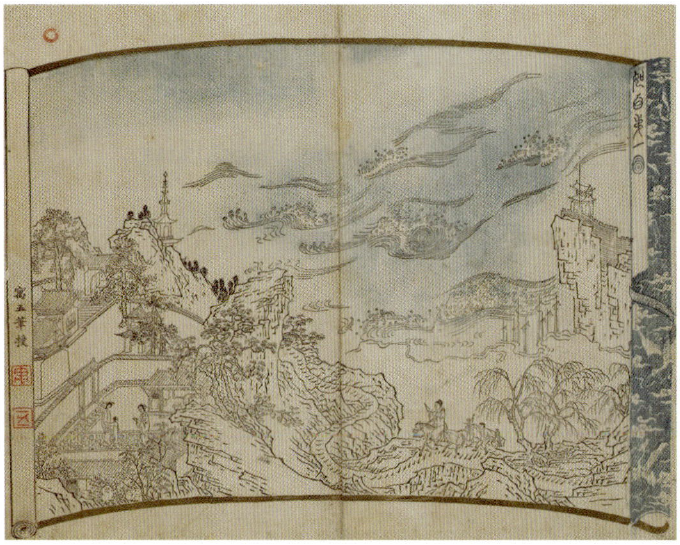

I.10
Min Qiji, publisher, Chinese, active in Wucheng (Huzhou), Zhejiang Province, 1580–after 1661
Student Zhang Questioning Oriole's Maid Crimson and Being Spied on by Monks from Romance of the Western Chamber (Xixiang ji), *Represented as a Fishbowl*, 1640
Album leaf 2 from a loose folio of twenty-one leaves, polychrome woodblock print, sheet: 10 1/32 × 12 11/16 in. (25.5 × 32.2 cm)
Museum für Ostasiatische Kunst, Cologne, R 62,1

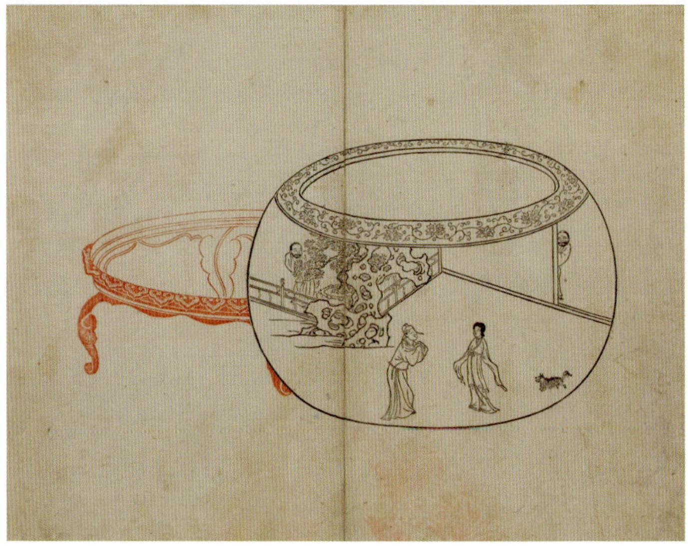

Over the next century, as the late Ming vogue for illustrated books in general, and editions of *Romance of the Western Chamber* in particular, reached its height, interest in complete pictorial narratives of the play waned. With the strengthening of the individual scene, both as a literary unit and as an independent performing excerpt, new fashions of representing the play took hold. Nonetheless, regardless of time period or medium, illustrations of *Romance of the Western Chamber* do tend to depict dramatic characters in a roughly naturalistic manner and setting, as in the 1498 edition, rather than in stage costume, hairstyle, and makeup.

From as early as the fourteenth century, scenes from the play were being painted on ceramics, and from the mid-seventeenth to early eighteenth century, *Romance of the Western Chamber* became the most popular theatrical story to be depicted on porcelain.[29] Woodblock illustrations are believed to be the main visual source for pictures from drama transferred to porcelain and other three-dimensional objects. As the art historian Meng-ching Ma has argued, however, there was also a feedback loop as illustrations of *Romance of the Western Chamber,* in turn, began to absorb design elements from the decorative arts, particularly in framing and the use of decorative motifs.[30] The best example of this trend is the set of color woodblock prints designed and produced by Min Qiji in 1640, now in the Museum für Ostasiatische Kunst in Cologne. Each of the twenty prints cleverly depicts an act of the play by imitating a different visual medium, from a handscroll (fig. I.9) and a ceramic fishbowl (fig. I.10) to a revolving zoetropic lantern (fig. I.11), and a puppet theater (fig. I.12).[31]

Similar sorts of games with material form and illusion were imported back onto three-dimensional objects, some depicting multiple scenes from the play like the rhinoceros horn cup from the Field Museum, in this exhibition (cat. 32), and others retaining the single scene format, like the eighteenth-century plate in *famille rose* (cat. 39). This plate, in the Philadelphia Museum of Art, shows a scene of Student Zhang jumping over the wall (part 3, act 3) superimposed on a handscroll in a trompe l'oeil fashion reminiscent of the Min Qiji print for part 1, act 1 (fig. I.9). Alternatively, a Qing dynasty bamboo wrist rest from the Metropolitan Museum, in the exhibition (cat. 38), dating from 1674 or 1734, is finely carved with Oriole reading Student Zhang's love letter in front of a screen (part 3, act 2). A wrist rest was customarily placed on a desk to support the hand holding the brush when writing a document, such as a letter, so in this sense the choice of this scene offers a witty take on the function of the object upon which it appears. The scene was a favorite for illustrators of *Romance of the Western Chamber* because of the opportunity it provided to show Oriole's maid Crimson spying on her mistress from the other side of the screen (fig. I.13). But the diameter of the wrist rest is too narrow to include the full screen or Crimson. Anyone looking at the wrist rest would immediately

I.11
Min Qiji, publisher, Chinese, active in Wucheng (Huzhou), Zhejiang Province, 1580–after 1661
Battle Scene on Horseback with an Acolyte Monk Chasing General Du, Who is Chasing the Bandit Flying Tiger Sun from Romance of the Western Chamber (Xixiang ji), *Represented as a Gyrating Zoetropic Lantern*, 1640
Album leaf 5 from a loose folio of twenty-one leaves, polychrome woodblock print, sheet: 10 1/32 × 12 11/16 in. (25.5 × 32.2 cm)
Museum für Ostasiatische Kunst, Cologne, R 62,1

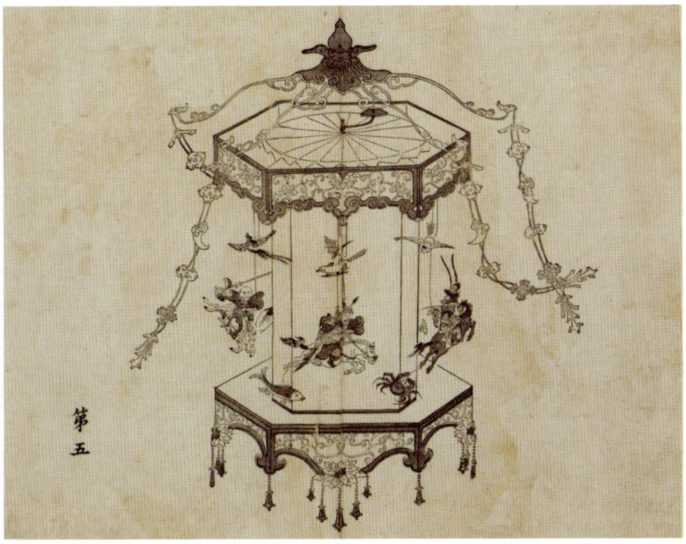

I.12
Min Qiji, publisher, Chinese, active in Wucheng (Huzhou), Zhejiang Province, 1580–after 1661
Crimson Conversing with the Rascal Zheng Heng, Student Zhang's Rival for Oriole's Hand in Marriage from Romance of the Western Chamber (Xixiang ji), *Represented as a Marionette Theater, with Oriole, Student Zhang, General Du, and the Abbot Puppets Hanging Offstage*, 1640
Album leaf 19 from a loose folio of twenty-one leaves, polychrome woodblock print, sheet: 10 1/32 × 12 11/16 in. (25.5 × 32.2 cm)
Museum für Ostasiatische Kunst, Cologne, R 62,1

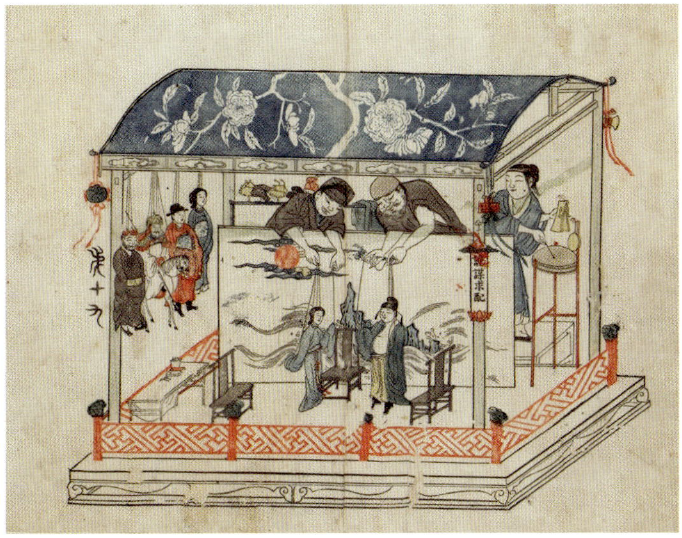

realize what was missing, however, and appreciate the joke that to use it meant positioning oneself in the place of the peeping maid looking over her mistress's shoulder.

Although it is rare to depict any scene from this play with the characters in stage costume before the late Qing, scholars have convincingly argued that changing performance practices did influence the pictorial representation of a scene in terms of gestures, poses, props, and even added episodes.[32] Nonetheless, such subtleties were certainly no longer comprehensible when *Romance of the Western Chamber* became a favorite pictorial subject for porcelain export ware and other decorative objects aimed at a foreign market in the late eighteenth and nineteenth centuries.[33] In these cases, the meaning of a dramatic scene or the auspicious symbols surrounding them is uniformly emptied of any specific meaning, becoming for the foreign beholder simply all-purpose decorative motifs signifying "chinoiserie."

Domestically, *Romance of the Western Chamber* remained a popular part of Chinese literary, visual, and performance culture. In the late nineteenth century, new Western printing technology came to China, and of course it was used to reproduce images of this and other plays. Amid the New Year prints with operatic themes collected by Laufer in 1902, and today in the American Museum of Natural History, are two polychrome lithographic prints of *Romance of the Western Chamber* illustrated in a radically different modern style (cats. 42, 43). Eight scenes from the play appear in comic book fashion, retelling the story to a new audience. The influence of performed excerpts is still evident in the selection of scenes in the two prints, but while Oriole's mother and Student Zhang are shown wearing traditional Ming-style garb, Oriole and Crimson are modishly dressed in the late Qing style of fin-de-siècle Shanghai. Such fashions were popularized in the new illustrated periodical press through columns with titles like "Ladies in Shanghai Style" (Huzhuang shinü).[34] As such, these two prints point forward to the important role that images of opera would play in the modern commercial visual culture of advertising, magazines, and film in Republican-era treaty port cities after the demise of the dynastic system. But that is a story for another exhibition.

Notes

1 Cited in David Johnson, "'Actions Speak Louder than Words': the Cultural Significance of Chinese Ritual Opera," in *Ritual Opera, Operatic Ritual: "Mu-lien Rescues His Mother" in Chinese Popular Culture*, ed. David Johnson (Berkeley: University of California IEAS Publications, 1989), p. 1.

2 See *Theater, Life, and the Afterlife: Tomb Décor of the Jin Dynasty from Shanxi*, ed. Shi Jinming and Willow Weilan Hai Chang (Beijing: Kexue chubanshe, 2012) and Jeehee Hong, "Virtual Theater of the Dead: Actor Figurines and Their Stage in Houma Tomb No. 1, Shanxi Province," *Artibus Asiae* 71/1 (2011), pp. 75–114.

3 To borrow Carolyn Abbate and Roger Parker's simple definition from *A History of Opera* (New York: Norton, 2012), p. 1: "Opera is a type of theatre in which most or all of the characters sing most or all of the time."

I.13
Chen Hongshou
Chinese, 1598–1652
Oriole Reading a Love-Letter from Student Zhang and Being Spied on by Maid Crimson from Act 10 of Romance of the Western Chamber (Xixiang ji), 1639 (Zhang Shenzhi edition)
Woodblock print book illustration

4 Cross-dressing has been a fundamental aspect of Chinese opera, although the practice has waxed and waned depending on the preferences of the ruling authority and elite patrons. Midway through their rule, for instance, the Qing emperors abolished the use of female entertainers at court, replacing them with eunuchs, and Peking opera grew up in the nineteenth century as an all-male theater because actresses were banned from the public stage in the capital until the twentieth century, when female stars began to emerge. Nonetheless, women continued to perform as actresses in other contexts and geographic locations, and some all-female genres of opera in the South are still popular today. Despite the glorification of top actors specializing in female roles like Mei Lanfang in the People's Republic of China after the 1949 revolution, the association of men playing women with homosexuality and effeminacy meant that the practice was abolished in the professional theater; it is now only gradually and sparingly being revived.

5 For this reason, analogies are sometimes drawn between Chinese opera and the commedia dell'arte, popular theater with its stock role-types and *lazzi,* improvised comic actions and routines.

6 The earliest known published score of operatic arias with traditional Chinese musical notation (*gongche pu*), *Fixed Rules for Southern Songs* (*Xinbian nanci dinglü*) dates to 1725, but for the most part, opera music was orally transmitted, and actors, instrumentalists, professional music teachers, and amateur connoisseurs played the pivotal creative roles in developing and shaping the music that was sung and played on stage.

7 In this respect, Chinese opera resembles German *singspiel* and the American musical.

8 Abbate and Parker, *A History of Opera*, p. 19.

9 On the rug and the architectural design of the Chinese stage, see Hay's essay in this catalogue.

10 Ordinarily an actor playing the Bodhisattva Guanyin or some other Buddhist deity should be seated on the throne upstage. It is possible that the throne has been left empty to symbolize the emperor.

11 Zhu Jiajin gives the figure of forty-nine opera stages, with performers visible on over twenty of them. See his "*Wanshou tu* zhong de xiqu biaoyan xieshi" [Realistic Depiction of Theater Performance in the Birthday Scrolls], in Zhu Jiajin, *Gugong tuishi lu* [Collected Essays upon my Retirement from the Palace Museum] (Beijing: Beijing chubanshe, 1998), vol. 2, p. 487.

12 Kangxi had the two-scroll painting of his sixtieth-birthday procession finely carved on woodblocks and printed in a 120-chapter book of tributes commemorating the event entitled *Magnificent Record of the Emperor's Birthday* (*Wanshou shengdian*).

13 Important precursors are the commemorative paintings of Kangxi and Qianlong's southern inspection tours, which also depict some open-air stages with opera performances, and the handscroll paintings of popular urban festivals. The Northern Song handscroll *Spring Festival Along the River* (*Qingming shanghe tu*) is the earliest and best-known example of this genre, but it is not until the Ming that we start to find opera stages represented in imitations of this scroll and other paintings of this sort. For examples, see Wu Zhao, *Zhuixun guoshi de yinyue zongji* [In Pursuit of Traces of Vanished Music: An Illustrated History of Chinese Music] (Beijing Dongfang chubanshe, 1999), pp. 320–31, 363.

14 Maxwell K. Hearn, catalogue entry no. 24 on *Copy of the Kangxi Emperor's Sixtieth Birthday Celebration, Scroll One*, in *China: The Three Emperors, 1662–1795,* eds. Evelyn Rawski and Jessica Rawson (London: Royal Academy of Arts , 2005), pp. 391–92.

15 Andrea Goldman, *Opera and the City: The Politics of Culture in Beijing, 1770–1900* (Stanford, Calif.: Stanford University Press, 2012), pp. 67–80.

16 The plaque above the entrance door reads: "Go Forth the Generals" (Chu jiang); the one above the exit door reads: "Go Inside the Ministers" (Ru xiang), an ancient phrase used to praise someone for being able to be a minister in court and a general on the field. It is unknown when the phrase became applied to theater. For use of the same plaques in the puppet theater, see Li-ling Hsiao, *The Eternal Present of the Past: Illustration, Theater, and Reading in the Wanli Period, 1573–1619* (Leiden: Brill, 2007), p. 111.

17 The 1987 film *Woman, Demon, Human* (*Ren gui qing*, dir. Huang Shuqin), a biopic of a rare female *jing* opera star who specialized in playing the painted face-role of Zhong Kui, offers sensational footage of an actress costuming herself as Zhong Kui.

18 Édouard Chavannes, *De l'expression des vœux dans l'art populaire Chinois* [The Expression of Auspicious Wishes in Chinese Popular Art] (Paris: Éditions Bossard, 1922). See also Elaine Spaulding's translation, *The Five Happinesses: Symbolism in Chinese Popular Art* (New York: Weatherhill, 1973).

19 The scene is "Startled by Beauty"; see Ni Yibin's essay in this catalogue. The reason for the presence of this scene on the pipa is uncertain; it may be an auspicious symbol for marital happiness or simply a decorative motif with no specific significance.

20 *Qingshou* is the opening play in the most widely published eighteenth-century collection of opera excerpts. See *Zhui baiqiu* [A Patched Cloak of White Fur], ed. Wang Xieru (Beijing: Zhonghua shuju, 1955), vol. 1, pp. 1–5. For late Qing imperial scripts and costumes for such plays, see *Junyue tianting: Gugong zhencang xiqu wenwu* [The Dragon's Stage: Chinese Opera Artifacts from the Palace Museum], ed. Chen Haoxing (Macau: Museu de Arte de Macau, 2008), vol. 2, pp. 186–207.

21 Like Kangxi, Qianlong had the two-scroll painting of his birthday procession printed as a woodblock album and included a 120-chapter commemorative edition of the event, which was titled *Magnificent Record of the Emperor's Eightieth Birthday (Baxun Wanshou shengdian),* and published by the palace in 1792. The Regenstein Library's copy of this edition is unfortunately incomplete and includes the printed version of the second scroll of the painting (chapter 78) but not the first (chapter 77). An explanatory text in the book identifies the scene as *The Three Star Deities Presenting Auspicious Gifts Being Performed on a Peach Stage* (*wei taoting nei yan sanxing xianrui ju).* See "Explanations of the Pictures" (*tushuo*), *Baxun wanshou shengdian* [Magnificent Record of the Emperor's Eightieth Birthday], in *Yingyin Wenyuange Siku quanshu* [Facsimile Reprint of the Imperial Four Treasuries Library] (Taipei: Shangwu yishuguan, 1983–1986), vol. 661, chap. 79, p. 250.

22 Ann Rosalind Jones and Peter Stallybrass likewise argue that costumes constituted by far the biggest capital investment for an acting troupe in Renaissance Europe. See their *Renaissance Clothing and the Materials of Memory* (Cambridge, England: Cambridge University Press, 2000), pp. 177–78.

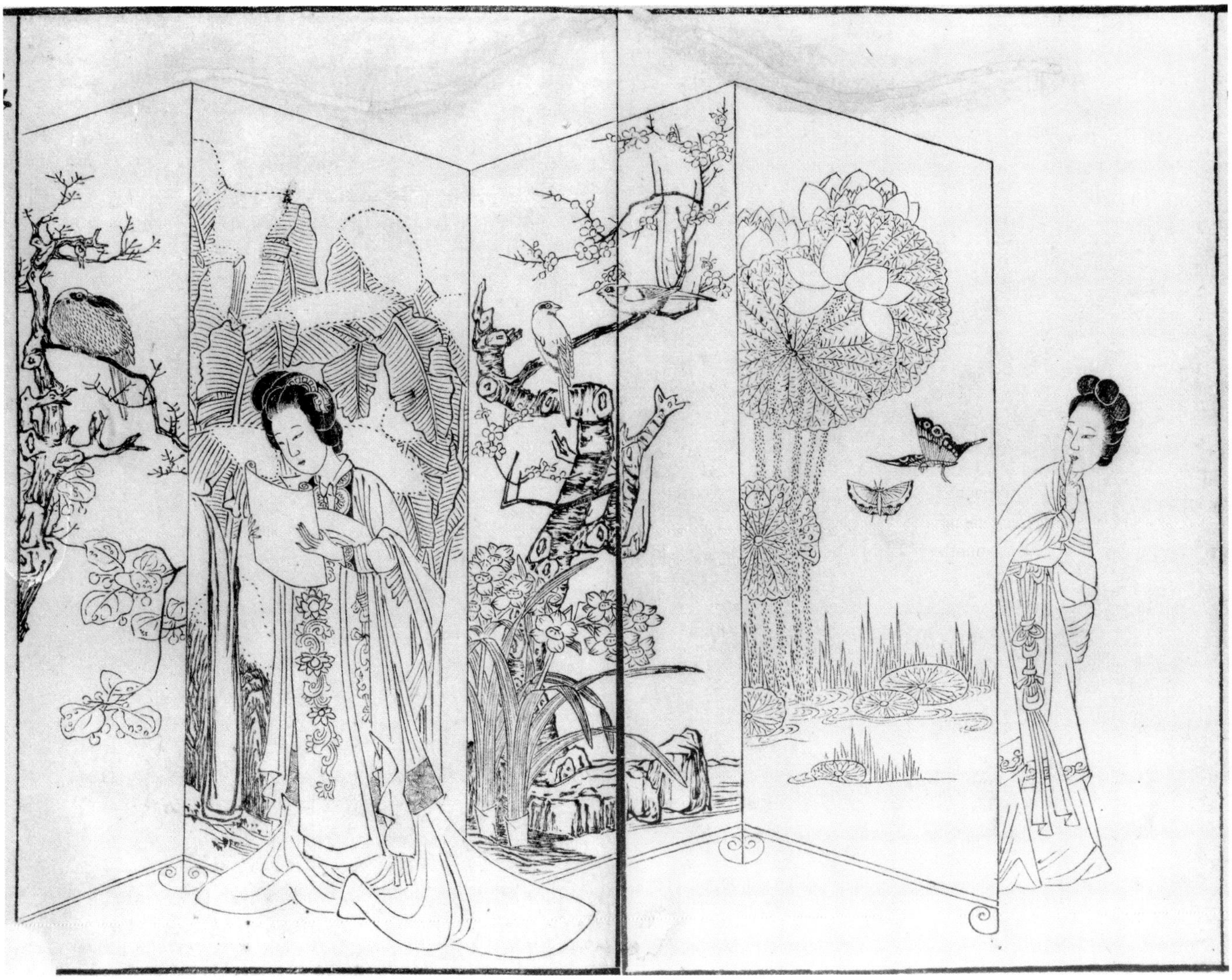

23 "Kong fu xixiang yiwu zongzhang" [A General Inventory of Costumes and Other Articles in the Stage Trunks Belonging to the Kong Clan] in *Kong fu dang'an xuanbian* [Edited Selections from the Kong Clan Archives] (Beijing: Zhonghua shuju, 1982), pp. 643–51.

24 Jonathan Hay, *Sensuous Surfaces: The Decorative Object in Early Modern China* (London: Reaktion Books, 2010), p. 67.

25 Hay, *Sensuous Surfaces,* p. 143.

26 For a translation of the tale, see James R. Hightower, "The Story of Ying-ying," in *The Columbia Anthology of Traditional Chinese Literature,* ed. Victor Mair (New York: Columbia University Press, 1994), pp. 851–61; for the *chantefable,* see Li-li Ch'en, *Master Tung's Western Chamber Romance* (New York: Columbia University Press, 1976); for the play, see Stephen H. West and Wilt L. Idema, *The Story of the Western Wing* (Berkeley, University of California Press, 1995).

27 West and Idema, "Introduction," *The Story of the Western Wing,* p. 3.

28 Zhu Jiajin, "*Wanshou tu* zhong de xiqu bianyan xieshi," p. 489, identifies this scene as a Kun opera. But this assumption is based on his knowledge that "Startled by Beauty" was part of the Kun opera repertory; there is nothing in the visual representation of the scene to indicate a specific performing genre.

29 Craig Clunas, "The West Chamber: A Literary Theme in Chinese Porcelain Decoration." *Transactions of the Oriental Ceramic Society* (1982), p. 79.

30 Meng-ching Ma, "Fragmentation and Framing of the Text: Visuality and Narrativity in the Late-Ming Illustrations to *The Story of the Western Wing*" (PhD diss., Stanford University, 2006).

31 The set opens with a portrait of the play's heroine Oriole to make a total of twenty-one prints. For an analysis of the transposition of media in these prints, see Wu Hung, *The Double Screen: Medium and Representation in Chinese Painting* (London: Reaktion Books, 1996), pp. 243–59; and Jennifer Purtle, "Scopic Frames: Devices for Seeing China c. 1640," *Art History* 33.1 (2010): pp. 54–73.

32 Yuming He, *Home and the World: Editing the "Glorious Ming" in Woodblock-Printed Books of the Sixteenth and Seventeenth Centuries* (Harvard University Asia Center, 2013), pp. 170–87; Li-ling Hsiao, *The Eternal Present of the Past*, pp. 87–174; and Ni Yibin's essay "The Iconic Variations of Two Scenes from *Romance of the Western Chamber*" in this catalogue.

33 Clunas, "The West Chamber," pp. 84–85.

34 Wu Youru, *Haishang baiyan tu* (The Pictures of One Hundred Shanghai Beauties), in *Wu Youru huabao: Shanghai Biyuan zhen cang* [A Treasury of Wu Youru's Drawing from the Shanghai Biyuan Collection (Shanghai: s.n., 1909?), vol. 7–8. The series was originally published in the column "Huzhuang Shinü" (Ladies in Shanghai Style) in *Feiyingge huabao* (Feiyingge Pictorial), 1890–93.

JONATHAN HAY

One

World-Making in Performance and Painting: An Intertwined History

In any figurative art, the making of a world requires the artist to generate not only an experience of space and time, but also a sense of place. Only place, through its necessary specificity, can convert generic illusionism into the illusion of a lived world.[1] In Chinese urban theater or opera, as it has come down to us today and as we know its history from primary sources (both textual and visual), it is possible to discern a single enduring template for world-making.[2] Through a combination of musically accompanied singing, dialogue, gesture, and acrobatics, costumed actors (male or female) delineate their characters in accordance with a limited number of role-types; the characters are the vehicle of a story, which develops within the constraints of a modular structure of acts or episodes. The full template has generated countless cultural and regional variations, of which a remarkable number can still be seen today. It has also given rise to shorthand forms that eschew costumes, musical accompaniment, and complex gestural movement, including, of course, acrobatics. The urban theatrical template crystallized in embryonic form under the Northern Song dynasty (960–1127) out of a diverse field of existing performance practices, some of which were of ancient vintage.[3]

The Terms of World-Making in Urban Theater

The earliest urban theater (*zaju*) took the form of single-act plays presented as the main attraction within a larger composite genre of performance, in groups of two or three.[4] Only one character in each play had a singing role (fig. 1.1). After the conquest of north China by Jurchen invaders in 1127, in both the Jurchen Jin–ruled north and the still Song-controlled South, groupings of single-act plays were gradually displaced by single four-act plays with one overarching narrative.[5] In North China only one character in each act was allowed to sing, while in the South the singing in each act came to be shared by two or more characters (fig. 1.2), a tradition

1.1

Chinese, Northern Song Dynasty (960–1127)

The Actress Ding Dusai, first quarter of the 12th century

Carved brick from a tomb, 11 13/16 x 2 21/32 in. (28.4 x 9.3 cm)

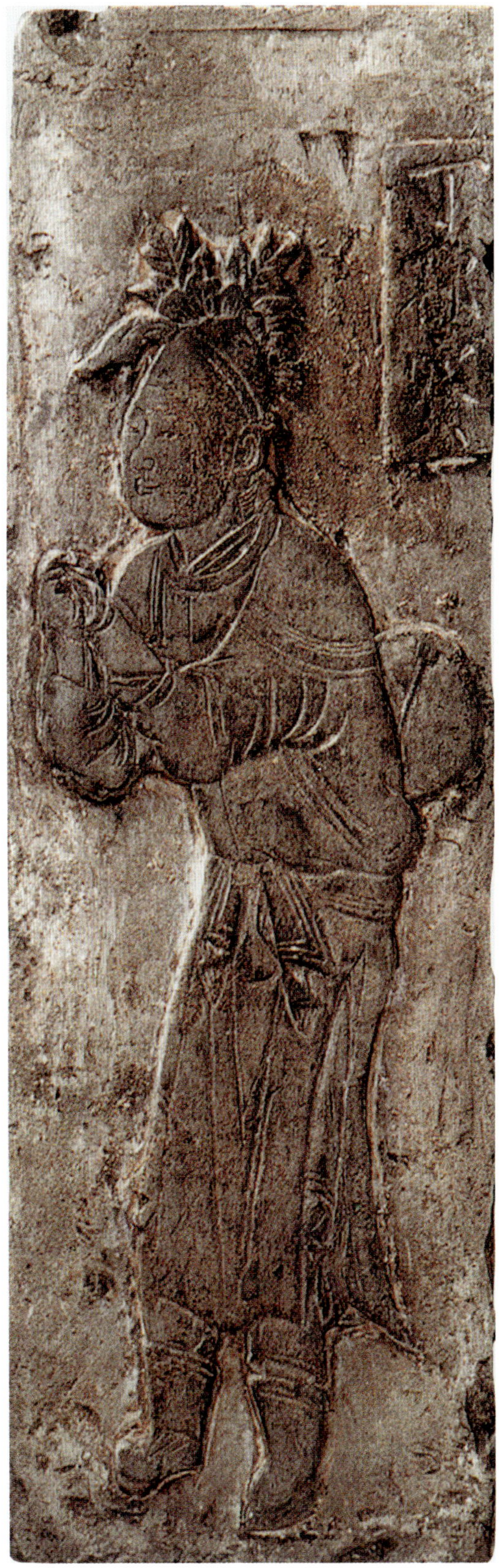

often distinguished by the name *nanxi*. The more complex southern approach was subsequently to become standard practice for all theatrical genres, even (during the Ming) northern-type zaju. A first transformation of the landscape of Chinese theater occurred in the mid-fourteenth century. On the one hand, the southern nanxi tradition vastly expanded the number of acts in a single play to several tens, giving rise to the new chuanqi genre. On the other, the equally flourishing four-act zaju on the northern model became popular in the South as well. The next big shift came in the course of the sixteenth century, when modes of meta-theater developed among Ming literati, the modes variously referring themselves to zaju, chuanqi, or a combination of the two. As discussed in more detail below, "literati theater," by analogy to literati painting, used an engagement with literary language and/or musical performance to distance itself from earlier theatrical engagement with storytelling and spectacle. On the side of musical performance, the most prestigious and enduring approach proved to be a system of tunes with distinctive instrumentation, pronunciation, and singing style involving a great deal of ornamentation known as *kunqu*. Under the Qing dynasty (1644–1911), kunqu eventually evolved into a theater genre of its own, still performed today. Through that kunqu genre, the influence of literati theater came to be reciprocally felt on the mainstream tradition of theater as storytelling and spectacle as it evolved under the Qing dynasty into the local opera (*huabu*, *bangzi*) and Peking opera genres.

Although ambitious world-making in theater soon came to be identified with the coherence of a single narrative in a multi-act play, its Northern Song roots lay in a shared horizon of human action that cut across the different narratives of separate one-act plays. This horizon, established through continuities of role-type, gesture, and scene-creating conventions and props, was the precondition, and was ultimately independent, of the narrative coherence that developed later.[6] It also underpinned the still later literati theater practice of presenting programs composed of highlights from different plays.

Urban theater since the Northern Song period also consistently respected three structural principles of world-making, principles that have less to do with style than with technical and conceptual craft.[7] This craft allows the actor to generate a world of space, time,

1.2
Chinese, Southern Song Dynasty (1127–1279)
Scene from a Zaju *Performance*, from a tomb dated 1204
Stone relief
Huangze Temple, Guangyuan county, Sichuan province

1.3
Chinese, Jin Dynasty (1115–1234)
Scene from a Zaju *Performance*, from a tomb dated 1135
Wall painting
Tomb, Tunliu county, Shanxi province

and place—a two-way portal between elsewhere at another time and the here and now of the audience.[8] The first principle is a commitment, shared with its village counterpart (discussed by David Johnson in his essay in this volume), to generating stage space outward from the performer's body rather than inward from a stage set.[9] The second principle complements the first: the actors establish an implied boundary that separates the observed world from the here and now of the living observer. As Wu Hung has noted for an analogous phenomenon in pictorial art, this separating boundary can be created in two very different ways, depending on whether the viewer is witness to a self-contained narrative (fig. 1.3), or confronts an icon that acknowledges the viewer's presence (fig. 1.4).[10] Just as complex pictorial artworks often combine narrative and iconic modes, the theater actor continually oscillates between the two. The iconic mode is most visible in asides to the audience and in the practice of striking and holding a pose (*liangxiang*). The degree to which the separating boundary is fixed or soluble, however, has varied historically.[11] The third principle operates on a compositional level, linking individual acts (and in the Northern Song period the separate single-act plays) in modular chain-like structures that repeatedly dissolve and reconstitute a sense of place (the *fenchang* or *huanchang* system), while simultaneously implying the cognitive continuity of a larger world in terms of a shared horizon of human action.

From a world-making viewpoint, because stage space is generated outward from the actor's body the fundamental stage element in urban theater has never been the stage itself. The function of a stage instead lies principally in its elevation, which makes the performance visible to a larger audience.[12] In China's recent theatrical history the basic stage element has been a mat or rug laid on the stage and located centrally on the vector joining the actor to the part of the audience directly in front of the stage; the orientation and symmetrical placement of theatrical furniture and actors reinforces this vector. Before the twentieth century, much of the audience saw the performance from the sides, but pictorial representations show that the same frontal orientation organized the actor's visual address to the audience, which was largely determined by ideal rather than actual spectatorship.[13] The history of onstage mats and rugs, though, is not well understood. Were they

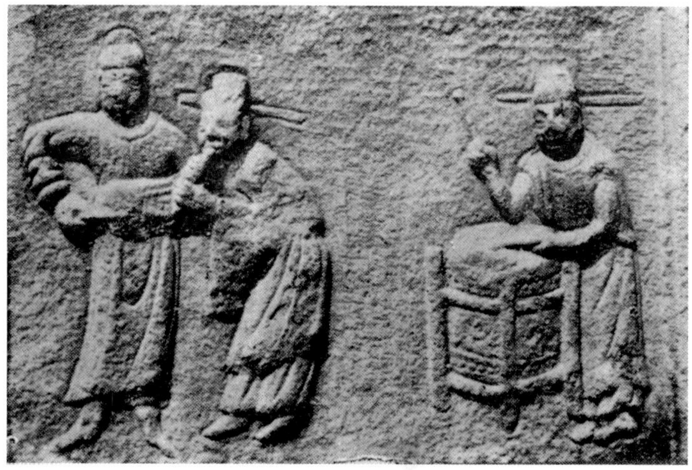

used from the beginning, or did the onstage floor covering replace a demarcated space that had previously been marked out on the stage surface in some other way?[14] It is known that around 1200 low-level theatrical performers sometimes traced out a performance space (*chang*) in the streets of Hangzhou, but we do not know if this was a substitution for a mat or rug, or represented a practice that these floor coverings later replaced.[15] It is certain, on the other hand, that by the late sixteenth century, if not sooner, it was common to center the performance on a mat or rug[16] for salon-style performances without an elevated stage in the intimate setting of a room in a private residence (an established practice since the Northern Song). Not certain, meanwhile, but probable, is that the organization of urban theatrical performance, with or without a stage, always took place in relation to a rectangular performance zone. Judging from theater practice today, this demarcated zone did not establish a space within which the actor moved; modern actors constantly cross the edges of the mat/rug. Most likely, the zone's main world-making function at the time was a formal one: to establish an implied center and central axis, and create a flexible implication of spatial recession.[17] The actors exploited these formal conventions to establish a sense of fictional place. In the marriage of mat/rug and actor in recent centuries, the former signifies the potential for a world to come into being; the actualization of a world depends on the actor's ability to generate space, time, and place with his or her body and on the audience's knowledge of the associated performance conventions. Some such system must have

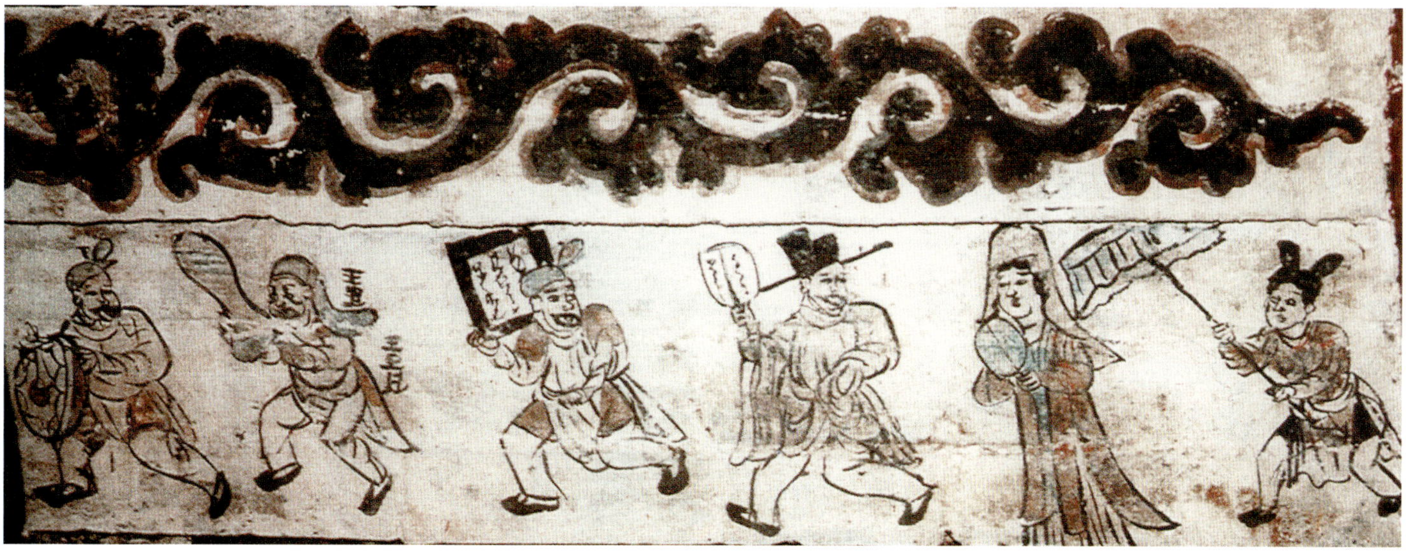

existed as early as the Northern Song as well; the fixed architectural stages that were introduced at that time have a rectangular floor plan that implies the existence of a small rectangular zone of world-making potential within the stage perimeter.[18]

Discontinuous Versus Continuous Performance

Although urban theater's terms of performance depend on spatial centering, this principle did not dominate all theater in Chinese history. Going back to a much earlier period, two performance genres of the Han dynasty (226 BCE–220 CE) evince a different principle. One is the heterogeneous entertainment genre of the "hundred performances," which met the leisure demands of an elite audience.[19] Han pictorial evidence from mortuary art suggests that the boundaries of this genre's performance space were probably quite elastic (fig. 1.5).[20] Artists often depict several kinds of performance going on simultaneously, and the performers are shown very close to, almost mingling with, their audience. Mats or rugs are rarely present, and when we do see them they concern only one performance among others. This disorderly "discontinuity," contrasting with the supremely orderly presentations of official ritual performance, seems to have been tied to a goal of constant change intended to induce excitement. In Zhang Heng's (78–139) "Rhapsody on the Western Capital" (*Xijing fu*), one reads that performance space could shrink or expand as necessary, and that performance wagons were used as moveable stages.[21] The long historical afterlife of the "hundred performances" genre saw it move out of wealthy households into increasingly public spaces, and eventually into the entertainment compounds of Northern Song Bianliang (Kaifeng today) where theater performances also took place. A second Han dynasty genre to consider is the popular exorcizing performance found in cities, towns, and villages that fused ritual with entertainment.[22] Such performances have persisted in Chinese social life (fig. 1.6). Even today, exorcizing performances can still be seen, especially in

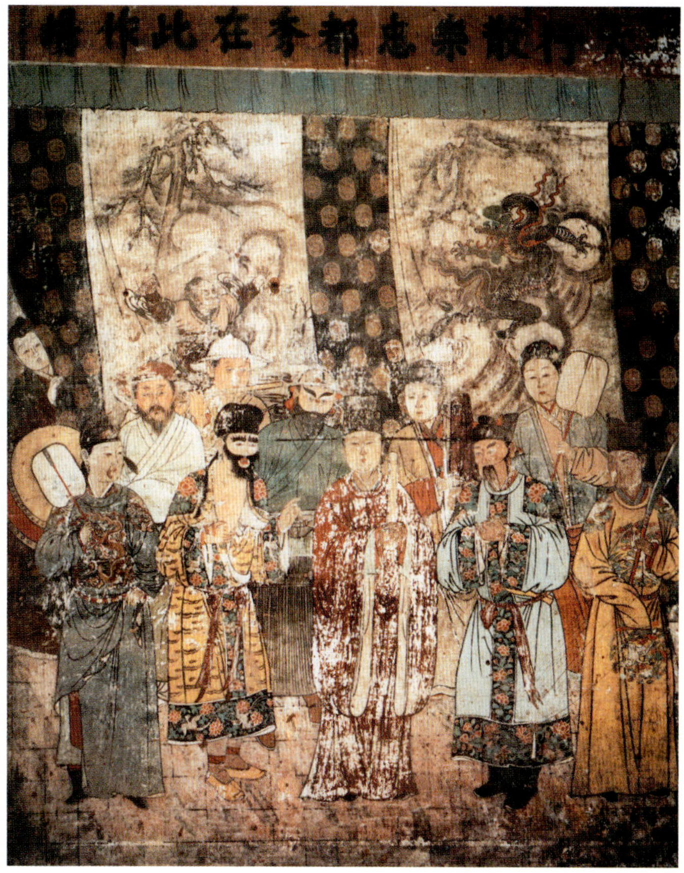

1.4
Chinese, Yuan Dynasty (1279–1368)
The Taihang Actress Zhongduxiu Standing Onstage, Costumed as an Official and Holding a Tablet of Office, Surrounded by Her Zaju *Troupe of Players and Musicians*, 1324
Wall painting, 153 7/16 × 122 13/16 in. (390 × 312 cm)
Prince Mingying's Hall, Guangsheng Temple, Hongdong county, Shanxi province

1.5
Chinese, Eastern Han Dynasty (25–220 CE)
A Baixi Performance in a Residence, n.d.
Molded brick from a tomb at Yangzishan, Chengdu, Sichuan province, 15 3/4 × 18 15/16 in. (40 × 48 cm)
Sichuan Museum

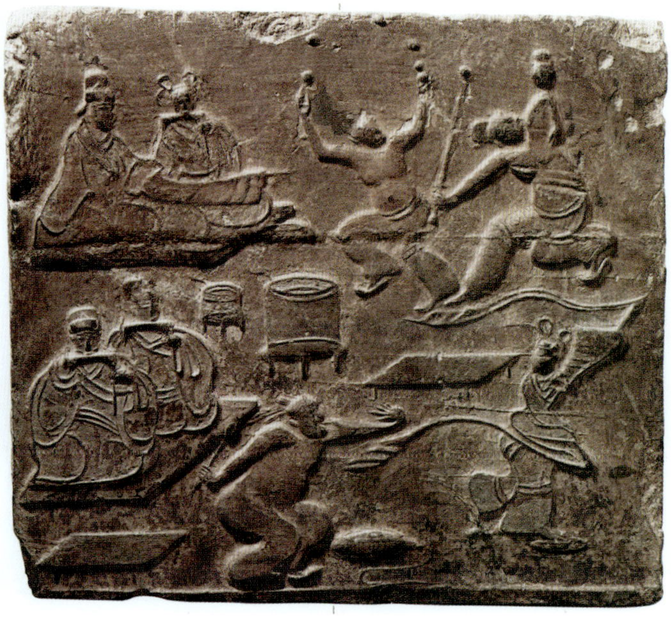

1.6
Chinese, Southern Song Dynasty (1127–1279)
Exorcizing Performance (Danuo tu), n.d.
Hanging scroll, ink and color on silk, 30 7/16 × 22 15/16 in. (67.4 × 59.2 cm)
Palace Museum, Beijing

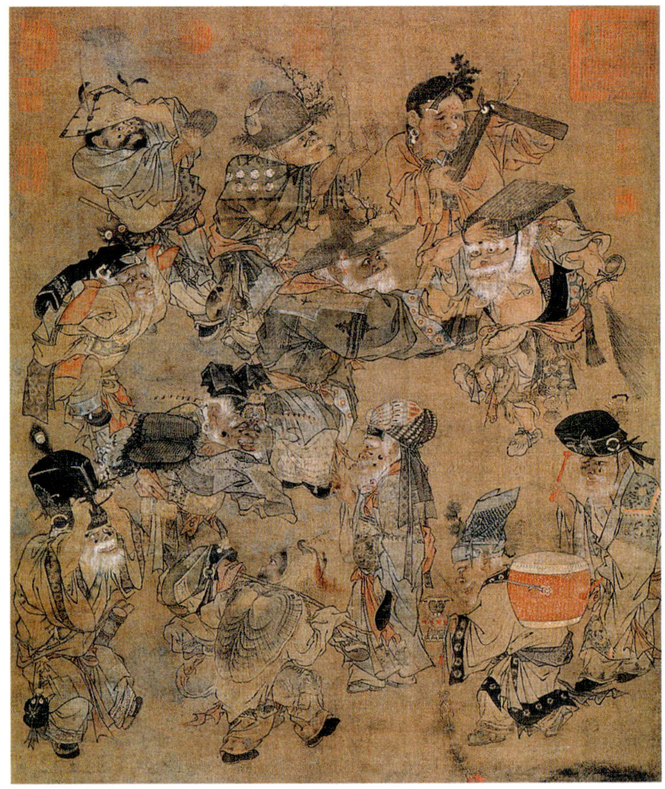

remote villages of south and south-central China, attracting a great deal of scholarly attention from drama theorists, theater historians, historians of religion, and anthropologists.[23] These scholars note the elasticity of the performance space, which extends out into the crowd. They also stress the extremely active participation of the audience, which at times renders the boundary between the world of the performance and the world of the audience completely porous, and also the discontinuity of performance genres, joined together in a serial structure whose units are of notably different sizes and durations. Exorcizing performances and related ritual theater, especially important during the New Year festival, were a basic feature of the Northern Song social world from which urban theater emerged.

Since the conventions of both the "hundred performances" and popular exorcizing performances privileged radical mutations of space and time conjured up by the performers, we can deduce that both genres are based on the same world-making principle of a nomadic or journeying body. The mutations demanded a compensating, highly active participation of the spectator's imagination, which took on its own nomadic, journeying character in order to ensure representational sense. Actor and spectator were thus to a much greater degree than in most theater (with the exception of village theater and late Ming literati theater, as discussed below) explicitly complicit *co*-creators of the performance's world. This co-creative dimension in turn gave performance a radically enactive character.

In contrast to the implicit continuity of a larger world that is characteristic of urban theater where the performer's body is centered within the performance space, the disjunctively mutational character of world-making in these ancient performance genres embraces discontinuity.[24] We are dealing with contrasting systems of continuous and discontinuous performance, which rarely interact except on village theater stages.[25] The question for us is not why Northern Song urban theater rejected the latter system in favor of the former, but rather, how it was able to do so. Here, one may speculate that the centered approach had ancient roots in court ritual, and was transferred over time into aristocratic entertainments that combined music, dance, and storytelling.[26] Tang dynasty (618–907) and later depictions of such entertainments show the dancers performing on circular mats. But those entertainment genres, which continued into the Song for a broader elite audience, lacked the means to articulate fully a shared horizon of human action.[27] It took until the Northern Song for the centered approach to evolve into

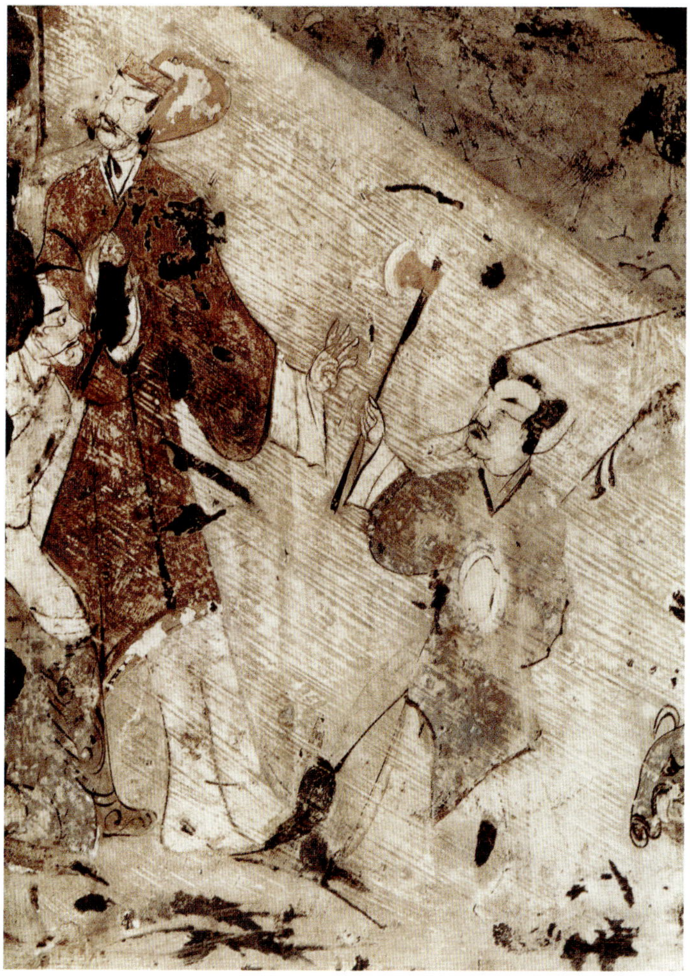

1.7
Chinese, Western Han Dynasty (202 BCE–9 CE)
Detail of Pediment with Scene of Passing the Axe, late 1st century BCE
Detail of right pediment from a multiple tile lintel and pediment from a tomb at Balitai in Luoyang, Henan province, hollow gray earthenware with colored pigment decoration, overall lintel dimensions: 28 7/8 × 94 3/4 in. (73.8 × 240.7 cm)
Museum of Fine Arts, Boston, Denman Waldo Ross Collection 25.10, 25.11, 25.12, 25.13, Gift of C. T. Loo. 25.190

a system of continuous performance (the urban theater) on the basis of that shared horizon, thereby developing its own separate capacity for world-making. To be sure, urban theater first declared itself within the immediate context of Northern Song programs of discontinuous performance adapted to commercial performance spaces in Bianliang (Kaifeng). In fact, it took its own initial name, *zaju* (variety play), from that context of discontinuity. Not surprisingly, therefore, urban theater borrowed many elements from older forms of discontinuous performance, including the actor's bodily generation of space, time, and place; paratactic composition; active co-creation by actor and audience; and a boundary porous enough to allow actors to address the audience directly. What makes urban theater distinctive, however, is that its conventions seem to have enforced a special and enduring contract between actor and audience.

This contract involves the alignment of the actor's body with a stable center and a recessional axis; a stable boundary; and the use of conventions to enforce cognitive coherence and leave the imagination of the spectator free to journey in interpretation. With the introduction of multi-act plays in the thirteenth century, the contract was expanded to include set pacing establishing a narrative continuum, but when compilations of excerpts became an alternative to single multi-act plays in late Ming literati theater, actors and spectators alike could still fall back on the earlier narrower contract. Whether in narrow or expanded form, the contract created a sense that a continuous onstage world existed beyond the fenchang discontinuities between scenes. It thus harmonized the onstage world with the here and now of the audience. As we shall now see, the origins of this contract lie outside the performance tradition, in secular painting.

From Performative Picturing to Pictorialized Performance

Painting and performance had a long history of interaction. Returning first briefly to the Han dynasty, in the first century BCE a new horizon of painting emerged that was associated with a double-sided innovation by painter-decorators. One of its crucial features was the pictorial creation of a psycho-physical field activated by the positioning, postures, and gestures of the representation's protagonists (fig. 1.7). But no less crucial was a new exploitation of the possibilities of material presence of the picture surface in the same paintings; these possibilities were caught up with the physicality of bodily gestures informing the traces of the brush. The two aspects were related, since the energy of the gestural brush traces resonated with the movement of the represented protagonists. This distinctive approach contrasts dramatically with that of earlier painted representations, which followed the structural logic of a graphemic mode of depiction whose origins lay in the use of picturing within a context of writing.[28] The radical innovations of the first century BCE by contrast pushed representation dramatically away from semiotic legibility toward the visceral enactment of an effect of presence, enlisting the beholder as active co-creator of a world. Moreover, this world accommodated radical disjunctions of place, which are fully exploited in the pictorial programs of tombs in the first and second centuries CE, where painting was often translated into stone engraving or molded bricks.

The new direction taken by painter-decorators was inseparable from the emergence of a heterogeneous urban elite during the Han period and from the existence of discontinuous performance as a point of reference. In earlier centuries, when painting was still predominantly under court and aristocratic patronage, discontinuous performance lay below the threshold of artistic awareness;

1.8
Chinese, Northern Song Dynasty (960–1126)
Tomb Interior with Wall Paintings Depicting a Kitchen Scene and Banquet, 1126
Northwest and north walls respectively, kitchen scene: 40 9/16 × 38 3/16 in. (103 × 97 cm), banquet scene: 41 5/16 × 37 in. (105 × 94 cm)
Li Village Tomb No. 1, Xin'an county, Henan province

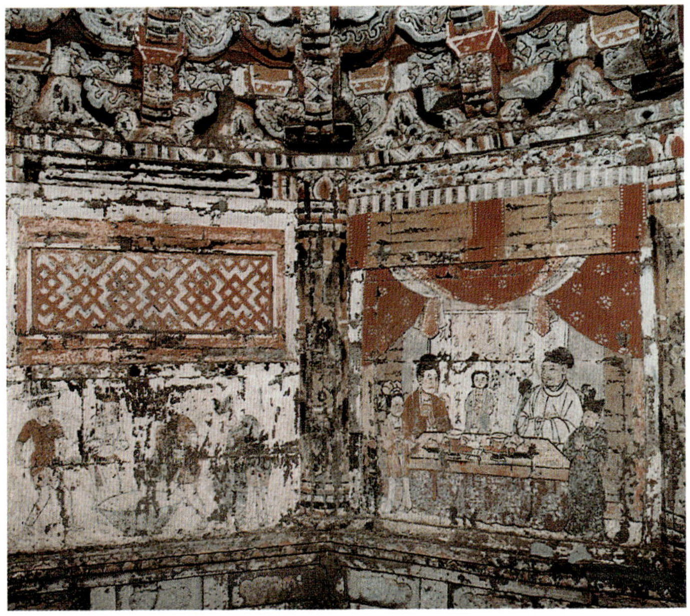

its absence of decorum may even have made it an anti-model for pictorial practice. Conversely, Han urban patronage, by calling on painter-decorators to evoke the psychophysical dimension of experience, made discontinuous performance visible and relevant as a model. Among the aspects of such performances to which Zhang Heng responded most strongly was his own visceral engagement with what he claimed to have seen: "After all this fun and excitement is over one feels spent and a little melancholy as well."[29] In painting, we see a similar attempt to engage the beholder's body and psyche by depicting human beings in lively action and interaction. Fundamental to this possibility was the way in which the depicted figure generated space around itself.[30] The painter-decorators of the first century BCE showed that the gestures of a human figure, if given a sufficiently dynamic quality in form and execution, would generate a larger space around the figure than previously possible and would also intensify the figure's temporal immediacy. In much the same way, they transformed the relations between figures. Earlier pictorial art had brought the self-generated spatial envelopes of individual motifs into relations that create larger, aggregative spaces. But in the first century BCE, with the added resources of gestural language and execution, painters were able to connect figures in a newly dynamic manner that paralleled the arts of performance. In my view, it is not plausible to attribute the invention of a dynamic gestural language wholly to painters when a similar language had long existed in discontinuous performance. Some pictorial themes of the time correspond to themes of discontinuous performance, and artists often depicted performances, and those facts together may be taken as partial confirmation of the primacy of performance.[31]

The later emergence of painting as its own tradition in the third or fourth century CE coincided with the new importance of Buddhism, which helped spur imaginary world-making in art as in performance.[32] Buddhas, pantheons, paradises, and stories all had to be visualized for a broad audience. The emergence of a tradition of painting, both religious and secular, under these conditions led to more complex and sophisticated pictorial world-making, in which the human figure remained the central element. The new reference points of rhetoric (in poetry, literature, and history writing) and metaphysics (in religious teaching) provided models for systematizing relational shifts of place.[33] Narrative world-making in painting, however, remained explicitly discontinuous, and appealed to an (imaginatively) journeying body.[34] Although the human figure was more than ever the painter's main subject, the original importance of performance practice for pictorial structure gradually became less visible, concealed under layers of translation into specific iconographic systems.[35] Reinforcing this cultural amnesia, in Tang religious icons the performer became present in a different way as a privileged reference point for the painter's execution of the image. Indeed, the common representation of performers during the Tang period can be understood as thematizing pictorially their new role as model for the artist's own performative approach to execution. Wu Daozi (about 710–760), for example, like the calligrapher Zhang Xu (active eighth century) and the poet Du Fu (712–770), is recorded to have taken inspiration from a sword dance.[36]

The amnesia with regard to performance's early world-making impact on pictorial art intensified after the mid-eighth century. As the art-commissioning elite diversified in the wake of a larger transformation of Chinese society, pictorial genres multiplied, and by the tenth century, landscape had displaced figure painting in importance. The creation of a space-time continuum in landscape painting in the course of the tenth century made it the most capacious of all genres, providing the cognitive ground against which

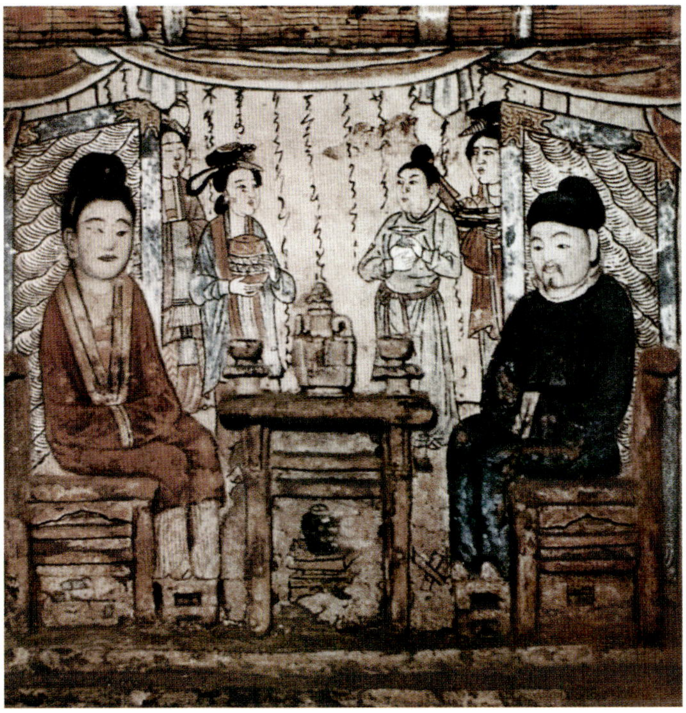

1.9
Chinese, Northern Song Dynasty (960–1127)
Couple Awaiting a Banquet, n.d.
West wall painting and painted relief, 35 7/16 × 53 3/16 in. (90 × 135 cm)
Baishazhen Tomb No. 1, Yuzhou, Henan province

other genres registered—sometimes literally so, as when figures were shown in a landscape setting. The continuum of landscape painting was partly preconditioned by the translation of the world-making systems of earlier figure painting into landscape terms.[37] Painters had always conceived landscape elements on the model of human figures, that is, as elements that could dynamically produce a larger, active envelope of space around them, and that made the translation possible. In this way, tenth-century artists imported into landscape painting the fundamental principles of world-making that had first been borrowed from the art of the performer so many centuries before.[38] However, this debt should not be allowed to obscure the fact that the creation of a continuum was a specifically pictorial contribution, tied to the possibilities of representational continuity offered by the landscape genre at this point in its development.

But if secular landscape defined a cognitive horizon of continuity for Northern Song art, that horizon affected theater only indirectly. The painters most likely to have been influential on eleventh-century theater are the artists who belonged to the same social world as actors, that is, the painters organized in workshops who were responsible for the ritual decoration of above-ground temples and below-ground tombs. These artists were above all figure painters. The paintings they produced under the Northern Song fused cognitive continuity (a shared horizon of human action) with compositional disjunction in ways that provide a direct model for urban theater (fig. 1.8).[39] Moreover, painting of this type provided models for other aspects of urban theater as well. The alignment of the actor's body with a stable center and a (usually closed off) recessional axis has its counterpart in ritual figure painting. The stable boundary between stage space and audience space, though undoubtedly encouraged by the introduction of architecturally fixed stages that projected into a closed rectangular audience space,[40] conceptually derived from the painter's paradigmatic identification of picture surface with screen. An innovation of elite painters of the tenth century, this equation of picture surface and screen was taken up by journeyman figure painters by the eleventh century at the latest (fig. 1.9).[41] The theater thus came into being under the Northern Song as a pictorialized version of performance, and it subsequently became even more pictorial once multi-act plays integrated narrative continuity as well.[42] Although the set pacing that established a visual continuum corresponding to narrative continuity undoubtedly derived partly from song-suite performance combining song, dance, and music, it owed just as great a debt to the landscape painter's pacing of the journeying imagination by means of paths and the placement of figures.[43] Painting's many-sided influence on urban theater could not but render the amnesia regarding painting's own earlier structural debt to performance arts even more complete.

Theater itself having been made pictorial, it is no wonder that that performance arts have regularly found their way back into painting, illustration, and pictorial decoration all the way down to the present. As this exhibition demonstrates, an entire pictorial universe developed through more or less faithful borrowings of themes, iconographies, role-types, and gestural language from the theater. It would not be difficult, moreover, to show that figural representation from the Northern Song on was often marked by theatrical conventions, even when the theme was not explicitly theatrical.[44]

Literati Painting, Literati Theater

Urban theater's deference to the model of painting was later to repeat itself, albeit very differently, in late Ming literati theater. While literati had long been active in the theater as playwrights, it was not until the late Ming dynasty (1368–1644) that literati values extended to the entirety of a theatrical experience. Late Ming and later literati commissioned, directed, or personally engaged in performances of chuanqi in the kunqu musical style. These performances depended on a core tradition of theater from whose

1.10
Collaborative Work.
Side A, right to left: Tan Fuying (Chinese, 1906–1977), Mei Lanfang (Chinese, 1894–1961), Zhou Xinfang (Chinese, 1895–1975), Cheng Yanqiu (Chinese, 1904–1958).
Side B, right to left: Yang Baosen (Chinese, 1910–1958), Shang Xiaoyun (Chinese, 1900–1976), Ma Lianliang (Chinese, 1901–1966), Xun Huisheng (Chinese, 1900–1968)
Fan with Painting and Calligraphy by Eight Famous Peking Opera Actors, n.d.
Ink and colors on paper, 7 15/16 × 20 7/16 in. (19 × 52 cm)

more popular manifestations they nonetheless deliberately distinguished themselves. In this regard, literati theater recalls and was surely inspired by literati painting, which had crystallized as a separate artistic tradition early in the fourteenth century.[45] In painting proper, the image is identified with the entire space of the painting; the painting is equal to its image field or imagescape. In literati painting, by contrast, the painted image is the center of a more complex artistic space involving writing and text as well, which is more inscriptional signscape than imagescape.[46] For its coherence, literati painting depends on the calligraphic brush trace, which mediates between text and image, between poetry and painting, bringing the different constituent practices of an inscriptional signscape into a stable overall relationship. In literati theater performance, the analogous mediating role was played by a sonic trace fusing language, pronunciation, and melody.[47] This sonic trace, tightly keyed to physical gesture, mediated between visual presence and narrative poetry.[48] But chuanqi were intended as much for literary circulation and publication as for performance. When they were read, it was instead the dramatic plays of linguistic register and imagery across sung poetry and spoken dialogue that mediated among performance, music, and text; one can perhaps speak here of a mediating semantic trace. Whether performed or read, literati theater opened up a space of operation across the media of theater, music, and text that was no less hybrid and contingent than the space that literati painting had opened up across painting, calligraphy, and text.[49]

Moreover, literati theater paralleled literati painting in its use of "deconstructive" practices, such as presenting a program of selected excerpts, usually chosen from a menu by the patron of the performance.[50] This common approach emerged around the same time as the small-album format in painting, which allowed literati artists to contrast styles and themes from one leaf to the next. This rediscovery of the artistic possibilities of disjunction built into both the theatrical program and the painting album a space of critical reflection appropriate to a literati meta-practice. Along different lines, a scholar of Ming theater, Sophie Volpp, has argued that the spectators of literati theater were imaginatively and often physically mobile. In this way the performance practices of seventeenth-century literati theater deconstructed the ontological boundary separating an imagined world from the lived world of the audience—a boundary inherited from the Northern Song that elsewhere in urban theater of the time was clearly understood, and that gradually hardened again.[51] Contemporary literati artists engaged in a similar deconstruction of pictorial boundary, sometimes in the name of a return to pre-Song dynasty pictorial practice, and sometimes to advance a claim for the ontological reality of what could only be imagined. All such theatrical and pictorial deconstructions of boundary belong to the same world of the late Ming elite. Their resonances with discontinuous performance and its pictorial analogues may be considered part of the larger late Ming rediscovery, sometimes across survivals of pre-Song practices in popular culture, of earlier possibilities that a normative Song tradition had closed off.[52]

Finally, reinforcing the parallel with literati painting, although the actor in literati theater certainly respected the inherited theatrical conventions of semiotic reference, his or her principal concern was to enact a metaphor-rich world of affect, feeling, and values in a manner that came closer to poetic declamation or musical performance than it did to the spectacle and rough populism of mainstream theater. The fact that shorthand versions of literati theater could also be performed out of costume in the practice known as *qingchang* (pure singing of arias), both by literati and by professional actors at a patron's request, brought theater even closer to the self-cultivating practice of the literati artist. The practice of "pure singing" later became part of the world of Peking opera as well in the nineteenth and twentieth centuries—an example of kunqu's reciprocal influence on mainstream forms of theater, which was equally operative in Peking opera's attention to pronunciation and ornamentation. Peking opera's own kunqu-mediated convergence with literati painting found its ultimate symbol in the twentieth-century practice of painting and calligraphy by celebrated actors (fig. 1.10).

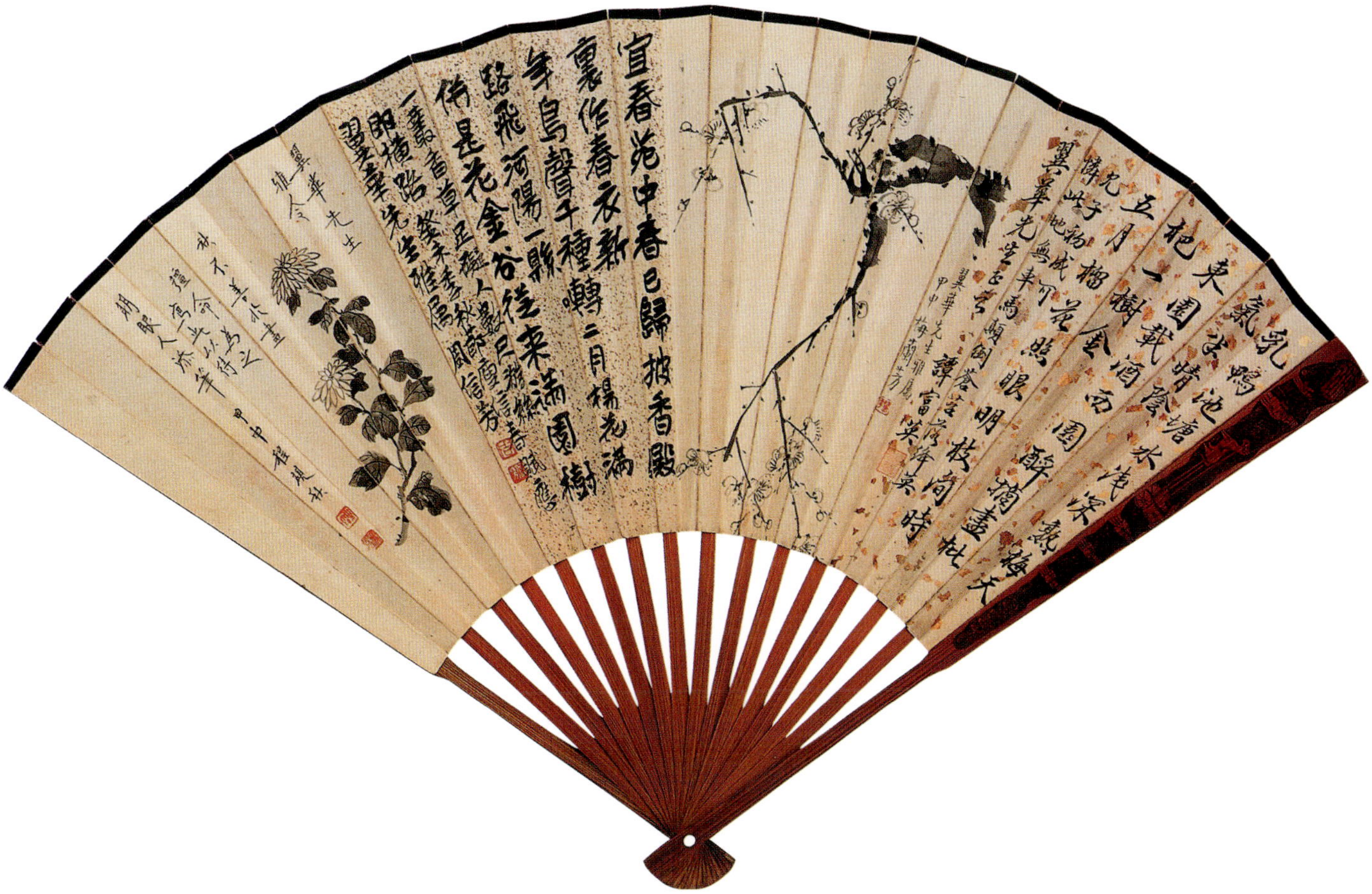

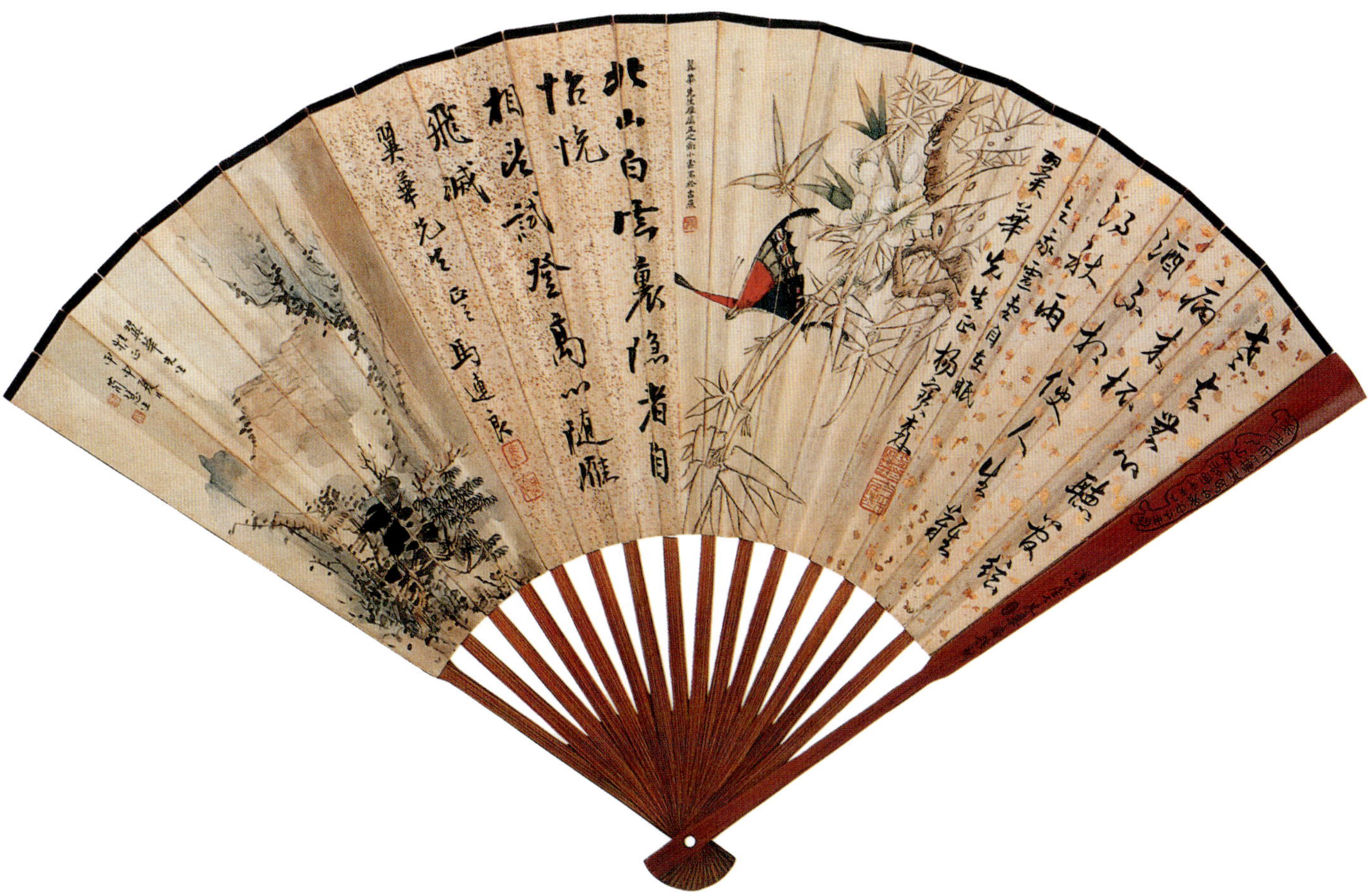

Notes

This essay is dedicated to Bo Songnian.

1 A focus on world-making makes possible a macrohistorical perspective on the dialogue between performance arts and pictorial art in China. In this essay I argue that at the moment of its emergence as a medium of pictorial representation in the first century BCE, painting was molded by the arts of performance. I also argue that more than a thousand years later, in the eleventh century CE, painting conversely impacted urban theater at the moment of the latter's emergence as its own art form. By putting these two widely separated historical moments of encounter together, I want to suggest that pictorial art and performance arts share an interwined history, still ongoing, that lies behind all the objects and images in this exhibition.

2 It is a question here of theater practiced in a context of urban values and not necessarily physically located in a town or city. I use the term "urban theater" in contradistinction to the "village theater" described by David Johnson in his essay for this catalogue. These were not, of course, neatly separated categories.

3 These older practices included performative storytelling, exorcizing performances, enactments of Buddhist stories, poetry, dance, martial arts, and the cultivation of breath and energy through movement. Also, the convention of placing the beginnings of theater in the early twelfth century reflects the fact that the major early source, Meng Yuanlao's *Dongjing meng Hua lu* [Dreaming of Splendors Past: The Eastern Capital], describes the Northern Song capital, Bianliang (Kaifeng), as it was at the end of the dynasty. The theatrical culture described in that text was clearly the fruit of a prior evolution during the eleventh century, for which an increasing body of archaeological evidence from the region around the Northern Song capital exists. See Zhang Guoqiang, "Cong Henan chutu wenwu kan Bei Song zaju de fazhan" [The Development of Northern Song *zaju* in the Light of Artifacts Excavated in Henan province], *Zhoukou shifan xueyuan xuebao*, no. 3 (2006): pp. 147–49.

4 The term *zaju* was variously used to refer to the composite program and to the single-act plays that were part of the program.

5 Under the Jin dynasty (1115–1234) the alternate name of *yuanben* was also used for *zaju*. In the Jin North, the development of the multi-act play came about through the incorporation into theater proper of a *ci*-based genre of storytelling and dance known as *zhugongdiao* ("all-keys-and-modes"), itself invented under the Northern Song. In the Song South, it involved instead the incorporation of the *qu*-based genre of storytelling and dance known as *daqu*. See Liao Ben, "Song Liao Jin daqu tukao" [A Study of the *Daqu* Pictures under the Song, Liao, and Jin Dynasties], *Zhongguo lishi wenwu*, no. 3 (2003): pp. 45–53.

6 In the context of literati theater, Li Yu (1611–1680?) discussed this shared horizon under the name of unity: "When I use the word *unity*, I don't simply mean that one scene follows another or that a single actor plays one character. Rather, I mean that the action of the play should be unified, coherent, and connected as the veins are by the blood that flows through them." Translation from Faye Chunfang Fei, ed. and trans., *Chinese Theories of Theater and Performance from Confucius to the Present* (Ann Arbor: University of Michigan Press, 1999), p. 80. I leave aside here the vexed question of how far the modular structure of Yuan and Ming readable chuanqi playtexts reflected performance practice. While the playtexts may have given greater emphasis to scene divisions, it seems improbable that performance practice could have done without them.

7 Style, as I restrictively use the term, denotes the dimension of form that makes an artwork identifiable (as the work of a culture, a period, a place, an artist, etc.); an artist will often deliberately adopt or invent a style for that purpose. Craft, by contrast, denotes the dimension of the artwork's form that embodies the artist's visual and material thinking; such thinking in and through form has both technical and conceptual aspects, which involve a reflection on the style or styles employed. The conflation of these two dimensions of form and artistic practice in a single concept of style was one of the originary moves of the modern discipline of art history.

8 Since terms have a way of taking on a life of their own, I should distinguish my use of the term "world-making" from Eugene Wang's in *Shaping the Lotus Sutra: Buddhist Visual Culture in Medieval China* (Seattle: University of Washington Press, 2005). For Wang, dealing with visual art alone, the worlds in question are essentially spatial. This allows him to treat visual images and programs as quasi-texts that unlike written and oral texts have a spatial rather than temporal logic but are similarly amenable to tropological exegesis. The importance of giving place and time equal importance along with space in a definition of world-making is that only by doing so can we acknowledge the latter's enactive dimension. For a good discussion of this question in relation to theater, see A Jia's remarks on the *fenchang* system in Fei, *Chinese Theories of Theater*, pp. 148–51.

9 In so doing, urban theater makes a virtue of the representational need to bring individual elements, whether human beings or not, into relation with each other in order to generate scenes of limited spatial extension and temporal duration. Because (in contrast to, say, a Song landscape painting) the relations among elements have precedence over the illusion of a preexisting world into which the elements would fit, the scenes have an explicitly contingent character.

10 Wu Hung, "What is *Bianxiang*?—On the Relationship between Dunhuang Art and Dunhuang Literature," *Harvard Journal of Asiatic Studies* 52/1 (1992): pp. 111–92.

11 "Soluble" is Sophie Volpp's term in *Worldly Stage: Theatricality in Seventeenth-Century China* (Cambridge, Mass.: Harvard University Press), p. 59. In her discussion of "Performance Practice and Stage Architecture," Volpp argues that the boundary was significantly more soluble in early seventeenth-century practice than at the end of the century.

12 On the history of theater stages, see Che Wenming, "Jin Yuan xitai yanjiu huigu" [An Overview of Research into Jin and Yuan Theater Stages], *Xiqu yanjiu*, no. 2 (2002): pp. 113–23.

13 Although there is plenty of evidence that theatrical performance spaces were viewed from different directions (See Volpp, *Worldly Stage*, pp. 71–77, for a discussion in relation to literati theater), I know of no

evidence that actors correspondingly made the visual address of the performance multi-vectorial.

14 Judging by the evidence of pictorial depictions, circular mats or rugs were used for individual dance performances at least as early as the seventh century.

15 As recorded by Zhou Nan (1159–1213), cited in translation (pp. 24–25) by William Dolby, "Early Chinese Plays and Theater," in *Chinese Theater from Its Origins to the Present Day*, edited by Colin Mackerras (Honolulu: University of Hawai'i Press, 1983), pp. 7–31; and in the original (p. 62) by Liu Nianci, "Song zaju Ding Dusai diaozhuan kao" [A Study on the Carved Brick Depicting the Song Actress Ding Dusai], *Wenwu*, no. 2 (1980): pp. 53–62.

16 See Liao Ben, "Tanghui yanju kao" [A Study of Salon-Style Performance], *Minzu yishu*, no. 2 (1997), pp. 105–119; Grant Shen, "Acting in the Private Theater of the Ming Dynasty," *Asian Theater Journal* 15/1 (1998): pp. 64–86; Sophie Volpp, *Worldly Stage*, pp. 63–71. Judith T. Zeitlin also points out (private communication) that rituals, too, as depicted in woodblock illustrations or paintings, were often carried out on rugs.

17 It also has the practical function of providing the actor with a more sympathetic surface on which to operate.

18 The stages were of two types. One was the temple stage, the earliest surviving example of which dates from 1157, but which are known to have been constructed as early as the early eleventh century. See Che Wenming, "Jin Yuan xitai yanjiu huigu"; "Bei Song 'wulou' beike de xin faxian" [A Newly Discovered Northern Song Dynasty "Performance Pavilion" Stele Inscription], *Wenxue yichan*, no. 5 (2011): pp. 144–47. The other was the *goulan* stage found in the *washe* entertainment compounds of Kaifeng and other cities, of which no examples survive. The latter was rectangular with a low railing around three sides, and projected out into a larger rectangular space for spectators. There is an extensive literature on *goulan* and the types of performance associated with them. I have found helpful the following: Huang Dahong, "Goulan: chuantong wenhua yu fojiao wenhua xianghu yingxiang de yige fanli" [*Goulan*: An Example of Mutual Influence between Traditional and Buddhist Culture], *Tang du xuekan*, no. 1, (2002): pp. 5–7; Song Yang, "Goulan de chuancheng yu mishi" [The Development and Decline of *Goulan*], *Zhongguo xiqu xueyuan xuebao*, no. 4 (2011): pp. 106–110; 100; Min Pan, "Bei Song Bianliang zaju chengshi juchang kaobian" [An Investigation into the Theaters of a *Zaju* City—Northern Song Bianliang], *Zhongguo xiqu xueyuan xuebao*, no. 2 (2012): pp. 122–25.

19 Although intended for an elite audience, the "hundred performances" must have been viewed by countless individuals of lower social standing as well: servants, soldiers, slaves, prostitutes, etc.

20 See Liao Ben, "Zhongguo zaoqi yan ju changsuo shulüe" [A Brief Account of the Early History of Theatrical Performance Spaces], *Wenwu*, no. 4 (1990): pp. 61–68; and, at much greater length, Xiao Kangda, *Han dai yuewu baixi yishu yanjiu* [Research on the Art Associated with Han Dynasty Musical and *Baixi* Performance] (revised edition, Beijing: Wenwu chubanshe, 2010). There are a great many depictions of performance in Han mortuary art. While these depictions certainly include visual tropes that can be credited to the rhetoric of representation, there are also the consistent references to performance practice noted here that recur in very different pictorial styles and formats and can thus be taken as evidence for elements of real-life practice.

21 Fei, *Chinese Theories of Theater*, pp. 24–25. As Eugene Wang points out (*Shaping the Lotus Sutra*, p. 191), although an imaginary description of a Western Han event, the text must be based on personal experience of contemporary performances.

22 It should be noted that there is not one audience of living viewers but two, since the performances are equally directed at the gods, which places the performer in a liminal position between this world and the beyond. This idea also survives strongly in village theater on temple stages (see David Johnson's essay in this catalogue), and in some regional traditions of urban theater. For urban theater, this is the case, for example, in Cantonese opera, where a cycle of performances begins with the ritualistic enactment of a pantheon of deities. Once all the deities are finally arrayed on stage facing the living audience, it is no longer clear who is being watched by whom. These enduring acknowledgments of a second, shadow audience in the beyond may help to explain why depictions of theatrical performance were incorporated into tomb decoration just when theater was first institutionalized as secular entertainment in the eleventh to thirteenth centuries. (See Jeehee Hong, "Virtual Theater of the Dead: Actor Figurines and Their Stage in Houma Tomb No. 1, Shanxi Province," *Artibus Asiae* 71/1 [2011]: pp. 75–114). It was in the nature of the actor's art to traverse a boundary between this world and another, be it a fictional world or the beyond. See also Judith T. Zeitlin's discussion of the stage door in *The Phantom Heroine: Ghosts and Gender in Seventeenth-Century Chinese Literature* (Honolulu: University of Hawai'i Press, 2007), chapter 4.

23 In English, see Yu Qiuyu, "Some Observations on the Aesthetics of Primitive Chinese Theater," *Asian Theater Journal* 6, no. 1 (1989): pp. 12–30; Feng Lide and Kevin Stuart, "Delighting the Gods in 1990: A Han Shehuo in Qinghai Province (PRC)," *Asian Theater Journal* 11, no. 1 (Spring 1994): pp. 35–63. Following a Marxist evolutionary paradigm, Chinese scholars have described such performances as "primitive theater," characterizing specific examples as "living fossils." The crudeness of these evolutionary terms inevitably inscribes such performances within a teleological narrative and flattens out the developmental history of the genre.

24 Jing Xinli, "Cong shixue jiaodu kan Song dai minjian biaoyan yishu ji gongting biaoyan yishu de xingshi tezheng" [A Consideration from a Historical Standpoint of the Formal Specificities of Popular and Court Performance Arts under the Song Dynasty], *Yishu baijia*, no. 7 (2006): pp. 97–99; Zou Dailan and Zheng Li, "Song dai baixi de yanchu yu jinhui," [The Performance and Interdiction of *Baixi* under the Song Dynasty], *Dianying pingjia*, no. 9 (2009): pp. 107–08.

25 See David Johnson's essay in this catalogue.

26 For the possibility of a pre-history of centered performance space associated with court ritual performances such as the Nuo exorcist rite under the Han and Eastern Zhou dynasties, see Min Tian, "Chinese Nuo and Japanese Noh: Nuo's Role in the Origination and Formation of Noh," *Comparative Drama* 37/3–4 (2003–04): pp. 343–60.

27 This is presumably one reason why *daqu* and *zhugongdiao* were absorbed into theater.

28 I owe the term "graphemic" to Lothar von Falkenhausen, who has noted connections to the pictographic imagery of Shang and early Zhou clan signs. ("Action and Image," pp. 70–73). In fourth- to second-century BCE paintings, the psychophysical reference is weak; figures, like other motifs, operate as narrative signs. The overall representation is meant to be deciphered or read rather than experienced.

29 See note 21.

30 The classic article on this as a theoretical problem is by Meyer Schapiro: "On Some Problems in the Semiotics of Visual Art: Field and Vehicle in Image-Signs," *Semiotica* 3 (1969): pp. 223–42.

31 The debt of pictorial art to performance may be greater still. In a continuous composition of the earlier graphemic type, a transitional motif such as a tree could, contextually, shift the reference of place. But the painters now made these shifts more dynamic and exciting, echoing the way in which the relational shifts of place in discontinuous performance had to be effected by human bodies alone. Zhang Heng made these shifts the very theme of his account of discontinuous performance. See note 21.

32 It was not until the third–fourth century CE that brush and representational purpose came to be closely associated with demarcated flat surfaces in the institutionalized formats of the handscroll, the screen, and the mural. In a context where artists were discovering the possibilities of subjectivity (as against the social personhood of an earlier period), the new association with a limited range of demarcated flat surfaces fully autonomized painting as a medium and allowed it to have a self-conscious history. Painting became its own tradition.

33 The influence of rhetoric is perhaps most clearly seen in a famous pictorial design of the early sixth century, the Nelson-Atkins Sarcophagus. For an illuminating study that identifies some of the rhetorical devices and interprets them in ontological terms, see Wu Hung, "The Transparent Stone: Inverted Vision and Binary Imagery in Medieval Chinese Art," *Representations* 46 (1994): pp. 58–86. The influence of metaphysics was, of course, everywhere visible in Buddhist pictorial icons.

34 For an attempt to map out some of these discontinuities in Buddhist art, see Wang, *Shaping the Lotus Sutra*. A useful discussion in this context is the section "Mystic Vision," pp. 292–310.

35 Wang (*ibid.*, 190–92) recognizes the connection to discontinuous performance. In line with his spatial interpretation of world-making (see note 8), however, Wang cites Zhang Heng's *Xijing fu* as a preamble to a discussion of landscape representations.

36 "In the Kaiyuan reign the General Pei Min excelled in sword dancing. Daozi watched Min dancing with the sword, and so observed the divine strength of its appearance and disappearance. When the dance was finished his wielding of the brush greatly improved." As recorded by Zhang Yanyuan, *Lidai minghua ji* [Record of Famous Painters of All the Dynasties], Book 9. Translation from Susan Bush and Hsio-yen Shih, *Early Chinese Texts on Painting* (Cambridge, Mass.: Harvard University Press, 1985), pp. 64–65. In a "feedback loop," Tang uses of dancing as a model for other kinds of artistic performance were later thematized in a performance current at the Southern Song court featuring Zhang Xu and Du Fu. See Jing Xinli, "Cong shixue jiaodu kan Song dai minjian biaoyan yishu ji gongting biaoyan yishu de xingshi tezheng."

37 For discussions, see John Hay, "Values and History in Chinese Painting, Part Two—The Hierarchic Evolution of Structure," *RES: Anthropology and Aesthetics* 7–8 (1984): pp. 103–36; Jonathan Hay, "*Interventions*: The Mediating Work of Art," *Art Bulletin* 89/3 (2007): p. 447.

38 The debt was not one that the class-conscious scholars of the late Tang and Northern Song chose to notice. Whereas the origins of pictorial art in writing were never forgotten, nowhere in the abundant art historical literature of the time does one see the importance of performance arts for painting acknowledged except as point of reference for the physical execution of an artwork.

39 There exist vivid demonstrations of the convergence between secular figure painting and theater in the Northern Song period in the form of brick relief depictions of secular figures in tombs, based on painted designs. The decorative programs of the tombs variously juxtapose ordinary people, actors, and scenes from plays, with the only continuity among the component scenes coming from their shared horizon of human action. For the most complete and varied program of this kind known to me, see Luoyang shi wenwu gongzuodui, "Luoyang Luolongqu Guanlinmiao Songdai zhuandiaomu fajue baogao [Report on the Excavation of a (Northern) Song Tomb with Carved Brick Decoration at Guanlin Temple in Luolung District, Luoyang], *Wenwu*, no. 8 (2011): pp. 31–46.

40 See note 18.

41 See Wu Hung, *The Double Screen: Medium and Representation in Chinese Painting* (London: Reaktion, 1996), especially pp. 102–68.

42 The same process of pictorialization can be observed in other areas of Northern Song visual culture. In the decorative arts, not only did pictorial designs derived directly from painting proliferate on object surfaces, but the forms, colors, and textures of objects also took their cue from the contemporary painting of subjects from nature. Even in architecture, which one might have thought impervious to a pictorial reading, a standard discourse analogized bracketing to floral imagery. See Feng Jiren, *Chinese Architecture and Metaphor: Song Culture in the Yingzao fashi Building Manual* (Honolulu: University of Hawai'i Press, 2012).

43 The two main kinds of song-suite performance—*daqu* and *zhugongdiao*—employed arias (*qu*) and short lyrics (*ci*) respectively, with different kinds of musical accompaniment in each case. In both performance genres, the song suite had the potential to convey a single overall story.

44 While the many identified depictions of actual performances and theatrical themes pose few problems, art historians have barely begun to identify all the unspecified theatrical themes in paintings and pictorial decoration, including in seemingly generic figural scenes. In some cases such scenes could refer to more than one play, which may be deliberate. Beyond theatrical themes, although it has long been known that typification and gestural language are fundamental to figure painting in general, the debt of pictorial conventions to the conventions of theater has never been systematically considered.

45 The great theorist of literati theater, Wang Jide (d. 1623) acknowledged the connection indirectly through an analogy between Yuan dynasty plays and literati painting: "The plays by Yuan dramatists contain a

great deal of anachronism. For example, Wang Wei put [the blossoms of] peony, hibiscus, and lotus in the same picture [even though each flower has a different blooming season]; he also sports palm trees in a scenic painting of snow. It is, of course, difficult to reason with a common person about this." Translation modified from Fei, *Chinese Theories of Theater*, p. 65. While it is certainly true that literati playwrights played a crucial role in Yuan dynasty theater, it was not until much later that literati values came to dominate not just the written script (around which Yuan actors engaged in much improvisation) but the performance as a whole. On Ming literati textual revision of Yuan playtexts to suit literati values, see Stephen West, "A Study in Appropriation: Zang Maoxun's Injustice to Dou E," *Journal of the American Oriental Society*, 111/2 (1991): pp. 283–302; and Patricia Sieber, *Theaters of Desire: Authors, Readers, and the Reproduction of Early Chinese Song-Drama, 1300–2000* (New York, Palgrave Macmillan, 2003).

46 From a theoretical standpoint, literati painting may be considered to be a paramedium relative to the medium of painting proper. For the concept of paramedium, see Jonathan Hay, "The Value of Forgery," *RES: Anthropology and Aesthetics* 53–54 (2008): pp. 5–19.

47 See Li-ling Hsiao, *The Eternal Present of the Past: Illustration, Theater, and Reading in the Wanli Period, 1573–1619* (Leiden: Brill, 2007), pp. 60ff.

48 As Jiao Xun (1763–1820) noted, "It is true that *kunqu*'s accents and tunes are delicate, soft, intricate, and harmonious, but the listeners can hardly understand what is being said without the help of a written script." Translation from Fei, *Chinese Theories of Theater*, p. 91.

49 Literati theater was thus another paramedium, relative to the medium of theater proper. See note 46. The difference, of course, is that literati painting was executed by literati, whereas literati theater was mostly performed by non-literati professionals.

50 See Sophie Volpp, *Worldly Stage: Theatricality in Seventeenth-Century China* (Cambridge, Mass.: Harvard University Press, 2011), pp. 66–67; Liao Ben, "Zhezi xi de chuxian" [On the Historical Emergence of Performances of Selected Scenes], *Yishu baijia*, no. 2 (2000): pp. 49–52.

51 See note 11.

52 The emblematic case is Dong Qichang's "invention" of Wang Wei's art as the fountainhead of the literati painting tradition through the reattribution of a relatively recent, archaistic painting to Wang Wei's hand. See Wen Fong, "*Rivers and Mountains after Snow (Chiang-shan hsüeh-chi):* Attributed to Wang Wei (699–759 CE)," *Archives of Asian Art*, 30 (1976–1977): pp. 6–33.

DAVID JOHNSON

Two

Opera Imagery in the Village

Opera imagery could be found everywhere in Chinese villages in late imperial times because opera had become a central part of village life. Well-to-do families hired actors or puppeteers to perform on special occasions in their homes, and everyone watched opera during temple festivals. Even small villages could have several temples, and it was not uncommon in more prosperous areas for a village to have ten or more. Each temple was dedicated to a particular god, though there might be shrines for a number of other deities in it. Gods had birthdays, one of the many ways in which they resembled people, and the birthday of a temple's chief god was the occasion for a great celebration. An elaborate program of rituals was carried out, usually over a three-day period, and operas were performed on a stage in the temple or nearby (or both) in close coordination with the rituals. The temple stage faced the main hall, where the statue of the principal deity or deities stood. The stage and the main hall were almost always on the central axis of the temple, and so the god looked directly at the stage. The operas were performed as offerings to the god, and the god had the best seat in the house. The villagers crowded into the courtyard between the stage and the main hall, or, if the temple did not have a stage, around a temporary stage that was constructed nearby. This was how Chinese villagers experienced opera—as an integral part of their ritual life.

More happened during temple festivals than rituals and operas: there were massive processions and temporary markets that could draw buyers and sellers from many miles away. There also might be supplemental entertainment: puppet operas, martial arts demonstrations, and dances. And families put on feasts for relatives and friends from villages round about. Festivals were the high points in the villagers' year, times of intense excitement and happiness. As the only form of professional entertainment available to villagers, operas would have been memorable whenever they were presented, but their impact was heightened because they were the central public part of a religious holiday. Moreover, the residents of a village could watch operas many times a year, so their influence on them was all the greater. One village may have had several important temples, each with its own festival. In addition, nearby villages also sponsored temple festivals. In the more densely populated regions people could in theory have had a chance to watch opera on average once every week or two, though in fact the festivals were not spread evenly through the year. In any case the cumulative impact of opera on country folk was enormous.

Opera began to be an essential part of the celebration of gods' birthdays in rural north China no later than the eleventh century, so by late imperial times it was deeply embedded in local culture.[1] *Dreaming of Splendors Past: The Eastern Capital* (*Dongjing menghua lu*), the twelfth-century description of the Song dynasty capital, Kaifeng, provides rich evidence on urban theater, and most historians of Chinese drama begin their story there. But the dates of stages in Shanxi province prove that at the very least, rural and urban opera emerged simultaneously. They were, however, fundamentally different, and remained so. Opera in Kaifeng and presumably in other large northern Chinese cities during the Song (960–1279) and Jin (1115–1234) dynasties was performed in theaters that charged admission.[2] The programs were in the nature of all-day variety shows, which included comedies and farces.[3] In the countryside, by contrast, operas were performed in or near temples, because that is where the stages were. It seems unlikely that admission was charged, because all the costs of the festivals at which operas were presented would have been borne by the villagers. We do not know what operas were performed, but since they must have been closely bound up with offering rituals and hence presented in a setting of high seriousness it would be very surprising if they were either farces or love stories. In short, rural opera at this early period was integrated into temple ceremonial, while urban opera was part of entertaining variety shows.

In late imperial times opera performances at rural temple festivals began with an exorcism of the stage, which thus became a sacred area. This was followed by the presentation of mimed ritual skits that were intended to expel evil influences and bring blessings to the village. Most of the full-scale operas had entirely secular subjects, but some were themselves rituals. There were short but intense pieces in which a demon or evil person was beheaded, and multi-day epics such as *Mulian Rescues His Mother* (*Mulian jiumu*) that dramatized the teachings of Buddhism and functioned as communal exorcisms in times of crisis. Shadow puppet opera in north China and string puppets in the southeast were particularly potent weapons against demonic forces. Performers in *Mulian* sometimes took the role of ritual specialists, and many people believed that puppets had magical powers.[4] All this gave rural opera exceptional symbolic weight.

However, operas performed on temple stages were limited to certain types: religious (few, but very important; examples are *Mulian Rescues His Mother* and *The Story of Xiangshan* [*Xiangshan ji*]), mythological/legendary (also not particularly numerous, but including some of the most popular stories, such as *Journey to the West* [*Xiyou ji*] and *The White Snake* [*Baishe zhuan*]), and, by far the most numerous, historical/martial. ("Historical/martial" because virtually all operas with historical subjects featured combat between warriors.) Farces, ribald or worse, were also performed at festival time but always at night, when there were no rituals. Love stories such as *Romance of the Western Chamber* (*Xixiang ji*), exceedingly popular in urban theaters, were never performed on rural temple stages.

Opera was not confined to the stage in village temple festivals. There were exorcistic performances in which an actor would leap off the stage, run through the village, and then be captured and brought back to the stage for punishment. Some operas used the village itself as a stage, as in *Crossing the Five Passes* (*Guo wuguan*), where each "pass" was a particular site in the village, or *Capturing the Yellow Demon* (*Zhuo huanggui*), a scripted performance in which an entire village was mobilized to hunt the demon down and hand him over for execution.[5]

In addition to actual operas, whether performed on stage or in the streets of the village, opera *imagery* was very much in evidence during village temple festivals. A great screen called the Flowery Offering (*Hua ji*), in one case 10 by 16 feet, constructed of tiles made of dough that had been elaborately carved and then deep fried until hard, was erected inside temples in southern Shanxi to separate the offering pavilion from the main hall. (The offering pavilion, if there was one, stood between the stage and the main hall.) Attached to the screen about 6 feet from the ground were scenes from opera, in which the characters were small figures finely crafted of clay

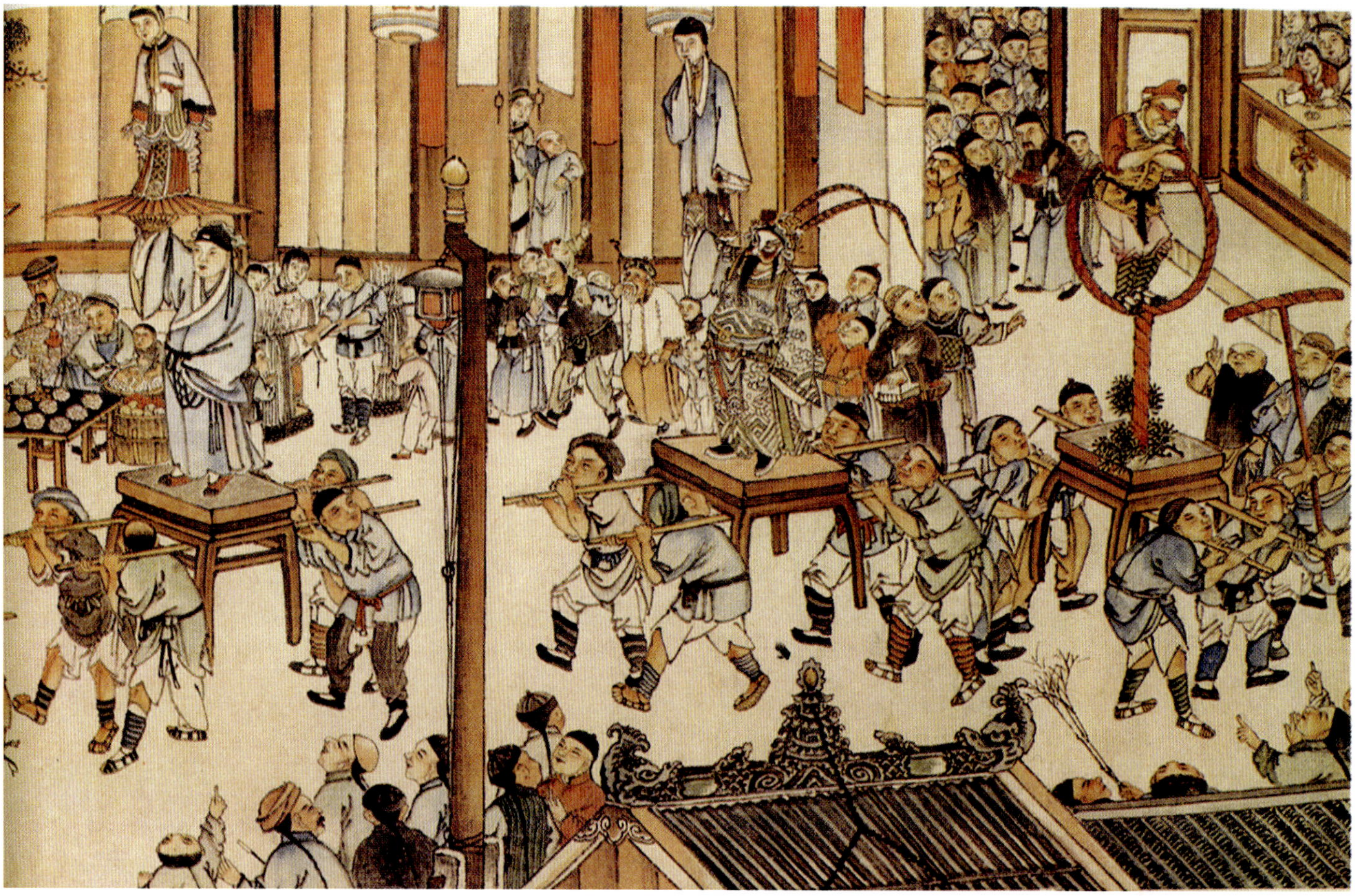

and paper. These scenes attracted crowds of onlookers who discussed them with enthusiasm.[6] Then in the massive processions that were an integral part of every temple festival, one of the most characteristic features was what we would call floats, platforms carried on men's shoulders, on which villagers were posed in scenes from operas. An exceptionally beautiful woodblock New Year print from the late Qing dynasty (1644–1911) shows what these floats looked like (fig. 2.1). The people on the floats are wearing elaborate opera costumes, with one figure seemingly holding another aloft. (Actually they were aided by a framework of iron rods hidden under their costumes.) This print was made in Sichuan province, but very similar floats were used in festival processions in southeastern Shanxi.[7]

Thus at festival time not only did the villagers have perhaps dozens of live operas and puppet operas to watch, they also saw representations of opera that were substantial creative works in their own right. And we can be sure that this intense saturation in opera was what the people wanted, since they had complete control over their own festivals.

Given all this, we can be sure that opera stories and opera imagery were central to the conceptual and imaginative worlds of ordinary people; opera supplied them with material to think and feel with. Thus it is no surprise to find that when villagers decorated their houses or temples, or when they needed patterns to embellish everyday objects like gowns and purses, they turned to opera imagery. Of course they used other types of imagery as well, including birds and flowers, auspicious symbols and scenes, didactic tableaux, and guardian deities, but opera imagery was very important, far more so than theatrical imagery ever was in non-elite art and decoration in Europe. By late imperial times opera had colonized the consciousness of the Chinese. The great story of their civilization presented itself to ordinary people in operatic guise, as did some of their central myths and legends.

New Year Pictures

The most important medium for the decoration of the interior of houses was woodblock prints, as discussed by Bo Songnian elsewhere in this catalogue. They are commonly called New Year pictures (*nianhua*) because they were usually purchased in the New Year season, when houses were cleaned from top to bottom. New Year pictures were generally printed on cheap paper with colors that did not last long, and so were ready to be replaced after a year. They were pasted on walls, windows (which themselves were made of paper), and on gates. Prints of the Stove God would be placed at the back of his shrine, above the stove, and prints of other deities would be placed on the family shrine and pasted up at key points around the house.[8]

2.1
Huang Ruigu
Chinese, 1866–1938
Detail of New Year Procession, Guangxu Reign (1875–1908)
Hand-colored woodblock print from Mianzhu county, Sichuan province,
18 ½ × 236 ¼ in. (47 × 600 cm)

2.2
Chinese, Qing Dynasty (1644–1911)
Scene from the Opera Crossroads Slope (Shizu po), n.d.
Polychrome woodblock print from Fuyang county, Anhui province,
7 ⅛ × 12 ⅜ in. (18.2 × 31.5 cm)

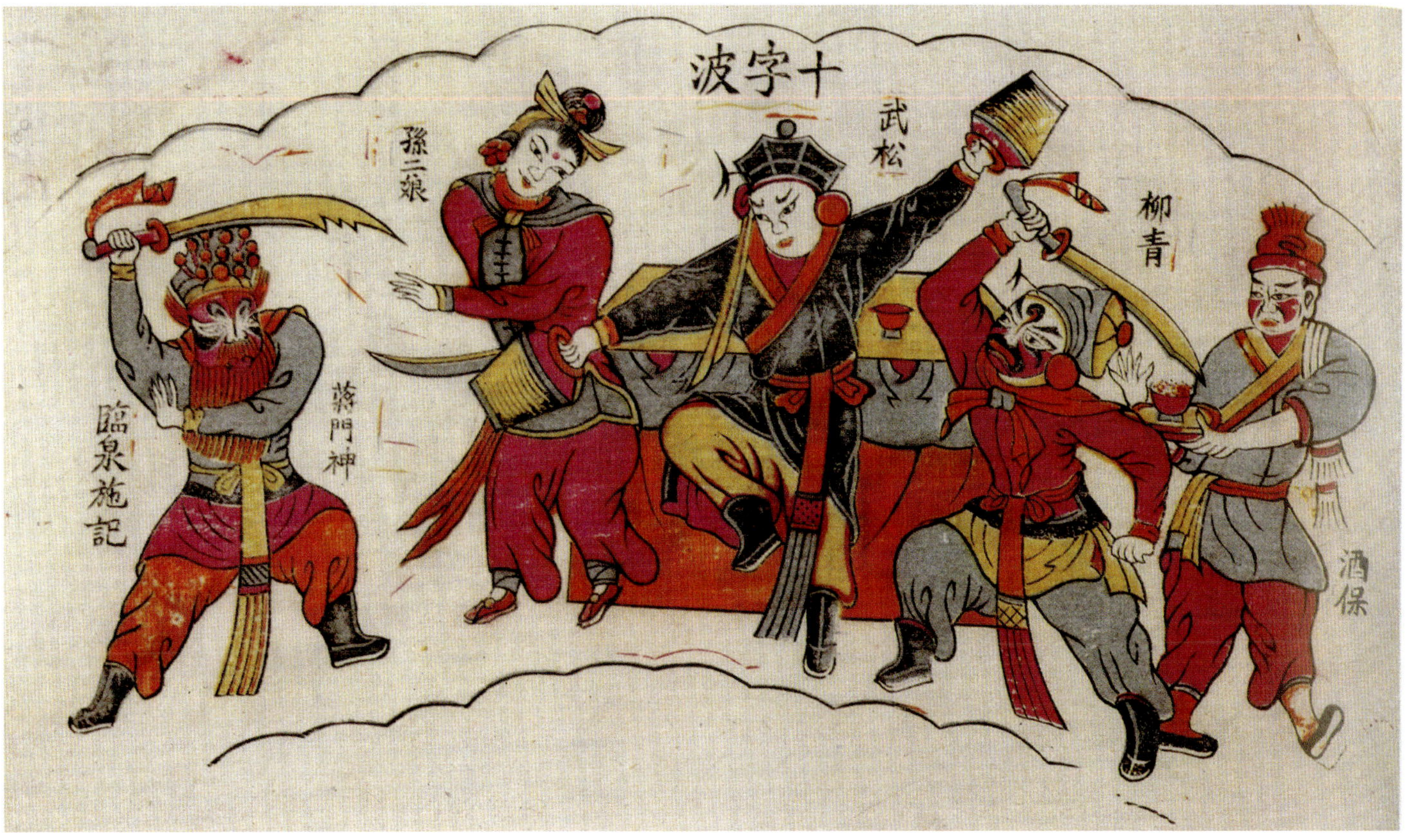

Making New Year pictures was a complex process that required skilled craftsmen. An ink drawing on thin paper of the entire image was pasted face down on a block of fine-grained wood. The carver cut away with great skill everything except the lines of the drawing. Then additional blocks were carved, one for each color. The prints were made by impressing first the outline (which looked like fig. 5.2 in Bo Songnian's essay) and then each successive color. Printers used simple but effective devices to maintain accurate registration as the blocks were changed. This folk industry was concentrated in numerous centers across China. Millions and millions of prints were sold every year, in shops and by peddlers. Because they were distributed so widely—they were as close as China came to a mass medium in the preindustrial era—they probably were the primary means by which opera imagery spread across China.

I have selected four prints out of hundreds that feature scenes from opera. They were chosen because they are visually striking, show different degrees of reliance on writing, and come from different print shops. The first is typical of opera prints because it has a title, *Crossroads Slope* (*Shizi po*), and identifies each of the figures in it[9] (fig. 2.2). The central figure is Wu Song, the famous fighter in the historical novel *The Water Margin* (*Shuihu zhuan*). In the opera Sun Erniang, the wife of the innkeeper at Crossroads Slope, attempts to murder Wu Song while he is in a drugged sleep. But he is only feigning sleep, and the two have a duel in the dark, Wu Song using two wine pots as weapons. After Sun is defeated her husband Zhang Qing arrives on the scene, learns Wu Song's identity, and becomes his sworn brother.[10]

The print departs from the opera in several interesting ways. It gives the painted-face figure on the right the name Liu Qing, not Zhang Qing. Moreover "Liu" appears to be Wu Song's main opponent, not Sun Erniang. Finally, the armed figure on the far left, Jiang Menshen, does not have a role in *Crossroads Slope* at all, but rather in an opera called *Joyful Grove* (*Kuaihuo lin*), which is based on an episode that comes two chapters later in *The Water Margin* than the incident at Crossroads Slope. *Joyful Grove* also features a brawl at an inn, this time between a genuinely drunk Wu Song and Jiang Menshen.

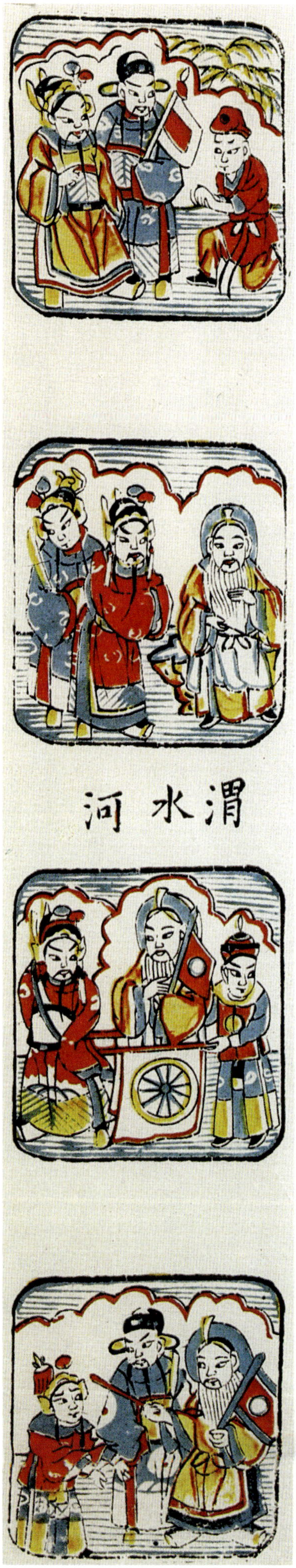

2.3
Chinese, Qing Dynasty (1644–1911)
Scenes from the Opera Weishui River (Weishui he), n.d.
Polychrome woodblock print from Wuqiang county, Hebei province,
$20\frac{1}{3} \times 3\frac{3}{4}$ in. (51.7 × 9.5 cm)

Thus the man who created the design for the print made three mistakes, all interesting: a mistake of the ear in the title; a mistake in the surname of one character; and the conflation of two operas featuring Wu Song fighting at an inn. The first is the sort of error found frequently in texts written by poorly educated men, but the other two suggest that this particular craftsman's memory played him false. He could not have made these mistakes if he had the novel at hand, or if he had recently seen either of the operas. But his reliance on his unaided memory in designing the print, which after all represented an investment of time and money, suggests paradoxically that he believed he knew the material well—that it was "in the air" so to speak. What we cannot know is whether the mistakes caused the print to have poor sales. But this raises the issue of who could read what was written on the prints, a major question I do not have space to deal with here.

Our second print, which is titled *Weishui River* (*Weishui he*) (fig. 2.3) differs considerably from *Crossroads Slope*. Prints of this type were pasted on paper windows near the large enclosed brick platforms called *kang*s found in houses all across rural north China, on which much household activity took place, especially in winter, when they were heated. *Weishui River* was made in Wuqiang, a village in Hebei province that specialized in New Year pictures. It is interesting because the designer evidently believed the opera would be so familiar that there was no need to identify the characters. And indeed we know that it was in the repertoire of Hebei local opera.[11]

The opera is set in the legend-rich period of the decline of the Shang dynasty and rise of the Zhou (about mid-eleventh century BCE), and probably drew on the popular novels *Plain Tale of King Wu's Conquest of King Zhou of Shang* (*Wuwang fa Zhou pinghua*) and *The Enfoeffment of the Gods* (*Fengshen yanyi*). In it, Ji Chang, the future King Wen of Zhou, dreams one night that a flying bear enters his tent. In the morning he divines to discover the meaning of the dream, and is told it means he will find a virtuous councillor. While on his quest to find this indispensable advisor he encounters a follower of the great sage Jiang Ziya, who takes him to the Weishui River, where Jiang is fishing. Ji makes him his prime minister and to further demonstrate his respect, seats the sage in a carriage and pulls it 808 steps, one step for each year the Zhou

2.4
Chinese, Late Qing Dynasty (1644–1911)
Scene from the Opera Dueling with Golden Claws (Duijin zhua), n.d.
Polychrome woodblock print from Kaifeng county, Henan province,
$9\frac{1}{10} \times 11\frac{1}{10}$ in. (23.1 × 28.1 cm)

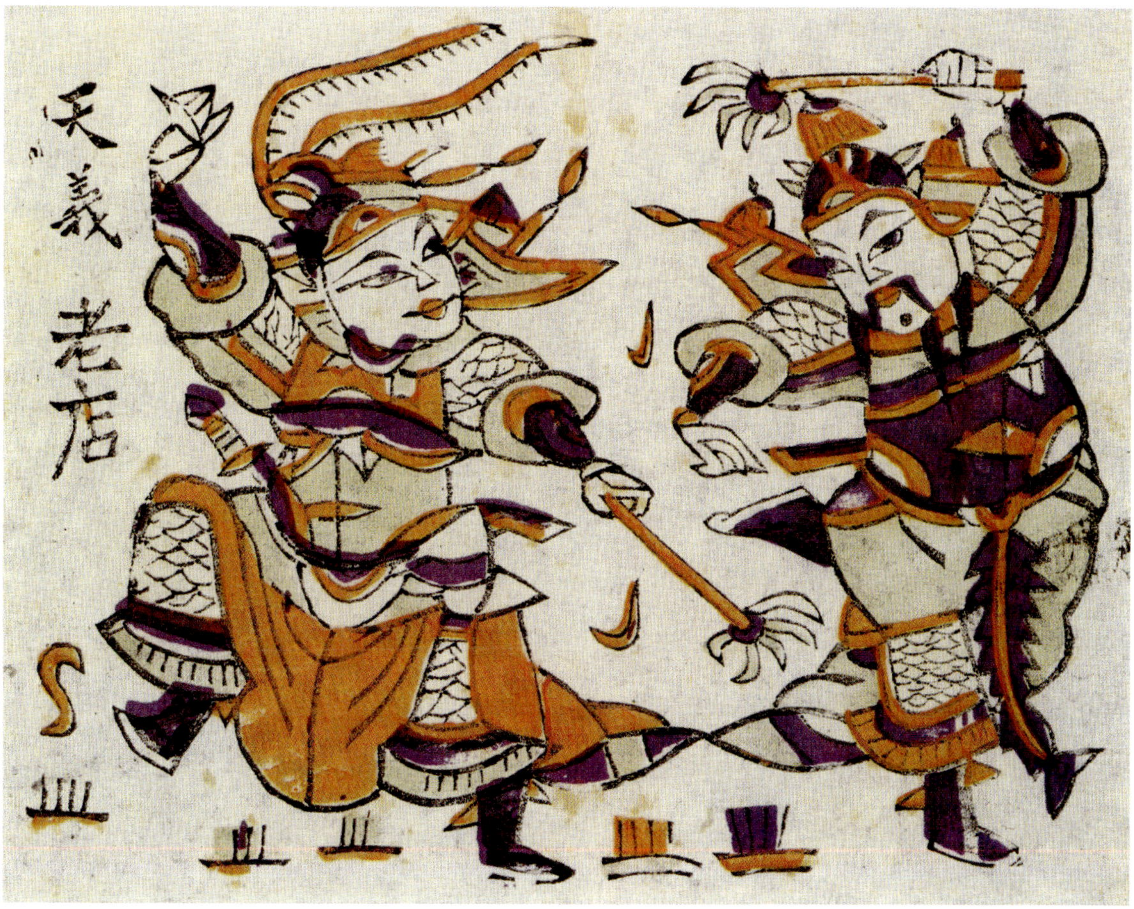

dynasty will endure, thanks to Jiang's founding counsel.[12] The print recounts the story's high points with images both simple and powerful. In the top picture we see Jin Chang, wearing a golden-yellow robe, being told of the whereabouts of Jiang Ziya. In the second, Ji, now in a red robe, is paying his respects to Jiang, whose fishing rod is just visible slanting across the bottom of his beard. In the third we see Ji pulling the sage in a carriage, represented by two pieces of cloth imprinted with wheels, just as on the stage. The last picture shows Jiang, still with the banner of office he held in the previous picture, advising the anxious Ji Chang.

In *Weishui River*, unlike *Crossroads Slope*, the designer carefully followed the story. The fishing rod and carriage are unmistakable visual clues, and the four scenes have a tidy narrative arc. But would the village woman who pasted this print up next to her kang have been able to tell the story to her children? The answer must be that she could have, to some reasonable degree of approximation. This in turn means that she, and others like her, given the title, would have recognized the story. And perhaps, thanks to the strong visual clues, she did not even need the title. How many stories would an uneducated peasant in seventeenth- or eighteenth-century France or Italy have been able to recognize on the basis of four simple pictures? Beyond stories from the Bible, probably not very many. This contrast between the One Great Story of medieval and early modern Europe and the thousands of stories in China after the Song dynasty points to one of the great differences in the popular cultures of the two civilizations.

The subject of the third print would seem to be rather difficult to identify, since it has neither title nor labels (the four characters on the left are the name of the shop that made it: "The old 'Heavenly Righteousness' printshop") (fig. 2.4). But there is an opera whose title suggests a connection with the picture—*Dueling with Golden Claws* (*Dui jin zhua*). Moreover, *Dueling with Golden Claws*

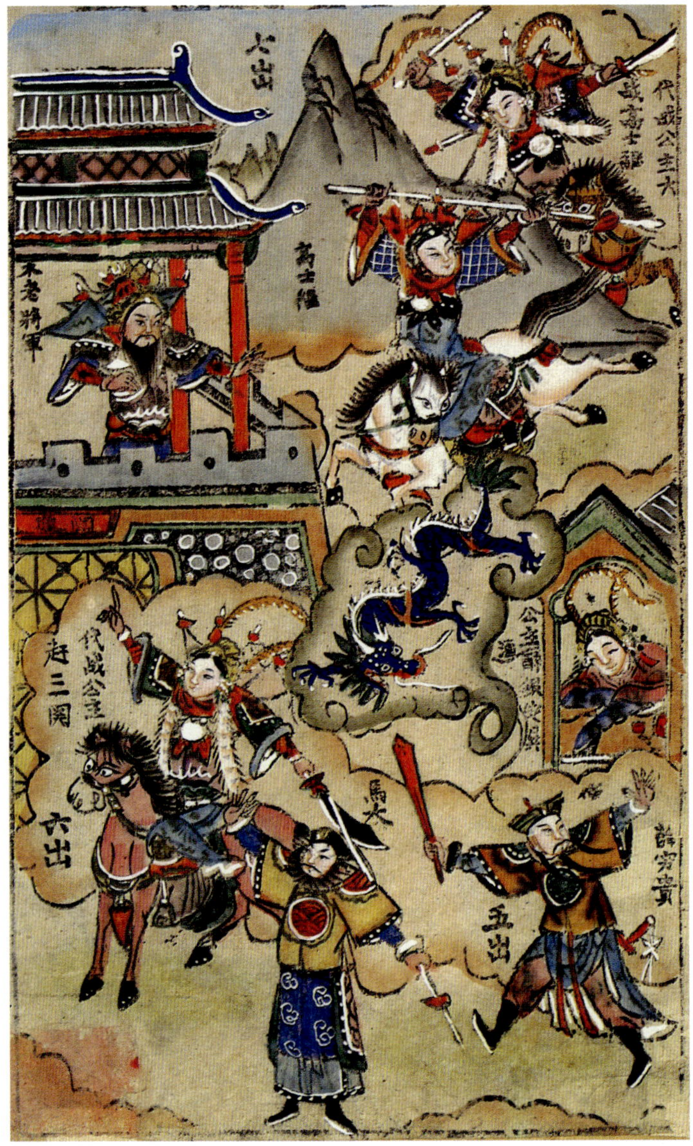

was in the repertoire of Henan opera, and Henan was the province where the print was made.[13] Although the story is set in the Three Kingdoms period (circa 220–65), it cannot be found in the great novel *Romance of the Three Kingdoms* (*Sanguo zhi yanyi*),[14] which confirms that our print was based on a local opera.[15] It tells of two brothers, Ma Chao and Ma Dai, each bequeathed one of a pair of unusual weapons that resembled backscratchers with pointed metal claws. Although they were separated for a long time during the wars of the Three Kingdoms period, the younger never abandoned his search for the elder. Hearing that someone named Ma Chao was at the birthday celebration of Liu Bei, one of the great heroes of the Three Kingdoms, Ma Dai went to Liu Bei's camp to see if it was his long-lost brother. Suspecting that he was an enemy, two of Liu's generals tried to prevent his entry, but Dai defeated them. Then Ma Chao came out to deal with the threat, whereupon each recognized the other's clawed weapon and the brothers were reunited.[16]

So although the print is untitled, the weapons provide unmistakable visual clues: the brothers are pictured at the moment they see their unique weapons and recognize each other. This is the defining moment in the opera, and for anyone who knew it, seeing the print would have called to mind the whole story, which was a good deal more complicated than my summary. Would that have been a large number of people? We cannot be certain, but surely within the regions in north China where the opera was performed, which included Shandong, Anhui, and Shanxi provinces in addition to Henan,[17] it must have been well-known; why else would it have been printed without a title? This print, pasted up by villagers in their rooms or on their gates,[18] is powerful evidence of the penetration of *local* opera, unmediated by one of the great novels or by Peking opera, into the consciousness of ordinary people.

The fourth print (fig. 2.5) is very different in form from the preceding three. It is the second of a set of four that show twelve scenes from the saga of Xue Pinggui, a warrior-hero who lived late in the Tang dynasty (618–907).[19] The prints tell the story of how Xue Pinggui kills a wild goose and discovers a letter tied to its leg. The letter, written in blood, is from his wife, Baochuan, telling him that she has been living in poverty for eighteen years faithfully waiting for his return. Xue thereupon leaves the kingdom of Western Liang, where he has ruled for many years, abandons his second wife, Princess Daizhan, and hurries back to Chang'an, where he is reunited with his faithful first wife, vanquishes his enemies at court, and takes the throne of the great Tang dynasty. Several authorities trace this story to a Qing dynasty *chantefable* called *The Story of the Golden Dragon-and-Phoenix Hairpin* (*Longfeng jinchai zhuan*).[20] *Chantefable*, an oral form, would have been more accessible than novels to people with little or no education, reminding us that operas whose plots can be found in well-known novels may actually have drawn on oral performance genres rather than the novels. The four prints have the overall title *Breaking Through Three Passes* (*Gan sanguan*), which must have been the title of the opera they were illustrating, even though that is the subject of only one of the prints' twelve scenes. There is an opera called *Breaking Through Three Passes*, but it deals with only the one episode.[21] The lack of fit between the title of the print and the story it tells, as well as the odd name given the protagonist, suggest that the print was based on a local opera that was not well-known.

Our print shows scenes five through seven of the twelve. The colors were added carefully by brush on an outline printed on fine

2.5
Tianjin, Yangliuqing (print workshop)
Chinese, Qing Dynasty (1644–1911)
Scenes from the Opera Breaking through Three Passes (Gan sanguan), n.d.
Hand-colored woodblock print

paper, which was the style of Yangliuqing, a famous printing center in Hebei province.[22] This hand-colored print must have cost more than the others we have looked at, and the abundance of writing—including not only the title and names of the characters but also the brief description of the scene that illustrates each numbered act—enhances the impression that the intended audience had a comfortable position in the hierarchy of wealth and education. For example, the text halfway up on the left says "Princess Daizhan Breaks Through Three Passes," and she is shown in full martial regalia elegantly commanding her troops to advance. Obviously these captions were intended to be read. This sets the print apart from the others we have looked at, which were visually much simpler and whose designers assumed the viewer would need few or no words to recognize the events being depicted.[23] Another feature that sets these prints apart from the others is the placement of their costumed figures not on an imagined stage, but rather in a landscape with palaces, gates, horses, distant mountains, and even a wild goose. Evidently neither designer nor viewer felt that opera characters were out of place in a naturalistic picture. For them, no deep difference existed between the stage and the world.

Unlike the other New Year pictures we have looked at, the set of four prints on *Breaking Through Three Passes*, one of which we have been considering, was more than a simple souvenir, so to speak. The story was not just alluded to but retold through key moments in each of twelve acts. Looking at the pictures and reading the text, the owner could privately re-experience the opera in considerable detail, and so can we. What did he or she see? In this particular set of scenes—the latter part of the whole saga—the love of Xue's two wives for him plays a prominent role. The letter, written in blood as a token of utmost sincerity, reminds the observer of Baochuan's eighteen years of patient suffering. Princess Daizhan pursues her beloved by fighting her way through three passes, and saves him when his enemies attack at the end. After he takes the throne, both women are given royal titles, and Baochuan's mother is also honored. Visually Xue is the most dominant figure, appearing in nine of the twelve scenes. But in only one is he shown fighting, and in that scene he is defeated. Princess Daizhan by contrast is shown leading her troops through the three passes and dueling successfully with the warrior who defeated Xue. Xue is the formal center of attention, but Daizhan, who appears in five scenes, is the active center of the prints. Women who were familiar with the opera and who had a certain amount of education may well have found this set of prints appealing, because they focus on heroines who are examplars of marital fidelity, romantic ardor, and martial prowess, and who in the end win honor, riches, and the man they love.

The four New Year pictures we have discussed came from Henan province, Anhui province, and two locations in Hebei province. They range from a simple picture of two warriors with neither setting nor words to identify them to an elaborate four-part picture composed of twelve tableaux, complete with descriptive labels, in which costumed actors move about in a (relatively) realistic setting. We know people bought them to decorate the places where they lived, to be *looked at*. The first three show how familiar the operas were to ordinary people; the last suggests how some prints might have embodied the fantasies of those who purchased them. Above all, these images suggest how deep and broad was the influence of opera on the consciousness of ordinary people.

New Year pictures were the most common way of depicting scenes from opera, but not the only way. Opera imagery came to be used in almost all the folk decorative arts; popular prints were the vector by which it spread. There are very simple examples of opera imagery in folk crafts, and some truly spectacular ones. Of these, the most remarkable are carvings in fired clay, wood, and stone that were used to decorate buildings.

Architectural Decoration

In late imperial times opera imagery appeared in the decorative schemes of a wide variety of buildings. It is obviously impossible to say just how common the practice was, but a pioneering article by the polymathic sinologist Wolfram Eberhard gives some interesting hints. In the mid-1960s he visited fifty temples in Taiwan and a few in Hong Kong to document the content of their decorations.[24] Out of a thousand "useable scenes" he found that 18 were "purely religious"; 114 concerned filial piety; 117 were "scenes from history"; 193 were "symbolic representations," for example of the Eight Immortals, the God of Long Life, cranes, lions, and pine trees; and 558 were "scenes from novels and plays."[25] This last number might well be an undercount, since some of the images Eberhard classi-

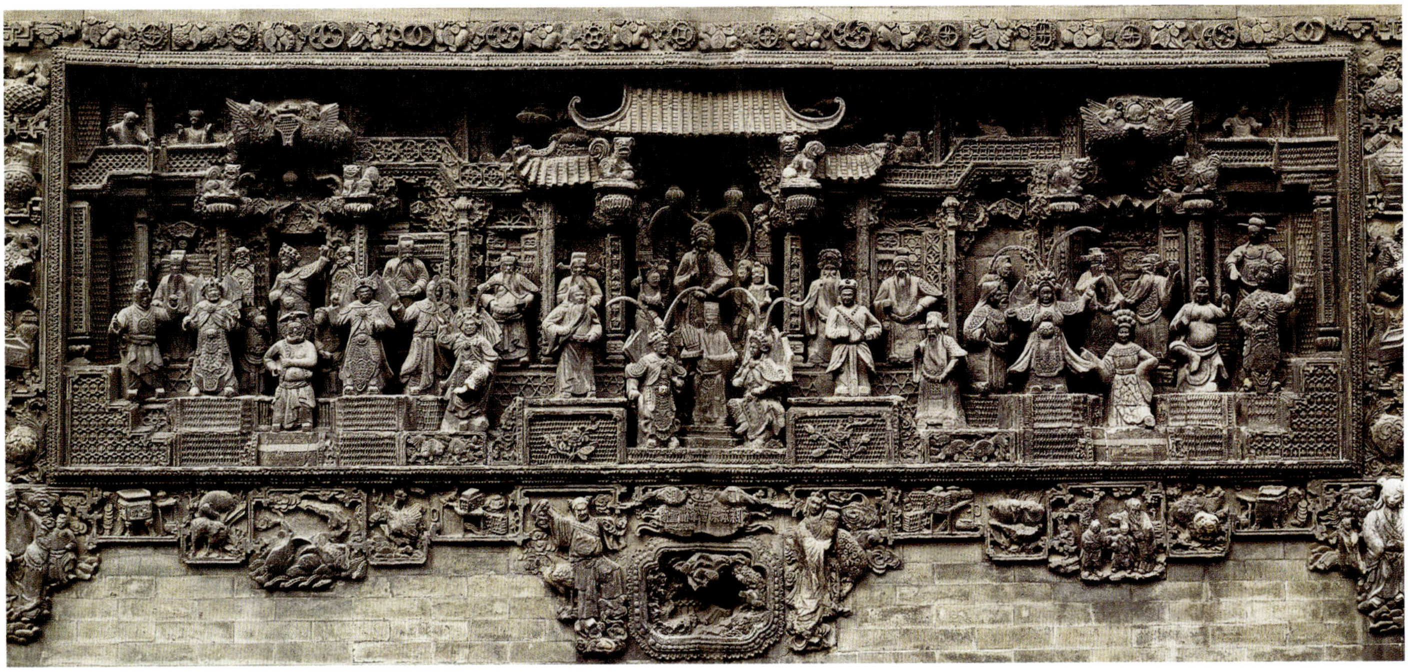

fied as historical could well have come from fiction or opera, as he himself states.[26] He does not say what proportion of the "scenes from novels and plays" came from plays, but he does tell us how he decided whether an image was derived from opera: if the figures wore opera costume, if the scene included the title of an opera, or if "the scene represented an event which was the central event of a famous play."[27] This is much the same method I used to determine whether a New Year picture was based on an opera.

Eberhard's findings were based on a small sample of temples, mostly from Taiwan, none of which was built before 1925, so they clearly cannot be taken as representative of China as a whole.[28] But opera imagery does indeed appear in the decorative programs of temples all over China, not to mention other buildings, such as guild halls and private dwellings. The spectacular example illustrated here was originally created for the ancestral hall of the Chen lineage in Guangzhou in southern China (fig. 2.6). Of carved brick, it is over 13 feet long. It is said to represent the heroes of *The Water Margin* in their headquarters, the Hall of the Assembled Righteous (*Juyi ting*), but there are no labels, either for the scene as a whole or for the individual figures.[29] The figures wear opera costumes, but are shown not on a stage but in front of the hall, with a few onlookers visible in the second story. Four figures and two attendants occupy the center; three of them, including the central and most senior one, wear military costume. The fourth, dressed as a high minister, carries what may be a crown. To each side of this central group a variety of figures are arranged, in three ranks. The rear-most one is composed of bearded elders wearing the officials' hats. (There are two exceptions, the figure with a rather exotic headdress looking to one side, second from the left, and the official on the far right.) In front of the elders is a rank of eight figures in two groups, most of whom appear to be generals or warriors. Particularly striking is the female general with her arms spread, in the middle of the right-hand group. The figure next to her, bare from the waist up, is also notable. In the front rank stand six figures. The two closest to the center of the piece, one a bearded elder and the other clean-shaven, are both dressed in civilian garb. The remaining four are a bearded barbarian with his strange cap, on the far left; then a warrior in full regalia; an older man in court dress; and a beautiful woman with the headdress of a princess, who is placed quite close to the female general.

The frieze is placed over the main entrance of the hall, facing out, and the figures, dressed in opera costumes, look directly at whoever passes through the gates. Clearly the leaders of the Chen lineage, who went to great expense to commission an expert sculptor to decorate an important part of their rebuilt ancestral temple, the ritual center of the lineage, felt it was right and proper that the work he created use the visual vocabulary of opera and very little else. Nor was this an unusual case, except perhaps in its scope. There are many similar published examples, in wood and stone as well as clay, and given the low prestige of such folk crafts many more must have gone unrecorded and indeed unpreserved.[30]

Woodblock prints and decorative carvings on temples and other buildings that made use of opera motifs were the products of professional craftsmen. There were other folk arts that were done by women in the home, at least originally, which also used imagery from opera. These included the sculpting of small figures out of clay or even hardened dough,[31] which unfortunately cannot be dealt with here, as well as embroidery and papercutting.

2.6
Chinese, Qing Dynasty (1644–1911)
Gathering of Heroes in the Hall of the Assembled Righteous (Juyi ting), from the Novel The Water Margin (Shuihu zhuan), Guangxu reign (1875–1908)
Frieze of carved brick from lintel over main entrance to the Chen Family Shrine, Guangzhou, Guangdong province, 78 ¾ × 160 ⅝ in. (200 × 408 cm)
Guangzhou Museum of Folk Crafts

2.7
Chinese, Late Qing Dynasty (1644–1911)
Purse with Scene from the Opera Fishing Kills a Family (Dayu sha jia), n.d.
Embroidered purse from Xinzhou county, Shanxi province, 5 ⅛ × 5 ⅛ in. (13 x 13 cm)
Collection of Peng Lixin

Embroidery

"Women in traditional China," according to the scholar Nancy Berliner, "were judged not by their beauty but by their embroidery skills, abilities believed to express the fine qualities of their inner natures." Moreover, embroidery traditionally was "one of the few ways a peasant woman could express and display her skills, her agility, her sense of beauty."[32] At the highest levels, such as temple hangings or priestly robes, Chinese embroidery reached a seemingly superhuman perfection, but even country women produced beautiful pieces that used silk thread and intricate stitches to create delicate shading and a wide variety of textures.[33] There are some fine examples in this exhibition (cats. 1, 33–36).

In Shanxi, scenes from opera were the most popular embroidery motifs.[34] But the imagery varied according to the object being embellished. For example, collars and hats for children, women's ear covers and shoes, and rank plaques on official robes seem not to have used opera imagery. But pillow ends, bed and table hangings, and nonofficial robes did use opera imagery, as can be seen in the woman's apron, the Daoist robe, and the woman's jacket in the exhibition (cats. 11, 27, 28). The example shown here, not in the exhibition, is a purse (fig. 2.7). It shows a scene from an opera that was in local opera repertoires all across north China. The plot material can be found in chapter 9 of the novel *Sequel to The Water Margin* (*Shuihu houzhuan*). A local strongman, Mountain Snake Ba, commands Xiao En, a poor fisherman, and his daughter Guiying to pay a fishing tax. Xiao En beats up the agent sent to collect the money and informs the local magistrate that Mountain Snake is levying an illegal tax. But the corrupt magistrate punishes Xiao and orders him to apologize to Mountain Snake. Unable to bear this injustice, Xiao En and Guiying cross the river at night and using the pretext of presenting to Mountain Snake the Pearl of Supreme Felicity, gain entrance to his house and slaughter his entire family.[35] In the scene embroidered on the purse we see Xiao En and Guiying crossing the river. He holds an oar, but behind his back the handle of his sword can be seen. Guiying is moving to the motion of the boat and smiling in anticipation of the bloody vengeance soon to be brought down upon their oppressor and his family. The expressions on the

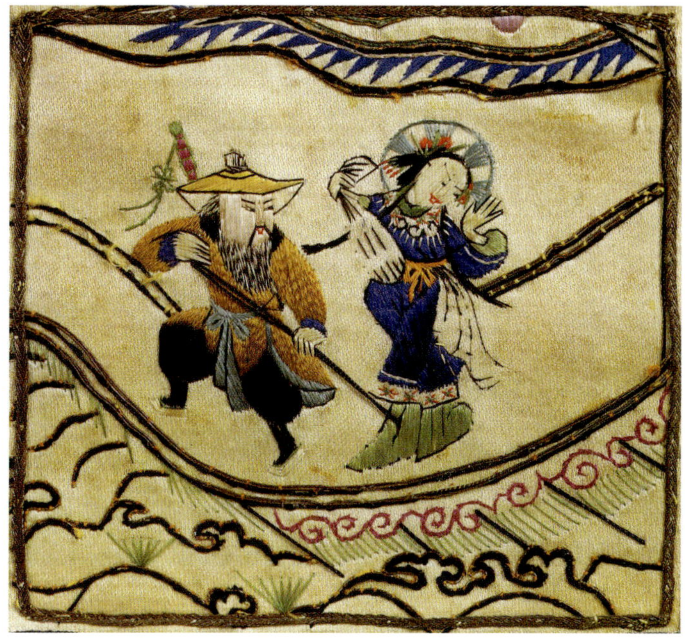

faces of Xiao En and Guiying, the balance and proportion of their bodies, and the poised energy of the piece as a whole are evidence of considerable artistic talent.

This opera is not set in a clear historical period, unlike those depicted in the works we looked at earlier. Village women may have found stories derived from fictionalized history such as *Romance of the Three Kingdoms* or historical romances such as *The Water Margin* less appealing than those that spoke directly to their personal circumstances, such as this one. But its theme—loathing for those who abuse power, whether officials or commoners—would have appealed to men and women alike.

Papercuts

Village women, perhaps older women in particular, who enjoyed a certain amount of leisure, made colorful decorations for their homes by cutting tissue paper into intricate patterns. When pasted on the paper-covered lattice windows of their homes they created a very beautiful effect, with the outside light shining through the thin brightly colored images. Papercuts did not have the cultural significance or practical usefulness of embroidery; they were purely and simply decorative. But the level of skill manifest in the best of them

2.8
Wang Laoshang, paper cutter
Chinese, 20th century
Eight Opera Characters, n.d.
Papercuts for windows from Weixian county, Hebei province
Collection of Lin Bandong

nearly matches that of the finest embroidery. Motifs from opera appear to have been less common in papercuts than in embroidery, though it is impossible to be sure, since the works were very fragile and survival in the home for more than a season must have been rare. Hence we should not be too quick to use the subject matter of extant papercuts to draw conclusions about the attitudes and values of their makers, since the taste of the men who collected traditional papercuts must have had a considerable influence on which examples survived.

Papercutting eventually became a village industry like printmaking, with men using knives and punches on workbenches to make many pieces at once. But originally women made papercuts as an amusing diversion, using scissors from their embroidery boxes on tissue-thin paper. I believe all the pieces reproduced here are of the latter type. Making large papercuts with traditional tools was difficult since the paper was held in the hand and it was hard to avoid tearing a complex lace-like piece as it neared completion. So smaller pieces, sometimes made in sets, probably were more common. The examples I have selected are of this sort (fig. 2.8). That a village woman, making papercuts to pass the time, chose to depict opera characters in addition to more obviously decorative subjects like flowers and butterflies, or symbols that would bring good luck, clearly demonstrates the depth of opera's influence on her, and other people like her, since she probably did not give much thought to the patterns she chose—they were immediately available to her consciousness.

In the patterns of both embroidery and papercuts we are as close to the symbolic world of individual villagers as it is possible to be, and they show that world was filled with opera imagery. Only one other system of imagery in China before the advent of mass media was as important, indeed more important: that relating to the realm of the divine and demonic powers. Buddhism, Daoism, village gods, and local cults each had their iconographies, which were familiar to all Chinese. We understand the relative importance of different kinds of religious iconography quite well. If we knew what proportion of opera imagery was derived from which operas, or types of opera, we would gain great insight into the attitudes and values of all Chinese in premodern times, especially villagers. To discover this will require close study of the entire range of popular iconography by students well versed in local opera. Judging on the basis of the very limited examples presented in this essay, however, opera imagery, for country folk, referred mostly to stories about people and events in certain epochs of Chinese history, such as the founding of the Zhou, the Three Kingdoms, the founding of the Tang, and the fall of Northern Song. A number of operas drew on a handful of near-mythical super-legends, such as those about the filial monk Mulian and the Tang dynasty monk Xuanzang and his journey to India, but clearly, history was the most important source.[36]

In the West, visual representations of past events are never composed of costumed actors moving in a stage set. If the subject is Biblical history, Jesus, the prophets, and the saints all look like living people and are placed in surroundings composed of realistic elements. Outside of the museums, in popular prints, it was the same. This was equally true of non-Biblical history. Pictures of the assassination of Julius Caesar, or of Marat, depict real people, not characters from a stage play. So too for scenes from mythology, a time out of time. Representations of stories from history and from most imaginative literature used the visual vocabulary of the stage in China and did not in Europe simply because drama was far more important in China than it was in Europe.

When Chinese villagers thought about the past they used the images that opera had given them. They imagined the great lords and warriors of history dressed like the actors they had seen on stage. Their mental picture of Napoleon would not have been like ours—little pot belly, hand thrust into the front of his coat, dark hair combed forward; they would have seen "Napoleon," his face depersonalized with makeup, wearing a costume quite unlike what real generals wore, and a gaudy headdress with two enormously long pheasant feathers. They saw role-types, not individuals. And just as individuality was dissolved out of the characters, so was contingency removed from the action, and specificity from the landscape.

In the European sense of history, events and individuals in the past have their places on an unbroken succession of years that reaches to the present. If a person or war or whatever cannot be *dated*, they are relegated to the realm of legend or myth. If we are to

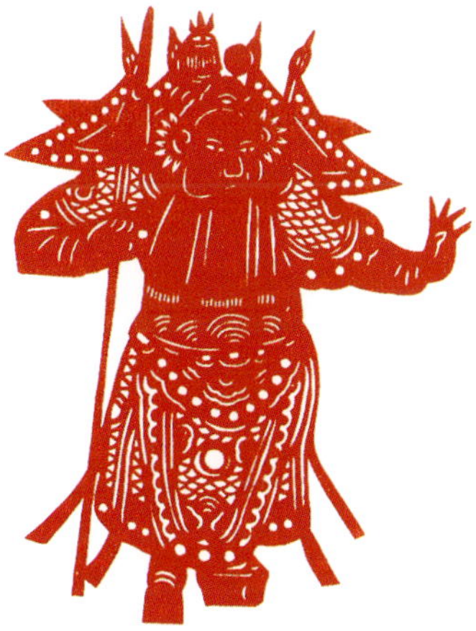
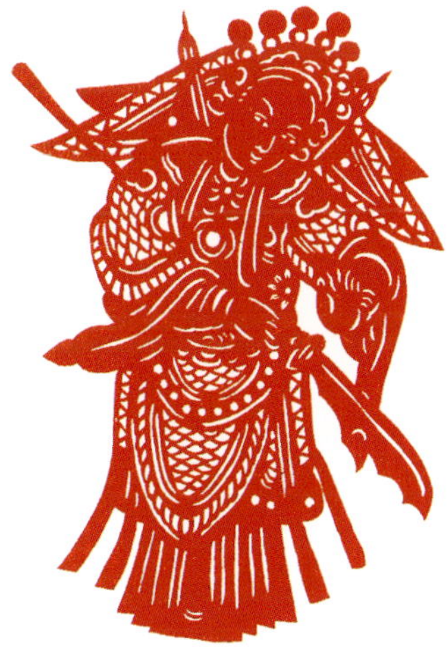
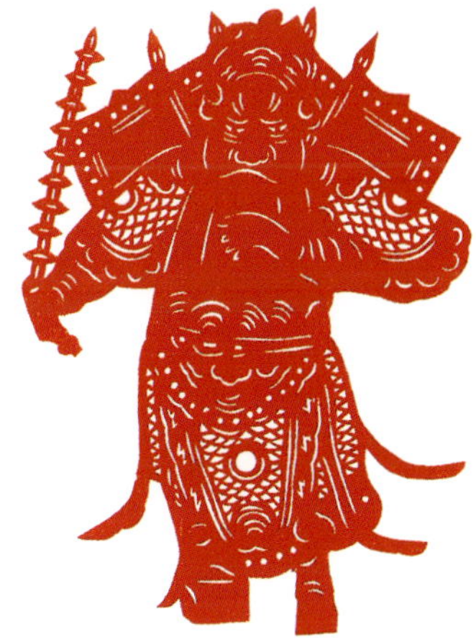
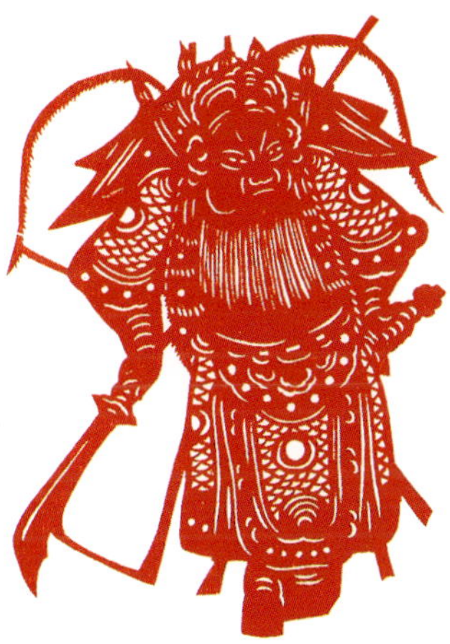
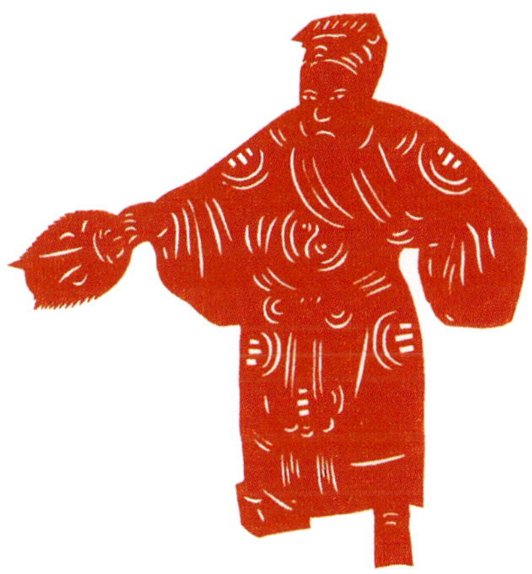
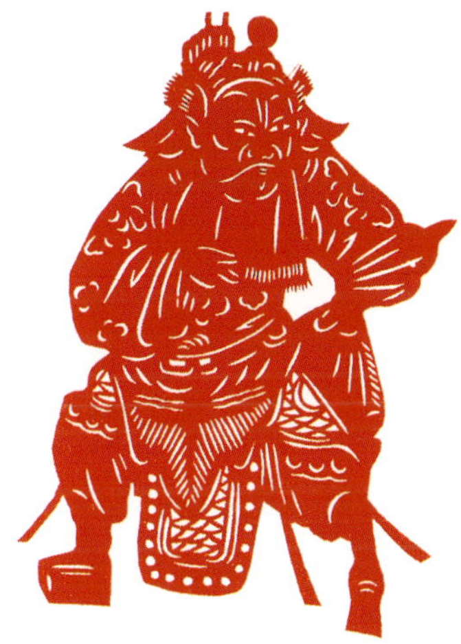
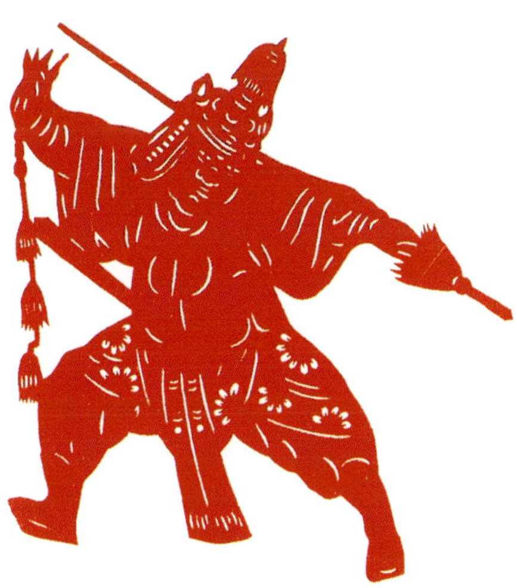
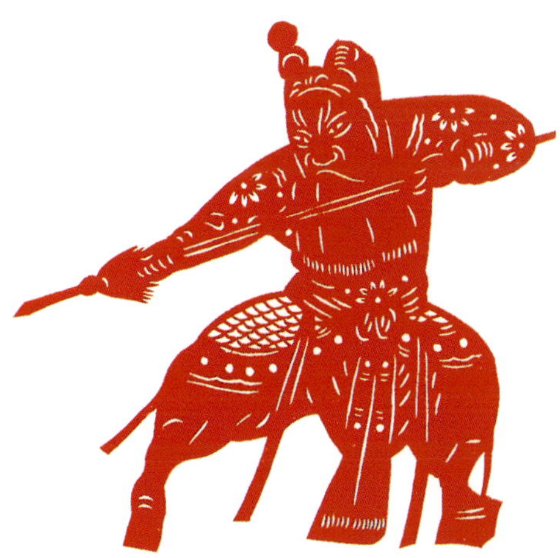

believe the evidence of popular iconography, for ordinary Chinese the past was not populated with people like themselves who lived on a chronological continuum that reached, unbroken, to the present. Rather history was a story, or more precisely a vast array of loosely linked systems of stories, told most memorably in operas. And these stories all had lessons to teach about personal integrity and the just use of power, about loyalty, respect for parents, and the whole range of practical ethics. The past as represented on stage, and as imagined by ordinary people, had an inner moral coherence by which the actions of living people were measured. Opera imagery in China ultimately points toward stories that embodied what was once, but no longer, the fundamental ethos of the culture.

Notes

1 See the list of early stages in David Johnson, *Spectacle and Sacrifice: The Ritual Foundations of Village Life in North China* (Cambridge, Mass.: Harvard University Asia Center, 2009), pp. 150–52.

2 The best early evidence for commercial urban theater is a short work called "A Country Bumpkin Knows Naught of the Theater" (circa 1220). It describes the payment of admission, the appearance of the theater, and part of a performance. Wilt Idema and Stephen H. West, *Chinese Theater 1100–1450, a Source Book* (Wiesbaden: Franz Steiner Verlag, 1982), pp. 187–89. There were more than fifty theaters in the Northern Song capital. (Ibid., p. 16.) It is possible that urban temples had annual festivals that included opera performances, but we know nothing about them, since the sources concentrate on entertainment in the pleasure quarters.

3 Ibid., p. 191. Though some of Idema and West's evidence comes from Yuan dynasty sources, they are explicitly concerned with pre-Yuan performance.

4 Fan Pen Li Chen, *Chinese Shadow Theatre: History, Popular Religion, and Women Warriors* (Montreal: McGill-Queen's University Press, 2007), p. 71.

5 *Crossing the Five Passes* was a popular opera in Shanxi that went by various names. For the version performed in Nanshe Village of Lucheng County, see Li Yuanxing, "Zhuishu Nanshe 'Tiao gui' " [On the "Provoking the Demon" Ritual of Nanshe Village], *Xiju ziliao* 15 xia, 462. For "Capturing the Yellow Demon," see Johnson, *Spectacle and Sacrifice*, pp. 111–18.

6 Johnson, *Spectacle and Sacrifice*, pp. 295–96.

7 Ibid., pp. 204–05, 292–93.

8 Prints were also used for other purposes, such as decorating fans. Wang Shucun, *Xiqu nianhua* [New Year Prints with Opera Themes] (Taibei: Hansheng zazhishe, 1990), p. 104.

9 There is a mistake in the title: the character for "wave (*bo*)" is used rather than the character for "slope (*po*)." In Northern Mandarin the words are near homophones; perhaps they were true homophones in Fuyang county, Anhui province, where the print was made.

10 See plot summaries in Tao Zhunqi, *Jingju jumu chutan* [Preliminary Study of the Repertoire of Peking Opera], rev. ed. (Beijing: Zhongguo xiju chubanshe, 1980), p. 243; Yang Mengheng et al., *Zhongguo bangzi xiju da cidian* [Great Dictionary of Chinese Bangzi Opera] (Taiyuan: Shanxi renmin chubanshe, 1991), pp. 355–56; Wang Shucun, ed., *Zhongguo meishu quanji: Huihua bian* vol. 21, *Minjian nianhua* [Complete Collection of Chinese Art, Painting Series, vol. 21: Popular Prints] (Beijing: Renmin meishu chubanshe, 1985), notes, p. 46.

11 Yang, *Zhongguo bangzi xiju da cidian*, p. 7; Tao, *Jingju jumu chutan*, p. 6.

12 Yang, *Zhongguo bangzi xiju da cidian*, 6–7; *Complete Collection: Popular Prints*, notes, p. 20; Qi Senhua et al., eds., *Zhongguo quxue da cidian* [Great Dictionary for Chinese Drama Research] (Hangzhou: Zhejiang jiaoyu chubanshe, 1997), p. 550.

13 *Complete Collection: Popular Prints*, notes, p. 32.

14 Ibid., notes, p. 93.

15 The opera's plot could in turn have originated in storytelling or *chantefable*, always a possibility with local operas that do not seem to have analogues in novels or printed stories. But evidence for this is lacking.

16 Yang, *Zhongguo bangzi xiju da cidian*, pp. 137–38.

17 Ibid., p. 138.

18 Feng Jicai, ed., *Zhongguo muban nianhua jicheng: Zhuxian zhen juan* [Collected Chinese Woodblock New Year Prints: Zhuxian Prefecture] (Beijing: Zhonghua shuju, 2006), p. 160.

19 The character used throughout the set for the "Ping" in Pinggui is a simplified form of a character pronounced "*qiong*" meaning "poor." Thus the protagonist has the rather odd given name Qionggui, "Poor-rich."

20 Qi, *Zhongguo qux ue da cidian*, p. 615, says the genre was drum-song (*guci*); Yang, *Zhongguo bangzi xiju da cidian*, p. 272, says it was stringed ballad storytelling (*tanci*). Both genres combine verse and prose, hence the *chantefable* label.

21 Tao, *Jingju jumu chutan*, p. 172; Qi, *Zhongguo qux ue da cidian*, p. 616. Note that an entirely different opera also has the title *The Story of the Dragon-and-Phoenix Hairpin*.

22 Li Zhiqiang et al., ed., *Zhongguo Yangliuqing muban nianhua ji* [Collection of Woodblock New Year Prints from Yangliuqing] (Tianjin: Tianjin Yangliuqing huashe, 1992), notes to plates, pp. 149–52.

23 There are some signs that the designer was not well educated. The characters for *dian* "palace, grand hall" and *hu* "tiger" are miswritten. And when Xue is said to invite the princess to drink wine the rather vulgar phrase *chi jiu* for "drink wine" is used, no way to speak to a woman of high rank.

24 Wolfram Eberhard, "Topics and Moral Values in Chinese Temple Decorations," *Journal of the American Oriental Society* 87 (1967), pp. 22–32.

25 Ibid., p. 25.

26 Ibid., p. 26.

27 Ibid., p. 30.

28 Ibid., p. 25.

29 Bo Songnian, ed., *Zhongguo minjian meishu quanji: Diaosu juan* [Complete Collection of Chinese Folk Art: Sculpture] (Beijing: Renmin meishu chubanshe, 2002), p. 102; Zhang Daoyi et al., ed., *Gudai jianzhu diaoke wenshi: Xiwen renwu* [Carved Decorations on Traditional Architecture: Opera Figures](Nanjing: Jiangsu meishu chubanshe, 2007), p. 12.

30 There is at least one recent book devoted entirely to architectural decoration with opera themes (*Gudai jianzhu*) and reproductions of such carvings can be found in a number of books on Chinese vernacular architecture and folk crafts.

31 Bo, *Diaosu*, pp. 1–76, 281–306, passim. Like many folk crafts, this one eventually was professionalized.

32 Nancy Berliner, *Chinese Folk Art* (Boston: New York Graphic Society, 1986), pp. 153, 160.

33 For the robes of Daoist priests, see Stephen Little, ed., *Taoism and the Arts of China* (Chicago: The Art Institute of Chicago, 2000). Note especially the detail of a robe on p. 188. See also the Daoist robe in the exhibition, discussed in Yuhang Li's essay in this catalogue.

34 Bo Songnian, ed., *Zhongguo minjian meishu quanji* vol. 4: *Shanxi* [Complete Collection of Chinese Folk Art, vol. 4: Shanxi Province] (Beijing: Renmin meishu chubanshe, 1993), p. 3. Whether this can be said of embroidery in other provinces I do not know.

35 Yang, *Zhongguo bangzi xiju da cidian*, p. 367; Tao, *Jingju jumu chutan*, p. 256. In some versions of the opera Xiao kills himself and Guiying escapes with the pearl to her mother-in-law's house.

36 One should perhaps say fictionalized history, since the sources opera drew on were oral storytelling and popular fiction, not formal works of history. But some popular historical fiction drew on dynastic histories, and oral traditions could have roots in actual events. Note that scenes from the nonhistorical romantic opera *Romance of the Western Chamber* (*Xixiang ji*), written originally for an elite audience, which appear a number of times in the exhibition, embellish objects that appear to have been intended for upper class consumers.

MEI MEI RADO

Three

Images of Opera Characters Related to the Qing Court

Theatrical performance constituted an essential part of Qing dynasty (1644–1911) palace entertainments, imperial ceremonies, and court rituals. Court theater ranged from large-scale, long dramas featuring spectacular pageantry and didactic themes to small-scale, private performances of selected episodes showcasing singing and acting skills. Several Manchu monarchs, notably the Qianlong emperor (r. 1736–1795), the Xianfeng emperor (r. 1851–1861), and the Empress Dowager Cixi (1835–1908), were enthusiastic lovers and promoters of opera. Their personal tastes had a profound impact on the stylistic and institutional developments of Qing opera. In particular, the Qing court played a crucial role in popularizing and refining the regional operatic styles in the capital, which evolved into the Peking opera as it is known today.

The vibrant theater culture in the Qing court left a rich visual legacy, as seen in a number of paintings, now in the Palace Museum, Beijing, and other collections, representing operatic scenes and dramatic characters. Several long handscroll paintings from the Kangxi (r. 1662–1722) and the Qianlong periods represent celebratory festivals during emperors' or empress dowagers' birthdays, in which theater performances took place on temporary stages along the route from the imperial palaces outside the city to the Forbidden City.[1] For example, in the scroll *Copy of The Kangxi Emperor's Sixtieth Birthday Celebration*, the performance scenes punctuate the street ceremonies and serve as intermittent visual climaxes that showcase magnificence and splendor (fig. 3.1). Another type of theatrical image produced in the Qing court represents stage tableaux composed of several characters and stage settings, strongly influenced by the visual style of popular woodblock prints, or New Year prints (*nianhua*) (fig. 3.2).[2] Popular theatrical prints made by the commercial workshops Yangliuqing in Tianjin also entered the palace collection.[3] The genre of imperial albums of stage tableaux shows strong compositional similarity with the Yangliuqing examples at

3.1
Unidentified Court Artists
Chinese, Qing Dynasty (1644–1911)
Detail of *Copy of the Kangxi Emperor's Sixtieth Birthday Celebration, Scroll Two*, late 18th century
Handscroll, ink and color on silk, 17 3/4 × 2499 in. (45 × 6347.5 cm)
The Palace Museum, Beijing

3.2
Chinese, Qing Dynasty (1644–1911)
Crossroads, late 19th century
Album leaf, ink and color on silk, 21 5/8 × 21 5/8 in. (55 × 55 cm)
The Palace Museum, Beijing

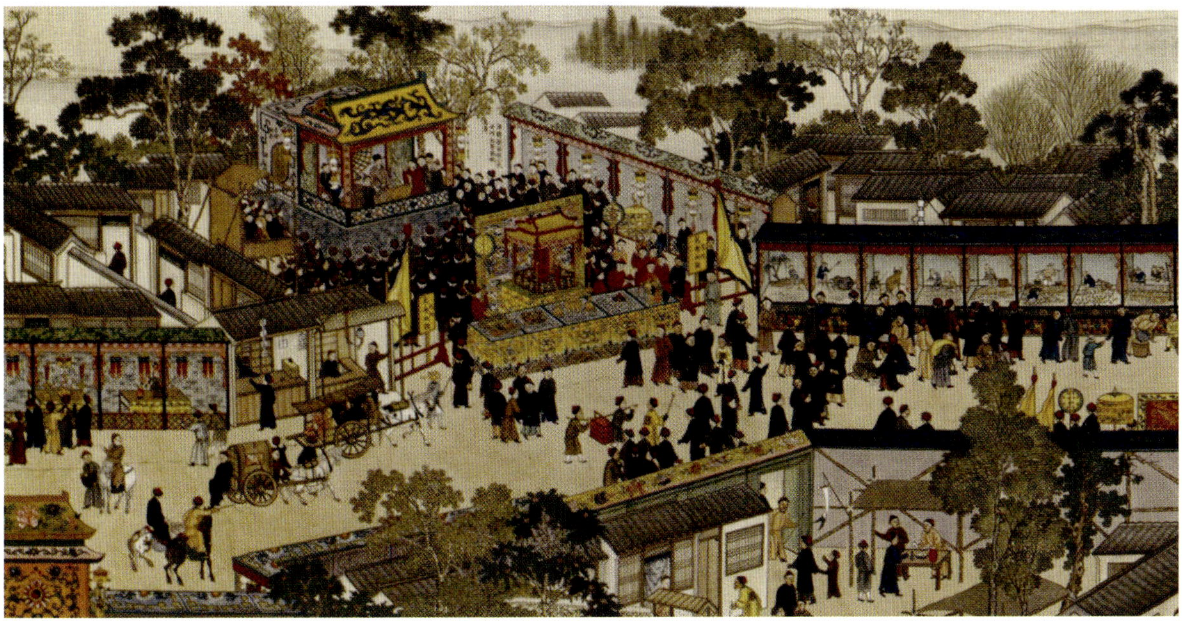

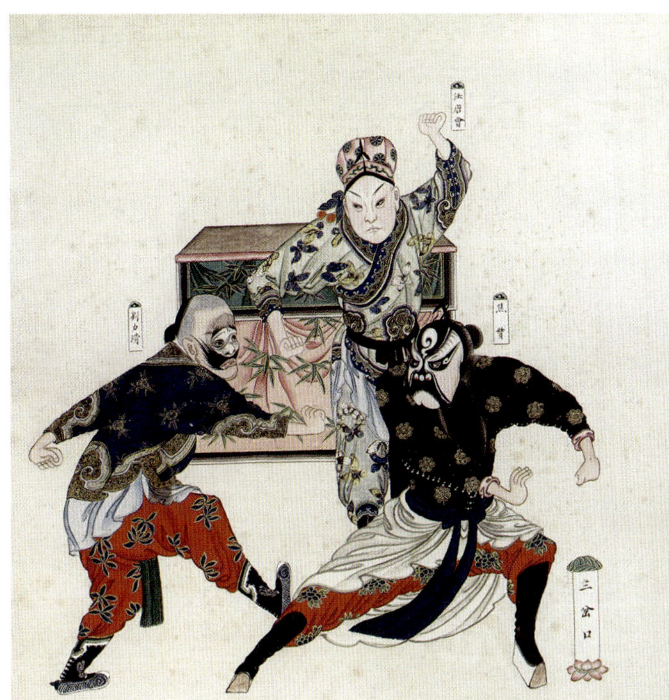

court. This resemblance bears witness to the interactions of theatrical visual culture between the palace and the outside in the late Qing period, which occurred in two directions. Some palace albums were reproduced by commercial publishers as well. For example, in 1879, the Shanghai-based Dianshizhai [the Touchstone Studio] made a photolithographic reproduction of the 1718 woodblock print version of the scroll *The Kangxi Emperor's Sixtieth Birthday Celebration*. The Dianshizhai editions were issued for both Chinese and Western audiences (cat. 8).[4]

The majority of the court-related theatrical images are serial portraits of stage characters mounted as albums or in loose leaves. Generally, they can be called "images of opera characters," as the play titles and characters' names are inscribed on these pictures. Surviving examples reveal their disparate representational modes and functional purposes. The four examples gathered from different sources consist of three visual types. The first one, which may be termed "mask image," shows detailed stage facial makeup (fig. 3.3, cat. 46). The second type illustrates dramatic characters in half-length portraits, both in the painting format (cat. 47) and as textile patchwork (fig. 3.4),[5] and the third category also depicts individual stage characters but in full-length (fig. 3.5).

On these pages I will discuss the court contexts of theatrical performance and analyze the visual modes as well as the possible functions of these characters' images, with a focus on the mask images and the half-length portrait paintings on display in the current exhibition. These characters' images were an important component of the opera culture in the Qing palace, attesting to a dynamic and diversified image-making practice centered on the court theater. As pictorial records, these images contain rich information on the performance repertoire, costumes, makeup, and acting styles, often serving as the complements or alternatives to ephemeral actual performances and less tangible textual documents such as stage directions and playbills. As painting representations, these images introduced new formulas to the theatrical visual tradition, synthesizing a variety of pictorial forms appropriated from other genres such as series of famous figures and informal portraits. Their representational modes also enable us to observe the relationships among role-types, actors, and dramatic characters in the operatic practice and cultural imagination of the period.

Qing Court Theater Performance

After a period of obscurity in the turbulent early Qing dynasty, court drama gained vitality by the 1680s, following the Kangxi emperor's success in quelling a series of political upheavals. In 1683, an extravagant performance of the *Maudgalyāyana* (Mulian) drama took place outside the palace, a public celebration of the defeat of the Ming loyalist forces in Taiwan.[6] This opera performance marked the consolidation and the prowess of the Manchu Empire. Throughout the Qing dynasty, the vicissitudes of court opera performance stood as a barometer of the rise and fall of Manchu power. The symbolic political significance of the court theater was intrinsically ambivalent. On the one hand, the magnificence and rectitude of the court drama partially shared the function of state ritual and music (*liyue*)—a signifier of dynastic stability and prosperity in Confucian ideology. On the other hand, the ruler's indulgence in extravagant performance could easily become a sign of the neglect of state duty and a manifestation of dynastic decadence.

In the late seventeenth century, Nanfu and Jingshan—two imperial offices in charge of the court drama within the Imperial Household Department—were established. Their exact founding dates and their activities during the Kangxi (1662–1722) and Yongzheng (1723–35) periods remain unclear due to the lack of early records.[7] Court drama flourished during the Qianlong period (1736–95), when the Qing Empire was at its pinnacle. Nanfu and Jingshan substantially enlarged their scale, with Nanfu developing into a sizable organization with over 1,000 persons (from about 100 in the Kangxi period)[8] and now including three inner schools (*neixue*), made up of eunuch actors, and two outer schools (*waixue*), comprising southern performers from the Lower Yangzi region and bannermen students.[9] Jingshan had a similar structure on a smaller scale. During the Jiaqing (1796–1820) and the Daoguang (1821–50) periods, when the financial and political power of the Qing Empire declined, the drama bureaus underwent significant downsizing. Jingshan was merged into Nanfu in 1821,[10] and in 1827, the Daoguang emperor abolished the outer schools and reorganized Nanfu into Shengping shu, or Bureau of Ascendant Peace.[11]

The number of performers gradually increased during the Xianfeng reign (1851–61), and outside actors regained permission to serve in the palace in 1860.[12] In October that year, English and French armies invaded Beijing during the Second Opium War (1856–60). Retreating to Rehe, the imperial hunting resort and summer residence about 150 miles from the capital, the Xianfeng emperor indulged himself in opera until his death in August 1861.[13] During the Guangxu period (1876–1908), court drama performance reached another peak, largely resulting from Empress Dowager Cixi's enthusiastic promotion. Aside from the eunuch actors serving in the Shengping shu, Cixi also founded her own private troupe—Universal Celebration (Putian tongqing).[14] In addition, famous troupes in residence in Beijing were frequently called to perform in the palace.[15] The revival of opera performance at court in the late nineteenth century may be viewed as part of Cixi's cultural ambition to reclaim the past glory of the high Qing dynasty.[16] But such excessiveness in spite of national crisis and economic deterioration inevitably proved to be a fatal symptom of a waning empire.

Court dramas were performed during four major types of occasions in the Qing dynasty—seasonal festivals throughout the year, such as the Lantern Festival and the Mid-Autumn Festival; imperial ceremonies in the Palace Hall, marking such occasions as royal engagements and weddings; birthdays of the emperors, empresses, and empress dowagers;[17] and the annual royal hunt in autumn at Rehe.[18] These events were highly ritualized occasions. The hunt at Rehe and the celebration of major imperial birthdays particularly functioned as diplomatic affairs for the Qing rulers to receive foreign envoys and audiences from Korea, Mongolia, and Central Asia. Exuberant theatrical performance served as a means to impress the visitors with the Qing Empire's splendor and strength.[19] The memoirs of foreign envoys contain some of the most vivid descriptions of high Qing court theater. For instance, the Korean scholar Park Jiwon (1737–1805), who visited Rehe in 1780 as part of the entourage of the Joseon court embassy for the Qianlong emperor's seventieth birthday, recounted in his travel diary:

> The thirteenth day of the Eighth Month is the birthday of His Imperial Majesty. Plays were performed for the three days before that date and the three days thereafter. . . .
>
> A stage had been built at the eastern side of the hunting lodge. [The separate floors of] the pavilion all had double eaves; they were so high that you could erect banners five *zhang* in height and so wide that they could accommodate myriads of people and that these people did not hinder each other during the decoration [of the stage] or the removal [of props]. The wooden imitation mountains to both sides of the stage were as high as the roof of the pavilion and were covered with jade trees and jasper woods; silk had been cut into flowers, and pearls had been strung together as fruits.
>
> Whenever a play was performed, those who took part in the performance were numbered by the hundreds. They were clad in gowns of brocade and embroidery and in each play they changed their costume but they always wore the garb of Chinese officials. Whenever the stage was decorated for a play, a brocade folding screen was placed on the stage, and not a sound was to be heard except for the shuffle of footsteps. When after a moment the screen was removed, [one saw] inside the pavilion the highest mountains, the broadest oceans, gnarly pine trees and a rising sun. This is what is called "the ninefold hymn." The songs were all in the mode of *la* and the music was loud and piercing as if sounded from heaven. . . . The accompanying instruments were the mouth-organ, the piccolo, the flute, the bells, the chimes, the lute and the zither—no drum was used, just a gong. In a moment mountains were moved and ocean replaced, without any misunderstanding or fault.[20]

The core repertoire of the court theater consisted of several full-scale, lengthy dramas with historical or mythical subject matter. Court academicians compiled them in the mid-eighteenth century by consolidating and refining popular plays from the early period. Called "grand plays" (*daxi*) or "serially performed palace plays" (*liantai benxi*), each of these dramas required several days and a cast of hundreds, even a thousand or more actors, to be performed in its entirety. Frequently performed grand plays, for example, included *Golden Norms for Exhorting Virtue* (*Quanshan jinke*) derived from *Maudgalyāyana, The Precious Raft of Ascendant Peace* (*Shengping baofa*) based on *Journey to the West* (*Xiyou ji*), *Annals of the Tripartition* (*Dingzhi chunqiu*) adapted from the stories of the Three Kingdoms (*Sanguo yanyi*), and *The Resplendent Picture of Loyalty and Righteousness* (*Zhongyi xuantu*) recounting the legends of *The Water Margin* (*Shuihu zhuan*).[21] All these court dramas contained mass pageantry scenes featuring lavish costumes, spectacular props, and sometimes, fanciful mechanical devices. In addition, there were about two hundred short plays—many of them celebratory pageants with auspicious themes—to be performed on various ceremonial occasions.[22] A number of popular plays incorporating repertoires of outside troupes, such as comic stories and romances, were also performed at court.[23] In the early nineteenth century, upon the dismissal of the outer schools and the downsizing of actors, full performance of the grand plays was discontinued at court. Instead, only selected episodes were performed.[24]

Before the nineteenth century, court drama was primarily tailored for *kunqiang*-style music, although some plays took the *yiqiang* style. An assortment of regional opera styles including *Qinqiang* and *pihuang*, collectively called *luantan* ("chaotic playing"), were regarded as vulgar by the court but were nonetheless present in the capital during the eighteenth century.[25] As well studied by theater scholars, the four famous Hui troupes sponsored by wealthy Anhui merchants arrived in Beijing from 1790 to 1803 and helped popularize the music style rooted in erhuang, which eventually led to the formation of the Peking opera in the later

3.3
Chinese, Qing Dynasty (1644–1911), Qianlong Period (1746–1795)
Design of Stage Makeup for An Escorting Ghost from the Play Golden Norms for Exhorting Virtue (Quanshan jinke), ca. 1746–95
Album leaf, ink and color on paper, 18 × 18 in. (46 × 46 cm)
The Field Museum, Chicago
121928

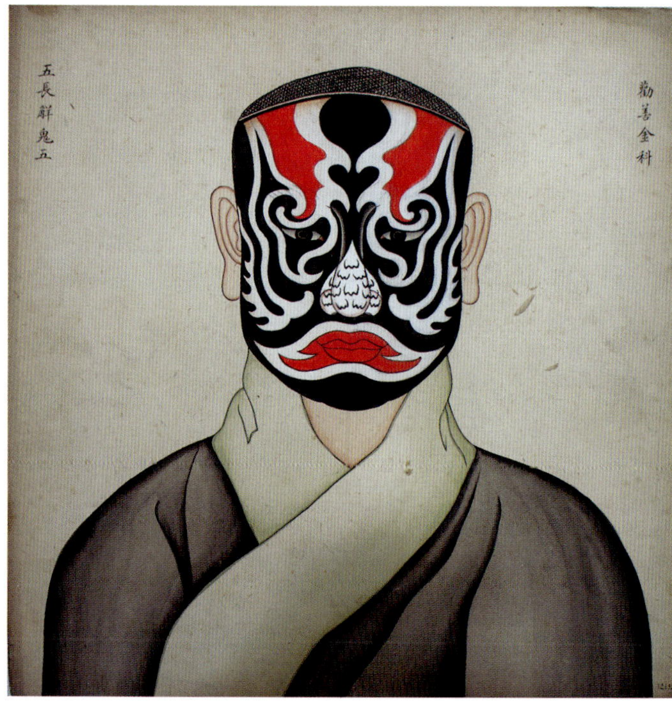

nineteenth century.[26] The earliest textual record showing luantan plays being performed at court dates to 1825, but only by 1860 were civilian opera instructors and students specializing in luantan largely recruited by Shengping shu.[27] From the 1880s onward when Cixi rose to power, her personal preference for the pihuang-style dramas resulted in their steady growth in the Qing court repertoire.[28] Cixi herself even organized a massive project to adapt the grand play *Elegant Music for a Brilliant Age* (*Zhaodai xiaoshao*)—stories of the female generals of the Yang clan—from the original kunqiang to pihuang tunes and texts.[29]

The last few decades of the nineteenth century saw increasingly closer interactions between the court and commercial troupes. Cixi frequently invited famous troupes and actors in Beijing to perform at court, who often adapted their scripts and performances to suit the court taste.[30] These court-related performances in turn spread new fashions outside the Forbidden City, contributing to the development of new acting styles and new repertoire among the commercial troupes. In some cases, court scripts even circulated outside the palace and were adopted by professional troupes.[31]

Mask Images

Seventy-nine leaves of mask images belonging to the same series are found today in the collections of the Field Museum, Chicago; Chinese National Academy of Arts, Beijing; and Samuel Herrup, a Massachusetts-based antique store. Berthold Laufer (1874–1934), a prominent anthropologist and specialist of Asian culture, purchased forty leaves from the series in Beijing between 1908 and 1910, which later entered the collection of the Field Museum (cat. 46). Each leaf shows a dramatic character in bust length with an elaborately painted, almost life-size face. The basic composition of all leaves follows the same model, repeating the formulaic sketch of face and garment, whereas the makeup is executed in full color and minute details. On some leaves, the makeup only covers the area above the mouth, to be joined by beards to complete the stage look. The upper edge of the makeup borders on a hair net. Each leaf bears the play title on the right and the character's name on the left. Wherever a beard is required, the type of beard to be used is specified below the character's name. For example, one of the forty Judges of the Nether world (*panguan*) performing in *Marvelous Tunes for Festivals* (*Jiejie haoyin*) takes a "red flying beard" (cat. 46.3).

The play titles appearing on the images range from grand plays such as *Golden Norms for Exhorting Virtue*, *The Precious Raft of Ascendant Peace*, *The Creation of the Gods* (*Fengshen tianban*), court festival plays collectively titled *Marvelous Tunes for Festivals*, to various popular dramas including *Jade Mandarin Ducks* (*Yu yuanyang*) by Zhou Gao (active circa 1650s) and *Coincidental Reunion* (*Qiao tuanyuan*) by Li Yu (1610–1680). The opera characters from the set of *Marvelous Tunes for Festivals* are all stamped with a red Chinese character on the top center—either the word *jie* (festival) or the word *shou* (birthday), which probably served to indicate the characters' associations with different ceremonial occasions. A few leaves bearing the names of short episodes are specified as "yiqiang" or "kunqiang." As seen in the unmounted set in the collection of the Field Museum, each leaf also has a number inscribed on the back,[32] with the highest number being 579, associated with the second rhinoceros spirit in the play *The Precious Raft of Ascendant Peace*. The number seems to correspond to the sequence of the characters of one play appearing on stage.[33] The number 579—by

3.4
Chinese, Qing Dynasty (1644–1911), Guang Xu Period (1875–1909)
The Character White Dragon from the Play Nazha Disturbing the Sea (Nazha naohai), 1875–1909
Album leaf, pasted textiles and ink on silk, 15 5/16 × 13 in. (39 × 33 cm)
The Palace Museum, Beijing

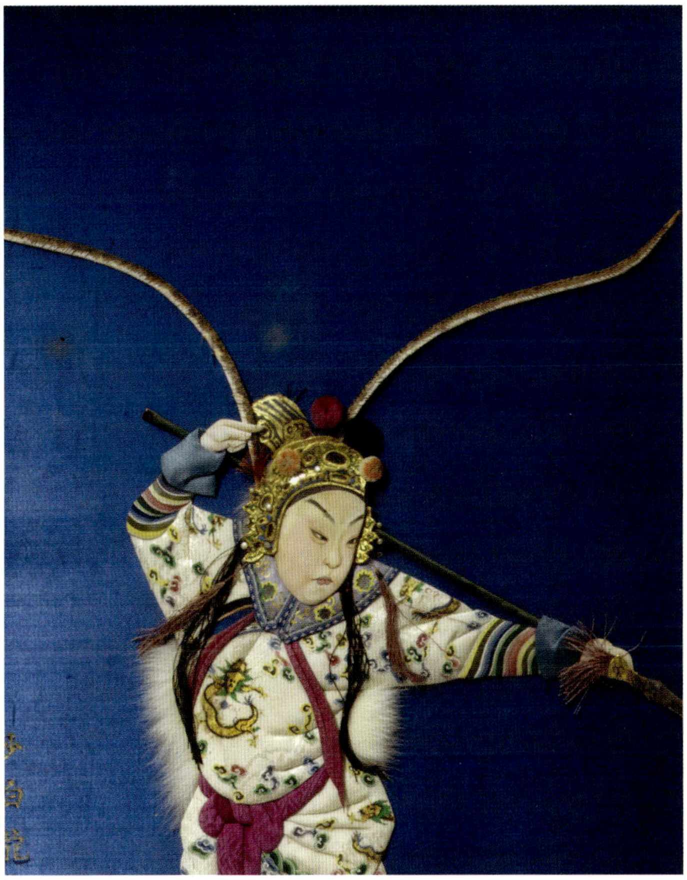

no means the highest in this play—attests to the massive scale of these performances. Based on the fact that these plays were court operas established in the mid-eighteenth century, the theater scholar Dai Yun correctly dates these mask images to the Qianlong period after 1746 and before 1795.[34] Given that the downsizing of the imperial theater bureaus beginning from the Jiaqing period did not permit the grand plays to be performed in their entirety any more, the date of mid- to late Qianlong period for these images seems logical.

Probably functioning as some master design plan of masks for easy reference and copying, these images were primarily intended to demonstrate stage makeup. Their grouping by ceremonial type or music style also suggests their practical use in performance management and their role as archival materials.

Qing court scripts of dramas usually contain detailed instructions on characters' stage costumes, written or printed in smaller size or in a different color to distinguish them from the main verses for singing and reciting, but information on the facial makeup and beard accessories is conspicuously and consistently missing from the texts. For example, the opening of the twentieth act of *Golden Norms for Exhorting Virtue* notes, "Minor [role-types] play the five supervising escorting ghosts, each wearing a ghost's hairpiece, a narrow-sleeved jacket with *mang*-type brocade, a tiger-skin soldier's drape, and a tiger-skin skirt, and each holding a weapon."[35] The stage image of an escorting demon is not complete without a painted face. As a leaf showing the makeup for "the fifth of the five supervising escorting ghosts" from the same play reveals, such masks featured bold patterns in contrasting black and white with red highlights to exaggerate the mouth and eyebrows (fig. 3.3). The mask images and the textual instructions on costume complemented each other in guiding the creation of a stage character.

A later manual on stage costume, *Instructions on Headgear and Clothing* (*Chuandai tigang*), datable to 1820 but very likely based on materials from the Qianlong period, also contains no information on characters' face painting.[36] It seems that stage makeup and costumes were conceived, prepared, and managed separately in the imperial theater bureau. As we know from the records of the Imperial Workshops, theatrical costumes used for palace performances were designed by court artists with imperial approval and then manufactured in Suzhou.[37] There is virtually no textual reference on the procedure of Qing court mask design and makeup artists. Mask images hence provide a precious record of this ephemeral visual phenomenon.

Most characters represented in the surviving mask paintings are supernatural figures such as judges of the underworld and attendants to deities. Exhibiting fanciful and flamboyant designs, the masks have vividly contrasting colors in bright shades and curling, flying patterns that enliven their faces with demonic qualities. Some designs highlight the mythical identities of the characters through a bold suppression of human facial features. For instance, Weiyueyan, one of the twenty-eight star deities, who is associated with the swallow, has a face entirely transformed into a black-and-white swallow against a red background (cat. 46.1). The bird's body and wings cover his nose and eyes, and its pointed beak is superimposed onto the human mouth. Also, inexhaustible variations mark the designs of the masks. Even for interchangeable roles, such as the eight attendant deities to the Goddess Nüwa, no two have anything resembling the same makeup. The impressive visual effect of this makeup on stage is described by the Qing scholar official Zhao Yi (1727–1814): "At times when all the gods and ghosts have assembled, there are thousands of masks but they all are completely different."[38]

Full-Length and Half-Length Images of Opera Characters

Serial images of characters from individual plays figure prominently among the extant theatrical paintings that could be linked to Qing court theater culture. There is only one known set of full-length portraits, as seen in two albums (in 100 leaves) in the collections of the Palace Museum, Beijing. The album represents forty-four plays, and under each play title, two to six main characters are depicted (figs. 3.5, 3.7, 3.8, 3.9).

Half-length images of dramatic characters have survived in quantity. Approximately 500 leaves in the same format are known today, scattered in various collections including the National Library of China (formerly the Beijing Library), the Chinese National Academy of Arts, and the Metropolitan Museum of Art, New York.[39] The Metropolitan Museum album, which has not previously attracted scholarly attention, was acquired by Alan Priest, then Curator of Chinese Art, in 1929 in Beijing. The size and the visual style of the images in this set are consistent with the widely published series from the National Library of China and the Chinese National Academy of Arts, and the mounting format of the Metropolitan Museum album is identical to that of the National Library of China album. All these details suggest a shared origin as part of a series that Chinese scholars conventionally call "the Shengpin shu albums."[40]

All plays depicted in the full-length sets, and most in the half-length sets, are luantan dramas, but in the half-length series, more personages are represented for each play. For instance, the 100 leaves of the Metropolitan Museum set depict only six plays. The drama repertoire and costumes shown in these albums can safely date them to the late Tongzhi and Guangxu periods (circa 1870s to 1900).

Unsigned and undated, full-length figure paintings were probably works by court painters serving in the Painting Academy (Ruyi

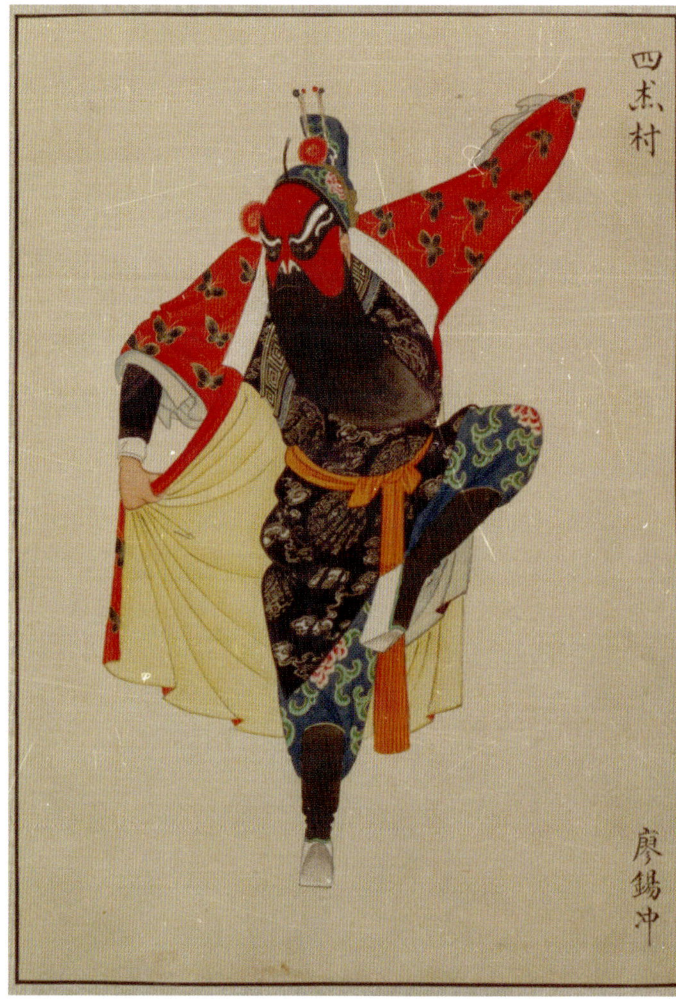

guan). Textual records from the imperial archives provide evidence that court painters produced a range of theatrical paintings. For example, the court artist Shen Zhenlin (active 1821–82) was asked to paint "operatic figures in eighteen leaves,"[41] and in 1891, a long handscroll depicting various scenes of theatrical performances was commissioned.[42] This full-length portrait album and a set of half-length portrait leaves of dramatic characters in the textile format (fig. 3.4) were stored in the Shoukang palace where Cixi resided.[43] They probably belonged to Cixi's private collection for her personal enjoyment.

The so-called Shengping shu albums of half-length portrait paintings have also been attributed to the court workshop.[44] The attribution is plausible to some extent. Their format and style closely resemble the textile set, attesting to the same court aesthetic. As I will elaborate below, these half-length portraits also exhibit some similarity to the full-length series in terms of the images' visual style and compositional strategy. The massive scale of this image-making project demonstrates the vibrant visual culture associated with luantan drama. Cixi—the keen opera lover and ambitious cultural promoter—may well have commissioned these pictures. However, a strong sense of formulaic reproduction characterizes these half-

3.5
Chinese, Qing Dynasty (1644–1911)
The Character Liao Xichong from the Play Four Heroes Village (Sijie cun), ca. 1870–1900
Album leaf, ink and color on silk
The Palace Museum, Beijing

length portraits and suggests a less sophisticated audience. Given the active exchanges of theater performances between the court and commercial troupes in the capital as well as the circulation of court painting style outside the palace, it is also possible that these albums were executed by an outside studio closely following the court model.[45] I suggest that we view these so-called Shengping shu albums as evidence of the extended influence Qing court theater taste had on visual culture during this time.

Interestingly, the opening page of each play in the half-length series bears the phrase "costume and makeup [shall] follow these [illustrations]."[46] Zhu Jiajin, a renowned scholar of Qing court art and culture, maintains that this note must have been added by antique dealers to enhance the sales value of these palace albums when they entered the market, as the personnel in charge of the theater wardrobe at court did not need illustrations to manage the stage costumes.[47] However, upon close examination of accessible examples—the Metropolitan Museum album and the set in the Chinese National Academy of Arts—on any given leaf that bears this phrase, its calligraphy style and ink tonality clearly do not display any difference from those of the title and character's name on the same page.[48] It is unlikely that they were added later. If the albums were originally created outside the palace to disseminate the stage fashion of court theater, the phrase might have been fully valid for advertising the authenticity of the information. But despite the meticulous depictions of costumes and makeup, these images would not have been used for stage instructions. First, the half-length portraits that only show the upper body do not provide adequate information on the costumes. Second, the images repeat certain formulae instead of creating individual models. The equivocal phrase "costume and makeup [shall] follow these [illustrations]" echoes the ambiguous purpose of these albums: the vivid pictorial quality of these images seems to suggest an artistic pursuit beyond the function of practical instruction, yet the minute attention to costume and makeup details and the extensive serialization also bestow the albums with a manual-like quality on the superficial level.

There are two ways that the half-length and full-length portraits are similar in composition. First, each leaf is composed with one character in the center against a blank background. Second, all figures turn slightly inward or outward, and figures on two facing leaves, although not necessarily two characters in the same scene, engage in a certain subtle interaction through their slightly crossed eyes or corresponding postures (cat. 47). The compositional plan carries an aesthetic dimension that further enhances the viewing experience, and the two albums share some of the same traits in the rendition of costumes and facial features. Costumes in both sets follow the same codes and formulae as contemporary stage dress. For example, the princess wears a cloud-shaped shoulder piece and a court robe with multiple decorative borders around the sleeves and two rows of streamers on the hem (figs. 3.6, 3.7). Surviving theater costumes confirm the realistic quality of this depiction (cat. 6). In addition, all figures are depicted in silk outfits with lavish embroidery despite their varying identities—a feature that reveals the court taste for extravagant display. The representations of the figures' faces in the two albums are also derived from the same pictorial model. For instance, the faces of the female lead (*dan*) are portrayed in the same oval shape consisting of elongated, curved eyebrows, tilted eyes outlined with two thin lines to indicate the creases, and half-opened lips only rouged on the lower center.

Despite these overall similarities, the full-length and the half-length portraits exhibit very different modes of conveying theatricality and engaging viewers. The former places much more emphasis on the theatrical action and dramatic narrative than the latter. In this set, each figure strikes a stage pose with the body either in motion or momentarily frozen with tension. For instance, the martial hero Liao Xichong in the play *Four Heroes Village* (*Sijie cun*) appears in a powerful and dynamic pose with his left knee bent forward, his right hand opening the robe, and his left arm thrown back (fig. 3.5). In the stage performance, this intimidating gesture often occurs right before the martial action, announcing hostility and challenge. It serves to accumulate force and accelerate tension. In another example, a monk sits on the floor with his palm pushing forward and his legs raised, as he quivers with fear (fig. 3.8). The image well captures the stage action of the character in the middle of a quick, backward movement in small steps, which represents defeat and horror. In this album, the theatrical narrative

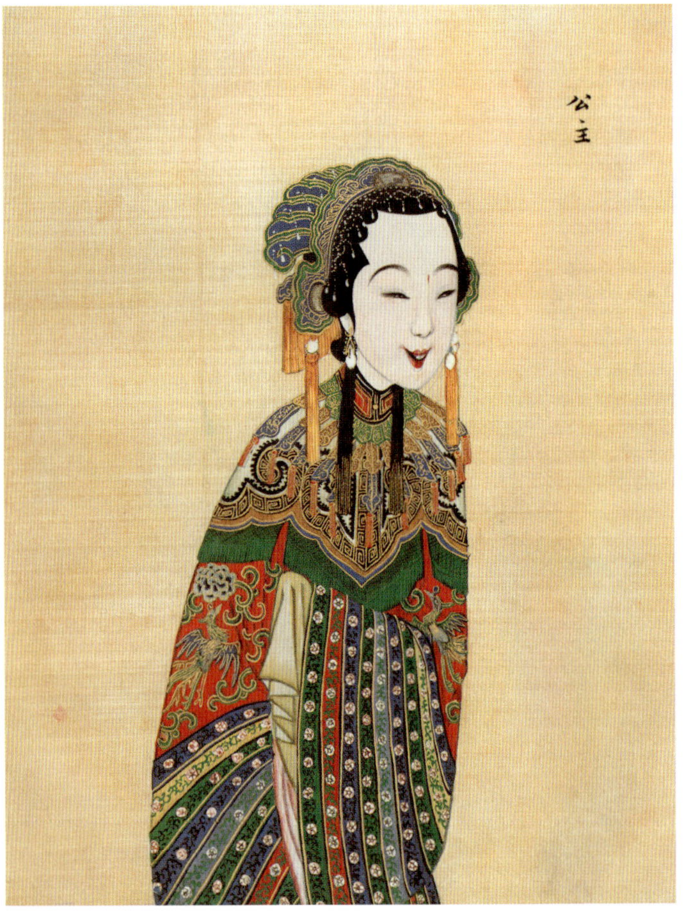

3.6
Chinese, Qing Dynasty (1644–1911)
The Character Princess in the Play The Bridge of Peace (Taiping qiao), ca. 1870–1900
Album leaf, ink and color on silk, painting: 10 3/8 × 8 1/4 in. (26.4 × 21 cm)
National Library of China

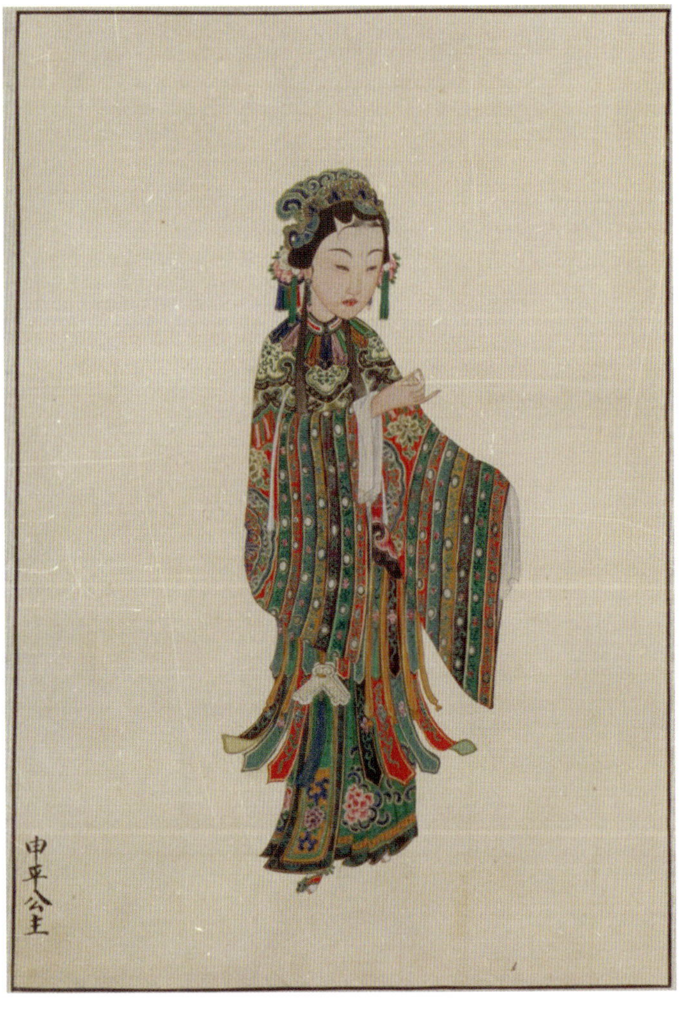

3.7
Chinese, Qing Dynasty (1644–1911)
The Character Princess Shenping from the Play Reed Marshes (Luhua dang), ca. 1870–1900
Album leaf, ink and color on silk
The Palace Museum, Beijing

3.8
Chinese, Qing Dynasty (1644–1911)
The Character Monk from the Play Beating the Drum (Da huagu), ca. 1870–1900
Album leaf, ink and color on silk
The Palace Museum, Beijing

3.9
Chinese, Qing Dynasty (1644–1911)
The Character Princess Tiejing from the Play Visiting Mother (Tanmu), ca. 1870–1900
Album leaf, ink and color on silk
The Palace Museum, Beijing

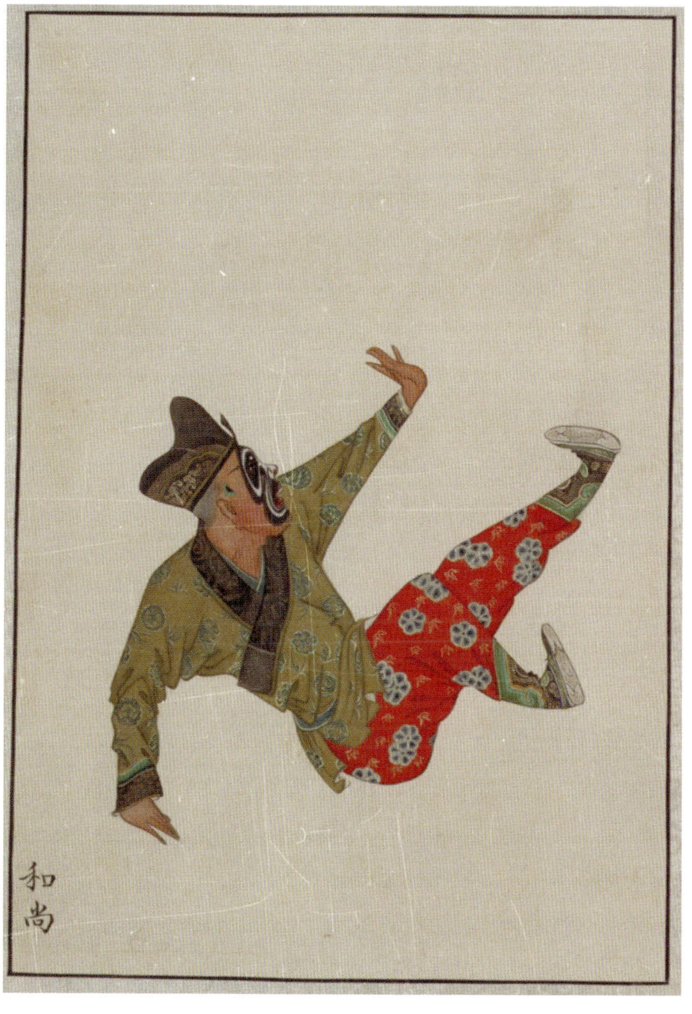

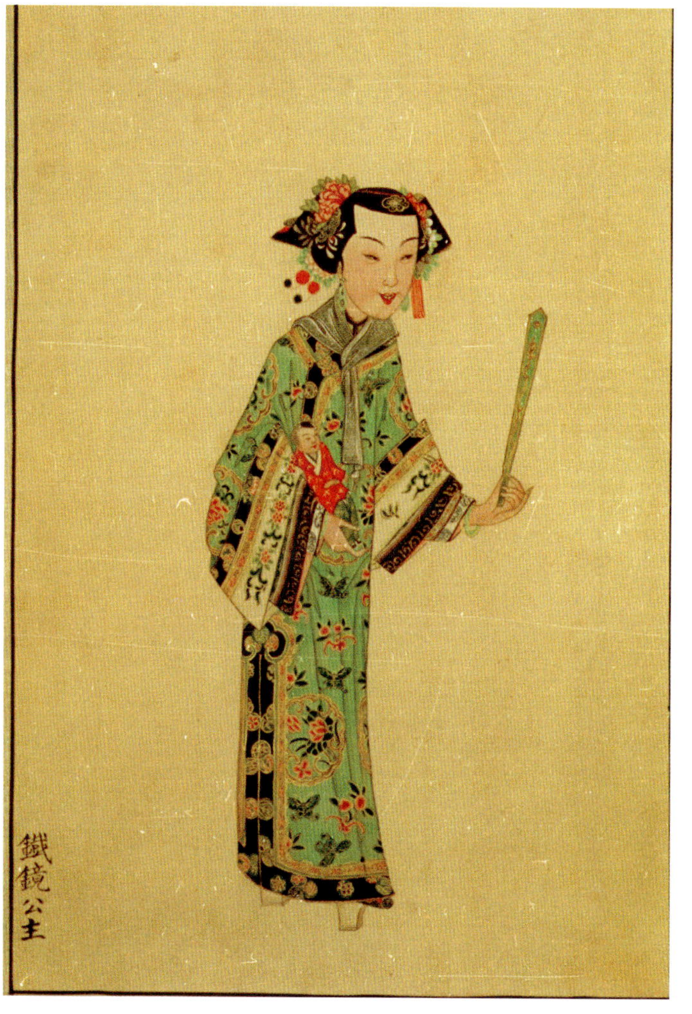

is condensed into the gestures and props of the characters. For example, Princess Tiejing in the play *Visiting Mother* (*Tanmu*) holds a baby doll in one hand and a border pass (*lingjian*) in the other (fig. 3.9). The entire play centers on how the princess helps her husband, Yang Silang, obtain a pass to enter Song territory and the consequences, while the baby pushes the plot forward at crucial moments. In short, the pictorial mode and representational strategy in this full-length portrait album provide visual clues that evoke the excitement of acting and the intrigue of pivotal plot elements in actual performance.

In comparison, the half-length format does not permit the figures to be shown in dramatic stage poses. They mostly stand in contrapposto with their gestures limited to stretching an arm or pointing a hand. Their props, such as a weapon or a symbolic object, though indicating a character's identity, are less effective in evoking the plots. In these portraits, the theatricality is mostly concentrated on the costumes and faces of the characters. The artists who painted these portraits clearly paid more attention to the brilliance of the decorative patterns of the figures' garments and makeup than to the coherence and credibility of their theatrical poses. In particular, hands are rendered in a rough way. Not only are the underdrawings visible in many cases, but also the hands are often disproportional, anatomically inaccurate, or very stiff. In addition, a sense of individuality true to each character is less

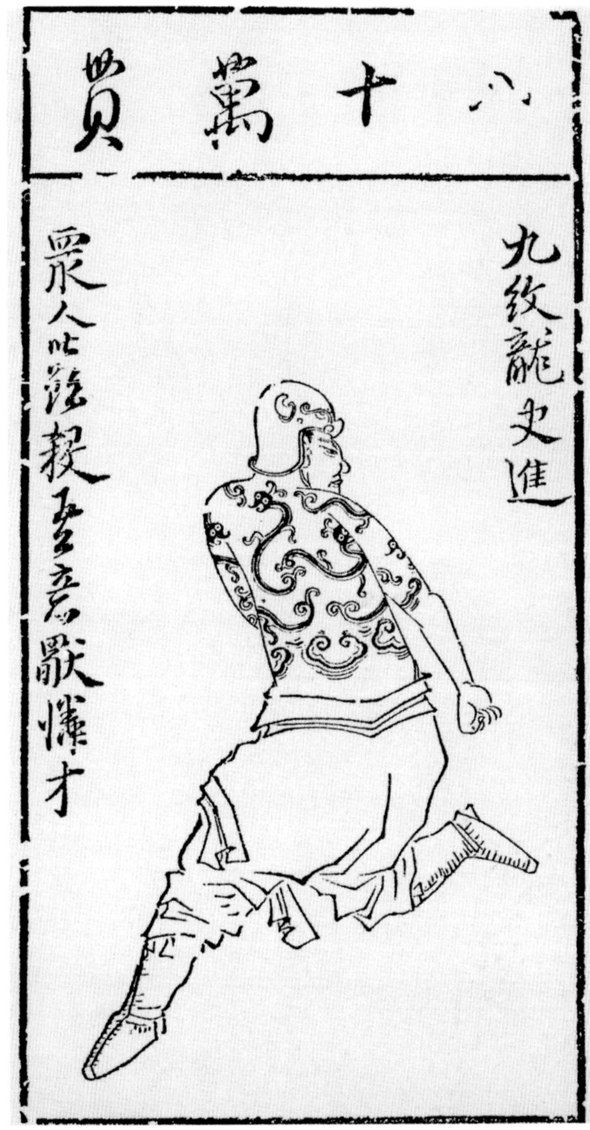

3.10
Chen Hongshou
Chinese, 1599–1652
The Character Shi Jin from the the *Novel* The Water Margin (Shuihu zhuan, alternately translated as Outlaws of the Marsh), 1633
Woodblock print, from a set of playing cards
Li Yimang Collection

visible in the half-length portraits than in the full-length series. Many characters, although bearing different names from different plays, are interchangeable with their nearly identical faces, poses, and costumes. It seems that each role-type is associated with a certain stereotyped mode of representation, and the entire series simply repeats these prototypes with slight variation each time to create a different personage. This feature points to a studio-based, mechanical mode of production. The repetition of magnificent details creates a lavish impression but the tendency to dwell on superficial aspects of theatricality suggests that these portraits were aimed at a less discriminating audience. According to Qing imperial archives, anecdotes, and eunuchs' memoirs, Cixi was a knowledgeable and demanding opera connoisseur.[49] It is unlikely that these half-length images would have matched her sophisticated taste and met her high standard.

Although these full-length and half-length character images adopt a portrait format, they are not likenesses of individual actors, but idealized and generic versions of contemporary stage roles. Serial representations of historical figures and imagined personages with formulaic features had a long tradition in Chinese visual art. While the origin may be traced to the imagery of wise and benevolent women (*lienü*), such as Gu Kaizhi's (344–405) famous scroll (a thirteenth-century copy), it was not until the late Ming and the Qing dynasties that this format flourished. One particularly popular genre is the "One Hundred Beauties" (*baimei tu*) series, which assembles a group of famous ladies from various historical, religious, and literary sources.[50] Contemporary courtesans also became the subject of serialized representation.[51] Illustrations of fictional characters drawn from literature emerged in the late Ming, with probably the most renowned example being a set of woodcut playing cards designed by Chen Hongshou (1599–1652) depicting personages from the novel *The Water Margin*. Each character occupies a blank leaf, and their poses are strongly reminiscent of stage performance (fig. 3.10).[52] By the nineteenth century, serial images of fictional figures abounded. The court artist Shen Zhenlin, for example, painted two albums of characters from *Strange Tales from a Chinese Studio* (*Liaozhai zhiyi*) and *Legends of Various States* (*Lieguozhi yanyi*).[53] Serialization in the visual field paralleled an intense interest in compiling manuals (*pu*) in the literary domain during the late Ming and Qing periods. The subjects of manuals extend from flowers and objects, to beautiful women and famous actors.[54] Pictorial serialization and literary compilation involved similar acts of selecting, grouping, and evaluating. Embedded in both processes was a connoisseurial effort to organize knowledge and to enforce order, thus symbolizing the power of possession.

In the Qing court context, the power of possession was in particular visualized through serialized illustrations of objects in the imperial collections and people under the control of the

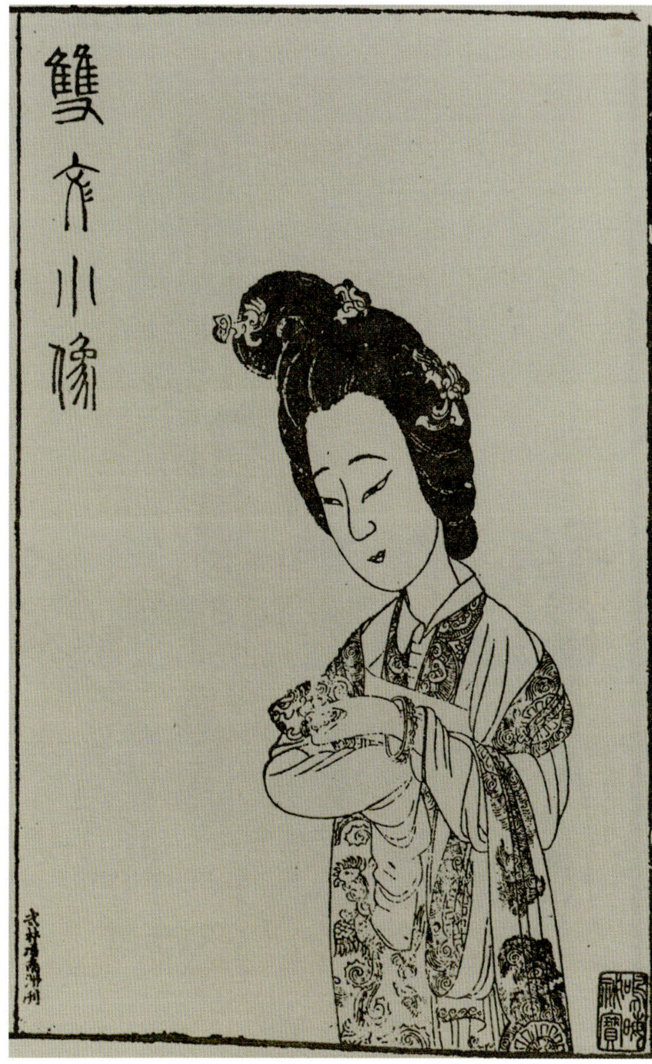

3.11
Chen Hongshou
Chinese, 1599–1652
Likeness of Oriele (Cui Yingying) from Romance of the Western Chamber (Xixiang ji), 1639
Woodblock print, frontispiece illustration from *Romance of the Western Chamber (Xixiang ji)*, 1639 Zhang Shenzhi edition

Manchu empire. The Qianlong emperor, for instance, commissioned a range of pictorial records of his antique collections, flowers, horses, and exotic animals and birds, as well as ethnic and foreign peoples.[55] At the current stage of research, nineteenth-century court painting practice is less clear to us. The serialized portraits of characters might have been conceived and perceived within the same visual tradition, serving to evoke imperial possession and connoisseurial control.

Serial representations of characters in stage costume also introduced a fresh visual mode to the repertoire of Chinese theatrical images. A survey of the Chinese painting tradition of theatrical figures is beyond the scope of this essay. In brief, early non-burial examples from the Song to Yuan periods, such as the album leaf *Zaju Performance* (*Zaju tu*) and the mural painting in the Guangsheng Monastery (1324) (fig. 1.4) that depict actors in theatrical costumes and poses, seem to focus on portraying the role-types rather than any specific scenes or dramatic characters. During the Ming and Qing dynasties, popular dramas such as *Romance of the Western Chamber* (*Xixiang ji*) and *The Peony Pavilion* (*Mudan ting*) were frequently illustrated in printed books. But these illustrations do not show the characters in stage costumes and instead depict them as social persons in daily settings (cat. 22). In other words, an imagined virtual world evoked by these illustrations overshadows the performative dimension of the drama. Dramatic personages depicted in their stage appearances are only seen in popular New Year prints and the late Qing examples of full-length and half-length character portraits associated with court theater culture. As I have already noted, these portraits of single characters incorporate the representations of the singularity of individual dramatic character as well as the generality of role-types. This new representational mode, with its emphasis on the performative aspect of drama, elicited a new visual experience that contributed to shaping the notion of Chinese theatricality.

The visual prototype and cultural implications of the half-length format also merits some discussion. Aside from their conventional association with ancestor portraits, the half-length format became increasingly popular in the subgenre of informal portraits, *xiaoxiang* ("small likeness"), from the late Ming through the Qing dynasties. As an alternative to the formal portrait that depicts a sitter in official dress and stiff pose, a xiaoxiang represents a sitter in casual clothing and in a private setting. The xiaoxiang genre provided a channel for male intellectuals to fashion and express their cultural identities. Half-length xiaoxiang, however, seem to be mostly associated with historical and fictional figures. This restriction may have to do with the deep-seated Chinese taboo against rendering the body of a living person in fragments. Fictional or legendary female figures were often depicted as half-length portraits in the xiaoxiang genre. For example, imagined half-length "small likenesses" of Cui Yingying and Du Liniang, the heroines of *Romance of the Western Chamber* and *The Peony Pavilion* respectively, frequently appear on the opening pages of printed drama books (fig. 3.11). Many figure paintings of the nineteenth century also depict imagined beauties against a blank background. Unlike the half-length male portraits in rigid full-frontal view that are usually associated with the imagery of wise men of the past (*xianxian*), these female half-length portraits depict generic beautiful women in sensual, sinuous poses, often in three-quarter profile, imparting a sense of intimacy and inviting close scrutiny. While the full-length character portraits

3.12
Chinese, Republican Period (1912–1949)
The Peking Opera Star Mei Lanfang as the White Snake, ca. 1920 (negative, probably later impression from 1930s–40s)
Silver nitrate photograph, 4 5/8 × 2 15/16 in. (11.8 × 7.5 cm)
Private Collection, Chicago

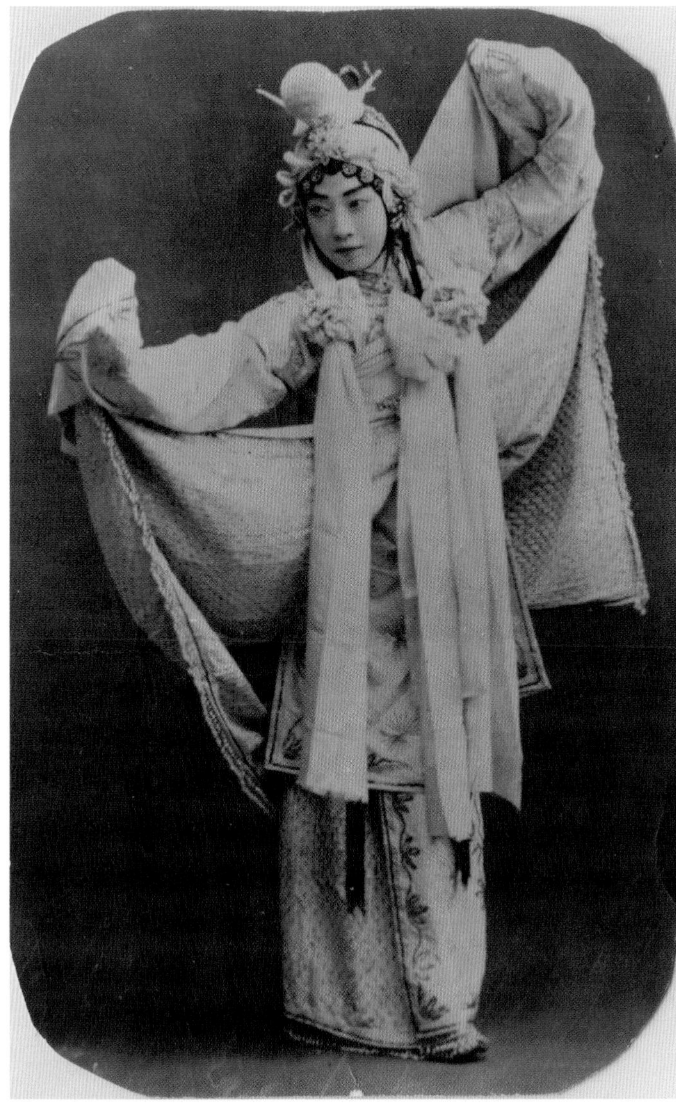

maintain a certain distance between the viewer and the figure, mimicking the viewing experience in the theater, the half-length series adopted the xiaoxiang visual tradition for imagined figures, creating a close-up visual experience that was more intimate and direct than viewing the actual performance.

Together the mask paintings and the full-length and half-length portraits of opera characters discussed here offer us a glance into Qing court theater visual culture and its extended influence. Each set from a different angle reveals perceptions and experiences of theatricality. The mask images intended for practical reference underscore theatricality as extravagant spectacle achieved through a massive parade of infinitely variable, fantastic makeup, while the full-length portraits represent theatricality as idealized synthesis of performance, plot, a character's personality, and a role-type's formulaic nature. As a less sophisticated adaptation of the full-length prototype yet with its distinct visual quality, the half-length series aimed to recapitulate the mode of the former but rather more effectively evokes theatricality through costume, excessive repetition of certain role-types, and implied intimate viewing experience.

Missing from (or rather, implicit in) all these representations is the dimension of the actor, an absence or allusiveness probably due to representational limitations. Or perhaps a certain visual code has been lost to us, as images of some famous actors well known to their patrons and fans might have been embedded in the images of opera characters, readily recognizable from certain characteristic poses or appearances.[56] This dimension of the actor did surface in photographic theatrical portraits in the early twentieth century. The visual mode of famous actors' photographs came under the influence of representations of stage characters in the late Qing dynasty, whereas the nature of this new medium introduced a fresh dimension of verisimilitude. As shown in a studio photo of Mei Lanfang (1894–1961) from around 1920, the Peking opera star in the stage costume of the incarnated White Snake spirit stands against a blank background and strikes a theatrical pose (fig. 3.12). Here the dramatic character that showcases his repertoire, the role-type that displays an operatic formula, along with the new element introduced by photography—the actor as star—are conflated in one picture to exemplify Chinese theatricality in its complete sense.

Notes

I am grateful to Mr. Liu Zhenghong, curator of court theater objects at the Palace Museum, Beijing; Mr. Liu Zhen, Professor of Chinese Theater at Chinese National Academy of Arts; Ms. Yuan-li Hou, conservator of Chinese paintings in the Department of Asian Art, the Metropolitan Museum of Art; and Mr. Jamie Kelly, Collections Manager in the Department of Anthropology, the Field Museum, for their assistance during my research for this essay.

1 The examples include *Kangxi liuxun wanshou tujuan* [Copy of The Kangxi Emperor's Sixtieth Birthday Celebration], 1713, *Chongqing Taihou liuxun wanshou tujuan* [The Empress Dowager Chongqing's Sixtieth Birthday Celebration], 1755–1757, and *Qianlong baxun wanshou tujuan* [The Qianlong Emperor's Eightieth Birthday Celebration], 1790. For a discus-

sion of the theater performance in some of these scrolls, see Zhu Jiajin, "Wanshou tu zhong de xiqu biaoyan xieshi" [Realistic Depiction of Theater Performance in the Birthday Scrolls], in Zhu Jiajin, *Gugong tuishi lu*, 2 vols. [Collected Essays upon my Retirement from the Palace Museum] (Beijing: Beijing chubanshe, 1998), 2: pp. 635–45.

2 Some of the album leaves in the collections of the Palace Museum, Beijing, are published in Haoxing Chen ed., *Junyue tianting: Gugong zhencang xiqu wenwu* [The Dragon's Stage: Chinese Opera Artifacts from the Palace Museum], exh. cat. (Macau: Museu de Arte de Macau, 2008).

3 Some examples of Yangliuqing theatrical prints in the palace collection are published in Chen, *Junyue tianting*.

4 The English version in the collection of the New York Public Library has a preface indicating that the publication was for the interest of "the European public." See *Wanshou shengdian, chuji* [*The Kangxi Emperor's Sixtieth Birthday Celebration*], vol. 4 (Shanghai: Dianshizhai, 1879).

5 Several portraits in the textile format are published in Chen, *Junyue tianting*.

6 See Dong Han (1624?–after 1697), *Chunxiang zhuibi* [Redundant Notes of Dong Han] (Juxiu tang, 1825), cited in Zhu Jiajin and Ding Ruqin, *Qingdai neiting yanju shimo kao* [Theater Performance in the Qing Court] (Beijing: Zhongguo shudian, 2007), pp. 7–8.

7 The earliest records that mention "Nanfu" and "Jingshan" date to 1686 and 1695, respectively, as seen in court files written in Manchu. But from 1681, Manchu files already showed various theater-related costs. See ibid., pp. 11–14.

8 Wang Zhizhang, *Qing Shengping shu zhilüe* [A Brief History of the Bureau of Ascendant Peace in the Qing Dynasty] (Shanghai: Shanghai shudian, 1991 [reprint, 1937]), p. 10; Ye Xiaoqing, "Imperial Institutions and Drama in the Qing Court," *The European Journal of East Asian Studies*, 2, no. 2 (Autumn 2003): p. 344.

9 Wang, *Qing Shengping shu*, pp. 9–10; Ye, "Imperial Institutions and Drama," p. 343.

10 Zhu and Ding, *Qingdai neiting yanju*, p. 125.

11 Ibid., p. 171.

12 Ibid., pp. 295, 301.

13 Ibid., pp. 303–18.

14 Ding Ruqin, *Qingdai neiting yanxi shihua* [History of Drama in the Qing Court] (Beijing: Zijincheng chubanshe, 1999), p. 27.

15 Zhu and Ding, *Qingdai neiting yanju*, pp. 399–402.

16 On Cixi's cultural projects emulating the Qianlong period, see Peng Ying-chen's talk "Reclaiming Past Glory: Antiquarian Trends in Late Nineteenth-Century Chinese Court Art," delivered in the 2013 annual meeting of the College Art Association, New York.

17 Zhaolian (1776–1833), *Xiaoting zalu* [Miscellaneous Notes of Xiaoting] (Beijing: Zhonghua shuju, 1997), pp. 377–78.

18 The annual Rehe hunting event was abolished in 1824. See Luo Yunzhi, *Qingdai Mulan weichang de tantao* [On the Mulan Hunting Ground of the Qing Dynasty] (Taipei: Wenshizhe chubanshe, 1989), p. 123.

19 For a discussion on court drama as diplomatic performance during the Qianlong period, see Liana Chen, "Ritual into Play: The Aesthetic Transformations of Qing Court Theatre" (PhD diss., Stanford University, 2009), chapter 3.

20 Park Jiwon, *Rehe riji* [Rehe Diary], 1784 (Shanghai: Shanghai shudian, 1997), p. 251. The English translation is quoted from Wilt Idema, "Performances on a Three-Tiered Stage: Court Theatre during the Qianlong Era," in Lutz Bieg, Erling von Mende, and Martina Siebert, eds., *Ad Seres et Tungusos–Festschrift für Martin Gumm zu seinem 65 Geburtstag am 25 Mai 1995* (Wiesbaden: Harrassowitz, 2000), p. 212.

21 Zhaolian, *Xiaoting zalu*, pp. 377–78.

22 Zhu Jiajin, "Qingdai neiting yanxi qingkuang zatan" [Remarks on Theater Performance in the Qing Imperial Court], in *Zhu Jiajin, Gugong tuishi lu*, vol. 2:, pp. 547–48.

23 Zhao Yang, "Qingdai gongting xiqu huodong zongshu" [Profile of Operas in the Qing Imperial Court], in Chen, *Junyue tianting*, vol. 3: p. 11.

24 Ibid., p. 11.

25 Zhu Jiajin, "Shengping shu shidai Kunqiang, Yiqiang luantan de shengshui kao" [On the Vicissitudes of Kunqiang Yiqiang, and Luantan in the Shengping Shu Period] in Zhu Jiajin, *Gugong tuishi lu*, vol. 2: p. 557.

26 For example, see Zhou Yibai, *Zhongguo xiju shi changbian* [History of Chinese Theater (Long Version)] (Shanghai: Shanghai shudian, 2004), pp. 469–91; Ma Shaobo et al., *Zhongguo jingju fazhan shi* [The Development of the Chinese Peking Opera] (Taipei: Shangding, 1992), vol. 1: pp. 24–34.

27 Zhu, "Shengping shu shidai," p. 561.

28 Ibid., pp. 564–72; see also Zhu Jiajin, "Qingdai luantan xi zai gongzhong fazhan de shiliao" [Historical Records on the Development of Luantan Dramas in the Qing Court], in Zhu Jiajin, *Gugong tuishi lu*, vol. 2: pp. 586–621.

29 Zhou Zhifu, "Zhaodai xiaoshao zhi sanzhong jiaoben [Three Scripts of Elegant Music for a Brilliant Age]," in *Juxue yuekan* [Studies on Theater Monthly] 3 (1934: 1).

30 Zhu, "Qingdai luantan xi," p. 619.

31 Ye, "Imperial Institutions and Drama," p. 363.

32 The Chinese National Academy of Arts images, to which I did not have access, also bear numbers on the back. See Dai Yun, "Qingdai Nanfu caihui xiju lianpu" [Qing Mask Images in Color from Nanfu, first part], in *Jingju wenhua* [Culture of Peking Opera] (2006: 4), p. 34. The Samuel Herrup set is framed so I was unable to see the back.

33 Dai Yun, *Quanshan jinke yanjiu* [Study on *Golden Norms for Exhorting Virtue*] (Beijing: Beijing shifan daxue chubanshe, 2006), p. 187.

34 Dai Yun, "Qingdai Nanfu caihui xiju lianpu II [Qing Mask Images in Color from Nanfu, second part]" in *Jingju wenhua* [Culture of Peking Opera] (2006: 5), p. 33.

35 Zhang Zhao et al., *Quanshan jinke* [Golden Norms for Exhorting Virtue], in Guben xiqu congkan [Collection of Ancient Editions of Drama], facsimile version, series 9, no. 5 (Beijing: Zhonghua shuju, 1964), 6: act 20. "雜扮五長解鬼，各戴鬼髮額，穿蟒箭袖，虎皮卒褂，繫虎皮裙，持器械。"

36 *Chuandai tigang* [Instructions on Headgear and Clothing], facsimile version, in *Gugong zhenben jikan* [Collection of Rare Editions in the Palace Museum], no. 690, *Gugong bowu yuan* [the Palace Museum, Beijing] (Haikou: Hainan chubanshe, 2000), pp. 236–84. On the date of *Chuandai tigang*, see Song Junhua, "Chuandai tigang yu Qingdai gongting yanju"

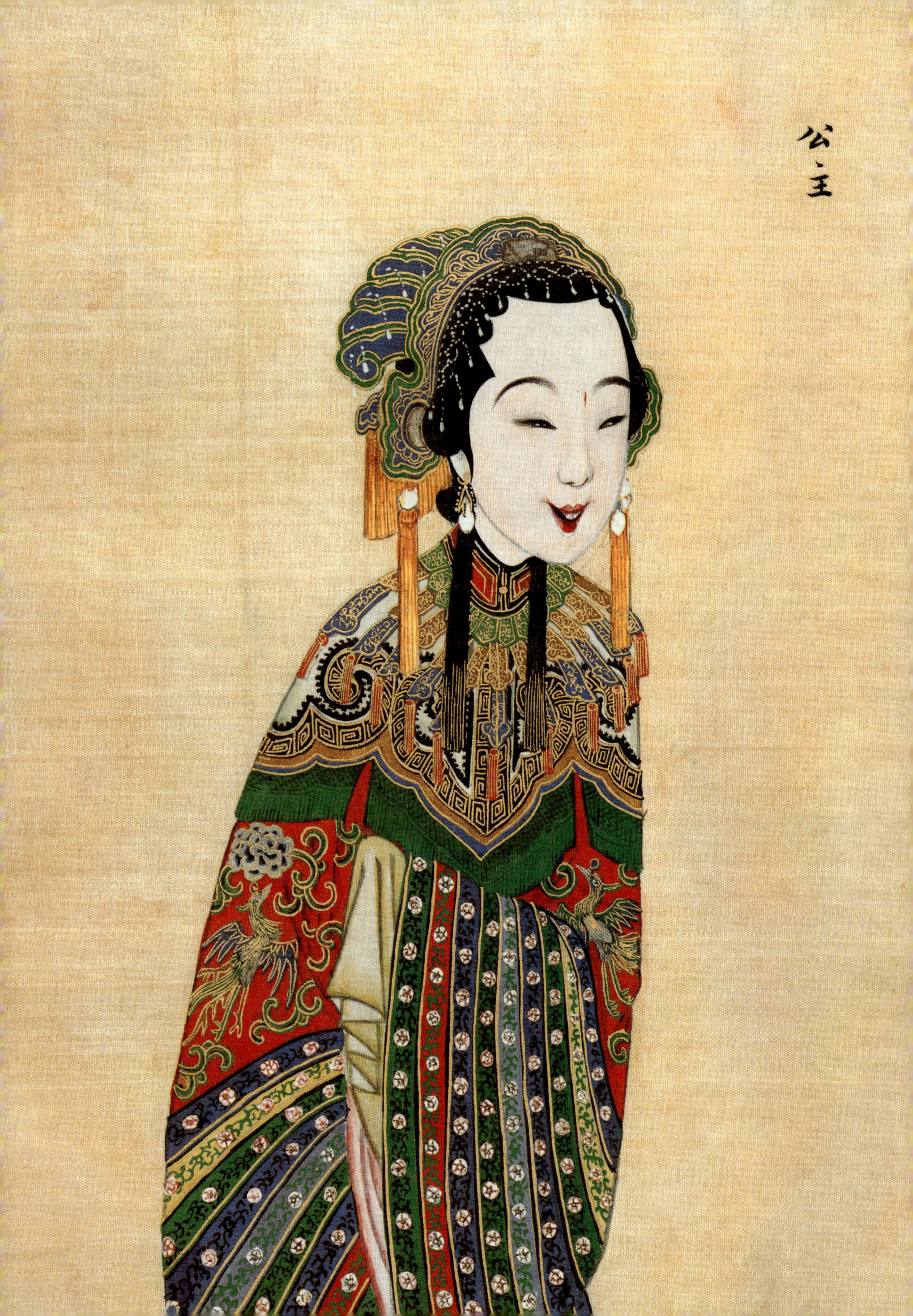
公主

[Chuandai tigang and Qing Court Theater Performance], in *Zhongshan Daxue xuebao* [Journal of Sun Yat-Sen University] 47: 4 (2007): pp. 22–23.

37 For the records, see Zhongguo diyi lishi dang'an guan [The China First Historical Archive] and Chinese University of Hong Kong Art Museum, *Qinggong neiwufu zaobanchu dang'an zonghui, Yongzheng–Qianlong* [Collected Files of the Workshops of the Imperial Household Department, 1723–95], 50 vols. (Beijing: Renmin chubanshe, 2005).

38 Zhao Yi, *Yanpu zaji* [Miscellaneous Notes from the Yanpu Studio] (Beijing: Zhonghua shuju, 1997), p. 11: "有時神鬼畢集，面具千百，無一相肖者." The English translation is quoted from Idema, "Performances on a Three-Tiered Stage," p. 209.

39 The theater scholar and Mei Lanfang's consultant, Qi Rushan, noted about 400 leaves that he had seen in the 1930s. See Yang Lianqi's preface to *Qinggong xichu renwu hua* [Theater Figure Paintings of the Qing Court], eds. Huang Ke and Yang Lianqi (Shijiazhuang: Huashan wenyi chubanshe, 2005), 1: p. 11. This number plus the 100 leaves at the Metropolitan Museum comes to about 500.

40 The albums in the Chinese National Academy of Arts have been remounted. Other published images do not show evidence of mounting.

41 Cited in Zhu, "Qingdai de xiqu fushi shiliao" [Historical Records on Qing Court Theater Costumes], in *Gugong tuishi lu*, 2: p. 653.

42 "Neiwufu zaoban chu gezuo zuocheng huoji qingdang" [Records of the Works of All Workshops in the Imperial Household Department], 1891, The China First Historical Archive, microfilm, no. 50, 3210–16.

43 Qingshi shanhou weiyuan hui, eds., *Gugong wupin diancha baogao* (1925–30), series 5, vol. 1, no. 1, "Shoukang gong" [Shoukang Palace], internal digital database in the Palace Museum, Beijing, accessed October 2012.

44 See Zhu, "Qingdai de xiqu fushi shiliao," p. 655; Zhu, preface to *Beijing tushuguan cang Shengping shu xiqu renwu huace* [Shengping Shu Paintings of Theatrical Figures in the Beijing Library], eds. Beijing tushuguan (Beijing: Beijing tushuguan, 1997), p. 1; Yang's preface to *Qinggong xichu renwu hua*, p, 6. The reason Zhu attributes these albums to the court workshop is that "we know that they are painted in the same style [as the full-length series in the Palace Museum] at first glance." See Zhu, "Qingdai de xiqu fushi shiliao," p. 655. As I discuss in this essay, the styles of these two series are quite different from each other.

45 Studies on late Qing court painters are still rudimentary at the current stage. For evidence of the influence of court-style theatrical paintings in commercial circles, see the paintings *Qunying hui* [Gathering of the Heroes] and *Hongni guan* [The Hongni Station] attributed to Shen Rongpu, who had a painting studio in the Qianmen area in Beijing. Both paintings are currently in the collection of the Chinese National Academy of Arts.

46 The phrase in Chinese: 穿戴臉兒俱照此樣.

47 Zhu, preface to *Beijing tushu guan cang Shengping shu xiqu renwu huace*, p. 1.

48 The images from the set in Chinese National Academy of Arts published in *Mei Lanfang cang xiqu shiliao tuji* have been retouched to remove this line. See *Mei Lanfang, cang xiqu shiliao tuji* [Theatrical Images in the Collection of Mei Lanfang], ed. Liu Zhanwen, 2 vols. (Shijiazhuang: Hebei jiaoyu chubanshe, 2002). For the reproductions of the original images, see Huang Ke and Yang Lianqi eds., *Qinggong xichu renwu hua*.

49 For example, see Zhu, "Taijian wangtan lu" [Interview with the Former Eunuch Geng Jinxi], in *Gugong tuishi lu*, 1: p. 421.

50 For a discussion of the *baimei tu* genre, see Wu Hung, "Beyond Stereotypes: The Twelve Beauties in Qing Court Art and *The Dream of the Red Chamber*," in Ellen Widmer and Kang-I Sun Chang, eds., *Writing Women in Late Imperial China* (Stanford, Calif.: Stanford University Press, 1997), pp. 322–31; Christine C. Y. Tan, "Chinese Print Culture and the Proliferation of 'One Hundred Beauties' Imagery," in Jerome Silbergeld et al., eds., *Bridges to Heaven: Essays on East Asian Art in Honor of Professor Wen C. Fong* (Princeton, N. J.: Princeton University Press, 2011), 2: pp. 813–26.

51 For example, see Wanyuzi (pseud.) ed., *Wuji baimei* [One Hundred Charming Beauties from Suzhou], preface 1617, facsimile version (Beijing: Beijing tushuguan chubanshe, 2002).

52 For a discussion on the theatricality in this set of playing cards, see Shi-yee Liu, "The World's a Stage: The Theatricality of Chen Hongshou's Figure Painting," *Ars Orientalis* 35 (2008): pp. 155–91, esp. pp. 159–61.

53 See Zhu, "Qingdai de xiqu fushi shiliao," p. 654.

54 For various manuals on famous actors compiled in the late eighteenth and nineteenth centuries, see Zhang Cixi, ed., *Qingdai Yandu liyuan shiliao: zheng xu bian* [Historical Records on the Theater Circle in Beijing: Original Series and Sequel], 1934–37, reprint (Beijing: Zhongguo xiju chuban she, 1988).

55 For example, see *Scroll of Antiques* (*Guwan tu*), dated to 1728, in the Sir Percival David Collection, British Museum; and *Official Tribute* (*Zhigong tu*), 1751–93, in the Palace Museum, Beijing, and other collections.

56 As Bo Songnian points out in his essay in this catalogue, some painters of New Year theatrical prints sketched from life during performances.

YUHANG LI

Four

Representing Theatricality on Textiles

During the mid to late Qing period (1644–1911), under the prevalent influence of Chinese opera and other performing arts, embroiderers and textile makers started to use clothing as a medium to convey theatrical motifs. Unlike objects that are primarily made for decorating space or being touched and handled, a garment is meant to be worn by a person and to adorn a human body and thus transmits codes for gender, style, color, symbolism, and function.[1] In the visual convention of Chinese clothing, regardless of whether something is a quotidian or ritual outfit, the patterns on a garment often indicate symbolic meanings associated with the wearer's social status, ritual context, and personal interests. For example, the large sums of bolts of uncut fabric and robes excavated from the Wanli emperor's (r. 1563–1620) tomb reveal that the Ming dynasty court used clothing with specific adornments representing seasonal changes throughout the year. For instance, during the Qingming Festival (Qingming jie), imperial women changed into *luo* or gauze robes patterned with an image of a maiden on a swing.[2] This decoration stands for the idea of going outside and enjoying greenery in the springtime. Fabric has been superimposed with meanings to signify social hierarchy and seasonal changes. When the images of theatrical figures are used to decorate a garment, however, there is no preexisting symbolic repertoire to which they belong. Theatrical figures therefore enrich the canon of decorative patterns on Chinese garments.[3] For the first time in China the social discourse of human relationship, such as morality and romance, is transmitted on the surface of attire.

First I will first sketch some preliminary observations on the impact of Chinese theatrical performance on clothing, and then I will focus on a Daoist liturgical robe made in the nineteenth century now in the collection of the Field Museum of Natural History, Chicago, and featured in this exhibition (cat. 27). The main source for the decoration on this robe has been identified as *The Pearl Pagoda* (*Zhenzhuta*).[4] Using this robe (hereafter cited as the *Pearl Pagoda* robe) as an example, I will discuss how the narrative of *The Pearl Pagoda* might have initiated the idea of designing it on a

Daoist robe and how literary, performing, and visual traditions are intertwined on a single material object. This robe also provides an unusual opportunity to examine the ways in which religious ideals and narratives of secular morality were artistically embodied on the surface of textiles in Qing China. In particular, the story of how a secular morality is depicted on a Daoist robe that usually represents Daoist celestial splendor will emerge, along with how a gendered space is constructed according to the form of a Daoist liturgical robe.

A Brief Survey of Garments with Theatrical Figures

In general, theatrical figures appear only on clothing intended for women or children, garments made by either individual female embroiderers or by professional workshops. Two kinds of designs with theatrical figures are used. In the first type, single or multiple vignettes from the same or different operas appear on a single costume. Figures are often represented in theatrical outfits, and their gestures provide clear reference to stage performances. The visual references for individual embroiderers to stitch such theatrical motifs usually come from embroidery manuals and New Year pictures (*nianhua*).[5] An embroidery manual is often an assemblage of different patterns, including scenes from various plays.[6] Multiple scenes appear for particularly popular dramas such as *Journey to the West* (*Xiyou ji*), but for most operas, only one representative image is selected. In order to assist embroiderers in transcribing the outline on fabric, a monochromic ink outline of the figure is printed and embroiderers have creative freedom to fill in the colors.[7]

The fragment of a woman's apron from the late Qing dynasty to the early Republican period from the American Museum of Natural History and in the exhibition provides an excellent example of this kind (cat. 11). On the lower back of the apron, against a black background, figures are fully embroidered with polychromic threads in Chinese knot stitches (*dazi xiu*) that express the Shanxi regional style.[8] Five characters in theatrical costumes are positioned on two different rugs. As Judith T. Zeitlin discusses in the introduction to this catalogue, using a rug to delineate theatrical space is both a theatrical and a visual convention in China.[9] However, the juxtaposition of two rugs in the same pictorial space is novel. Accommodating the symmetric principle of patterns on Chinese clothing, a pair of phoenixes and flowers appear above the figures. Meanwhile one figure in the middle mediates between the groups on either side of him, reinforcing the narratives and linking the two sections to one another.

The arrangement of figures represents an episode from the historical drama *Fortress with a Beaded Curtain* (*Zhulian zhai*).[10] Staged in both Peking opera and Shanxi clapper opera (*bangzi*), this play has two protagonists, Li Keyong (856–908) and his son Li Cunxu (885–926), who have been associated with Shanxi local history since the tenth century. The first figure on the left, Cheng Jingsi, the minister of the Ministry of Personnel for the court of the Tang emperor Xizong (862–888), is trying to persuade the person next to him, the military governor Li Keyong, who is of Shatuo Turkish origin, to return to assist him against the Huang Chao (?–884) rebellion. Resentful of the Tang emperor, Li Keyong declines the request. His son Li Cunxu, positioned between the two rugs, is more sympathetic to Cheng Jingsi, but fails in his attempt to help Cheng. Li Cunxu then tries to convince his imperial mothers Madam Cao (Caoshi) and Madam Liu (Liushi) to aid him in his quest by using his henpecked father's fear of his wives. On the apron, the woman in a military outfit and pheasant feather headdress most likely represents Madam Cao. The contrast between Li Keyong and his wife Madam Cao is vividly captured as Li just stretches his right (proper) hand, seeming to express his unwillingness to help while Madam Cao holds a command tablet to assume the position of a military commander. Historical and legendary woman warriors and martial art fighters abounded in various operas during the Qing period; the popularity of these characters can be observed in New Year pictures in this exhibition (cats. 14–16). Madam Cao in *Fortress with a Beaded Curtain* represents a woman's power over her husband in both domestic life and public affairs. Depicting such an image on a woman's garment widens the scope of symbols that represent the feminine ideal in pre-modern China.

In contrast, the second type of theatrical motif usually shows a set of sequential pictorial units of a relatively longer narrative, which is often taken from a southern drama (*chuanqi*) or stringed ballad (*tanci*) storytelling. One robe could contain eight, ten, or twelve episodes. Sometimes, the edge of the robe bears a different operatic story. The narrative could be a rather complete account as

4.1
Chinese, Late Qing Dynasty (1644–1911)
Woman's Summer Jacket with Eight Scenes from Romance of the Western Chamber (Xixiang ji), late 19th–early 20th century
Silk, gilt paper-wrapped thread, and bands of machine ribbon, employing gauze weave, embroidery (petit point satin), machine weaving, and appliqué, 55 × 35 in. (139.7 × 88.9 cm)
Honolulu Museum of Art, Gift of Sybil K. Paris (Mrs. Irvine Paris), 1994
7697.1

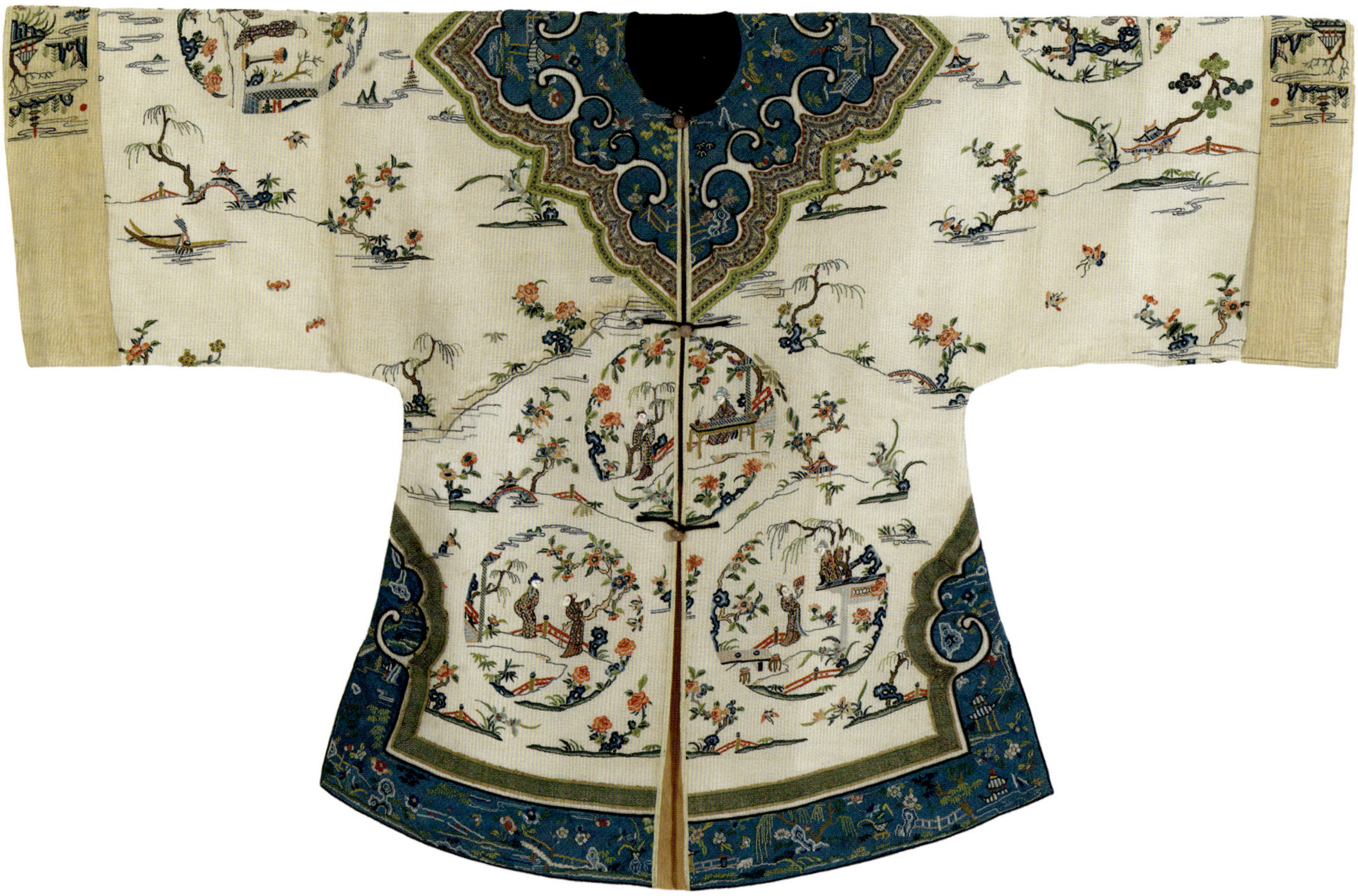

we will see in the case of the *Pearl Pagoda* robe, but sometimes, it is just an assemblage of vignettes, with no story line. Chinese literary historian Dore Levy has proposed the idea of vignettism to argue that the logic of both Chinese literary and visual narratives is based on "a succession of lyric tableaux" rather than "a dynamic temporal sequence."[11] Levy's observation provides an important perspective for understanding narrative robes in the context of a larger literary and visual tradition in China. However, a more direct influence contributing to this type of narrative robe is probably the popularity of performing opera as excerpts or independent acts (*zhezi xi*).

Theatrical imagery on a robe raises important questions about how to organize a pictorial narrative on a garment regardless of whether the narrative is complete or a series of discrete episodes.[12] Like other media such as ceramics, every piece of clothing is a three-dimensional object upon which a pictorial narrative has to be expressed spatially according to the physical form, fashion, and usability of the garment. The selection and arrangement of the story will also reflect personal preference or the popularity of a certain act.

The remarkable nineteenth-century woman's jacket from the Jordan Schnitzer Museum of Art, Eugene, Oregon, in this exhibition depicts two completely different narratives: *Dream of the Red Chamber* (*Honglou meng*) on the main body of the garment and *The White Snake* (*Baishe zhuan*) along the borders (cat. 28).[13] Both pictorial narratives have been influenced by their popular adaptation as chuanqi play and tanci performance in the late nineteenth century.[14] On Chinese garments, the border often frames the image on the main body.[15] As Yunfei Shao's research indicates (cat. 28), the border depicting *The White Snake* is also used as a topographical space to represent the White Snake descending from Mount Emei embroidered on the neckline to the water motif embroidered on the bottom edge. However, the logic of the arrangement of the ten episodes from *Dream of the Red Chamber* on the robe remains unclear.

The selection of these ten episodes was probably influenced by adaptions of *Dream of the Red Chamber* into popular performing genres at the time, including chuanqi plays, tanci storytelling, and *sanqu* (non-operatic arias).[16] The arrangement of these episodes might not follow internal narrative logic but be related to the popularity of certain acts in actual performances at the time, or they might simply be arranged according to personal preference.

Unlike the first type of theatrical motif where the figures wear theatrical costumes on stage, figures in a sequential pictorial narrative are usually portrayed wearing regular clothes and in a naturalistic setting, as in illustrations from printed editions of chuanqi and tanci.[17] However, the number of figures and the composition might be altered according to the limitation of the size and visual convention of a pattern on a textile. For instance, unlike *Romance of the Western Chamber* (*Xixiang ji*) that appears on various objects in this exhibition (cats. 30–37, 40, 42, 43), the woman's jacket with eight scenes of *Romance of the Western Chamber* from the Honolulu Museum of Art has only two figures in each roundel. With fewer characters, each individual character is given more prominence (fig. 4.1).[18]

Both the *Dream of the Red Chamber* robe and the *Pearl Pagoda* robe call our attention to the association of tanci performance with the production of a narrative robe. Scholars nowadays usually differentiate two types of tanci.[19] The first, literary tanci, which resembles novels, began to be written in part by women for women readers beginning in the seventeenth century.[20] The second, performed tanci, is a type of professional oral storytelling that includes sung verse accompanied by musical instruments, but it also circulated in manuscript and print with role-types for different characters indicated in the text. In performances, the storyteller usually impersonates different roles by changing his or her voice and manner. Tanci storytellers of both sexes could perform in public storytelling establishments and private households in the eighteenth and nineteenth century, though the Qing government banned female storytellers from public performance spaces during certain reigns.[21] Women could invite female storytellers to their private household to perform for an all-female audience.[22] Both tanci performance and the luxury textile industry, particularly the production of slit silk tapestry (*kesi*) used in the *Pearl Pagoda* robe, are centered in Suzhou.[23] As we have seen in the case of the *Fortress with a Beaded Curtain* apron from Shanxi province, which depicts theatrical figures that may derive from Shanxi clapper opera, it was common to combine local textile forms and technologies with local genres of popular performance.

It is unclear who would wear narrative robes with theatrical figures, since both women's jackets for daily use and special occasions have survived. The *Dream of the Red Chamber* jacket and the *Pearl Pagoda* robe are not ordinary types of clothing for daily use. The former is in the style of a *dapo yi*, a theatrical jacket worn by female clowns, while the latter is in the form of a Daoist ritual robe. In the late Qing courtesan novel *The Illusion of Romance* (*Fengyue meng*), a courtesan tanci performer named Yuexiang is portrayed as wearing a jacket and using a fan decorated with scenes from *Dream of the Red Chamber* while performing a dramatic song (*qu*) narrating an episode from *Dream of the Red Chamber*.[24] Though there is no description in the novel of the courtesan using her garment and her fan as part of her performance, it seems clear that she is using her attire and accessory in some self-referential fashion. This episode in the novel allows us to speculate that the *Dream of the Red Chamber* jacket and the *Pearl Pagoda* robe might have been worn during a tanci performance.

The Physical Structure of the *Pearl Pagoda* Robe

The *Pearl Pagoda* robe is a full-length garment with the center front opening fastened with one brass button (cat. 27).[25] The straight sleeves end in square cuffs and the slits start from the midpoints of each side. It is in the style of one common type of Daoist ritual vestment called a *fayi* or *fafu*.[26] Based on the study of extant Daoist liturgical robes in European and North American collections, Chinese textile art historian Verity Wilson points out that there are two basic types of Daoist liturgical robes: the *jiangyi*, a word having two different written forms, "red robe" or "mantle of descent," and *daopao* or Daoist robe. The *jiangyi* is a sleeveless gown and *daopao* is a sleeved garment. In general, jiangyi's rank is higher than daopao.[27] For instance, as Wilson explains, "When a Grand Master wears a robe of descent, his cantors dress in the sleeved gown. When the master dons the sleeved gown, his assistants wear a plain black or orange robe, sometimes edged with a narrow contrasting

4.2
Chinese, Qing Dynasty (1644–1911)
New Year Print with Scenes from The Pearl Pagoda, Part I (Zhenzhuta qianben), 18th century
Polychrome woodblock print

piping."[28] However, during the Ming and Qing periods, there are no scriptures that entail the difference between jiangyi and daopao. The surviving examples reveal that both types of Daoist robes share similar patterns.[29]

The body and the borders of the garment are made of red silk using the weaving technique of kesi.[30] The main pattern on the body consists of eight roundels arranged symmetrically with respect to left and right on the front, back, shoulder, and back of the sleeves. In each roundel, a different figural composition appears in varied architectural settings and landscapes. They are woven in a multitude of colors on a white background contrasting with the red color of the robe. Gold metal-wrapped threads adorn rocks and small articles, and the figures and architectural settings are outlined in ink. The combination of weaving, drawing, and sometimes embroidery is common in the production of kesi fabrics in the nineteenth century. The eight roundels are surrounded by patterns of bats and clouds, which symbolize abundant happiness, in different shades of blue. Eight Daoist attributes—calabashes, swords, fish-shaped musical instruments, fans, flower baskets, flutes, jade-castanets, and lotus flowers—are doubled to form pairs and mapped symmetrically along the central opening from the front bottom and continue along the central line at the back.

All the edges are trimmed with borders of kesi silk material as well. The longest strip forms the upper chest border and collar. It is decorated with the male Spirit of Longevity (*shougong*) holding a staff with a calabash at left and his counterpart, the female Spirit of Longevity (*shoupo*), holding a horsetail whisk (*fuchen*) on the right. Their difference in gender is enhanced by sets of birds and attendants, who appear above and below them—a crane and a boy at the left and a phoenix and a girl at the right. The lower parts of the borders are decorated with the Two Immortals of Peace and Harmony (*Hehe erxian*).

The lower edge is trimmed with yellow panels of two dragons in profile facing each other, a design which often appeared on the lower borders of a Daoist robe. Flying above the waves, the dragons are separated by a tiny mountain with a bat above it. The design on the back lower edge is identical. On the back of the two yellow sleeve-cuffs, eight Daoist immortals are divided into two groups, which are lined up vertically and surrounded by rocks and trees. From top to bottom on the left are Zhang Guolao, He Xiangu, Han Xiangzi, and Tie Guai Li, and from top to bottom on the right are Zhong Lihan, Lü Dongbin, Lan Caihe, and Cao Guojiu. All the immortals and symbols denote longevity.

On the back of this garment, the neckband is rendered in dark blue silk and adorned with a Buddha sitting on a lotus flower. He wears a red robe, and a yellow halo hangs above him as the flower's stem rises above the waves. This image replaces the representations of the supreme Daoist deities known as the Three Divine Teachers that are often rendered in the same location on a Daoist robe. Below the Buddha, midway on the back of the robe, a round embroidered appliqué depicts a seven-storied palace with three gates, the standard symbol of Daoist heaven on a regular Daoist robe.[31] A pair of cranes hovering above the clouds faces the focal point of the palace surrounded by rayed lines, flames, and sixteen gold discs—the Chinese convention for representing stars and constellations worshiped in Daoism. Compared to most Daoist ritual robes where twenty-four, twenty-eight, or thirty-six constellations appear, far fewer constellations appear on this robe.[32]

The Story of *The Pearl Pagoda*

The Pearl Pagoda was one of the most popular tanci performed in the lower Yangzi delta during the Qing dynasty, and it is still widely enjoyed in south China today.[33] The author of the story is unknown. Surviving printed editions are usually attributed to certain famous tanci performers. Though the basic storylines are the same, performers could alter episodes.[34] The 1781 edition, *The Complete Story of Filial and Righteous True Traces of The Pearl Pagoda* (*Xiaoyi zhenji Zhenzhuta quanzhuan*, hereafter *The Pearl Pagoda*), with a preface by Zhou Shushi, is one of the earliest Pearl Pagoda texts.[35] Zhou was one of the best-known storytellers of *The Pearl Pagoda* in the eighteenth century, and this printed text is believed to have been modified based on his performances. However, during the mid-nineteenth century when the *Pearl Pagoda* robe was made, Ma Rufei was considered the most successful and influential tanci storyteller of *The Pearl Pagoda*.[36]

The story describes a young man, Fang Qing from a high official family, who experienced turmoil after his father was framed by an enemy at the court and wrongly executed. Hoping to continue his

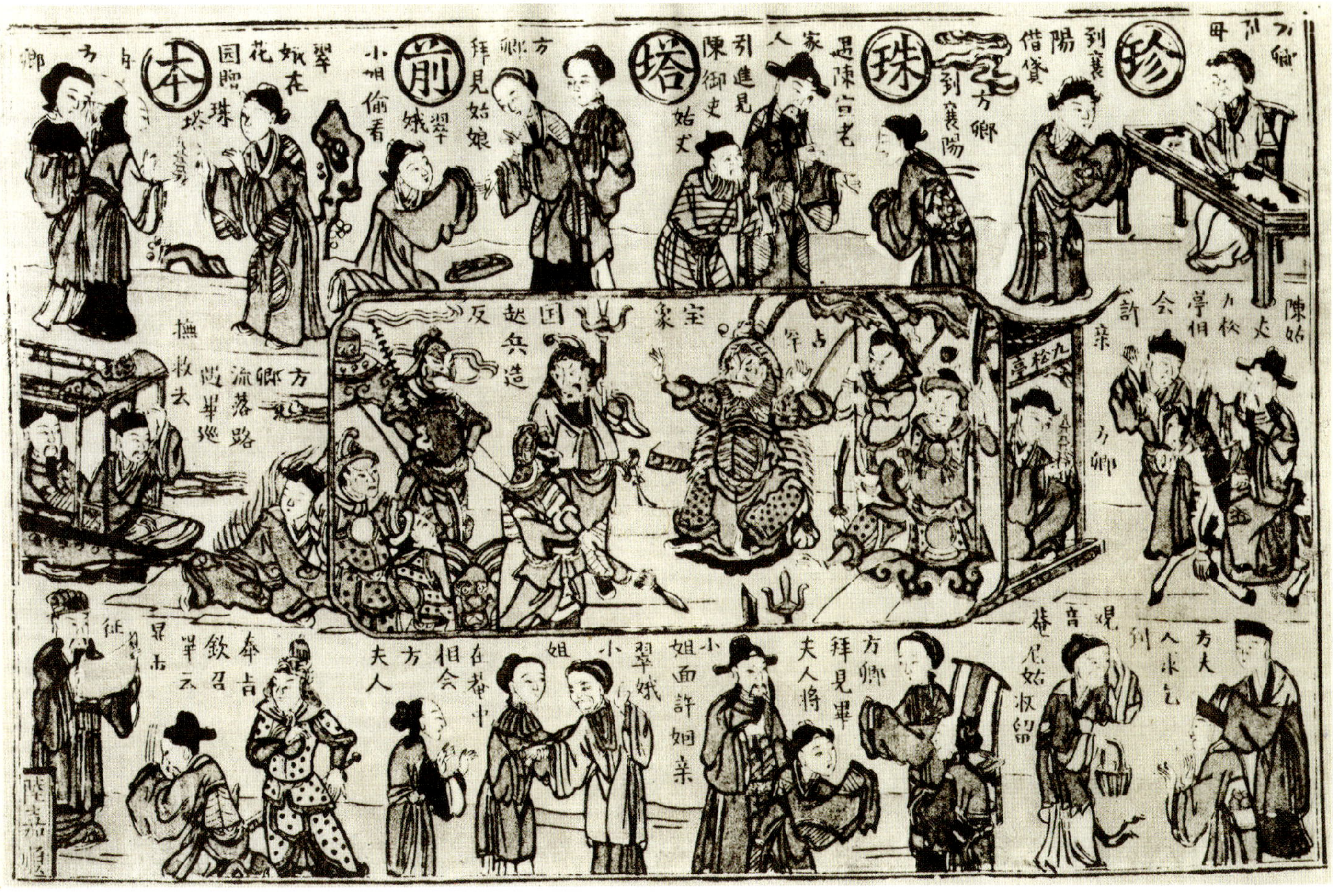

study for the civil service exams, he travels to ask his aunt Madam Chen for help, but to his surprise, his aunt not only refuses him any assistance but also humiliates him. Her daughter, his cousin Chen Cui-e, secretly helps Fang by giving him a small pearl pagoda as a keepsake, while his uncle promises him her hand in marriage. On the way to the capital, Fang is robbed but rescued by Minister Bi Yunxian. Impressed by Fang's intelligence, Minister Bi promises his sister Bi Xiujin to Fang in marriage. One year later, Fang Qing achieves first place in the official exams and is appointed minister of inspection. He then happily marries his fiancées.

On the surface, *The Pearl Pagoda* follows the plot of a traditional romantic comedy with love matches between the cultivated daughters of elite families and young male candidates for the imperial examinations. More importantly, however, this narrative combines romance with three religions: the Buddhist ideal of karmic effect, Confucian family ethics of virtuous conduct for women, and Daoist practices of divination and magical power. Hence, the *Pearl Pagoda* robe provides a good test case to study how an oral/literary tradition is transferred onto a particular type of material object, in this case, a Daoist robe. In this process, Confucian morality is still conveyed through the narrative on the robe, but the two key Buddhist elements in the story, the pearl pagoda and the bodhisattva Guanyin, have disappeared. Daoism moves from being a minor part of the story to a set of ideas literally woven into the fabric of the narrative and shaping the material conditions used to tell the narrative. From this perspective, it is fair to say that Daoism, which is only a minor literary motif in the original story, becomes the catalyst that shapes the arrangement and meaning of the episodes on the robe, and in so doing, fundamentally alters the proportional relation between the three religions in the narrative.

Constructing a Narrative on a Daoist Robe

The most common medium used to visualize *The Pearl Pagoda* in the late Qing dynasty are woodblock prints that include both book illustration and New Year pictures. Book illustrations, which are typically arranged at the beginning of the text, depict individual characters from *The Pearl Pagoda* as full-length portraits. Each figure is rendered in simple ink outline in an empty space with the name of the opera character inscribed on the top right of the image.[37] New Year pictures of *The Pearl Pagoda*, however, provide a concrete narrative. A complete version or selected episodes are divided into two equal parts and arranged on two separate sheets commonly titled *The Pearl Pagoda, Part I* (*Zhenzhuta qianben*) and *The Pearl Pagoda, Part II* (*Zhenzhuta houben*). As a New Year picture of part 1 from the mid-Qing period demonstrates, on each of these sheets, following the format of the rectangular border, episodes are arranged in two or three rows, and in each row, scenes are juxtaposed sequentially side by side from right to left. The only exception is that a climactic

4.3
Panorama view of the *Pearl Pagoda* Robe (cat. 27).

4.4
Outline diagram of overall view of the *Pearl Pagoda* Robe (cat. 27).

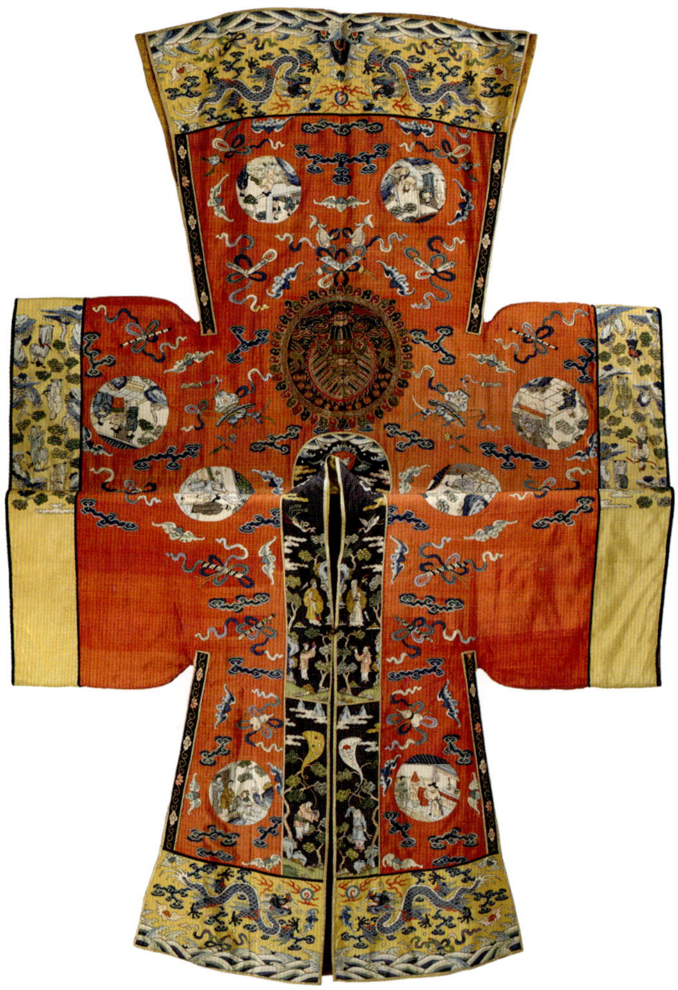

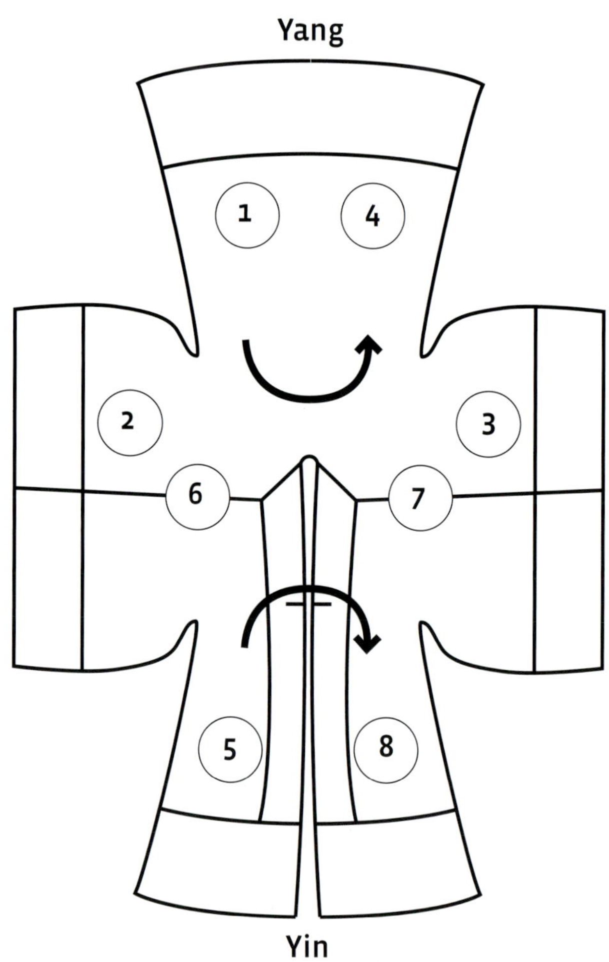

scene is sometime elaborated with more figures and positioned in the center of the sheet and thus does not follow the chronological order of the narrative (fig. 4.2).[38] By contrast, the Daoist ritual robe reconstitutes this linear narrative onto a three-dimensional object and builds a new temporal structure for the operatic episodes. Furthermore, the scenes on the robe are ordered according to one type of Daoist robe: two on the lower front, two on the shoulders, two on the back sleeves, and two on the lower back. Unlike Western garments, which are often tailored to the human body and created by draping fabric onto a three-dimensional form shaped like the human body, the process for constructing a Chinese garment begins with the design of the raw material. The entire shape of the garment, including sleeves and neckline, and the robe's decorative patterns are first programmed on sketches used in the weaving of the cloth. When the weaving is complete, the garment appears as a single, flat piece of two-dimensional art. The *Pearl Pagoda* robe is made of two long strips that were stitched together and then folded in the middle to form a front and back. This means that if we flip out the back of this robe, we gain a panoramic view of the robe as well as the textile (fig. 4.3). Although it is impossible to view the front and back of the finished robe simultaneously, on the conceptual level of design and also on the practical level of textile making, the front and back are conceived as a unified composition.

Once we see the robe as a whole, the eight roundels become the most distinctive patterns on this two-dimensional space. The sequence of episodes from the opera depicted in the roundels is: (1) Meeting Madam Chen, (2) At Mr. Bi's Home, (3) The Rebellion of Baoxiang Country, (4) Receiving the Imperial Edict to Conquer the Rebellion, (5) Meeting Her Mother-in-Law at the Guanyin Nunnery, (6) Singing Songs of the Dao, (7) Fang Qing Meeting His Mother, and (8) The Wedding. The two scenes of Minister Bi quelling the rebellion on the robe are not included in *The Pearl Pagoda* tanci text. Since combat scenes are often added in an oral performance to attract the attention of an audience, it is possible that the *Pearl Pagoda* robe and the aforementioned woodblock prints were directly influenced by the performance tradition. In any case, we can see that the four roundels, including the two on the shoulder, depict episodes 5 through 8. The four roundels on the back of the robe cover episodes 1 through 4 (fig. 4.4). Observing this sequence prompts

4.5
Chinese, Qing Dynasty (1644–1911)
Daoist Robe (Daopao), 19th century
Silk satin embroidered with silk and gold thread, 50 3/8 × 65 9/16 in. (128 cm × 166.5cm)
Victoria and Albert Museum, London, Purchase
1620-1901

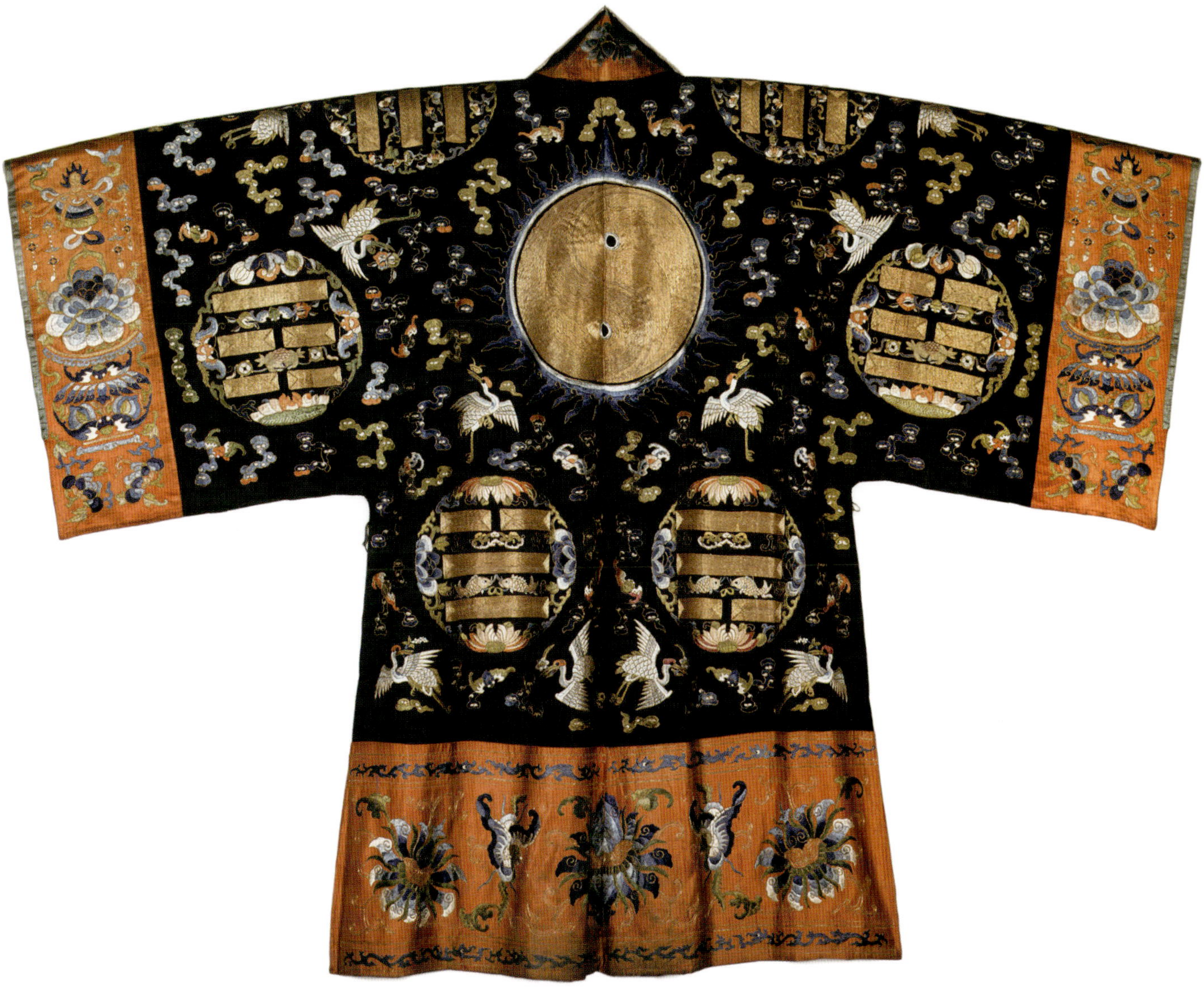

three questions: What is the visual logic of arranging these eight roundels/scenarios? Why does the sequence of the episodes read clockwise on the front and counterclockwise on the back? And why does the story start on the back rather than the front of this robe?

The answers lie in the visual conventions and format of a Daoist robe. The use of the eight roundels and the way that they are positioned on this robe resemble the arrangement of a pattern made up of eight trigrams (*bagua*) found on Daoist liturgical robes. Two examples from the nineteenth century can be drawn for comparison to the *Pearl Pagoda* robe: one from the Victoria and Albert Museum collection (fig. 4.5) and one from the Minneapolis Institute of Arts collection that is dated to 1861.[39] On the backs of both Daoist robes, the eight trigrams are arranged in the same position as on the *Pearl Pagoda* robe: two on the lower front, two on the shoulders, two on the back sleeves, and two on the lower back. Nonetheless, although the topography of eight trigrams employed on a Daoist robe might be similar, the way of arranging the sequence of trigrams is not the same.

In Daoist cosmology, the circle of eight trigrams represents the fundamental principles of the universe. Each trigram is composed of three lines, and each line is either solid or broken. A solid line symbolizes *yang*, while broken lines stand for *yin*. The combinations

4.6a–b

Prior Heaven Eight Trigrams and Great Ultimate diagram.

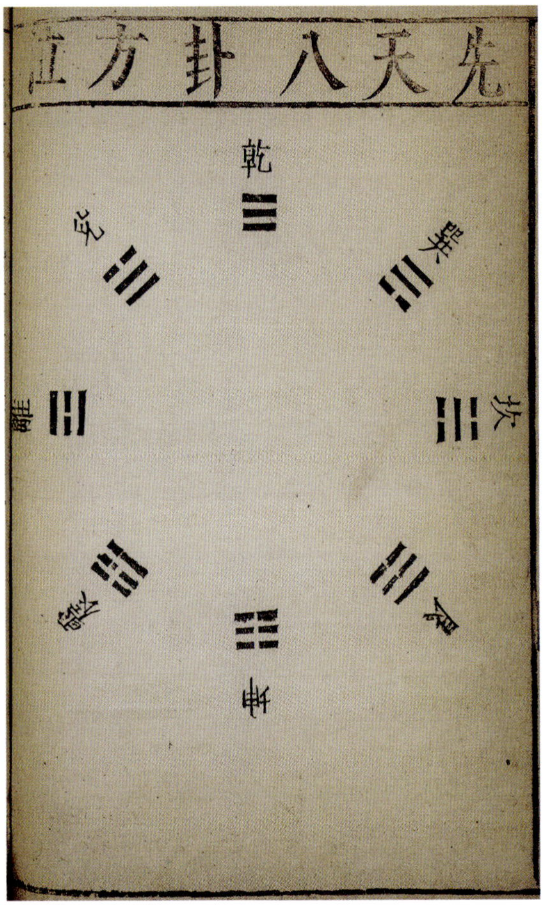

4.6a

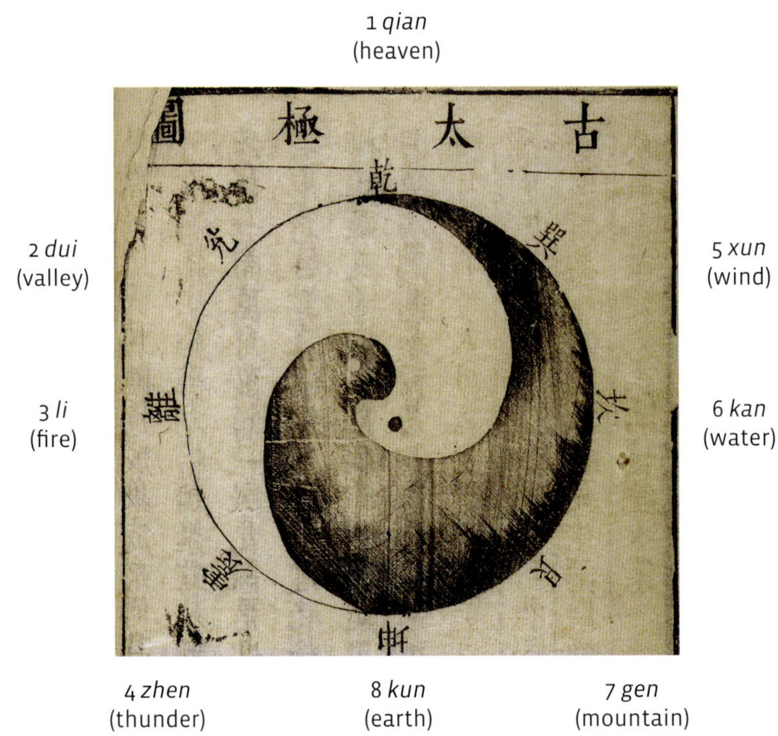

4.6b

of these broken and unbroken lines symbolize yin, yang, and the intermediary phases in the cycle from yin to yang and back.[40] The Daoist *Book of Changes* (*Yijing*) arranges the trigrams in paired combinations of yin and yang to form sixty-four hexagrams.[41] The ordering of the eight trigram circles comes in two basic arrangements: the Prior Heaven Arrangement of the Eight Trigrams (*xiantian bagua*) attributed to the mythical sage Fu Xi, and the Posterior Heaven Arrangement of the Eight Trigrams (*houtian bagua*) associated with Wen Wang, the King of Zhou (r. late twelfth to early eleventh century BCE). The former represents heavenly influences and the latter stands for earthly influences. The arrangement of the eight episodes on the *Pearl Pagoda* robe closely follows the Prior Heaven Eight Trigrams. In this arrangement, eight trigrams can be numbered from one to eight according to the degree of yang and from the extreme yang to the extreme yin: (1) heaven (*qian*), (2) valley (*dui*), (3) fire (*li*), (4) thunder (*zhen*), (5) wind (*xun*), (6) water (*kan*), (7) mountain (*gen*), and (8) earth (*kun*) (fig. 4.6a). When the Prior Heaven Eight Trigrams circle is mingled with the Diagram of the Great Ultimate (*taiji tu*), another configuration showing the movement from yang to yin and back, we can observe that the trigrams *qian*, *dui*, *li*, and *zhen* are on the side of the white half circle, which stands for the yang or masculine world. In other words, the numbers 1 to 4 are on the yang side of the diagram. Trigrams *xun*, *kan*, *gen*, and *kun*, numbered from 5 to 8, are on the half circle in black symbolizing the yin or feminine world (fig. 4.6b). Moreover, *qian*, which stands for heaven and ultimate yang, and *kun*, which represents earth and ultimate yin, form the vertical north-south axis. Following this sequence and comparing it to the eight episodes on the robe, we find that episodes 1–4, which are on the back, represent yang force, and episodes 5–8, which are on the front, represent yin force. To begin with, the sequence of the roundels on the back goes counterclockwise—exactly the way in which the four triagrams on the yang side of the *Taiji* (great ultimate) diagram are read. Similarly, the sequence of the four episdodes on the front goes clockwise, which is the also the same order in which the four trigrams on the yin side of the Taiji diagram are read.

But why does the arrangement of the eight episodes follow the Prior Heaven Eight trigram, rather than other versions of the trigrams? In the literary text of *The Pearl Pagoda*, in chapter one, Fang Qing meets a Daoist master named Xu Xixian, who makes predictions concerning his official career and marriage destiny. Thus from the very beginning, Daoist Xu serves as a supernatural power who can provide a holistic view of Fang's future. As part of the prognostication, Master Xu asks Fang to select a trigram and as he does so, recites: "Today Fang Ziwen [Fang Qing] from Henan, holds his palms together and burns incense and prays for one out of the sixty-four trigrams. . . . this is the *ditiantai* trigram."[42] The "Heaven-Earth-Peace" *ditiantai* trigram basically refers to the yin force on the top and yang force on the bottom. Since I have shown that the front of the *Pearl Pagoda* robe represents the yin or feminine world and the back of the robe represents the yang or masculine world, if we rotate the robe 180 degrees, it matches the Heaven-Earth-Peace trigram exactly with yang on the bottom and yin on the top. More interestingly, in chapter one of the *Pearl Pagoda* text, when Daoist Xu appears, he is described as wearing a "crane mantle of descent" (*hechang*), another term for a sleeveless Daoist ritual vestment. Since Daoist Xu is not conducting any ritual ceremonies in his fortune-teller shop when he meets Fang Qing, he would be wearing a regular Daoist robe rather than a "mantle of descent, " so the term *hechang* is being used imprecisely here. Because the eight episodes on the robe represent the whole story of *The Pearl Pagoda*, the Daoist robe becomes a vehicle to visualize Daoist Xu's prediction of Fang Qing's whole life. More importantly, unlike illustrations of the *Pearl Pagoda* images in woodblock prints, which are a conventional medium for transmitting an operatic or tanci story, there was no prior tradition of representing a narrative and secular people on a Daoist robe. Most figures appearing on Daoist robes are various Daoist celestial beings who represent a generalized universe. The production of Daoist robes increased dramatically and underwent a period of artistic refinement during the eighteenth and nineteenth centuries. Although there are some particular symbols associated with Daoist robes, such as the roundel of the Daoist celestial palace, surviving Daoist robes display no fixed design or pattern.[43] It is therefore highly possible that the selection of a Daoist robe as the article of clothing on which to depict the narrative of *The Pearl Pagoda* was inspired by the role of the Daoist Xu and his divination of Fang Qing's eight trigrams in the story of *The Pearl Pagoda* itself.

Constructing a Gendered Space on a Daoist Robe

Here the Heaven-Earth-Peace trigram makes us think further about the gendered space represented on the Daoist robe as a material object. In most cases, Daoist liturgical robes are worn during a Daoist ritual ceremony. While performing rituals, the grand master usually faces an altar and displays his back to the audiences, which means that the back of a Daoist robe is more significant than the front. As seen in the illustration of a well-known Chinese novel titled *The Plum in the Golden Vase* (*Jin Ping Mei*), which shows a priest wearing a Daoist liturgical robe while conducting a funerary ritual in a wealthy household (fig. 4.7), the back of a Daoist liturgical robe is considered the exterior side and faces the audience, so we often see the most important symbols rendered on the back instead of on the front.[44] The fronts of some Daoist robes are not even decorated.[45] Thus the arrangement of images of the male protagonists Fang Qing and Mr. Bi, and even the Liao rebellion, on the back of the robe not only corresponds to the Daoist ideal of the male world positioned in the cosmos rather than in the domestic world, but also on a conceptual level reflects the practice of an image being displayed in public. The images of the female protagonists, however, face inward. In other words, the conventional Chinese idea that male and female spaces are separate and correlate with the divisions between heaven and earth, exterior and interior, and public and private is embodied on the back and front of the Daoist robe.

Indeed, episode 5 (Meeting Her Mother-in-Law) on the *Pearl Pagoda* robe actually happens before episode 4 (Receiving the Imperial Edict to Conquer the Rebellion). The aforementioned woodblock prints of *The Pearl Pagoda* (fig. 4.2) show that Fang's cousin Chen Cui-e had met his mother in the Guanyin nunnery before Bi Yunxian received the imperial edict to subdue the rebellion in Baoxiang country. But in order to correlate the cosmological

4.7

Chinese, Qing Dynasty (1644–1911)

Ximen Asks the Daoist Huang to Hold a Memorial Service for His Sixth Mistress Ping from the Novel The Plum in the Golden Vase (Jin Ping Mei), 17th century

Album leaf, ink and colors on silk, $15\frac{3}{4} \times 12\frac{1}{4}$ in. (38.7 × 31.1 cm)

The Nelson-Atkins Museum of Art, Kansas City, Missouri, Purchase: the Uhlmann Family Fund, F83-4/1

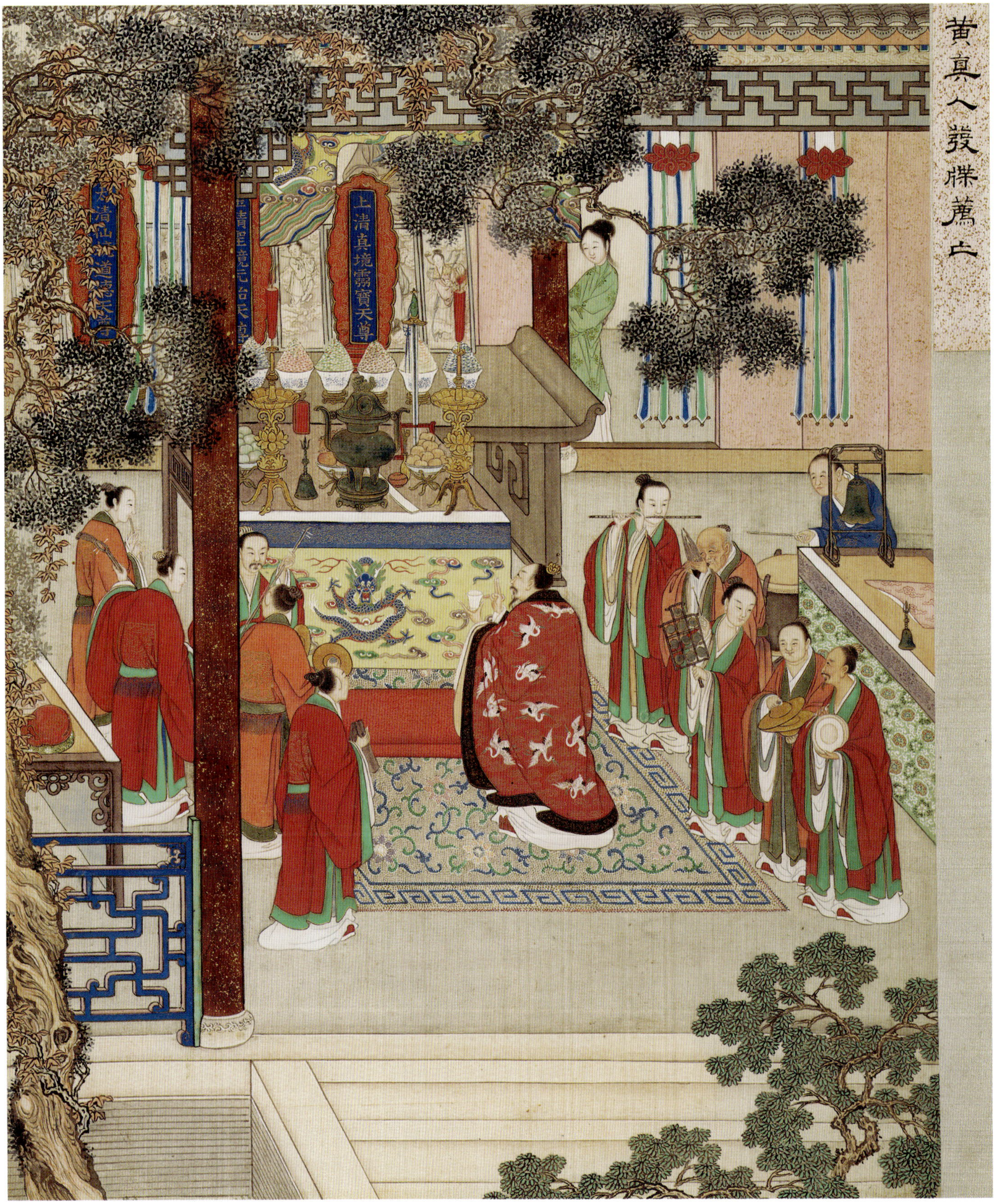

principle of yang and yin with the image of male and female, the designer of the *Pearl Pagoda* robe tried to reconstruct the whole of the eight episodic roundels according to this division. This scenario is doubly secured by arranging two yang trigrams [episode 1 (*qian*) and 4 (*zhen*)] on the back and two yin trigrams [episode 5 (*xun*) and 8 (*kun*)] on the front. Episode 5 (Meeting Her Mother-in-Law) shows a young woman kneeling in front of an old lady who is stepping out of a door (fig. 4.4, roundel 5). This image could signify that when Fang Qing's mother was sheltered in a Buddhist nunnery, both his fiancée Chen Cui-e and Bi Xiujin met their future mother-in-law in the nunnery and secretly helped her. As a result of their being generous to their future mother-in-law, after Fang Qing was successful in his official career, he happily married both women, as shown in episode 8 (The Wedding) represented on the lower right on the front of the robe. Although Fang Qing also appears in this scene, the two brides are covered by their red wedding veils, their concealed faces occupying the center of this scene (fig. 4.4, roundel 8). The main theme of this roundel is perhaps not just that Fang Qing had the good fortune to marry two women but that the two virtuous women could modestly share one husband together. The literary source of this story indeed describes how both Chen Cui-e and Bi Xiujin tried to give up the title of principal wife to allow the other to have the honor. Even on their wedding night, they each tried to let the other one sleep with their husband first. In the end, poor Fang Qing ended up having to sleep alone on his wedding night.

Though the protagonist of *The Pearl Pagoda* is a male, the didactic message of the story is clearly directed toward women. One important theme in this tanci is how to be a righteous mother, aunt, wife, and daughter-in-law. This model of virtuous female conduct, which transcends class distinctions, helps account for the story's extreme popularity during the Qing dynasty. Juxtaposing a scene of a virtuous daughter-in-law with a scene of a virtuous wife on the front of this robe delivered a strong message, which makes the front side as important as the back in this case. Or we can say the garment reverses the usual ritual function of the Daoist robe by making the back the most important side. Hence in a secular context, the two distinctive female scenes on the front of the robe reverse the gender hierarchy of an iconic Daoist robe, and they become the most visible imagery on this robe.

Though this robe follows some visual conventions of a Daoist ritual robe, it is still unclear whether this robe was actually made for ritual purposes, since no existing Daoist ritual vestment portrays a narrative. There are instances in which women wore Daoist robes for special occasions.[46] It is possible, as I have already speculated, that the *Pearl Pagoda* robe might have been used by a tanci storyteller. Given that most surviving narrative robes are women's garments, this article of clothing might have been made for or used by a woman. Another possibility is that this robe may have been produced as a luxurious gift for someone's birthday celebration. Apart from *The Pearl Pagoda* story, the remaining symbols on this robe are all related to longevity, and perhaps the form of a Daoist robe itself was used as an auspicious object for celebrating longevity.

Notes

1 The exceptions are the unisex dragon robes used by the Qing court. Chuimei Ho and Bennet Bronson, *Splendors of China's Forbidden City: The Glorious Reign of Emperor Qianlong.* (London and New York: Merrell; Chicago: The Field Museum of Natural History, 2004), pp. 66–71.

2 Chen Juanjuan and Huang Nengfu, "Silk Fabrics of the Ming Dynasty," in Dieter Kuhn, ed., *Chinese Silk* (New Haven, Conn.: Yale University Press, 2012), pp. 416–17.

3 Kuang Yanghua, "Minjian cixiu xiqu ticai yanjiu," [Study on Opera Subjects Adopted in Folk Embroideries] MA thesis, Donghua daxue, 2007.

4 I would like to express my gratitude to Prof. Bo Songnian for helping to identifying the subject matter on this robe.

5 For the discussion of how women used New Year pictures in their embroidery, see David Johnson's article "Opera Imagery in the Village" in this catalogue.

6 Pan Lusheng, *Fu benzi* [Booklet of Good Fortune] (Shijiazhuang: Hebei meishu chubanshe, 2003), pp. 77–92.

7 Embroidery Manual, late Qing period, private collection.

8 Zhang Qing and Duan Gaifang eds., *Shanxi xiqu cixiu* [Theatrical Embroideries in Shanxi] (Harbin: Heilongjiang chubanshe, 1999).

9 Judith T. Zeitlin, Introduction to this catalogue.

10 I would like to express my gratitude to Bo Songnian for helping me to identify the subject matter.

11 Dore Levy, *Ideal and Actual in the Story of the Stone* (New York: Columbia University Press, 1999), p. 3.

12 The idea of using a robe as an image-bearer can be traced back to sixth-century China. It first appeared on the freestanding statues of Dharmadhàtu Buddha. The stone carved robe worn by the Buddha served as a pictorial space to represent Buddha's manifestations of all existence in different realms. See Katherine R. Tsiang, "Embodiments of Buddhist Texts in Early Medieval Chinese Visual Culture," in Wu Hung and Katherine R. Tsiang, eds., *Body and Face in Chinese Visual Culture* (Cambridge, Mass.: Harvard University Asia Center and Harvard University

Press, 2005), pp.49–78. However, it was not until the late Ming to the Qing period that an actual garment, more precisely a Daoist liturgical robe, became the actual physical form for visualizing a complicated Daoist cosmology constructed through various symbols and immortals. Stephen Little, *Taoism and the Arts of China* (Chicago: The Art Institute of Chicago; Berkeley: University of California Press, 2000), p. 195.

13 One more example with a possible *Dream of the Red Chamber* motif can be found in the collection of the Minneapolis Institute of Arts. See Robert D. Jacobsen, *Imperial Silks: Ch'ing Dynasty Textiles in the Minneapolis Institute of Arts*, vol. 1 (Minneapolis: Minneapolis Institute of Arts, 2000), pp. 514–15. It also contains ten roundels.

14 Yunfei Shao, "Spectacular Prop: Study of a Female Jacket in Jordan Schnitzer Museum of Art," unpublished paper. Also see her entry on the *Dream of the Red Chamber* robe in this catalogue.

15 The production process for borders is complicated and most of these borders could be purchased in commercial shops.

16 Shao, "Spectacular Prop," pp. 3–7.

17 This is only a general observation. There is also an example of figures rendered in theatrical costume. See *Woman's Informal Robe* (acc. no. 1979.107) in the collection of the Metropolitan Museum of Art, New York.

18 More examples of narrative robes decorated with scenes from *Romance of the Western Chamber* can be found in other collections, such as the "Chinese Woman's Unofficial Informal Robe," published in Jacobsen, *Imperial Silks*, pp. 526–27.

19 Marina H. Sung, "T'an-Tz'u and T'an-Tz'u Narratives." T'oung Pao LXXIX (1993): pp. 1–22. 3–7; Mark Bender, "Tan-ci, Wen-ci, Chang-ci." *CLEAR* 6 (1984): pp. 121–24. Bender distinguishes between literary tanci (*wen-ci*) and performed tanci (*chang-ci)* as two separate categories and traditions.

20 Hu Siao-chen, *Cainü cheye weimian: Jindai zhongguo nüxing xushi wenxue de xingqi* [Burning the Midnight Oil: The Rise of Female Narrative in Early Modern China] (Taibei: Maitian, 2003).

21 Female tanci performers can be traced back to the Ming dynasty. The majority of female tanci performers from this period were blind. Only after the Daoguang period (1821–1850) did unimpaired women start to perform in the public storytelling hall, and sometimes with a male performer. See Aying, "Nütanci xiaozhi," [Records of Woman's Tanci] in Aying *quanji* [Aying's Complete Works] (Hefei: Anhui jiaoyu chubanshe, 2003), vol. 7, pp. 405–27. For an in-depth discussion of female tanci performers in late imperial China, see Zhou Wei, *Jiyi yu xingbie: Wanqing yilai Jiangnan nütanci yanjiu* [Skill and Gender: Research on the Female Tanci in the Jiangnan Area Since Late Qing] (Shanghai: Shanghai renmin chubanshe, 2010), pp. 60–94.

22 In the novels and dramas from the Qing period, blind female tanci performers are often described as being invited to a private household to perform for women. The subjects they perform are not only historical and moralistic stories of filial piety and virtuous women, but also include contemporary affairs. Zhou Wei, ibid., pp. 63–72.

23 Tanci also spread to nearby areas such as Yangzhou, Songjiang, Changzhou, Jiaxing, Huzhou, and Taicangzhou.

24 Shao, "Spectacular Prop," pp. 14–15. For a general introduction to *Fengyue meng*, see Patrick Hanan, "Fengyue meng and the Courtesan Novel." *Harvard Journal of Asiatic Studies,* 1998: 2, pp. 345–72.

25 A regular Daoist robe should be fastened with two silk ties.

26 The regulation of Daoist ritual robes can be traced back to the Six Dynasties in Lu Xiujing's "Lu xianxiang daomen kelüe" [Master Lu's Summary of Daoist Liturgy] in Zhang Jiyu, ed., *Zhonghua daozang* [Daoist Canon of China] (Beijing: Huaxia chubanshe, 2004), vol. 8, pp. 556–59. One detailed discussion of Daoist robes is from the Tang dynasty (618–907). Zhang Wanfu not only recorded different ranked robes with different names but also indicated the cap and skirt used for each rank. Apparently, the Daoist liturgical robe was only one part of a whole set of ritual vestments. See Zhang Wanfu, "Sandong fafu kejiewen" [Treatise on the Code of Ritual Vestments for the Entire Liturgy] in Daozang [Daoist Canon] (Beijing. Wenwu chubanshe, Shanghai: Shanghai shudian, Tianjin: Tianji guji chubanshe, 1988), vol. 18, pp. 228–31. The regulation of Daoist liturgical robes is also complicated with respect to different periods, localities, and Daoist sects. See Livia Kohn, *Monastic Life in Medieval Daoism: A Cross-Cultural Perspective* (Honolulu: University of Hawai'i Press), pp. 140–71. Livia Kohn, trans., *The Daoist Monastic Manual: A Translation of the Fengdao Kejie* (Oxford: Oxford University Press, 2004), pp. 119–22. For the discussion of the tern *fayi* or *fafu*, see Zhang Dandan, "Chuanshi daojiao fayi tuxiang yanjiu zhi yuluoxiao tai" [Study of the Iconography of Yuluoxiao tai on the Inherited Daoist Ritual Robes], *Daojiao wenhua yanjiu zhongxin tongxun*, issue 25, and Verity Wilson, "Cosmic Raiment: Taoist Traditions of Liturgical Clothing," *Orientations* (May 1995): p. 47. The earliest Daoist liturgical robe is found in a tomb of a Daoist named Yan Deyuan, dated to the year of 1189 or 1190 near Datong, Shanxi province. Both types of *jiangyi* and *daopao* are found in this tomb. See Datongshi bowuguan, "Datongshi Yan Deyuan mu fajue jianbao" [Excavated Report of Yan Deyuan's Tomb in Datong], *Wenwu*, 4 (1978): pp. 1–13, and Wilson, "Cosmic Raiment," p.44.

27 John Lagerwey, *Taoist Ritual in Chinese Society and History* (New York: Macmillan Publishing Company, 1987), pp. 291–92.

28 Wilson, "Cosmic Raiment," p. 44.

29 I would like to thank Dandan Zhang for calling my attention to the ambiguity about *jiangyi* and *daopao*.

30 The red has faded to tangerine.

31 As Susan Huang points out, the Daoist iconography of the seven-storied palace is similar to the diagram of Buddhist cosmology called Three Worlds and Nine Lands (*sanjie jiudi*) used in the Tang period. See Shih-shan Susan Huang, *Picturing the True Form: Daoist Visual Culture in Traditional China* (Cambridge, Mass.: Harvard University Press, 2012), pp. 98–102. For a fruitful discussion of this subject, see Zhang, "Chuanshi daojiao fayi tuxiang yanjiu zhi yuluoxiao tai."

32 Zhang, "Chuanshi daojiao fayi tuxiang yanjiu zhi yuluoxiao tai."

33 People from the Suzhou area in Jiangsu province believe that *The Pearl Pagoda* is based on a real story of a high official and a native of Tongli county in Suzhou, Chen Wangdao (1526–1576). According to a Tongli

gazetteer, Chen Wangdao had a *jinshi* degree and achieved the rank of highest official as Administer of Inspection for Nanjing during the Wanli reign (1573–1620). The male protagonist is widely believed to hail from a nearby county. An inventory catalogue of the dowry from the Chen family was found in the Republican period and "a pearl pagoda" is listed on the first page. Contemporary Tongli natives such as Fan Yanqiao use this as evidence to prove the connection between the Chen family and *The Pearl Pagoda*. Many places mentioned in the play are believed to be identical with sites in Tongli. For instance, Tongli also has a nunnery called Baiyunan an (White Cloud Nunnery), which is an important place in *The Pearl Pagoda*. The old residence of the Chen family also remains. In order to realize the connection between the Chen family and *The Pearl Pagoda*, the local government of Tongli has renovated the Chen family's house and promoted it into a tourist site called the Scenic District of *The Pearl Pagoda* (*Zhenzhuta jingqu*). Whether this *Pearl Pagoda* robe has anything to do with the Chen family or Tongli county is still unclear and warrants further investigation. See Fan Yanqiao, *Cha yan xie* [Tea, Tobacco and Rest] (Shanghai: Zhongfu shuju, 1933).

34 For an in-depth research on the musical aspect of the *Pearl Pagoda* tanci performance, see Sun Hui-ya, "Suzhou tanci Zhenzhuta yanjiu" [Study of Suzhou Tanci Pearl Pagoda], MA thesis, Guoli Taiwan shifan daxue, 1985. For an analysis of the narrative, see Fang Ssu-ju, "Tanci Zhenzhuta yanjiu" [Study of Tanci Pearl Pagoda], MA thesis, Guoli zhongyang daxue, 2011.

35 The 1781 edition was recorded in the catalogue of Aying's collection of various editions of *The Pearl Pagoda*; see Aying, "Ma rufei de Zhenzhuta ji qita" [Ma Rufei's Pearl Pagoda and Other Related Issues] in Aying, *Quanji* (Hefeishi: Anhui jiaoyu chubanshe, 2003–2006), vol. 7, pp. 249–50. For a comparison of different editions of *The Pearl Pagoda*, see Ling Jingyan, "*Zhenzhuta geben yitong kao*" [Investigation into the Similarities and Dissimilarities of Various Editions of *The Pearl Pagoda*] (*Pingtan yanjiu ziliao*, diyiji, 1957). Zhao Jingshen, "Zhenzhuta" [The Pearl Pagoda] in *Tanci kaozheng* [Evidential Research on Tanci], pp. 66–75. I have mainly consulted the 1849 edition titled *Xiaoyi zhenji Zhenzhuta* (hereafter Zhenzhuta [1849]) published by Sanhuai tang in Weiyang in 1849. A facsimile reproduction of this edition can be found in *Xuxiu siku quanshu* [Sequel to Complete Collection of the Four Treasuries] (Shanghai: Shanghai guji chubanshe, 1995–2002), vol. 1, 745, pp. 433–571.

36 Aying, "Ma rufei de Zhenzhuta ji qita," pp. 244–58.

37 There are ten portrait illustrations in the 1849 edition of *The Pearl Pagoda*, see *Pearl Pagoda* (1849), pp. 436–38. For a discussion of the images of opera characters, see Mei Mei Rado's essay "Images of Opera Characters Related to the Qing Court," in this catalogue.

38 For a discussion of a different layout on a *Pearl Pagoda* New Year picture, see Boris Riftin, "Chinese Performing Arts and Popular Prints," in Vibeke Børdahl and Margaret B. Wan, eds., *The Interplay of the Oral and the Written in Chinese Popular Literature* (Copenhagen: NIAS; Abingdon: Marston [distributor], 2010), pp. 187–239, 212–15.

39 See "Taoist Priest's Robe (Tao Pao)," in Jacobsen, *Imperial Silks*, pp. 426–27.

40 Schuyler Cammann, "The Eight Trigrams: Variants and Their Uses," in *History of Religions*, 29, pp. 301–17. Poul Anderson, "Guideline to the Eight Trigrams," *Occasional Paper 6* (Copenhagen, 1990): pp. 13–30. The Eight Trigrams have long been incorporated into Chinese religion. Eugene Wang, "What Do Trigrams Have to Do with Buddhas? The Northern Liang (397–439) Stupas as a Hybrid Spatial Model." *RES: Anthropology and Aesthetics*, 35 (Spring 1999), pp. 71–91. Maggie C. K. Wan, "Motifs with an Intention: Reading the Eight Trigrams on Official Porcelain of the Jiajing Period (1522–1566)."*Artibus Asiae*, 63/2 (2003): pp. 191–221.

41 *Yi Jing* [Book of Changes] (Su Yong annot., Beijing: Beijing daxue chubanshe, 1989).

42 "(老生曰) 今有河南方子文,稽首焚香. 禱告八八六十四卦內求一卦.........此乃地天泰卦," *Zhenzhuta* (1849), p. 440.

43 Zhang, "Chuanshi daojiao fayi tuxiang yanjiu zhi yuluoxiao tai."

44 Little, *Taoism and the Arts of China*, p. 193.

45 See the "Robe of Descent" (*jiangyi*) from the collection of the Victoria and Albert Museum, London (acc. no. T.91-1928). Also see Wilson, "Cosmic Raiment," pp. 44–45.

46 Mao Wenfang, "Yige Qing guige de shijiao—Gu Taiqing (1799–1877) huaxiang tiyong xilun" [The Analysis of Inscriptions on Paintings—Viewpoints on Regentry Woman Gu Taiqing (1799–1877), Qing dynasty]. *Wen yu zhe* [Literature & Philosophy], 8 (2006.6): pp. 417–74.

BO SONGNIAN

Five

Operatic Images in Popular New Year Prints

Chinese Opera has deep footings in vernacular culture. Watching plays and listening to oral storytelling performances have long constituted a principal form of popular entertainment. While opera itself is a time-bound medium that can be savored only by attending a performance, the fixed images in works of art allow for more long-term appreciation. Thus a great number of operatic images have appeared in Chinese popular art, especially in New Year pictures (*nianhua*), a genre of decorative woodblock prints produced for the Chinese New Year celebrations.[1] In fact, aside from auspicious images intended to ward off evil and bring good fortune, a considerable proportion of these pictures are taken up with theatrical subject matter. In an age before television, such artworks projected much-loved scenes from the stage onto the walls of people's living quarters and time and again fulfilled their aesthetic desires.[2]

The history of operatic New Year pictures can, at the earliest, be traced back to works of Song dynasty (960–1279) seasonal paintings such as *The Five Auspicious Omens* and *The Great Exorcist Rite*, with their scenes from the popular exorcizing performances discussed by Jonathan Hay in his essay in this catalogue. By the Ming and Qing dynasties (1368–1911), an unprecedented surge in the sheer range and number of popular operatic forms contributed to the flourishing of theatrical New Year picture designs. Although many theatrical images are evident in surviving early Qing dynasty woodblock New Year prints, there is greater emphasis on reproducing popular figures within easily recognizable storylines. *The Garden of Auspicious Herbs* (*Ruicao yuan*) from Yangliuqing in Tianjin, and the New Year picture *Jinshan Monastery* (*Jinshan si*) from Suzhou, for instance, are simply attractive illustrations of the heroine White Snake and her foil Green Snake from *The White Snake* (*Baishe zhuan*) (fig. 5.1). The story of the bond between the White Snake and the Green Snake indebted to her, with both serpents assuming human form, and their fight to save the White Snake's human love Xu Xian from an evil Buddhist monk named Fahai (Ocean of Dharma), was one of the most popular tales in late imperial China and was adapted across a wide range of media (cats. 28, 29).

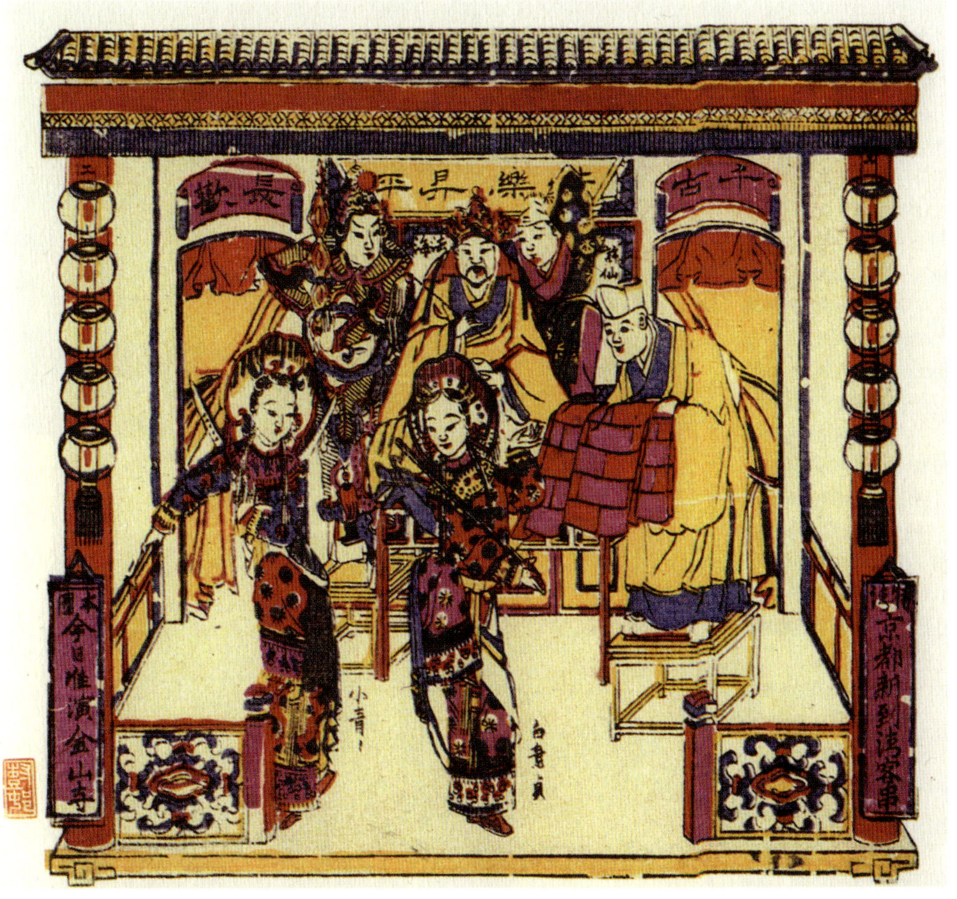

5.1
Suzhou, Taohuawu (print workshop)
Chinese, Qing Dynasty (1644–1911)
Jinshan [Gold Mountain] Monastery (Jinshan si), n.d.
Polychrome woodblock print

With a heightened interest in the theater, however, images that better allowed viewers to recall the pleasures of attending a performance became more and more popular. The Suzhou Taohuawu image *Jinshan Monastery*, for example, represents the scene of a performance on a stage from the late Qing dynasty . The illustration realistically depicts both the columns and balustrade of the stage and the rear stage doors through which actors make their entrances and exits. Illuminated lanterns hang in a chain along both sides of the stage, along with a sign that has been specifically inscribed: "Welcoming a New Amateur Troupe of Guest Performers at Special Invitation from the Capital." Onstage, an impassioned White Snake has returned to Jinshan Monastery to reclaim her human husband Xu Xian with whom her fate is intertwined, but the intractable Buddhist priest Fahai will not relent. Fahai along with some young monks and his prisoner Xu Xian are all standing on tables and chairs as they would on stage to create the impression of the tall peak of Jinshan (Gold Mountain). We see Green Snake and White Snake clutching her precious sword in her hand, as though the climactic scene—in which the White Snake tries to free her husband Xu Xian from the monastery as it floods with water—is just about to unfold. These types of New Year pictures were tantamount to bringing the stage into people's homes and were received enthusiastically.

Another Taohuawu New Year image, *Mount Fenghuang (Fenghuang shan)*, depicts a particularly interesting theatrical scene (cat. 00)[3] During the Qing dynasty (1644–1911), women were prohibited from either performing publicly in plays or attending public theaters as spectators. This ban was first broken in Shanghai. Toward the end of the Qing dynasty we find the emergence of troupes composed of young women, referred to at the time as "Pussycat Opera" (*Mao'er xi*.) For the most part, these troupes plied their trade in small theaters or on makeshift stages in private residences and brothels. This print bears the specific inscription "Pussycat Opera at Tan Garden in Qingyangdi" and thus apparently depicts the scene of a performance in a courtesan house. The audience of intermingled men and women sit around the small stage as young courtesans in opulent attire entertain them. Another scene illustrates a client beckoning to the performing girls. The focus of the image is not so much the content of the play, but rather a reflection of the social atmosphere and the vicissitudes of life in a courtesan house.

Peking opera (*jingju*), the most prominent form of traditional Chinese theater, first took shape in the capital Beijing but had spread to Shanghai by the late 1860s. Two different styles of Peking opera, the Beijing School (*Jingpai*) and the Shanghai School (*Haipai*) emerged as a result of the different tastes of the respective local audiences. The Beijing School tended to place more importance on the appeal of singing and the elegance of measured performances, while Shanghai audiences preferred lively spectacles with exciting twists and turns. Consequently, we can speak of a contrast between "listening to opera" in Beijing and the experience of

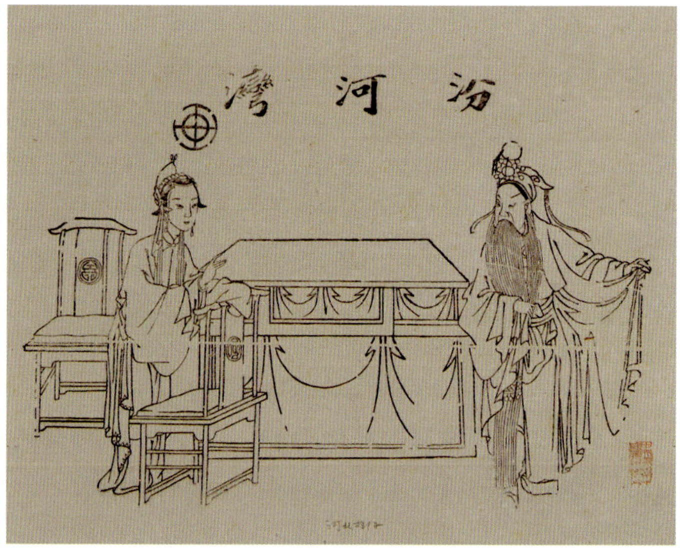

5.2
Tianjin, Yangliuqing (print workshop)
Chinese, Qing Dynasty (1644–1911)
Fenhe Cove (Fenhe wan), n.d.
Woodblock print
Central Academy of Fine Arts Library, Beijing

"watching opera" for the audiences of Shanghai. These distinctive aesthetic traits are clearly reflected in the differences between the Yangliuqing prints from Tianjin in the North and the Taohuawu prints from Suzhou in the South.

At the same time that Beijing came to possess a considerable number of famous actors and popular plays, the Yangliuqing firm in Tianjin would hire renowned artists to take their pens and paper with them to the theater to make draft sketches of performances and venues. These New Year prints vividly capture scenes of actors performing onstage. The strict requirements for costumes and gestures are caught with near faultless accuracy, sometimes to such a degree that one can recognize not only the opera and the aria within it, but also the specific lines the actor is singing. Take for instance a print of the play *Fenhe Cove* (*Fenhe wan*) that depicts a famous general of the Tang dynasty, Xue Rengui (614–683), who had left home on military campaigns for eighteen years, returning to meet his wife (fig. 5.2). The two figures in this image are separated by a chair, which symbolizes the door of the house, as the actor dressed as Xue Rengui appears to be midway through an aria about his experiences during his eighteen-year absence, endeavoring to win back his wife's trust. The character's gestures in this image are particularly evocative. Hundreds of images of this type still exist.

In Shanghai, more raucous spectacles drew audiences to Peking opera. Martial characters in combat plays would normally take to the stage one at a time in accordance with their parts in specific storylines, but New Year prints went further in creating rich and lively effects through depicting many different martial characters grouped together onstage regardless of the plot. The late Qing Shanghai print *The Capturing of Shi Wengong from the Zeng Family District* (*Zengtou shi huoqin Shi Wengong*), for instance, depicts the episode of the famous outlaws of the Marshes of Mount Liang from the popular novel *The Water Margin* (*Shuihu zhuan*) seizing the enemy militia instructor Shi Wengong (fig. 5.3).[4] Onstage, aside from a few rank-and-file troops and small-time crooks, the only heroes from Mount Liang that are present ought to be Li Kui, Lin Chong, Lu Junyi, Yan Qing, Wu Song, and, and in the last act, Ruan Xiao'er and Ruan Xiaowu, who take to the water to seize Shi Wengong. In the center of the print, however, Lu Junyi and Shi Wengong are locked in deep battle, while other characters from the Mount Liang marshes fill the surrounding space. Among these figures are Li Li, Zhang Heng, Zhang Shun, and the two female generals Hu Sanniang and Sister Gu, who do not appear in the original version of the story but whose presence heightens the palpable fervor of the scene. Similarly, the Shanghai New Year print *The Great Upsurge of Mount Liang, or Subduing Guan Sheng* (*Daxing Liangshan soufu Guan Sheng*) depicts the figure of Guan Sheng, an imperial general who eventually defects to join the outlaws of the marsh, flanked by other characters, falling to the ground and being seized (cat. 51). Of particular note in this image are three tables stacked upon each other, in preparation for the climactic moment when Guan Sheng performs a thrilling backflip from the top of the stack, symbolizing his signature fall from the mountaintop.

The Suzhou Taohuawu print *Seizing Lady Nine Flowers at the Tavern of Delusion* (*Miren guan zhuona Jiuhua niang*), an episode from the late Qing novel *The Cases of Judge Peng* (*Peng gong'an*), was a popular play for the role of the martial heroine on the Shanghai stage (cat. 14). This play presents the story of the capture of the violent and promiscuous female bandit Lady Nine Flowers (Jiuhua niang). The image depicts a group of martial heroes and the figure of Lady Nine Flowers locked in battle: the characters wear distinctive costumes and makeup, and their gestures are rendered in graphic detail. In the center of the print a bed with curtains indicates the interior of a room, while figures stand at both sides on tables and chairs suggesting that bandits are closing in on her from the rooftop. On a horizontal beam above the stage, two actors are performing extremely demanding moves. Such scenes of skilled martial arts actors seeming to fly off the eaves and climb down walls clearly evoke some of the hair-raising antics characteristic of Shanghai School performances.

The Suzhou print *Wu Song Kills His Sister-in-Law and Flees to Mount Liang* (*Wu Song sha sao shang Liangshan*) breaks away from the constraints of time and space altogether (cat. 50). The print

5.3
Shanghai
Chinese, Qing Dynasty (1644–1911)
The Capturing of Shi Wengong from the Zeng Family (Zengtou shi huoqin Shi Wengong), n.d.
Polychrome woodblock print
American Museum of Natural History, New York
Asia/0574 A45

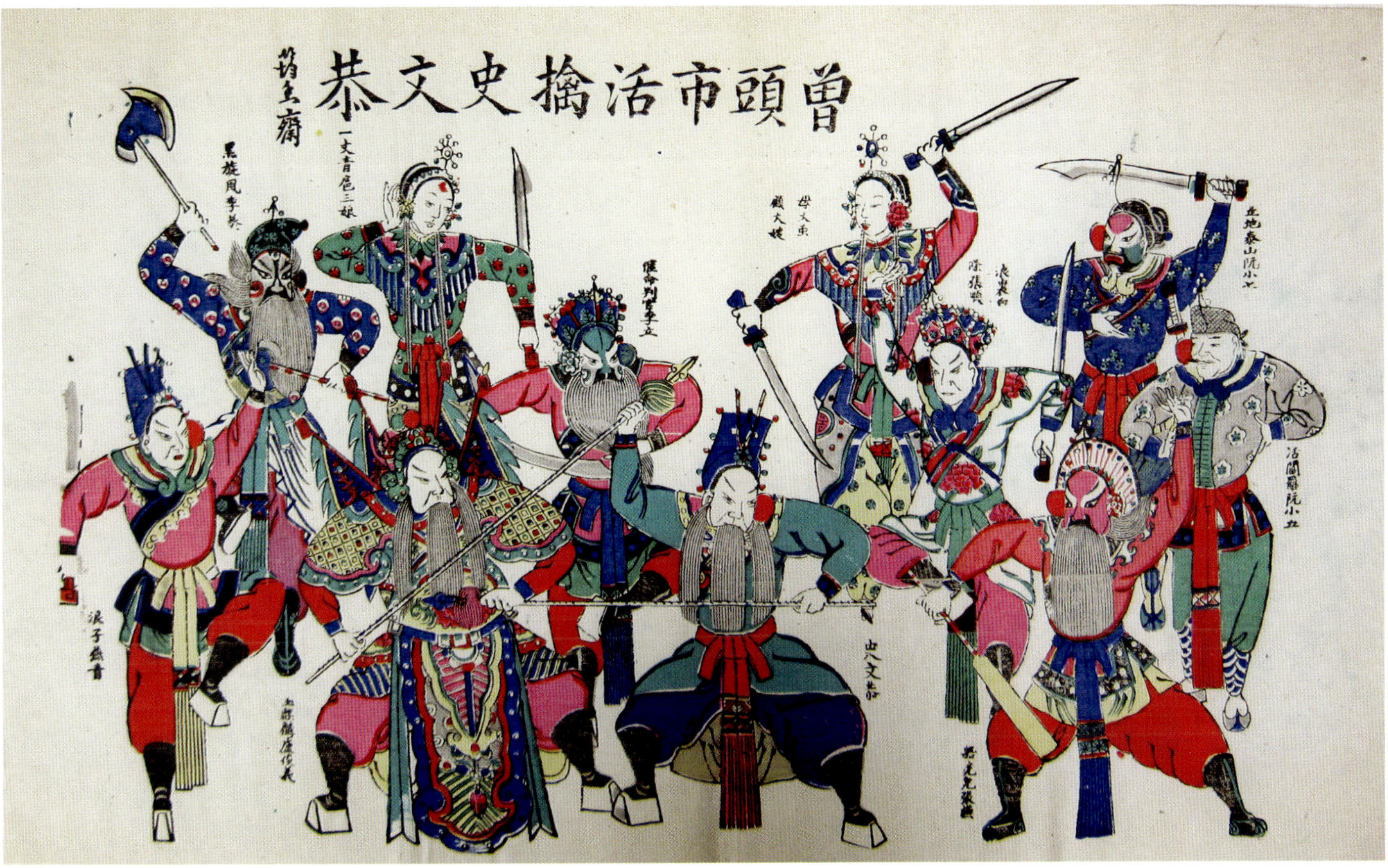

simultaneously depicts the two infamous scenes of the hero Wu Song killing his adulterous sister-in-law Pan Jinlian at his ancestral hall and Ximen Qing, Pan's rakish lover, drinking wine at the Lion Tavern. This print warrants our close attention because it integrates different parts of the original narrative. The composition, for example, depicts the dead spirit of Wu Song's brother, the dwarf Wu Dalang, who was murdered at the hands of Pan and her paramour, demanding Ximen Qing's life in revenge. This representation foreshadows the ending of the play in which the playboy Ximen Qing is fated to die under Wu Song's sword. Later in this play there is indeed an act in which Wu Song and Ximen Qing are fighting each other and Wu Dalang's spirit comes to Wu Song's aid.

Also famed for its convoluted narratives designed to draw in audiences, the Shanghai School Peking opera has many lengthy plays within the repertory that could last anywhere from ten days to a fortnight, such as the tale popularized by the martial arts novel *The Three Heroes and Five Gallants* (*Sanxia wuyi*) titled "Replacing the Infant Heir Apparent with a Civet Cat" and "The Investiture of the Gods," a loose adaptation from a Ming dynasty vernacular novel of the same name. New Year prints reflected the contemporary popularity of these plays through a comic book–style format that could include multiple images on a single page and thus represent a series of linked scenes. The Suzhou print *The Complete Series of the Civet Cat Exchanged for the Real Heir Apparent* (*Quanben luomaofeng limao huan zhenzhu*) consists of eight pictures depicting episodes from the story of Consort Liu and Guo Huai's conspiracy against Empress Dowager Li from their swapping a skinned cat for the infant that she had just given birth to, right up to the scene twenty years later when Judge Bao, the legendary incorruptible magistrate from the Song, clears up this case of injustice, welcomes Empress Dowager Li back to court, and executes the treacherous Guo Huai (fig. 5.4).[5] The pictures are labeled "Cooking up an evil plan to switch the heir apparent with a civet cat," "Judge Bao meeting the Empress Dowager in the Tianqi Temple," and "Vindicating the Empress

5.4
Suzhou, Taohuawu (print workshop)
Chinese, Qing Dynasty (1644–1911)
The Complete Series of the Civet Cat Exchanged for the Real Heir Apparent (Luo mao feng limao huan zhenzhu), n.d.
Polychrome woodblock print
Suzhou Art and Design Technology Institute Library, Suzhou

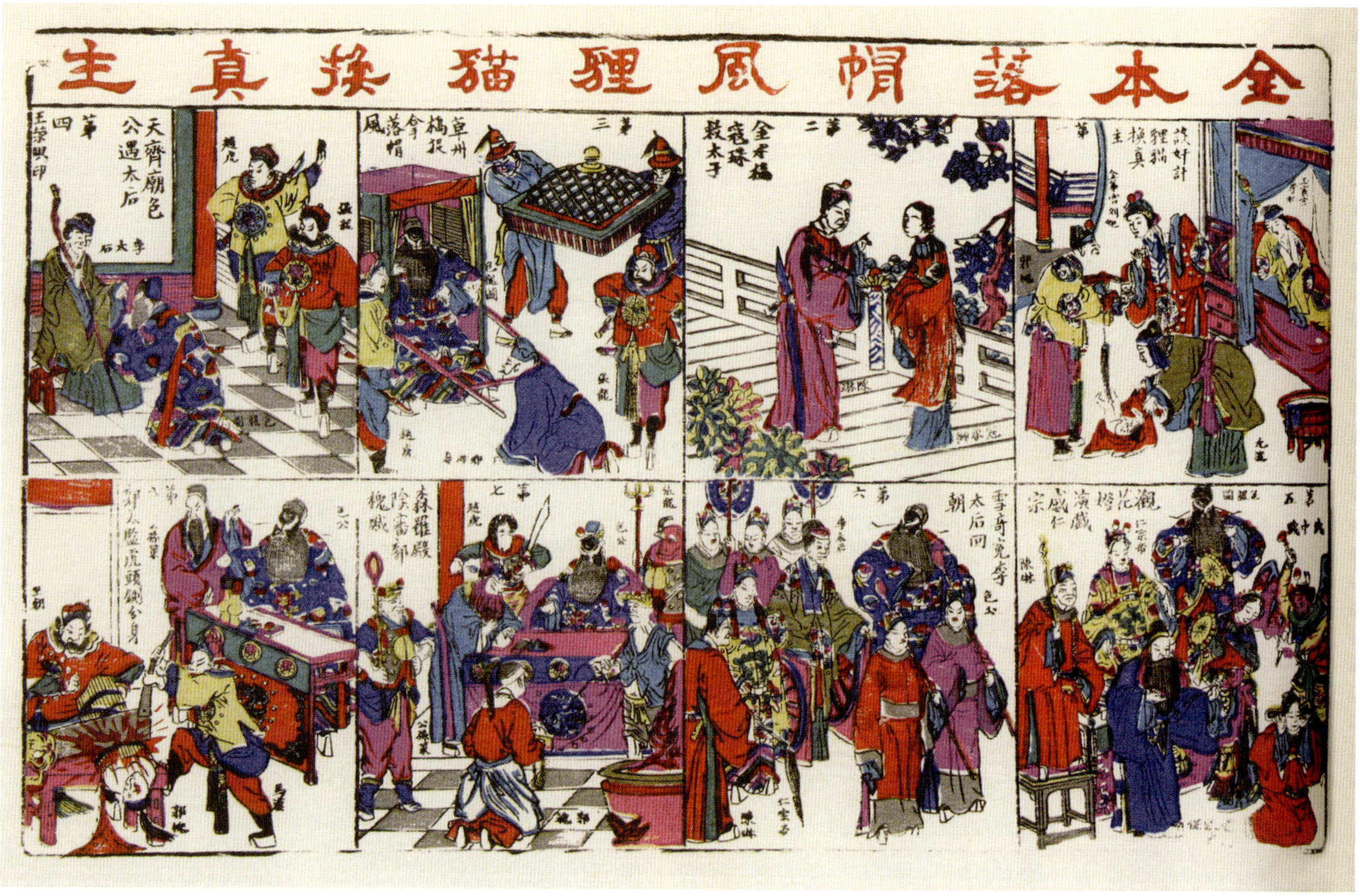

Dowager and returning her to court." These lines, aside from their function as captions, can also be read as markers of important episodes in the series of plays and as advertisements for the acts that a troupe might perform.[6]

The rich tradition of Chinese popular opera shares deep and inextricable bonds with vernacular fiction and oral storytelling. Works of popular fiction, with their sprawling narratives, spread to the lowest levels of society through oral storytelling. Often these stories were then further adapted into dramas and depicted in New Year prints to be appreciated and enjoyed by even larger audiences. New Year prints with scenes from works of widely known novels like *Romance of the Three Kingdoms* (*Sanguo zhi yanyi*) and *The Cases of Judge Shi* (*Shi gong'an*) include realistic depictions of scenery within which the narrative unfolds; in order to give greater prominence to the visual appearance of the characters, however, they are rendered in "operatic" fashion: striking and holding poses as if they were onstage with the stock painted face masks of actors. When these vernacular novels are adapted into the dramatic medium and transformed into brilliant performances, however, the New Year print depictions emphasize the scenery of the stage as well. The New Year picture (published by Yangliuqing) *Seizing Xie Hu at the Gui'de Station* takes up the plot of chapter 165 of *The Cases of Judge Shi*. In this woodblock print, the buildings and garden are presented realistically (fig. 5.5). Both parties have started fighting inside and outside of the residence as figures are seen closing in to capture them from the rooftop. However, the rendition in another print titled *Seizing Xie Hu at the Maozhou Temple* completely imitates theatrical scenery with stage pillars and hanging lanterns (fig. 5.6). Zhu Guangzu, and the criminal Xie Hu, whom he is trying to capture, are standing on tables striking and holding poses, which

5.5
Tianjin, Yangliuqing (print workshop)
Chinese, Qing Dynasty (1644–1911)
Seizing Xie Hu at the Gui'de Station (Guide yi na Xie Hu), n.d.
Woodblock print
Central Academy of Fine Arts Library, Beijing

5.6
Tianjin, Yangliuqing (print workshop)
Chinese, Qing Dynasty (1644–1911)
Seizing Xie Hu at the Maozhou Temple (Maozhou miao na Xie Hu), n.d.
Woodblock print
Central Academy of Fine Arts Library, Beijing

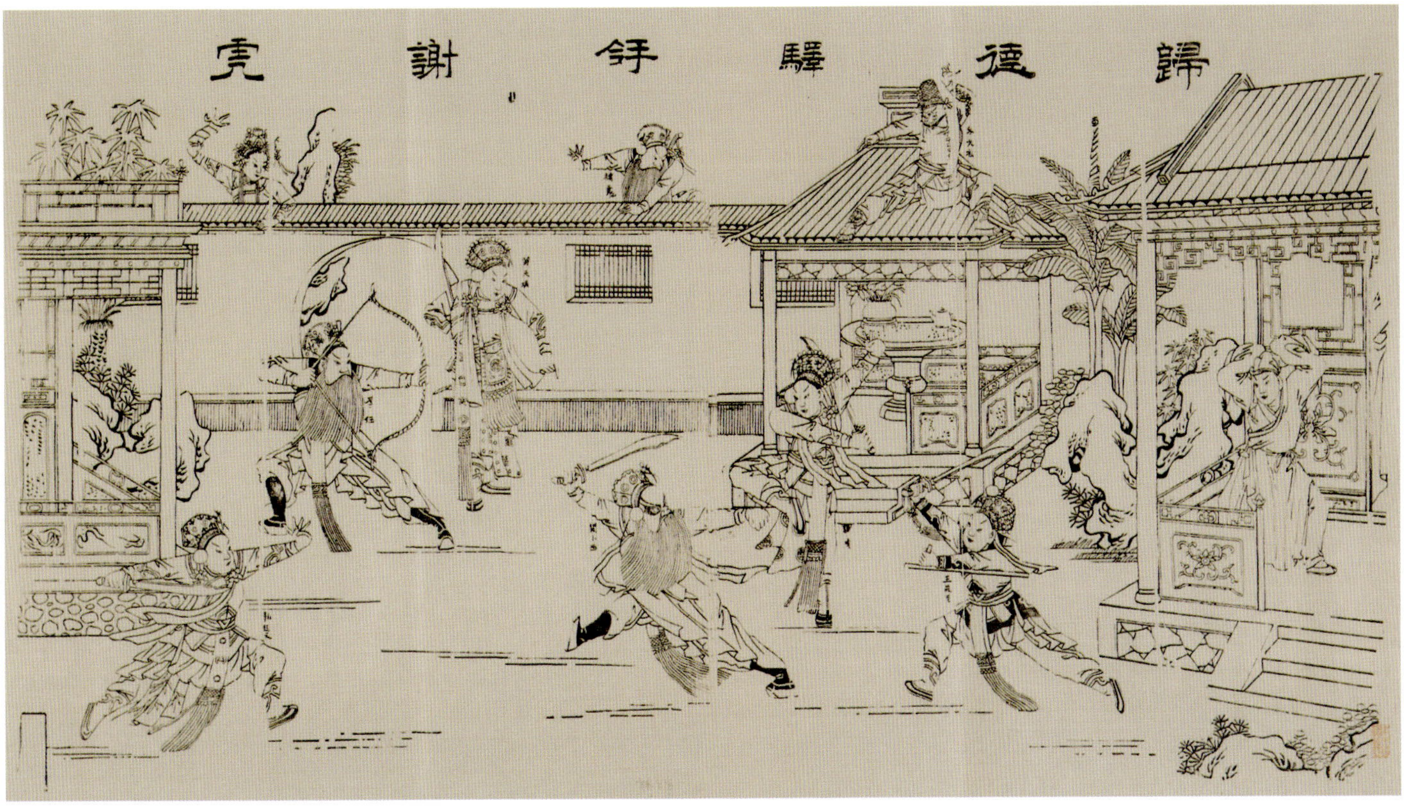

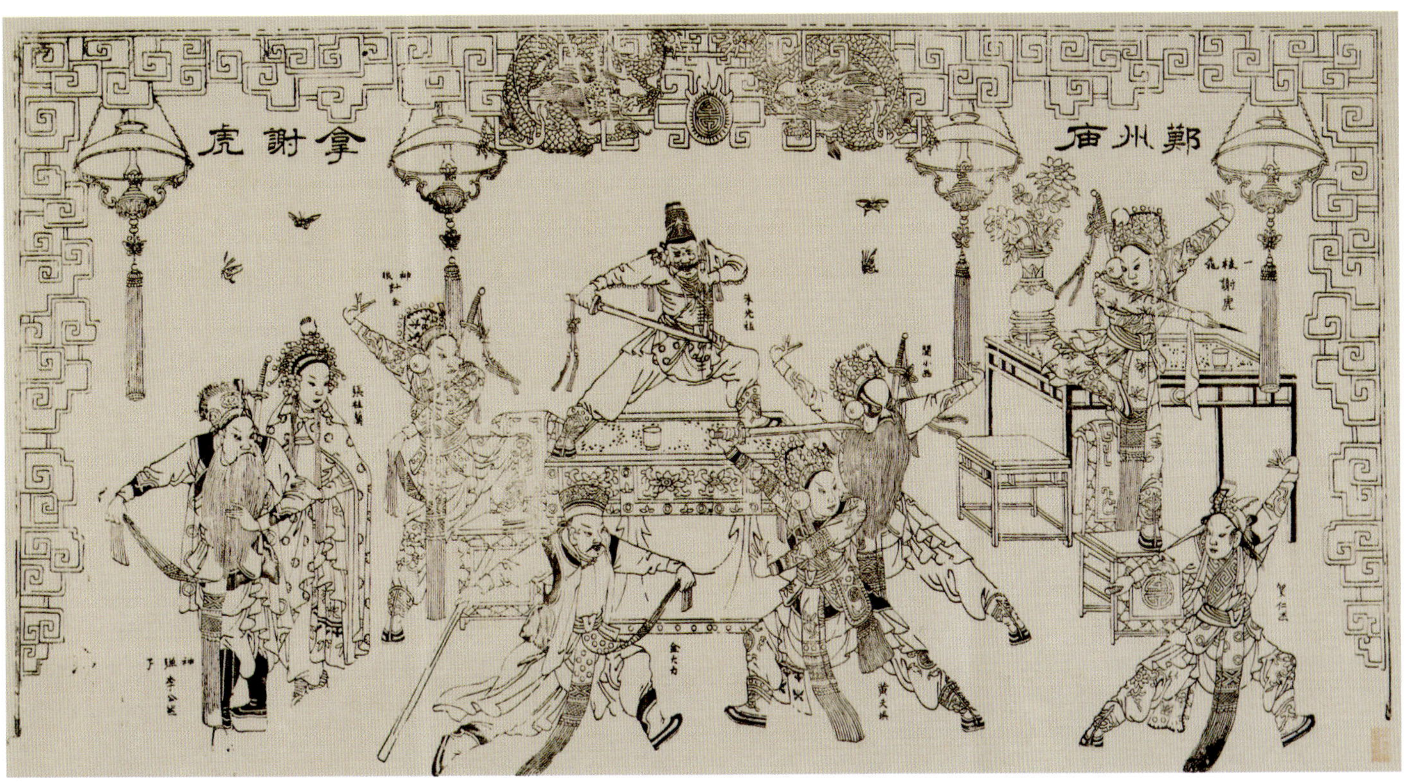

5.7
Wuqiang
Chinese, Qing Dynasty (1644–1911)
Door-Gods (Menshen), n.d
Two polychrome woodblock prints
Wuqiang Museum of New Year Pictures, Hebei

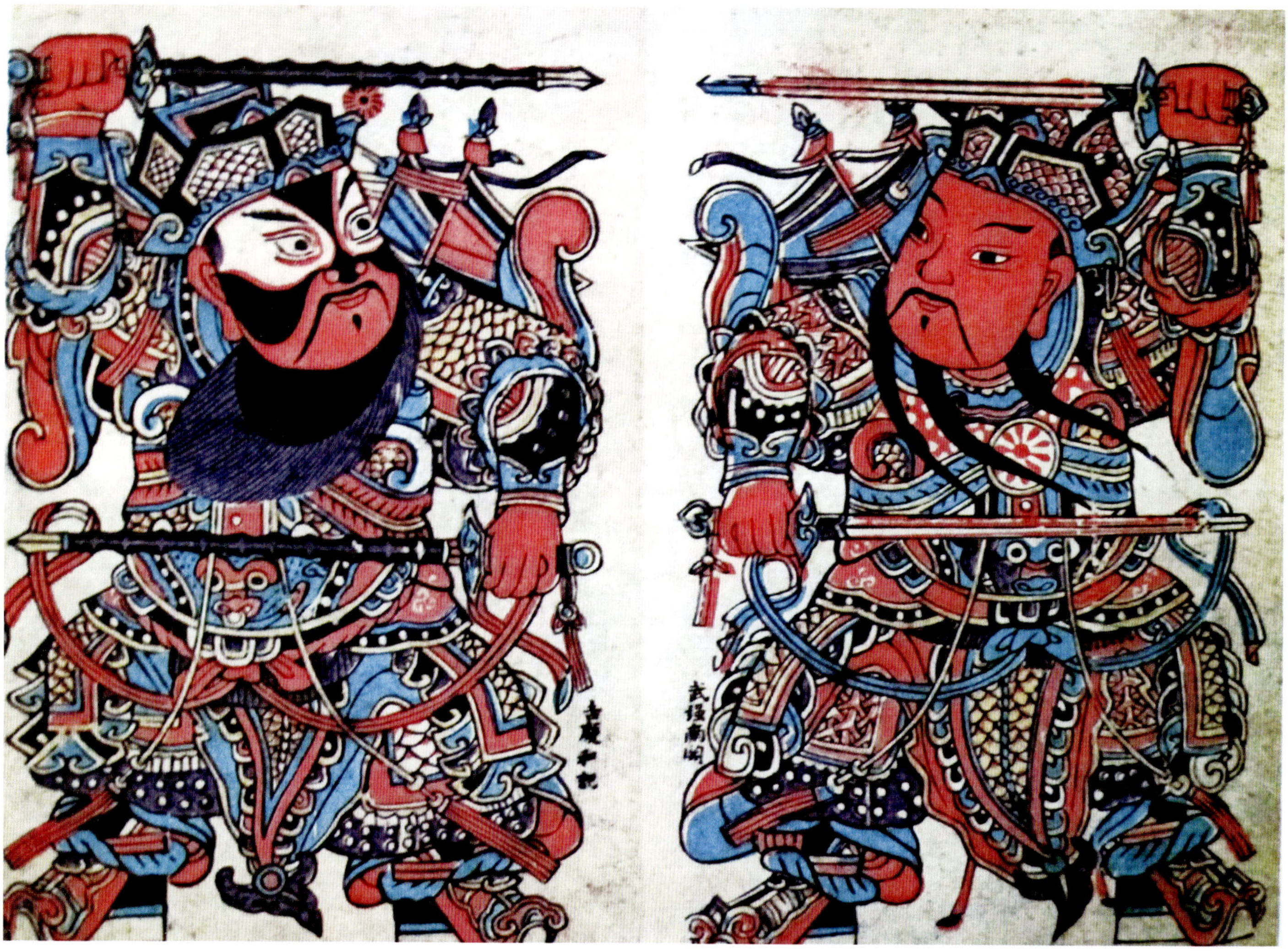

symbolize that they have already jumped onto the rooftop. Our attention here is thus pointedly directed toward the lively spectacle of the play in performance.

Images of characters from the opera also influenced the representation of divinities from the pantheon of popular religion, especially the Divine Steed, offered as a sacrifice during New Year celebrations. In the North, the Wuqiang prints of Qin Shubao (died 638) and Yuchi Jingde (585–658), both Tang generals whose legendary bravery led to their later apotheosis as door-gods, not only incorporate features of face masks from opera, but are even made to look like they are doing theatrical dance moves (fig. 5.7). The celestial and terrestrial deities, the Four Generals of the Heavenly Palaces, also appear as though they are wearing dramatic face-masks (fig. 5.8). And in New Year prints, the gestures of the infamous demon queller Zhong Kui wielding his sword and dancing closely resemble the poses he strikes and holds in the many stage plays about him. The New Year prints from Henan (published by Zhuxianzhen) moreover, use images of characters from drama to decorate and embellish door fronts. In doing so, these images completely transform apotropaic door-gods into participants in the spectacle of a theatrical performance.

At the arrival of the spring festival marking the new year, the doors and the interiors of houses were plastered all over with operatic New Year images. A profusion of vivid colors with alluring and

5.8
Wuqiang
Chinese, Qing Dynasty (1644–1911)
Images of All the Spirits of Heaven and Earth (Tiandi quanshen xiang), n.d.
Polychrome woodblock print
Wuqiang Museum of New Year Pictures, Hebei

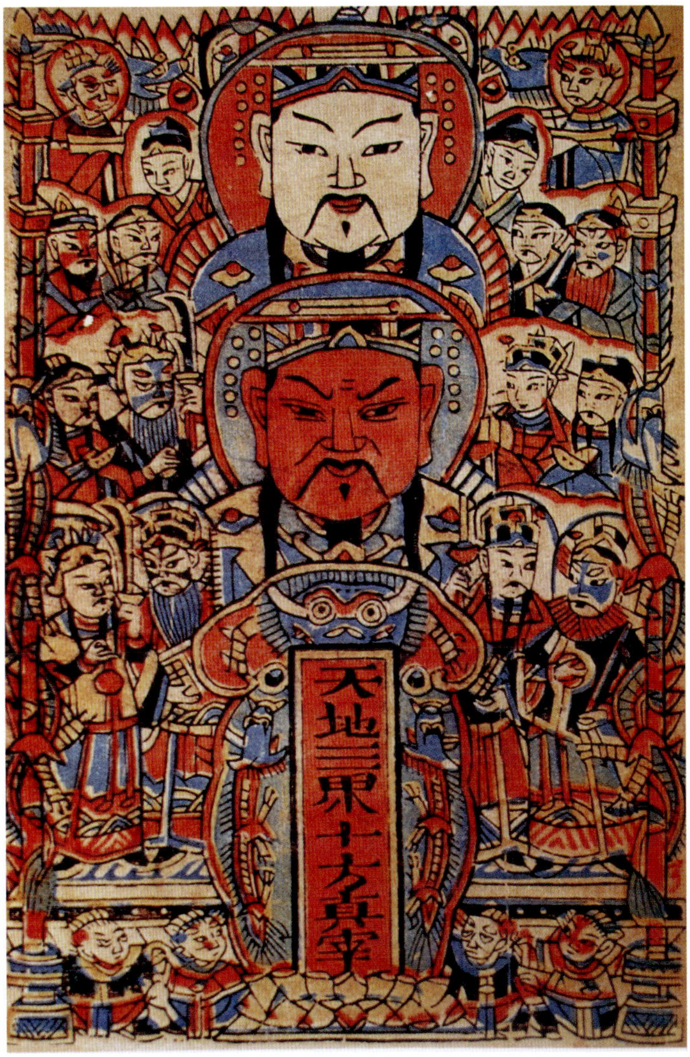

expressive figures from compelling story lines made viewers feel as if they had entered an enchanted theatrical garden. Reflecting popular affection for opera, artisans would adapt their techniques to fit the aesthetic preferences of the theater-going public. As such, a great number of these operatic New Year prints leave us with precious visual evidence of performances from the past and have come to possess significant historical and artistic value.

Notes

1 For an introduction to this genre of decorative prints, see James A Flath, *The Cult of Happiness: Nianhua, Art, and History in Rural North China* (Seattle: University of Washington Press, 2004).

2 New Year pictures were created in a range of formats, from matching flower and bird couplets and square paper prints to prints for main halls, partition screens, beside and above windows, and around the hearth. For more details on types of *nianhua*, see Zhang Daoyi, "Nianhua lilun" [A Discussion of Some Examples of New Year Prints], *Dongnan daxue xuebao*" [Periodical of Dongnan University], 5, no. 1 (2003): pp. 67–73.

3 Other New Year opera prints with images of the stage that I have observed include "Qiao yinyuan (Coincidental Marriage)," "Dian Qiuxiang (Pointing at Qiuxiang)," "Shi yuzhuo (Picking up the Jade Bracelet)," "Shou Jiang Wei (Subduing Jiang Wei)," and "Zhaojun chusai (Zhaojun Departs for the Frontier)," along with another seven or eight titles.

4 For an introduction to the novel, see Wai-Yee Li, "Full-Length Vernacular Fiction," in *The Columbia History of Chinese Literature*, ed. V. Mair (New York: Columbia University Press, 2001), especially pp. 626–32. For a full English translation of this classic novel, see John and Alex Dent-Young, *The Marshes of Mount Liang: A New Translation of the Shuihu zhuan or Water Margin of Shi Nai'an and Luo Guanzhong*, 5 vols. (Hong Kong: Chinese University Press, 1994).

5 For more on Judge Bao, see Wilt L. Idema, *Judge Bao and the Rule of Law: Eight Ballad-Stories from the Period 1250–1450* (Singapore: World Scientific, 2010).

6 There are descriptions of New Year prints being sold in a market in a Qianlong period stringed ballad (*tanci*) called *Xianzhuang hui*, which is discussed in Zheng Zhenduo, *Zhongguo gudai muke hua xuan ji* [Selected Works of Chinese Ancient Woodblock Prints]. (Beijing: Renmin meishu chubanshe, 1985), vol. 9, pp. 92–93. Zheng suggests that the seller is trying to promote new prints by mentioning the theater, troupe, and actors from the Suzhou or Yangzhou area. There is also a short essay by A Ying on this topic, "Nianhua de jiaomai" [Vendor Cries for New Year Prints], in Aying, *Aying wenji* [The Writings of Aying], vol. 2 (Beijing: Sanlian shudian, 1979), vol. 2: p. 860.

NI YIBIN

Six

The Iconographic Variations of Two Scenes from *Romance of the Western Chamber*

Several of the works included in *Performing Images: Opera in Chinese Visual Culture* come out of the iconographic tradition of depicting scenes from the opera *Romance of the Western Chamber* (*Xixiang ji*) and reflect how popular images were adopted, altered, and reproduced in late imperial China. The artists who made these works naturally had to respond to the challenges of their patrons' demands, the limitations and advantages imposed by the materials and techniques available, and the social constraints of their time and place. In particular, when producing images from a literary work like *Romance of the Western Chamber* (hereafter *Western Chamber*), artists would unintentionally, as well as intentionally, manifest their understanding or misunderstanding of the original play, its stage performance, and the iconographic traditions already associated with it.

The First Encounter Scene

Of all the *Western Chamber* illustrations, *Startled by Beauty* (*Jingyan*), which depicts the two lovers' initial encounter in the temple, enjoyed the most widespread currency. On an album leaf attributed to Qiu Ying (Chinese, circa 1494–1552), but likely a later work by an anonymous artist and now in the C. V. Starr East Asian Library, Berkeley (fig. 6.1), the scene is set in a courtyard in front of a grand hall built on a raised platform with a railed staircase leading to the ground. Bushes bloom in the foreground, enhancing the amorous ambience. On the left, Student Zhang (Zhang sheng) is mesmerized by the beauty of Oriole (Yingying); he simply cannot take his eyes off her. Meanwhile the monk Dharma Wit (Huiming) is trying to pull him away by the arm, indicating that Zhang's prolonged staring *is* rather rude. On the right, Oriole, wearing a scarlet undergarment and a patterned silk skirt with a lighter-colored sash over her arm, fingers a sprig of flowers picked from the garden. Aware of a male stranger's anxious gaze on her mistress, the maid Crimson (Hongniang) scrambles to shield Oriole from Zhang with

6.1
Chinese, Late Qing Dynasty (1644–1911)
Formerly attributed to Qiu Ying, Chinese, ca. 1494–1552
Scene from Romance of the Western Chamber (Xixiang ji), n.d.
Album leaf, ink and color on silk, 14 9/16 × 13 in. (37 × 33cm)
Courtesy of the C. V. Starr East Asian Library, University of California, Berkeley

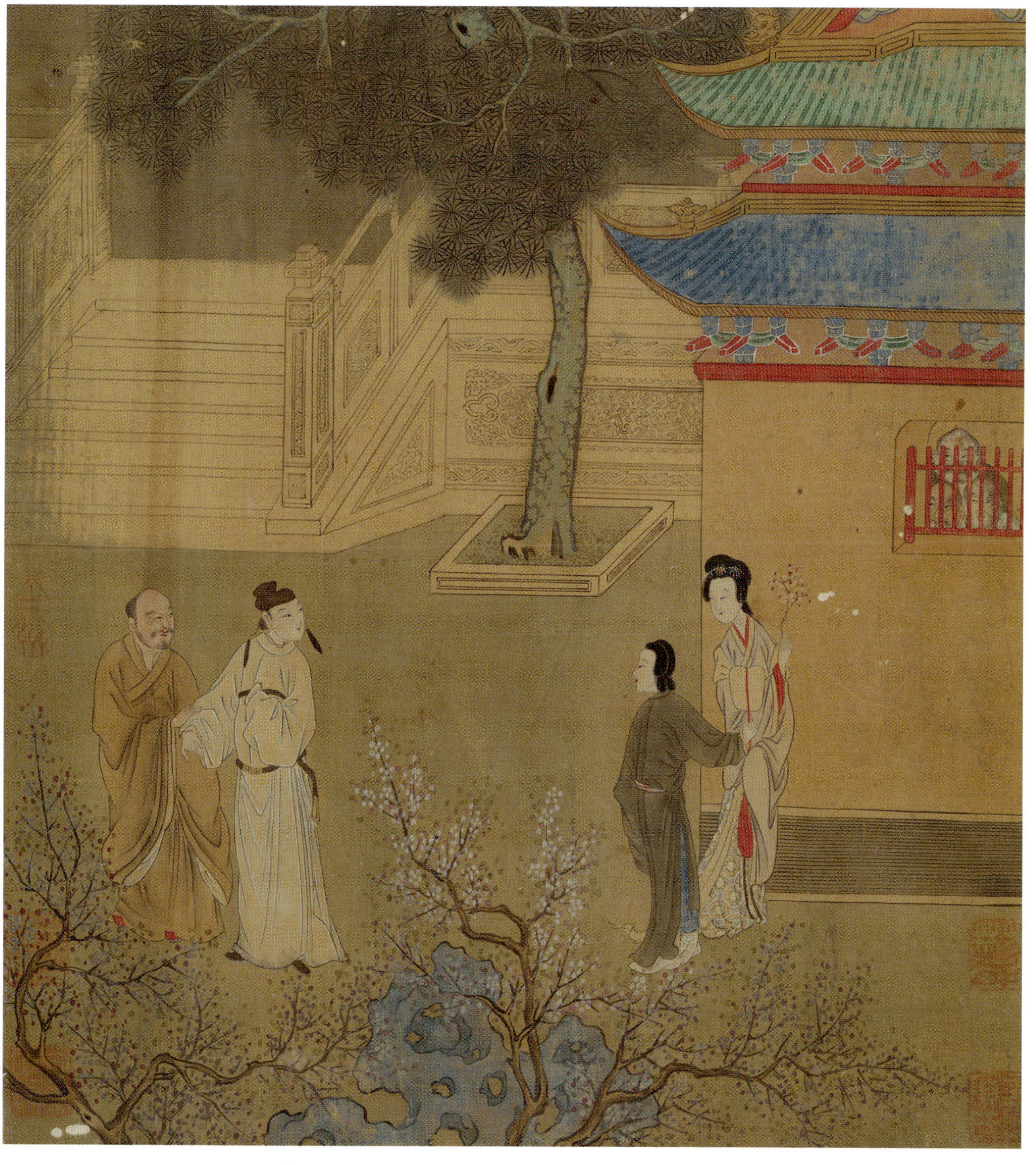

her gauze fan and tries to hurry Oriole away in order to avoid any scandal.[1] Before her departure, however, Oriole turns around, casting a glance at Zhang. It is a rare chance for a young lady to see a fine young man in her closely protected environment, and naturally her curiosity overcomes her sense of propriety. The eyes of Oriole and Zhang meet, and their fate is sealed.

The Berkeley album leaf follows one of the Western Chamber iconographic traditions that portrays Oriole turning to cast a glance at Zhang, which can be traced back to a woodblock print illustration in the 1610 Qifengguan edition of the play (fig. 6.2). Comparing the two, we see a clear resemblance in the relation and postures between the figures in the two versions, although the positions of

6.2
Chinese, Qing Dynasty (1644–1911)
Scene from Romance of the Western Chamber (Xixiang ji), 1610
Woodblock print book illustration from *The Yuan Northern Edition of the Illustrated Story of Romance of the Western Chamber (Yuanben chuxiang Bei Xixiang ji)* by Wang Shifu (ca. 1250–1300), 1610 Qifengguan edition, 8 5/32 × 5 15/32 in. (20.7 × 13.9 cm)
Shanghai Library, Shanghai, 787531-32

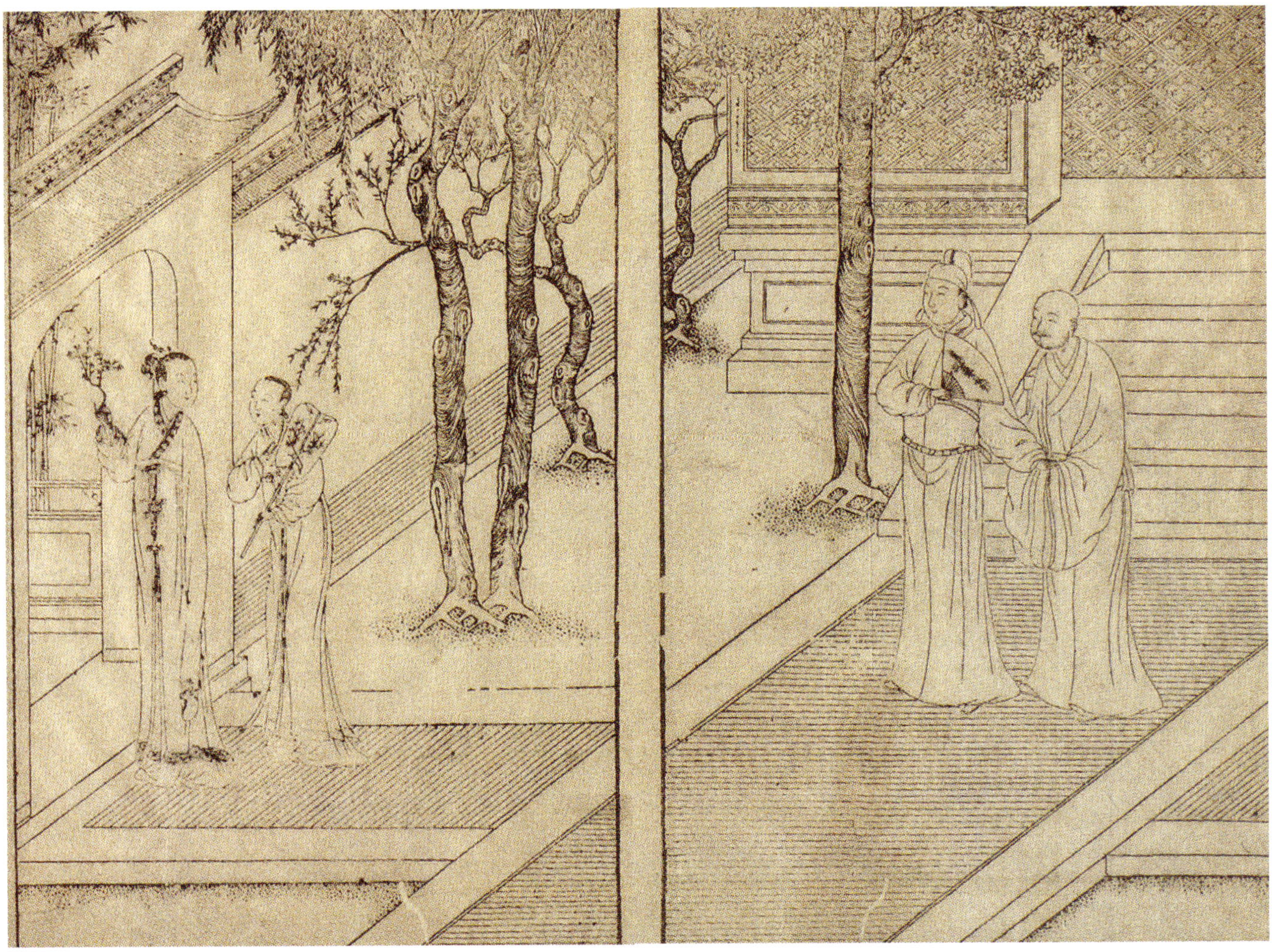

the figures are reversed.[2] Mirror images like this are common among different versions of the same theme, especially those that are rendered in different media, such as painting and prints or painting and lithograph.[3]

Zhang is not always so lucky as to meet Oriole's eyes in illustrations of the scene. In late imperial China, a lady was not supposed to look at a male stranger in the eye or to return his look. The rules of propriety strongly influenced artists' portrayals of ladies in respectable media. Hence, the majority of the *Startled by Beauty* scenes have Oriole either averting her eyes from Zhang or hiding her face behind her fan, as shown in many extant examples, two of which are noted here: a vase in the Philadelphia Museum of Art (fig. 6.3) and a plaque on a pipa lute in the Metropolitan Museum of Art, New York (fig. 6.4).[4] Chinese artists were not interested in linear perspective until quite recently, nor did they like covering a person's face in a picture. As a result, in these examples the fan appears either beside or below Oriole's face, signifying the shielding of her face from the male strangers nearby.

In the original northern recension of *Romance of the Western Chamber*, Oriole is said to be "twirling a flowering sprig" in this scene[5] and, correspondingly, there are *Startled by Beauty* images with Oriole holding the sprig. It seems that the version with Oriole hiding her face behind a folding fan in her hand initially appeared on a porcelain painting from the Kangxi reign (1662–1722), most probably under the influence of a new fashion in stage performance, in which a folding fan or gauze fan replaced the sprig as Oriole's prop. A very similar design is also found on one side of a Kangxi lantern in the National Gallery of Art, Washington, DC

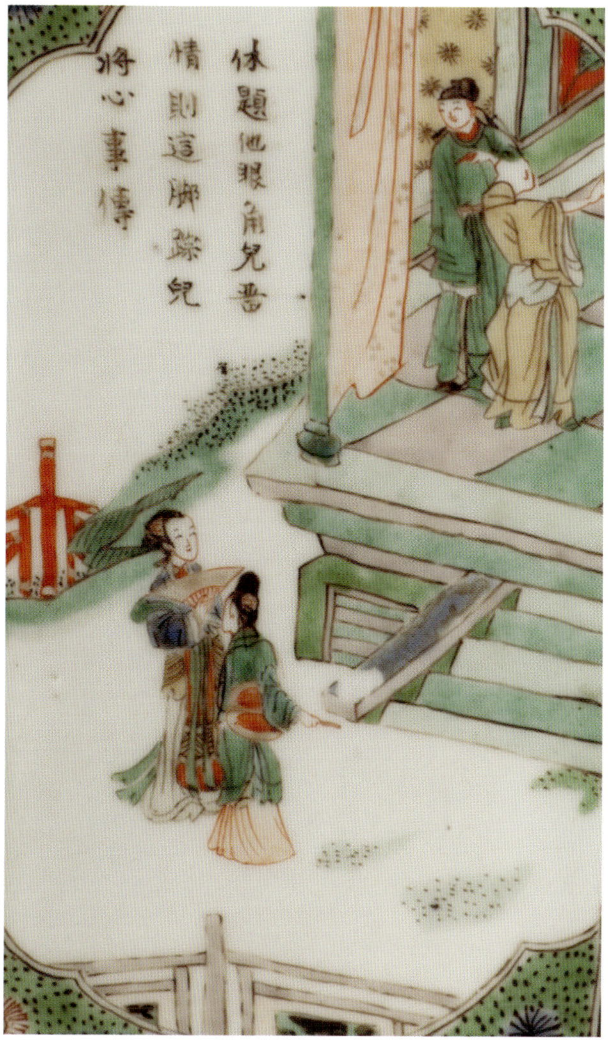

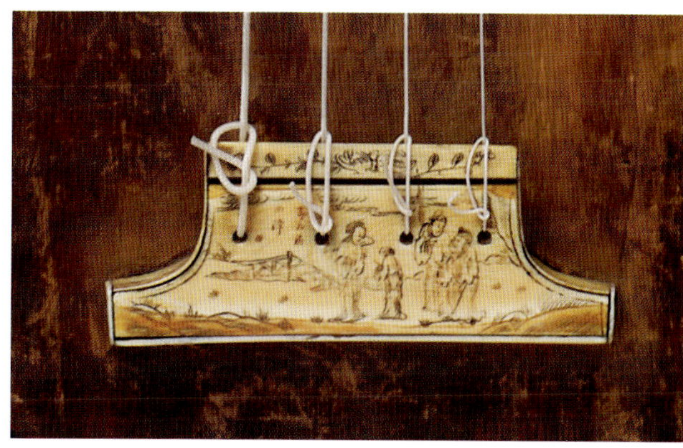

6.3

Detail of cat. 30: *Hexagonal Vase Depicting Scenes from* Romance of the Western Chamber Chamber (Xixiang ji).

6.4

Detail of cat. 5: *Pipa with String Holder Engraved with "Startled by Beauty" Scene from* Romance of the Western Chamber (Xixiang ji).

6.5

Chinese, Qing Dynasty (1644–1911), Kangxi Period (1662–1722)
Hexagonal Lantern (detail), late 17th–early 18th century
Porcelain with overglaze enamel decoration, 11¼ × 7½ in. (28.5 × 19 cm)
National Gallery of Art, Washington, DC, Widener Collection
1942.9.586

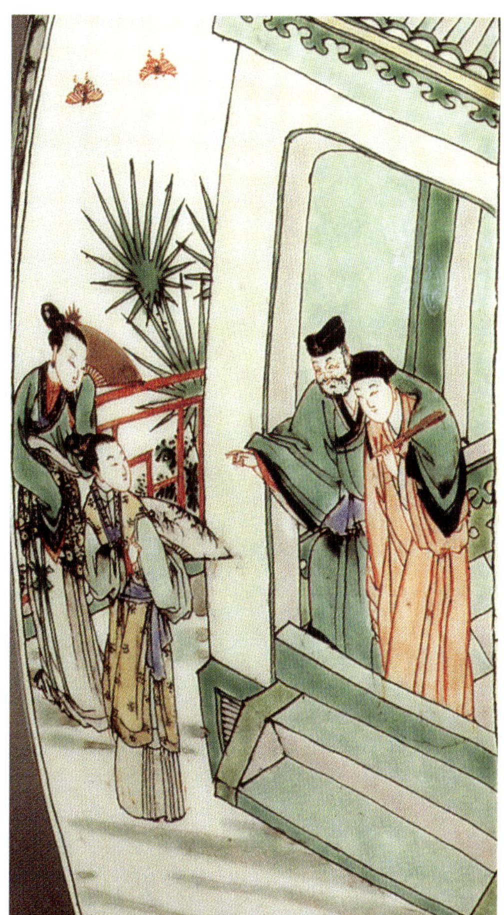

(fig. 6.5),[6] which is most probably a predecessor of the late Qing faceted vase from the Philadelphia Museum of Art in the exhibition (cat. 30). On the lantern, however, the folding fan is gilded.

When compared with the Berkeley album leaf, the illustration on the Philadelphia late Qing vase places the men high up on the terrace to look down upon the women in the courtyard, which actually represents an important subtype of the *Startled by Beauty* scene. This design may not have been a conscious choice; rather, it is very probably the result of successive modifications to the scene during the transfer of the image and its reproduction by various artists. On the late Qing vase, Zhang is depicted turning around to fix his eyes onto Oriole despite the fact that the monk beside him is trying to guide his attention to some architectural features of the buildings. One of the forerunners of this image is a woodblock print designed for a later sixteenth-century edition of *Romance of the Western Chamber* (fig.6.6)[7], since in both pictures the posture of each character looks almost the same, except that Oriole holds a sprig in the book illustration. Some later artists who catered to a more affluent community chose to elaborate details that might impress the potential patron or meet the patron's need for luxury.[8] In this case, a later version, also in the form of a woodblock print

6.6
Liu Ciquan, designer and carver
Chinese, active Ming Dynasty (1368–1644), Wanli Period (1572–1620)
Scene from Romance of the Western Chamber (Xixiang ji), n.d.
Woodblock print book illustration from *The Re-Collated Northern Edition of Romance of the Western Chamber (Chongjiao Bei Xixiang ji)*
by Wang Shifu (ca. 1250–1300)
Mukyukai Library, Tenri, Nara

6.7
Chinese, Ming Dynasty (1368–1644), Chongzhen Period (1627–1644)
Scene from Romance of the Western Chamber (Xixiang ji), n.d.
Woodblock print book illustration from *The Newly Carved Mr. Wei-Zhongxue Commented* Romance of the Western Chamber (*Xinke Wei Zhongxue xiansheng pidian* Xixiang ji) by Wang Shifu (ca. 1250–1300)
National Central Library, Taiwan

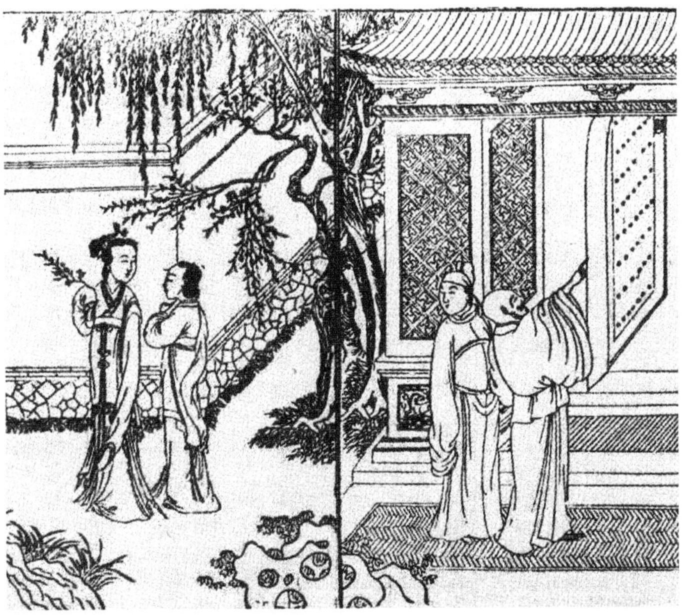

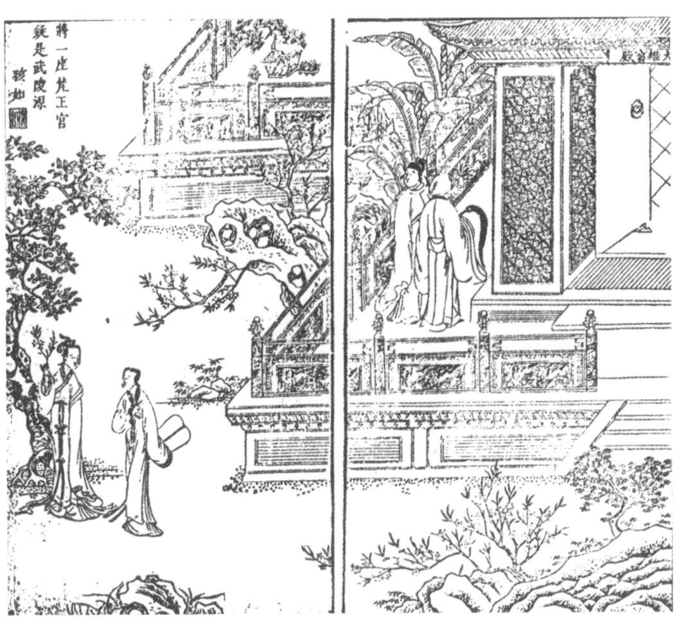

6.8
Chinese, Ming Dynasty (1368–1644), Chongzhen Period (1627–1644)
Scene from A String of Pearls (Zhuji lian), n.d.
Woodblock print book illustration from *A String of Pearls (Zhuji lian)*
by Wang Shifu (ca. 1250–1300)

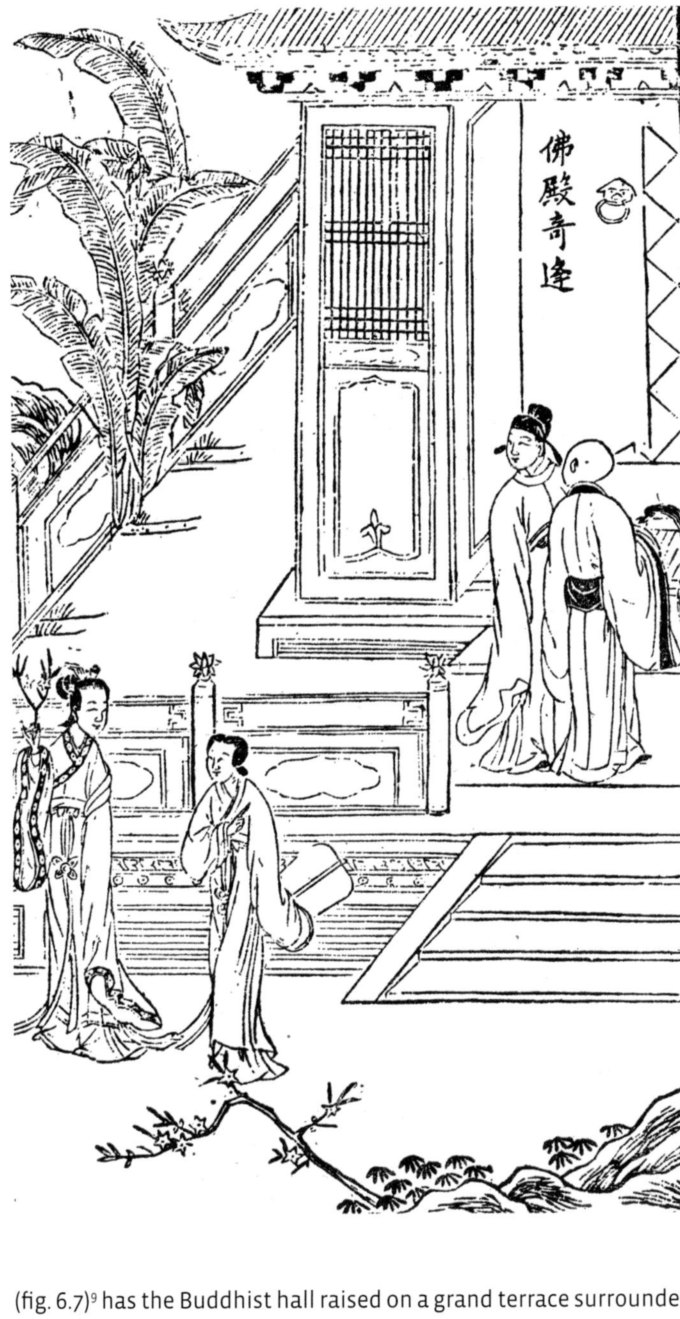

(fig. 6.7)[9] has the Buddhist hall raised on a grand terrace surrounded by an ornate balustrade: Zhang and the monk are lifted onto the terrace, while Oriole and her maid remain on the ground. A still later Ming woodblock print version of this illustration from a literary anthology reduced it from two pages to one in order to cut down the production cost, resulting in a closer, sharply contrasted "male-up-female-down" composition (fig. 6.8)[10] from which the porcelain painter may well have drawn inspiration.

6.9
Cat. 33: "*Startled by Beauty" Scene from* Romance of the Western Chamber (Xixiang ji).
Courtesy of the Division of Anthropology, American Museum of Natural History
70.3/7027 B

6.10
Chinese, Ming Dynasty (1368–1644)
Scene from Romance of the Western Chamber (Xixiang ji), n.d.
Woodblock print book illustration from *Master Dong's Story of Romance of the Western Chamber* (*Dong jieyuan* Xixiang ji) punctuated by Yang Shen and collated by Huang Jiahui

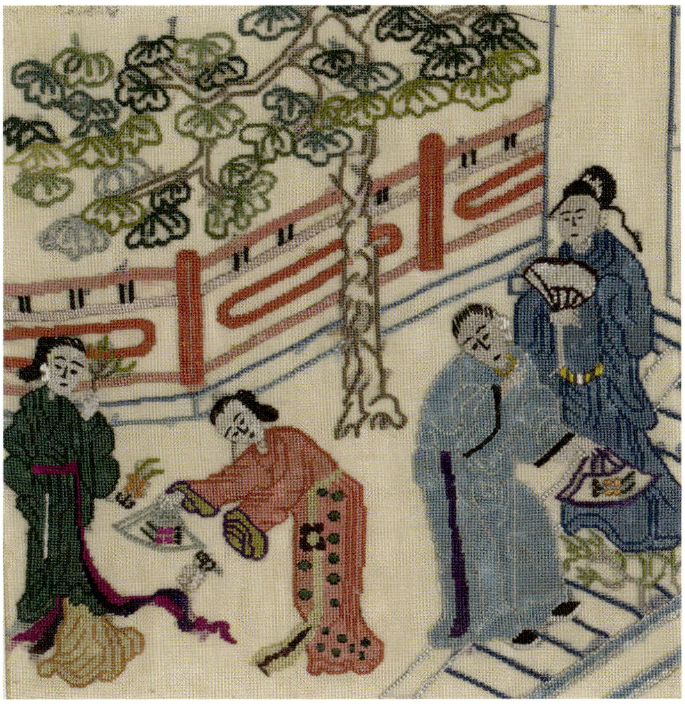

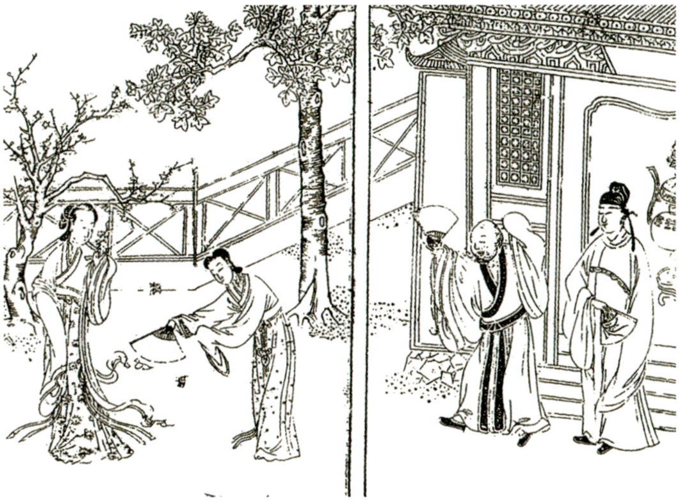

As instances of transmission multiply, information becomes increasingly corrupted or altered, and with dissemination and reproduction pictures deviate further and further from their predecessors. The *Startled by Beauty* scene on an embroidered textile square from the American Museum of Natural History Museum, New York, in the exhibition (fig. 6.9) includes a detail of Crimson waving her folding fan at butterflies, which seems to shock the monk and almost steals the show from the protagonists Zhang and Oriole.

The artist who adopted this detail may have seen such a scenario performed on stage. The stage performance, in turn, may have been based on the southern adaptation of the play text (*Nan xixiang ji*) from around 1522, which is attributed to Li Rihua.[11] In this text, there is a new line uttered by Crimson that uses the metaphor of "mad bees and wild butterflies hovering around" (*kuangfeng langdie wu pianqian*) to hint to Oriole that there are lascivious men nearby.[12] As a result, some stage productions may well have had Crimson act out the line by waving her fan as if she were driving away those bees and butterflies. Such a detail was captured by a Ming book illustrator, who had the advantage over the actor performing on stage: he could actually depict butterflies in the scene (fig. 6.10).[13] Apparently, the embroidered image in New York was modeled after the book illustration. On yet another *Startled by Beauty* scene woven on a slit silk tapestry (*kesi*) scroll in the collection of the Honolulu Museum of Art (fig. 6.11), the obviously disarrayed composition in the embroidered image seems to have been corrected with a concentric arrangement, in which Crimson and the monk bend over a pair of mating butterflies in the center and the two protagonists are pushed to the periphery. Also notice that the sprig in Oriole's hand in both the book illustration and the embroidery square has evolved into a folding fan on the kesi scroll. In this way another new subtype was added to the repertoire of depictions of *Startled by Beauty*. Other examples of this subtype include one from the Kangxi period in the Butler Family Collection, England,[14] and one from the following Yongzheng period (circa 1725–30) in the Taft Museum, Cincinnati.[15]

Further deviation occurs in a version of the scene incised on an ivory plaque attached as a string holder on a pipa in the Metropolitan Museum of Art (fig. 6.4). Oriole stands on the left, modestly raising a folding fan in front of her face. Since I believe this iconographic detail to have appeared no earlier than the Kangxi period, and the pipa itself is thought to date from the late Ming dynasty it is possible that this plaque was added later. Crimson is portrayed here like a small child because the artist may have

6.11
Chinese, Late Qing Dynasty (1644–1911)
Gracious Living in a Garden Compound, 19th century
Slit silk tapestry weave (*kesi*) and painting on silk mounted as a handscroll, 14 ½ × 80 ½ in. (36.8 × 204.5 cm)
Honolulu Museum of Art, Bequest of John Gregg Allerton, 1991
6285.1

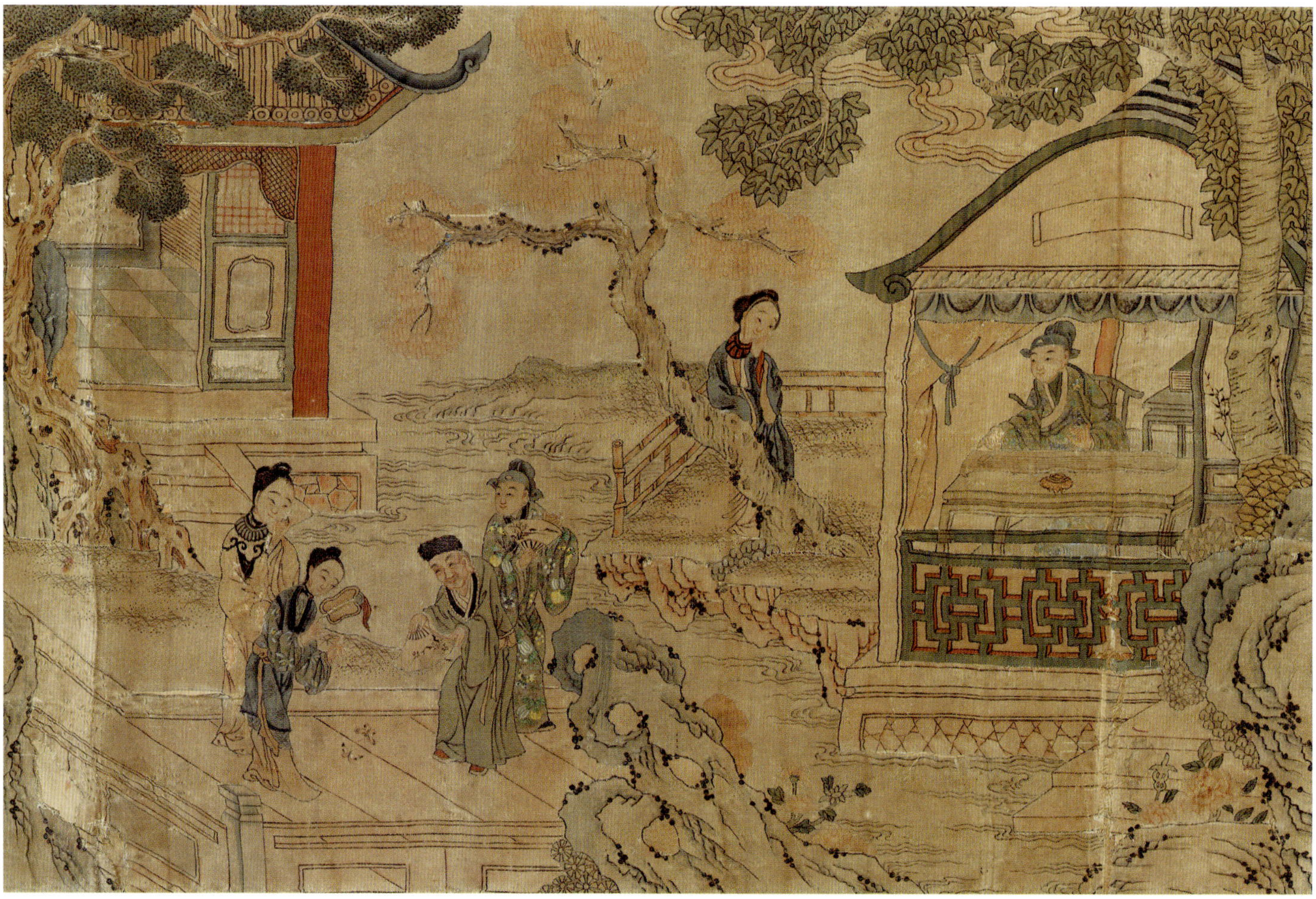

consciously followed the convention that a smaller figure in scale could indicate Crimson's lower social status, as did the illustrator for the 1498 edition of the play, the earliest extant imprint.[16] This can be regarded as a somewhat degenerated version because Scholar Zhang in the picture no longer fixes his gaze on Oriole, which is a quintessential characteristic of the original scene. In the process of adoption and reproduction, artists would gradually lose track of the story that a popular scene had been meant to represent, and some of the scene's essential features would get twisted or even lost. The corresponding scene on the rhinoceros horn cup from the Field Museum of Natural History, Chicago, in the exhibition (fig. 6.12) is also a typical example of this sort of degeneration. Very probably due to the restraints of having to accommodate the four characters in a very limited area, the horn carver had to arrange Zhang and the monk on one side of the Buddha Hall, while placing the two women on the other side. This arrangement on a curved surface makes it barely possible for Zhang to eye Oriole. The carver has completely given up portraying Zhang according to the story and has turned him to face the opposite direction.

One reason why Oriole does not hide behind a fan in the Berkeley album leaf discussed above may be that the album was created for private viewing by male connoisseurs, making such immodesty acceptable, even desirable. Sure enough, another rare example of the scene with a staring-back Oriole appears on a blue and white porcelain *gu* vase in the Butler Family Collection, where the scene is explicitly connected with the pleasure quarters (cat. 10). The title of the song inscribed on the vase is "Courtesans Practice the Art of the Theater" (Qinglou jiaoyan liyuan). The painting on the vase thus records a theatrical scene in a late-Ming garden where four sing-song girls rehearse in full swing. The girls all look

6.12
Detail of cat. 32: *Rhinoceros Horn with Scenes from* Romance of the Western Chamber (Xixiang ji).

6.13
Chinese, Late Qing Dynasty (1644–1911)
Formerly attributed to Qiu Ying, Chinese, ca. 1494–1552
Scene from Romance of the Western Chamber (Xixiang ji), n.d.
Album leaf, ink and color on silk, 14 9/16 × 13 in. (37 × 33cm)
Courtesy of the C. V. Starr East Asian Library, University of California, Berkeley

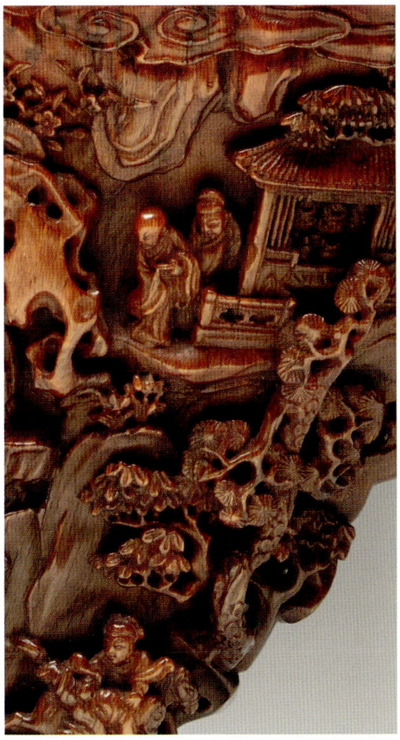

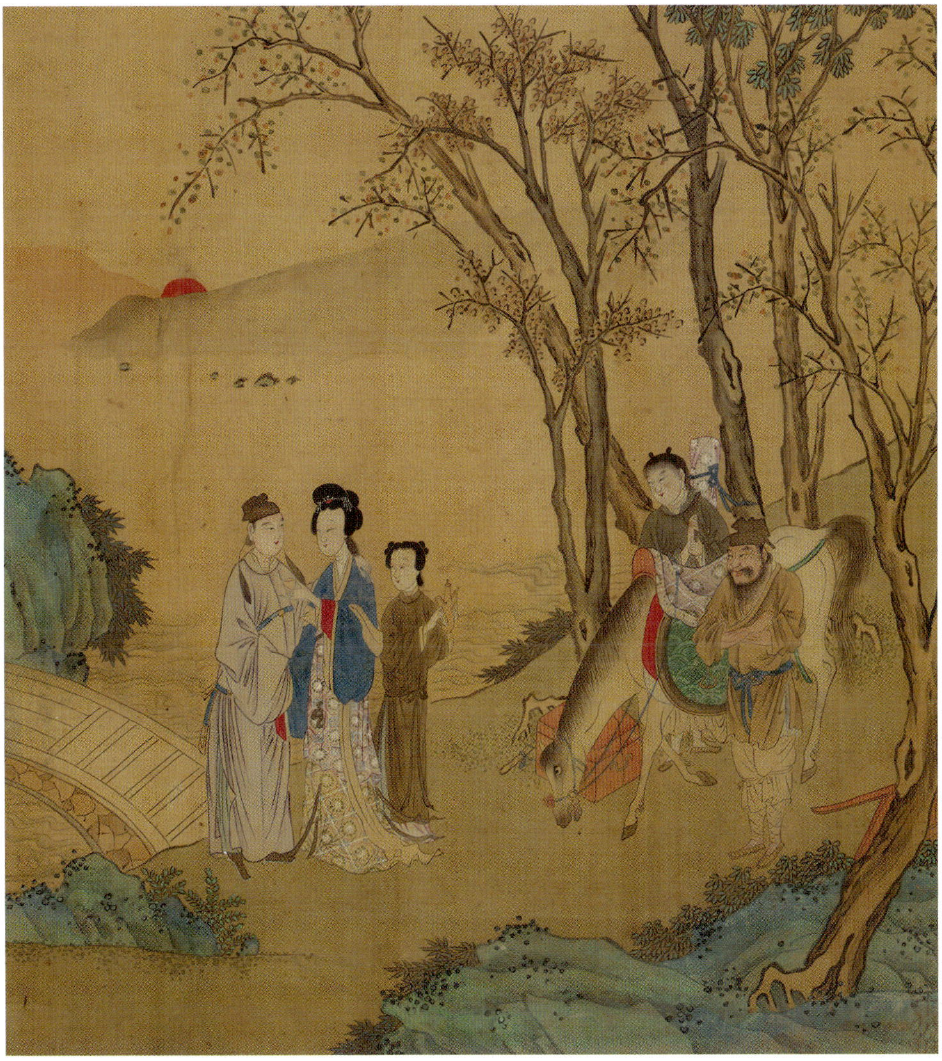

slender and the two male roles are distinguished by the monk's tiara and Zhang's mesh hat with two wings, in addition to their male-style robes. The austere setting has just a plain carpet on the grass and a four-fold white screen as the backdrop. Beside the carpet additional costumes for other acts hang from a clothes rack. Two musicians retreat behind a huge rock, one standing and playing the flute and the other sitting and beating a hand drum. Scripts sit on a minimalist Ming-style square table, within reach of the actresses and musicians. This image stands out among examples discussed in this essay because the others are pictorial representations of narrative scenes in the story of *Romance of the Western Chamber*, while this one depicts performers rehearsing an act of the play. Images of a recognizable scene of performance from such an early date are rare, so this example sheds welcome light on our understanding of theatrical production in late imperial China.[17]

The Farewell Scene

After his first encounter with Oriole, Zhang begins his tenacious pursuit of his goddess and wins her heart. When the love is eventually consummated, Oriole's mother insists that Zhang must pass the civil service examination in the capital before he will be permitted to marry Oriole. Zhang's departure for the capital when the two lovers bid farewell became a very popular scene for illustration in a variety of media.

6.14
Detail of cat. 30: *Hexagonal Vase Depicting Scenes from* Romance of the Western Chamber Chamber (Xixiang ji).

6.15a–b
Details of cat. 31: *Pair of Matching Fans with Multiple Scenes from* Romance of the Western Chamber (Xixiang ji).

6.16a–b
Details of cat. 32: *Rhinoceros Horn with Scenes from* Romance of the Western Chamber (Xixiang ji).

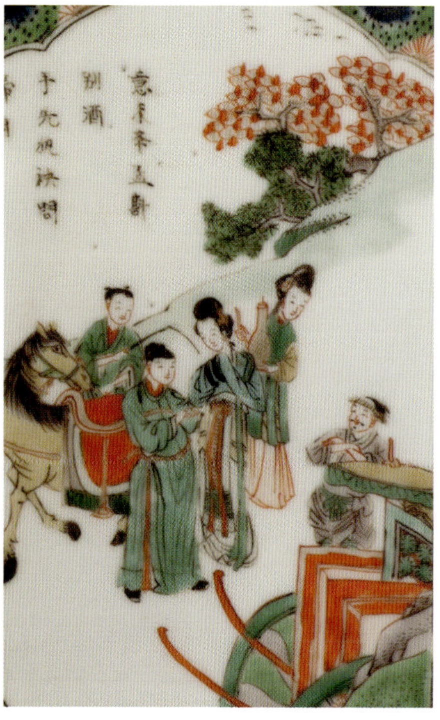

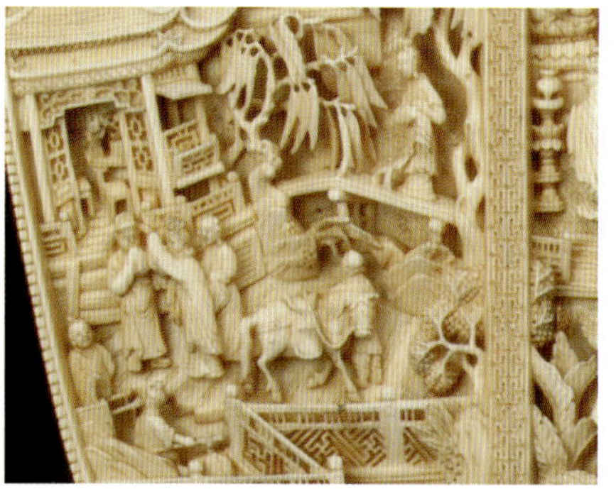

6.15a

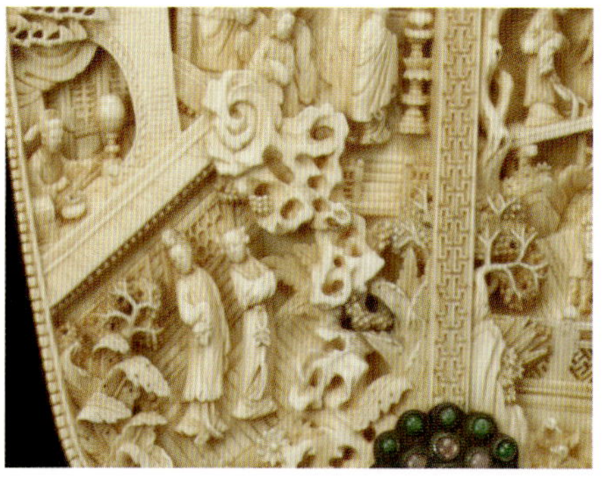

6.15b

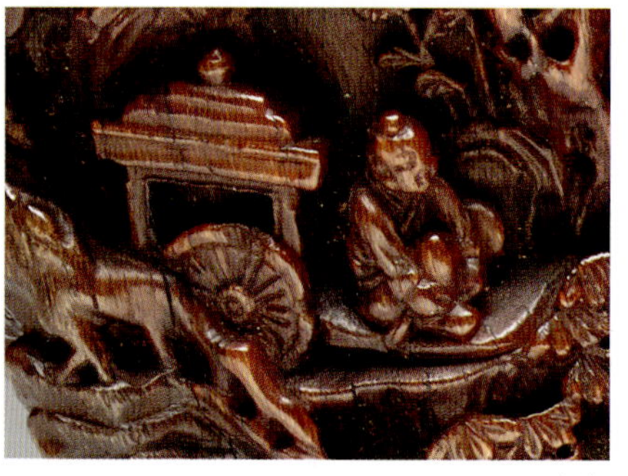

6.16a

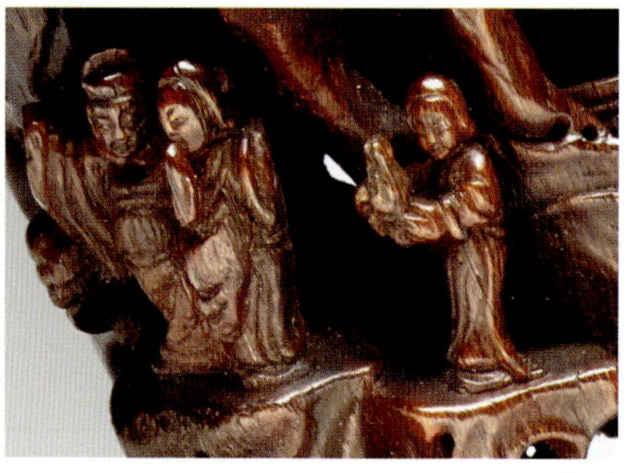

6.16b

The farewell scene in the Berkeley album (fig. 6.13) is a prototypical example, possessing all the conventional features of the scene: the couple standing close to each other with Oriole handing the wine cup to Zhang, Crimson holding a wine ewer ready to serve, Zhang's pageboy carrying a wrapped *qin* zither on his back waiting beside the luggage trunk and the horse, Oriole's sedan cart driver folding his arms in front of his chest, one red handle of the sedan cart sticking out of the bush, and a stone bridge leading to the highway on which Zhang is to start his journey.

The same scene is also found on the late Qing dynasty faceted vase in Philadelphia (cat. 30), in the center of which Zhang and Oriole are bidding farewell to each other by raising clasped hands, with the wine cup nowhere to be seen (fig. 6.14). Crimson still holds the ewer, but the pageboy waves a whip while the bearded driver stands by with folded arms. Oriole's wheeled sedan chair with a canopy on top is clearly visible. The narrow facet of the vase leaves no room for the bridge. In the sky high above, however, an upside-down V-shaped wild geese formation has been added to reinforce the sense of separation of loved ones, since such wild geese imagery was traditionally used to allude to the melancholy of departure.

An artist's ability and imagination naturally leave marks on a work, causing details to vary in different examples of the same scene. On the pair of ivory fans from the Asian Art Museum, San Francisco in the exhibition (cat. 31), the detail of the lovers shedding tears overtly enhances the heart-breaking sadness of departure (figs. 6.15a–b). Raising one or both long sleeves to one's eyes or covering one's face with one's hands is a conventional means in Chinese pictorial art to indicate crying;[18] both the San Francisco ivory fan and Chicago horn cup carvers made a special point to show Oriole's expression of emotion by explicitly depicting her raised long sleeves (figs. 6.16a–c). Crimson's prop in this scene, the wine ewer, is omitted on the ivory fan, while she still holds it on the horn cup.

However, on the kesi scroll in Honolulu (fig. 6.17), Crimson's tray carries two cups without the ewer. There are two signs that indicate the kesi scroll is of a relatively later date: the person who is responsible for the sedan chair has become a woman with a sun hat, and Zhang's groom turns out to be a chubby baby, both changes largely due to multiple whimsical improvisations.

In this context, the iconographic content on a high-end tapestry valance in the collection of the Art Institute of Chicago (fig. 6.18) can

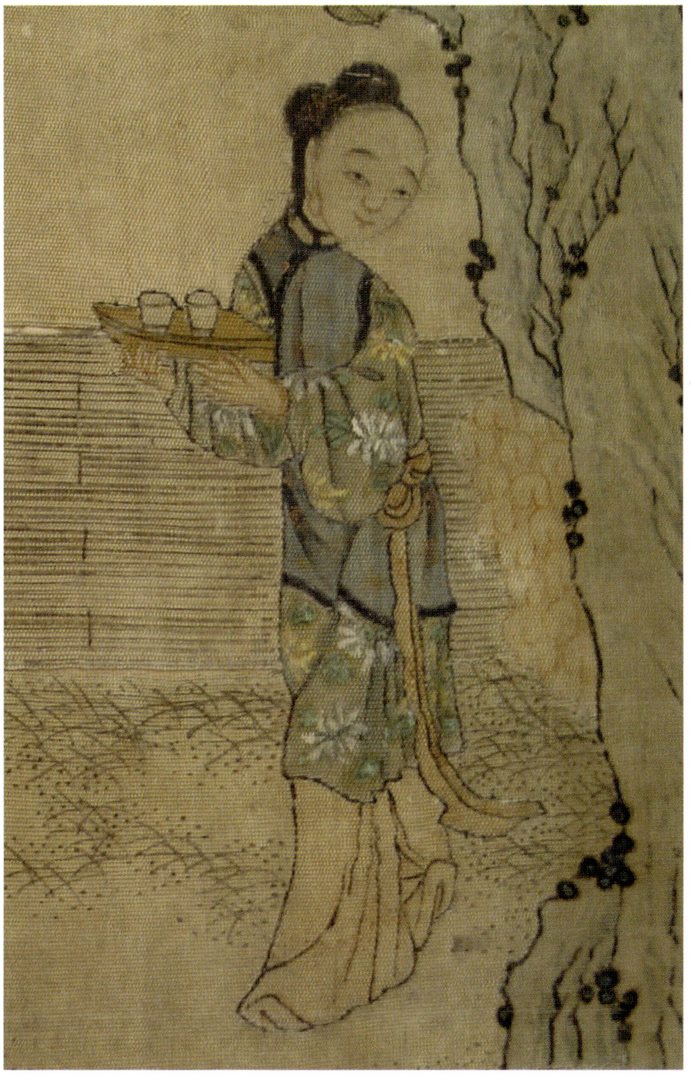

6.17
Detail of fig. 6.11: *Gracious Living in a Garden Compound.*

be duly clarified.[19] On the panel, the group on the far left is the focus of the drama: near the stone bridge that leads to the road out of town, a fashionably dressed woman with a sash over her arms and a man in a red robe and a black mesh hat are holding each other's hand and talking intimately to each other. Nearby, a plainly dressed lady's maid is carrying a wine ewer on a tray, ready for her mistress to serve the man a farewell cup. On the right, a groom stands beside a horse waiting for his master to embark on a journey; next to him a bearded hunchbacked man in armor looks on. Compared with the examples of the departure scene in *Romance of the Western Chamber* discussed so far, this picture can be reasonably identified as a version of the same theme, even though the attire of the groom and Oriole's sedan cart driver has been upgraded. The two formerly peasant-like characters in the picture have been transformed: the groom is dressed like a shop assistant in a formal long robe, and the bearded man, who usually stands by the sedan chair with folded arms and rolled-up sleeves, now wears full military armor.

These two popular scenes from *Romance of the Western Chamber* show how, in relation to their literary source, narrative images evolve with varied perceptions and abilities of artists, range of materials used, different requirements of patrons, and with the increase of instances of image transfer and reproduction. I have highlighted some dialogues among the visual narrative, the narrator, and the audience. Clarifying these issues helps us better understand the environment in which these images were created—and the lives of those who produced and consumed them.

Notes

1 One of the earliest examples of the scene in which Crimson tries to shield Oriole from the male strangers with her fan is seen in a woodblock illustration of a late sixteenth- or early seventeenth-century edition of the play. For an example, see Stephen H. West and Wilt L. Idema, eds. and trans., *The Moon and the Zither: Romance of the Western Chamber* (Berkeley: University of California Press, 1991), p. 449.

2 The image is reprinted in *Xixiang ji renwuhua xuan* [Selected Illustrations of the Story of the Western Wing] (Shanghai: Shanghai shuhua chubanshe, 1986), n.p.

3 For a Western example of mirror images, see a Venus and Adonis painting by Titian (circa 1477–1576) and an engraving of the same theme rendered by Robert Strange in 1769. The painting is published in John Walker, *National Gallery of Art, Washington* (New York: Harry N. Abrams, 1984), p. 213, and, the print is published in Harold E. Wethey, *The Paintings of Titian*, vol. III (London: National Gallery, 1969–1975), plate 95.

4 The third example, not in this exhibition, in which Oriole hides her face behind her folding fan, is found on a *kesi* scroll from the Honolulu Museum of Art (acc. no. 6285.1).

5 West and Idema, *The Moon and the Zither*, p. 177.

6 The side of the lantern is published in Virginia Bower et al., *The Collections of the National Gallery of Art Systematic Catalogue, Decorative Arts, Part II: Far Eastern Ceramics and Paintings, Persian and Indian Rugs and Carpets* (Oxford: Oxford University Press, 1998), p. 213, with the description "Two men stand in the doorway of a pavilion and look out at two young women holding fans. The older of the two men is bearded and has one arm around the younger man, who holds a fan."

7 See an example printed in Hsu Wen-chin, "Fictional Scenes on Chinese Transitional Porcelain (1620–circa 1683) and Their Sources of Decoration," *Bulletin of the Museum of Far Eastern Antiquities, Stockholm*, no. 58 (1986): p. 105.

8 See, for example, the various versions of the biblical scene of the Adoration of the Magi throughout history. A comparison can be made between the image on the Sepulchral Stone of Severa engraved about the end of the third century CE, in which the containers of the gifts look like three plain plates, and a painting by Andrea Mantegna (1431–1506) in the collection of the J. Paul Getty Museum, in which a Chinese blue-and-white porcelain cup was presented to hold gold coins, a deliberate match between the precious metal and the then fashionable high-tech ware. The Roman stone carving is published in Asian Civilizations Museum, Singapore, *Journey of Faith: Art & History from the Vatican Collections* (Singapore: Asian Civilizations Museum, 2005), p. 56. The painting can be

6.18

Chinese, Qing Dynasty (1644–1911), Jiaqing Period (1796–1820)

Valance (?) with Parting Scene from Romance of the Western Chamber (Xixiang ji), 1799

Slit silk tapestry weave (*kesi*) with block-printed cotton, painted silk, and gold-leaf-over-lacquered-paper-strip-wrapped silk, 44 3/4 × 49 5/8 in. (113.4 × 126cm)

The Art Institute of Chicago, Gift of Mrs. William J. Calhoun

1937.817

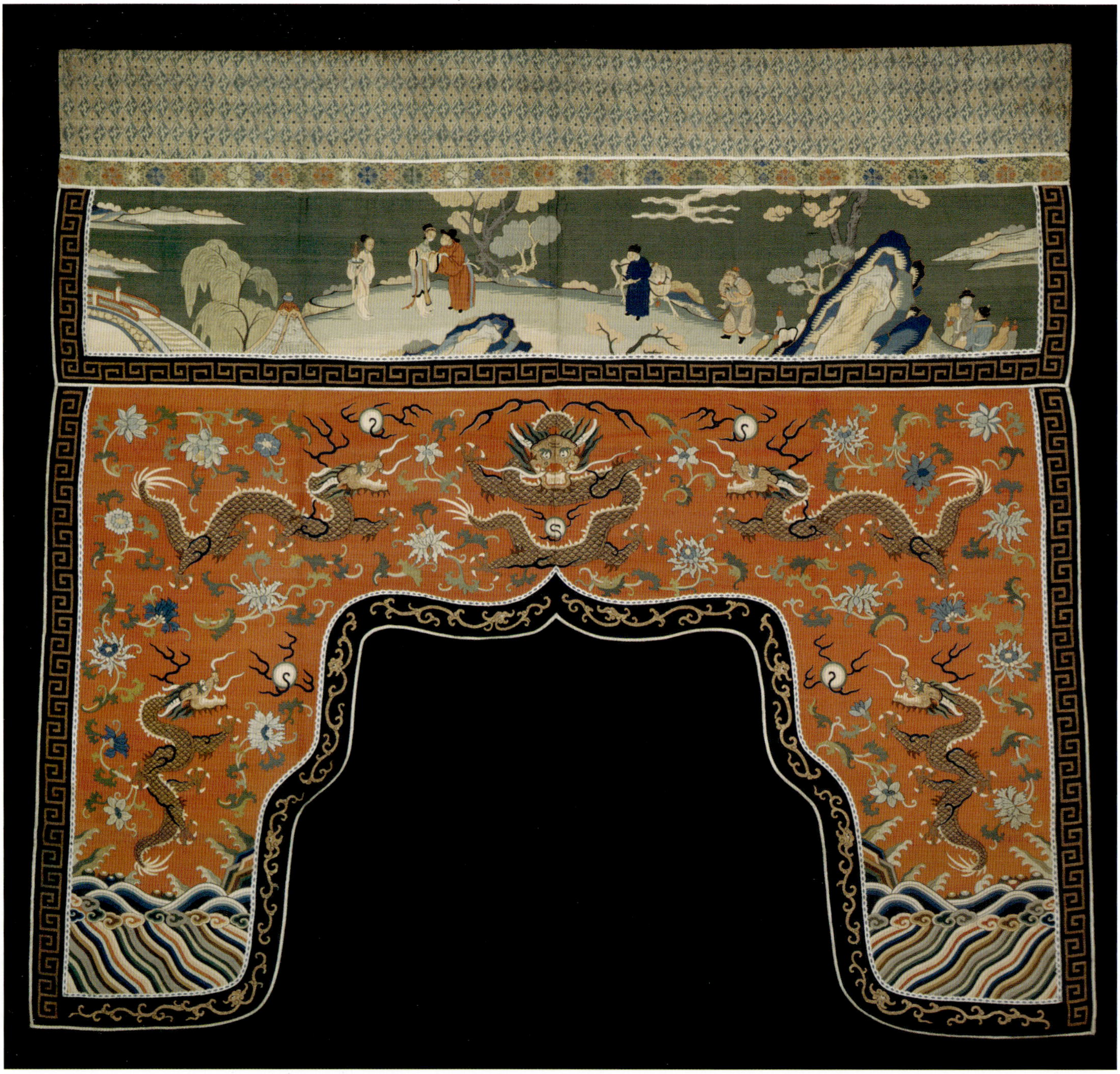

found from the J. Paul Getty Museum website http://www.getty.edu/art/gettyguide/artObjectDetails?artobj=900, last access May 10, 2013.

9 Reprint in Zhou Wu et al., eds., *Riben cang Zhongguo gu banhua zhenpin* [Highlights of Ancient Chinese Woodblock Prints in Japanese Collections] (Nanjing: Jiangsu meishu chubanshe, 1999), p. 230.

10 Reprint in Fu Xihua, ed., *Zhongguo gudian wenxue banhua xuanji* [Selected Woodblock Prints from Classical Chinese Literature] (Shanghai: Shanghai renmin meishu chubanshe, 1981), 2: p. 644.

11 See Zhang Shuying, "Notes on the Punctuation and Collation of the Southern Version of Xixiang ji," in Li Rihua, *Nan Xixiang ji* [Southern-version of Xixiang ji] (Beijing: Zhonghua shuju, 2000), p. 1.

12 Li Rihua, *Nan Xixiang ji*, p. 9.

13 Reprinted in Wu Xixian, ed., *Suojian Zhongguo gudai xiaoshuo xiqu banben tulu* [A Collection of the Illustrations in Encountered Chinese Traditional Fiction and Drama], 4, part B, Traditional Drama I (Beijing: Quanguo tushuguan wenxian suowei fuzhi zhongxin, 1995), pp. 173f.

14 See Sir Michael Butler, Margaret Medley, and Stephen Little, *Seventeenth-Century Chinese Porcelain from the Butler Family Collection* (Alexandria, Va.: Art Services International, 1990), plate 125.

15 The scene is incorrectly identified as "illustrat[ing] the episode 'The Interruption of the Religious Service," from the novel Xi Xiang Ji, or The Romance of the Western Chamber," in Edward J. Sullivan and Ruth Krueger Meyer, *The Taft Museum: Its History and Collections, Vol. II* (New York: Hudson Hills Press, 1995), p. 675. This misidentification is based on another misidentification in Sheila Keppel, *China in 1700: Kangxi Porcelains at the Taft Museum*, exh. cat. (Cincinnati, Ohio: Taft Museum, 1988), p. 12.

16 Wang Shifu (circa 1250–1300), *Xinkan qimiao quanxiang zhushi Xixiang ji* [Recently Published Completely Illustrated and Annotated Romance of the Western Chamber,], reprinted in *Guben xiqu congkan chuji [1]* [An Anthology of Ancient Editions of Drama] (Shanghai: Commercial Press, 1954). Also see examples in West and Idema, *The Moon and the Zither*, plates 8, 12, 13.

17 The author discusses the iconography and the iconological significance of the scene on this vase in Michael Butler et al., *Treasures from an Unknown Reign: Shunzhi Porcelain 1644–1661* (Alexandria, Va.: Art Services International in association with the University of Washington Press, 2002), p. 186, and Ni Yibin, *Kantu shuoci* (Looking At Porcelain and Talking About Pictures) (Beijing: Zhonghua shuju, 2008), pp. 20ff.

18 See an example of brick figures in one of the Twenty-Four Models of Filial Piety in *Ancient Taoist Art From Shanxi Province* (Hong Kong: University Museum and Art Gallery, The University of Hong Kong, 2003), p. 88; another example can be found on a ceramic pillow made during the Jin dynasty (1115–1234), in Ye Zhemin et al. eds., *Zhongguo cizhou yao* [Cizhou Kilns in China] (Shijiazhuang: Hebei meishu chubanshe, 2009), 2: p. 234.

19 It has been identified as "a narrative scene of a woman and servant with a barbarian chieftain, probably a reference to the story of Lady Wenji, who was abducted by nomads in the second century BCE and forced to live on the Central-Asian steppes for twelve years," in John E. Vollmer, *Clothed to Rule the Universe: Ming and Qing Dynasty Textiles at The Art Institute of Chicago*, Art Institute of Chicago Museum Studies, 26, no. 2 (Chicago: The Art Institute of Chicago, 2000), p. 39.

WU HUNG

Seven

Inspired by the Opera: Reimagining Traditional Opera in Contemporary Chinese Photography and Video

The exhibition *Performing Images: Opera in Chinese Visual Culture* demonstrates that opera played a crucial role in shaping traditional Chinese visual culture and its artistic vocabulary. But what followed that influence? Did opera's impact on Chinese visual art persist after China entered the modern era? No comprehensive study has been conducted to answer this question, although some recent research projects have revealed the continuous infiltration of opera into multiple modern art forms.[1] Inspired by these studies, I have curated a small show of selected works of contemporary Chinese photography and video to supplement the main exhibition.[2] Each of the four artists whose work is featured in this additional presentation derives specific elements from traditional opera, but each of them works for a different purpose.

All four artists—Liu Wei, Liu Zheng, Cui Xiuwen, and Chen Qiulin—emerged in the mid- and late 1990s, when a trend of contemporary Chinese art called "experimental art" reached the height of its development.[3] One important goal of this trend was to expand artistic means beyond conventional media, and during this period "experimental photography" (*shiyan sheying*) divorced itself from mainstream art photography, and video art also developed into an independent field.[4] Another primary objective of experimental art was to explore new sources of visual language. Unsatisfied with the simple borrowing of influential Western styles, many experimental artists sought inspiration from traditional art and visual culture, dismantling the medium-based division between Chinese-style painting (*guohua*) and Western-style painting (*xihua*). Compared with ink and oil, the main media of these two painting traditions, photography and video, are not strictly culturally specific.

When experimental artists fused traditional images with these new art forms, they identified their works as both "Chinese" and "contemporary," and in this context these artists rediscovered the traditional opera.

Liu Wei: The Shadow of History

When Liu Wei (b. 1965) participated in the exhibition *Between Past and Future: New Photography and Video from China* in 2004, he made this statement about his series of ten photographs titled *The Forbidden City*:

> I was born in the time of the Cultural Revolution, and my life as a child was full of images of combat. One of my favorite childhood memories is of playing with puppets. In fact, the puppets unconsciously conveyed the emotions and stories of the puppeteers. . . . Puppets and humans mirror each other. The grand Forbidden City provides the arena for the puppets to act out the manipulated fate of human beings. The scenes not only illustrate apathy, lying hearts, and emotional intrigue, but also remind us of the uncontrollable fates locked into such scenes.[5]

These words also describe the video in the current exhibition, which is a byproduct of the same project and shares the same title (*Zijincheng,* 2000). Unlike the photographic series, which displays still theatrical puppets in various settings, the video, which has never been exhibited before, connects these images into a lyrical rumination on China's bygone history. It starts by introducing three puppets one by one: a middle-aged, mustached man, probably a general; a proud young scholar; and a female character with "willow-leaf" eyebrows and a gentle expression. With carved and painted wood heads but empty cloth torsos, these are "glove puppets," or "cloth bag puppets" (*budai kuilei*) in Chinese. Originating in the southeastern province of Fujian during the seventeenth century, it then became a popular dramatic form in Guangdong and Taiwan as well. At the time of performance, the puppeteer inserts his hand into a puppet's costume and engineers its movements. Since the video does not show any trace of a puppeteer, Liu Wei must have staged and recorded the performance separately and inserted the images into architectural settings with the help of digital technology.

After introducing the three characters, the video fills the screen with a decaying wall. Shot frontally, it is like an open book; its eroding bricks resemble columns of Chinese characters. This image will reappear nine more times in the video, dividing the mini epic into ten tight sections. Since each section begins and ends with the wall, one senses that the story continually emerges from and vanishes into it. Without any dialogue or voiceover explicating the narrative, the wall takes on the meaning of history itself, inspiring memories and also silencing them.

The grand view of the Forbidden City follows the wall's initial appearance. The three puppets enter again, marching energetically in front of the imperial palace. The next section introduces a fourth puppet character, a villain, whose evil disposition is signified by his distorted mouth and nearly vertical eyebrows. He confronts the other figures and seems to overpower them (fig. 7.1). We are reminded of Liu Wei's remembrance of the Cultural Revolution as an endless political "combat," and of his statement that "the grand Forbidden City provides the arena for the puppets to act out the manipulated fate of human beings."

The villain's triumph sets a melancholy tone for the rest of the video, which evolves around the themes of isolation, impotence, and death. The female figure becomes the sole character of the story: she walks silently before the wall, which at one point grows infinitely behind her shrinking body. Two sequences of landscape scenes then transport her to a mournful, desolate poetic space—first a lotus pond filled with the last remaining leaves and then a wasteland with weeds shaking in a chilly wind. Momentarily she stretches her arms toward the sky and her spirit seems to ascend to heaven. But eventually she is trapped in the Forbidden City, walking in the vast courtyard and casting her lonely shadow on the ruined pavement. The video ends with her empty, discarded body lying on the ground.

Liu Wei's other video in the exhibition, a comical yet pessimistic piece that he created the following year, is a continuation of *The Forbidden City*. Called *The Shadow* (*Yingzi,* 2001), it has a prelude that links the two videos and also frames the second work: one of the puppets marches toward the onlooker while casting a deep shadow on the ruined wall. Once the shadow spreads over the entire screen, a contemporary person emerges as the video's

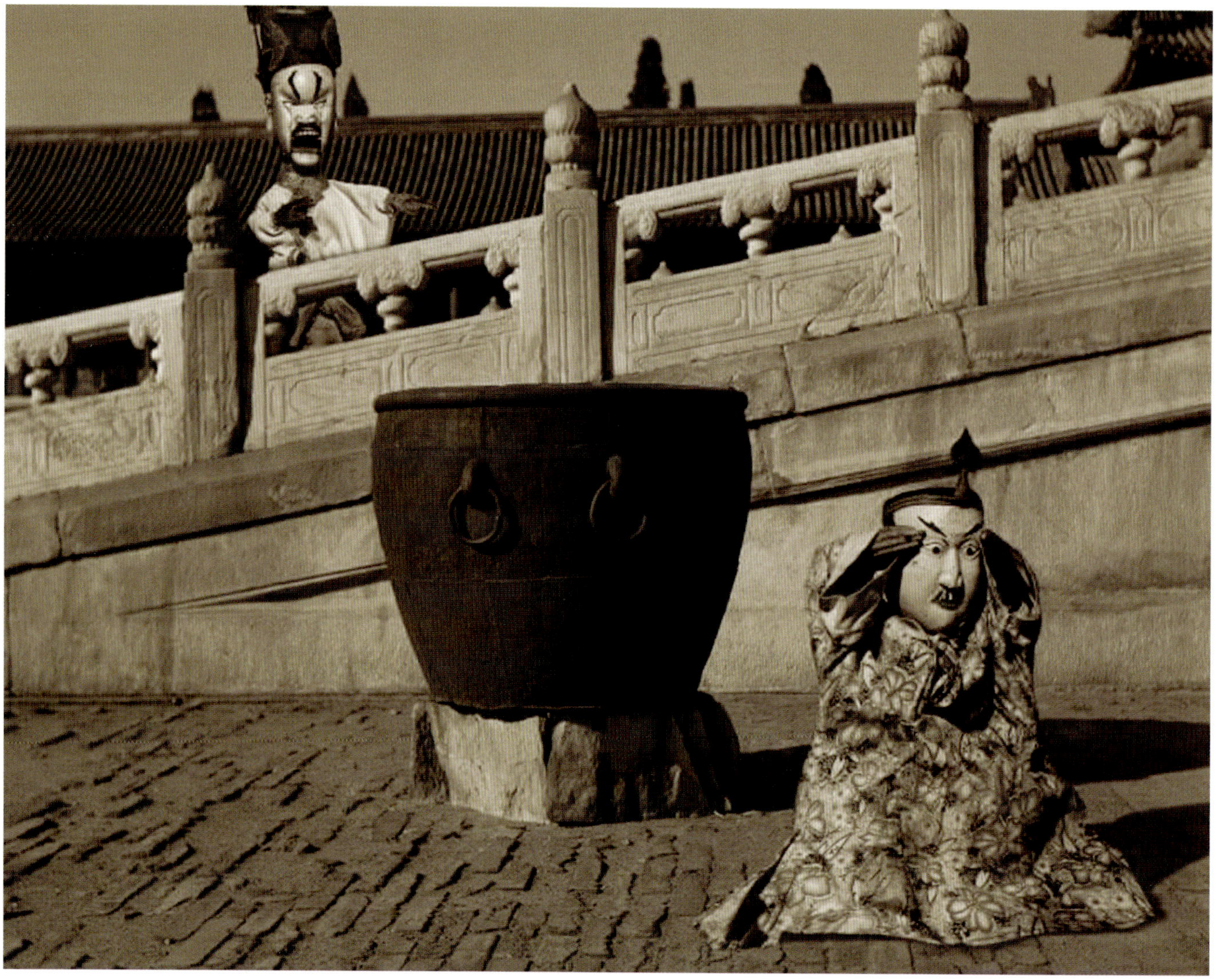

central figure; the message seems to be, as a popular Chinese epigram goes, "the living always live in the shadow of the past." This person, the artist himself, then becomes the subject of two kinds of metamorphosis, merging either into history or the present. In two repeated sections of the video, he stands before the old wall and transforms himself into each of the four puppets by changing his facial expression (fig. 7.2). In other sections, his face is distorted—squeezed or stretched—by some invisible forces surrounding him, finally dissolving into the hazy atmosphere of a sprawling modern Chinese city. His final disappearance seems to echo the demise of the puppet in the first video.[6]

Chen Qiulin: Finding Reality in Opera

Chen Qiulin's (b. 1975) two videos in the exhibition are also concerned with death, but her subject is the impact of China's economic development on the environment. Differing from Liu Wei's metaphorical use of basic drama role-types, Chen Qiulin finds parallels between reality and famous historical plays, and interweaves two such plays with her account of the transformation of her homeland brought about by the construction of the Three Gorges Dam. The largest hydroelectric project in human history, the construction of the dam stirred up controversy from the very beginning, with its advocates expecting it to generate clean energy crucial for China's economic growth, and its critics emphasizing the human cost and environmental damage. Growing up in Wanxian on the upper reaches of the Three Gorges, Chen Qiulin became deeply engaged in this debate and created four videos from 2002 to 2007 to voice her reactions. *Rhapsody on Farewell* (*Bie fu*, 2002) and *River, River* (*Jianghe shui*, 2005) are the first two in the series.[7]

Rhapsody on Farewell begins with two sequences of images that rapidly intersect. One sequence shows the demolition of an old building on the bank of the Yangzi River; the other focuses on Chen's transformation into a Peking opera character named Consort Yu (Yu Meiren), a tragic heroine in the play *The King Bids Farewell to His Mistress* (*Bawang bie ji*), better known in the West as *Farewell My Concubine*. The story relates how in 207 BCE, Xiang Yu, the powerful king of Western Chu, had resigned himself to defeat in competing for the central power. Cornered and unable to retreat further,

7.1
Liu Wei
Chinese, b. 1965
Still from The Forbidden City, 2000
Video, running time 5:30
Courtesy of the artist

7.2
Liu Wei
Chinese, b. 1965
Still from The Shadow, 2001
Video, running time 2:47
Courtesy of the artist

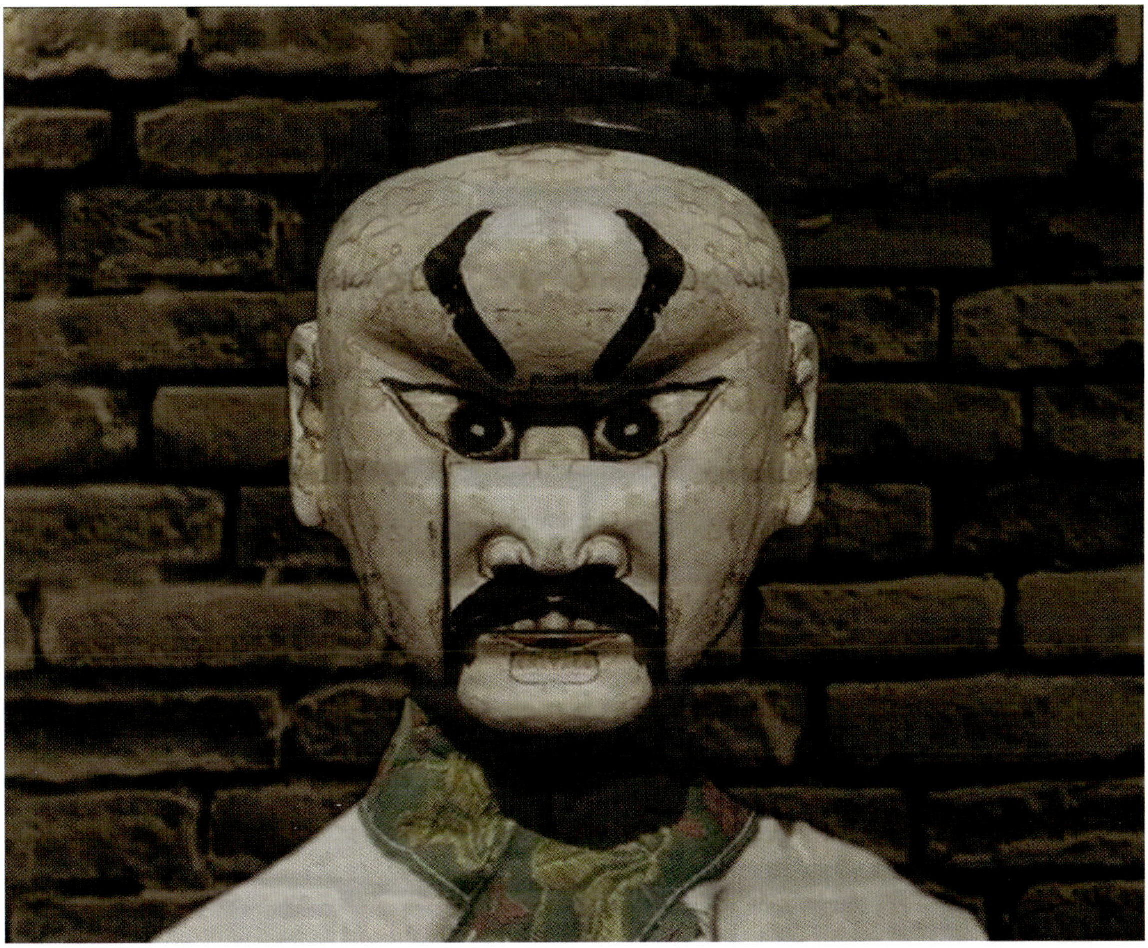

Consort Yu danced her last dance for her lord and then committed suicide. An intertitle written in Chen Qiulin's first-person voice explicates the relationship between these two sequences:

> In August 2002, I went back to my hometown Wanxian. In the ruins of the city torn up for the upcoming construction of the Three Gorges Reservoir, I experienced again the joy, happiness, despair, and tears in my memory. Only then did I truly feel a kind of unspeakable feeling, a feeling that blood is thicker than water. During the following thirteen days, our group of eight traveled through Wanxian, Yunyang, Fengjie, Wushan, and finally entered the old town of Dachang located in the hinterland of the Three Gorges. Borrowing from *Farewell My Concubine*, a Peking opera that I have cherished since childhood, I made this work *Rhapsody on Farewell*.

It then becomes clear that the two sequences of images are both about death, and their constant intersection implies the interchangeability between the death of a place and the death of a woman. As the video continues, we witness the violence inflicted upon the whole city and its impact on people's lives, while Consort Yu's story unfolds to its climax. These two narrative threads are connected by the figure of the artist herself, who appears in different guises as Consort Yu in the historical play (fig. 7.3), as a phantom swirling amid ruined houses, and as a little girl filmed in black and white running through the frame. Instead of constituting a clear story line, these fragmentary images heighten the feeling of dislocation and trauma.

Such confusion and bitterness, however, largely disappears from *River, River*, in which the construction of new Wanxian is carried out at full speed. By 2005, the Three Gorges Project had entered

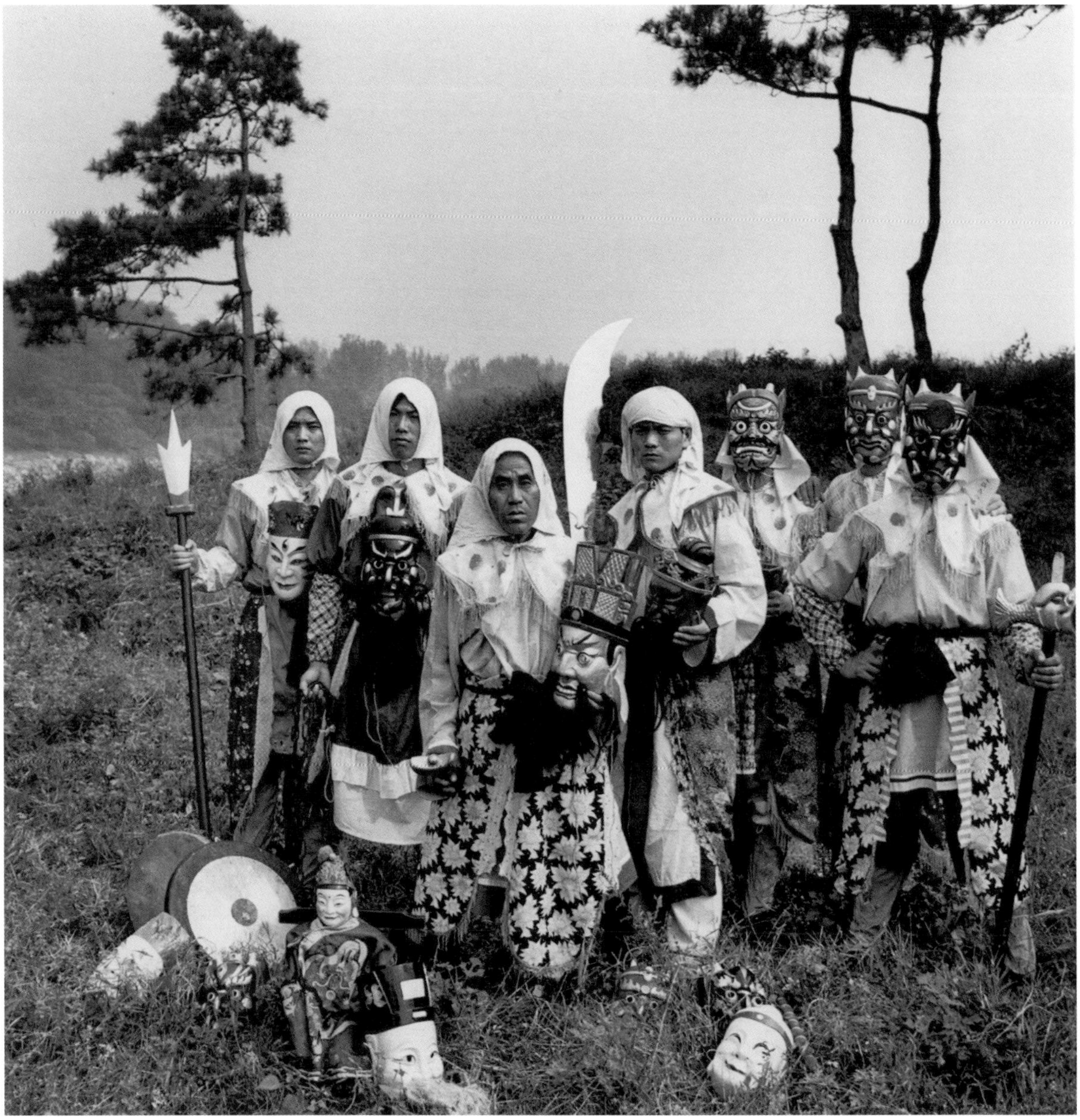

amateur performers in cross-gender roles, whom he encountered by chance:

> One day in 1995, I ran into a strange team of performers in a subway station in Beijing. There were forty to fifty of them, all dressed in colorful costumes and wearing heavy makeup. Most of them were quite old; only a few were middle-aged. They told me that they came from Qinhuangdao, in northern Hebei. Because the government had lowered the age of retirement to sixty or even fifty-five, they now found themselves jobless and with nothing to do in their lives. So they formed a touring *yangge ju* [a folk theatrical genre popular in northern China] troupe to amuse themselves and to earn some money. Some low-budget clubs and hotels hire them, because the customers love to see old guys dancing in young girls' outfits.
>
> I followed them to the place where they were going to perform that night—an underground theater remodeled from an air-raid shelter built in the early seventies. I couldn't bring myself to watch them perform. Several actors asked me to take their portraits. The one in this picture was actually seventy-two years old. A younger one, also dressed in female clothes, held my hand and saw me off at the entrance.[9]

The old man in the picture wears a wig and is dressed like a young girl (fig. 7.6). Kneeling cross-legged in a challenging pose, he looks into the camera lens with a half-teasing expression. A cigarette dangles from his lips. The actor in figure 7.7 is perhaps the "younger one" mentioned in Liu Zheng's passage—the tiled wall behind him identifies the setting as the same underground space. His costume suggests that he is impersonating an empress or princess: the phoenix in the jeweled headdress is a conventional symbol of female royalty. But his heavy makeup stresses the angularity of his face, and his intense, piercing gaze would overpower any onlooker. Instead of displaying feminine beauty, the photograph is energized by the tension between the actor's masculinity and the female role that he plays.

7.5
Liu Zheng (Chinese, born 1969)
A Nuo Opera Performing Troup, Nan Feng, Jiangxi Province, 2000
From *My Countrymen (Guoren*, alternately translated as *The Chinese*) series
Gelatin silver print, image: $14\frac{9}{16} \times 14\frac{9}{16}$ in. (37 × 37 cm), sheet: 24 × 20 in. (61 × 50.8 cm)
Courtesy of the artist

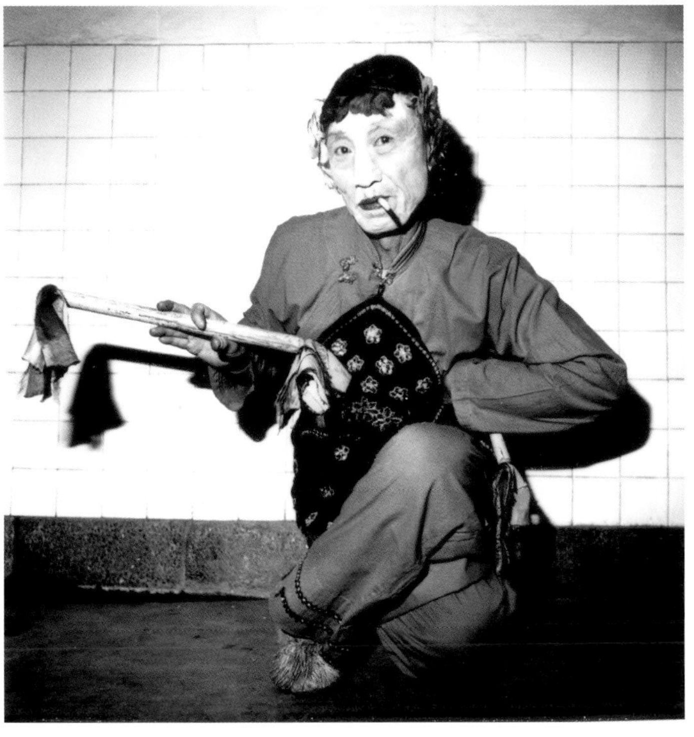

7.6
Liu Zheng (Chinese, born 1969)
An Old Peking Opera Actor Playing a Female Role, Beijing, 1995 (negative, this impression printed 2007)
From *My Countrymen* (*Guoren*, alternately translated as *The Chinese*) series
Gelatin silver print, image: $14\frac{9}{16} \times 14\frac{9}{16}$ in. (37 × 37 cm), sheet: 24 × 20 in. (61 × 50.8 cm)
The David and Alfred Smart Museum of Art, Purchase, Paul and Miriam Kirkley Fund for Acquisitions
2013.25

7.7
Liu Zheng (Chinese, born 1969)
An Old Actor Playing a Female Role, Beijing, 1998
Gelatin silver print, image: $14\frac{9}{16} \times 14\frac{9}{16}$ in. (37 × 37 cm), sheet: 24 × 20 in. (61 × 50.8 cm)
Courtesy of the artist

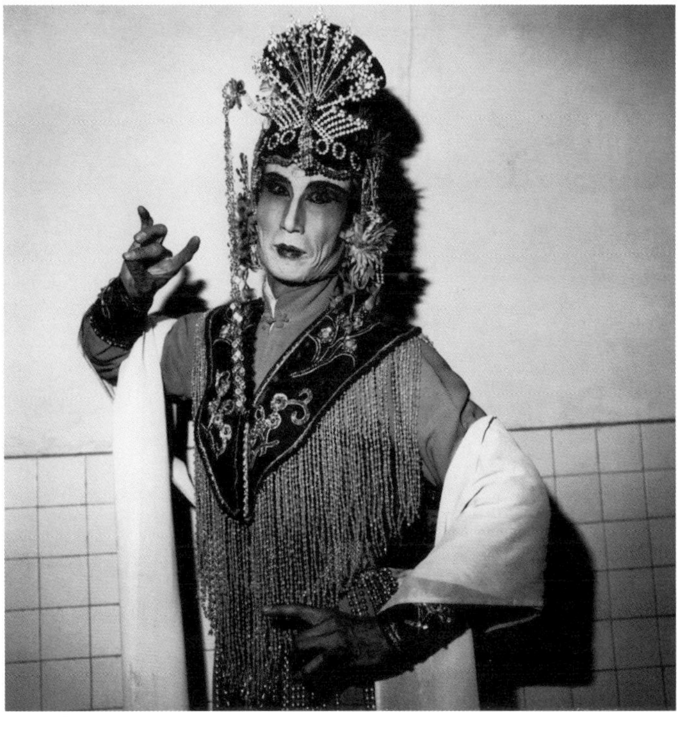

In making these two portraits, Liu Zheng adopted certain conventions of "opera photography" (*xiqu sheying*), a photographic genre that developed in the late nineteenth and early twentieth centuries. Departing from the ethnographic mode, this type of photograph represents one actor or a group of actors striking and holding studied poses for a sustained moment, known as *liangxiang* in traditional terminology. Often produced in photo studios, such images exhibit theatrical movements with a sculptural quality. Skilled retouching on the negatives further erased traces of gender impersonation and helped produce "perfect" images of famous stars. Liu Zheng's actor portraits embody this tradition but turn it upside down, as they never intend to idealize but always venture into the realm of the uncanny. He professes that what he tries to capture is a particular subjectivity that is "simultaneously real and surreal, both here and not here."[10] The aged amateur performers in these photos have neither jobs nor steady incomes, and their cross-dressed theatrical roles reinforce their marginality in society. Anthropologists have characterized such people as *liminal* because "they are marginal to society—poised perhaps to enter, but still outside its boundaries."[11] In Liu Zheng's photos they yearn for fictional identities but can never erase the gap between fantasy and reality. In this way, by revealing what costume and makeup *cannot* disguise and transform, these images present in fact the antithesis of conventional opera photography.

Cui Xiuwen: Internalizing Opera

Finally, the two videos by Cui Xiuwen (b. 1970) differ from the other works in that they do not refer to traditional opera directly, either to role-types or to famous plays. Indeed, it is by no means clear whether the artist consciously borrowed elements from the opera while creating these videos. Rather, their connections with traditional opera are detected on a deeper, aesthetic level, in their

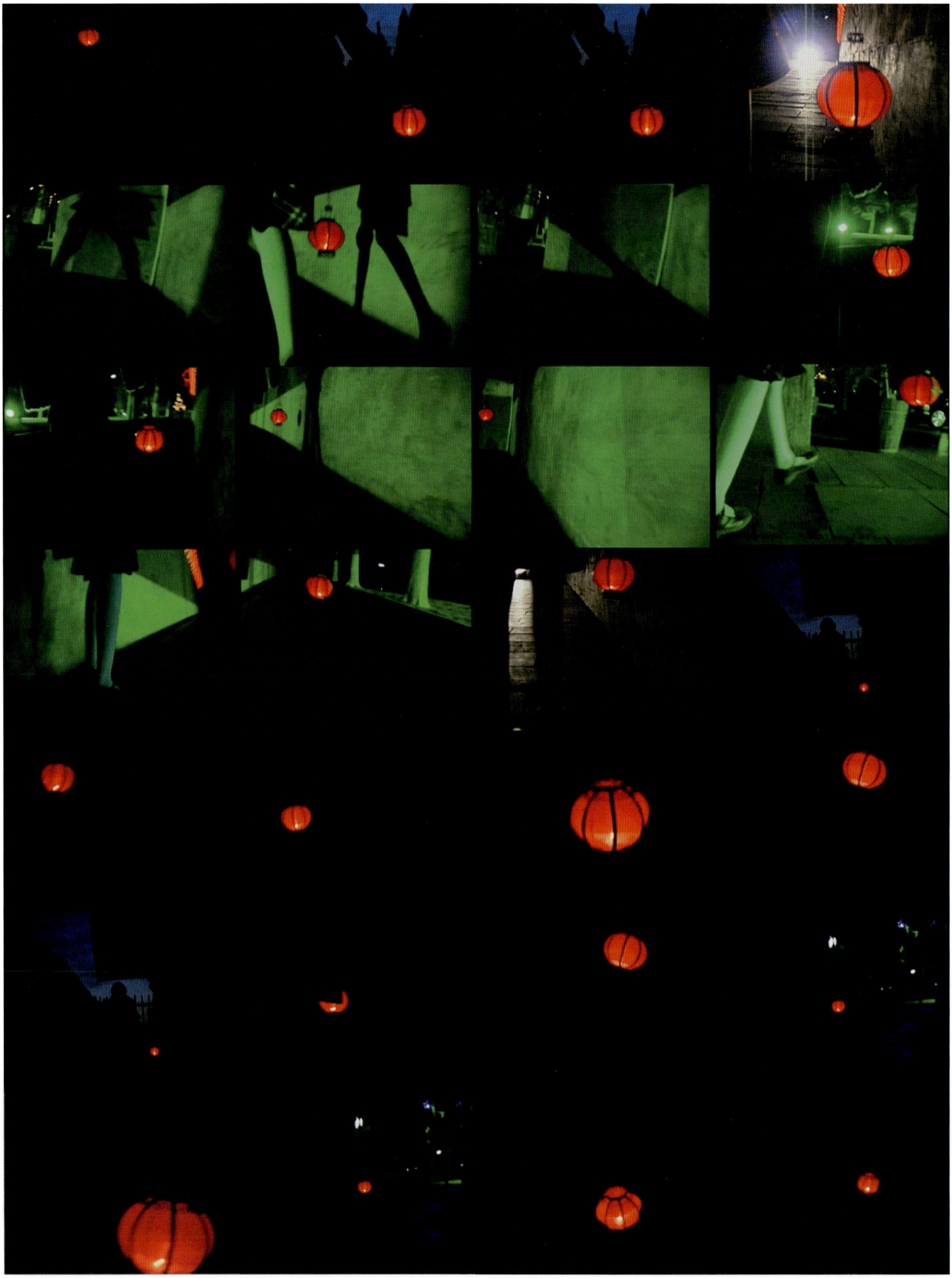

7.8
Cui Xiuwen
Chinese, b. 1970
Still from Drifting Lantern, 2005
Video, running time 23:21
Courtesy of the artist

strong performative quality, use of symbolic props, the sensitivity to gesture and costume. Moreover, Cui Xiuwen is one of the most outspoken female artists in China and has consistently made works to demonstrate the unique creative power of women. Both videos demonstrate this effort.

Drifting Lantern (*Piaodeng*, 2005) is a slow, meditative visual journey without dramatic happenings. What it presents, for most of its twenty-three minutes, is the vermillion silhouette of a drifting lantern moving in darkness in unpredictable patterns, seemingly guided by an invisible force (fig. 7.8). Circular and covered with red silk, this lantern is not a practical lighting device used in daily life. Called a "palace-style lantern" (*gongdeng*), it is an indispensible element of holiday decoration and also frequently adorns the stage. Making such a theatrical prop into the central image of the video, Cui Xiuwen plays up a convention in the traditional theater, which is the highly symbolic and economical use of props. As scholars have often noted, peripheral objects in Chinese opera often signify the presence of larger objects or the environment: a whip is used metonymically to indicate a horse and an oar symbolizes a boat on a river.[12] In Cui Xiuwen's video, the drifting lantern summarizes her childhood memory of life as a long, tenuous nocturnal journey. The surrounding darkness swallows up all shapes, including the traveler's own presence. Only a beautiful lantern glows, allowing the traveler to catch glimpses of the world from an intimate distance.[13]

TOOT (2001)[14] originated from an earlier installation/performance that was never publicly exhibited. Created in 1996, this earlier work consisted of three elements: an empty room, a chair, and the artist's body; the chair and the pipes were wrapped in white toilet paper.[15] Its minimalist use of furniture and performer bring to mind a traditional Chinese stage, in which a single scene frequently consists of just a lone actor sitting in a chair. Five years later Cui Xiuwen transformed this early work into *TOOT* for a workshop on homosexuality held in Beijing and sponsored by the Ford Foundation: because of Cui Xiuwen's long-term engagement with issues of sexuality, the organizers of the workshop invited her to develop an art project for the event. This context explains, at least partially, the intensification of the visual language in the new work, effectively heightening the conflicting notions of anonymity versus individuality, bondage versus freedom, concealing versus revealing, and violence versus lyricism.

After a friend backed out from performing for the video (because of the required nudity), Cui Xiuwen took on the role herself and went to a commercial hair salon to have her head shaved (an event that was recorded as part of the art project). Compared with the 1996 piece, *TOOT* is even more economical in visual imagery: the chair and architectural space are both gone; the only means the artist has now is her body and rolls of toilet paper, which she uses to turn herself into an immobile object. This object is in the making when the video starts: we see parts of an unknown bulk rotate rapidly while being enswathed by a white bandage. The fast, rising sound of the pipa musical accompaniment adds a sense of urgency and conjures the impression of a theatrical performance. Moments later, the camera pulls away and exposes the entirety of the bulk: a mummy-like figure standing rigidly in the middle of an empty, pitch-dark space. As the pipa's voice becomes softer and more lyrical, we notice that something is beginning to happen to this lifeless shape: water silently spreads on its surface, darkening the head and then the shoulders and upper body. For a while, it seems that the figure is melting from the inside. But we soon realize that a soft, shapeless rain is washing the bandage off. The camera zooms in and we see the figure faintly breathing under the wet tissue. Suddenly she opens her arms with a dramatic movement that breaks the last vestiges of bondage, as if she were about to fly away (fig. 7.9).

Recalling her experience during the performance, Cui Xiulin likens it to the final movement of the cicada sloughing its skin, thus providing a key to understanding the whole video and linking it to China's cultural heritage.[16] Climbing slowly out of the earth, emerging painfully from its former body, shedding an empty shell and flying into the sky, the cicada became the most celebrated metaphor for transformation in ancient China. Numerous cicada images in painting, carving, and decorative art symbolized the most desirable consequence of any transformation—the state of immortality wherein a body transcended its former being and became eternal. The same yearning enlivens Cui Xiuwen's work, but through the new resources of visual technology and contemporary art.

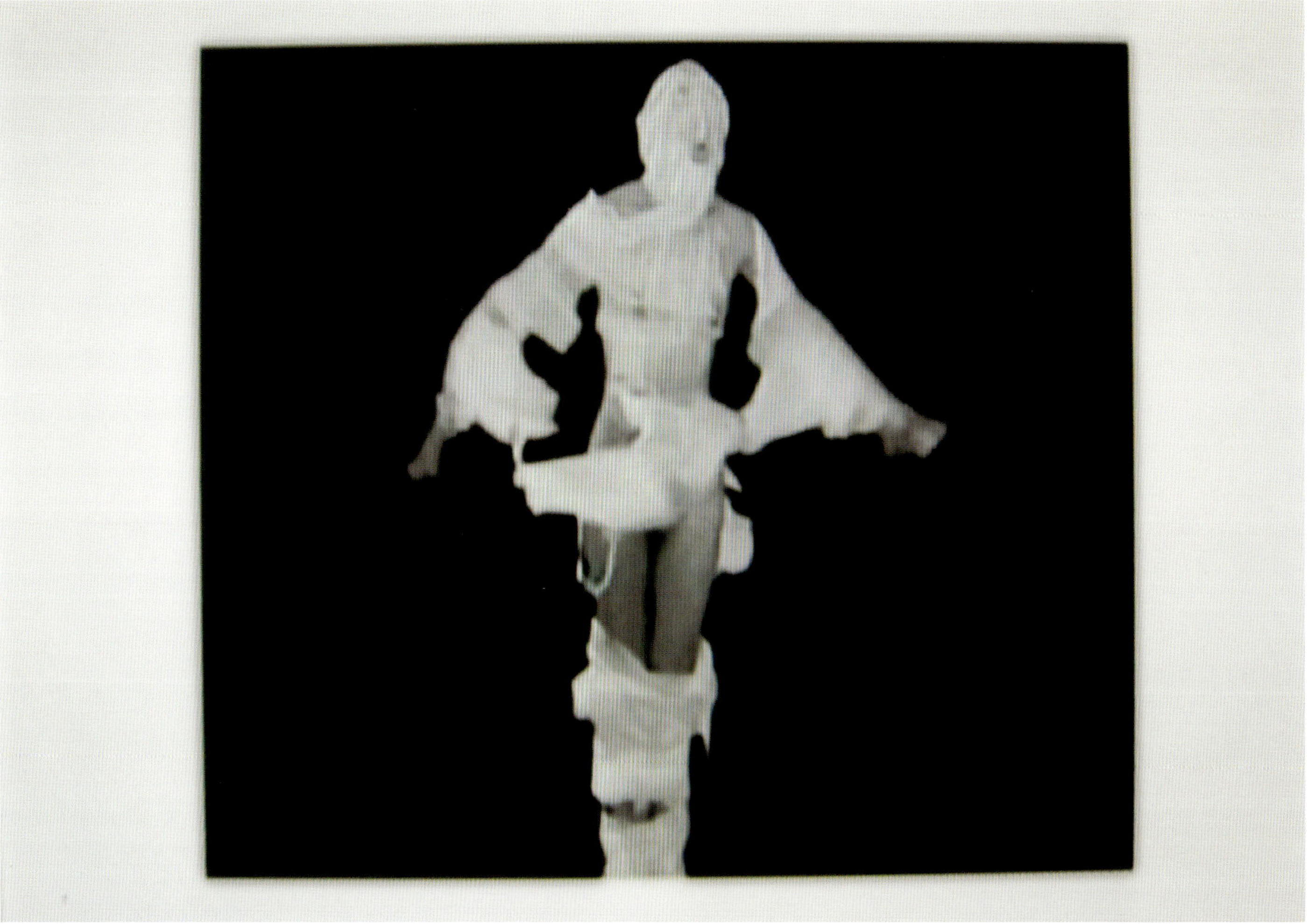

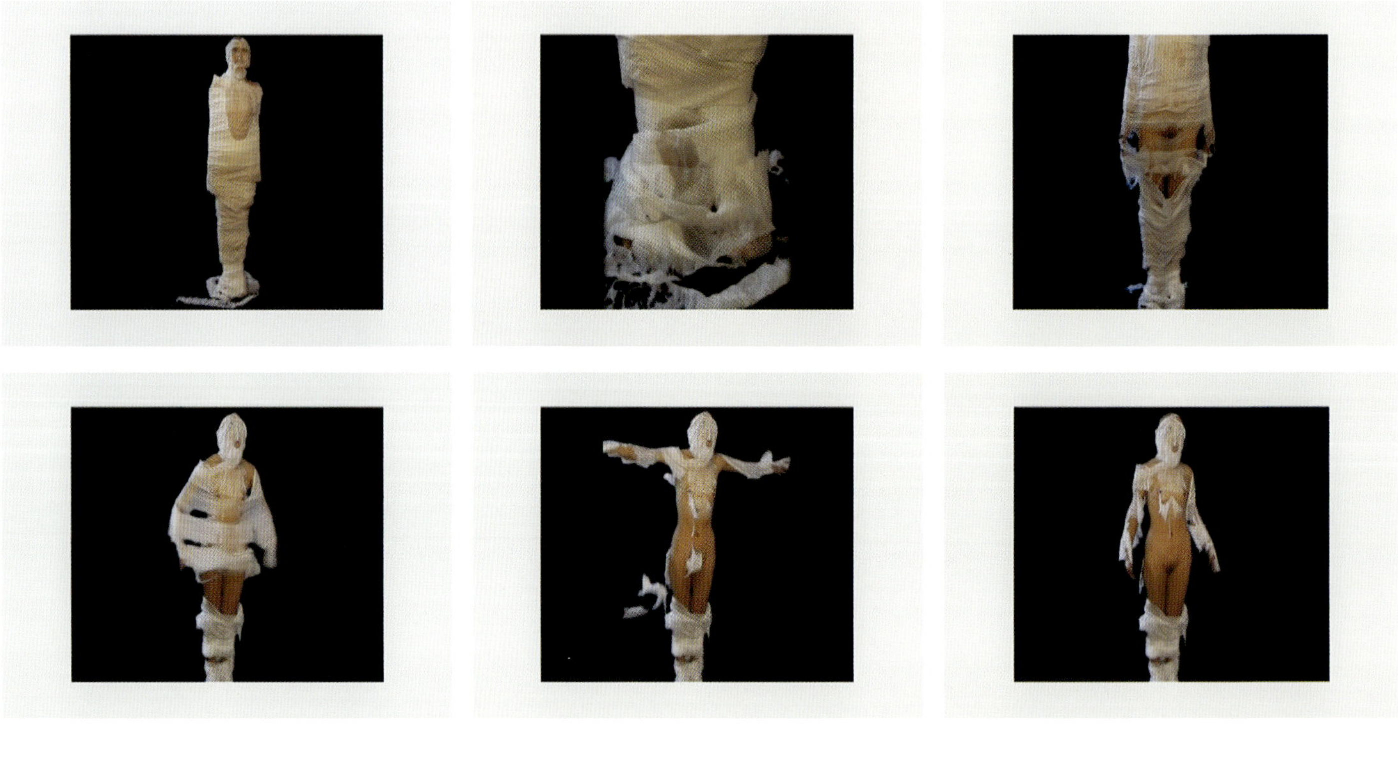

7.9
Cui Xiuwen
Chinese, b. 1970
Stills from TOOT, 2001
Video, running time 3:12
Courtesy of the artist

Notes

1 For example, Catherine Yeh demonstrates how the rise of professional actors as "stars" in the late nineteenth to early twentieth century stimulated new types of images in photography and print culture. See her articles, "Where Is the Center of Cultural Production?—The Rise of the Actor to National Stardom and the Beijing/Shanghai Challenge (1860s–1910s)," *Late Imperial China* 25.2 (December 2004): pp. 74–118; "Refined Beauty, New Woman, Dynamic Heroine or Fighter for the Nation? Perceptions of China in the Programme Selection for Mei Lanfang's Performances in Japan (1919), the United States (1930) and the Soviet Union (1935)," *European Journal of East Asian Studies* 6.1 (2007): pp. 75–102. In a special issue of the *Opera Quarterley,* edited by Judith T. Zeitlin and Paola Iovene, nine authors discuss how traditional operas were transformed into a powerful cinematic genre in the twentieth century, especially after 1950. "Chinese Opera Film," special issue of *The Opera Quarterly* 26/2–3 (Spring/Summer 2010). Scholars like Paul Clark and Xiaomei Chen have also written at length about the profound impact of the Cultural Revolution "model operas" on other visual forms. See Clark, *The Chinese Cultural Revolution: A History* (Cambridge: Cambridge University Press, 2008); Chen, *Acting the Right Part: Political Theater and Popular Drama in Contemporary China* (Honolulu: University of Hawai'i Press, 2002).

2 *Inspired by the Opera: Contemporary Chinese Video and Photography*, Smart Museum of Art, The University of Chicago, February 13–June 15, 2014.

3 For a general discussion of Experimental Chinese Art in the 1990s, see Wu Hung, "Introduction: A Decade of Chinese Experimental Art (1990–2000)," in Wu Hung, ed., *Reinterpretation: A Decade of Experimental Chinese Art (1990–2000)* (Guangzhou: Guangdong Museum of Art, 2002), pp. 10–19.

4 For discussions of the development of these two art forms in 1990s China, see Wu Meichun and Qiu Zhijie, "The Rise and Development of Video Art and the Maturity of New Media Art," in ibid., pp. 51–59; Wu Hung, "Between Past and Future: A Brief History of Contemporary Chinese Photography," in Wu Hung and Christopher Phillips, *Between Past and Future: New Photography and Video from China* (Chicago and New York: Smart Museum of Art and International Center of Photography, 2004), pp. 11–36.

5 Cited in Wu and Phillips, *Between Past and Future*, p. 208.

6 Liu Wei's statement in 2004 about *The Forbidden City* includes this passage: "China is experiencing a tremendous change that has exerted great influence on Chinese people and confronted them with physical and psychological pressures. When we are obsessed with vehement struggles, do we control the games of combat, or visa versa?" Ibid., p. 208. *The Shadow* seems to raise the same question.

7 The other two videos are *Color Lines* (*Caidai*, 2006) and *The Garden* (*Huayuan*, 2007). For an introduction to Chen Qiulin and these four videos, see Wu Hung, *Displacement: The Three Gorges Dam and Contemporary Chinese Art* (Chicago: Smart Museum of Art, 2008), pp. 56–81.

8 For a discussion of this significance of Liu Zheng's *My Countrymen*, see Wu Hung, "Photographing Deformity: Liu Zheng and His Photo Series *My Countrymen*," *Public Culture* 13.3 (Fall 2001): pp. 399–428; reprinted in Wu Hung, *Wu Hung on Contemporary Chinese Artists* (Hong Kong: Timezone 8, 2009), pp. 71–82.

9 Interview of Liu Zheng conducted by the author in 1998. Cited in ibid., p. 410.

10 Cited in Bingman [psued.], "The Chinese at the Turn of the New Millennium: A Review of Liu Zheng's Photographic Series 'The Chinese'" (manuscript, n.d.).

11 Robert F. Murphy, et al., "Physical Disability and Social Liminality," *Social Science and Medicine 26* (1987): p. 237.

12 Elizabeth Wichmann, *Listening to Theatre: The Aural Dimension of Beijing Opera* (Honolulu: University of Hawai'i Press, 1991), p. 6.

13 About the relationship between this video and her childhood memory, see Cui Xiaowen, "Piaodeng" [Drifting Lantern], in Cui Xiuwen, *Simi kongjian* [Private Space] (Hunan meishu chubanshe, 2006), pp. 46–48.

14 According to the artist, this title does not have a specific meaning. It actually combines the names of two girls who assisted in the video's production, who called themselves TT and OO. Cui Xiuwen, "TOOT," in Cui, *Simi kongjian*, p. 45.

15 Ibid., p. 38.

16 Ibid., p. 44.

Catalogue of the Exhibition

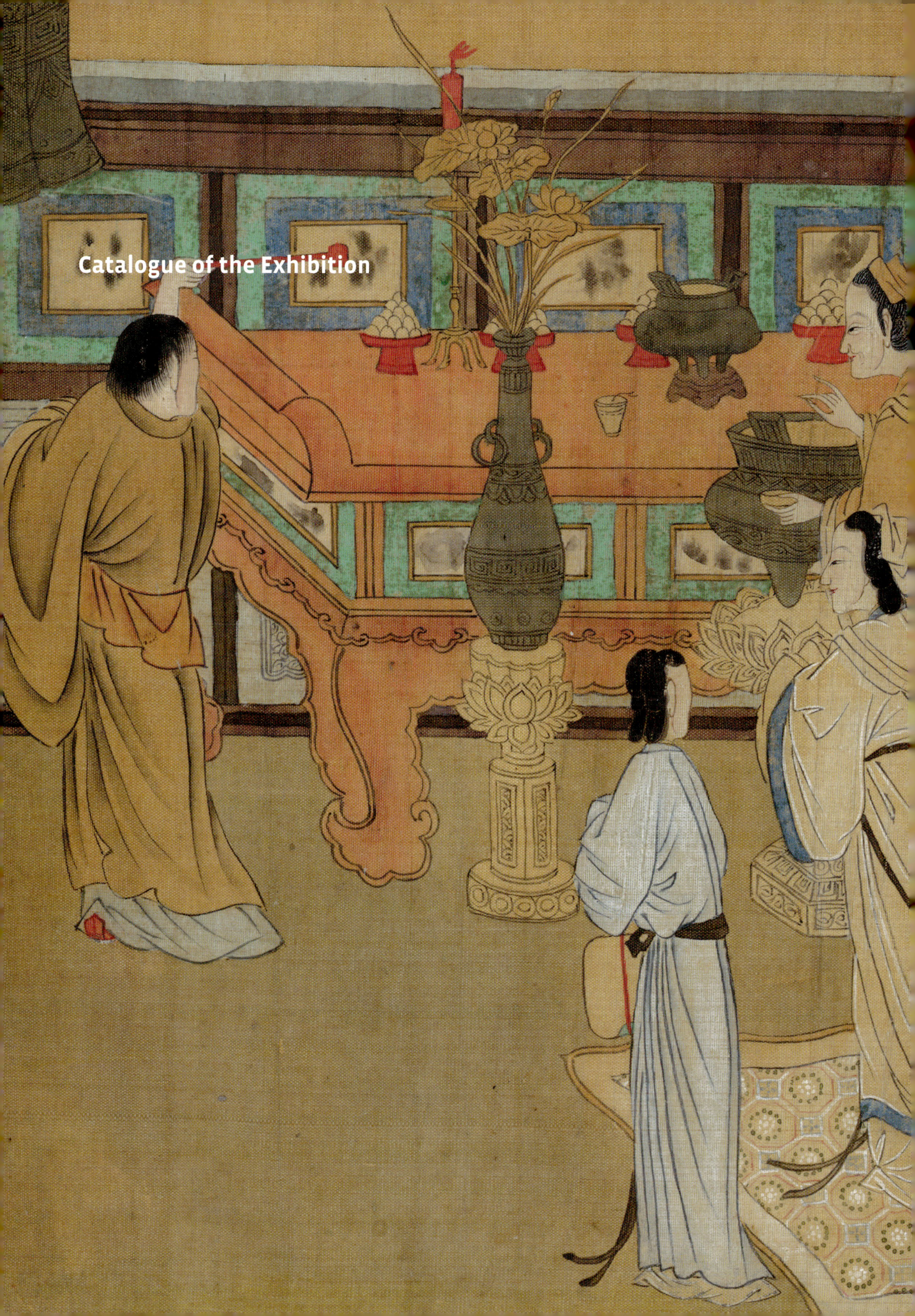

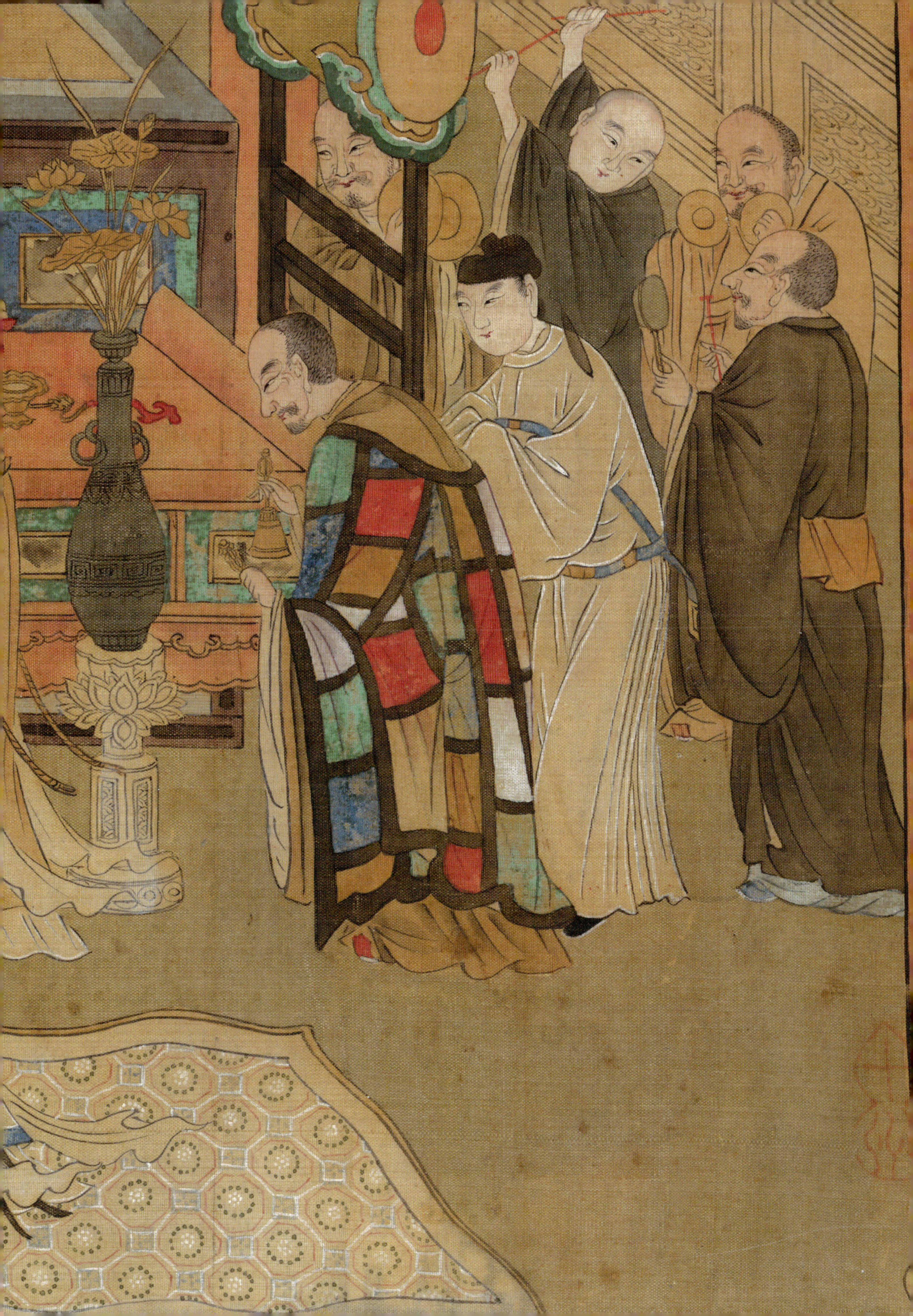

One

A Multiplicity of Forms

In the dramatic entertainments of late imperial China, virtually all the characters sing for most of the performance, making the term "opera" applicable to all traditional Chinese theatrical works. During the Ming (1368–1644) and Qing (1644–1911) dynasties, opera performance was an integral part of social and ritual life and enjoyed widespread popularity throughout the realm, from the village to the city to the court. Familiarity with the basic performing conventions and repertory of plots and roles constituted a common culture across class, occupation, gender, and region. Operatic characters and stories therefore appeared as images and motifs on a broad spectrum of media and objects, including scroll paintings, illustrated books and popular prints, painted fans, ceramics, textiles, musical instruments, carved bibelots, architectural ornaments, snuff bottles, miniature dioramas, playing cards, and eventually, photography, advertising, and film.

With the exception of two scroll paintings, none of the objects in this exhibition belongs to the narrow province of what was traditionally considered fine arts. Representations related to opera instead belonged to the wider category of a popular, shared visual culture, from products like painted albums and printed books produced by imperial workshops to luxury goods fashioned by skilled craftsmen of expensive materials like ivory, rhinoceros horn, porcelain, lacquer, or silk tapestry. Depictions of opera were even more prevalent in ephemera like cheap commercial prints and homemade embroideries. This multiplicity of forms attests to the power that opera wielded in shaping the visual imagination and material landscape of late imperial China.

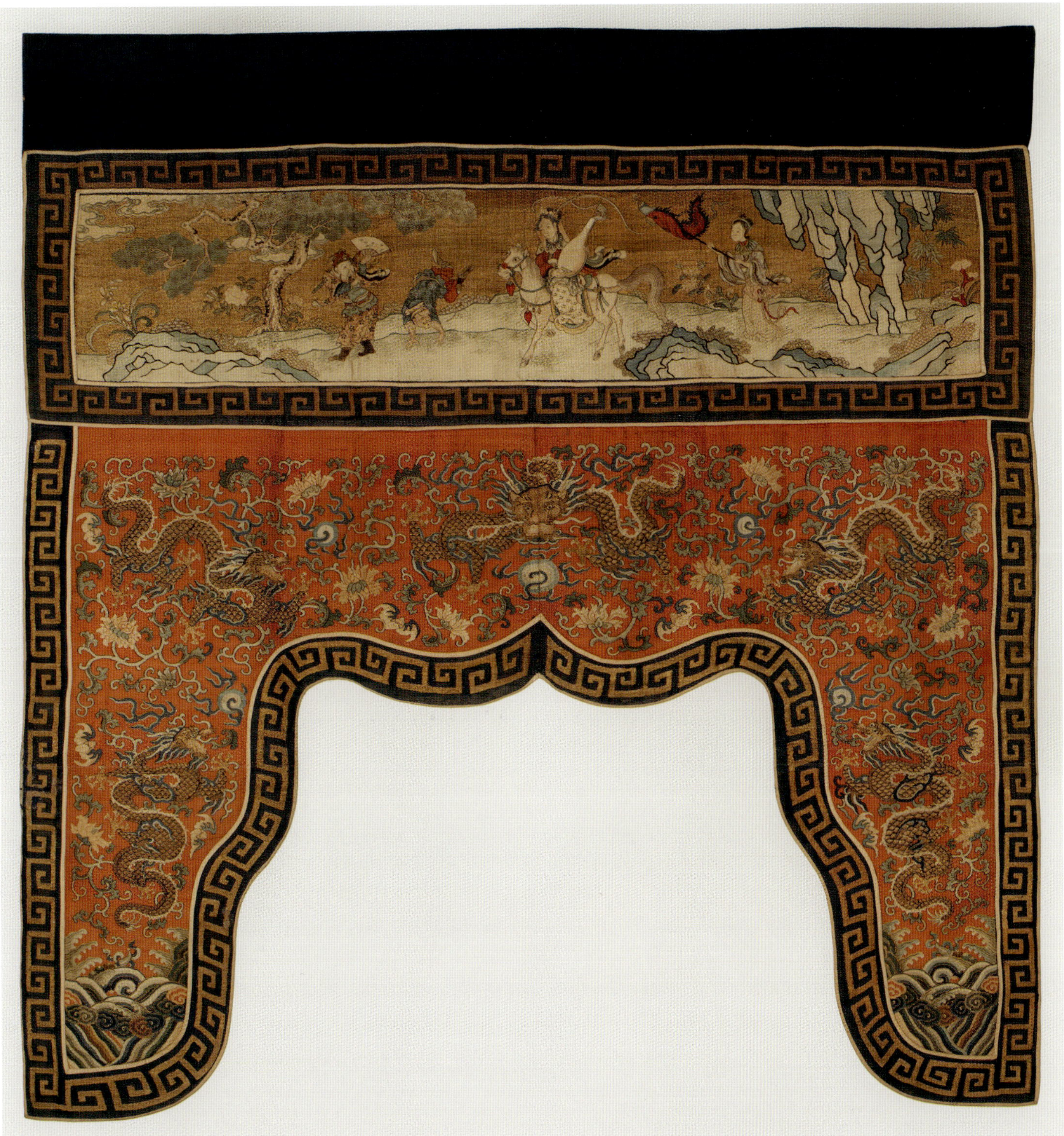

Cat. 1
Chinese, Qing Dynasty (1644–1911)
Altar Hanging with Acrobatic Figures (Wang Zhaojun Story), 18th–19th century
Slit silk tapestry (*kesi*) with brocade borders, overall: 45 1/4 x 43 3/8 in. (108.9 x 100 cm), textile only: 41 x 41 in. (104.1 x 104.1 cm)
Asian Art Museum, Gift of Carlotta Mabury
B81M28

This hanging consists of a rectangular top panel and a curved lower section, both outlined by decorative bands featuring gold meander patterns on a dark blue ground. Gold metallic threads, used generously in the kesi panels and borders, indicate that this textile was a luxury item.

The upper panel represents the procession of a lady on horseback, accompanied by her entourage. Although the scene is set in an outdoor landscape, the figures' postures and costumes recall theater performance on a stage. Two comic figures lead the procession. They are striking dramatic poses, with one turning back to flutter a fan and the other assuming an acrobatic upside-down gesture. The lady on horseback carries a pipa lute and wears a theatrical headdress with two long feathers—two details that reveal her identity as Wang Zhaojun, a palace lady at the court of Emperor Yuandi (76–33 BCE) of the Western Han dynasty, who was betrothed to the leader of the Xiongnu on the northern frontier as part of a peace treaty in 33 BCE.[1]

One of the most popular legends in Chinese history, the story of Zhaojun inspired numerous literary works and visual representations. The pipa lute had been associated with the image of Zhaojun in the literary imagination since the Yuan dynasty (1271–1368), first through the Yuan play *Autumn in the Han Palace* (*Hangong qiu*) by Ma Zhiyuan (1250–circa 1321) and later reinforced by several Ming dramas, notably *Lamenting on the Pipa* (*Diao pipa*) by You Tong (1618–1704). An instrument often poetically associated with female loneliness and grievance, the pipa highlights Zhaojun's sorrow over parting with the Han emperor and being far away from her homeland. By the Ming dynasty (1368–1644), the painting genre of beautiful women (*meiren hua*) had firmly established the visual cliché of representing Zhaojun carrying the pipa.[2] Another symbol often associated with Zhaojun—the long feather tail (*lingzi*)—first appeared in play illustrations in the Wanli period (1573–1620) of the Ming dynasty.[3] In the Qing dynasty (1644–1911), a feathered headdress on stage often functioned to indicate the identity of a non-Han character.[4] In this textile hanging, the headgear evokes Zhaojun's identity as a consort of a barbarian ruler.

The inverted arch in stylized curves of the lower portion suggests that this textile may have been intended as a hanging over an altar or an offering table. Textiles cut in the same shape and decorated with dragon and wave motifs were used both in Daoist and Buddhist ritual space during the Qing dynasty. In an early eighteenth-century illustration of a scene from the novel *The Plum in the Golden Vase* (*Jin Ping Mei*), which depicts a Daoist memorial service held in the house of Ximen Qing (fig. 4.7), the lower part of a hanging that frames an altar for tablet and offering vessels shows the same shape and design. Another example—a highly similar valance in the collection of the Art Institute of Chicago—bears an inscription dated to 1799 and indicates that it belonged to a Buddhist temple.[5]—MEI MEI RADO

1 Ban Gu, *Han shu* (Beijing: Zhonghua shuju, 1962), vol. 11, p. 3,803.
2 For example, see attributed to Qiu Ying (1498–1552), *Exceptional Beauties of A Thousand Years* (*Qianqiu jueyan tu*), collection of the National Museum of China. For a Yuan example, see a blue and white porcelain jar representing Zhaojun and her attendants in the Idemitsu Museum, Japan.
3 For example, see the illustration of *Hangong qiu* [Autumn in the Han Palace], in the Guqu zhai edition of *Gu zaju* [Ancient Plays], Wanli period (1573–1620).
4 Meng Yao, *Zhongguo xiju shi* [History of Chinese Theater] (Taipei: Zhuanji wenxue chubanshe, 1979), p. 497.
5 See Christa C. Mayer Thurman, "Introduction," in *Clothed to Rule the Universe: Ming and Qing Dynasty Textiles at The Art Institute of Chicago* (Chicago: The Art Institute of Chicago in association with University of Washington Press, 2000), p. 39.

Cat. 2

Chinese, Qing Dynasty (1644–1912), Kangxi Period (1662–1722)
Plate with Horseback Battle Scenes from Generals of the Xue Family (Xuejia jiang), ca. 1662–1722
Porcelain with underglaze blue and white decoration, diameter: 13 5/8 in (34.6 cm)
Asian Art Museum, The Avery Brundage Collection
B60P39

The base of this plate bears the mark "made during the Chenghua reign of the great Ming" (*Da Ming Chenghua nian zhi*) inside a double circle. This Chenghua (1465–1487) mark does not necessarily indicate a forgery, but rather abides by the Kangxi emperor's 1682 ban on the use of his name on export porcelains.[1] The back of the body and rim are adorned with six large *ruyi* scepters and four sprays of flowering plums, conventional auspicious garnitures.

While the back of the dish is relatively nondescript, the front is a merry-go-round of martial action. Despite initial appearances, these scenes illustrate a romance. Upon the central panel, Fan Lihua, a Turkic princess famed for her martial prowess, encounters Xue Dingshan, the son of a famous Chinese general, in battle and falls in love at first sight. Although the fighters are on horseback, their accoutrements evoke a staged performance. Fan Lihua sports the general's helmet adorned with pheasant tail feathers appropriate to her role-type and to her barbarian identity, and both riders are trailed by pages wielding military banners.

Six panels around the rim enable these indefatigable fighters to face off three times, buffered from one another's blows by a bold diaper of chevrons and an interlocking Buddhist swastika lattice pattern. A nearly identical rim design is found on Kangxi blue and white plates featuring

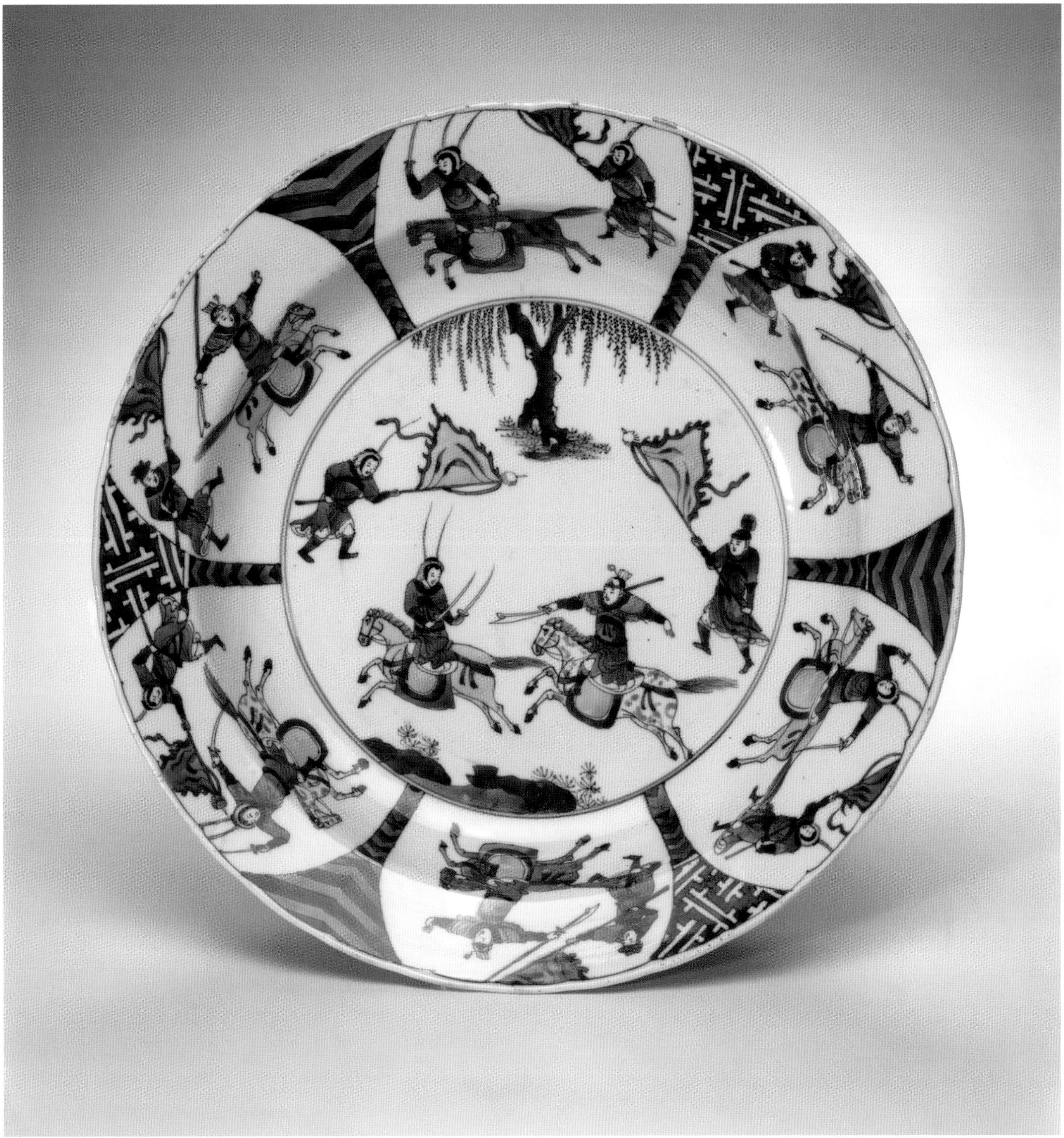

2

other illustrations,[2] but this plate takes advantage of the six-panelled rim's narrative potential. Although these rim scenes appear to be simple repetitions of the battle scene in the center, they likely correspond to Fan Lihua's three attempts to capture Xue Dingshan and woo him into marriage. Unfortunately, Xue escapes each time, and much drama ensues before the two are happily united. The Shanghai Museum contains a strikingly similar plate. —ALIA BREITWIESER

1 David Sanctuary Howard, *The Choice of the Private Trader: The Private Market in Chinese Export Porcelain illustrated from the Hodroff Collection* (London: Zwemmer, 1994).

2 For instance, a "washer in the shape of petals with ladies in underglaze blue" at the National Palace Museum in Taipei, museum acc. no. 1872.

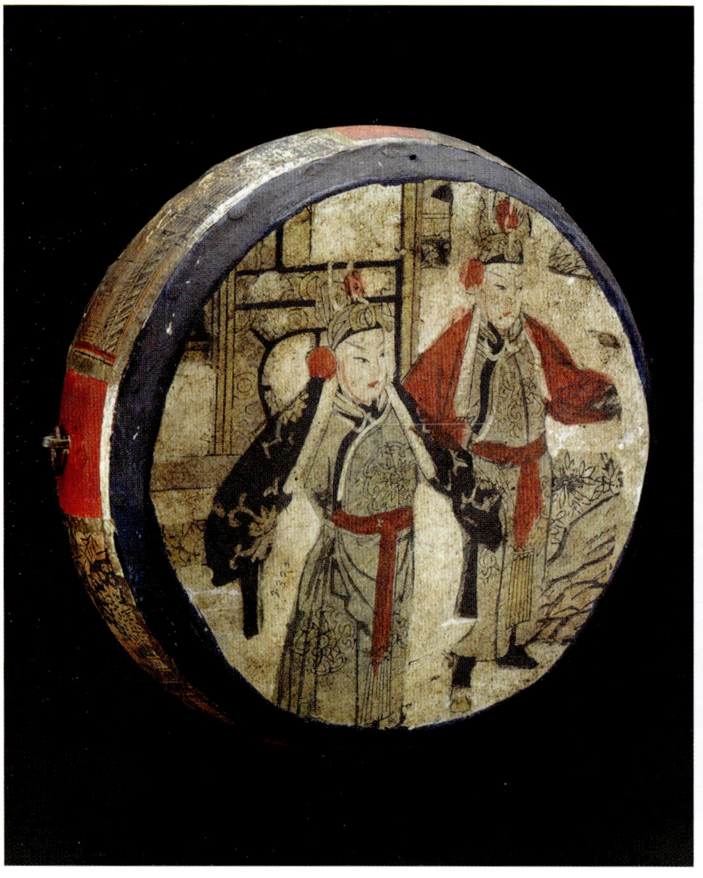 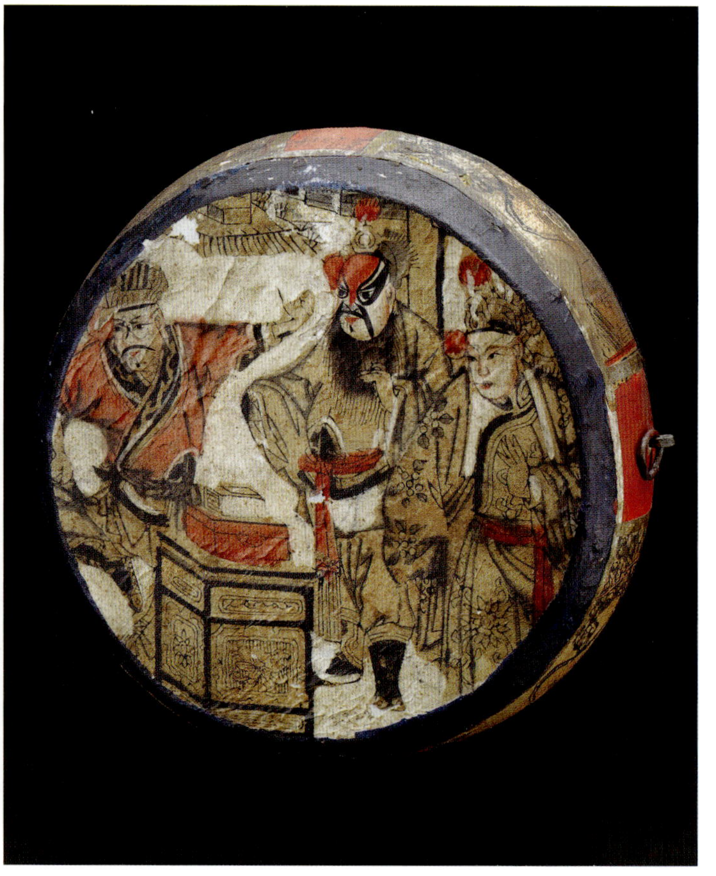

Cat. 3

Chinese, Late Qing Dynasty (1644–1911)
Drum with Martial Figures from the Peking Opera Jiang Gan Steals the Letter (Jiang Gan tou shu), 19th century (before 1889)
Mixed media, diameter: 8 ¼ in. (21 cm), depth: D: 2 ½ in. (6.4 cm)
Lent by The Metropolitan Museum of Art, The Crosby Brown Collection of Musical Instruments, 1889, 89.4.2322

In Peking opera, percussive sound dominates the action. Different rhythmic patterns announce the entrance and exits of characters, spur on fighting scenes, and punctuate the striking and holding of poses (*liangxiang*). And even though the high-pitched two-stringed fiddle called the *jinghu* is the principal instrument that accompanies the singing, the chief percussionist leads the orchestra.

The decorative covering on this small drum indicates that it was made for display rather than playing. A New Year print (*nianhua*) has been carefully cut into two circles and pasted over the top and bottom drumheads, and then further accented with dabs of paint. Too fragile to have ever been struck, the paper surface on each head shows evidence of natural deterioration. The sides of the drum's wooden shell are embellished with four identical woodblock landscape prints separated by red painted panels. Two metal rings hanging from two sides of the shell would have enabled the drum to be suspended or carried in some fashion.

The top drumhead shows a scene from the Peking opera *Jiang Gan Steals the Letter* (Jiang Gan tou shu), which is based on an episode from chapter 45 of the fourteenth-century historical novel *Romance of the Three Kingdoms* (*Sanguo yanyi*). This episode comes right before the famous Battle of Red Cliffs (208/209 CE), in which the allied forces of the states of Wu and Shu decisively thwart the state of Wei's attempt to conquer southern China. The two armies are camped on opposite sides of the Yangzi River. The warlord Cao Cao, commander of Wei, sends Jiang Gan to spy on Zhou Yu, the commander of the Wu forces, because he knows Jiang Gan and Zhou Yu are old friends. Zhou Yu immediately grasps Cao Cao's intention and devises a counter strategy. He forges a letter of surrender from Cao Cao's two chief admirals and then entices Jiang Gan to steal it. When Jiang Gan returns and presents the stolen letter, Cao Cao is so angry that he immediately executes the two admirals, which contributes to Wei's defeat in the battle.

On the left side of the picture, Jiang Gan, played as a clown role-type (*chou*) wearing white makeup across his nose, a black mustache, and a red jacket, raises one arm to steal the letter, which is concealed inside the book on the table. On the far right, Zhou Yu, played as a martial young male lead (*wu sheng*), holds up his palm as if to block him. He is wearing a flowery robe and not clad in armor because the scene is taking place in his sleeping quarters. The fluffy red balls on his hat, though not part of the costume worn by this role today, resemble those adorning the headdresses of martial male leads in the late nineteenth-century *Album of One Hundred Portraits of Opera Characters* from the Metropolitan Museum of Art, New York (see cat. 47). Between Jiang Gan and Zhou Yu stands a painted face role-type (*hualian*), who is pulling on his beard. This might be Huang Gai, a low-ranking general who plays a minor role in the episode.

The bottom drumhead features two additional martial young male leads with fluffy red balls on their headdresses and dressed similarly to Zhou Yuan. Their identities are unclear.

—JUDITH T. ZEITLIN

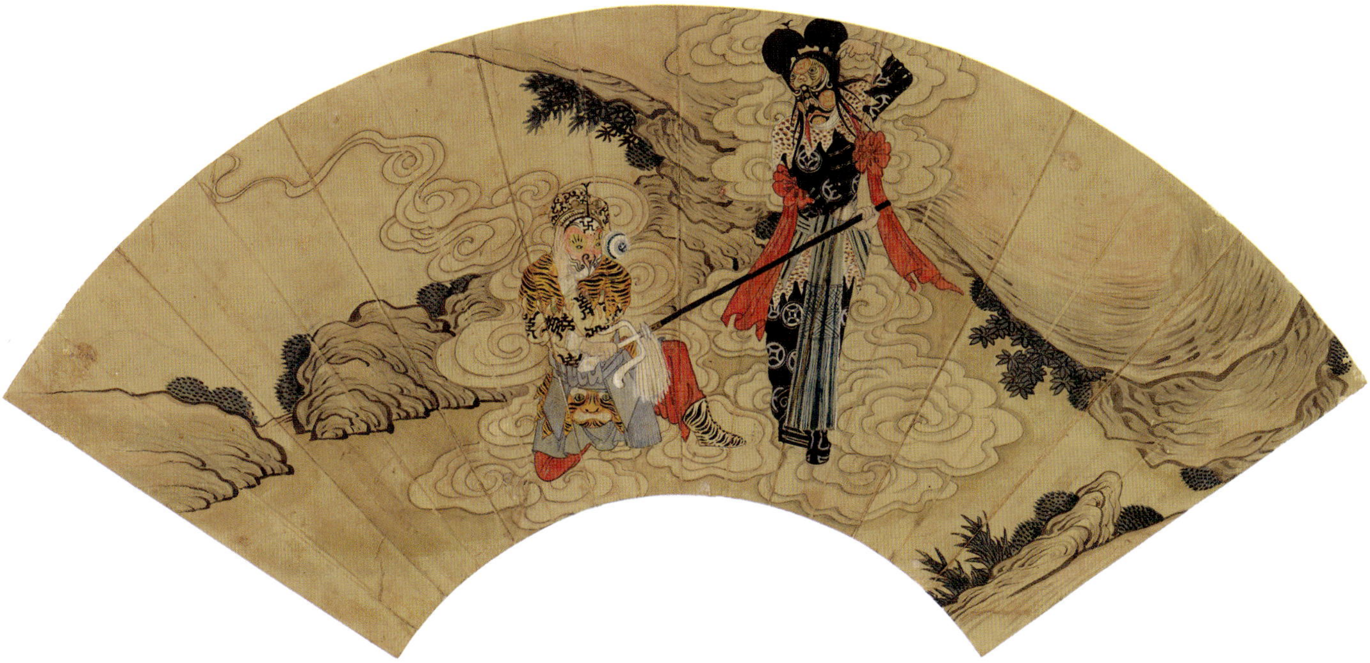

Cat. 4

Chinese, Qing Dynasty (1644–1911)
Fan Painting with Peking Opera Scene from The Leopard Demon (Jinqian bao, also known as Red Plum Mountain [Hongmei shan]), 19th century
Folding fan mounted as album leaf, ink and colors on gold paper, 6 7/8 x 19 15/16 in. (17.5 x 50.6 cm)
Museum of Fine Arts, Boston, John Ware Willard Fund, 1983.122

This fan depicts a scene from *The Leopard Demon* (*Jinqian bao*), also called *Red Plum Mountain* (*Hongmei shan*), a Peking opera based on the legends surrounding the seventh-century pilgrimage of the monk Tripitika (Tang sanzang) to India to bring back Buddhist scriptures to China. Although this particular story cannot be found in the famous sixteenth-century novel *Journey to the West* (*Xiyou ji*), it follows the general theme of countless episodes in the many narrative and dramatic treatments of Tripitika's journey and the supernatural disciples who protect him on his way. The plot always involves a demon that is terrorizing the residents of a certain area. In this painting, as Tripitika is passing through the region of Red Plum Mountain, Monkey, his faithful and able disciple, fights the monster and subdues him. The play starts with the Leopard Demon, who has made his lair in Red Plum Mountain, setting his eyes on a pretty maiden, Miss Deng, and ordering his minions to ask the girl's family for her hand. The Deng family, in dismay and despair, pleads for aid from Tripitika's entourage when they happen to stop by. Monkey concocts a scheme: he asks his fellow disciple Pigsy to play the role of Miss Deng, while he himself dresses up as Miss Deng's maid. At night when the Leopard comes to the wedding chamber, the two ambush him, but the Leopard manages to escape and returns with his demonic legions. Monkey again fails to subdue him in battle, and eventually has to accept help from the celestial army to capture the Leopard and take him away.[1]

The villainous Leopard, who is in fact the star of the play, displays dazzling martial skills even superior to Monkey's. The role became a star vehicle for many of the most famous twentieth-century *jing* (painted-face) performers. In this painting, the Leopard is depicted in an upright stance while Monkey is half kneeling on the floor. Wielding a trident, he is on the offensive, and Monkey is portrayed in a subordinate position. The leopard skin the Leopard wears as a shawl and also as an apron, as well as the coin (*jinqian*) design on his black costume (an informal robe called a *xuezi*) and on his facial makeup, make plain his identity. The red bow and ribbon draped over his shoulder, on the other hand, is the celebratory bridegroom outfit he sports in anticipation of his blissful wedding night. Monkey is wearing his signature tiger skin vest and apron and the auspicious Buddhist swastika (卍) symbol on his facial makeup.

Like the other fan paintings in the series (cats. 53, 54), the scene has a naturalistic background. Here the setting seems to be in front of or inside the Leopard's cave. Following a common pictorial convention, clouds enshroud both characters to indicate their supernatural identity. The clouds mirror the fantastic shapes of the rocks, heightening the fantastical setting of the story. Their spiral form also reflects the long and spectacular fight scene, during which the two exchange blows. Monkey's cloud, however, seems to taper off to the left, suggesting either he has arrived from outside of this space, or he is about to retreat from it.

It is extremely unlikely that smoke was used to evoke clouds on stage in Chinese opera before the twentieth century, but the famous actor Mei Lanfang (1894–1961) introduced smoke to create clouds during his experiments with new forms of stagecraft. It is said that his modern opera *Goddess of the Luo River* (*Luoshen*) used clouds on stage when it was performed in Shanghai in the 1920s. We can perhaps catch a glimpse of this stage effect in his 1955 feature film of this opera, in which clouds were used extensively to convey the supernatural identity of the characters.

—MIA YINXING LIU

1 For a plot synopsis and published editions of this play, see Wang Senran, *Zhongguo jumu cidian* [Dictionary of Chinese Opera Titles] (Shijiazhuang: Hebei jiaoyu chubanshe, 1997), p. 395.

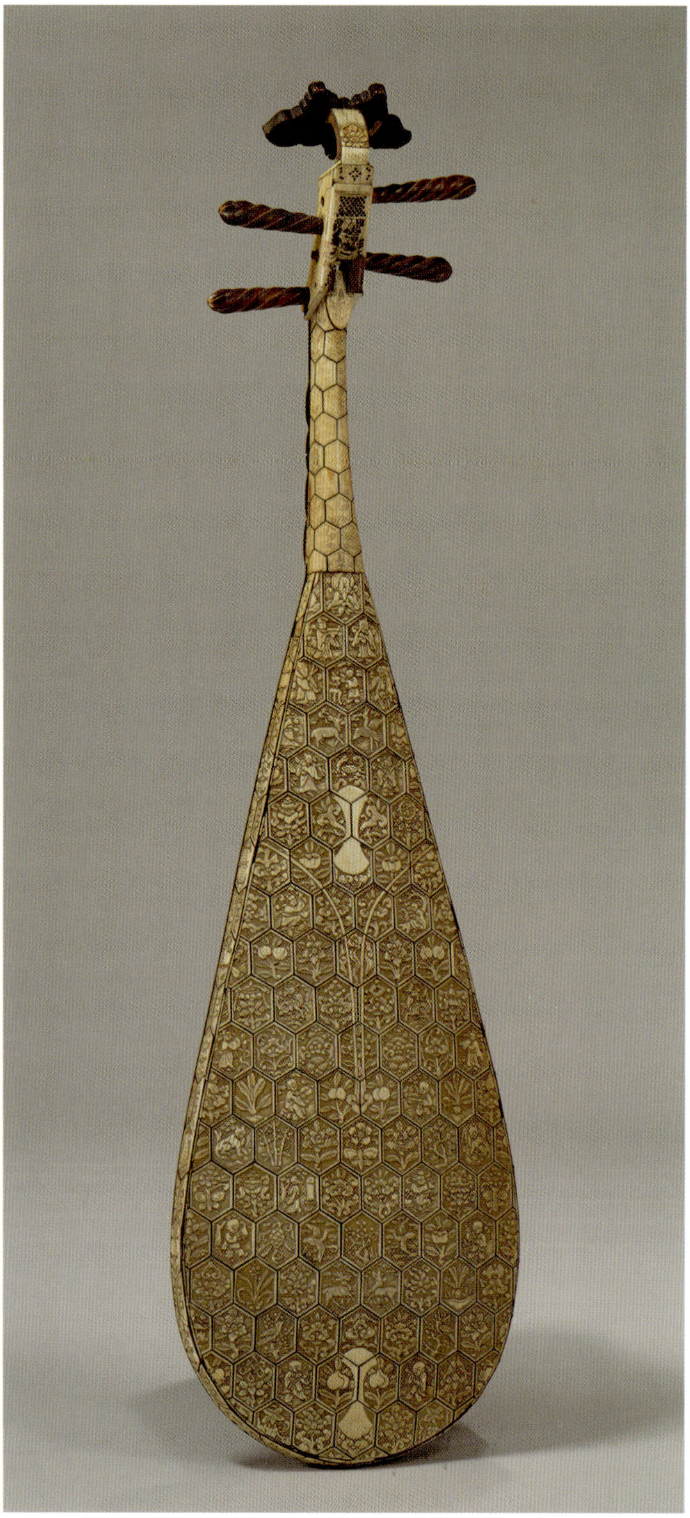

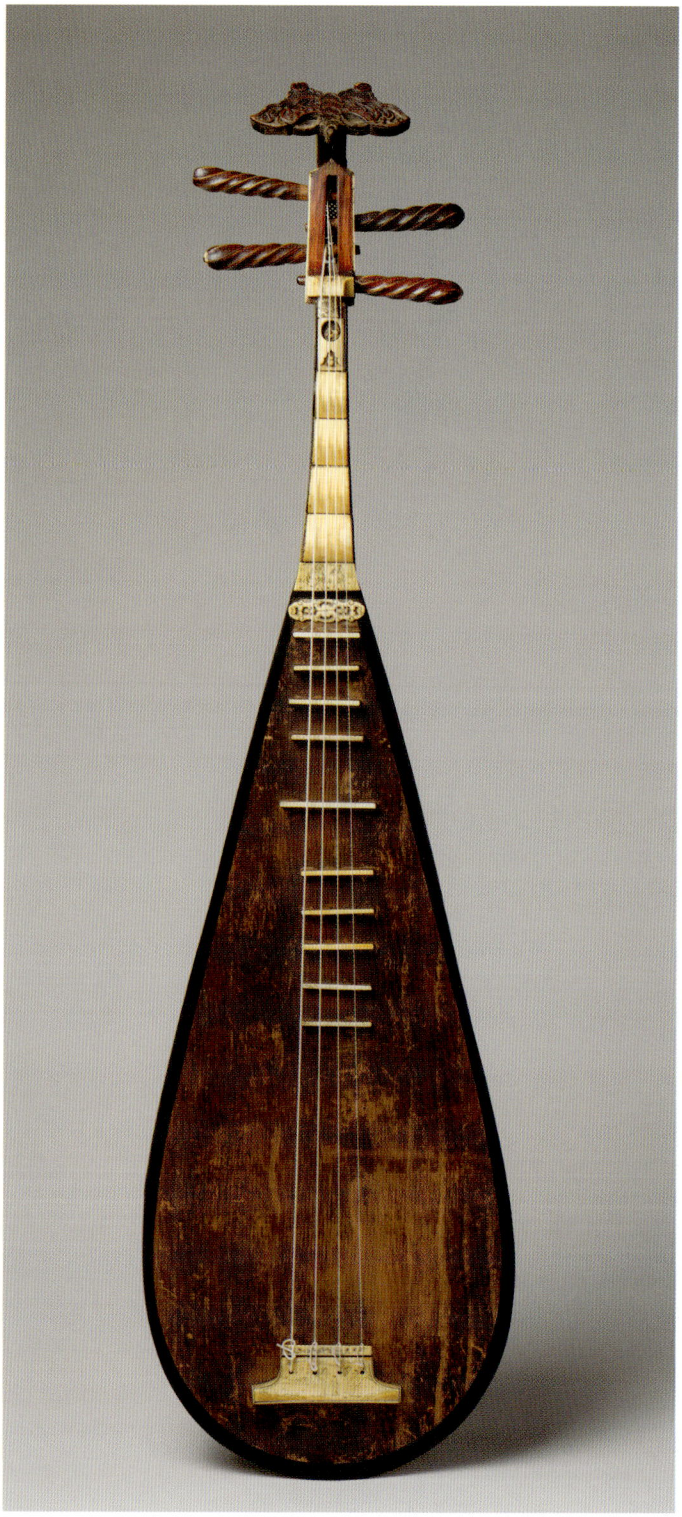

Cat. 5
Chinese, Late Ming Dynasty (1368–1644)
Pipa with String Holder Engraved with "Startled by Beauty" Scene from Romance of the Western Chamber (Xixiang ji),
late 16th–17th century
Wood, ivory, bone, and silk, overall:
37 x 9 15/16 x 1 1/8 in. (94 x 25.3 x 2.9 cm)
Lent by The Metropolitan Museum of Art,
Bequest of Mary Stillman Harkness, 1950
50.145.74

This beautiful Chinese lute is one of very few *pipa* still in existence believed to date from the late Ming dynasty (roughly 1580–1644). The unusually rich and profuse decoration, superb level of craftsmanship, and extensive use of costly ivory indicate that this instrument was manufactured as a luxury good. Changes in both design and playing technique had revolutionized the pipa during the Ming, which went from being held transversely and played with a plectrum to being held upright and plucked with the fingernails. The pipa was sometimes played as a solo instrument or in an instrumental ensemble, but it was particularly popular as an accompaniment for the voice, especially in performances of operatic arias and stringed ballad storytelling (*tanci*). Although many male virtuosi and professional music teachers specialized in the instrument, the pipa was above all associated with female musicians in the Chinese literary and pictorial traditions (see cat. 1). In theory, the beauty of the instrument complemented the beauty of the player, which in turn enhanced the beauty of the music for the audience.

The flat, pear-shaped back of the instrument is covered with a diaper pattern made of about 120 ivory hexagons carved with auspicious motifs, including the eight immortals, deer and cranes, little boys, a *ruyi* scepter, and silver ingots. This diaper pattern not only wittily recalls the brocade covering used to protect stringed instruments,[1] but also serves as an auspicious motif in its own right because the pattern follows the contour and markings of a tortoise shell, another symbol of longevity. The wooden head of the instrument is carved into the shape of a bat or a butterfly, with *yin-yang* symbols on the wings. Each of these creatures is a visual pun—the bat (fu[a]) is a homophone for happiness (fu[b]), and the butterfly (die[a]) is both a homophone for octogenarian (die[b]) and a symbol of romance.

On the front of the instrument are four upper frets of bone and ten lower frets of bamboo. Two cunningly carved ivory creatures, a spider (*xi*) and a bird, most likely a magpie (*xi que*), are inset in a roundel on the fingerboard. Based again on visual punning, the two probably form the rebus "double happiness" (*shuang xi*), the emblem of marriage. In addition, almost every possible surface or crevice on the instrument is adorned with geometric patterns or flowers. The main exception is the wooden belly, which has scratches and is worn around the string holder, suggesting that despite the instrument's lavish ornamentation and precious materials, it may have been played in the past and was not simply for display.

On the belly we find a trapezoidal ivory string holder engraved with a free and fluid rendering of the "Struck by Beauty" scene from *Romance of the Western Chamber* (*Xixiang ji*) (as identified by Ni Yibin in his catalogue essay). On the right, Student Zhang and the Abbot seem to be talking among themselves, while on the left, Oriole and the smaller figure of her maid Crimson (whose back is turned) seem studiously oblivious to the two men. A few clouds and some rudiments of plants, rocks, and a railing evoke the temple setting. A line of verse in cursive script reads, "Spring floods fill the four seas." This caption comes from the first line of a well-known verse on the four seasons attributed to the early painter Gu Kaizhi (circa 344–406 CE).[2] The connection between this line and the scene is tenuous, but since the word "spring" in Chinese also signifies "love," and "floods" evoke "clouds and rain"—the most common poetic euphemism for sex—the caption might be reinforcing the amorous theme of the play. If so, we might tentatively interpret the narrative scene on the plaque as expressing yet another auspicious wish, in this case for marital happiness and offspring. —JUDITH T. ZEITLIN

1 Jonathan Hay, *Sensuous Surfaces: The Decorative Object in Early Modern China.* (London: Reaktion Books; Honolulu: University of Hawai'i Press, 2010), pp. 368–69.
2 The poem is recorded in an early Tang imperial compendium from 624 CE. See *Yiwen leiju* [A Classified Collection of Literary Writing], comp. Ouyang Xun (Shanghai: Shanghai guji chubanshe, 1982), *juan* 3, p. 42.

Two

Stage and Spectacle

Chinese opera owes its appeal as much to visual display as to musical virtuosity. Famous as spectacle, this composite art form boasts colorful costumes, painted faces, and decorative props, and physical movement is as fundamental as voice. Actors are trained to master an extensive repertory of stylized gestures, mimed actions, dance steps, and sometimes even acrobatics and martial arts. Since the traditional stage did not demand any scenery, built set, or stage machinery for special effects, however, the mise-en-scène was very simple. The emptiness of the stage allowed for a remarkable flexibility in performance venues.

In no way limited to the palace or commercial playhouse, opera was performed almost everywhere during the Qing dynasty (1644–1911), especially during festivals: on temporary open-air stages or permanent ones, many attached to temples, in private salons and gardens, at restaurants and even brothels. For operatic performances held at banquets in private homes, a rug in the middle of a hall surrounded by tables and chairs for the guests easily became a makeshift theater. Ordinarily, however, an operatic stage required not just a performing space marked by a small rug but a specially constructed raised platform. During the Qing period, the typical theater featured a three-quarter thrust stage, open box frame, inscribed pillars on either side, and a low balustrade separating the actors from the audience.

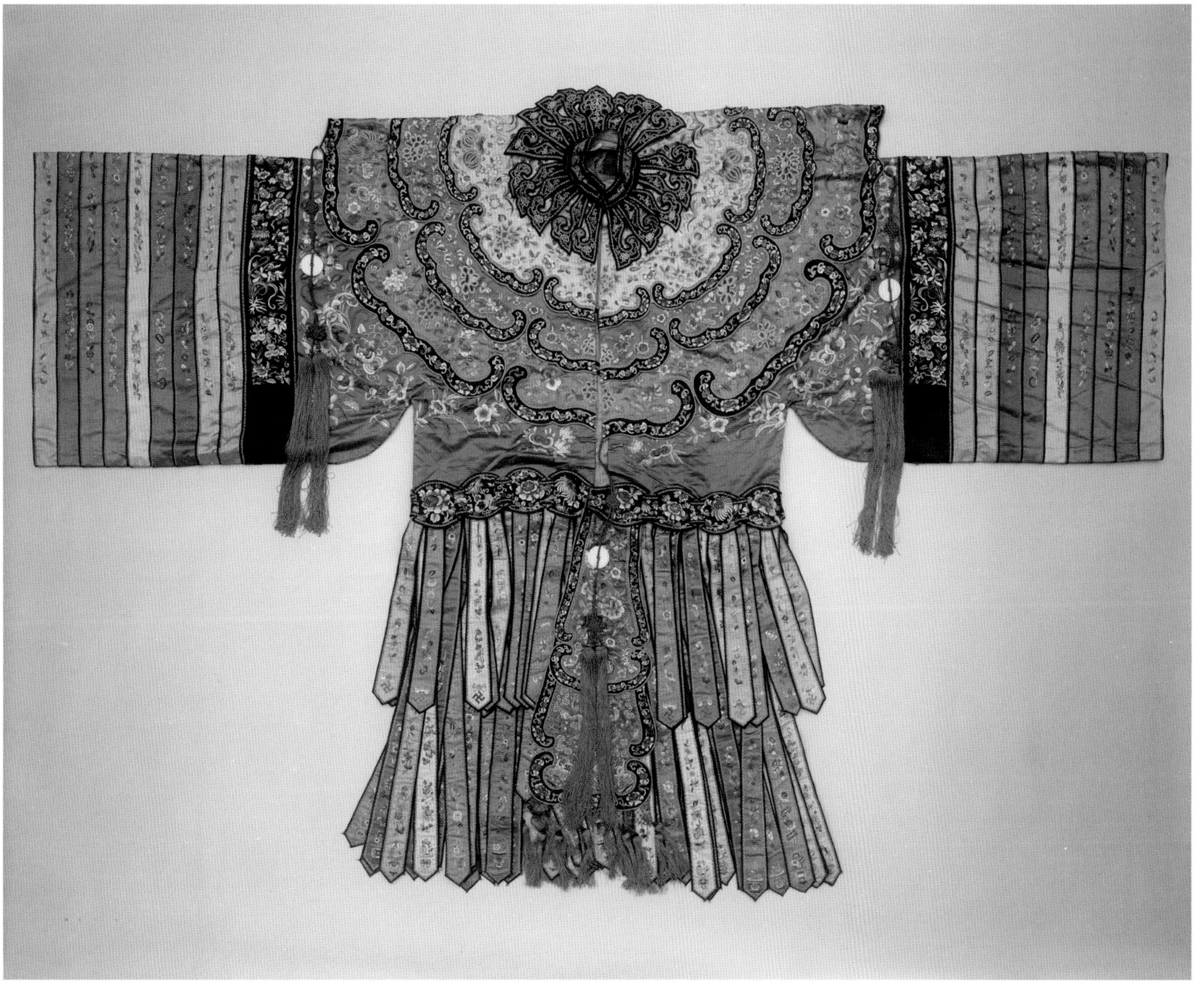

Cat. 6
Chinese, Late Qing Dynasty (1644–1911)
Theatrical Court Gown (Gongyi),
late 19th century
Silk satin with embroidery, 38 x 80 in.
(96.5 x 203.2 cm)
Lent by The Metropolitan Museum of Art, Gift of John A. Bross, 1970
1970.274

During the Qing dynasty (1644–1911), especially since the eighteenth century, Chinese theater costumes developed an extremely elaborate system. Specified by type, opera costumes and accessories were highly stylized and coded, conveying messages about an individual character's identity and quality that were embedded in the associated role-type. For example, a demure female type wore a dark robe, which distinguished her from the young maiden type, who typically wore colorful embroidered robes, while a coquettish type, usually in the role of a maid, courtesan, or shrewish lower-class woman, wore a blouse-and-trousers ensemble. In Chinese opera where stage settings were simple and sparse, the costume played a central role in creating visual spectacle. While the imperial court no doubt commissioned the most luxurious opera costumes, wealthy merchant households and influential commercial troupes competed with the court fashion for extravagance and opulence.

This theatrical robe with ornate decorations would have made a dazzling showpiece. Over a simple cut with a round neckline and central opening, layers of densely embroidered froufrou in bright colors largely conceal the red satin garment beneath. Three tiers of shoulder pieces cut in a curved *ruyi* shape—known as "cloud shoulders" (*yunjian*)—extend over the upper body and are further accentuated by a circular neckpiece. The enlarged sleeves, each featuring nine thin stripes in alternating shades of yellow, green, pink, blue, red, orange, etc., are joined to the main body by a thicker band with blue and white embroidery on a dark ground. Below the waistband, which is stitched in folds to create a wavy pattern, the skirt consists of two layers, each formed by a number of narrow, short streamers with pointed tips. Their alternating colors and embroidery echo those of the sleeve bands. A long panel embroidered with peony, dragon, and sea wave motifs, is draped on the center of the skirt. In addition, tassels and jade pendants adorn the shoulders and skirt. The style of the robe does not resemble contemporary Manchu or Han dress but represents a free adaptation

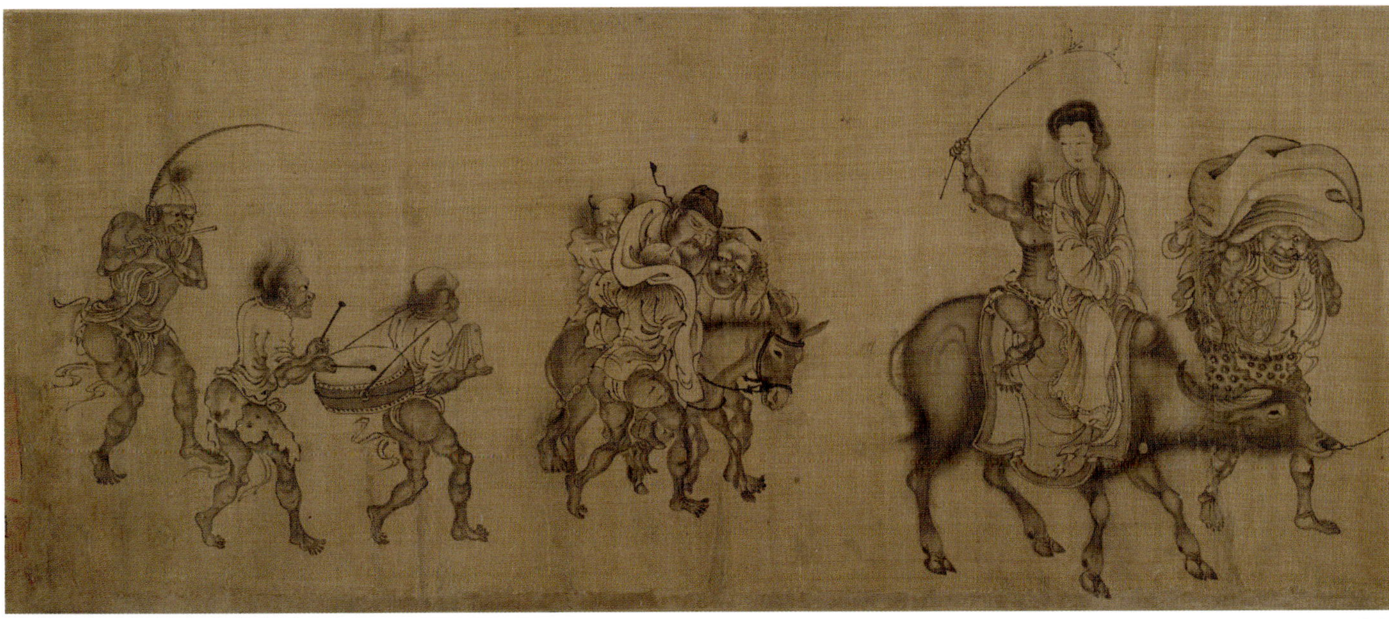

Detail

of female ceremonial gear of the Ming dynasty (1368–1644) with additional fanciful details.

Termed a "court gown" (*gongyi* or *gongzhuang*), this type of robe in Qing opera was mainly reserved for the role of a princess. Two theater portraits datable to the late Tongzhi and Guangxu periods (circa 1870s to 1900) illustrate the princess characters in *luantan* (precursor of Peking opera) plays dressed in highly similar costumes (see figs. 3.6, 3.7). A pictorial representation of a court gown in the exhibition appears on Fourth Sister Zhang (Zhang Sijie) in the New Year print *Fourth Sister Zhang Secretly Presents Money Trees* (cat. 15). Such a costume reveals this character's true identity as the daughter of the Jade Emperor (Yuhuang dadi). The role of an imperial consort might also adopt a court gown on an informal occasion, with the most famous example being Consort Yang (Yang Guifei) of Emperor Minghuang of the Tang dynasty (618–907) performing a drunken dance in such a robe. By extension, less ornate court gowns with simpler shoulder pieces and sleeve bands were worn by female immortal and aristocratic lady roles to highlight their divine or noble identities. In addition to showcasing extravagance, abundant ornaments on a court gown would have created a spectacular visual effect when the actress was dancing or moving, with the swaying streamers, sleeves, and pendants turning into a colorful swirl.

The calf length of this robe suggests that it was to be worn over a skirt, as shown in one of the aforementioned portraits and the New Year print. In the early twentieth century, the court gown evolved into a full-length version in modern Peking opera, as seen on today's stage.[1]
—MEI MEI RADO

1 For example, see Qi Rushan, *Hangtou kuitou* [Costume and Headdress], p. 10, and *Guoju jianyan tu'an* [Brief Illustrations of Peking Opera], "Illustration of Costumes, II," Beijing: Guoju xuehui, 1935, facsimile reprint, in *Qi Rushan quanji* [Collected Works of Qi Rushan], vol. 1 (Taipei: Qi Rushan xiansheng yizhu bianyin weiyuanhui), 1964.

Cat. 7

Yan Geng
Chinese, active late 13th century
The Demon Queller Zhong Kui Marrying Off His Sister, n.d.
Handscroll, ink on silk, 9 5/8 x 99 3/4 in. (24.4 x 253.4 cm)
Lent by The Metropolitan Museum of Art, Purchase, The Dillon Fund Gift and Rogers Fund, 1990
1990.134

Zhong Kui has long captured the Chinese cultural imagination as a central figure in popular stories, folk dramas, ritual pageants, and the visual arts. He acquired legendary status during the reign of Emperor Minghuang (r. 713–756) of the Tang dynasty (619–907), when the emperor miraculously recovered from illness after dreaming of Zhong Kui expelling a malignant demon. To commemorate this event, the emperor ordered the master painter Wu Daozi (689–after 755) to paint the demon queller's portrait.[1] From that time on, portraits of Zhong Kui were believed to exorcise evil spirits. By the Southern Song dynasty

(1127–1279), images of Zhong Kui were hung on front doors during the lunar New Year, and figures costumed as Zhong Kui and his escorts paraded through the streets to simultaneously entertain and ward off evil spirits.

Various versions of Zhong Kui have collectively shaped the popular image of this legendary deity: a tragic and failed scholar in his former life; a chivalric and impetuous hero with a frightening, hideous visage; and a comic drunkard. A new character—Zhong Kui's younger sister—appeared in paintings around the tenth century,[2] and by the Southern Song dynasty, she was included in the New Year exorcising procession.[3] Although its origin is not clear, the legend of Zhong Kui marrying off his sister has been a popular subject since the thirteenth century. Representations and performances of this tale may have served as visual or corporeal reenactments of a benedictory word play, for the phrase "marrying off one's sister" (*jiamei*[a]) puns on "sending away evil spirits" (*jiamei*[b]).

This humorous handscroll by an obscure professional painter may well have been inspired by contemporary New Year street pageants. Led by a gong-beating herald and with clapper, drum, and flute players bringing up the rear, mischievous demons in the troupe show off their acrobatic skills and feats of martial prowess. Near the end of the scroll comes the climax of the procession—the beautiful bride, followed by the drunk Zhong Kui, immediately identifiable by his wobbly official hat and gourd-shaped wine container. The demons' grotesque musculature and rough clothing highlight their strangeness. Zhong Kui himself is turned into a comic caricature, his robe rendered in expressively twisting lines to suggest a state of helpless stupor.

A similar scroll from roughly the same period is the *New Year's Eve Excursion of Zhong Kui* by Yan Hui (active circa 1270–after 1324) at the Cleveland Museum of Art. Although Zhong Kui's sister does not appear in the Cleveland scroll, the two illustrations may have shared common models in painting manuals for the depiction of figures. As exemplified by Gong Kai's (1222–after 1304) painting *Zhong Kui Traveling* in the Freer Gallery of Art in Washington, DC, contemporary literati explored the theme of this legend as a means of expressing political commentary. The Metropolitan Museum and Cleveland scrolls, however, clearly demonstrate a different artistic practice, wherein inspiration and production were deeply associated with traditions of popular theatrical spectacle. —MEI MEI RADO

1 Zhou Yao (841–912), "Meng wu Zhongkui fu" [Rhymed Prose on Dreaming of the Dancing Zhong Kui], in Li Fang et al. eds., *Wenyuan yinghua* [Anthology of Excellent Literary Works] (Beijing: Zhonghua shuju, 1966), vol. 1, p. 434; Shen Kuo (1031–1095). *Mengxi bitan, bu bitan* [Brush Talks from Dream Brook, Additional Talks] (written around 1086–1093), in *Xin jiaozheng Mengxi bitan* [Newly Collated and Annotated *Brush Talks from A Dream Brook*] (Beijing: Zhonghua shuju, 1959), p. 986.

2 In *Xuanhe huapu* [Treatise on Painting Written During the Xuanhe Reign] (1120), Portraits of Zhong Kui's younger sister are listed under the repertories of several painters active in the Five Dynasties and early Northern Song, including Zhou Wenju (circa 907–975), Shi Que (active Five Dynasties-early Northern Song), and Huang Quan (903–965).

3 Wu Zimu (active circa 1240–1274), *Mengliang Lu* [Dreams of the Former Capital], in *Dongjing menghua lu wai sizhong* [Dreams of the Splendor of the Eastern Capital, and Four Other Works] (Taipei: Dali chubanshe, 1980), p. 181. See also Sherman Lee, "Yan Hui, Zhong Kui, Demons and the New Year," *Artibus Asiae* 53: 1/2 (1993), p. 211.

Cat. 8

Shanghai, Dianshizhai [the Touchstone Studio]
Chinese, Qing Dynasty (1644–1911)
Four Theater Scenes with Actors Performing for the Kangxi Emperor's Sixtieth Birthday Celebration, 1879
Photo-lithographic prints after original woodblock-printed palace (Neifu) edition of 1718, four book illustrations on facing pages, one from each volume, from *Magnificent Record of the Emperor's Birthday, First Installment (Wanshou shengdian, chuji 1–4 juan)*, 1879 edition
Loan from The East Asian Collection, University of Chicago Library
2789.3213

On April 11, 1713, the day before his sixtieth birthday, the Kangxi emperor (r. 1662–1722) made a symbolic homecoming from his Garden of Joyous Spring (Changchun yuan) in the northwestern suburbs of Beijing to the Forbidden City. Elaborate festivities were set up along the entire nine or so miles (fifteen kilometers) of his route, including a remarkable array of open-air stages for opera performance. To commemorate the celebration, the emperor ordered his court painters to create a visual record of the procession. The huge painting they prepared under the supervision of Wang Yuanqi (1642–1715)—two handscrolls of color on silk some 262 feet (80 meters) long—was completed in 1717. The panoramic processional scenes of this painting were in turn painstakingly carved on woodblocks and included in an enormous book of written tributes titled *Magnificent Record of the Emperor's Birthday* (*Wanshou shengdian*), which was printed by the palace in 1718.[1] Images of the birthday celebration were not made accessible to the general public, however, until 1879 when the Dianshizhai print workshop in Shanghai took advantage of the new technology of photolithography to bring out a cheap

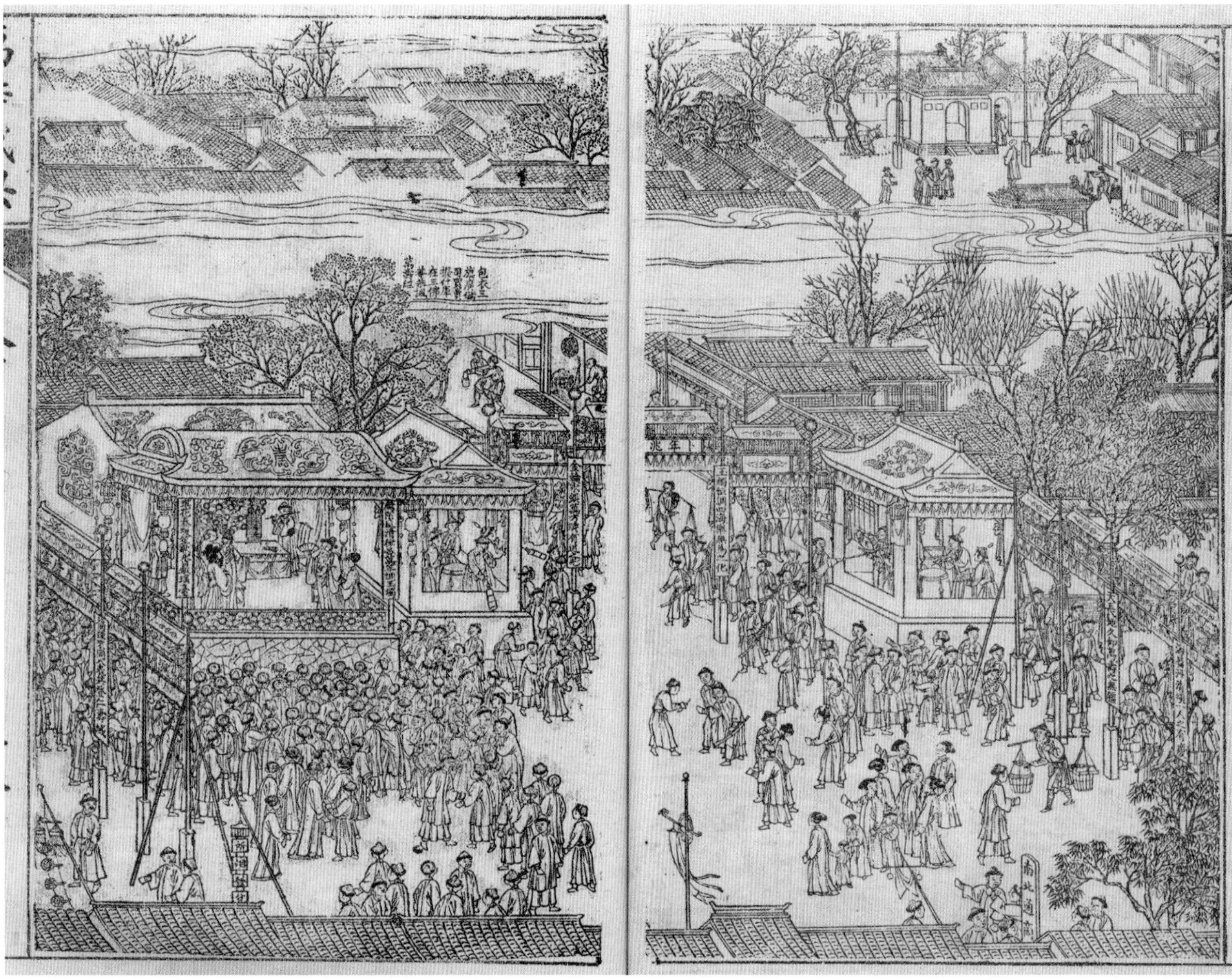

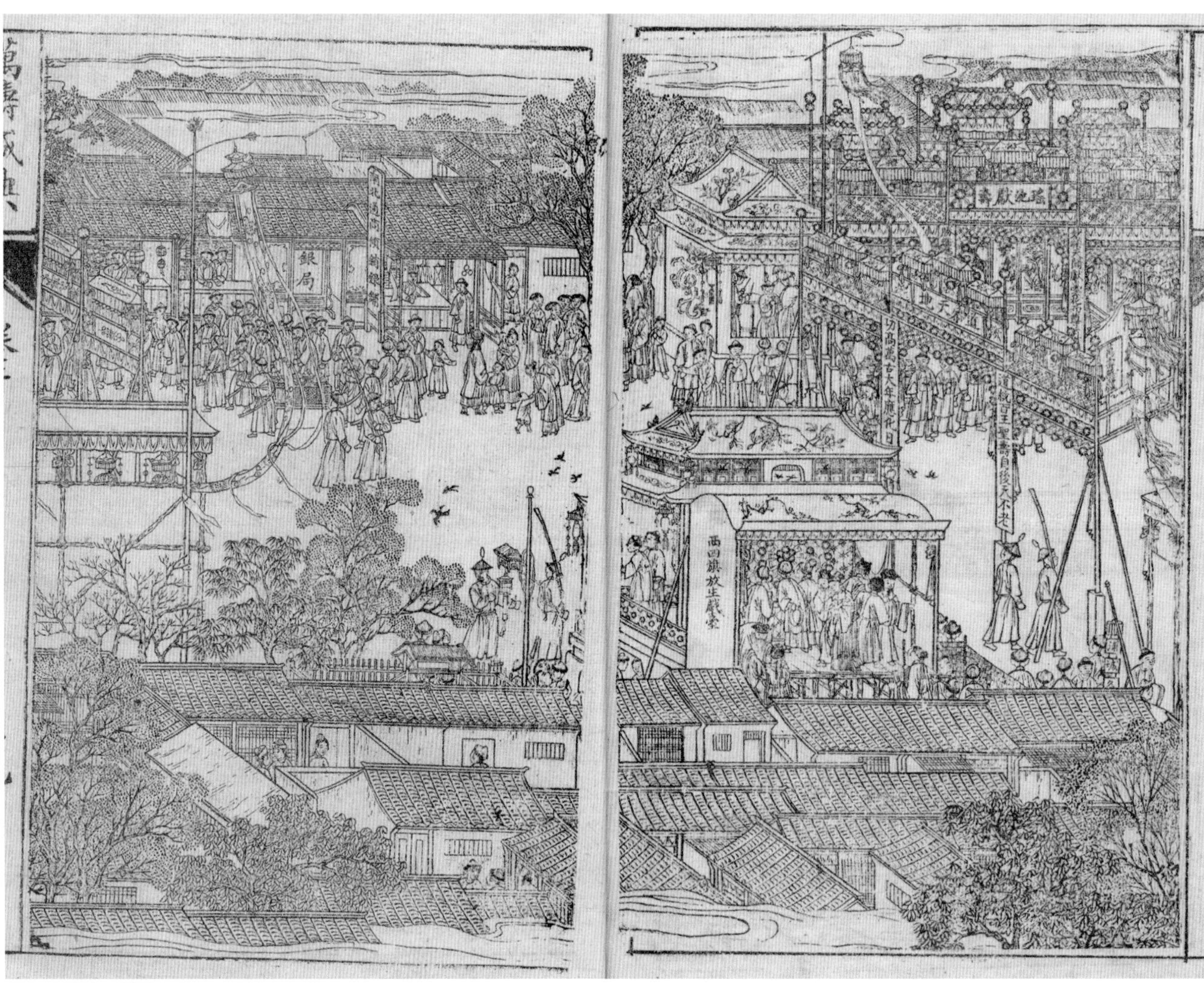

8.1 (top) and 8.2 (bottom)

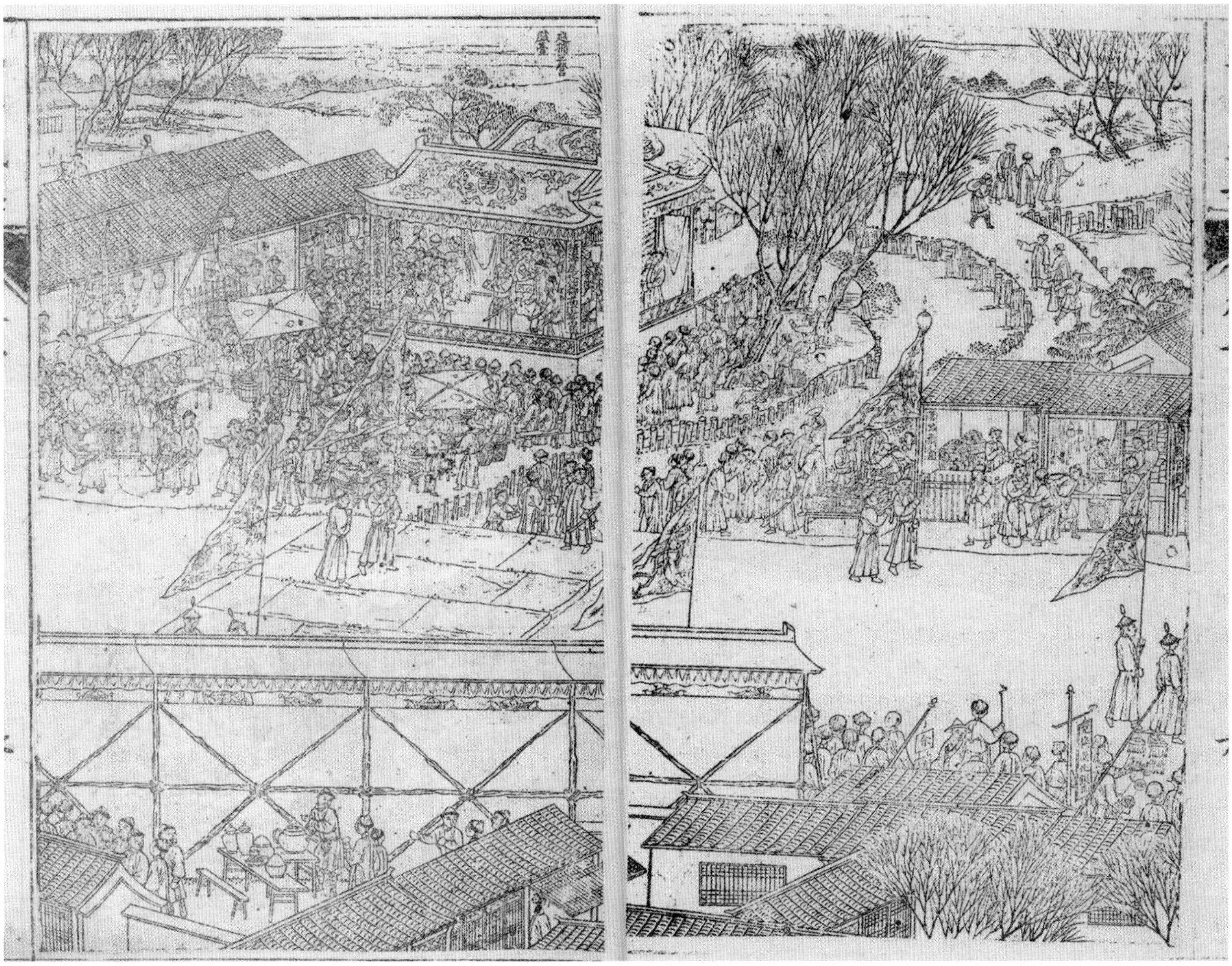

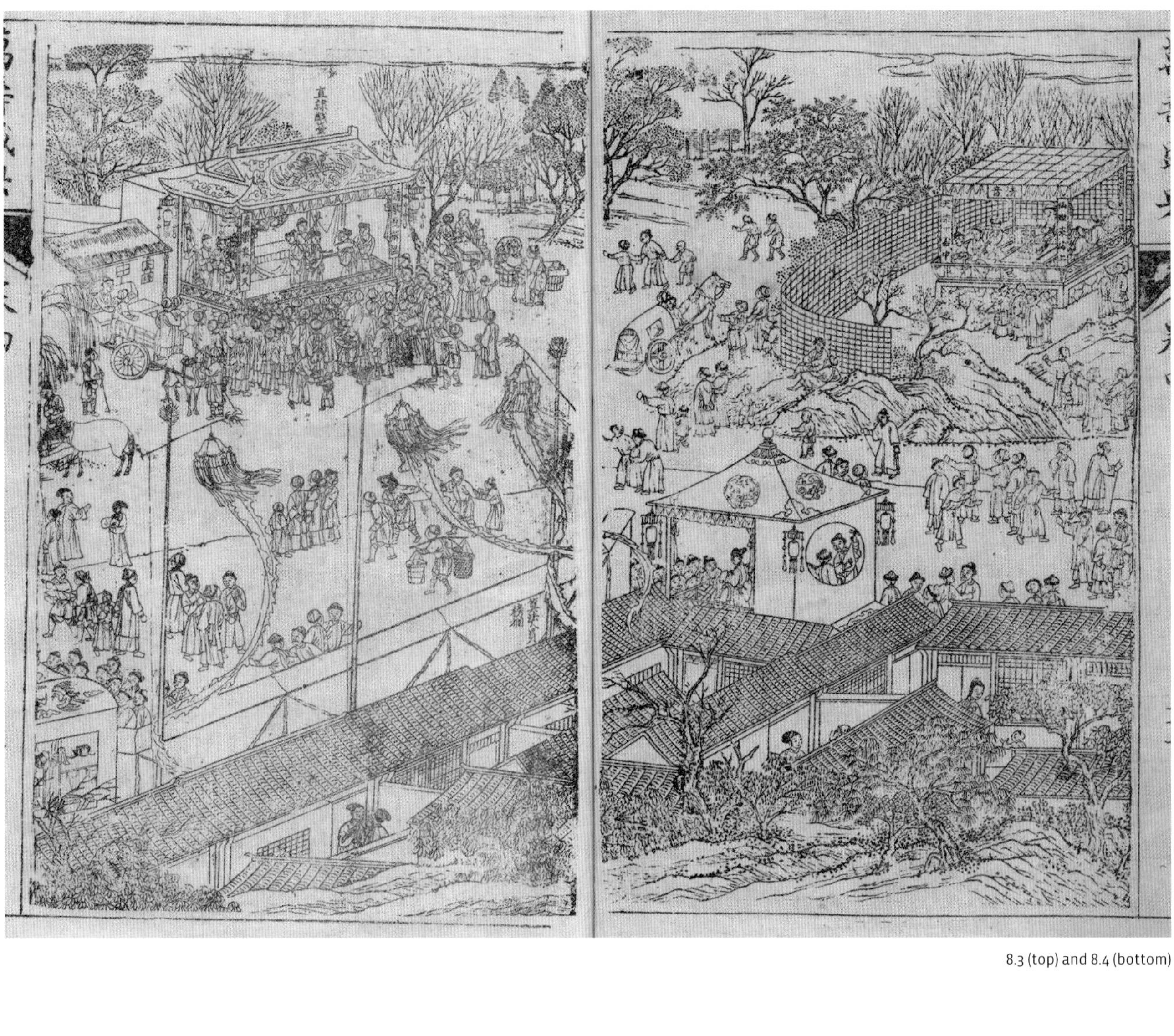

8.3 (top) and 8.4 (bottom)

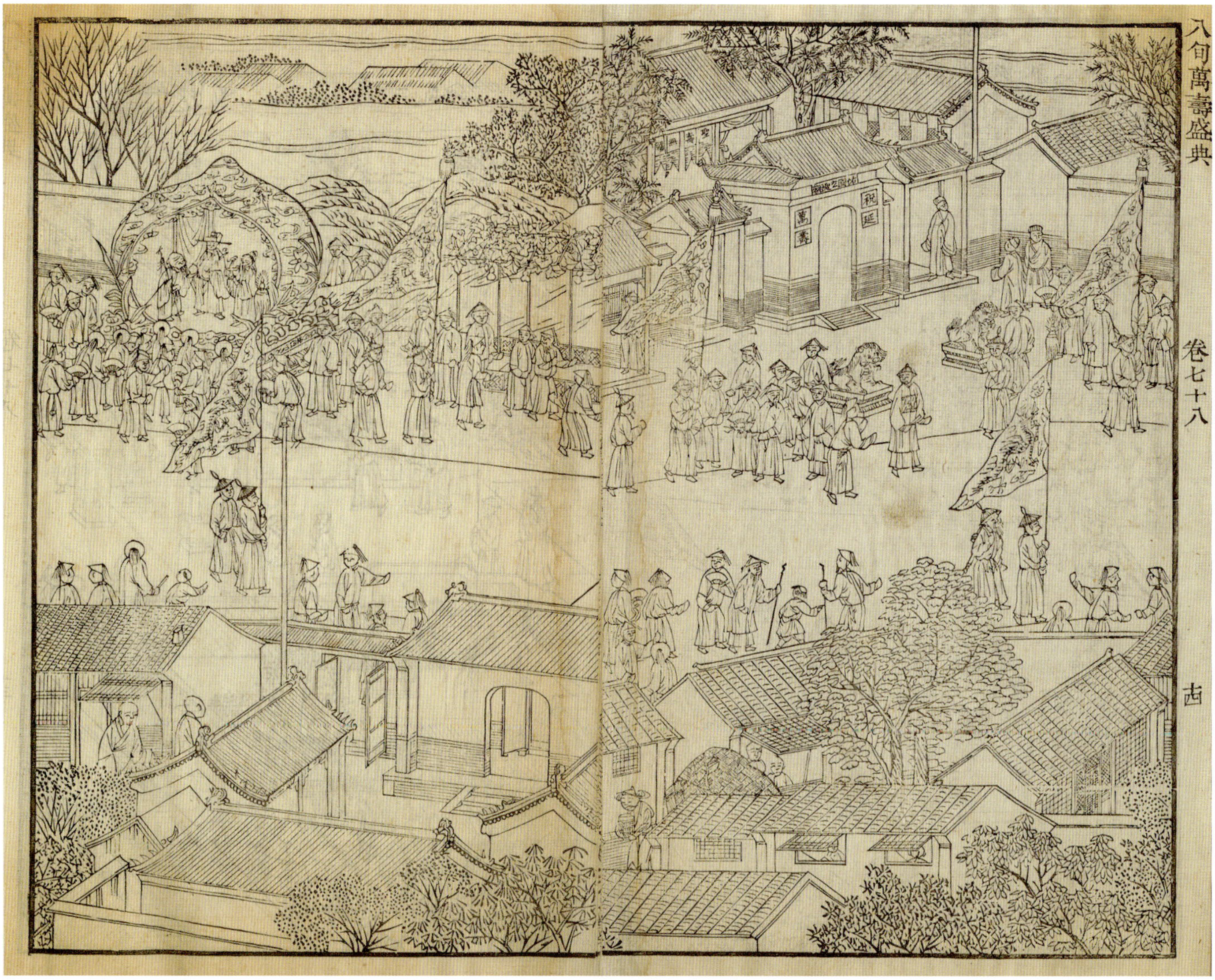

9a

pocket edition based on the palace imprint *Magnificent Record of the Emperor's Birthday, First Collection* (*Wanshou shengdian, chuji*). All four string-bound booklets in this miniature edition are included in the exhibition.

For symbolic reasons, pictures of an imperial homecoming to the capital conventionally show the procession going from left to right, that is, opposite to the right to left direction in which Chinese scrolls and books are traditionally read. This means both the handscroll and print versions of the Kangxi birthday pictures open from inside the Forbidden City, the journey's endpoint, and close with the Garden of Joyous Spring, the journey's starting point (see Judith T. Zeitlin's introduction in this catalogue).

Booklet I. The lively illustration selected from the first booklet (cat. 8.1) presents a full frontal view of an elaborate stage draped with cloth painted with auspicious symbols and couplets. A performance of *Drinking Tea* (*Chi cha*), a popular excerpt from the Kun opera repertory, is in full swing.[2] Adapted from *The Cry of the Phoenix* (*Mingfeng ji*), an influential Ming dynasty (1368–1644) historical drama denouncing the crimes of the corrupt grand secretary Yan Song (1480–1565), the scene on stage shows two groups of actors playing officials with a flute accompanist standing upstage. A group of spectators, mainly men, but also including some women and children, mill about on the street, watching the performers, talking among themselves, and shopping. Musical ensembles are playing on two smaller stages, while a Buddhist temple complex is visible in the background.

Booklet II. In the illustration from the second booklet (cat. 8.2), a backstage view of the theater sponsored by the Buddhist Releasing Life Society of the Western Fourth Bannerman Regiment (Xi siqi fangsheng xitai) dominates the right side of the page (on this stage see Zeitlin's introduction) along with a series of ceremonial gateways.[3] On the opposite side of the page, city folk congregate in front of a bank and pawnshop in the background while we glimpse some household interiors and their inhabitants in the foreground.

Booklet III. The illustration from the third booklet (cat. 8.3) shows a stage sponsored by the Three Constable Brigades of the Capital (Xunbu sanying xitai), which straddles the page divide. On the left, the stage is embedded in a cluster of little food stalls and outdoor cafes with customers seated under umbrellas or seated on benches to enjoy the show. On the right, spectators are standing under some trees and watching the play, while further right a grain shop and a money-changing stall are doing a brisk business.

Booklet IV. The illustration from the fourth booklet (cat. 8.4) shows a theater sponsored by Zhili province (today mostly subsumed into modern Hebei province) on the top of the left hand page. A performance of the "Startled by

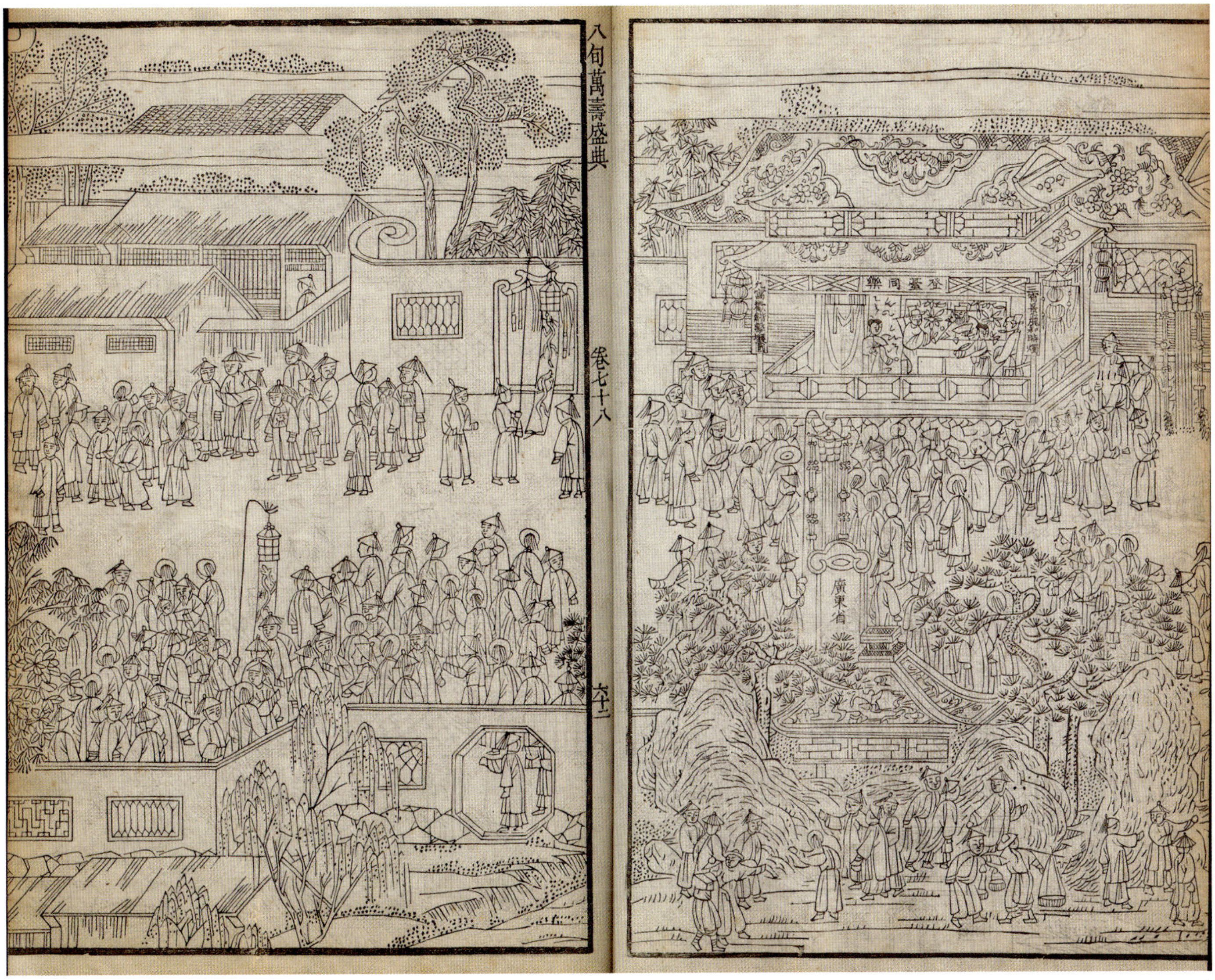

9b

Beauty" scene from *Romance of the Western Chamber* (*Xixiang ji*) is in process.[4] On the right, Student Zhang, flanked by the Abbot, is holding a fan as he gazes toward Oriole, who is modestly shielding her face with a fan as her maid Crimson stands besides her. A string accompanist is partly visible behind them. On the left side of the stage, two more musicians are seated; the one in front is striking a drum while behind them someone backstage is lifting the entrance door curtain and peeking out. We glimpse a partial view of the backstage of another theater on the bottom left of the page, but only a few hats and beards and some male spectators are visible. On the right side page two more stages can be seen. In the upper right hand corner a musical ensemble is playing in one that bears the placard "Pure Tones" (*qingyin*), while the mid ground offers a sideways view of an actor performing on another stage, with a male pipa player visible through a cutout on the back wall. As befits a suburban panorama, more draft animals, carts, and foliage add to the relaxed atmosphere of this final scene. —JUDITH T. ZEITLIN

1 See Maxwell K. Hearn's entry in *China: the Three Emperors,* ed. Evelyn Rawski and Jessica Rawson (London: Royal Academy of Arts, 2005), entry 243, pp. 391–92. A sequence from *Copy of the Kangxi Emperor's Sixtieth Birthday Celebration, Scroll One,* is reproduced on pp. 100–05.

2 The scene is identified in Zhu Jiajin and Ding Ru'qin, *Qingdai neiting yanju shimo kao* (Beijing: Zhongguo shudian, 2007), color plate 6.

3 Releasing Life Societies were dedicated to freeing living creatures like birds or fish in order to gain karmic merit.

4 This scene is identified and described in Zhu Jiajin, "Wanshou tu zhong de xiqu biaoyan xieshi [Realistic Depiction of Theater Performance in the Birthday Scrolls], in Zhu Jiajin ed., *Gugong tuishi lu* [Collected Essays upon my Retirement from the Palace Museum] (Beijing: Beijing chubanshe, 1998), vol. 2, p. 489.

Cats. 9a–b

Chinese, Qing Dynasty (1644–1911)
Street Theaters with Actors Performing for the Qianlong Emperor's Eightieth Birthday Celebration, 1792
Two woodblock book illustrations on facing pages, from volume two of the woodblock book *The Magnificent Ceremony for Longevity of Ten Thousand Years, Celebrating the Eightieth Anniversary* (*Baxun wanshou shengdian*), 1792 palace (Neifu) edition
Loan from The East Asian Collection, University of Chicago Library
T2829.8024

The Kangxi emperor's sixtieth birthday festivities launched a vogue for imperial birthday processions commemorated in paintings, notably for his grandson the Qianlong emperor (r. 1736–1795), whose own eightieth birthday received the same fanfare on September 21, 1790.[1] Like his grandfather, Qianlong also had the events depicted on a two-scroll painting of his birthday celebration and then finely carved on woodblocks and printed as two volumes of a huge commemorative book of tributes. Qianlong's book was titled *The Magnificent Record of the Emperor's Eightieth Birthday* (*Baxun wanshou shengdian*) and published in a palace (Neifu) edition in 1792 (cat. 8). The second volume of the pictures in this edition—depicting the suburban leg of the procession from Qianlong's famous Garden of Perfect Brightness (Yuanming yuan) to the Due West Gate (Xizhi men) of the city of Beijing—is in the exhibition.

The imperial birthday festivities are regarded as milestones in the history of Chinese opera for facilitating cross-pollination between different regional genres and the introduction of commoner (*minjian*) styles into the palace. Qianlong's eightieth birthday, in particular, is hailed as the founding event in the creation of Peking opera, which developed out of the synthesis that emerged after troupes from Anhui province, who had come for the celebration, stayed on permanently in the capital.

Compared to the Kangxi birthday pictures, however, the Qianlong birthday pictures illustrate fewer stages, and the spectators consist primarily of officials. Although the pictures do include some shop scenes, the street scenes are generally more subdued, while in keeping with an overall stricter decorum, women are shown only in domestic interiors and do not mingle publicly with the men outside.

The first illustration in the volume on view (cat. 9a: chapter 78, pp. 13b–14a) shows a theater fancifully designed in the shape of a peach, the symbol of long life, with auspicious cloud images adorning the outside of this unusual structure. On the stage inside, the ceremonial opera *Three Heavenly Stars of Happiness, Wealth, and Longevity* (*Fu, Lu, Shou*) is underway. The old man with an outsize bald forehead who is leaning on a staff and proffering a large peach is the God of Longevity. In the middle, clad in the costume of a high official and holding a long *ruyi* scepter is the God of Happiness, while next to him stands the God of Wealth, with an auspicious *lingzhi* fungus in his hand. In the foreground, a Buddhist monastery stands open with two Buddhist monks visible inside the compound.

The second illustration (cat. 9b: chapter. 78, pp. 61b–62a) depicts a large theater sponsored by Guangdong province and set inside a garden landscape of rockery and pines. With its double roof and hipped gables, the theater looks much more solidly built than the comparable structures seemingly made of wood and cloth in the Kangxi birthday pictures. The scene on stage shows three scholars or officials sitting at a table as two female characters entertain them. A group of male spectators surround the stage, most of them with their backs to us. On the opposite page, near a curved wall cunningly shaped like a scroll, officials stand around in clumps, while a larger group of officials stands in front of another zigzag wall. —JUDITH T. ZEITLIN

1 See Maxwell K. Hearn's entry in *China: the Three Emperors,* ed. Evelyn Rawski and Jessica Rawson (London: Royal Academy of Arts, 2005), entry 25, pp. 392–93. A sequence from *The Qianlong Emperor's Eightieth Birthday Celebration, Scroll Two,* is reproduced on pp. 106–09.

Cat. 10

Chinese, Qing Dynasty (1644–1911), Shunzhi Period (1644–1661)

Gu-Shaped Vase with Courtesans Rehearsing a Scene from "Startled by Beauty" (Part 1, Act 1) from Romance of the Western Chamber (Xixiang ji), ca. 1645–55

Porcelain with underglaze blue and white decoration, height: 17 5/16 in. (44 cm), diameter at rim: 8 1/16 in. (20.5 cm), diameter at base: 5 29/32 in. (15 cm)

The Butler Family Collection

This blue and white vase produced at Jingdezhen in the form of an ancient ritual bronze vessel called a *gu* is divided into three registers, with a design of tapering veined leaves on the bottom and an arrangement of cut flowers and fruit—peony, lotus, and pomegranate—in the middle. But it is the unusual figurative scene on the large upper register that dominates our attention.

Four costumed performers in a southern-style garden are rehearsing an opera scene on a simple salon-type stage, which is made of a light blue rug spread on the ground enclosed by a white screen on three sides. On another side of the vase, two male musicians, a transverse flute (*dizi*) player, and a percussionist are accompanying them. The presence of the clothes draped on the rack beside the rug and the absence of any audience indicate that this is a dress rehearsal; the book placed on the table behind the flutist—most likely a script or songbook—subtly reinforces the point.[1]

The scene they are performing is "Startled by Beauty" from *Romance of the Western Chamber* (*Xixiang ji*). (See Ni Yibin's essay and the play's synopsis in this publication.) The male character in the peaked triangular hat raising his finger in the air is the abbot. He has just been showing the temple grounds to Student Zhang, the male lead, who is doffing a fan, his back turned to the viewer, as he gazes at Oriole, the female lead,

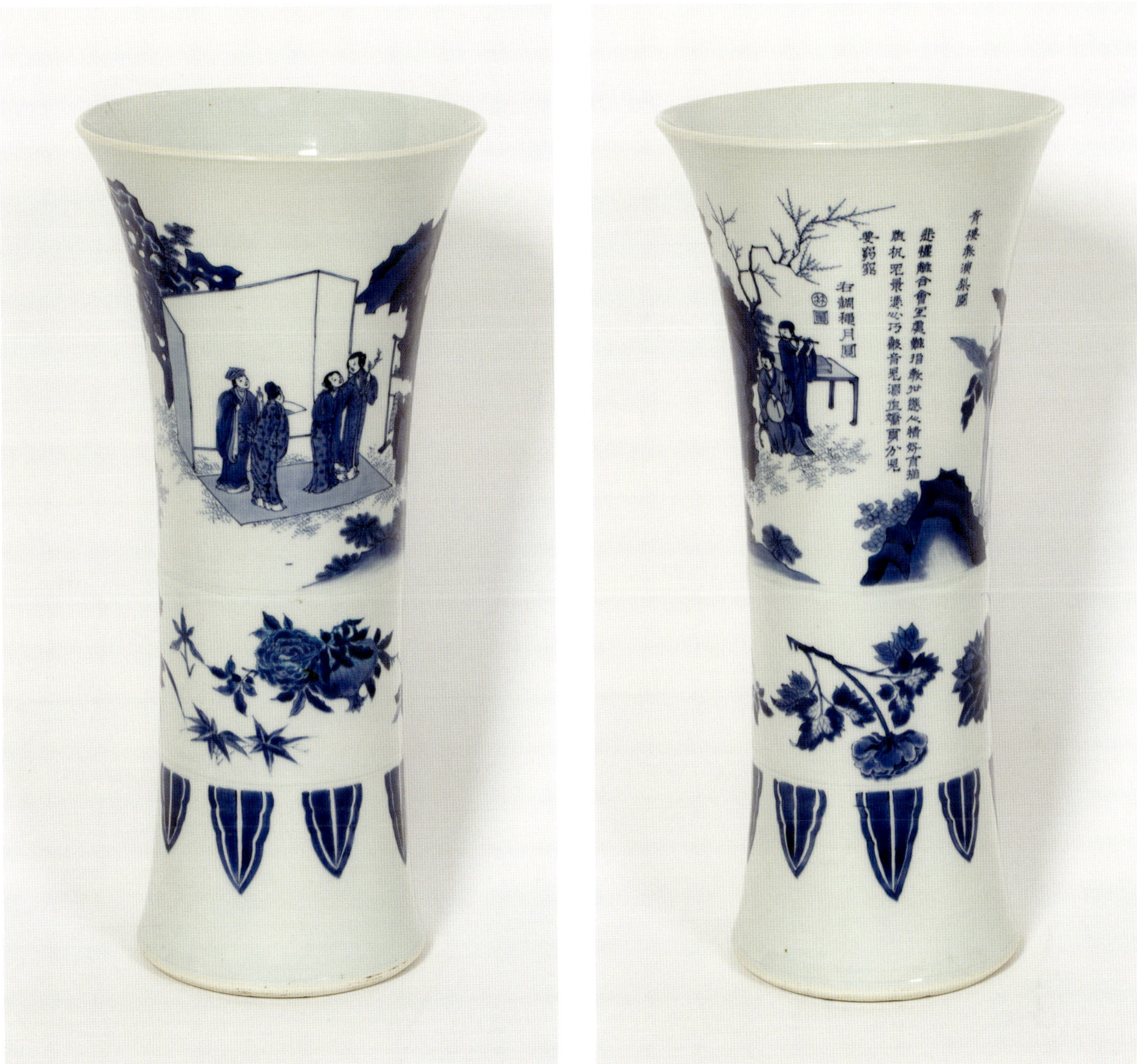

10

with whom he has fallen in love at first sight. Oriole, the tall female figure, is holding a sprig of flowers as she gazes back at him. Her maid Crimson (conventionally pictured as smaller than her mistress) is looking up at her quizzically as she leans in protectively to shield her from the men.

The scene is being performed as Kun opera, which the inclusion of the flute player—the signature instrument in this musical genre—unmistakably indicates. The austere elegance of the garden setting with its towering scholar rocks, banana trees, and unadorned "pure screen" all connote the prestigious refinement of literati taste, which was closely associated with Kun opera, the theatrical entertainment of choice for the elite during this period.[2] Such elegant gardens were not only constructed in upper-class homes but were also characteristic of top courtesan houses, which catered to this clientele. By the mid-seventeenth century when this vase was made, however, these markers of literati discernment had been largely assimilated into popular taste.

To the right of the musicians, the lyrics to a short aria are inscribed in clerical script calligraphy. The aria is set to the tune "Full Autumn Moon" (Qiuyue yuan) and titled "Courtesans Practice the Art of the Theater" (Qinglou jiaoyan liyuan).[3] By this time, the professions of courtesan and actor had essentially bifurcated, though they remained linked. The thrust of the inscribed aria is to blur the boundaries between the two since both professions require mastering the arts of deception and expediency. Underlying the lyrics is the commonplace notion in this period that "all the world's a stage." The analogy here implies criticism of the false, hypocritical roles that the respectable people (especially literati and officials) assume, making them no better than debased actors or courtesans.[4]

The aria goes:[5]

Where joy and sorrow, parting and reunion[6] resonate—that's hard to teach.
But the ways of the world and human feelings are easy to portray.
Just act as the situation demands and rely on your quick wit.
Make your voice sweet and your postures graceful.

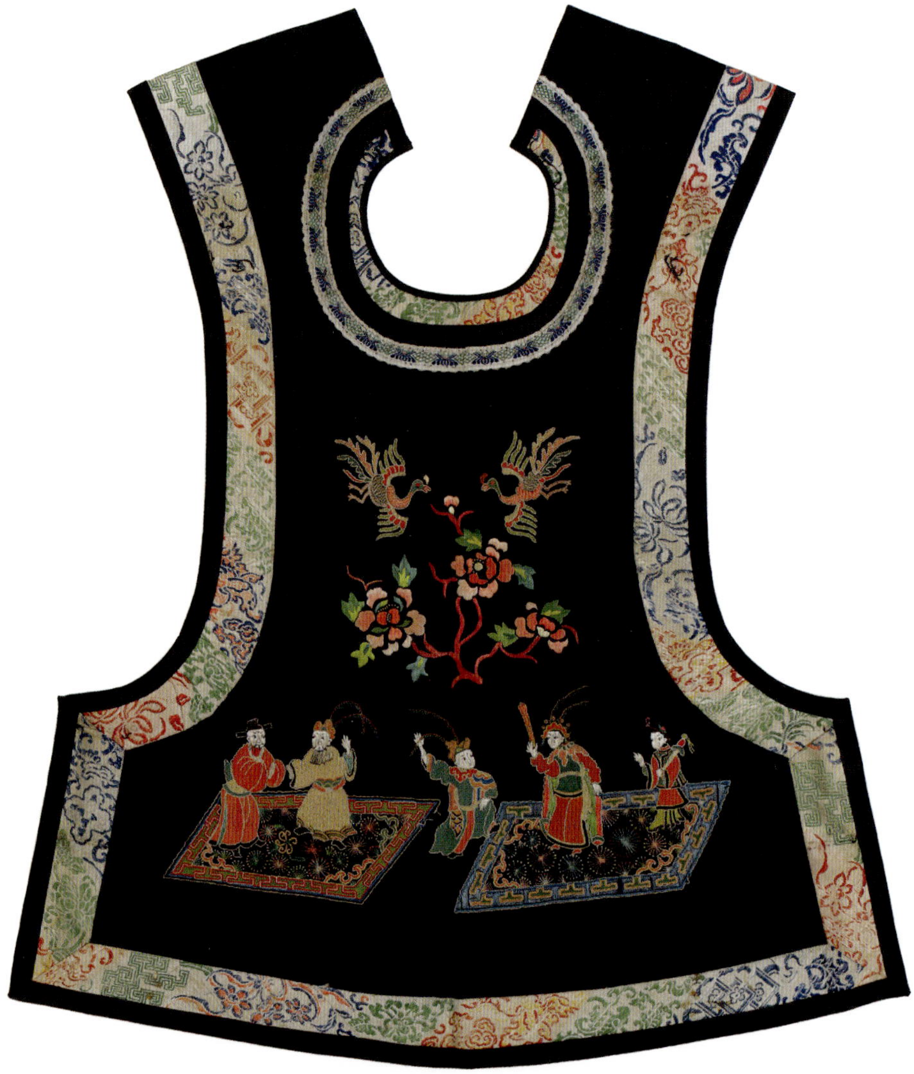

Underneath the inscription, two small seals in the same clerical script appear, the character for "bamboo" (*zhu*) set inside a circle and the character for "shadow" (*ying*) set inside a square. This insignia is found on other porcelain wares produced at Jingdezhen from the 1640s to 1660s and, like a logo, probably identified the kiln that produced them.[7]—JUDITH T. ZEITLIN

1 Judith T. Zeitlin, "'Notes of Flesh' and the Courtesan's Song in China," in *The Courtesan's Arts: Cross-Cultural Perspectives*, eds. Martha Feldman and Bonnie Gordon (Oxford and New York: Oxford University Press, 2006), pp. 92–94.

2 On the "pure screen" as a motif in literati paintings that is transported into the popular realm in the late sixteenth century, see Wu Hung, *The Double Screen: Medium and Representation in Chinese Painting* (London: Reaktion Books, 1996), pp. 183–87.

3 The title is deliberately ambiguous since the term for practice (*jiaoyan)* means both "to rehearse" and "to instruct" while the poetic term used for "courtesans"—Green Bower (*qinglou)*—also means "a courtesan house" and the poetic term for "the theater"—Pear Garden (*liyuan*)—also means actors. So the title might also be understood to imply "Actors Rehearsing in a Courtesan House" or "Courtesans Instruct Actors How to Act."

4 On this theme , see Sophie Volpp, *Worldly Stage: Theatricality in Seventeenth-Century China* (Cambridge, Mass.: Harvard University Asia Center, 2011).

5 The Chinese characters for the inscribed aria are 青樓教演梨園_悲歡離合會宜處，難指教。世態人情好自描。隨機兒景憑心巧，聲音兒須作嬌，身分兒要窈窕. 右調秋月圓.

6 The phrase "joy and sorrow, parting and reunion" is commonly used to describe both the abrupt workings of fate and the twists and turns required of a dramatic plot.

7 Qianshen Bai, "Inscriptions, Calligraphy, and Seals on Jingdezhen Porcelains from the Shunzhi Era," in *Treasures from an Unknown Realm: Shunzhi Porcelain, 1644–1661*, eds. Michael Butler, Julia B. Curtis, and Stephen Little (Alexandria, Va.: Art Services International, 2002), p. 61.

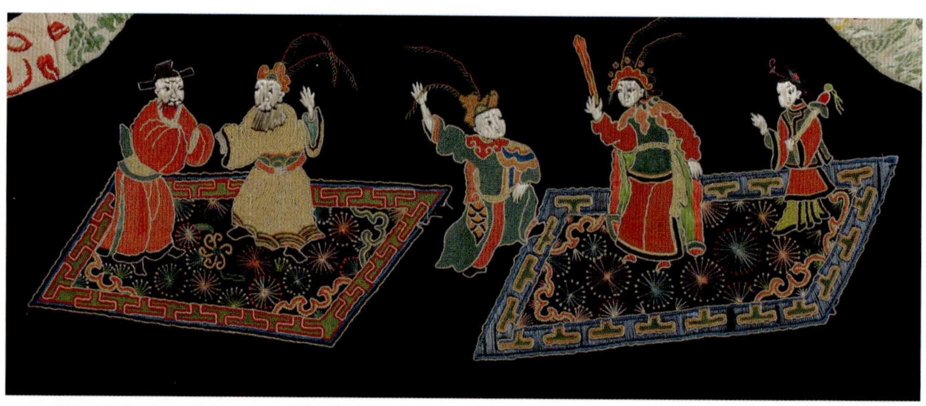

11

Cat. 11
Shanxi Province
Chinese, Qing Dynasty (1644–1911)
Woman's Apron with Two Scenes Performed on Rugs from Fortress with a Beaded Curtain (Zhulian zhai), n.d.
Embroidered textile in the knot stitch (*dazu xiu*) technique, 24 3/4 x 22 in. (63.5 x 55.7 cm)
Courtesy of the Division of Anthropology, American Museum of Natural History
70.3/6800

For a discussion of this work see essay 4 in this volume, "Representing Theatricality on Textiles" by Yuhang Li.

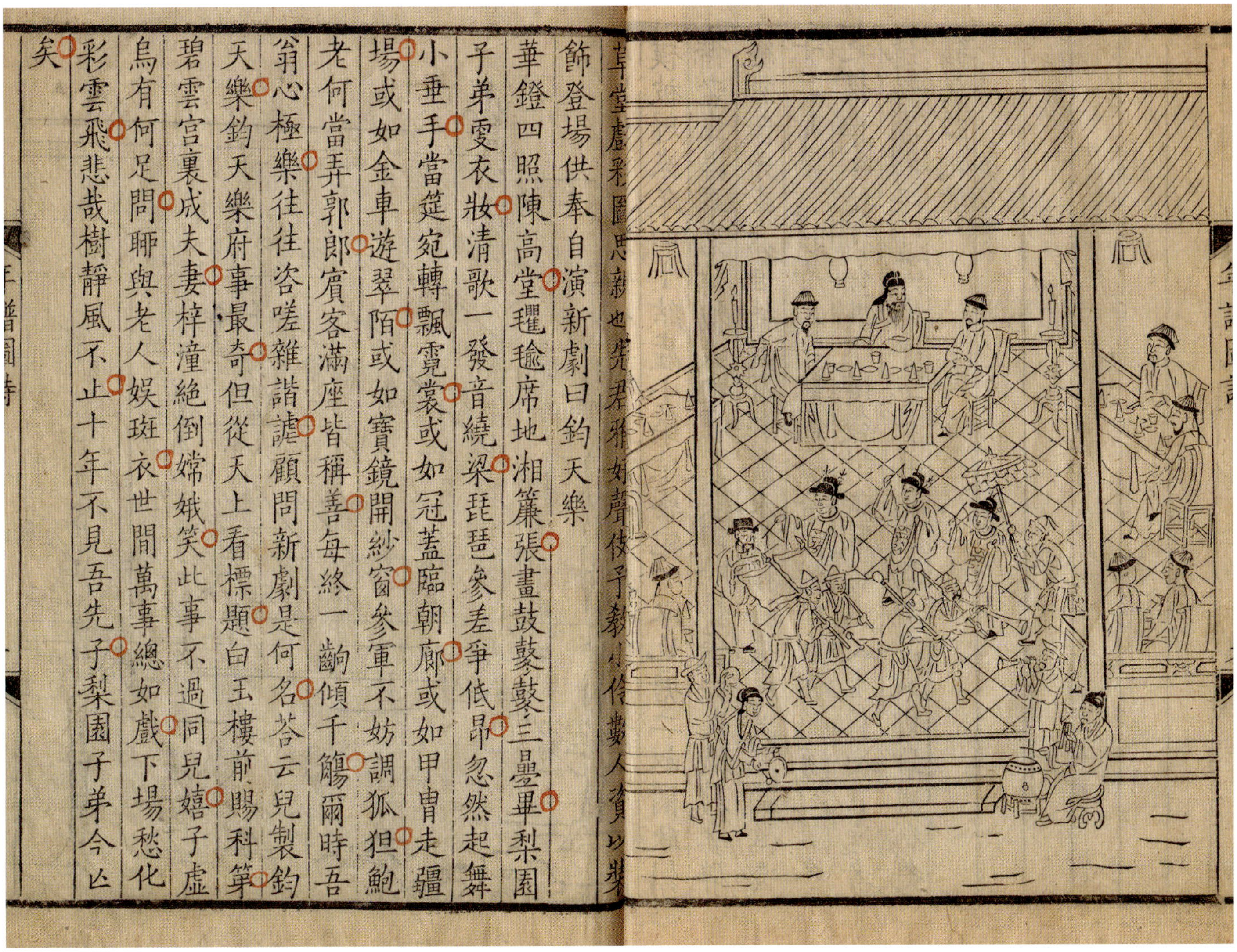

草堂戲綵圖思親也先君雅好聲伎予教小伶數人資以裝
飾登場供奉自演新劇曰鈞天樂
華鐙四照陳高堂氍毹席地湘簾張畫鼓鼕鼕三疊畢梨園
子弟變衣妝清歌一發音繞梁琵琶參差爭低昂忽然起舞
小垂手當筵宛轉飄霓裳或如冠蓋臨朝廊或如甲冑走疆
場或如金車遊翠陌或如寶鏡開紗窗參軍不妨調狐狸鮑
老何當弄郭郎賓客滿座皆稱善每終一齣傾千觴爾時吾
翁心極樂往往咨嗟雜諧謔顧問新劇是何名荅云兒製鈞
天樂鈞天樂府事最奇但從天上看標題白玉樓前賜科第
碧雲宮裏成夫妻梓潼絕倒嫦娥笑此事不過同兒嬉子虛
烏有何足問聊與老人娛斑衣世間萬事總如戲下場愁化
彩雲飛悲哉樹靜風不止十年不見吾先子梨園子弟今亡
矣

Cat. 12

You Tong, author and possible illustration designer
Chinese, 1618–1704
Filial Entertainment in the Thatched Hall: The First Performance of Celestial Court Music (*Juntian yue*), possibly 1694–1722
Woodblock book text and illustration on facing pages from *An Autobiography in Pictures and Verse* (*Nianpu tushi*) included in *The Complete Works of You Tong* (*Xitang quanji*), Qing dynasty, possibly Kangxi reign (1694–1722) edition, box 4, booklet 20, pp. 9b–10a
On Loan from The Joseph Regenstein Library, University of Chicago
T5445.1982

This picture is part of an unusual illustrated memoir created by the distinguished playwright, poet, and historian You Tong (1618–1704), who was also a devotee of Daoism. He selected sixteen important moments or aspects of his life, and then made or commissioned a drawing and wrote an accompanying poem for each of them. The autobiography bears a preface dated 1694, which probably means that it was completed when You Tong was already in his late seventies and published not long afterward. The scene here shows the 1657 premiere of his play *Celestial Court Music* (*Juntian yue*) being performed as a Kun opera for his father at the family home in Suzhou. This romantic comedy (*chuanqi*) of thirty-two acts is divided into two distinct parts. Part 1 takes place in the corrupt contemporary world and culminates with the hero's failure at the civil service examinations, the death of his beloved, and his suicide. Part 2 shifts to heaven—the paradise of wish fulfillment—and reverses all the injustices and tragedies of part 1 to produce the happy ending required of the genre: success in the examinations, marriage, and in this case, immortality for hero, heroine, and his friends to boot.

The illustration shows the opera being staged for guests at a private banquet with a household troupe of actors, the kind of theatrical entertainment most common among the Chinese elite during this period. Within the hall the spectators are seated at tables arranged in a semi-circle, with the head table placed in the center at the back. The central figure at the head table, in a black hat and bushy beard, must be You Tong's father, with You Tong sitting next to him, probably to the right. In the middle of the room the actors are performing the beginning of part 2, the triumphant procession in heaven for the hero who has taken first place in the celestial examinations. We recognize him as the figure on the left because of the two sprigs adorning his scholar's hat—a sign of the top graduate. He is wearing an official robe and holding a whip to symbolize that he is on horseback. The other two actors costumed in scholar's hats and official robes and holding whips are his friends, the winners of second and third place in the examinations. Various extras in peaked caps wield pennants, a canopy, and a long trumpet (*laba*) as props to fill out the procession. Below, the orchestra is playing the raucous music appropriate for a parade: on the left, cymbals and gong, and on the right, drum, clappers, and the Chinese oboe (*suona*).

You Tong captions the picture "Filial Entertainment in the Thatched Hall: Thinking of My Father" (*Caotang xicai tu: Si fu*). Not surprisingly, his accompanying text is deeply nostalgic as he remembers his dead father at an event that had taken place nearly forty years before. The poem supplies details missing from the visual representation of the scene and vividly evokes for us the delights of watching a private opera performance at a literati banquet during the early Qing dynasty. The last two lines allude to the commonplace notion of the world as a stage but he gives it a Daoist spin, so that death, our exit from the theater of life, holds the hope of an entrance onto another transcendent realm of existence.

The full text is translated below:

> My late father deeply loved the opera. I outfitted a small troupe of actors to put on a performance of my new play in his honor, which was entitled *Celestial Court Music*.
>
> Brightly colored lanterns are strung, lighting the main hall.
> On the floor the performing rug is spread, the speckled screens are set.
> Rat-a-tat-tat! The painted drum strikes three times.
> Here come the actors of "The Pear Garden"[1] clad in costume.
> Once the singing starts, the pure tones soar "around the rafters,"[2]
> As the notes of the pipa's *tremolo* jump from high to low.
> Suddenly the dance of "Dangling Sleeves" begins,
> Twirling and swirling, "Rainbow Skirts" flutter at the feast.[3]
> At times it's as though high officials are attending court,
> At times like warriors in armor running on the battlefield.
> At times like a gilded carriage traveling over green paths,
> At times as though a mirror is uncovered at my lady's window.
> The adjutant has license to tease the female lead and the official
> So why can't the play-leader play tricks on the clown?[4]
> From their seats all the guests shout "Bravo!"
> At the end of each act they drain a thousand cups.
> At that time my father, how overjoyed he was.
> He kept sighing with admiration mixed with amusement.
> "What is this new play called?" he asks
> I reply: "*Celestial Court Music*, composed by your son."
> In *Celestial Court Music*, the most amazing events transpire!
> The civil examinations are given in Heaven.
> The top degrees are awarded in the White Jade Tower.
> Hero and heroine are wed in the Blue Cloud Palace.
> The Divine Lord of Letters bursts out laughing, the Moon Goddess is in stitches.[5]
> This story is nothing more than a childish game.
> No need to ask whether it's of the "Sir Fantasy" or "Mr. Nonexistent" type.[6]
> It was just something I did to amuse my aged father.
> Everything that happens in this world is like a play.
> When we exit the stage, sorrow vanishes and rainbow clouds fly.
>
> How sad! The trees stay still but the wind never stops. Ten years already since last I saw my father. The actors too are dead and gone now.

—JUDITH T. ZEITLIN

1 "Pear Garden" (Liyuan) alludes to the musical entertainment division at the eighth-century court of the Tang emperor Xuanzong, and is a common literary term for an acting troupe during the Ming and Qing.

2 There is a story in the third-century *Book of Liezi* about a female singer whose voice was so powerful that the notes lingered "around the rafters" for three days. The phrase is a cliché used to describe fine singing.

3 Both "Dangling Sleeves" (Xiao chuishou) and "Rainbow Skirts" (Nishang) are famous Tang dynasty court dances. Here these allusions also nicely evoke the graceful movements of the actors' flowing sleeves and skirts on stage.

4 You Tong is showing off his erudition by using archaic role-type names from Tang, Jin, and Yuan dynasty drama. The "adjutant" (*canjun*) is a comic butt role from early farces; the character written for "female lead" (*dan*) is an obscure variant; and the *gu*, the role of an official in Yuan drama, is written as *hu*, another archaic variant. Both "play-leader" (*baolao*) and "clown" (*guolang*) are archaic Song dynasty role-types associated with the puppet theater.

5 "The Divine Lord of Letters" is Zitong, the Daoist god Wenchang, who is in charge of examinations and official posts. "The Moon Goddess" is Chang'e, who is also associated with the examinations because in Chinese mythology a cassia tree grows on the moon and "breaking off the cassia branch" is a poetic metaphor for passing the exams.

6 "Sir Fantasy" (Zixu) and "Mr. Nonexistent" (Wuyou) are the names of allegorical characters in a prose-poem by Sima Xiangru (circa 179–117 BCE), and came to signify playful fictional writing.

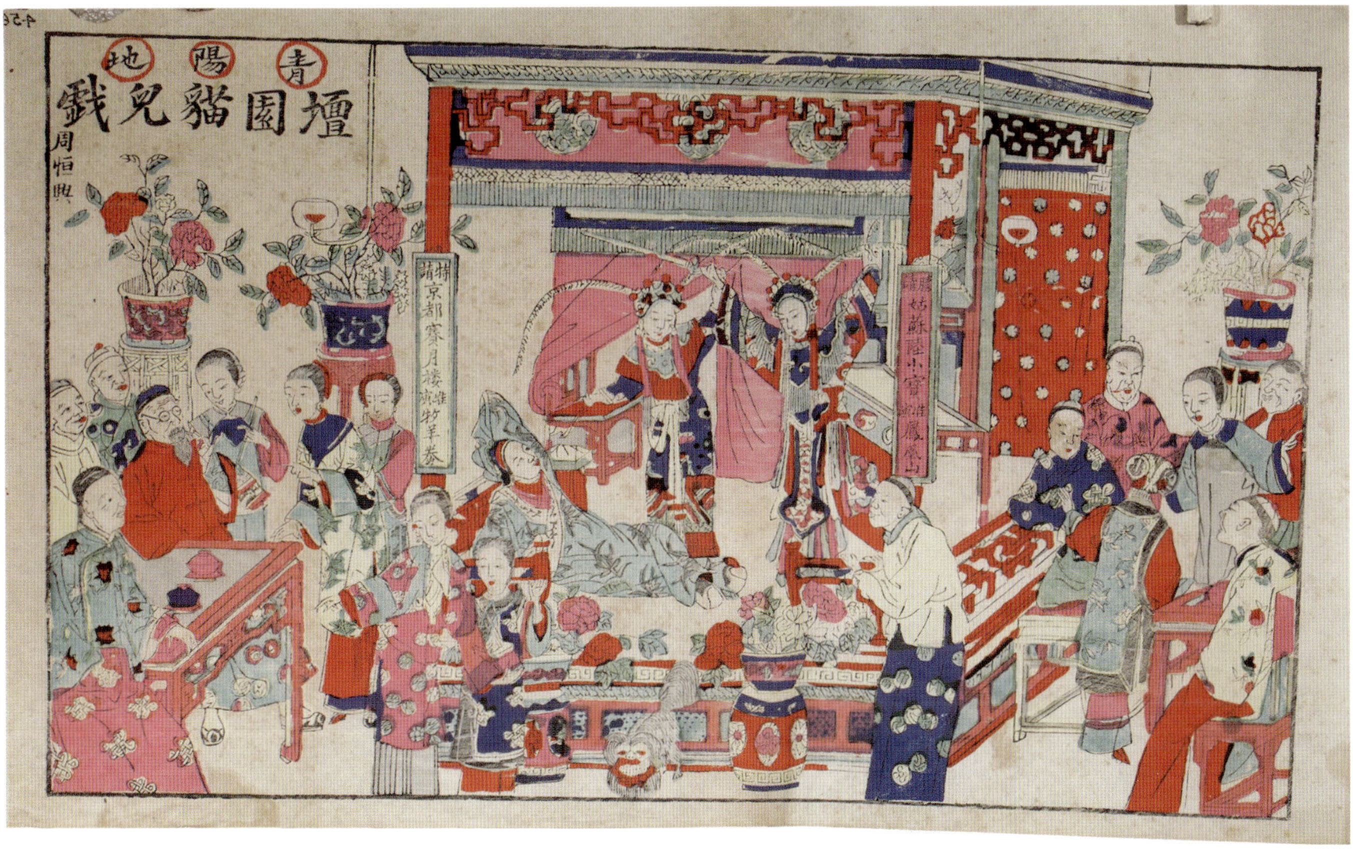

Cat. 13

Shanghai, Zhou Hengxing (print workshop)
Chinese, Late Qing Dynasty (1644–1911)
Pussycat Opera at Tan Garden, 1902
Polychrome woodblock print, 21 7/16 x 12 13/32 in. (54.5 x 31.5 cm)
Courtesy of the Division of Anthropology, American Museum of Natural History
70/4561 A59

This New Year print (*nianhua*) was purchased by Berthold Laufer in 1902. As with other popular woodblock prints in the Taohuawu style, a palette of bright colors—hot pink, red, yellow, blue, and azure—dominates. A three-part inscription identifies the type of opera and performance venue: "Pussycat Opera at Tan Garden" (Tanyuan Mao'er xi); location: "Qingyangdi" (in red circles), the Japanese Concession in Suzhou; and the name of the workshop that made the print: "Zhou Hengxing" (in small vertical characters), which, like other Suzhou printmakers, had moved their operations to Shanghai after the Taiping Rebellion (1850–64). Pussycat Opera was an all-female theater that became fashionable in the late Qing, especially in the Shanghai area. It was performed on small temporary stages in courtesan establishments and private homes as well as in public theaters.

At the center of the print is a rectangular stage with an elaborately decorated base, a short balustrade, two red columns, and blue upper beams. A pair of partly open pink curtains hanging in the middle of the stage may indicate not so much backstage space as an available empty room. The first half of the couplet on the left column advertises, "By special invitation, Sai Yuelou from Beijing will perform *The Morality Tale of a Shepherdess* (*Muyang juan*)," while the second half of the couplet on the right column boasts, "[We] successfully invited Lu Xiaobao from Gusu [Suzhou] to perform *Phoenix Mountain* (*Fenghuang shan*)."

The opera being performed on the stage is *Broken Bridge* (*Duanqiao*) from *The White Snake* (*Baishe zhuan*), in which the pregnant White Snake is trying to protect her husband Xu Xian from being killed by her maid Green Snake for having previously betrayed the two women, both snake spirits in human form. (See Judith T. Zeitlin's introduction and Bo Songnian's essay in this catalogue.) The actress playing the young male lead is lying on the ground in a theatrical pose while the actress playing the female lead White Snake grabs the wrist of the actress playing Green Snake, who menacingly brandishes her sword.

The performance is clearly taking place in a courtesan establishment, with up-to-date gas lamps lit on either side of the stage to indicate a nocturnal setting. As described in Han Banqing's contemporaneous novel *The Sing-Song Girls of Shanghai* (*Haishang hua*), the picture's composition emphasizes the intimacy and eroticism of Pussycat Opera performances. There is no clear boundary between the performing space and the audience. A small dog is frolicking in front of the stage. The male spectators are sitting, standing, and lounging freely, accompanied by beautiful young women, who are dressed in the chicest late-Qing Shanghai fashion as they flirt and wait on the men. A man standing in a pale jacket holds onto the stage railing while two other men in blue and pink robes lean casually against it. Few of those attending the opera focus on the stage. The man sitting in the right corner is watching the performance, but the two men by the railing are looking at the women in the opposite direction. The actions of the young women also contribute to the sensuality of the atmosphere: the woman on the right holds out a water tobacco pipe while the one on the left seems to be unbuttoning the top of her jacket. —NAIXI FENG

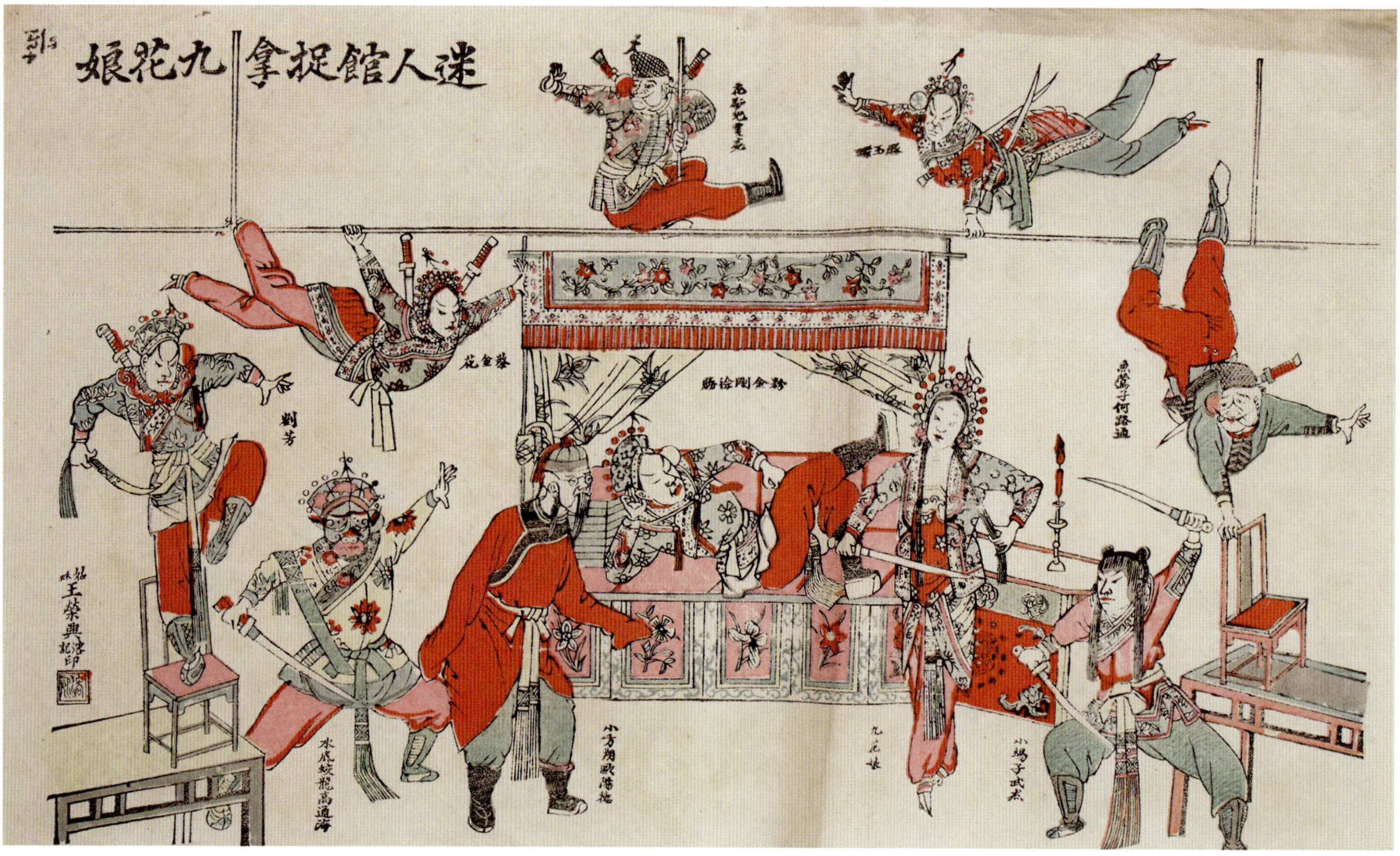

14

Cat. 14

Shanghai, Wang Rongxing Rongi (print workshop)
Chinese, Late Qing Dynasty (1644–1911)
Seizing Lady Nine Flowers at the Tavern of Delusion (*Miren guan zhuona Jiuhua niang*), 1902
Polychrome woodblock print, $21\frac{13}{16} \times 12\frac{13}{32}$ in. (55.5 × 31.5 cm)
Courtesy of the Division of Anthropology, American Museum of Natural History
70/4561 A14

For a discussion of this work see essay 5 in this volume, "Operatic Images in Popular New Year Prints" by Bo Songnian.

Cat. 15

Shanghai, Wenyizhai (print workshop)
Chinese, Late Qing Dynasty (1644–1911)
Shanghai New Year Print Depicting the Opera Excerpt "Fourth Sister Zhang Secretly Presents Money Trees" (Zhang Sijie sizeng yaoqianshu), 1902
Polychrome woodblock print, $20\frac{11}{16} \times 12\frac{3}{16}$ in. (52.5 × 31 cm)
Courtesy of the Division of Anthropology, American Museum of Natural History
70/4837 A26

As the title at the top of this New Year print shows, this scene is taken from an opera excerpt called "Fourth Sister Zhang Secretly Presents Money Trees" (*Zhang Sijie sizeng yaoqianshu*). Set in the Song dynasty (960–1279), the story follows one of the Jade emperor's daughters in heaven, the goddess Fourth Sister Zhang, who longs for earthly love and descends to the mortal world, where she marries a poor scholar named Cui Wenrui. She miraculously creates money trees and brings enormous fortune to her husband's family. A local rich man, Squire Wang (Wang Yuanwai), jealous of Cui's sudden wealth, accuses Cui of stealing and has him arrested. Fourth Sister Zhang consequently breaks into jail and rescues her husband. Judge Bao investigates the case and sends the famous generals from the Yang family to capture Fourth Sister Zhang, but they fail in their attempt. Judge Bao then visits heaven to plead for help from the Jade Emperor. Eventually the Jade Emperor sends his heavenly soldiers, including the boy warrior Nezha, down to earth, but none of them can defeat Fourth Sister Zhang. Finally, the Jade Emperor's other daughters persuade their sister to give up life on earth and bring her husband back with her to the immortal world.

The historical Fourth Sister Zhang was originally the daughter of a hunter who led a thirteen-year rebellion in the Lüliang area in Shanxi during the Yuan period (1271–1368) and was killed by the Mongol government. This play is one of many myths that commemorate her posthumously. Fourth Sister Zhang's legend, however, was transposed to a different historical period and blended with several popular legends such as that of the Weaving Girl and Herd Boy, Judge Bao, the Yang Family Generals, and others. Theatrical performances of her exploits are usually based on the romantic comedy (*chuanqi*) *Story of a Heavenly Destiny* (*Tianyuan ji*) written by an anonymous playwright some

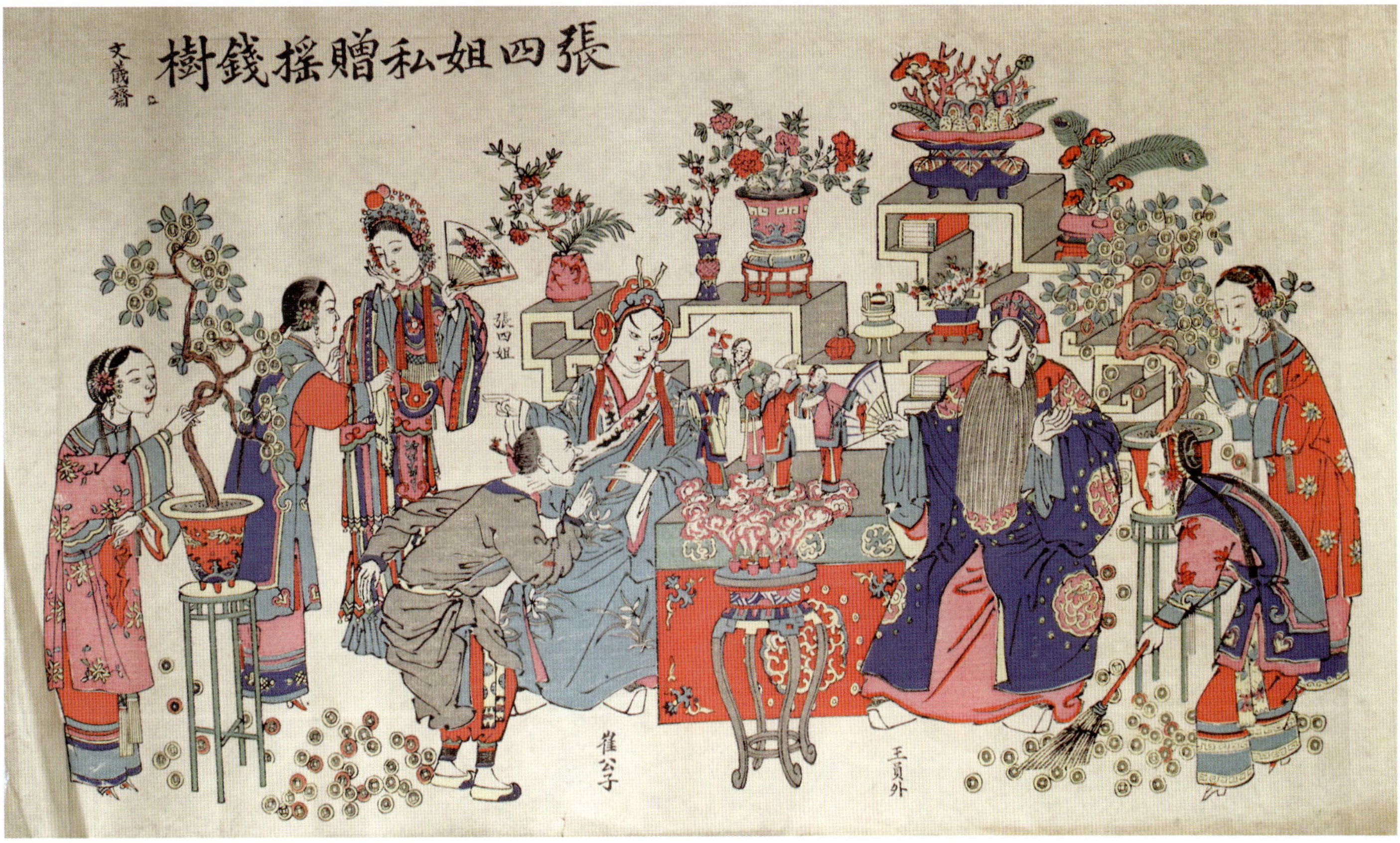

15

time during the Ming (1368–1644) and Qing (1644–1911) periods. The original play text has been lost, but legends of Fourth Sister Zhang have survived in many other popular media, including precious scrolls (*baojuan*), drum lyrics (*guci*), storytelling, Peking opera, and various regional opera genres.[1] This and the other New Year woodblock print depicting a scene with Fourth Sister Zhang in this exhibition (cat. 16) demonstrate both how this story was performed as a Peking opera in late-Qing Shanghai and how stage performance is fantasized and visualized in New Year prints.

This print depicts the moment when Squire Wang visits Cui to spy on him and witnesses various miracles at Cui's house. In the foreground on each side, two ladies in fashionable late-Qing women's jackets shake coins from potted money trees. A serving girl is busy sweeping up coins with a broom. At the back, a curio shelf laden with potted treasure plants and auspicious flowers in vibrant colors also attests to the Cui family's wealth. Sitting to the right of a square table, Squire Wang is represented as a *jing* role-type in a white painted face to indicate his treacherous personality and a long gray beard. Scholar Cui, positioned opposite Wang, is depicted as a young scholar (the *xiaosheng* role-type) with a folding fan in his left hand. He points with the index and middle fingers of his right hand to a woman standing beside him. The lady wears a colorful palace garment (*gongzhuang*), which indicates her noble status as the daughter of the Jade Emperor.

In an actual performance, Fourth Sister Zhang would probably remain offstage during this scene. After drinking wine, Cui becomes drunk. Without his wife's consent, he asks a servant to show Wang some magical cups brought by Fourth Sister Zhang from heaven. From the cups, four miniature female musicians and dancers rise on clouds and play music. Like the other women shown here, their hairdos, tiny feet, jackets, and trousers reflect late-Qing fashion. Squire Wang stares at them with his hands raised to express his astonishment. It is unlikely such a miraculous performance within a performance could have been realized on stage. Hence, this New Year print enables viewers to behold a performance that could never be realized in actual theatrical space.

This story spread widely and is represented in diverse ways in different regional New Year prints. For instance, one late-Qing New Year print from Mianzhu in Sichuan takes Fourth Sister Zhang and Cui Wenrui out of their theatrical context and uses them as symbols of wealth. Transformed into an iconic image, the money tree now occupies a prominent visual position[2] and includes two little boys—one in the tree picking coins, one standing under the tree receiving coins and presenting them to Cui Wenrui—additions that imply both prosperity and the continuity of the family line. —YUHANG LI

1 Che Xilun comp., *Zhongguo baojuan zongmu* [Catalogue of Chinese Precious Scrolls] (Beijing: Beijing Yanshan chubanshe, 2000), pp. 262–63, 375–76. Also see *Xinke Cui Wenrui Zhang Sijie nanyin quanben* [Newly Published Complete Version of the Southern Music of Cui Wenrui and Zhang Sijie], Guangzhou Yiwen tang, Danzhu tang edition, facsimile reprint in *Su wenxue congkan* [Folk Literature Series] (Taibei: Xinwenfeng chuban gongsi, 2006), vol. 460, pp. 425–80.

2 Wang Shucun, *Xichu nianhua* [Theatrical New Year Pictures] (Taibei: Hansheng zazhi she, 1990), p. 154.

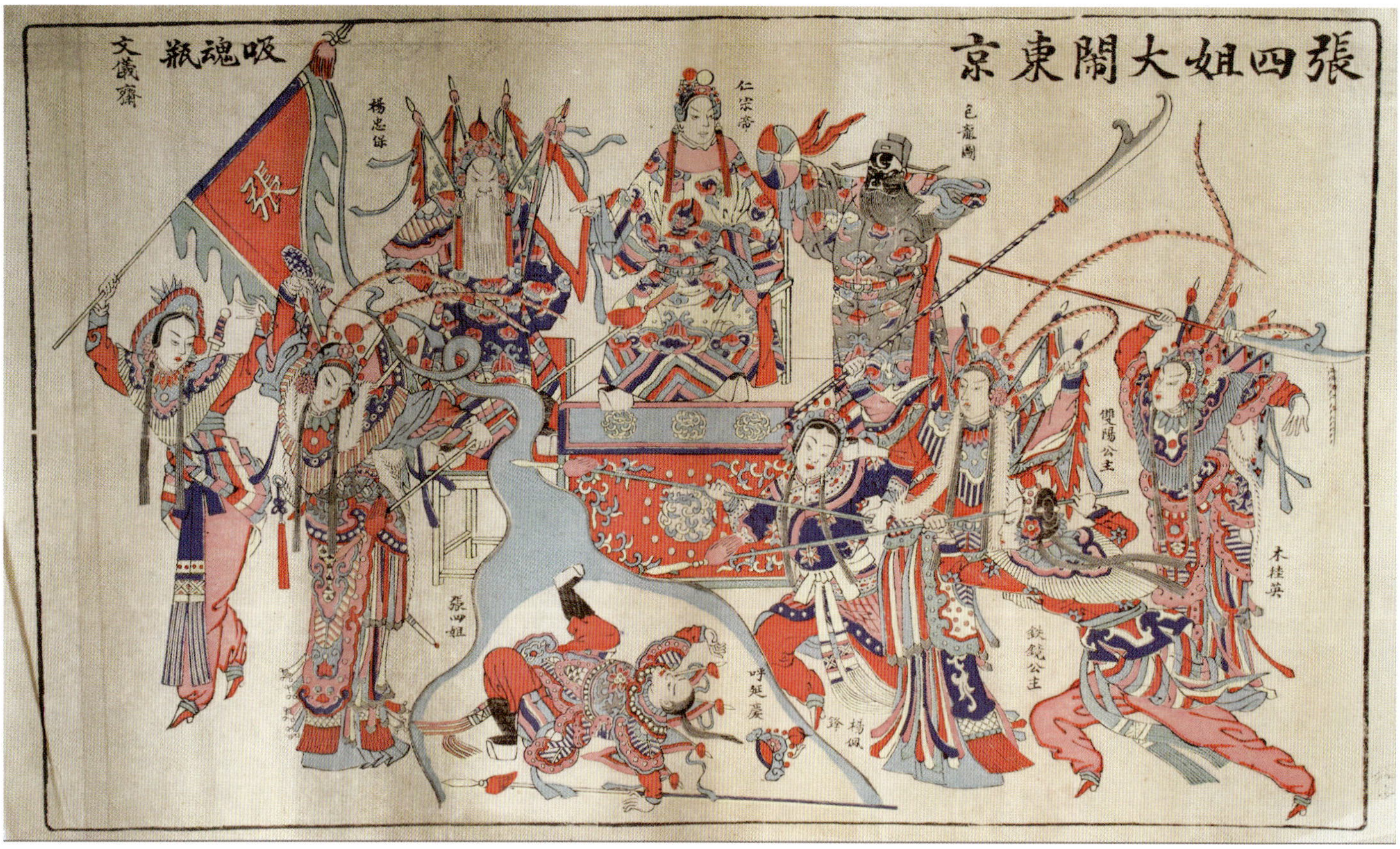

Cat. 16

Shanghai, Wenyizhai (print workshop)
Chinese, Late Qing Dynasty (1644–1911)
New Year Print Depicting "The Soul-Sucking Bottle" (Xihun ping) Scene from Fourth Sister Zhang Wreaks Havoc in the Eastern Capital (Zhang Sijie danao Dongjing), late 19th or early 20th century
Polychrome woodblock print, 20 7/16 x 12 3/16 in. (52 x 31 cm)
Courtesy of the Division of Anthropology, American Museum of Natural History
70/4837 A27

The title *Fourth Sister Zhang Wreaks Havoc in the Eastern Capital* (*Zhang Sijie danao Dongjing*) is positioned in the top right corner of this New Year print, while the subtitle "The Soul-Sucking Bottle" (Xihun ping) is inscribed in the top left in a smaller font, and the name of the print workshop Wenyizhai, runs vertically to the left of the subtitle. Wenyizhai, one of the oldest printing houses in the old Jiaochang area in Shanghai during the nineteenth century, was founded by Xiang Mengjiao, a painter from Taohuawu in Suzhou, the most influential New Year printmaking center in the lower Yangzi River during the Ming (1368–1644) and Qing (1644–1911) periods. After the Taiping rebels seized Suzhou in the 1860s, a number of New Year print studios moved to Shanghai to avoid the turmoil of the war. Both "Fourth Sister Zhang Secretly Presents Money Trees" (Zhang Sijie sizeng yaoqianshu, cat. 15, hereafter, "Money Tree") and "The Soul-Sucking Bottle" maintain Taohuawu's palette of vibrant pinks, reds, and blues. At the same time, the subject matter and pictorial composition of busy combat scenes also reflect what was then in vogue in Shanghai.

This print may not technically form a pair with "Money Tree" since their framing devices are different. In the opera, however, "The Soul-Sucking Bottle" scene does immediately follow "Money Tree." After Fourth Sister Zhang rescues her husband Cui Wenrui from prison, her seemingly heroic act alarms the Song court. Emperor Renzong (r. 1022–1063) orders his generals from the famous Yang family to capture Fourth Sister Zhang. In the background of this print, Emperor Renzong, wearing a yellow dragon robe and sitting in a chair atop a table, occupies the highest point on stage, thus indicating his status as commander-in-chief. Piling furniture upstage to represent a hill or a terrace for watching a battle (*guanzhan tai*) as depicted here is a Chinese theatrical convention (for another representation, see cat. 51). This convention enabled a few pieces of stage furniture to be economically reused for multiple functions. In the picture, Judge Bao and the chief general Yang Zongbao stand on chairs on either side of the emperor. Judge Bao is portrayed with his signature black painted face, the gauze hat of judges and prime ministers (*xiangsha mao*), and a black civil official robe. He lifts his long black beard with one hand and holds a circular prop in the other. His raised arms and the lines on his sleeves effectively express agitation. Compared to Judge Bao, Yang Zongbao (mistakenly identified by an inscription as Yang Zhongbao) seems calm. Yang Zongbao's costume looks awkward, since only his right shoulder, right arm, and the four triangle flag (*kaoqi*) on his back are regular components of a general's stage armor (*kao*). The rest of his body is clad in a cloud-patterned blue civil robe. His left arm holds the square-shaped white flag with red border typical of a commander-in-chief in the theater. It is unclear why the designer of the picture took the liberty of costuming a character in a half military-half civilian outfit that would never appear in an actual operatic performance.

Beneath these male gazes, the fighting scene in the foreground involves mostly women. Fourth Sister Zhang is second from the left. On the far left, her attendant holds a banner with the character "Zhang." Their opposing camp on the right includes Huyan Qing, the male figure tumbling to the ground in the middle, and four woman warriors, from left to right: Yang Peifeng, Princess Tiejing (Tiejing gongzhu), Princess Shuangyang (Shuangyang gongzhu), and Mu Guiying. These female martial role-types are portrayed wearing two types of costumes. The higher-ranking women warriors Fourth Sister Zhang, Mu Guiying, and Princess Shuangyang are all depicted in elaborate sets of women's armor (*nükao*). Such costuming usually includes a full-length garment consisting of several pieces with four flags affixed to the back. They are also adorned with accessories such as cloud collars edged with fringes, multicolored pastel streamers, foxtail furs, and helmets with furry balls and long pheasant feathers. The lower ranking warriors such as Zhang's attendant, Princess Tiejing, and Yang Peifeng sport the much simpler outfit of a martial woman combat fighter (*duanda wudan*), which consists of a jacket, a short waist wrapper, and trousers.

The focal point of this print is the scene between Fourth Sister Zhang and the well-known general Huyan Qing. Zhang employs her magic soul-sucking bottle against her enemy. Failing against this supernatural power, Huyan falls to the ground face up. His spear and helmet drop on the ground, and his hair loosens embarrassingly. He balances upon his left hand and foot, a theatrical gesture used to express the act of falling. His right hand and foot stretch out as if to resist the force pulling him into the bottle. Fourth Sister Zhang holds the magical blue and white bottle above her head. The ink outline and light blue color encircling Huyan Qing make manifest the bottle's invisible soul-sucking power. This depiction enables viewers to imagine that Huyan cannot escape the bottle's force. The swirling ink outline indicates the bottle's movement, possibly suggesting that, in an actual stage performance, the actor playing Zhang would sweep the bottle toward Huyan several times. In contemporary performance, the actor playing Huyan simultaneously spins around rapidly to express the soul-sucking force, and then exits the stage to indicate his disappearing into the bottle. Supernatural weapons such as the soul-sucking bottle are recurring objects in both the novels and dramas of late imperial China, and are associated with the descent of heavenly beings to the mortal world. Because of this magical weapon, Fourth Sister Zhang is undefeatable. —YUHANG LI

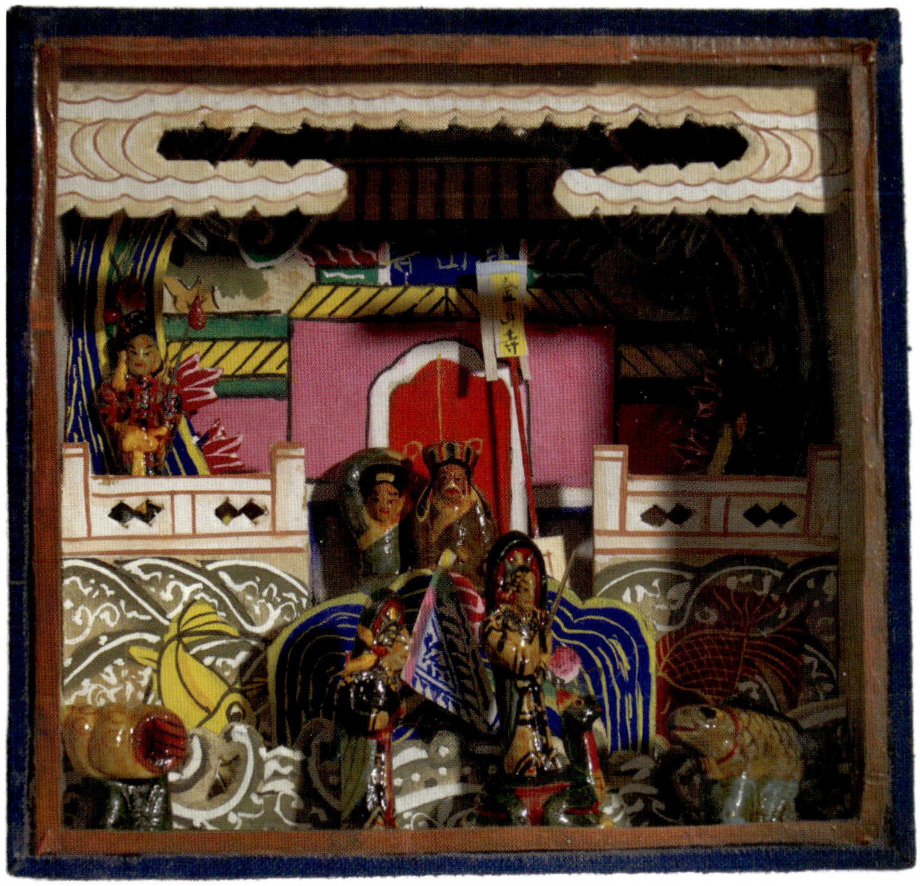

17

Cats. 17, 18, 19, 20, 21

Chinese, Late Qing Dynasty (1644–1911)

Five Opera Scene Diorama Boxes, early 20th century (1903 or before)

Cloth, wood, glass, paper, clay, lacquer, bamboo, wool, and pigment, dimensions vary

Courtesy of the Division of Anthropology, American Museum of Natural History

The American Museum of Natural History holds fifty-nine opera scene dioramas, five of which are included in the present exhibition. Acquired by Berthold Laufer in Canton in 1903, these dioramas reflect the popularity of Peking opera in the great port city, where wealthy merchants from different regions patronized various operatic traditions. Each box provides the stage for transforming a life-size, live-action performance into a memorable moment in miniature, complete with figurines in recognizable costumes and stage makeup.

Made of paper embellished with mixed media, each diorama is carefully decorated to emphasize a moment that is not so much narrative as theatrical. Brightly colored backdrops, structural features, and stage props lend a limited, stage-like depth to the scene within the diorama space. The miniature performers are sculpted from clay and painted with gold faces and brightly patterned robes. Figures playing *jing* (painted-face) role-types have patterned face paint.

Made of cheap materials, such miniature dioramas were ephemera, and no other boxes of this exact type have come to light. A comparable example is a set of twenty-eight opera-themed diorama boxes in Pingyao, Shanxi province. The Pingyao boxes were made in 1904, but are much larger[1] than those from Canton and are of much higher quality. A named craftsman produced the dioramas at the behest of a Pingyao paper shop for display in a public municipal space during the Lantern Festival (on the fifteenth day of the first lunar month).[2]

It is unclear for what purpose the Cantonese dioramas were made—perhaps as souvenirs, display items, or even toys—but viewers would have been able to recognize the scene featured in each box by virtue of a small placard labeling the opera, the figures' costumes and gestures, stage props, and backdrops. Since each box has a glass cover that opens, viewers could play with the mini theater inside and appreciate the scene at close hand. —NAIXI FENG

Cat. 17

Opera Scene Diorama Box: Water Battle Scene also known as Gold Mountain Temple (Jinshan si) from The White Snake (Baishe zhuan)
2 9/16 x 4 15/16 x 17/32 in. (6.5 x 12.5 x 11.5 cm)
70/10974

This diorama depicts the water battle scene from *The White Snake* (*Baishe zhuan*), a popular play known as *Gold Mountain Temple* (*Jinshan si*) in the Peking opera tradition. The pregnant heroine White Snake and her maid Green Snake lead an army of sea creatures to rescue White Snake's

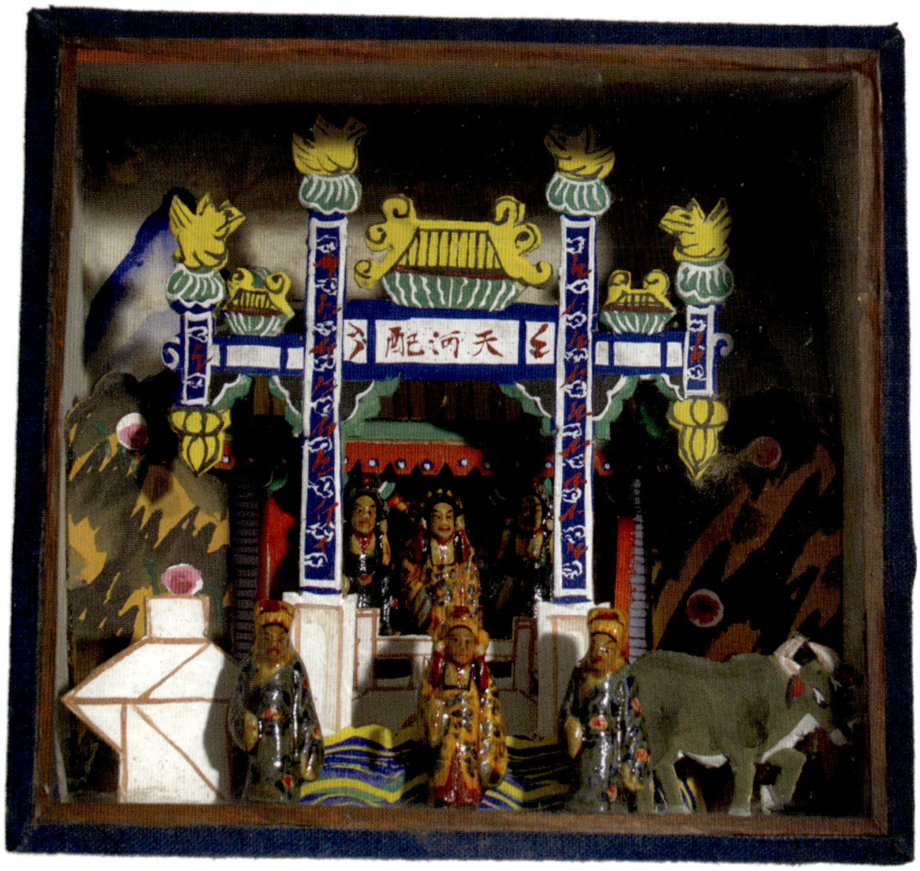

18

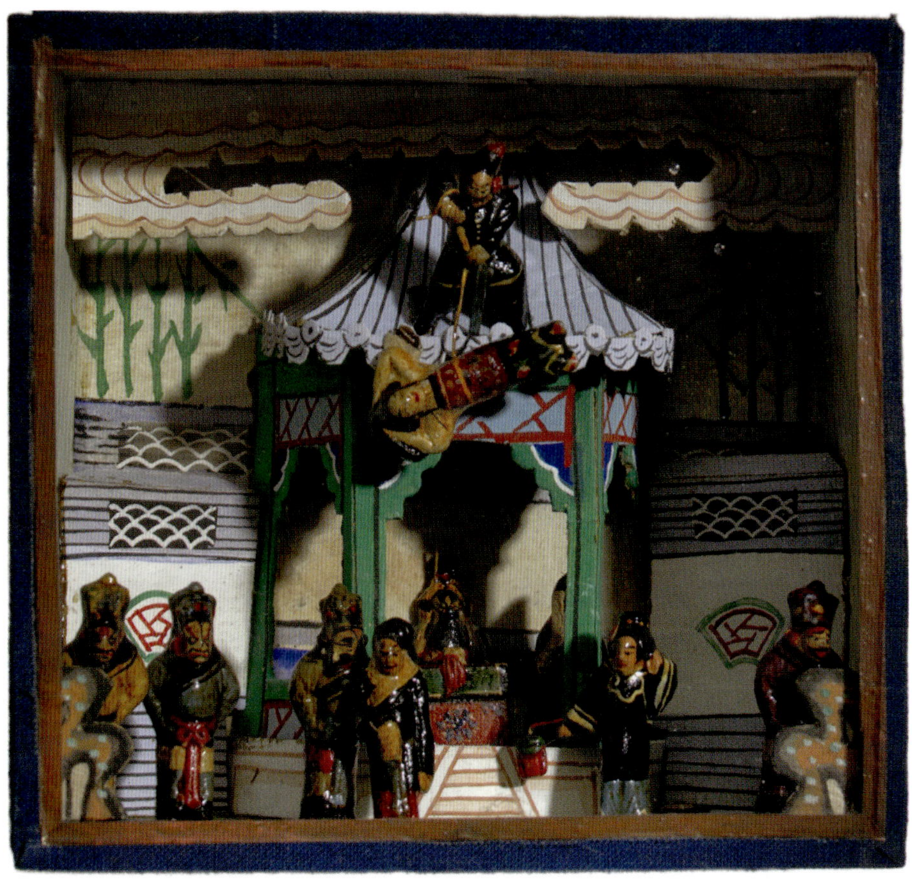

20

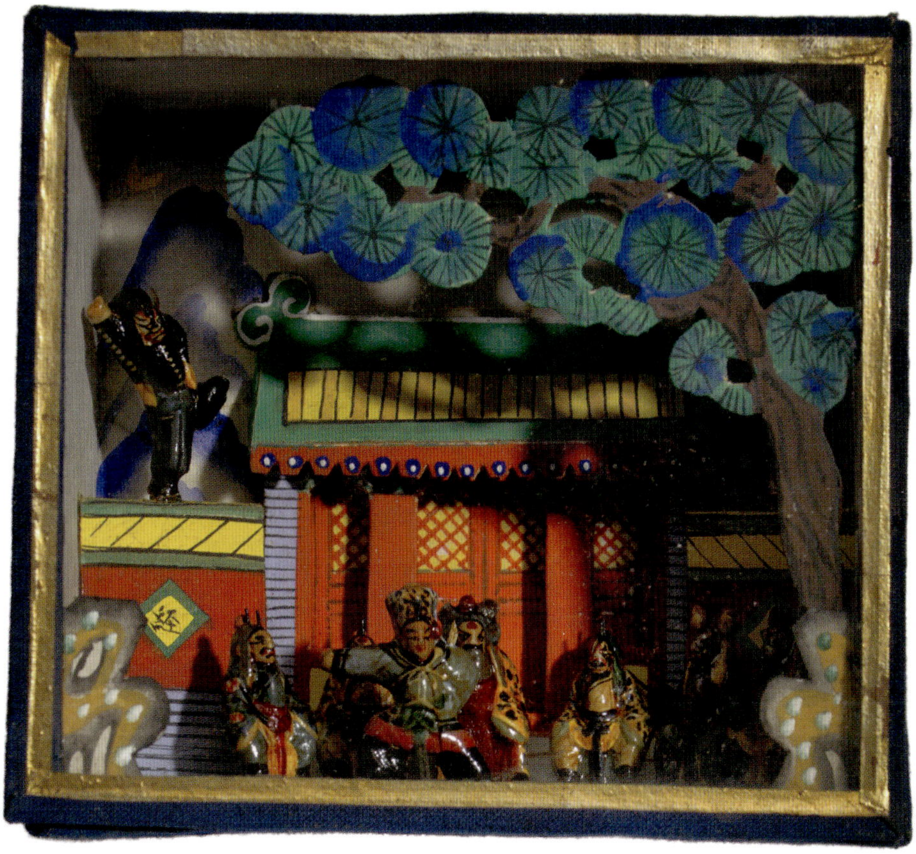

19

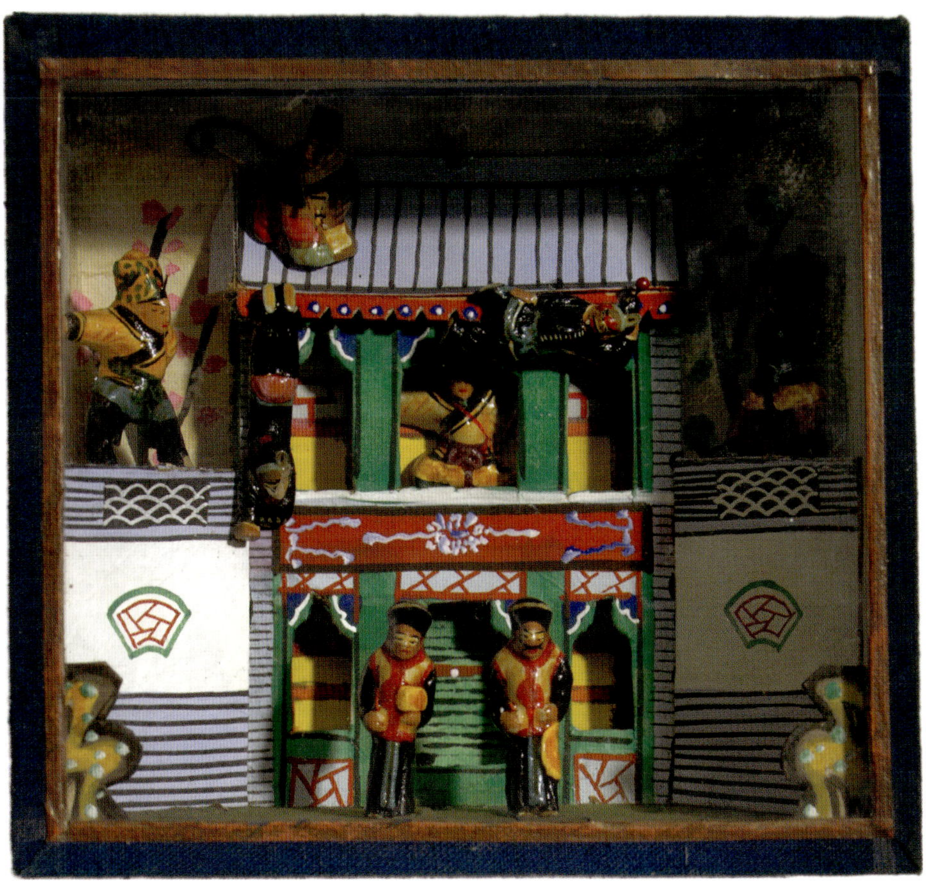

21

human husband Xu Xian from the malevolent Monk Fahai (see also cat. 29). The temple facade, clearly identifiable by a blue placard inscribed *Gold Mountain Temple*, provides a backdrop. In the foreground, wearing a white robe, White Snake rides a turtle upon a churning sea and wields a sword. Behind her, Green Snake brandishes a military flag. A blue piece of paper, perhaps representing a wave, rises behind the two female figures. Wearing a scholar's black cap, Xu Xian stands behind the blue mass and raises his right sleeve in fear. Monk Fahai (with a painted face) stands beside Xu Xian. Two guards stand on either side of the temple gate behind a paper balustrade. —NAIXI FENG

Cat. 18

Opera Scene Diorama Box: Milky Way Lovers (Tianhe pei)

$2\frac{33}{64} \times 4\frac{59}{64} \times 4\frac{17}{32}$ in. (6.4 x 12.5 x 11.5 cm)

70/10977

This diorama displays *Milky Way Lovers* (*Tianhe pei*), an opera based on the myth of the Herd Boy (Niulang) and Weaving Girl (Zhinü) constellations. The Weaving Girl, the youngest daughter of the divine Queen Mother of the West, descends into the human world where she falls in love with and marries a young herd boy. Infuriated, the Queen Mother separates the couple by banishing them to the sky and flinging the Milky Way between them. Only once a year can the two lovers meet by crossing a magpie bridge that spans the Milky Way. The diorama shows a ritual gate made of paper painted with bright colors, with the play's title written on the central board of the gate. The Herd Boy, wearing a golden robe and hat, stands flanked by two serving men in green robes. His ox appears on the right. Upstage, three immortals are behind him, facing the audience. —NAIXI FENG

Cat. 19

Opera Scene Diorama Box: The Copper Net (Tongwang zhen)
$2\frac{33}{64} \times 4\frac{59}{64} \times 4\frac{17}{32}$ in. (6.4 x 12.5 x 11.5 cm)
70/10990

This diorama depicts the opera *The Copper Net* (*Tongwang zhen*), which is based on an episode from the late nineteenth-century novel *The Seven Heroes and Five Gallants* (*Sanxia wuyi*). In this scene, the hero Bai Yutang has secretly entered the palace of the evil prince of Xiangyang (who is plotting to rebel and usurp the throne) to retrieve stolen evidence of the prince's criminal intent. After Bai is trapped and killed in the palace's diabolical copper net, however, his heroic friends vow to avenge his death and finally succeed in quelling the rebellion. In this scene, Bai Yutang, played as a *wusheng* (young martial male lead) stands in front with several *jing* (painted-face) role-types standing behind him. Another jing figure in black is jumping from the left wall. The brilliant contrast of bright colors—the green pine tree, red gate, and yellow roofs—enhances the diorama's visual appeal. —NAIXI FENG

Cat. 20

Opera Scene Diorama Box: The Nine Dragon Cup (Jiulong bei)
$2\frac{33}{64} \times 4\frac{59}{64} \times 4\frac{17}{32}$ in. (6.4 x 12.5 x 11.5 cm)
70/10986

This diorama represents *The Nine Dragon Cup* (*Jiulong bei*), a famous play in the martial clown's (*wuchou*) repertory, based on a complicated episode from the popular novel *The Cases of Judge Peng* (*Peng gong'an*). In the opera, Yang Xiangwu first steals the Emperor Kangxi's precious Nine Dragon Cup, which is later stolen from him in turn and enters Zou Yinglong's possession. In order to help Huang Santai, whom the emperor has ordered to retrieve the cup, Yang uses various strategies to persuade Zou to return it. In the diorama, the clown Yang Xiangwu, clad in black, stands on the roof of the pavilion dangling another man from a rope in an attempt to steal the cup. Looking shocked at Yang's actions, the other characters stand or sit around the pavilion. —NAIXI FENG

Cat. 21

Opera Scene Diorama Box: "The City of Sizhou" (Sizhou cheng) from Journey to the West (Xiyou ji)
$2\frac{33}{64} \times 4\frac{59}{64} \times 4\frac{17}{32}$ in. (6.4 x 12.5 x 11.5 cm)
70/10988

This diorama depicts *The City of Sizhou* (*Sizhou cheng*) from *Journey to the West* (*Xiyou ji*). In the opera, Monkey journeys to India as the disciple of the Buddhist monk Tripitika (Tang sanzang), and encounters a water demon who unleashes a flood on Sizhou. Monkey bravely fights the demon and eventually rescues the city and its people. A battle scene takes place downstage; behind, the high city wall divides the stage into an upper and lower register. Several role-types populate the scene: a *laosheng* (mature male lead), a *xiaosheng* (young male lead), and a *jing* (painted-face role) stand upon the wall, while two jing actors with yellow and green faces fight in the space below. —NAIXI FENG

1 $39\frac{3}{8} \times 27\frac{9}{16} \times 23\frac{5}{8}$ in. (100 x 70 x 60 cm)
2 For reproductions, see Zhang Linyu, *Shanxi xiju tushi* [An Illustrated History of Shanxi Drama] (Taiyuan: Shanxi renmin chubanshe, 2002), vol. 1, pp. 312–14.

Three

Picturing the Play

For much of its history (from mainly the thirteenth to eighteenth centuries), Chinese opera attracted talented writers, developing an important textual tradition of dramatic literature produced not only for the viewing audience, but also for the reader. Plays were widely published and reprinted in multiple formats, many of them beautifully illustrated, for a large reading public. Many of these woodblock illustrations rank among the finest examples of Chinese graphic art and served as important sources for designs on decorative objects. In most cases, book illustrations published during the Ming (1368–1644) and Qing (1644–1911) dynasties that represent a scene from a play do so as if it were a chapter in a novel, not as it would be presented on stage. Dramatic characters are shown wearing regular clothes, not theatrical costume or makeup, and the scenery is rendered naturalistically, not as stage furniture.

Due to the length of Ming and Qing plays—a romantic comedy (*chuanqi*) could easily run over forty acts—the distance between text and performance in Chinese opera is unusually great, and a tradition of performing a varied program of single-scene "excerpts" (*zhezi xi*) became the norm. On decorative objects, the influence of staging excerpts is most apparent in two ways of picturing a play: either as a sequence of independent scenes arranged across a single item or as an intense focus on one emblematic scene occupying the whole of an item.

Cat. 22
Chinese, Ming Dynasty (1368–1644)
Two Book Illustrations for The Soul's Return (Huanhun ji) (The Peony Pavilion [Mudan ting]) *in* Four Plays with New Lyrics from the Hall of the Jade-White Camellia (Yumingtang xinci sizhong): *"The Interrupted Dream" (Jingmeng)* (verso) and *"Seeking a Matchmaker" (Yangmei)* (recto), 1618
Two woodblock book illustrations on facing pages from the 1618 revised and abridged version of *The Peony Pavilion (Mudan ting)* by Zang Maoxun (1550–1620) published in his Zang Jinshu Diaochong guan (Carving Insect House) edition of Tang Xianzu's (1550–1616) *Four Plays with New Lyrics from the Hall of the Jade-White Camellia* (*Yumingtang xinci sizhong*)
C. V. Starr East Asian Library, Berkeley, California
5686.1618

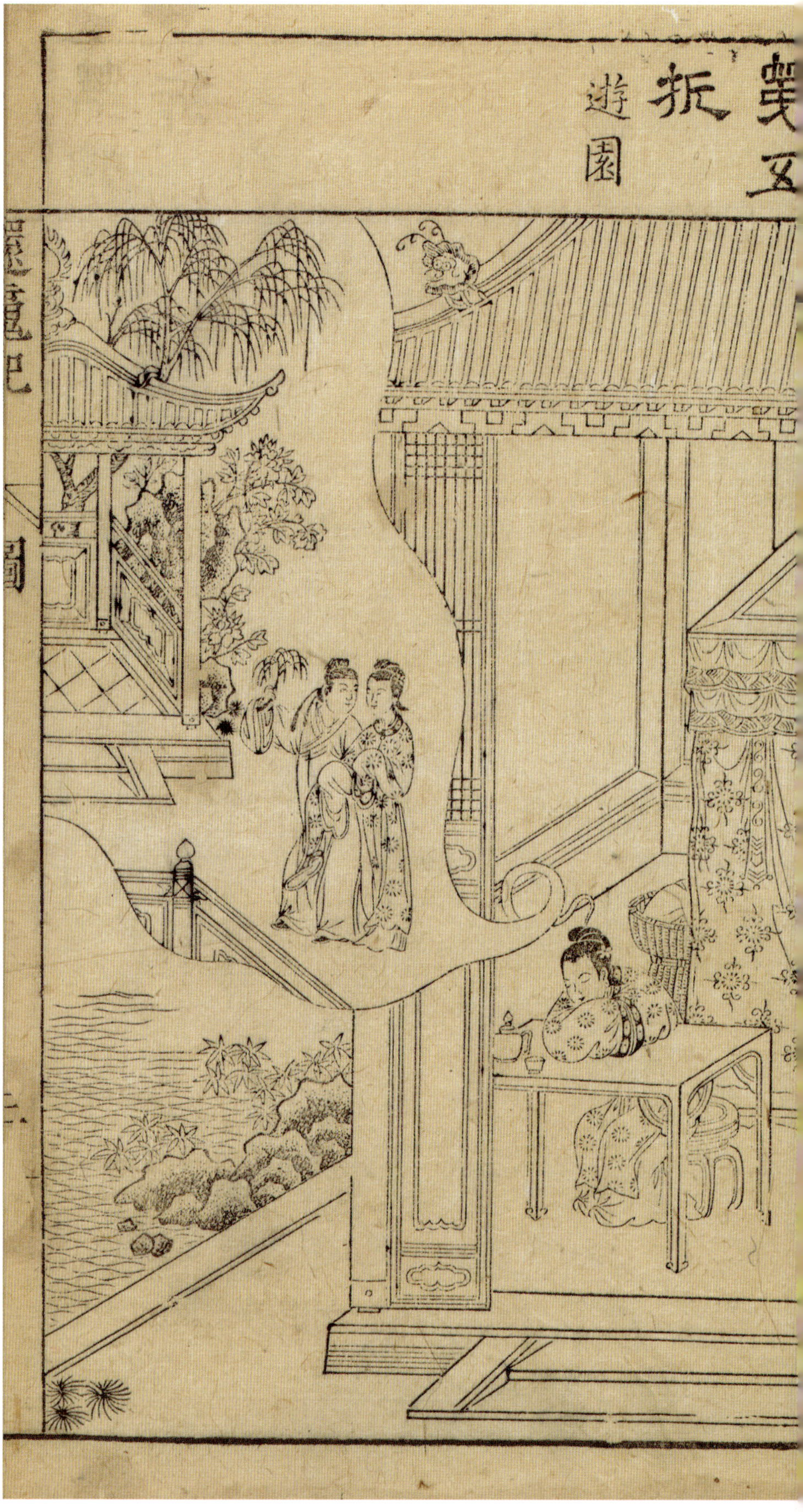

These adjacent pages illustrate two scenes from Tang Xianzu's (1550–1616) masterpiece *The Peony Pavilion* (Mudan ting), a romantic comedy (*chuanqi*) in fifty-five acts, which he completed in 1598. The play was a lasting success, not only on the Kun opera stage, but also with the reading public. The woodblock illustrations here come from the heavily abridged and revised version of the play by Zang Maoxun (1550–1620), which he published under its alternative title *The Soul's Return* (*Huanhun ji*) in his complete edition of Tang's four major plays in 1618.

The Peony Pavilion tells the story of Du Liniang, the beautiful, sheltered daughter of a high official, whose adolescent feelings of sexual desire are stirred after she wanders through the springtime garden behind their compound. Upon returning to her room, she falls asleep and dreams of a handsome young examination candidate named Liu Mengmei, who ravishes her in the garden. When she awakens, overcome with longing, she falls ill with a wasting disease, and after painting her self-portrait, she pines away and dies. Both the portrait and her body are buried in the garden, which her grief-stricken parents turn into a shrine to consecrate her memory. But the dead woman's desire is still so strong that three years later she returns from the underworld as a ghost to seek the young man from her dream. She finds him in the vicinity of her shrine, and the two enter into a passionate affair. (Coincidentally, he had earlier discovered her self-portrait at the shrine and fallen in love with it.) After they pledge their love forever, she reveals to him that

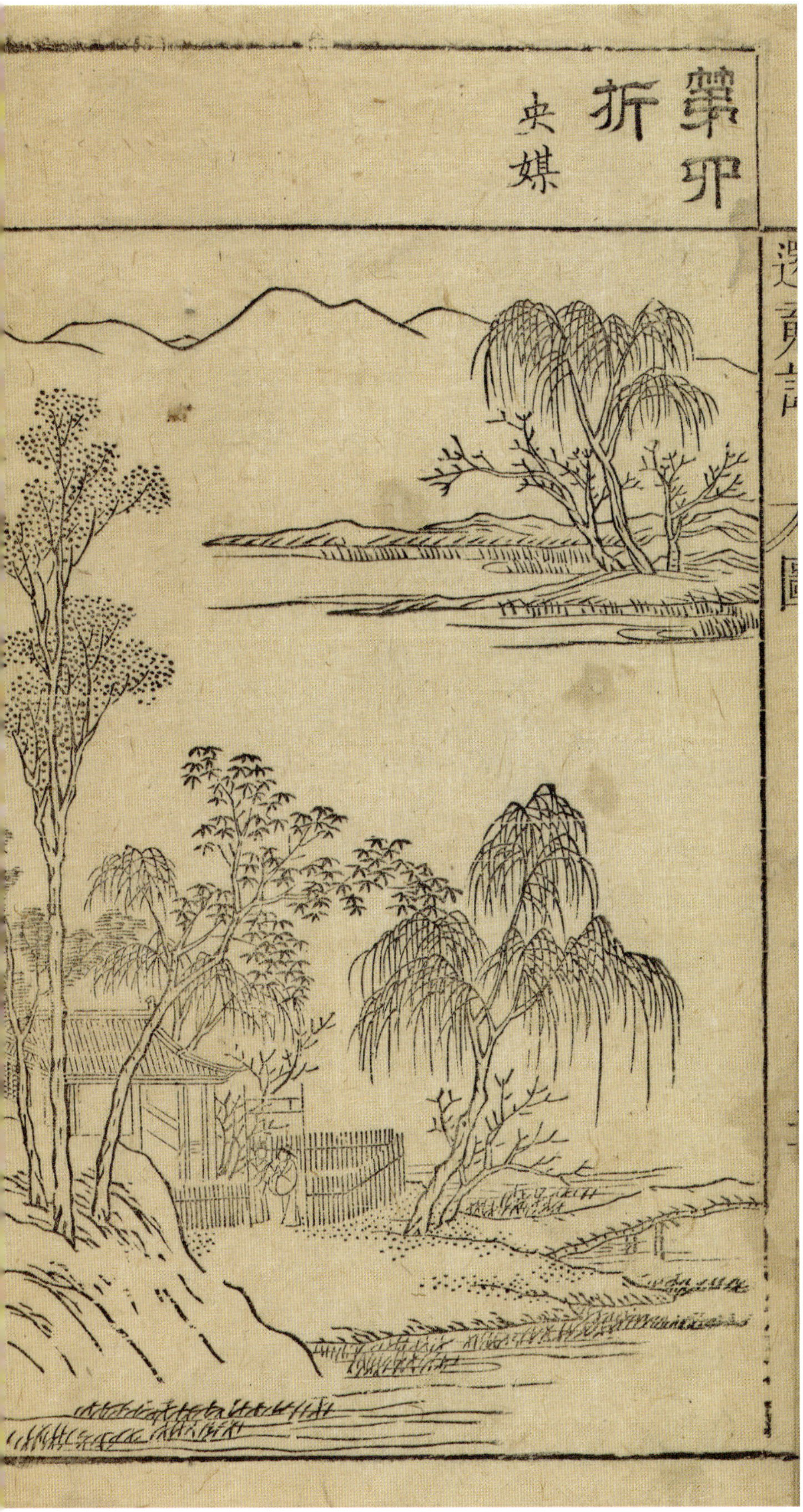

she is actually a ghost, imploring him to exhume her remains so that she may be resurrected. Once he brings her back to life, they elope, and after he passes the highest palace examination, her resurrection and their secret marriage are officially sanctioned by imperial decree.

The illustration on the left depicts the most famous act from the play, "The Interrupted Dream" (Jingmeng). By the mid-eighteenth century, the stage tradition had split this act into two separate excerpts that could be performed independently or together, the first called "Wandering in the Garden" (Youyuan) and the second called "The Interrupted Dream." Even today, these two excerpts remain fundamental pieces in the Kun opera repertory. Although the Zang edition uses the title "Wandering in the Garden," his revision keeps both parts of the original act and includes the dream sequence.

The finely carved illustration shows Du Liniang drowsing at a low table in her bedroom, as described in the play, her chin resting on her arms. A dream bubble delicately swirls upward from her head. Inside it, two smaller figures are standing in a garden, a young man in a scholar's robe and hat and a young woman wearing the identical flowered dress and hairstyle as the sleeper. The two lean close together with entwined sleeves as they gaze tenderly at each other. The man holds a willow branch in one hand. This prop, specified in the play's stage directions, is the clue to Liu Mengmei's as yet unrevealed identity: Liu, his surname, means "willow." A willow tree arches over the roof of the garden pavilion behind them, echoing the curved shape of the willow branch in his hand. The floral pattern on the curtains covering the bed behind the dreaming Du Liniang echo the floral pattern on her dress and allude to the shower of flower petals that will eventually interrupt the love-making in her dream and awaken her.

As in most woodblock illustrations of plays published during the Ming and Qing dynasties, this scene is represented as it would be in a novel, not as it would be on stage. Dramatic characters are shown wearing regular clothes, not theatrical costume or makeup, and the scenery is rendered naturalistically, not as stage furniture. The use of the bubble, a longstanding convention in Chinese pictorial art, enables the representation of the dreamer and her dream to appear simultaneously in a single composition. On stage, as written in the play, Du Liniang would first have to act out falling asleep, then arise to join Liu Mengmei for the dream, then resume her sleeping pose to awaken. Nonetheless, this illustration incorporates three clear borrowings from stage performance: the sleeping pose at the table, the holding of the willow prop, and the action of intertwining sleeves.

The illustration on the adjacent page for act 4 adopts a completely different format, which emphasizes landscape representation rather than the Zang edition's usual focus on human figures and story. In fact, the printer may have even borrowed the illustration from another book and simply inserted it here in error or to cut corners. The scene is labeled "Yangmei" (Seeking a Matchmaker), a title that does not correspond to act 4 in Zang's revision or to any scene associated with *The Peony Pavilion*. —JUDITH T. ZEITLIN

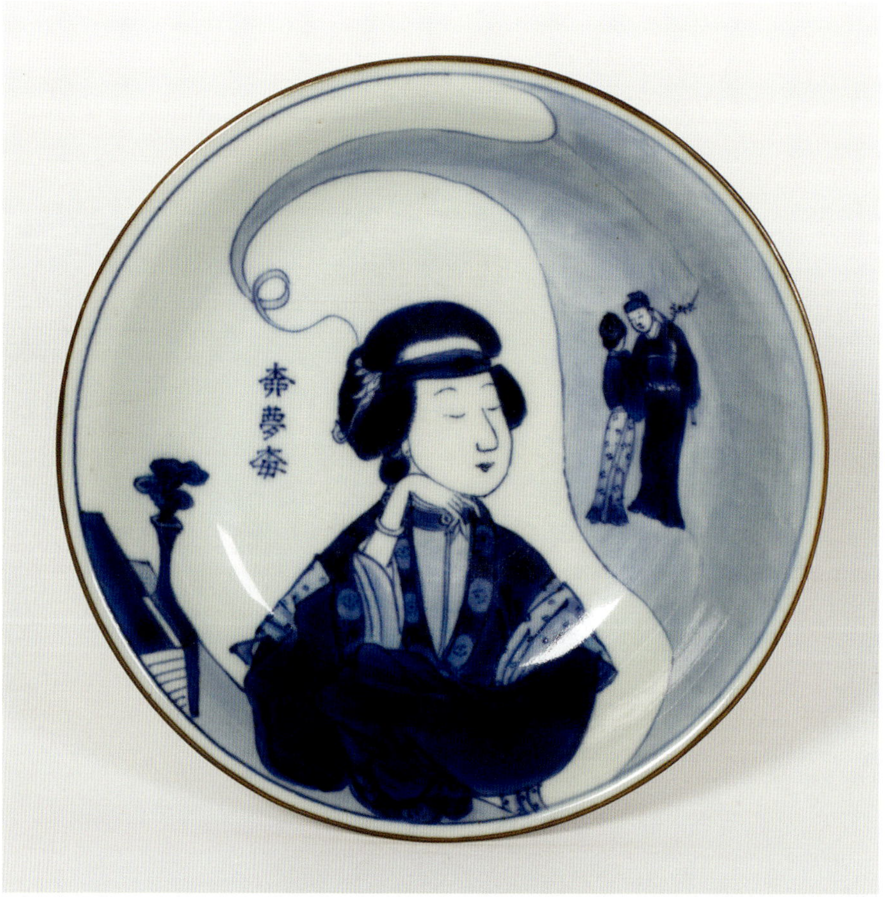

Cat. 23

Chinese, Qing Dynasty (1644–1911), Shunzhi Period (1644–1661) or early Kangxi Period (1662–1722)

Deep Dish with Du Liniang Dreaming of Her Lover Liu Mengmei from The Peony Pavilion (Mudan ting), ca. 1655–65

Porcelain with underglaze blue and white decoration, height: 1 3/4 in. (4.5 cm), diameter of rim: 6 5/16 in. (16 cm)

Sir Michael Butler Collection

On this blue and white porcelain dish from Jingdezhen, Du Liniang, the heroine of *The Peony Pavilion* (*Mudan ting*), rests her chin on her hand, with her eyes closed, a bemused expression on her face, and a pale blue dream bubble swirling from her head. She wears a fashionable, long-sleeved robe that is open at the neck to reveal a white garment inside with a collar trimmed in blue, and both a fillet (*lezi*) and a hairpin with flower petals adorn her hair. The bracelet on her delicate arm emerging from a silk sleeve accentuates the beauty of her slender fingers, which curl into a lotus shape. Her elbows lean gracefully on a low table, where a boxed book signals her literary talent and a vase holds a cloud-shaped mushroom. A three-character inscription in clerical script appears on her left. Ordinarily such an inscription would identify the main figure in the scene, but here it names instead the figure that occupies her mind: Liu Mengmei. She dreamed him up, and then dreamed he made love to her in a garden. In the bubble he is holding his trademark prop of a willow branch—his surname "Liu" means willow—and bending tenderly toward Du Liniang's avatar, whose sprigged skirt echoes the pattern on the wrap draped over the shoulders of her dreaming self.

Yet is she really dreaming? The composition on the dish is clearly indebted to woodblock illustrations of the "Interrupted Dream" (Jingmeng) scene in printed editions of the play (see cat. 22). But in these and most other illustrations of someone dreaming, the convention is to show the sleeper with his or head down on a table, or with the face at least partially concealed. Here, by contrast, the visual focus of the composition is Du Liniang's face positioned in the dead center of the dish, while the dream bubble includes no trace of the scene's usual garden setting. As a result, although Du Liniang's eyes are closed, she does not appear to be sleeping so much as fantasizing, to be recalling her dream rather than actually experiencing it. The streamlined composition makes the most of the dish's limited space and round contours. The effect is to turn the dish into a large peephole into Du Liniang and her innermost thoughts.[1]

On the back of the dish a six-character mark in a double circle on the glazed base reads: "The Jiajing reign period [1522–1546] of the Great Ming" (Da Ming Jiajing nianhao). Both the apocryphal date and the simple landscape scene painted on the back are typical of Shunzhi and very early Kangxi porcelains. —JUDITH T. ZEITLIN

1 The dish's composition recalls a style of late Ming and early Qing illustration in which a scene is depicted within the confines of a round circle. Although some printed woodblock editions of plays employed this style, including a few editions of *Romance of the Western Chamber* (*Xixiang ji*), *The Peony Pavilion*—at least based on the extant evidence—was not among them.

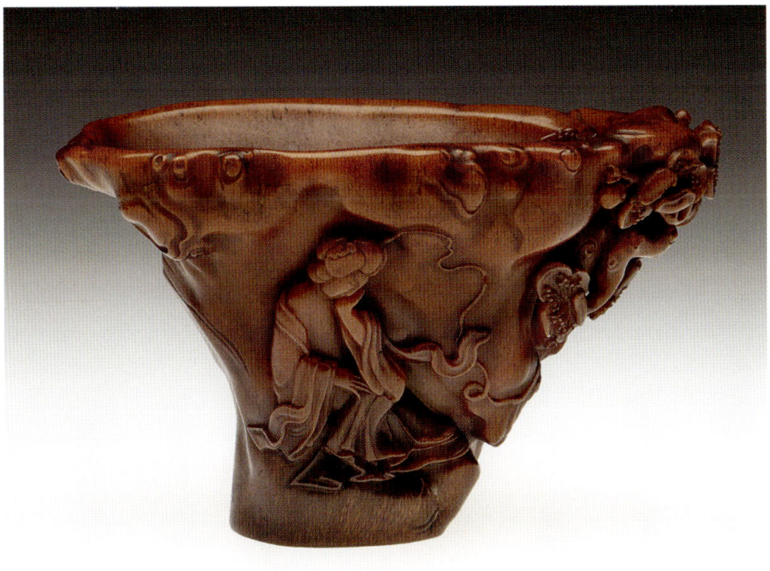

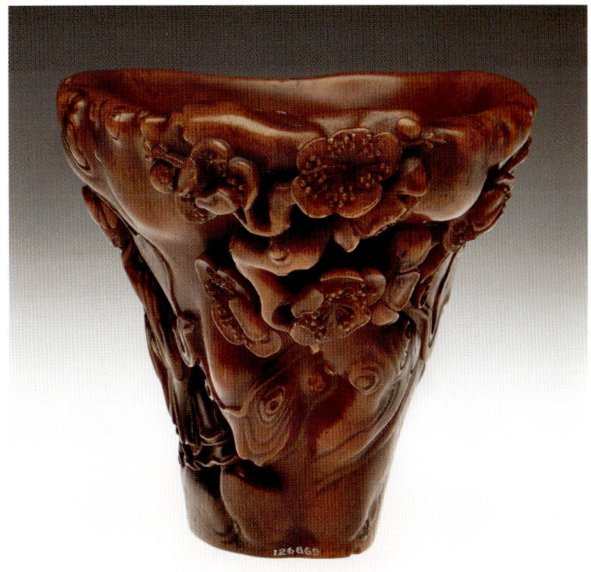

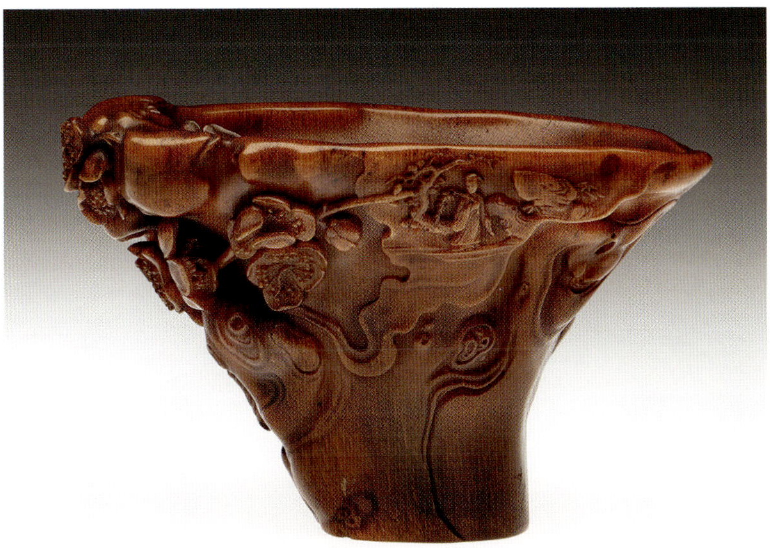

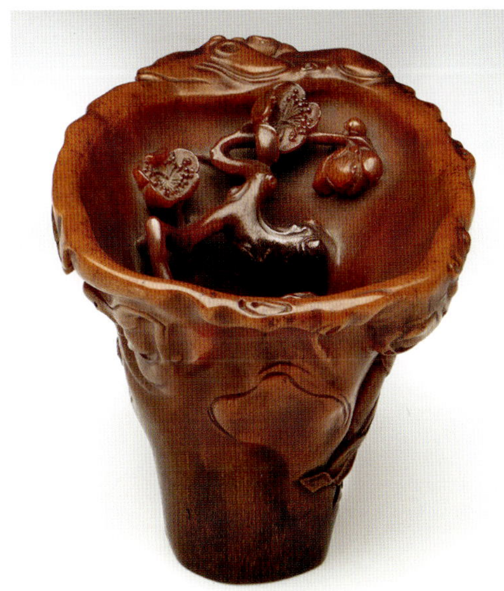

Cat. 24

Chinese, Qing Dynasty (1644–1911)
Rhinoceros Horn Cup with a Scene from The Peony Pavilion (Mudan ting), probably 17th century
Carved rhinoceros horn, height: 3¾ in. (9.5 cm)
The Field Museum, Chicago
126869

Artifacts made of precious imported rhinoceros horn were prized as luxury goods in late imperial China, but this cup's lustrous surface, rich color, and imaginative carving make it a particularly fine example of the artistry achieved with this material during the seventeenth century. Although inspired by woodblock illustrations of "The Interrupted Dream" from *The Peony Pavilion* (*Mudan ting*) (see cat. 22), the design has been adapted to both the cup's three-dimensional form and the symbolic properties of rhinoceros horn.

On one side of the cup, Du Liniang, the heroine of the play, dozes with her tilted face nestled in the palm of one hand, while her other hand rests on her lap. As in the blue and white dish from the Sir Michael Butler Collection, England (cat. 23), a wrap is draped over her shoulders, but here the right end flies up to intersect with the beginning of the dream bubble spiraling out like an umbilical cord from her elegant coiffure. Both wrap and spiral point to the right, beckoning the viewer to rotate the cup in that direction to follow her dream.

On the upper edge of the reverse side we spy a tiny Liu Mengmei, Du Liniang's lover from her dream, standing in a tiny garden containing a tree, a garden rock, and a clump of bamboo within a cloud-shaped bubble. All alone in this setting, he is looking to the left, in the direction of the spiral and the invisible dreamer. He holds his usual, identifying willow branch—his surname "Liu" means willow—but here the artist has cleverly worked in the rest of his name—

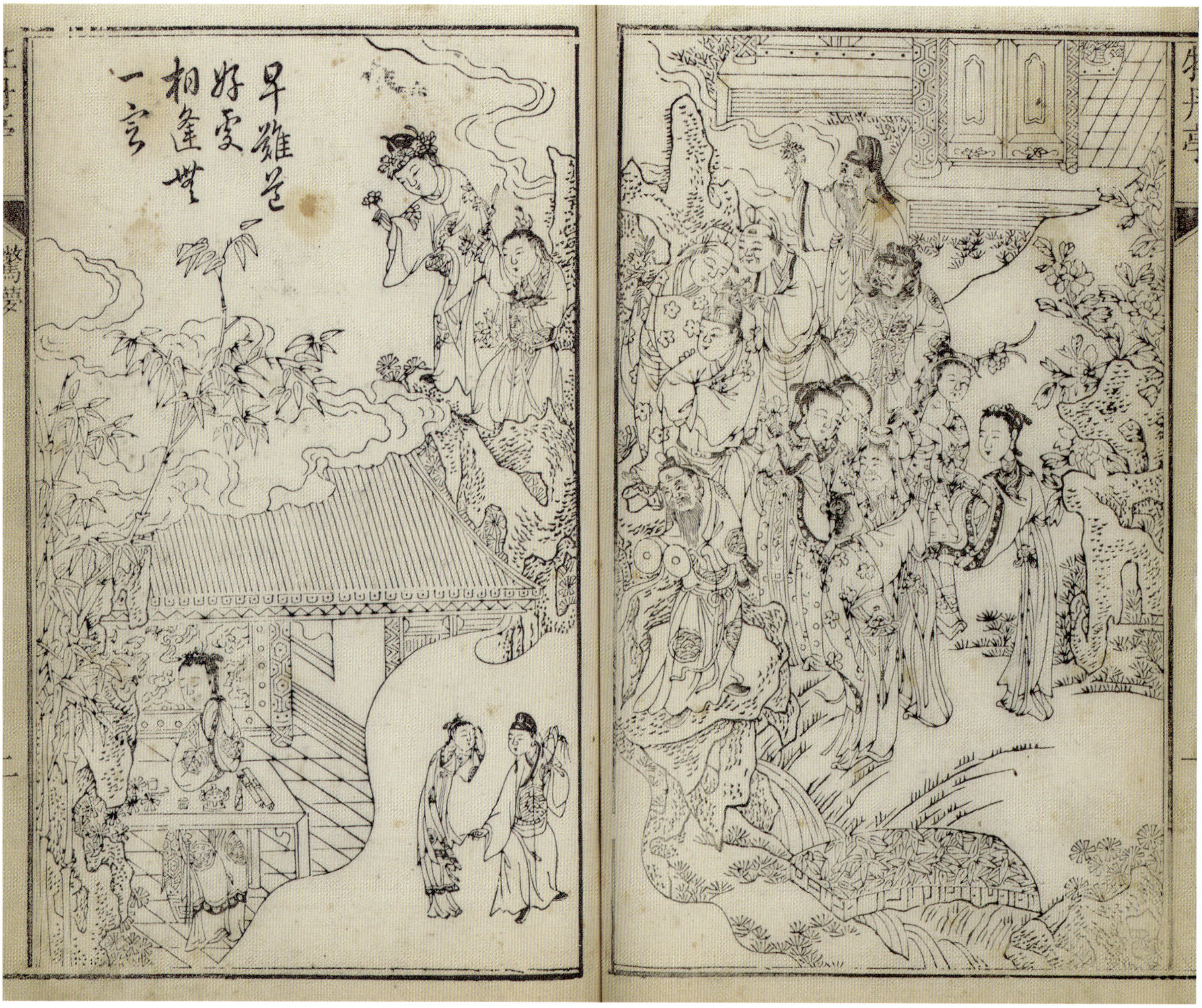

25

"Mengmei" means "Dream of Plum" (*prunus mumei*)—to become the main decorative motif of the cup.[1] The fine-grained, chestnut-hued surface has been carved to mimic a tree trunk with knots and whorls and branches that follow the cup's contours up to the lip. Plum blossoms cluster all over, some spilling into the bowl of the cup. Since the flowering plum is closely associated with beautiful women in Chinese literature and art, the extensive use of this botanical image evokes Du Liniang as well as Liu Mengmei.

Renowned for its magical and aphrodisiacal properties, rhinoceros horn itself became a poetic metaphor for love. According to legend, the finest specimens had a white line running through them from end to end. Rhinoceros horn therefore came to symbolize the spiritual resonance between two souls, as immortalized in this famous line by the Tang poet Li Shangyin (circa 813–858 CE): "For hearts the one minute thread from root to tip of the magic horn."[2] The symbolic meaning of rhinoceros horn thus made it especially appropriate as a medium to represent the dream lovers of *The Peony Pavilion*.

—JUDITH T. ZEITLIN

1 For another example of a seventeenth-century rhinoceros horn cup carved with a plum blossom motif, see Thomas Fok (Huo Mantang), *Connoisseurship of Rhinoceros Horn Carving in China [Zhongguo xijiao diaoke zhenshang]* (Hong Kong: Daye gongsi, 1999), p. 164, plate 112.

2 Li Shangyin, "Untitled Poem" (Wuti) in *Poems of the Late T'ang*, trans. A. C. Graham (Harmondsworth, England: Penguin Books, 1965), p. 148.

Cat. 25

Chinese, Late Qing Dynasty (1644–1911)
Two Book Illustrations for "Heaped Blossoms" (Duihua) Interlude, Adapted from The Peony Pavilion (Mudan ting) *in* Record for Parsing Notes and Mirroring Great Performances (Shenyin jiangu lu), by 1834
Two woodblock book illustrations on facing pages from the book with textile binding, *Record for Parsing Notes and Mirroring Great Performances* (*Shenyin jiangu lu*), compiled by Qinyinweng (pseud.)
Courtesy of the C. V. Starr East Asian Library, Berkeley, California
6756.3084

This two-page woodblock illustration of the "Heaped Blossoms" (Duihua) interlude adapted from *The Peony Pavilion* (*Mudan ting*) comes from a nineteenth-century collection of miscellaneous opera excerpts (*zhezi xi*) titled *A Record for Parsing Notes and Mirroring Great Performances* (*Shenyin jiangu lu*). Published miscellanies were one of the most common formats for the circulation of dramatic texts during the Ming (1368–1644) and Qing dynasties (1644–1911). Historians of Chinese opera consider printed miscellanies of excerpts to be better indicators of actual theatrical performances than complete editions of romantic comedies (*chuanqi*), which typically ran from thirty to forty acts and were probably only rarely staged in full. In the case of a fifty-five act play like *The Peony Pavilion,* which the playwright Tang Xianzu completed in 1598, we do not even know if it was *ever* performed in its entirety during the Ming or Qing period. By at least the eighteenth century, when the production of new plays ebbed in importance and a repertory system took firm hold, performing excerpts rather than full-length plays had become the norm in theaters and private households outside the court.

This illustration from *A Record of Parsing Notes and Mirroring Great Performances* shows the marked impact of Qing stage practice on "The Interrupted Dream" (Jingmeng), act 10 from *The Peony Pavilion*.[1] It had become customary to split this act into two independent excerpts that could also be performed together, "Wandering in the Garden" (Youyuan) and "The Interrupted Dream." To bridge the gap, actors began adding the interlude known as "Heaped Blossoms," represented in this edition as an illustration inserted between the texts of these two excerpts. The cursive inscription on the upper left is the line the heroine Du Liniang and the hero Liu Mengmei sing together right before he forcibly takes her offstage to make love in the dream: "But do not say, in this lovely place we should meet and speak no word."[2]

Tang Xianzu's original scene featured a single Chief Flower Spirit (Huashen) who scatters flower petals after the lovers re-enter the stage to gently awaken Du Liniang from her dream. By the nineteenth century when this edition was published, however, a spectacular procession of at least a dozen Flower Spirit attendants had become the rule on stage, a practice still followed in performances today.

On the bottom left of the illustration, we see Du Liniang drowsing at her table. Inside the blank space of the dream bubble, Liu Mengmei brandishes his willow branch over his shoulder and tugs at Du Liniang's robe, as she modestly shields her face with her hand. Unlike other illustrations of this scene, which clearly show the bubble originating from Du Liniang, here the source is a bearded old man—a painted face (*jing*) role—who is wielding two round bronze mirrors like magnets to draw the two lovers into the dream together. This is the God of Sleep (Shuimoshen), sometimes called the God of Dreams (Mengshen), another staple of the Qing performance tradition. The crowd of Flower Spirit attendants dominate the garden, each holding a flower as a self-identifying prop and represented as different role-types. In the top right corner of the left page, Chief Flower Spirit, crowned with a wreath of flowers, prepares to rain petals onto the dreaming lovers.

—JUDITH T. ZEITLIN

1 The discussion of this illustration and its relation to Qing stage practice is deeply indebted to Catherine C. Swatek, *Peony Pavilion Onstage: Four Centuries in the Career of a Chinese Drama* (Ann Arbor: University of Michigan Center for Chinese Studies, 2002), pp. 109–12.

2 Cyril Birch's translation, quoted in Swatek, *Peony Pavilion Onstage*, p. 110. The Chinese text reads: 早難道這好處相逢無一言.

Cat. 26

Suzhou, Ding Liangxian (print workshop)
Chinese, Qing Dynasty (1644–1911), Kangxi Period (1662–1722)
Tea Picker's Song for the Twelve Months, late 17th–early 18th century
Polychrome woodblock print, image: 13 ¼ x 10 ⅞ in. (33.7 x 27.6 cm)
Lent by The Metropolitan Museum of Art, Rogers Fund, 1923
CP3

This print is signed "Made by Ding Liangxian of Gusu [Suzhou]." A seventeenth-century Catholic printmaker, Ding Liangxian was a prominent member of the Ding family workshop in Suzhou and famous for his flower-and-bird painting. An almost identical print, but curiously printed on both sides of the paper, is now in the British Museum, London (acc. no. 1991,1015,0.1). The color palette of the one-sided print from the Metropolitan Museum of Art, New York, in this exhibition is more muted, without the yellows, pinks, greens, and blues of the British Museum version.

The print illustrates verses from a tea picker's song for the twelve months of the year. It consists of three scenes featuring verses for the tenth, eleventh, and twelfth months, according to the Chinese lunar calendar. This print is the last in a set of four prints, which would have been viewed sequentially from right to left. Unfortunately, the prints for the other nine months are lost.

The genre of tea picker's songs had long been popular in southern China where the climate is suitable for tea growing. Although varying according to region, the basic formula is that each of the twelve months is assigned a heptasyllabic quatrain (a four-line verse with seven characters per line), which opens with the name of the month and a seasonal observation, and is then followed by three lines alluding to a well-known story. Such stories initially derived from history or legend but were retold and embellished in multiple forms, including adaptations for the stage and ballad storytelling.

The scene for the tenth month, in the picture's lower register, is based on the southern drama tradition of *The Orphan of Zhao* (*Zhaoshi guer*).[1] In the seventh century BCE, during the rule of Duke Ling in the state of Jin, the evil general Tu'an Gu has his rival the prime minister Zhao Dun killed and then exterminates his entire clan. Only Zhao Shuo, the prime minister's son, who is married to the duke's daughter, the princess (De'an gongzhu), escapes because his loyal retainer Zhou Jian, who happens to be the spitting image of Zhao Shuo, volunteers to die in his place. The princess in captivity gives birth to a son, who is smuggled out of the palace and grows up ignorant of his true identity as "the Orphan of Zhao." When the orphan comes of age and learns his true identity, he murders General Tu'an and avenges his family's massacre. He is then reunited with both his parents for the happy ending mandated by southern drama convention.

The scene illustrates an early episode in the play in which Zhao Shuo earns the impoverished Zhou Jian's eternal devotion by paying off his debt at a wine shop and taking him into his service. In the picture, Zhao Shuo and the princess are celebrating the lantern festival on the second floor of a decorated wine shop. Zhao is leaning out and watching Zhou on the street below being hounded by the wine shop owner, Mistress Wang (Wangpo), for the money he owes her.

The inscribed verse reads:

> Tea plucking in November, when the snow whirls in the sky.
> Zhou Jian, who bought wine on credit as he watched the Lantern Fair,
> Later gave up his life for Zhao Shuo.
> The Orphan of Zhao avenged blood with blood.[2]

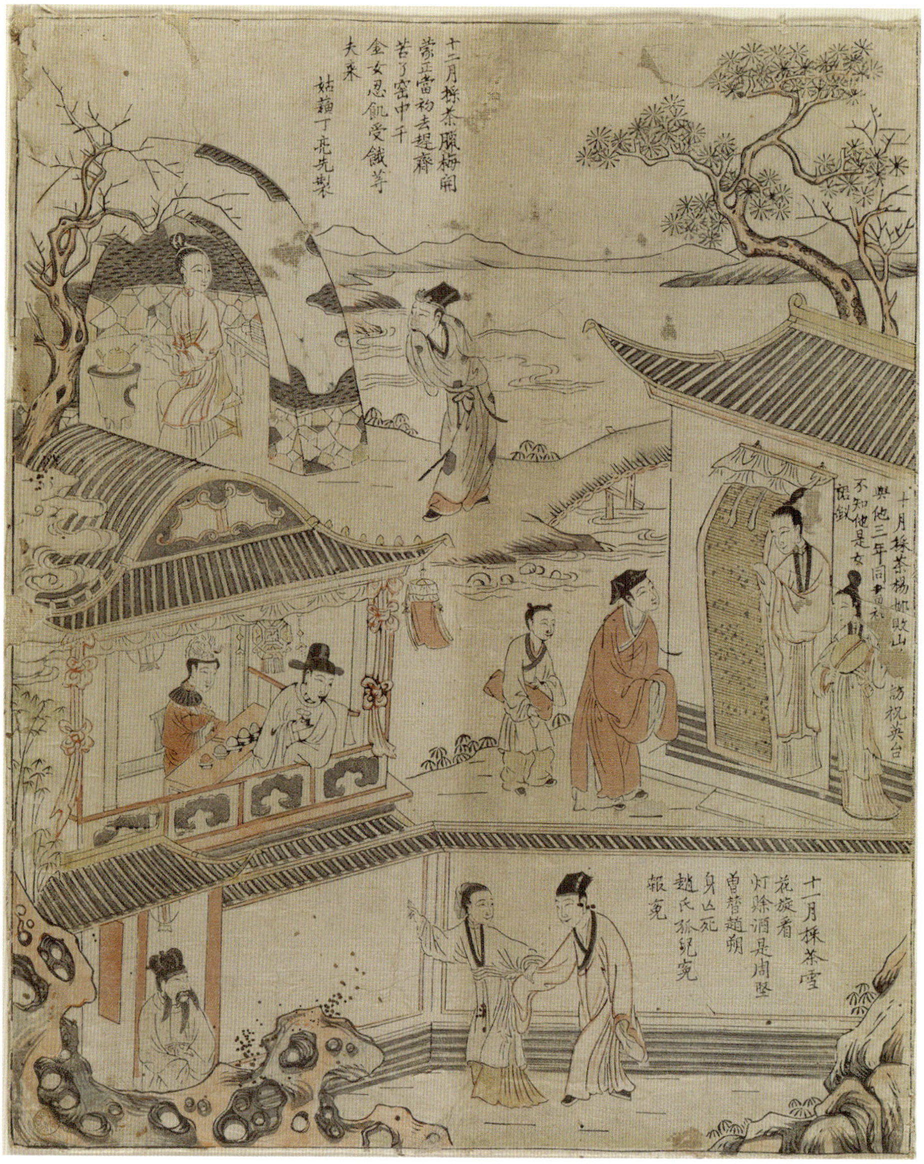

26

The scene for the eleventh month comes from the romantic legend of Liang Shanbo and Zhu Yingtai. The heroine, Zhu Yingtai, is a girl from a wealthy family who disguises herself as a boy and journeys far from home in order to attend school. There she falls in love with a fellow pupil, Liang Shanbo. They live together as best friends for three years, but only after she has left school does he discover her true identity. He immediately rushes off to her house to propose but it is too late. Her parents have already betrothed her to another man. Grief-stricken, Liang dies of love for her and is buried nearby. On Zhu's wedding day, as her bridal sedan is passing by Liang's grave, the tomb cracks open and she jumps inside and perishes. Later two butterflies—the couple transformed and reunited—are discovered flying around the tomb.[3]

The print's middle register shows Liang, dressed in a scholar's cap and robe, and accompanied by a page boy holding his bedroll, bowing in greeting to Zhu, who is now outfitted in a woman's gown and hair-do. As befits her status as a well-born maiden, she is standing behind a curtained door while a maid holding a fan stands at attention outside. Zhu is lifting the speckled bamboo blind and gazing back intently at Liang to show their mutual love.

The inscription reads:

> Tea plucking in the eleventh month, when poplar and willow lose their leaves
> Liang Shanbo went to visit[4] Zhu Yingtai.
> Together they attended school for three years,
> But he never realized Zhu was a girl.[5]

The scene for the twelfth month comes from *The Dilapidated Kiln* (*Poyao ji*), a southern romantic comedy (*chuanqi*) about Lü Mengzheng (circa 946–1011), a poor scholar who eventually rose to become prime minister during the Song dynasty.[6] At the beginning of the play, the prime minister Liu Mao agrees to allow his daughter Qianjin to choose her own bridegroom. She selects Lü, but when her father learns how impoverished this man is, he reneges on the agreement. Despite her father's opposition, Qianjin insists on marrying Lü, so the prime minister disowns her and drives her away. The couple is so poor that they have to make their home in an abandoned kiln and Lü is forced to beg for food at temple sacrifices.

In the picture's upper register, the virtuous Qianjin, clad only in thin garments, sits inside the mouth of a dilapidated kiln, holding her hands toward a teapot on the stove for warmth. She is turning her head to look at her husband, who has just come home and is gazing toward her. He wears a patched robe, a typical stage costume for a destitute scholar, and is holding his sleeves up to his mouth in a theatrical gesture of sorrow and distress.

The inscription reads:

> Tea plucking in December, when the winter plum is blooming.
> Early on, Mengzheng went to beg for food at a temple sacrifice,
> While his wife Qianjin suffered from hunger as she waited for him in the old kiln.[7]

This print offers an early example of a composition often found in rectangular vertical New Year pictures from the mid-Qing dynasty onward. Such prints either contain multiple narratives or a single narrative with multiple episodes. The composition of this print follows the basic structure of a landscape painting with a foreground, middle ground, and far ground. The arrangement of scenes with the twelfth month on the top, the tenth month in the middle, and the eleventh month on the bottom does not follow chronological order, but is rather based on a spatial, pictorial logic. At the bottom of the print, a long wall with a gate stretches across the foreground. In front of it, Mistress Wang is not only trying to drag Zhou Jian back into the building as the episode demands, but is also leading viewers to be drawn inside and up to the balcony where Zhao Shuo and the princess are sitting. We are now level with the second story, that of Liang Boshan and Zhu Yingtai, who are meeting at her house on the right, which also forms part of the architectural compound created by the wall on the first level. However, when we look up to glimpse what's behind Zhu's house, we find not a private courtyard, but the horizon of an open landscape in the far ground, which fits the setting of *The Dilapidated Kiln* on the top level very well. The green tree in the right upper corner and the bare tree in the left upper corner help balance the overall pictorial composition, but their contrast also expresses the seasonal change from fall to winter in the three months covered in the print. —RANTING JIANG, JUDITH T. ZEITLIN, AND YUHANG LI

1 The famous story of the Orphan of Zhao's revenge is recorded in various early Chinese histories. The scene illustrated here, which is absent from the Yuan northern version of the play, comes from an anonymous late Ming–early Qing *chuanqi* play titled *The Story of Eight Righteous People* (*Bayi ji*) or its early Ming southern drama (*nanxi*) precursor, *The Story of the Orphan of Zhao* (*Zhaoshi guer ji*). See Guo Yingde, *Ming Qing chuanqi zonglu* [A Comprehensive Catalogue of Ming and Qing Romantic Comedy] (Shijiazhuang: Hebei jiaoyu chubanshe, 1997), pp. 322–24.

2 The text of the Chinese verse for the tenth month reads 十一月採茶雪花旋，看燈賒酒是周堅，曾替趙朔身亡死，趙氏孤兒冤報冤.

3 On the evolution of the legend and its adaptation into ballad storytelling and drama in the late imperial period, see Wilt L. Idema, "Introduction," in *The Butterfly Lovers: The Legend of Liang Shanbo and Zhu Yingtai: Four Versions, with Related Texts* (Indianapolis: Hackett, 2010), pp. xi–xxxii.

4 Two characters in the inscribed verse are illegible in the Metropolitan Museum of Art print because of damage. These missing characters (*Bo qu* [Bo went]) have been retrieved from the British Museum print, which is intact.

5 The text of the Chinese verse for the eleventh month reads 十二月採茶臘梅開，蒙正當初去趕齋，苦了窯中千金女，忍饑挨餓等夫來.

6 On this sixteenth-century play, which also circulated in a redacted version titled *Romance of a Colorful Two-Storied Chamber* (*Cailou ji*), see Guo Yingde, *Ming Qing chuanqi zonglu*, pp. 282-84.

7 Her name literally means "a thousand pieces of gold," which is a set phrase that denotes the daughter of a rich and noble family. The text of the Chinese verse for the twelfth month reads 十二月採茶臘梅開，蒙正當初去趕齋，苦了窯中千金女，忍饑挨餓等夫來.

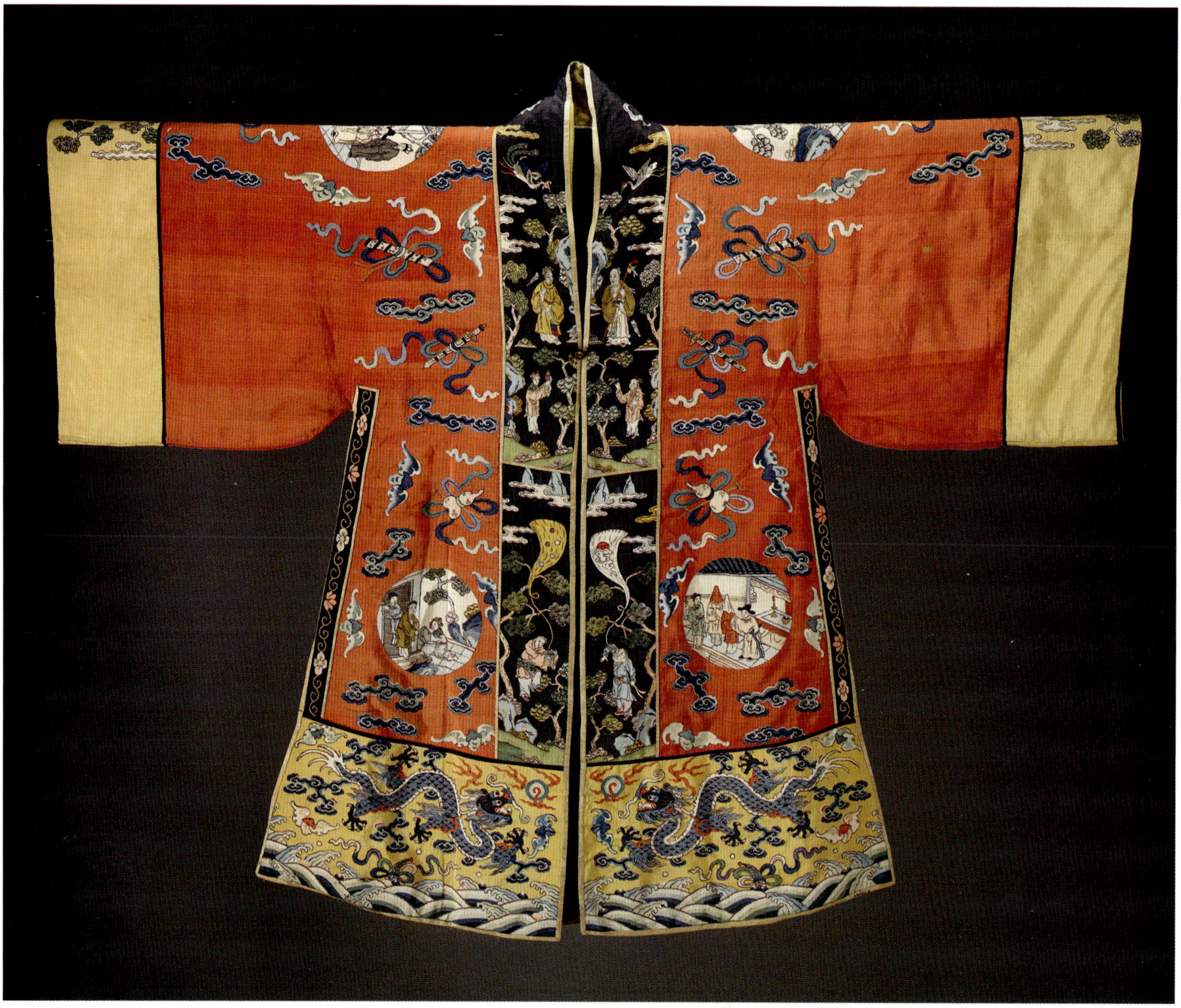

Cat. 27

Chinese, Qing Dynasty (1644–1911)

Robe with Scenes from The Pearl Pagoda (Zhenzhuta), 18th century

Embroidered slit silk tapestry (*kesi*)

60 × 68 in. (152.5 × 173 cm)

The Field Museum, Chicago

235024

For a discussion of this work see essay 4 in this volume, “Representing Theatricality on Textiles” by Yuhang Li.

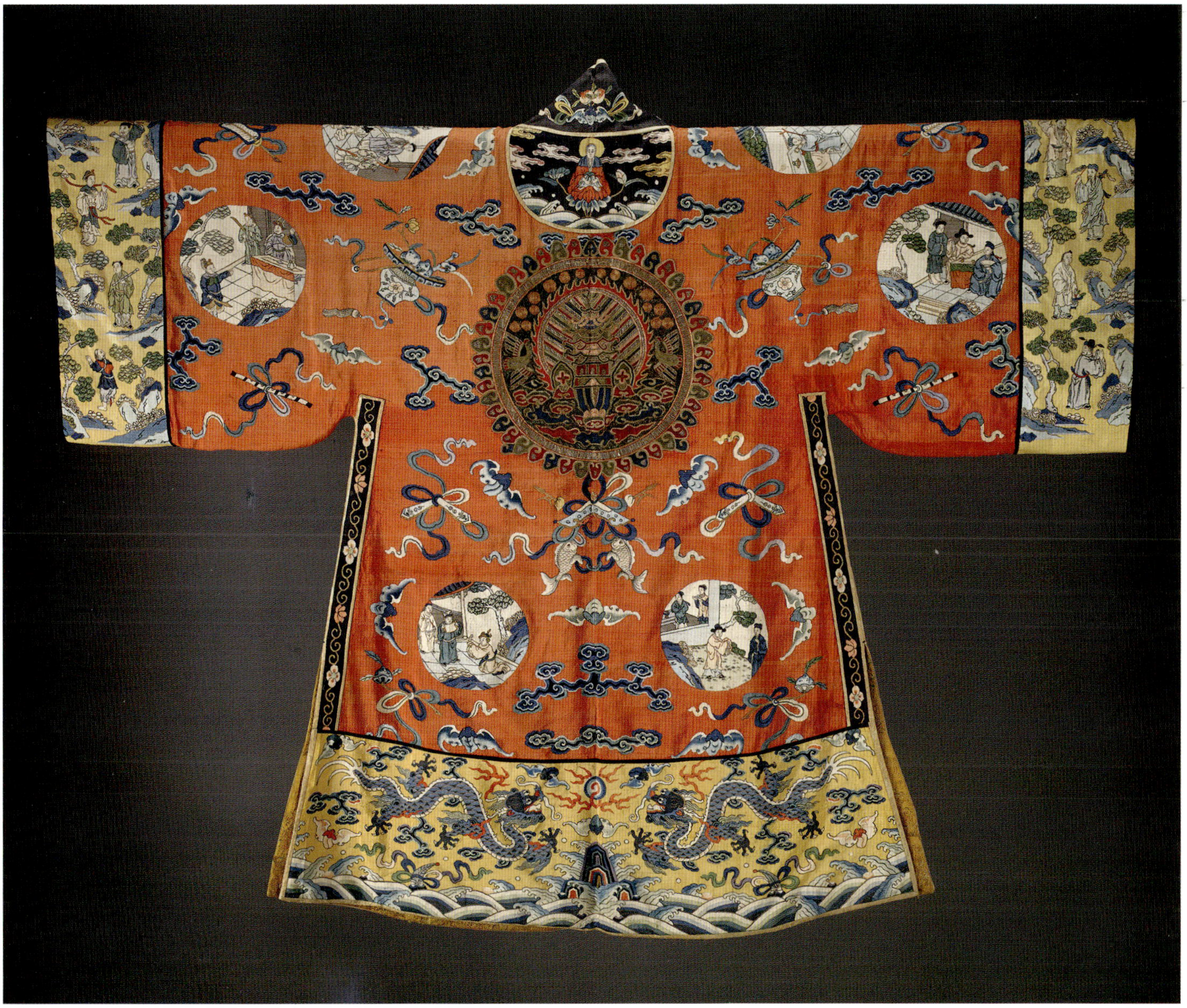

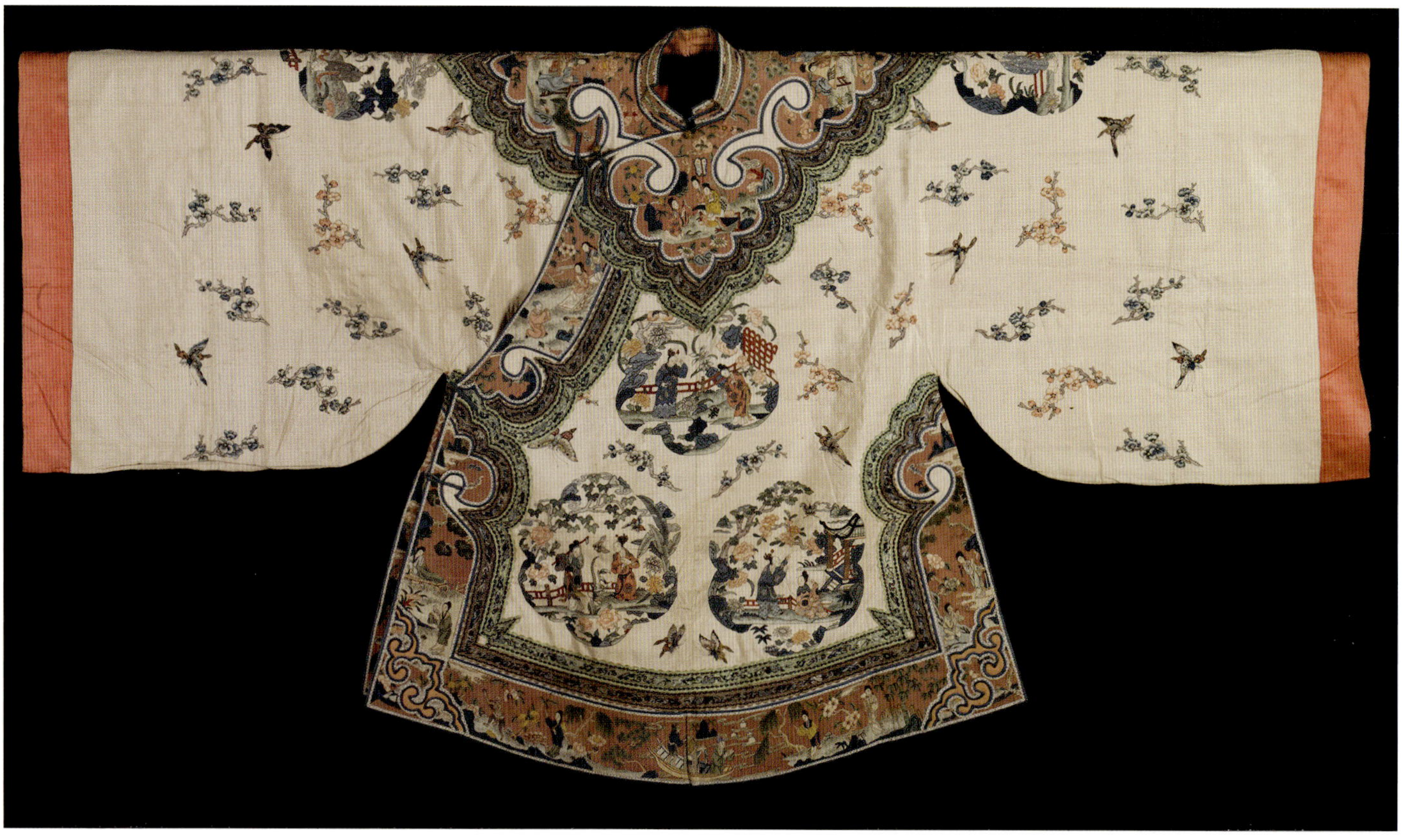

Cat. 28

Chinese, Late Qing Dynasty (1644–1911)
Woman's Nonofficial Formal Jacket, 1875–1900
Slit silk tapestry (*kesi*) patterned with silk and gold-wrapped thread, 37 ½ x 68 in. (95.2 x 172.8 cm)
Jordan Schnitzer Museum of Art, Murray Warner Collection of Oriental Art
MWCH45:11

This large jacket has red cuffs and a round collar with a zigzag neckline extending to the chest. It opens with the lapel beneath the right arm and is decorated with multiple colors against a white surface. The front and back of the robe is beautifully embellished with silk and gold-wrapped thread. The right lapel of the jacket and the lower border are embroidered with illustrations of *The White Snake* (*Baishe zhuan*) set against a red ground. The front and back of the garment below the neckline to the midsection are decorated with three scenes each from the novel *Dream of the Red Chamber* (*Honglou meng*); four additional scenes from this novel appear on and under each arm.[1]

The format of a woven garment restricted yet also considerably enhanced the illustrations. Within the constraint of a small roundel, a given scene could hold only two figures, so the craftsman seems to have selected scenes with a minimum number of characters from the play and ignored the grandiose and crowded acts. In "Dai-yu Burying Flowers" (scene 8), for example, Dai-yu holds a hoe over her shoulder and looks back at Bao-yu on the right. Holding a fan, he leans toward her, thus forming an interactive circle. Trees, flowers, and butterflies fill the remaining space.

In another scene, the little actress Charmante scratches the Chinese character *qiang* (rose) on the ground (scene 7). In the novel, Bao-yu peeps from outside the garden to spy on Charmante, but here he is depicted next to her. The girl, wearing an elaborately embroidered dress, is leaning down to write on the ground and lightly covering her heart with her right hand as she lowers her left one to write. Clearly, she is immersed in her own emotions, unaware of Bao-yu's existence. The latter, in a blue formal outfit, and in a gesture suggesting curiosity, looks directly at Charmante. Placed in the center of the front of the jacket, the two characters are divided by the central line of the jacket itself. The contrasting colors and the repeated motif of red handrails and trees and flowers connect the separate roundels. Gold threads woven into the silk highlight architectural details such as pillars and handrails, thus creating a sense of space through tonal variation.

The arrangement of the *White Snake* scenes functions as a framing device for the whole composition. The thirteen scenes lay a symbolic spatial framework that accords with the shape of the jacket, forming the sky above, mountains on each side, land on the lower part, and water in the lowest central part. The selection of scenes

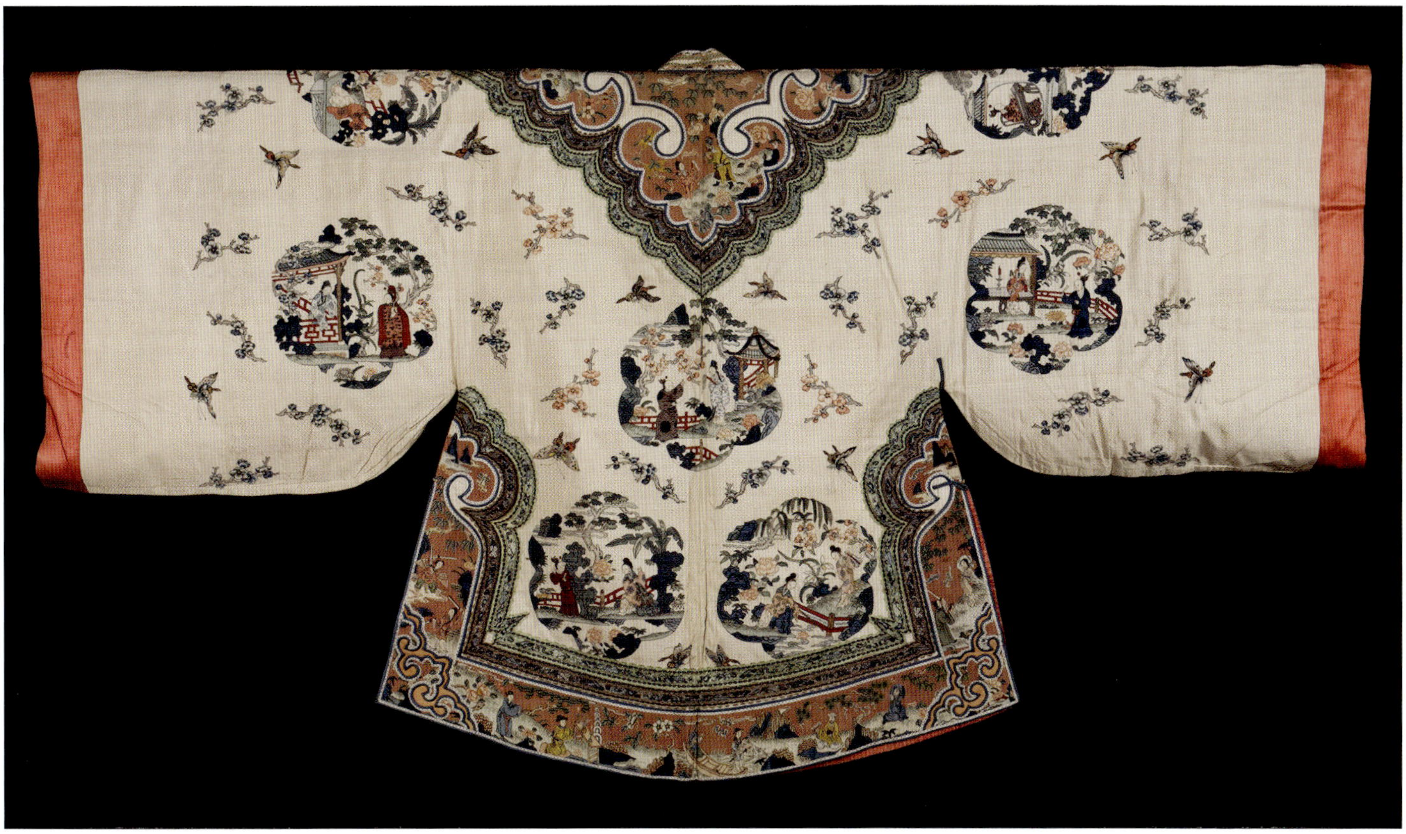

corresponds to their popularity as subject matter in late Qing dynasty (1644–1911) printed plays and *tanci* (stringed ballad storytelling), woodblock prints, and actual theater performances.[2] In terms of composition and iconography, the depictions on the robe most closely resemble the late Qing woodblock illustrations for Chen Yuqian's tanci version *The Illustrated Story of the Righteous Snake Spirit* (*Xiuxiang yiyao zhuan*).[3] The selection and iconography of *Red Chamber* scenes on the garment also show the clear influence of woodblock illustrations to popular adaptations of the novel into *chuanqi* plays (romantic comedies) and tanci.[4]

This jacket might have been used as a costume for an opera or tanci performance. There are records of robes of similar form and design being worn on stage in Kun opera productions.[5] However, a contemporary account from the nineteenth-century novel *Romantic Illusions* (*Fengyue meng*) suggests another possible function and context for the jacket. In it, the author describes a courtesan putting on a gown decorated with scenes from *Dream of the Red Chamber* and then singing tanci lyrics related to these scenes to entertain a group of male guests at a party.[6]—YUNFEI SHAO

1 See diagrams accompanying this entry for the arrangement of scenes.

2 For influence from play texts, see Fang Chengpei, *Leifengta chuanqi* [Legend of the Leifeng Pagoda] (Taipei: Dongfang wenhua shuju, 1951); for influence from late Qing New Year prints and opera performance, see Feng Jicai, *Zhongguo muban nianhua jicheng* [Collection of Chinese Woodblock New Year Prints] (Beijing: Zhonghua shuju, 2004), Wuqiang volume, p.78 and Fengxiang volume, p.183. See also Bo Songnian's essay in this catalogue.

3 Compare scenes 1, 5, 12, 13, 20, 21 ,22 with illustrations of the same (or similar) titles in Chen Yuqian, *Xiuxiang yiyao zhuan* [Illustrated Story of the Righteous Snake Spirit] (Shanghai: Langhuan shuzhuang, 1898).

4 The selection of scenes was influenced by two late Qing dramatic adaptations of the novel, *Honglou meng chuanqi* [*Dream of the Red Chamber*: A Romantic Comedy] and *Honglou meng santao* [Selected Scenes from *Dream of the Red Chamber*], reprinted in Hong Zhenkuai, *Honglou meng guhua lu* [Collection of Traditional Illustrations to *Dream of the Red Chamber*] (Hong Kong: Zhonghua Shuju Youxian gongsi, 2006), and by various *tanci* adaptations reprinted in Hu Wenbin, *Honglou meng shuochang ji* [Collected Chantefable Lyrics on the *Dream of the Red Chamber*] (Shenyang: Chunfeng wenyi chubanshe, 1985) and Liu Caonan, ed., *Honglou meng tanci kaipian ji* [Collected Chantefable Overtures Inspired by *Dream of the Red Chamber*] (Beijing: Xueyuan chubanshe, 2003).

5 Similar garments are recorded in Liu Yuemei, *Zhongguo Kunqu yixiang* [Kun Opera Costumes] (Shanghai: Shanghai cishu chubanshe, 2010). According to Zeng Changsheng (*Kunqu chuandai* [Kun Opera Apparel] (Suzhou: Suzhou xiqu yanjiushi, 1963), this kind of costume was used for female clown roles in Kun opera.

6 Anonymous, *Fengyue meng* [*Romantic Illusions*] (Beijing: Zhongguo wenlian chubanshe, 1985), pp. 35–36; trans. Patrick Hanan, *Courtesans and Opium: Romantic Illusions of the Fool of Yangzhou*, chapter 5, pp. 40–42.

Scenes illustrated on the robe:

The White Snake

1 Traces of the Immortals
2 Broken Bridge
3 Giving Birth to a Son
4 Robbing the Treasury
5 Meeting on a Boat
6 Summoning Green Snake
12 The Dragon Boat Festival
13 Sealing the Alms Bowl
14 Leaving the Mountain
20 Fighting for the Magic Herb
21 A Sacrifice in Front of the Pagoda
22 Water Battle
23 Banishing the Taoist Priest
24 The Dragon Boat Festival
25 Closing the Alms Bowl

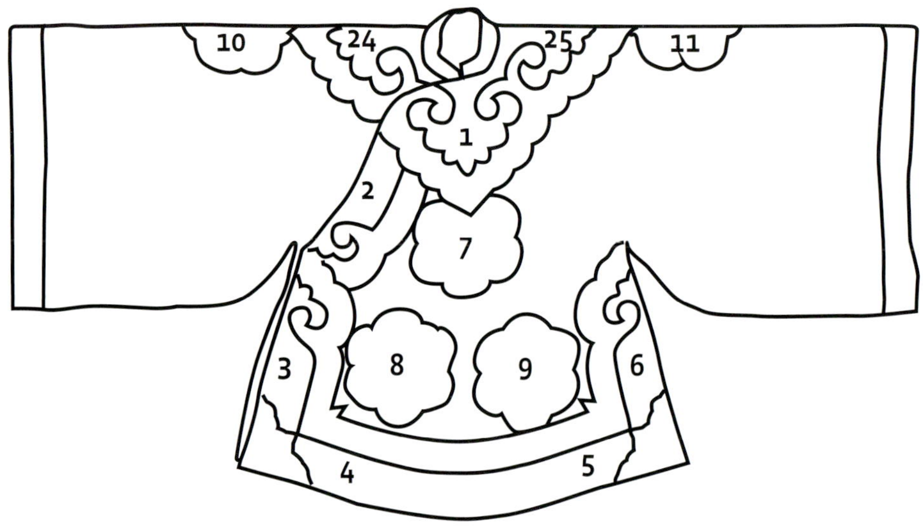

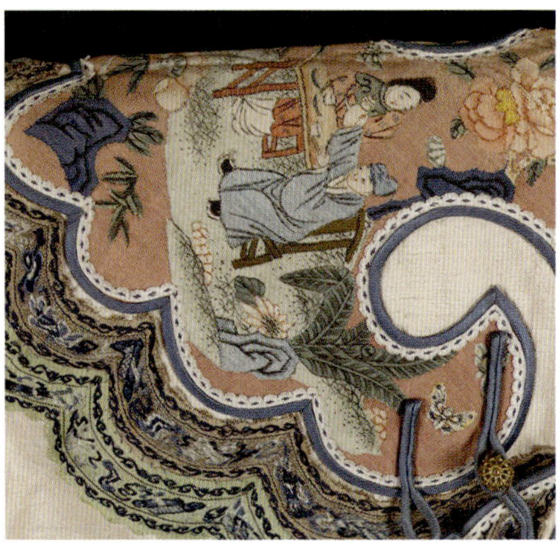

Scene 24

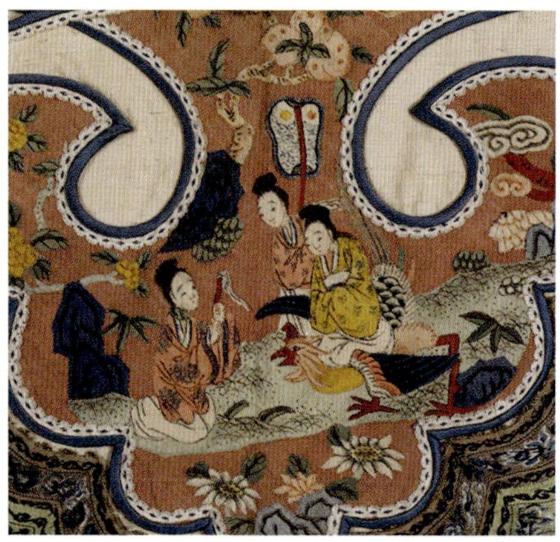

Scene 1 (center)

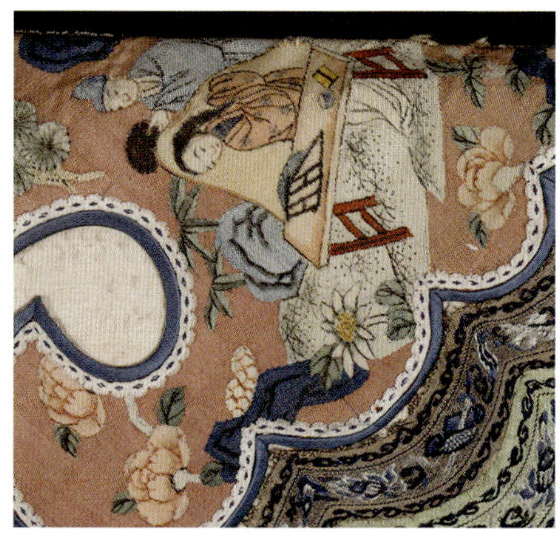

Scene 25

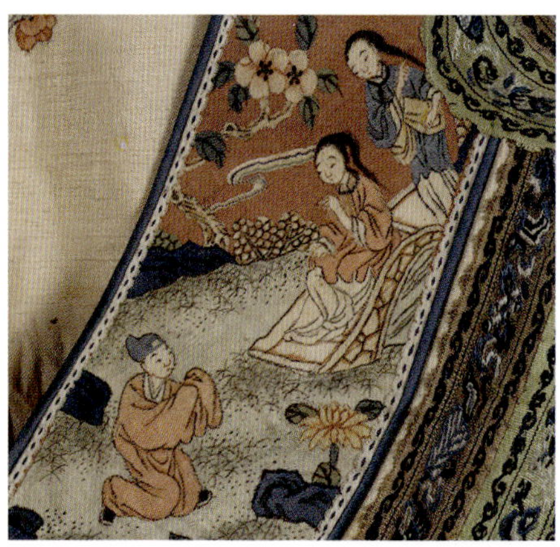

Scene 2

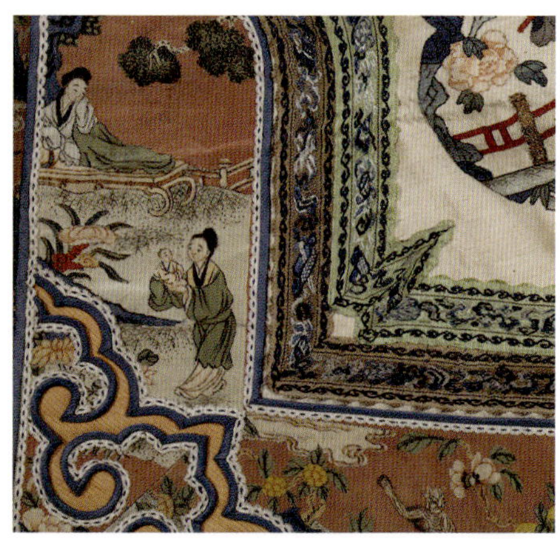

Scene 3

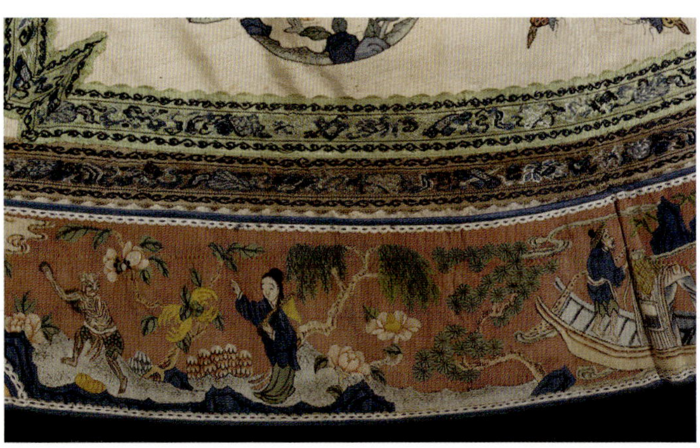

Scene 4

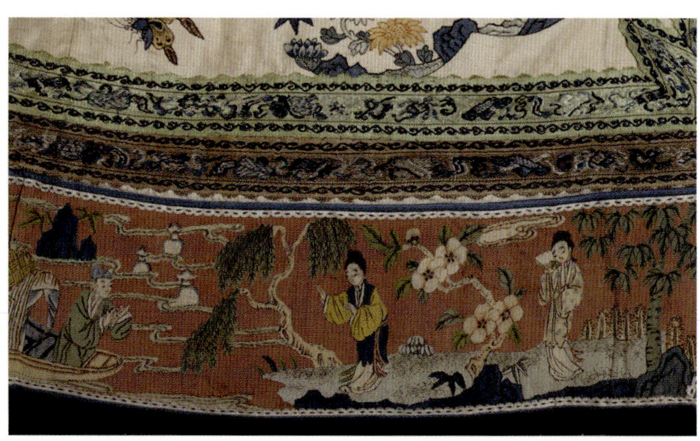

Scene 5

Dream of the Red Chamber

7 Charmante Scratching the Character *qiang*
8 Dai-yu Burying Flowers
9 Bao-yu Flying a Kite
10 Bao-yu Playing the Zither
11 Xiang-yun Sleeping on a Peony-Petal Pillow
15 Adamantina Taken by Evil Spirits
16 Bao-yu Getting a Branch of Red Plum in Green Bower Hermitage
17 Bao-yu Composing "Invocation to a Hibiscus Spirit"
18 Skybright Repairing a Peacock Gold Snowcape
19 Beauties Fishing

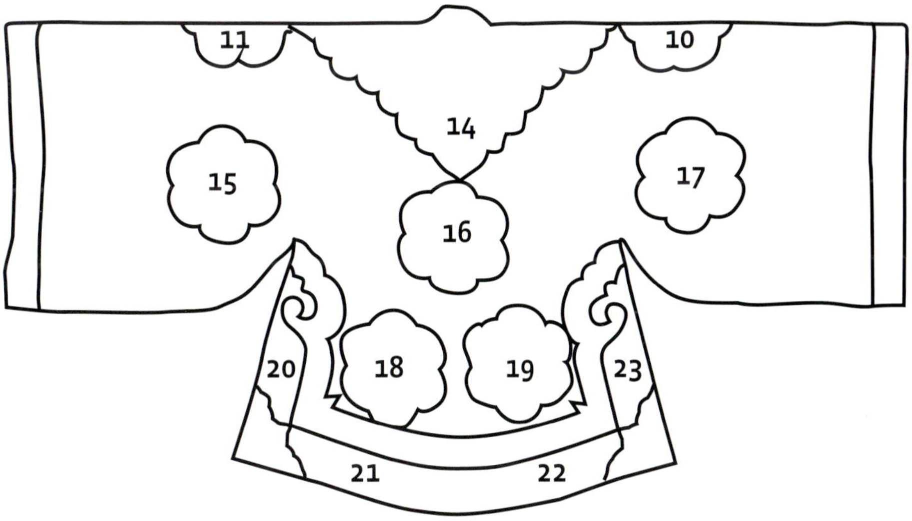

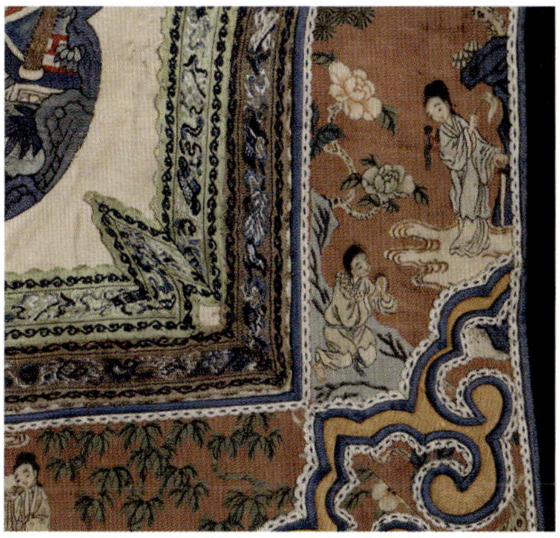

Scene 6

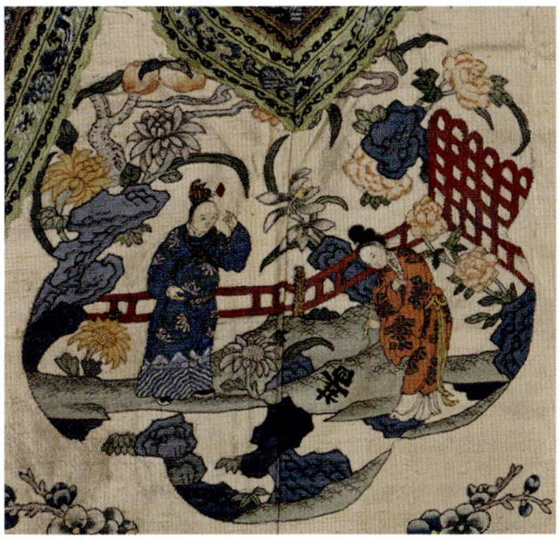

Scene 7

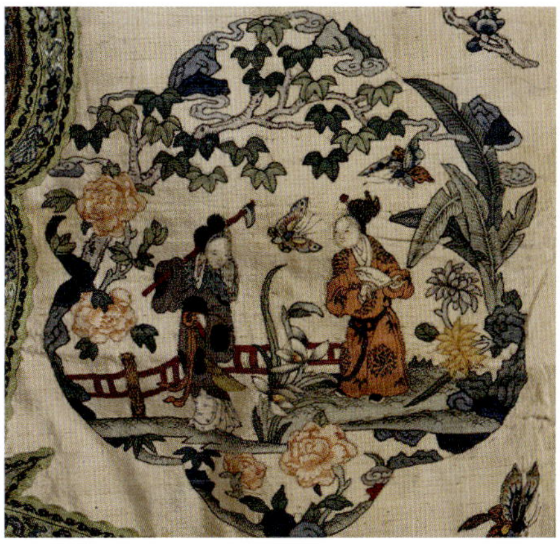

Scene 8

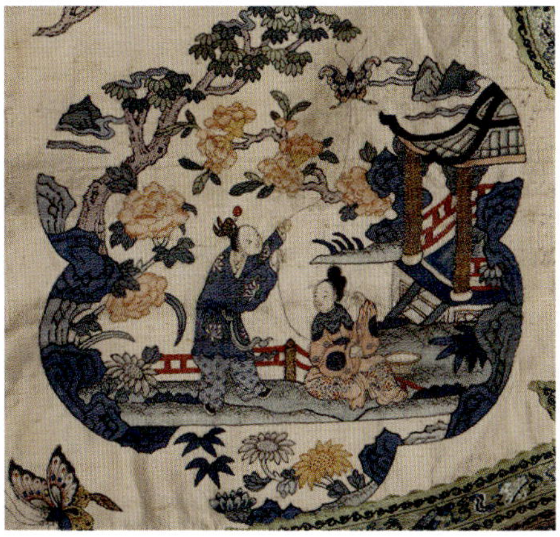

Scene 9

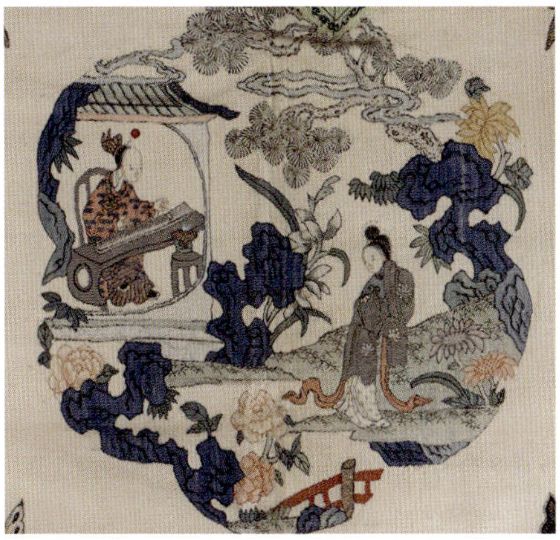

Scene 10

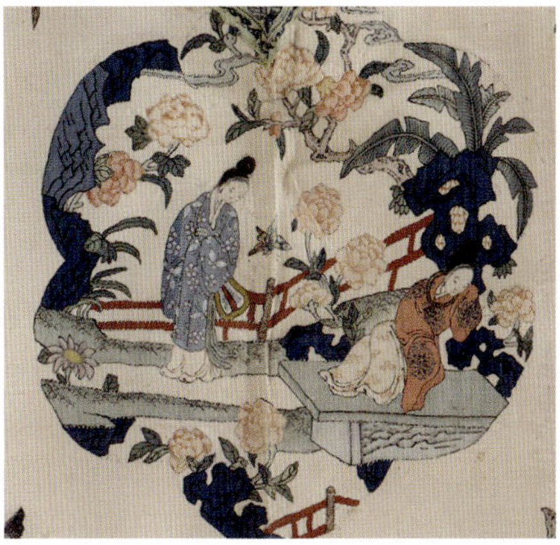

Scene 11

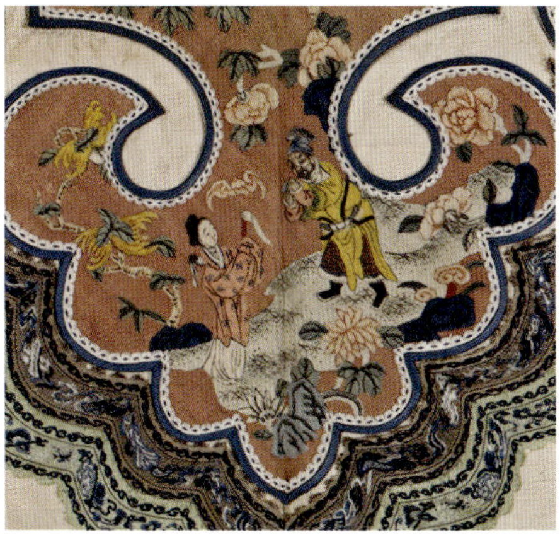

Scene 14

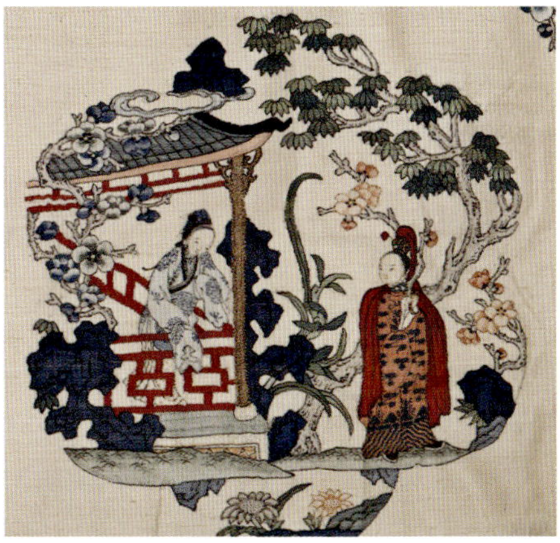

Scene 15

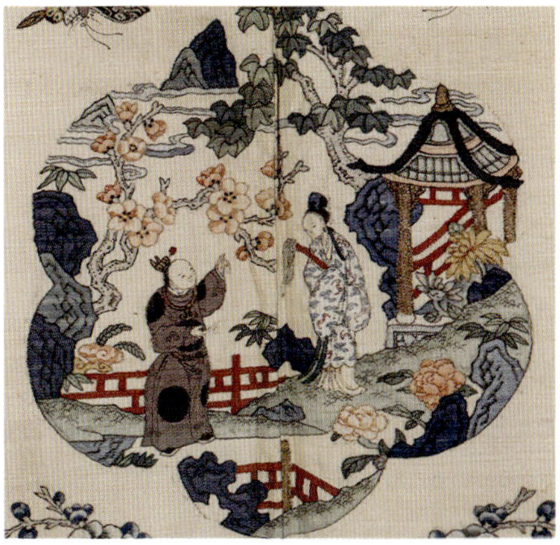

Scene 16

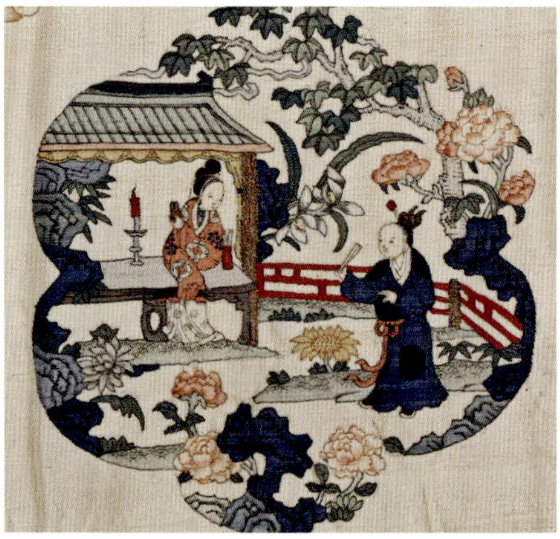

Scene 17

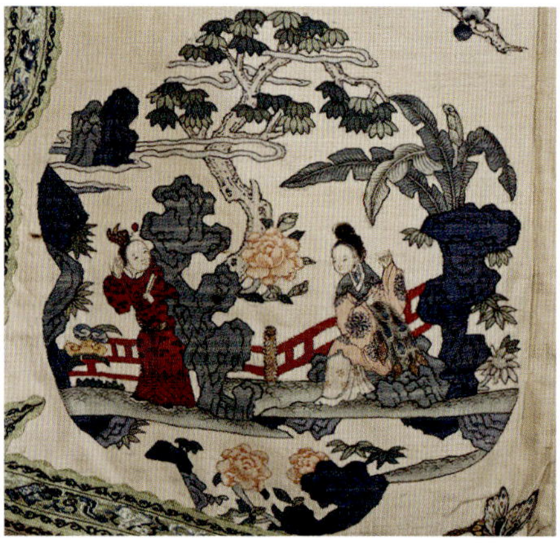

Scene 18

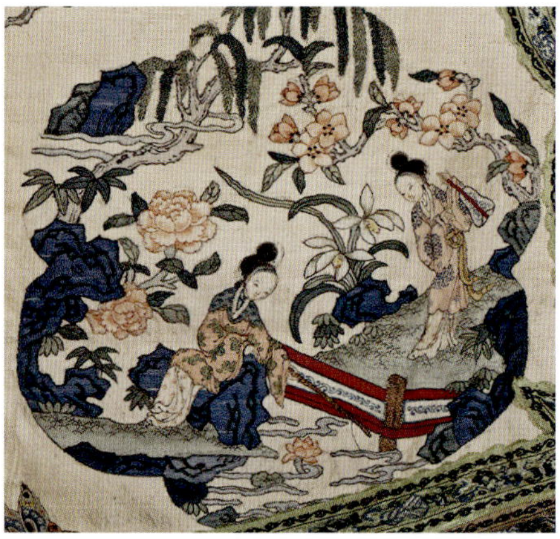

Scene 19

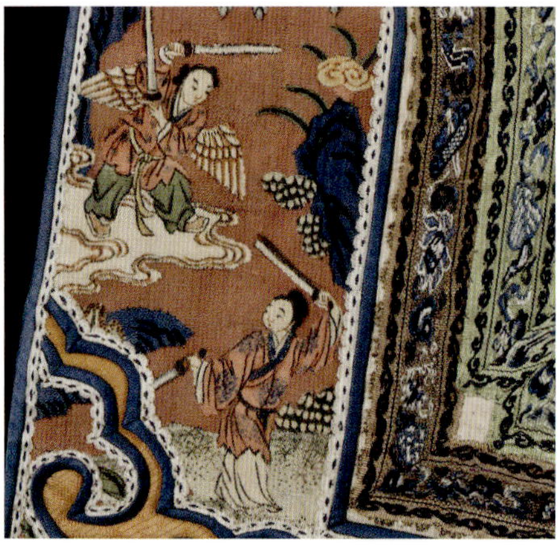

Scene 20

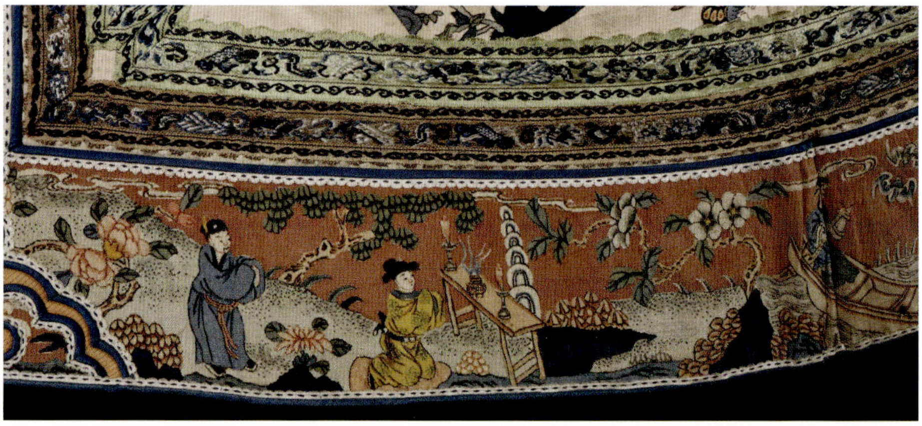

Scene 21

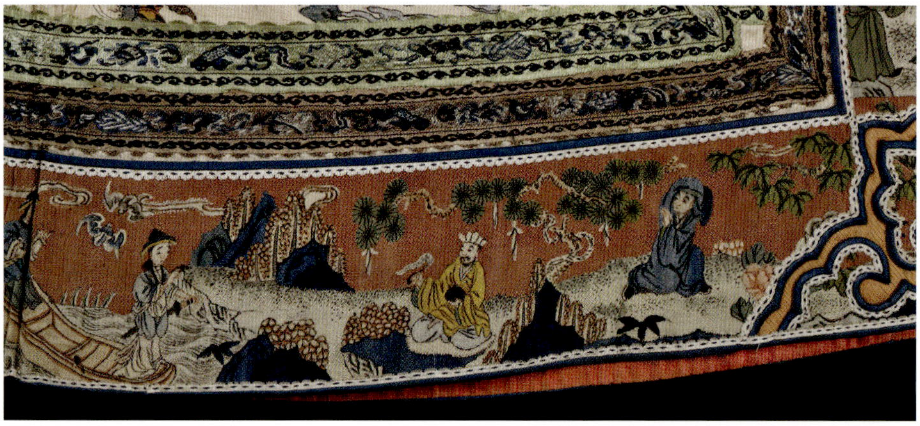

Scene 22

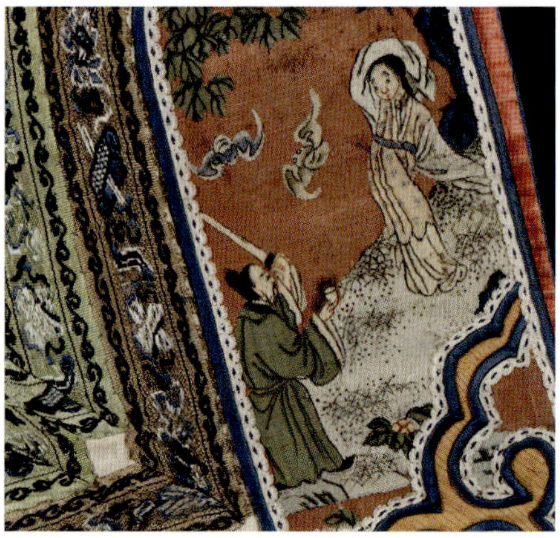

Scene 23

Cat. 29

Chinese, Qing Dynasty (1644–1911)

Cup with the Water Battle Scene from The White Snake (Baishe zhuan), first half of the 19th century

Porcelain with overglaze polychrome enamel decoration, height: 2 3/8 in. (6 cm), diameter: 4 3/8 in. (11.1 cm)

Lent by The Metropolitan Museum of Art, Purchase by subscription, 1879

79.2.1281

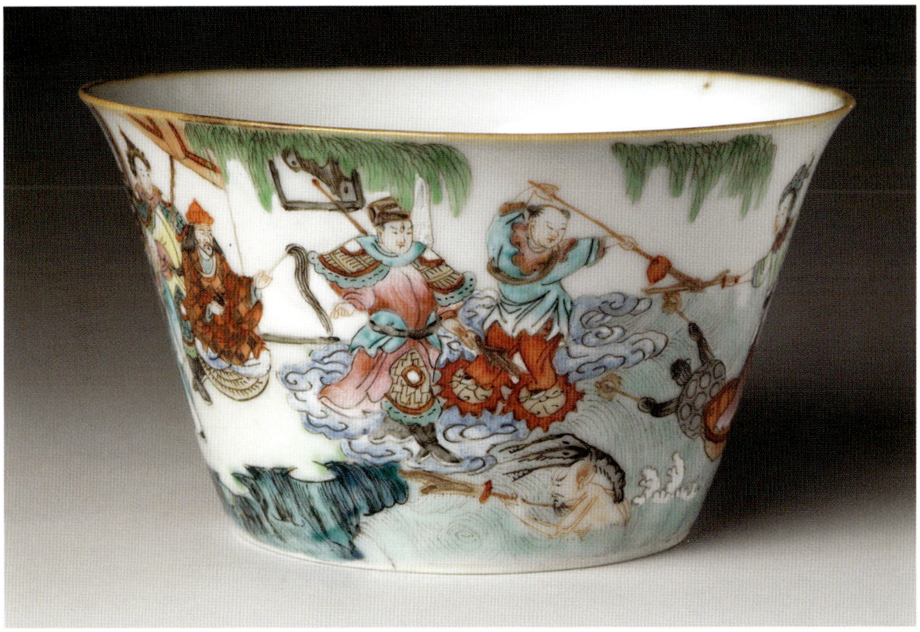

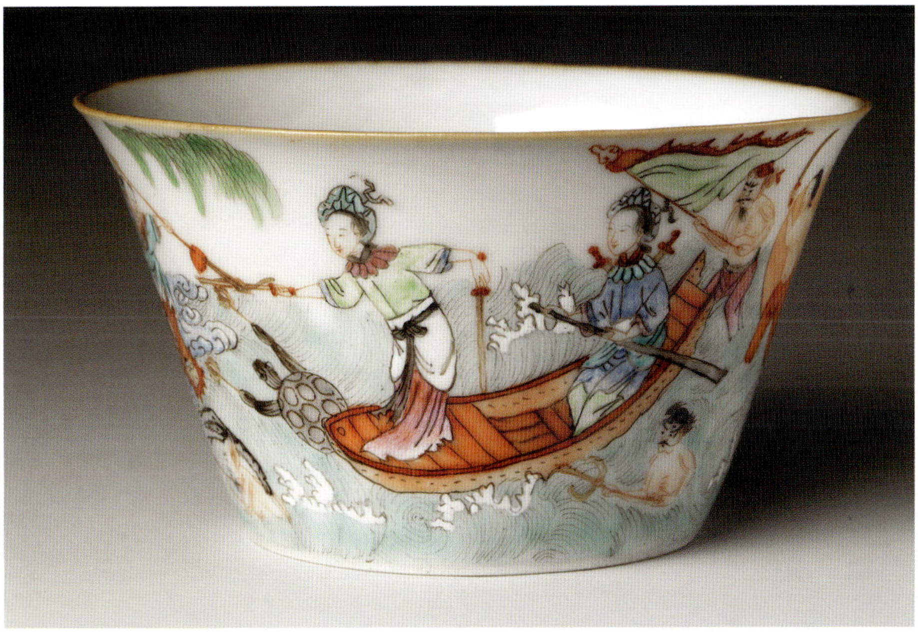

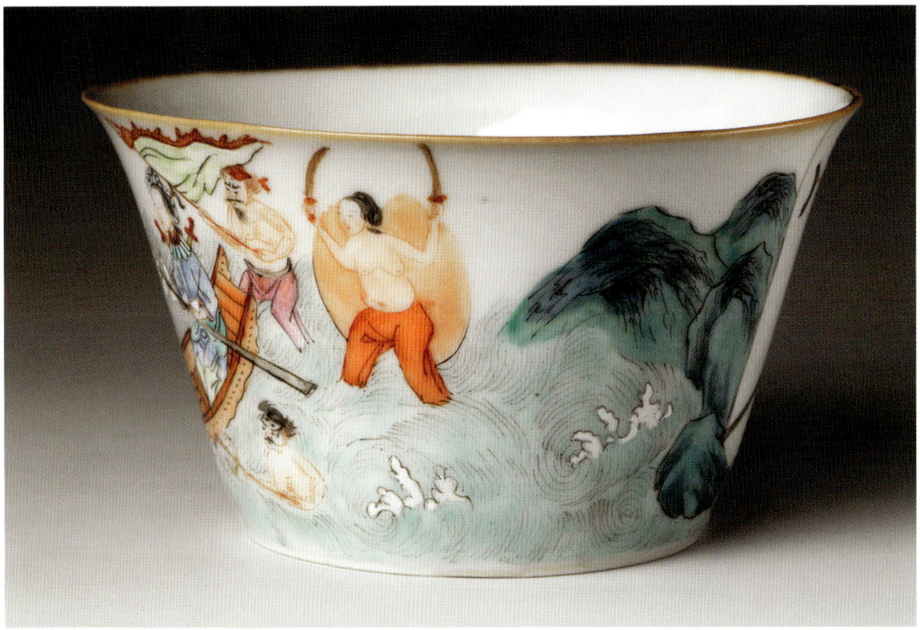

The painting on this small porcelain drinking cup depicts the water battle episode from *The White Snake* (*Baishe zhuan*), a folktale that was a popular subject for opera and storytelling performance. The technique of painting porcelains with overglaze polychrome enamels produced soft but vivid colors on a white surface. The use of contrasting colors dramatizes the scene and also resembles the chromatic visual effects in contemporary theater performance. The horizontal ground line of the painted scenes follows the curved shape of the cup. Fully two-thirds of the cup's outer surface is decorated with scenes that take place in water, echoing the liquid content inside the drinking cup.

The cup illustrates the climax of the story. In the Water Battle (Shuidou), Madame White Snake (Baishe) and her maid, Green Snake (Qingshe), water snake spirits who have assumed human form, fight against Monk Fahai in order to rescue White Snake's mortal husband Xu Xian. In the focal center of the scene, Green Snake, clad in a green top and pink skirt, fights with Nezha, the divine child-warrior riding on his wind-and-fire wheels. White Snake, who is pregnant, reclines in the boat and steers it. Surrounding them is the aquatic battalion that Green Snake has summoned in her defense: a clam spirit brandishing twin swords to the far right, a fish spirit holding up a banner, and a crab spirit, trident

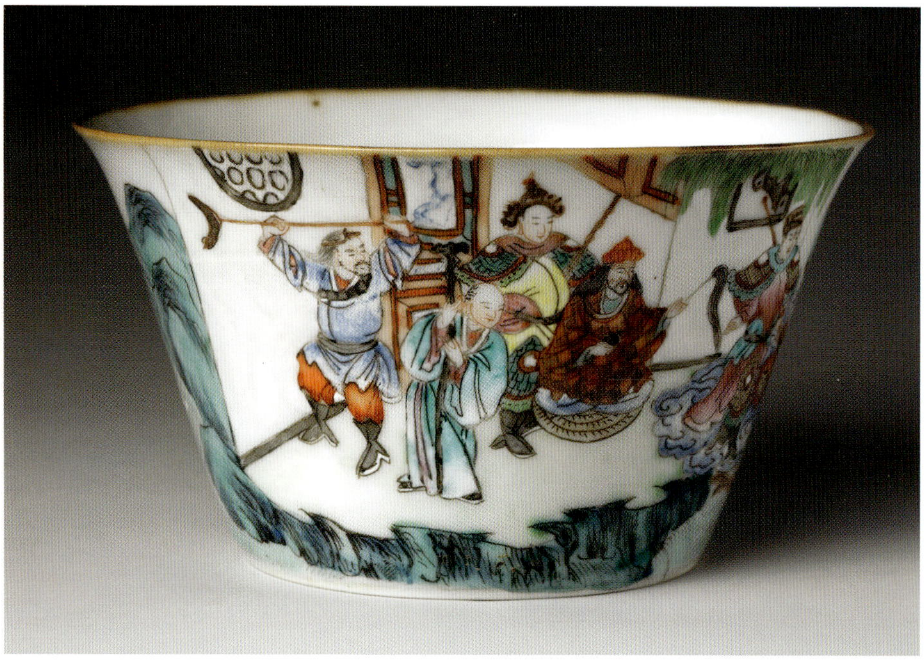

in hand, below the boat. A turtle spirit and a prawn spirit are fighting alongside Green Snake. On their opponents' side, Monk Fahai, sitting on his woven mat in Gold Mountain Temple (Jinshan si) with fly-whisk in hand, has also called for reinforcements. Behind Nezha, the mighty god Erlang shen, standing on clouds, his third eye just visible on his forehead, has joined the fray. The Bodhisattva Weituo (Skanda) stands behind Fahai. Another monk stands next to Fahai, holding the latter's staff, while a monastery guardian spirit (sengqielan) hoists a weapon with a crescent-shaped blade. This Buddhist fighting force wields invincible power against the two serpent ladies and their crustacean allies. The picture echoes the tension of the narrative by placing the heavily armored male warriors on land and rock, with the more vulnerable females on water.

The legend of the White Snake has a long history and was performed, depicted, and retold in many forms and media. The combination of the White Snake together with celestial guards and Buddhist deities, especially Nezha, Weituo, and Erlang shen, was common in operatic and storytelling versions of the Water Battle. The sea creatures, which are portrayed as human actors in costume, clearly show the mark of stage practice. In surviving nineteenth-century New Year prints, we find similar scenes and motifs (see fig. 5.1 of Gold Mountain Temple in Bo Songnian's essay in this catalogue and other collections of New Year prints).[1] The composition, costumes, and props, especially the iconography of the sea warriors and the Buddhist forces on the cup all imply the influence of contemporary opera performance. —YUNFEI SHAO

1 Feng Jicai, *Zhongguo muban nianhua jicheng* [*Collected Chinese Woodblock New Year Prints*] (Beijing: Zhonghua shuju, 2004), vol 3: Wuqiang, p. 78; vol. 10: Fengxiang, p. 183.

Four

Romance of the Western Chamber

Romance of the Western Chamber (*Xixiang ji*) began as a Tang dynasty tale written in the early ninth century CE, but it was the Yuan dynasty playwright Wang Shifu's adaptation of the story into a long northern drama (*zaju*) during the second half of the thirteenth century that turned it into the most beloved Chinese romantic comedy of all time. The play, which runs twenty-one acts, tells the love story of the handsome and talented Student Zhang and the beautiful and intelligent Oriole, who meet when both are staying at the Monastery of Universal Salvation. When local bandits menace the monastery, Oriole's widowed mother promises her daughter to any man who can protect them. Zhang saves them by getting a message to his friend General Du, who defeats the bandits. But Oriole's mother unaccountably reneges on her promise. With Oriole's pert maid Crimson serving as go-between, Zhang and Oriole manage to spend the night together and become lovers. Eventually Oriole's mother consents to the marriage but only if Zhang first passes the civil service examinations. Fortunately, he takes top place in the exams, and the play concludes with the joyful celebration of the couple's wedding at the monastery.

During the Ming (1368–1644) and Qing (1644–1911) dynasties, more than 100 different woodblock editions of the play were published, many of them illustrated, dwarfing the popularity of any other play in Chinese print history. From as early as the fourteenth century, when scenes from *Romance of the Western Chamber* began to be painted on porcelain, woodblock illustrations have served as the main visual source for depictions of the play on decorative objects. In the late eighteenth and nineteenth centuries, the play became a favorite subject for porcelain export ware and other items of *chinoiserie* aimed at a foreign market.

Domestically, the play remained a popular part of Chinese literary, visual, and performance culture throughout its long existence. As an opera adapted for multiple genres and formats over the course of its history, *Romance of the Western Chamber* persists in the performance repertory and can still be seen in stage and film versions today.

Cat. 30

Chinese, Qing Dynasty (1644–1911)
Hexagonal Vase Depicting Scenes from Romance of the Western Chamber (Xixiang ji), 19th century
Porcelain with famille verte overglaze enamel decoration, 20 1/2 x 6 7/8 in. (52.1 x 17.5 cm)
Philadelphia Museum of Art: The Alfred and Margaret Caspary Memorial Gift, 1955
1955-50-390

Each side of this hexagonal, famille verte vase contains two large cartouches against a diaper of red and blue flowers on a speckled green ground. In the upper register, a curved border with scalloped corners frames the image; in the lower register, small flourishes embellish the corners of an otherwise rectangular cartouche. The floral diaper also covers the shoulders, which are separated from the neck by a double border of *ruyi* scepters. Four auspicious characters in alternating red and blue decorate the outside of the neck. Inside the rim, two butterflies and a wasp hover over a blank ground.

This vase previously belonged to the collection of Sir Leonard Gow VIII (1859–1936), a Scottish shipping magnate whose collection of Chinese porcelain was renowned for its Kangxi period (1662–1722) wares. Although recently identified as a nineteenth-century work, this vase has a speckled green ground that appears on many eighteenth-century export porcelains. Likewise, scenes from *Romance of the Western Chamber* (*Xixiang ji*) are not uncommon on exported Kangxi wares.

Far less common are porcelains depicting such a great number of scenes. Exceptions include a matching famille verte bowl and saucer, both illustrating twenty-five scenes in chronological order, and a blue and white Jingdezhen vase presenting twenty scenes. Interestingly, these works, both of which are Kangxi wares, contain several scenes strikingly similar in composition. Their designers likely drew upon related visual sources, such as one of the many illustrated editions of the opera or a pictorial manual for popular designs.

The hexagonal vase is unique in its presentation of twelve scenes from eleven acts of the opera—in no discernable order. Either unacquainted or unconcerned with the opera's plot sequence, the designer may have based his selection of scenes on an assortment of acts in a contemporary anthology. Such anthologies took into consideration that many Chinese operas were too long to be frequently performed in their entirety and that patrons of operatic troupes requested assorted scenes.

Another distinctive feature of this vase is that each scene includes an inscription, eight of which draw on arias from the northern version of the opera. Two others adapt lines from other versions. Still two others, accompanying part 4, acts 3 and 4, employ lines from a long cycle of poems titled "Exquisite Poems on Oriole and Student Zhang in Pudong" (Pudong Cui Zhang zhuyu shi), which appears as an appendix in an edition of the northern version of the opera.[1] The inscription for act 3 describes the lovers' parting: "Desires unfinished, raising a cup and pouring a farewell drink; clasping a sleeve, asking the date of return."[2] The inscription for act 4 accidentally combines lines from two poems in the cycle, producing a nonsensical combination to describe Student Zhang: "Baggage temporarily stowed at Xiao temple, he suddenly dreams that Oriole comes to the inn."[3] Such an error may attest to the illiteracy of the artist who decorated the vase.

Two cartouches illustrate part 3, act 3, "Repudiating the Letter." While one of these, Zhang's clambering over the garden wall to meet Oriole, is a common motif on Qing porcelains, the image of Oriole entering the garden to burn incense at night is unusual. The inscription describes Oriole in Crimson's words: "Golden lotuses trample peony sprouts; jade hairpins catch on the brier-rose trellis."[4] This depiction draws our attention to a special visual quality of this vase: whereas the scenes depicted in the aforementioned porcelains are densely colored and contain many landscape features, the scenes of this vase are more minimalist and evoke a staged space.

The decorative elements of this vase convey auspicious meanings. *Ruiyi,* the name for the scepters dividing the neck and shoulders of the vase , means "according to your wishes," and imitate the shape of *lingzhi*, a fungus traditionally associated with longevity. The highly stylized characters on the neck also express good wishes. The character for longevity, *shou*, has over a hundred stylized forms, and often appears on traditional decorative products, such as ceramics, textiles, and carvings.

The insects on the rim probably serve a more romantic function. Because women are associated with flowers, depictions of insects and flowers often signify romance. This is a suitable motif to accompany *Romance of the Western Chamber*, which takes place in the garden-like setting of a Buddhist monastery. The opera itself may also have been regarded as a lucky motif, and not only for its happy ending: the scene in which Zhang and Oriole consummate their love is not an act of empty sensuality, but one of procreation, and thus it evokes the good fortune of bearing children. —ALIA BREITWIESER

1 See *Xinkan kaozheng quanxiang pingshi Bei Xixiang ji* [All-New, Revised, Complete Annotated Northern Version of *Romance of the Western Chamber*], in *Guojia tushuguan cang Xixiang ji shanben congkan* [Rare Editions of *Romance of the Western Chamber* in the Collection of the National Library of China, facsimile series] (Beijing: National Library of China, 2011), vol. 8, pp. 1–332.

2 Ibid., p. 325.

3 Ibid., line 1, p. 313 and line 2, p. 326.

4 Wang Shifu, *The Story of the Western Wing*, trans. Stephen H. West and Wilt L. Idema (Berkeley: The University of California Press, 1995), p. 210.

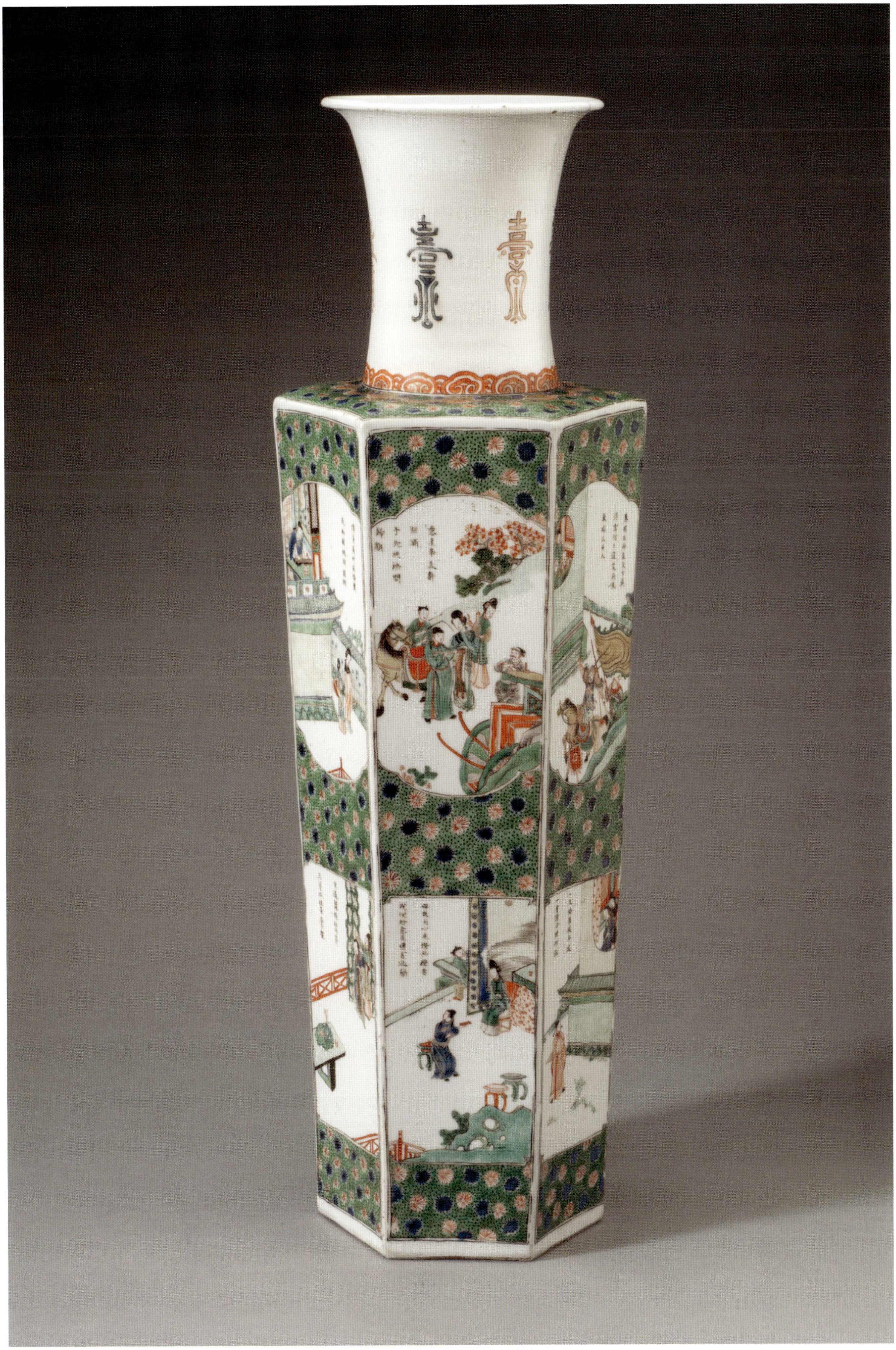

Guide to Scenes in Their Two-Tier Order on Each Facet of the Vase

Part 1, Act 1
Startled by Beauty
It's not necessary to say, "The corners of her eyes, there she lets passion linger," Because this footprint relays all the feelings of her heart. (121)

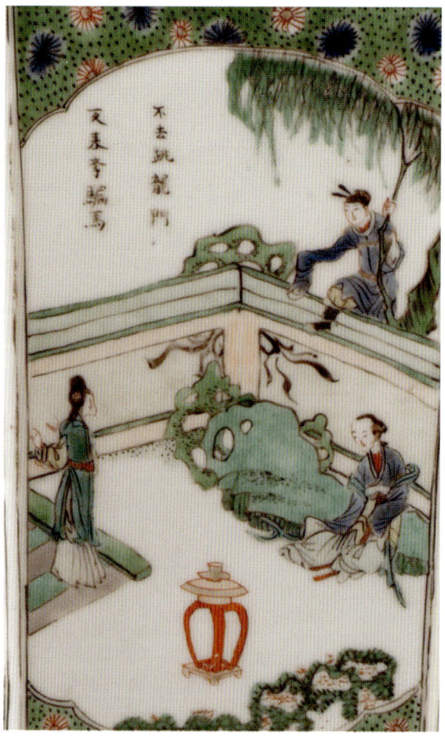

Part 3, Act 3
Repudiating the Letter
Not going to jump the dragon gate, You come to study mounting a mare.

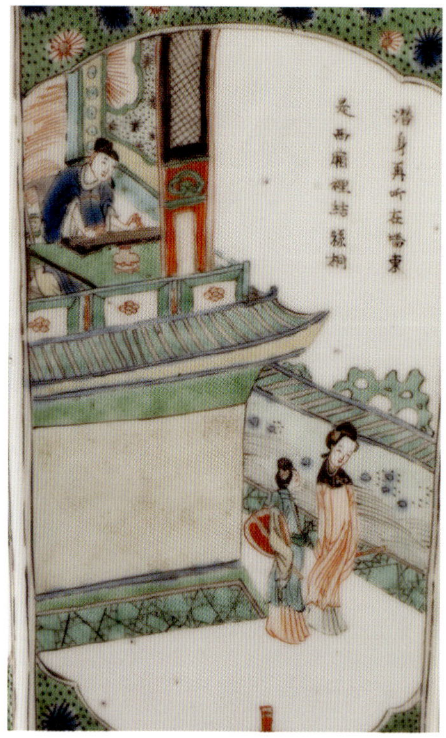

Part 2, Act 4
Sentiments of the Zither
Concealed, I listen again, east of the wall; It's someone tuning zither strings in the Western Wing.

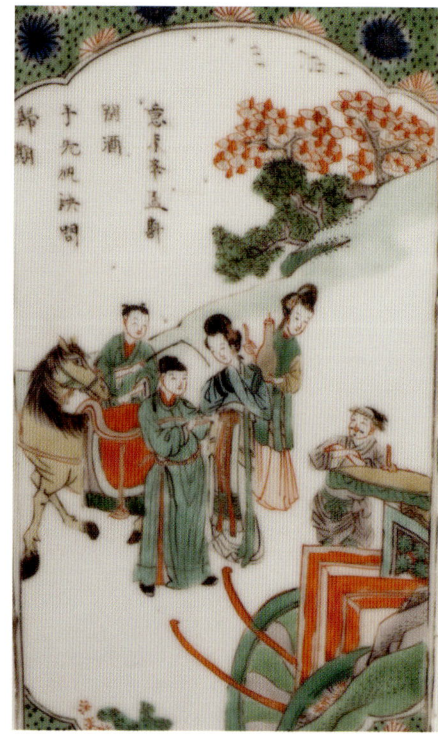

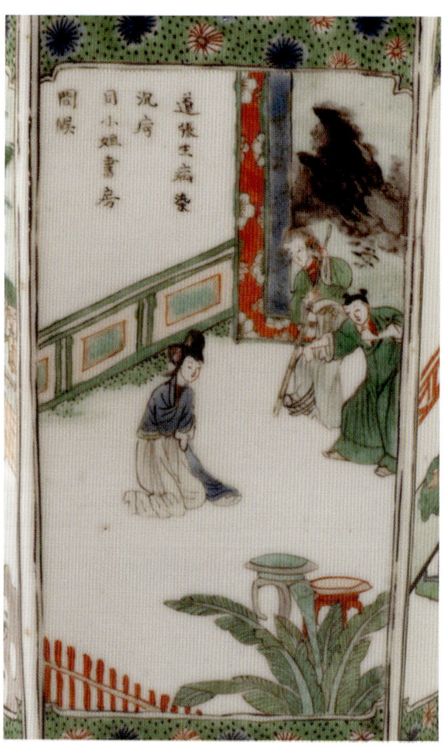

Part 1, Act 2
Guest Lodgings
Just rent me out the smallest guest room or a monk's cell, Then I'll be living just opposite that lovable wretch of mine. (125)

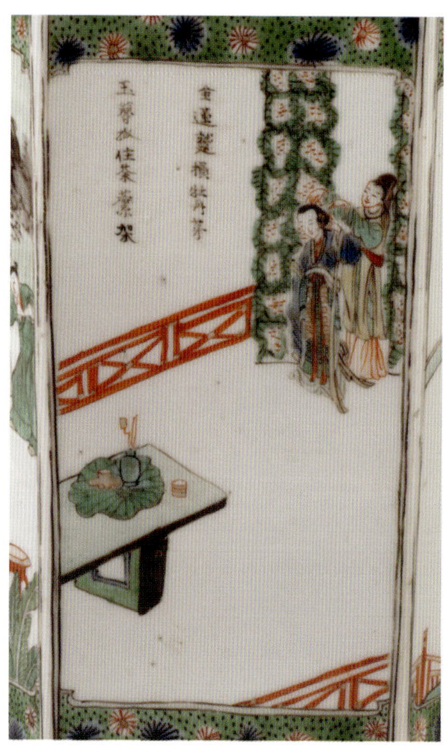

Part 4, Act 2
Interrogating the Girl
Reporting Student Zhang's serious illness, I accompanied Miss to the study to ask after him.

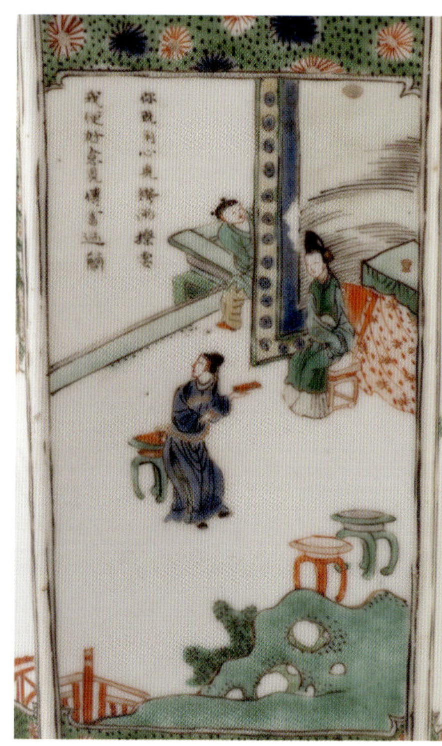

Part 3, Act 3
Repudiating the Letter
Her golden lotuses trample sprouts of peonies, Her jade hairpins catch on the brier-rose trellis. (210)

Part 4, Act 3

Tears at a Banquet

Desires unfinished, raising a cup and pouring a farewell drink; Clasping her sleeve, she asks when he will return.

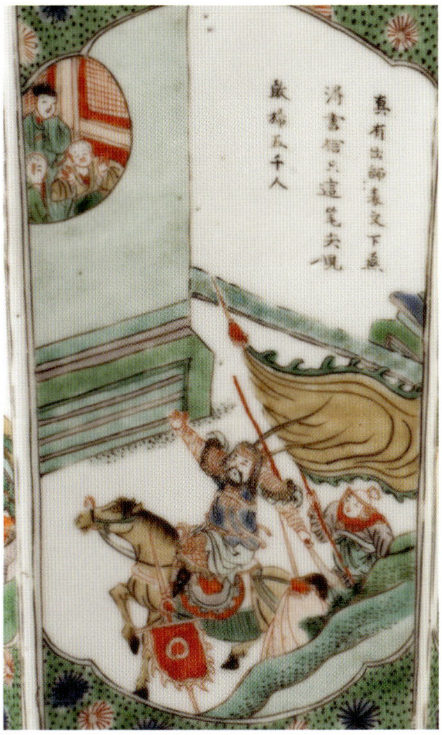

Part 2, Act 1

Alarm at the Monastery

Truly capable of a "Rescript to Send Out the Army" and a "Letter to Order Yan", Only with such a brush-tip could one dare to wipe out five thousand men!

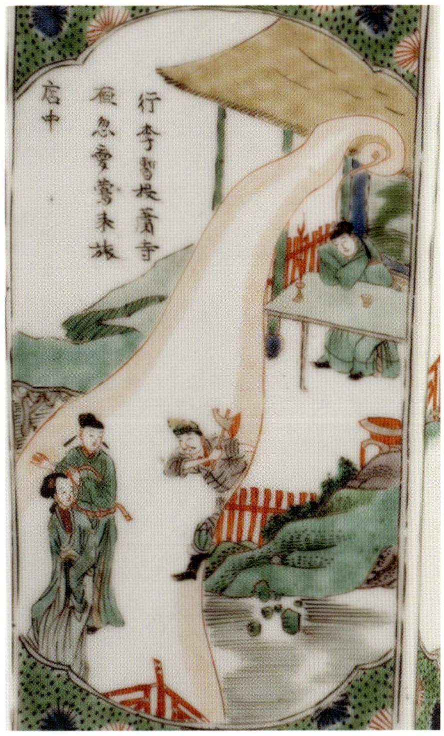

Part 4, Act 4

Startled in a Dream

Baggage temporarily stowed at Xiao Temple, he suddenly dreams Oriole has come to the inn. Should be: A lonely candle flickers, his eyes grow dim; he suddenly dreams Oriole has come to the inn.

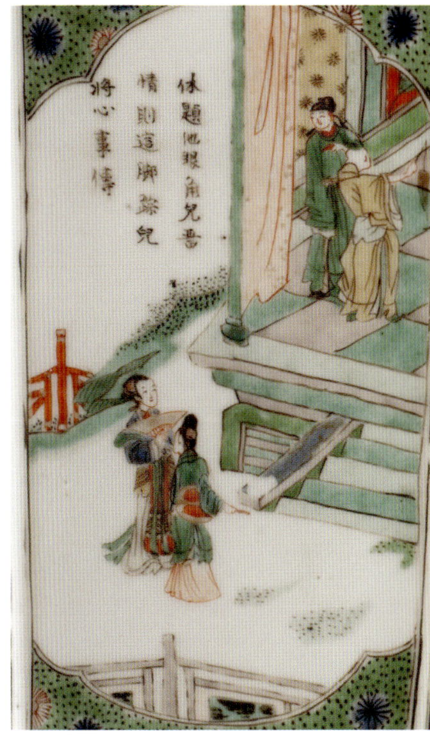

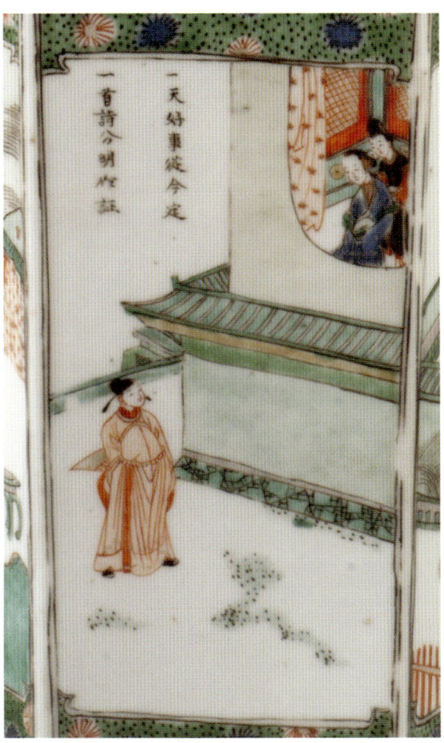

Part 3, Act 2

Commotion Over a Letter

You purposely stirred up rain and clouds, while I graciously delivered messages.

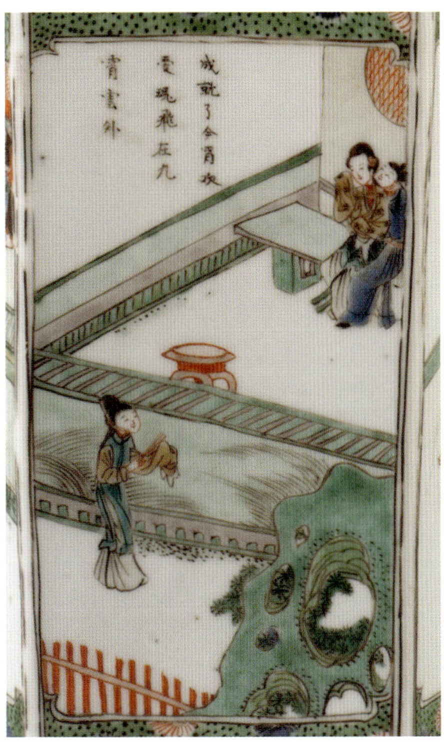

Part 1, Act 3

Matching Verses

The happiness of that day has now been fixed: A single poem is clear evidence. (143)

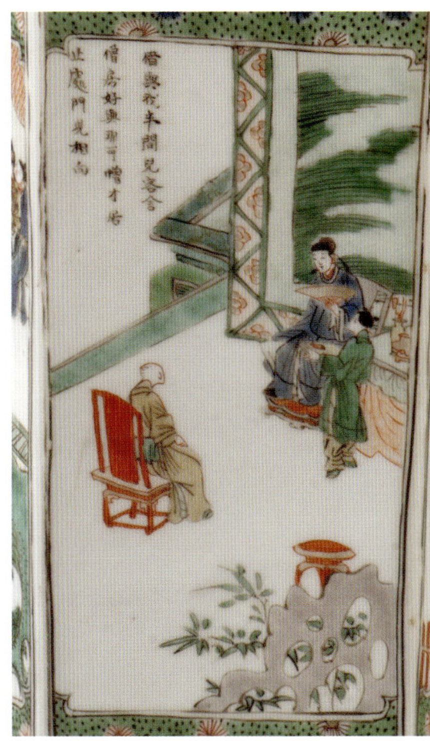

Part 4, Act 1

Responding to the Letter

Consummating tonight's joyous affections, My soul flies beyond the highest heavens.

Cat. 31

Chinese, Late Qing Dynasty (1644–1911)
Pair of Matching Fans with Multiple Scenes from Romance of the Western Chamber (Xixiang ji), 1800–1911
Carved ivory, inlaid gemstones, metal hinges, and silk tassels, each overall: 48 x 10 in. (122.5 x 25.3 cm); each fan without tassel: 19 x 10 in. (48.3 x 25.3cm)
Asian Art Museum, Gift of Mr. and Mrs. Herbert J. Fahnestock
1992.93.1-2

In the Qing dynasty (1644–1911) artisans in the southern treaty port of Guangzhou (Canton) developed an intricate style that became popular not only in the imperial court, but also in Europe. Guangzhou ivory carvings were usually bleached to enhance their whiteness and were also known for having inlaid materials such as jade and sandalwood. This pair of ivory fans, with their delicate carvings on both sides, impressively white hue, and inlaid gemstones, might have been produced in Guangzhou for the tourist market.

The shape of the fans imitates that of the palm-leaf fan popular during the Wei and Jin dynasties (220–420). Their size and weight indicate that these ornately carved objects were meant not for practical use but for display. Their front panels depict six scenes from *Romance of the Western Chamber* (*Xixiang ji*), three that take place inside the monastery and three that occur outside. A straight central line demarcates this division of inner and outer spaces, while alongside it different trees, buildings, and balustrades remain on their side of the boundary to suggest a shift of space. Most interestingly the scenes are arranged so that each fan is a mirror image of the other.

Starting from the bottom and keyed to the numbered diagram at right, the scenes within the temple are (1) Student Zhang playing the zither; (2) the Buddhist ceremony for Oriole's deceased father; and (3) Madam Cui's chastisement of Crimson. Read in the same direction, the scenes on the other side of the central line are (4) the lovers' sad farewell banquet; (5) Zhang's dream in which Oriole is abducted by the bandit Flying Tiger Sun; and (6) Zhang's triumphant return after he has passed the examinations. This arrangement of the scenes shows that the designer did not follow the play's linear narrative.

All six scenes employ popular elements whose precedents may be found in printed illustrations and other depictions of *Romance of the Western Chamber*, but with some minor changes. For example, in the farewell scene, the ivory fan emphasizes Oriole's emotional expression by depicting her raised sleeves. Raising one or both sleeves up to one's nose or covering the face with one's hands conventionally indicates crying—a detail that further enhances the heart-breaking sadness of separation. Roughly the same design is found on the rhinoceros horn cup from the Field Museum, Chicago, also included in the exhibition (cat. 32).

The backs of the fans are meticulously carved with zigzag bamboo mat patterns, and both fans bear the same fraudulent inscription above the handles: "Shi Yao respectfully presents [this ivory fan] in the year Dingwei during the Chenghua reign period [1457]."

The craftsman cleverly gave material form to the literal meanings of the expression *heshan*[a] (matching or joined fans), which implies two sides or people fitting each other perfectly. When the twin fans are put together, a romantic story with a happy ending is concealed by the ordinary mat patterns on their exterior surfaces. *Heshan* (matched or closed fans) is also a homonym for the term *heshan*[b] (kind and amiable), which adds a sense of harmony to the objects.

A pair of late nineteenth-century ivory fans of comparable shape and dimensions, but with different depictions (a carving of the Queen Mother of the West and other deities on the front and an incised narrative scene on the back) may be found at the Sir Victor Sassoon Chinese Ivories Trust, England. —RANTING JIANG, JUDITH T. ZEITLIN, AND YUHANG LI

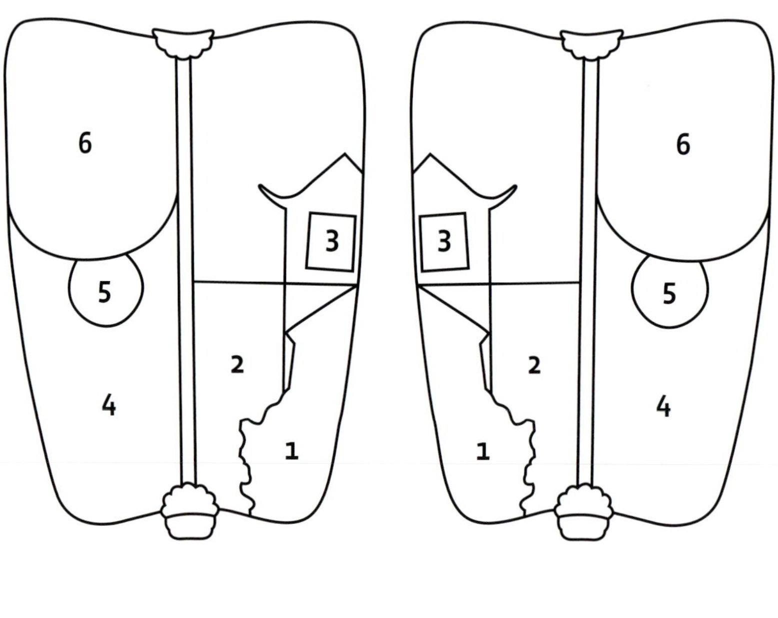

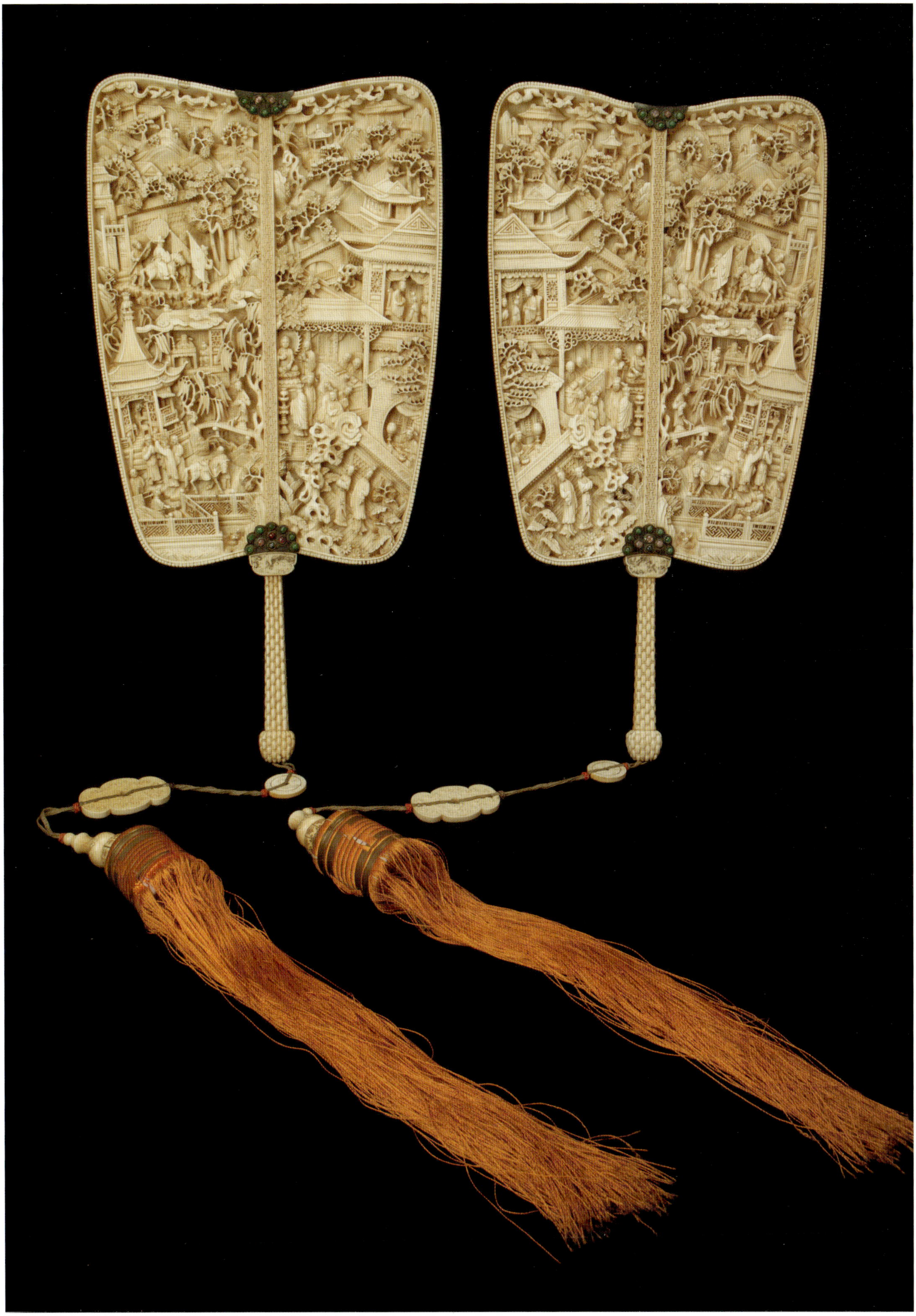

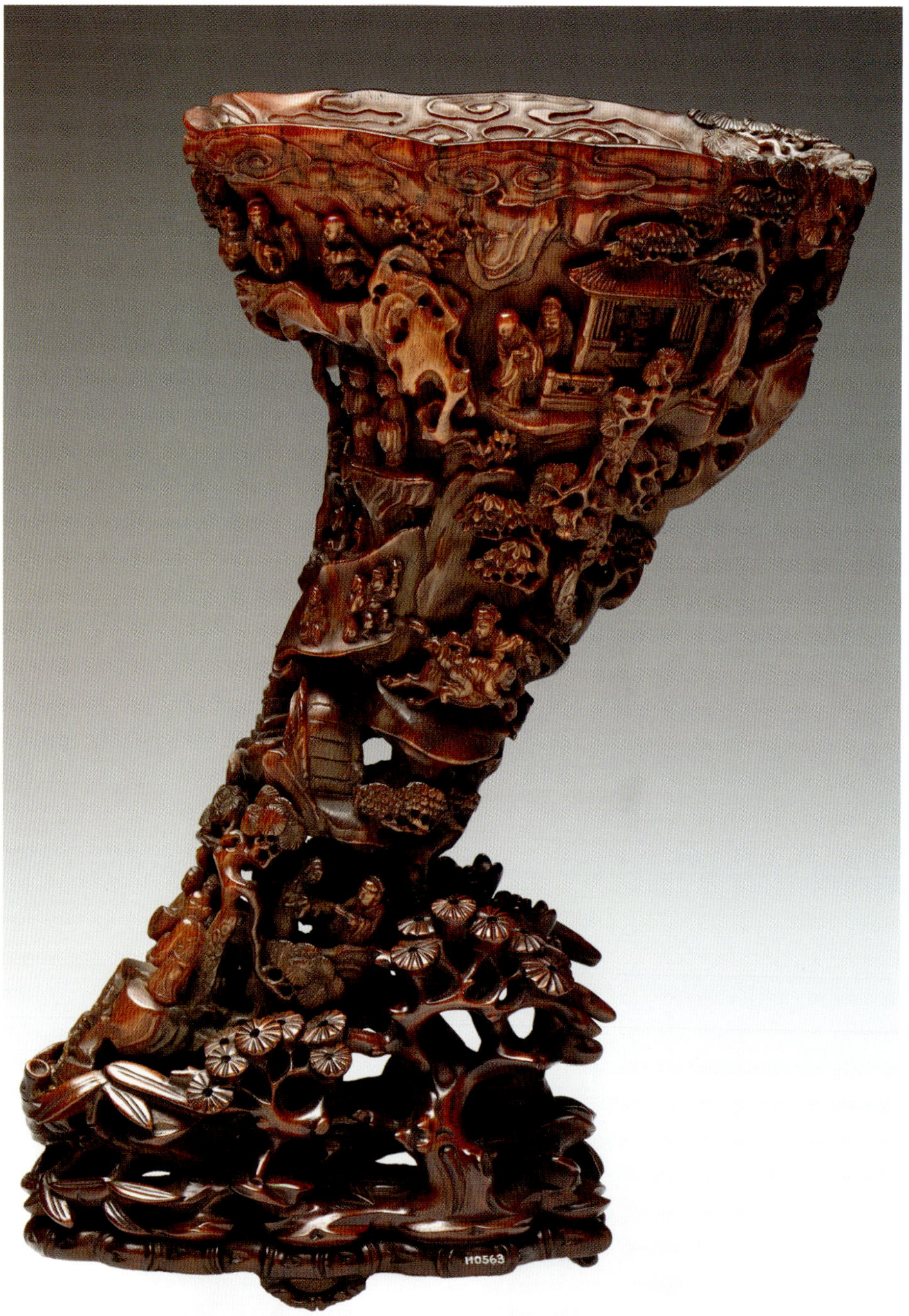

Cat. 32
Chinese, Qing Dynasty (1644–1911)
Rhinoceros Horn Cup with Scenes from Romance of the Western Chamber (Xixiang ji), n.d.
Carved rhinoceros horn, height: 10 in. (25.5 cm)
The Field Museum, Chicago
110563

The impressive size of this rhinoceros horn cup, along with its lustrous chestnut hue and ornate carving, would have made it a luxury item even during its own time. Too heavy to stand on its own, the cup is supported by three branch-shaped lobes rising out of a wooden base. The base is delicately carved into branches of pine, flowering plum, and bamboo, evoking in combination the three friends of winter (*suihan sanyou*), a traditional symbol of scholarly virtue.

Rhinoceros horn cups much simpler in form were used in the imperial court during the early Ming dynasty (1368–1644). Over the course of the Ming and Qing dynasties (1644–1911), international trade enabled the increased importation of rhinoceros horn from South Asian and African markets. During this time, beautifully carved cups and bowls featuring bird and flower motifs, literary scenes, and other designs grew in popularity outside the court.[1]

The cup bears an inscription that reads, "Scenes from *Romance of the Western Chamber* (*Xixiang tu*)," thus indicating the thematic content of its carvings. The design features fifteen scenes,[2] which are not arranged chronologically but instead organized according to a unique pictorial logic. This design effectively adapts the narrative contents to the material demands and shape of this largely preformed natural medium.

The main body of the cup has been carved to depict a towering pine growing among rocks and extending to the clouds, an auspicious image implying longevity. Beyond their symbolic function, the tree and rocks also serve to frame and divide the scenes into two registers. The upper register contains the bulk of the scenes, which focus on romantic events occurring in the Monastery of Universal Salvation, where most of the play takes place. The lower register, which occupies the narrow end of the horn, depicts the small handful of scenes that occur outside the monastery walls.

Whereas most of the cup is crowded with scenes, its spine depicts only the monastery gate nestled among a mass of thick pine and rocks, thus symbolizing the entrance and end-point of both the story and the viewer's experience. The abbot stands nearby with his staff in hand as though he were receiving or sending off a visitor. A striking contrast between these natural objects carved in high relief and the relatively flat temple gate and abbot presents the temple as a paradise far from the mortal world and emphasizes the illusionistic nature of this romance and its dramatic moments.

Although the cup does not depict the events of the opera in precise chronological order, it presents popular scenes in readily recognizable formats. To the right of the gate,

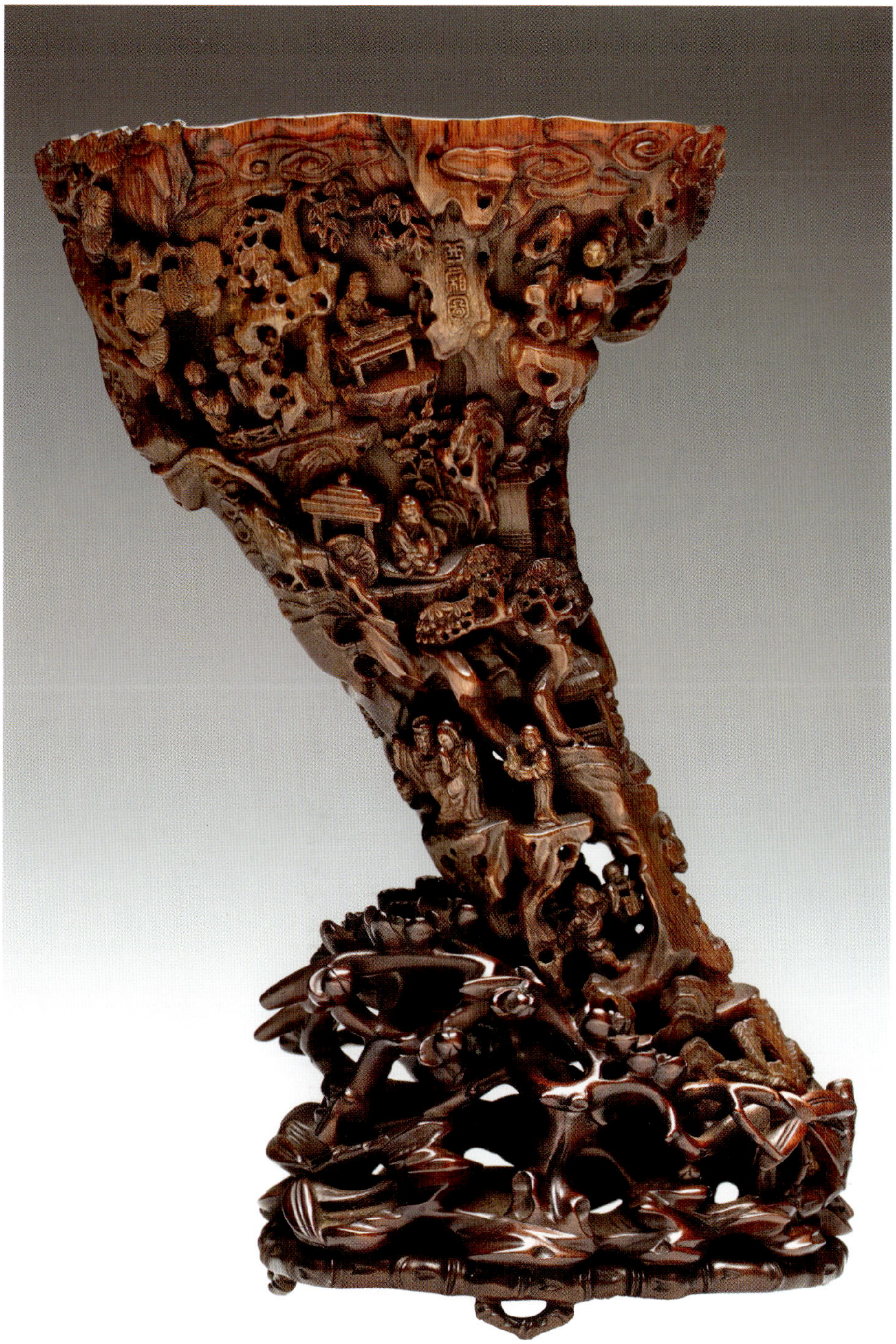

page provide sufficient visual context to identify Zhang, Oriole, and Crimson. Similarly, the designer's rendition of "Startled in a Dream" depicts Zhang asleep at a table in a small inn beside a bridge. The dream bubble illustrates bandits stealing Oriole away, a clever but nearly ubiquitous visual device in renditions of this scene.

Another large rhinoceros horn cup presents a similar combination of scenes from *Romance of the Western Chamber* and might originate from the same workshop or artist. The two cups have comparable poses and arrangements.[3]

—RANTING JIANG

1 Patricia Bjaaland Welch, *Chinese Art: A Guide to Motifs and Visual Imagery* (Tokyo: Tuttle Publishing, 2008), pp. 143–44.
2 See accompanying diagram.
3 "A Very Large Carved Rhinoceros Horn Libation Cup," *Fine Chinese Ceramics and Works of Art: Hong Kong, October 8, 2006* (Hong Kong: Sotheby's, 2006), pp. 260–61. See also Thomas Hok (Huo Mantang), *Connoisseurship of Rhinoceros Horn Carving in China* (*Zhongguo xijiao diaoke zhenshang*) (Hong Kong: Daye gongsi, 1999), p. 191, plate 138. Hok erroneously identifies the scenes on the cup as belonging to *The Peony Pavilion* (*Mudan ting*) rather than to *Romance of the Western Chamber* (*Xixiang ji*).

Crimson and Oriole listen surreptitiously as Student Zhang plays his zither, which rests on a table before him. Oriole covers her face with her fan in a gesture that conveys her emotional excitement. To the right, just beside the inscription, Oriole sits and reads Zhang's love letter as Crimson peers over her shoulder. Just below and to the right, the viewer encounters one of the most popular and recognizable illustrations from the *Western Chamber*, Zhang jumping over a wall for a romantic tryst with Oriole. As in so many other depictions of this scene, Oriole is stationed beside a rockery and an incense stand, oblivious to the acrobatic feat behind her. Another familiar element is the willow tree that Zhang uses to pull himself up before leaping across the wall.

The legibility of this visual conglomeration of romantic moments relies on popular depictions such as those in printed editions of the opera and on porcelains. In the lower register, two especially popular scenes often appeared in highly varied configurations, but always with the same figural elements. For instance, in the illustration of "Tears at a Banquet," the manned carriage, wine vessel, small pagoda, and waiting

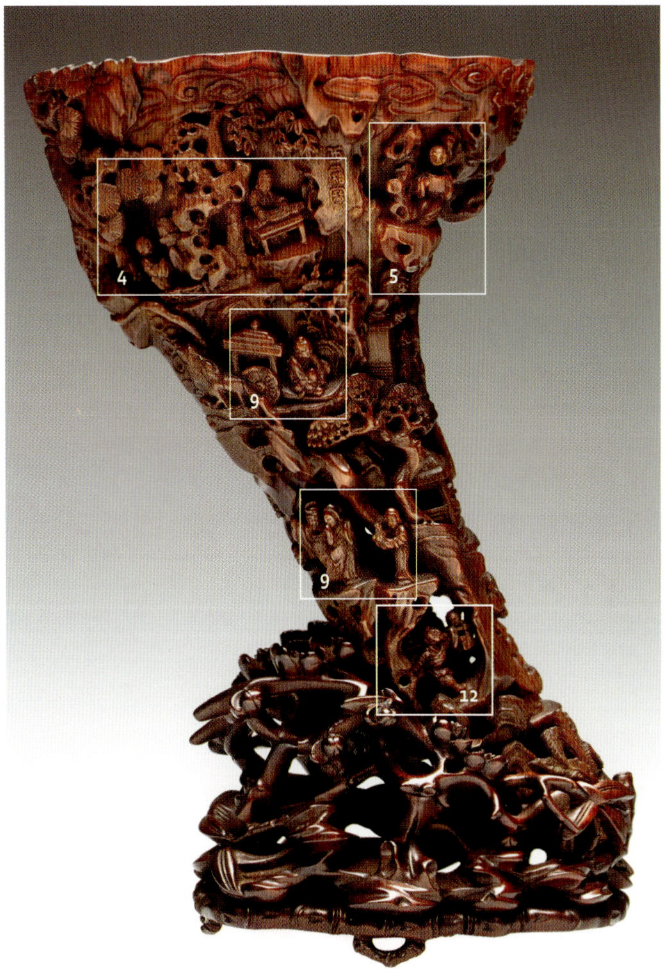

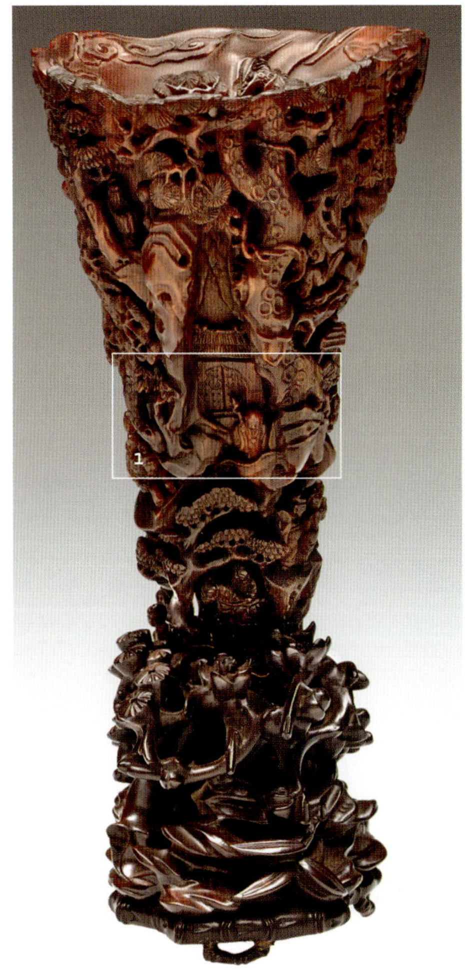

Key

1 Abbot at the Monastery Gate
2 Startled by Beauty
3 Monk Huiming Departs to Deliver the Message
4 Sentiments of the Zither
5 Commotion Over a Letter
6 Student Zhang Jumps Over the Wall
7 Oriole Burns Incense at Night
8 Exchanging Poems
9 Tears at a Banquet
10 Startled in a Dream
11 General Du Defeats the Bandits
12 A Glittering Report of Success in the Exams
13 A Brocade Missive on Sorrowful Parting
14 Oriole and Zhang's Wedding

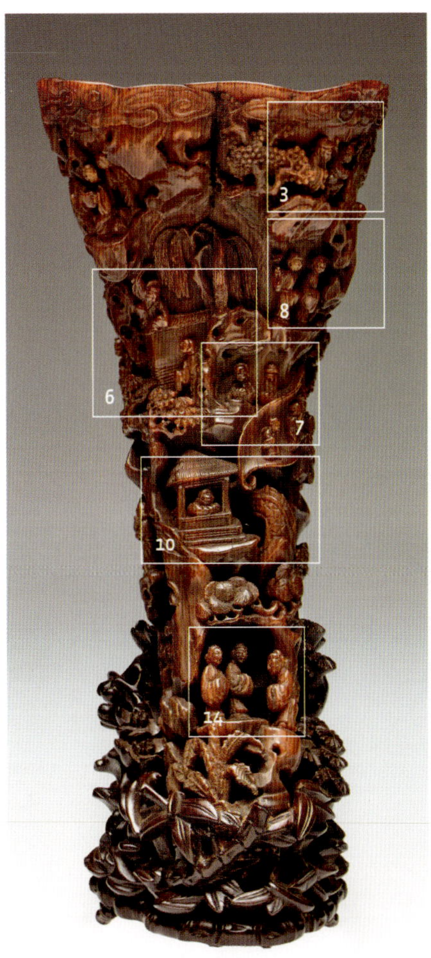

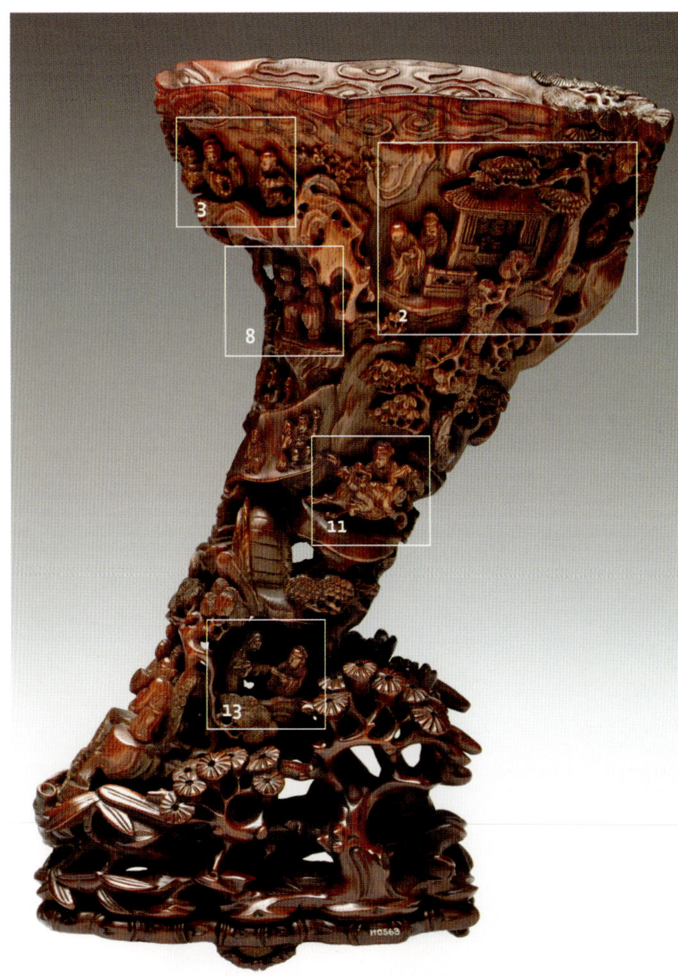

Cat. 33

Chinese, Qing Dynasty (1644–1911)

Pillow End: "Startled by Beauty" (Part 1, Act 1) from Romance of the Western Chamber (Xixiang ji), n.d.

Polychrome silk threads embroidered on white gauze, 6 1/32 x 6 1/6 in. (15.3 x 15.4 cm)

Courtesy of the Division of Anthropology, American Museum of Natural History

70.3/7027 B

Cat. 34

Chinese, Qing Dynasty (1644–1911)

Pillow End: "Commotion Over a Letter" (Part 3, Act 2) from Romance of the Western Chamber (Xixiang ji), n.d.

Polychrome silk threads embroidered on white gauze, 6 x 6 1/6 in. (15.2 x 15.4 cm)

Courtesy of the Division of Anthropology, American Museum of Natural History

70.3/7027 A

Cat. 35

Chinese, Qing Dynasty (1644–1911)

Pillow End: "Playing Chess" from Romance of the Western Chamber (Xixiang ji), n.d.

Polychrome silk threads embroidered on white gauze, 6 1/8 x 6 3/8 in. (15.6 x 16.2 cm)

Courtesy of the Division of Anthropology, American Museum of Natural History

70.3/7027 I

Cat. 36

Chinese, Qing Dynasty (1644–1911)

Pillow End: "Startled in a Dream" (Part 4, Act 4) from Romance of the Western Chamber (Xixiang ji), n.d.

Polychrome silk threads embroidered on white gauze, 6 1/8 x 6 3/8 in. (15.6 x 16.2 cm)

Courtesy of the Division of Anthropology, American Museum of Natural History

70.3/7027 H

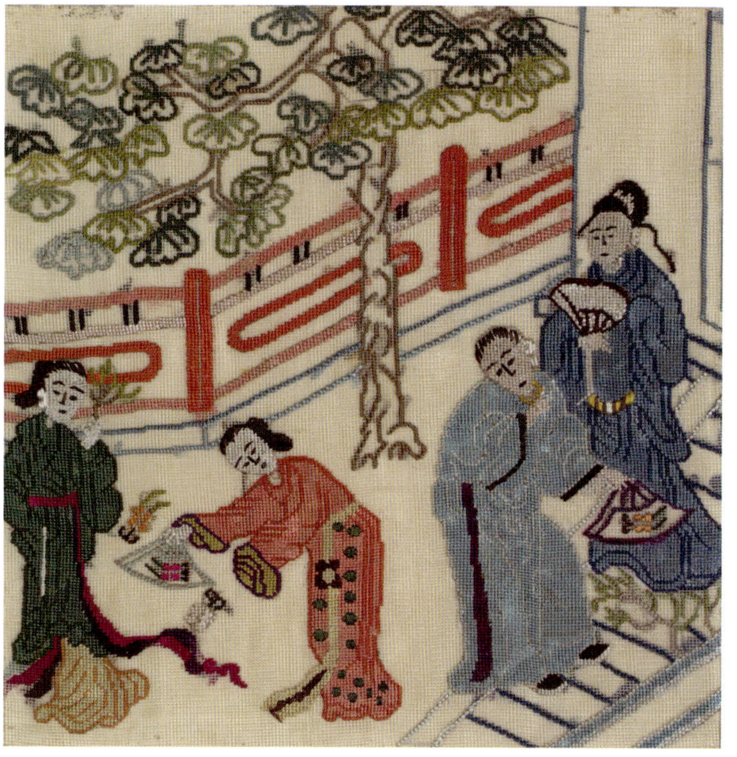

33

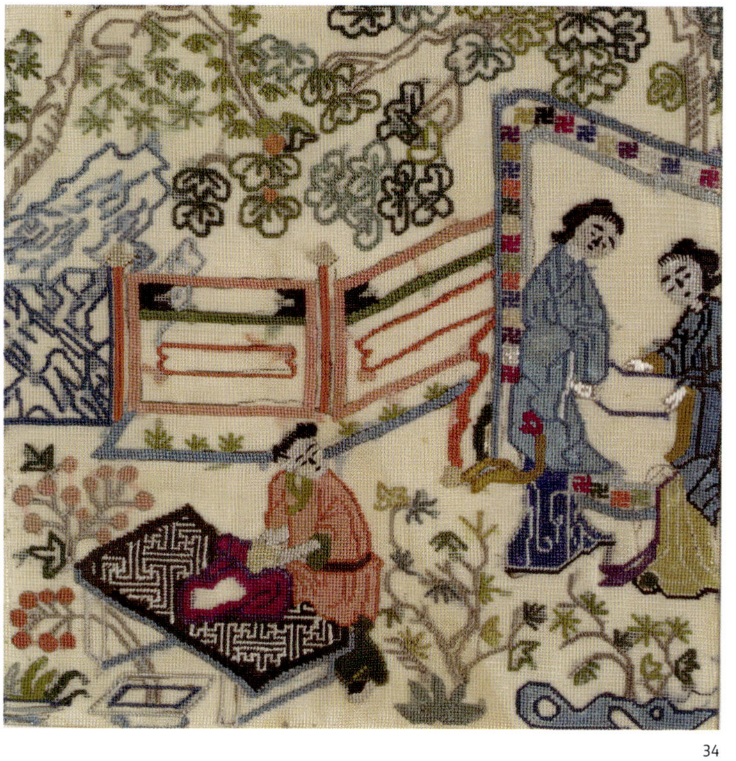

34

The four embroidered square pieces in this exhibition are probably examples of pillow-end embroidery (*zhending xiu*). Traditional Chinese pillows are made from a wide range of materials including wood, ceramic, metal, bamboo, jade, lacquer, and textiles, depending on the social and historical context. Usually associated with the user's stage in the life cycle, pillow designs reflect individual taste, health, and gender. The patterns adorning pillows favor auspicious motifs that inspire good dreams and harmonious love lives for those who sleep upon them. Fabric pillows, usually filled with a sturdy mixture of buckwheat husks and herbs, were most common during late imperial China, and most often fabricated by women.

In the erotic paintings and vernacular stories of the Ming (1368–1644) and Qing (1644–1911) dynasties, pillows are often depicted as rectangular cushions covered with fabric, with embroidered square pieces on each end. Sometimes these decorative pillow ends include romantic

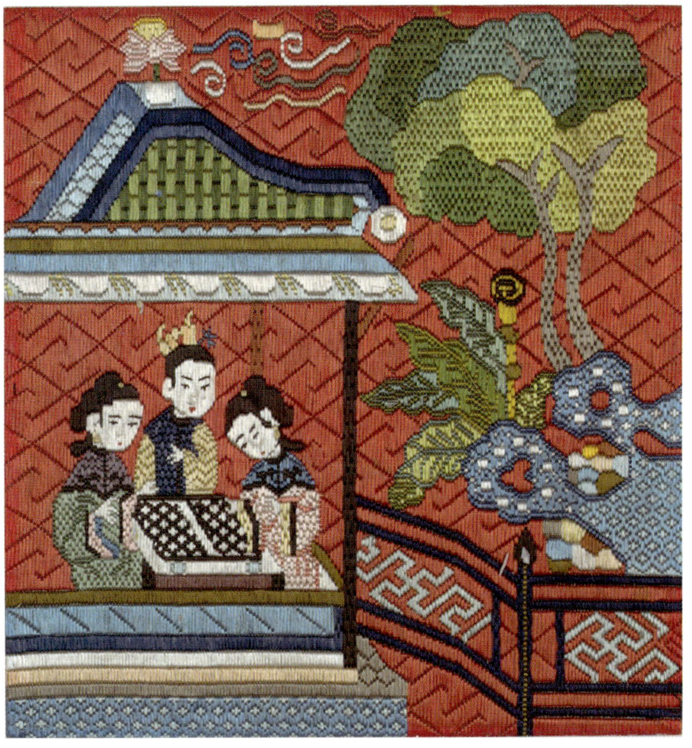

35

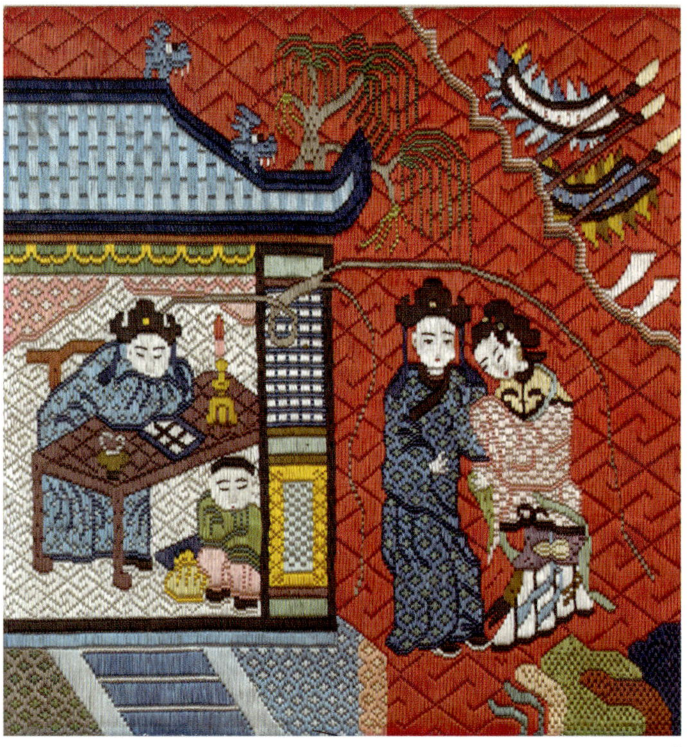

36

symbols signifying the eroticism of the accompanying scene. Indeed, in the case of *Romance of the Western Chamber* (*Xixiang ji*), a mandarin-duck pillow (*yuanyang zhen*) notably alludes not only to the love affair between Student Zhang and Oriole but also to Crimson's thoughtfulness as a maid. In part 3, act 4, for example, after noticing that Zhang uses only a jasper zither as a pillow, Crimson kindly suggests that Oriole bring a mandarin-duck pillow and a kingfisher-feather coverlet to Zhang's place so that the two of them will be comfortable during their first night together. The mandarin-duck pillow refers to a pillow decorated on either end with mandarin ducks, a traditional symbol of a felicitous union. In part 4, act 1, Crimson passes the lovers' bedding to Zhang before Oriole enters his room. Then, at the beginning of their lovemaking, a very shy Oriole grasps the mandarin-duck pillow, an action Zhang finds particularly enticing. In the material context of a pillow—an intimate object evoking amorous relations—imagery culled from *Romance of the Western Chamber* differs from abstract symbols such as mandarin ducks, which signify romance in general. The owner of the pillows could thus look to the human figures in *Romance of Western Chamber* as tangible representations of passion.

Like other media featuring images from *Romance of the Western Chamber*, these pieces have compositions associated with woodblock print traditions rather than stage performance, but the logic behind this particular pairing of scenes remains unclear. One set of pillow ends usually consists of four pieces that decorate the ends of two pillows. In this set, all four pieces were made with essentially the same technique; the embroidery thread penetrates the space between warps or wefts according to the required length of the stitch. In these pillow ends, however, the scenes "Startled by Beauty" and "Commotion Over a Letter" rely on "partly counted embroidery" (*nasha*), in which much of the ground fabric remains uncovered (cats. 33, 34), while "Playing Chess" and "Startled in a Dream" on the other set demonstrate "full count embroidery" (*najin*), in which the embroidered pattern covers the surface of the gauze fabric (cats. 35, 36). Contrasting with the neutral hues in the first pair, vibrant red, blue, green, and pink silk threads form the images on the second. An amateur probably made the two nasha pieces, since the charcoal pattern lines are still visible on the white gauze background, while the perfect, rigid stitches on the najin set indicate the work of either a skilled amateur or a commercial embroidery shop. —YUHANG LI

Cat. 37

Chinese, Late Qing Dynasty (1644–1911)
Formerly attributed to Qiu Ying,
Chinese, ca. 1494–1552
Two Scenes from Romance of the Western Chamber (Xixiang ji): *"The Disrupted Ceremony" (Part 1, Act 4) and "Further Anticipation" (Part 3, Act 4)*, 19th century
Two leaves from an album of 21 Scenes from *Romance of the Western Chamber (Xixiang ji)*, ink and color on silk, each: 14 9/16 x 13 in. (37 x 33 cm)
Courtesy of the C. V. Starr East Asian Library, University of California, Berkeley

These leaves are from an album of paintings accompanying text from the northern style *Romance of the Western Chamber* (*Xixiang ji*). Decorative elements are colorfully rendered in conventional forms recognizable from commercial painting manuals. Each illustration faces just one page of text comprising an entire act from the drama, omitting all stage directions and spoken lines, but retaining a poetic combination of romantic images and metered arias.[1] Such painted album editions of dramas and fiction were available during the Ming (1368–1644) and Qing (1644–1911) dynasties as higher-end alternatives to woodblock-printed editions.

The National Library of China in Beijing contains an album identical to this one in content and format. Both albums are attributed to Qiu Ying (circa 1494–1592), a professional artist esteemed, with Shen Zhou, Tang Yin, and Wen Zhengming, as one of the Four Great Masters of the Ming dynasty. While the National Library's album is painted in the fine and engaging style characteristic of Qiu Ying, the Berkeley album's attribution is spurious, a means of advertising employed by commercial publishers to appeal to a moderately wealthy clientele.[2]

The first of these two illustrations depicts part 1, act 4, "The Disrupted Ceremony" (cat. 37.1). Like so many of its contemporaries, it presents conventional elements from Student Zhang's arias: mists surrounding the temple's roof-tiles; incense smoke condensing above the hall; monks playing dharma drums, bronze clappers, and bells.[3] Zhang stands to the right of the abbot, clad in a colorful *kasaya* (*jiasha*). Madame Cui makes an offering before the altar. Oriole, flanked by Crimson, stands on a patterned carpet in the center of the picture.

The carpet, a traditional component of the Buddhist prayer hall, is often included in depictions of this scene. Here, it provides a stage for Oriole, as one of Zhang's arias describes all eyes on her.[4] Similar patterned carpets called *qushu* appear in other Ming-dynasty illustrations to designate performance areas.[5] The inclusion of a carpet in this scene thus blurs the line between ritual and dramatic performance.

The Qiu Ying album in Beijing lets landscape and architectural elements dominate each scene; the Berkeley album, however, focuses on the characters and their actions. The text of the second album leaf, which depicts part 3, act 4, "Further Anticipation" (cat. 37.2) reads in part:

> Your body lies covered by a strip of cotton sheet,
> Your head is pillowed on your three-foot jasper zither.[6]

In this act, Crimson calls upon the love-sick Zhang with a prescription from Oriole. Zhang,

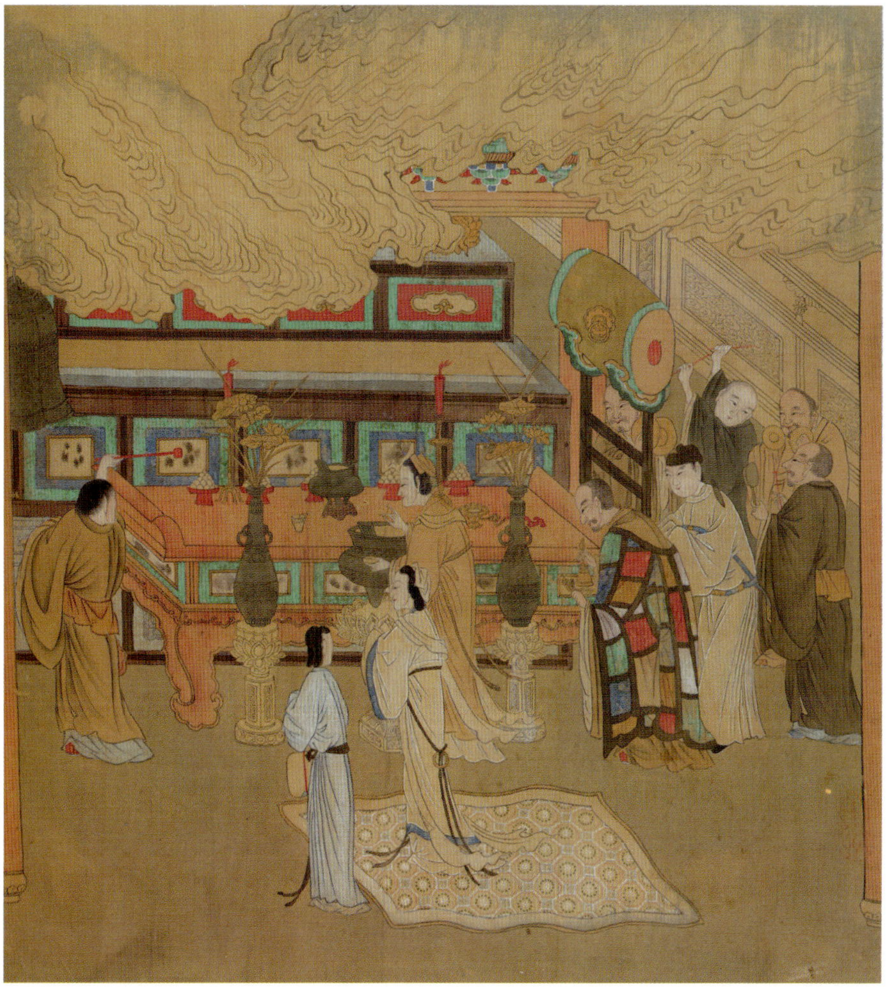

37.1

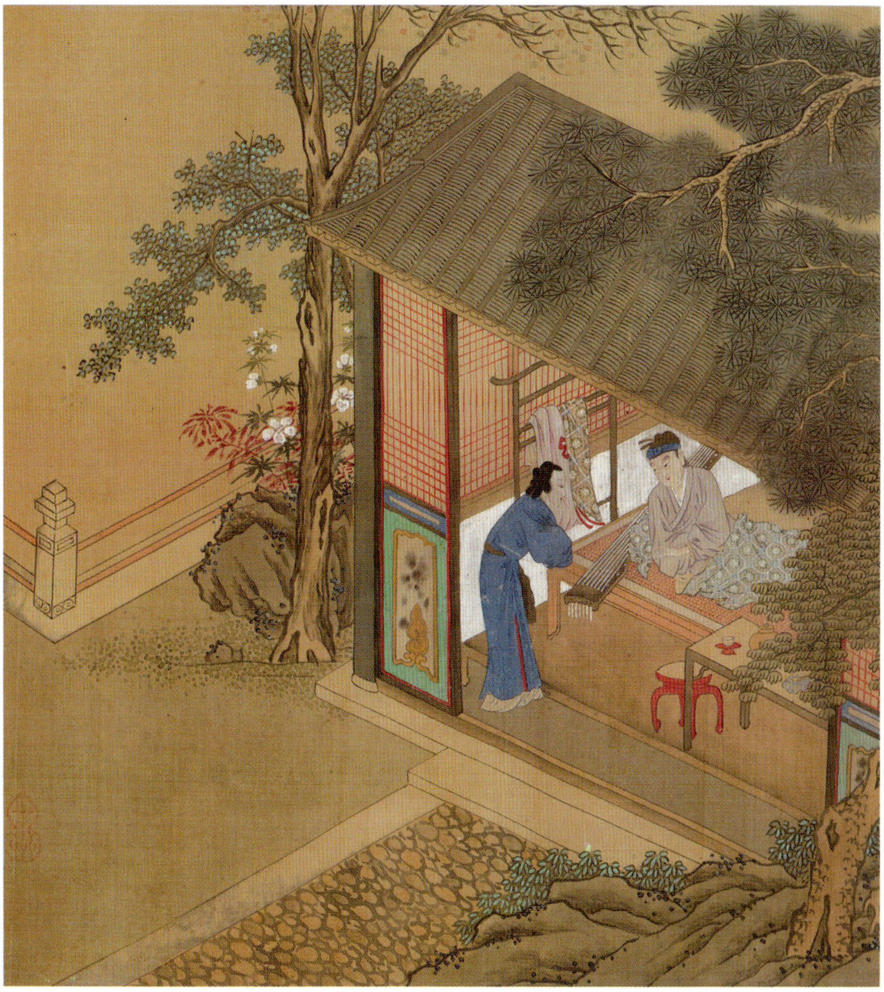

37.2

wearing a headband indicative of a sick person, reads the "prescription," which is in fact Oriole's written promise to pay him a visit in the evening to consummate their romance. —ALIA BREITWIESER

1 *Qiu Wen hezhi Xixiang ji tuce* [Qiu Ying and Wen Zhengming's Collaborative Pictorial Album of *Romance of the Western Chamber]*, in *Guben Xixiang ji huiji, chuji* [Collected Old Editions of *Romance of the Western Chamber*, first series] (Beijing: Guojia tushuguan chubanshe, 2011), vol. 9, pp. 493–538.
2 Robert E. Hegel, *Reading Illustrated Fiction in Late Imperial China* (Stanford, Calif.: Stanford University Press, 1998), p. 278.
3 Wang Shifu, *The Story of the Western Wing*, trans. Stephen H. West and Wilt L. Idema (Berkeley: University of California Press, 1995), p. 144.
4 Ibid., p. 146.
5 See, for example, Grace Wu, "Le mobilier dans les intérieurs Ming," in Jean-François Jarrige et al., *Ming: The Golden Age of Chinese Furniture* (Paris: Réunion des Musées Nationaux, 2003), p. 33.
6 Wang, *The Story of the Western Wing*, p. 221.

Cat. 38

Chinese, Qing Dynasty (1644–1911),
Kangxi Period (1662–1722) or
Yongzheng Period (1722–1735)
Wrist Rest with Letter-Reading Scene (Part 2, Act 3) from Romance of the Western Chamber (Xixiang ji), 1674 or 1734
Carved bamboo, 8 1/8 x 2 1/8 x 1/2 in.
(20.6 x 5.4 x 1.3 cm)
Lent by The Metropolitan Museum of Art, Purchase, Elizabeth M. Riley Bequest, 2006
2006.237

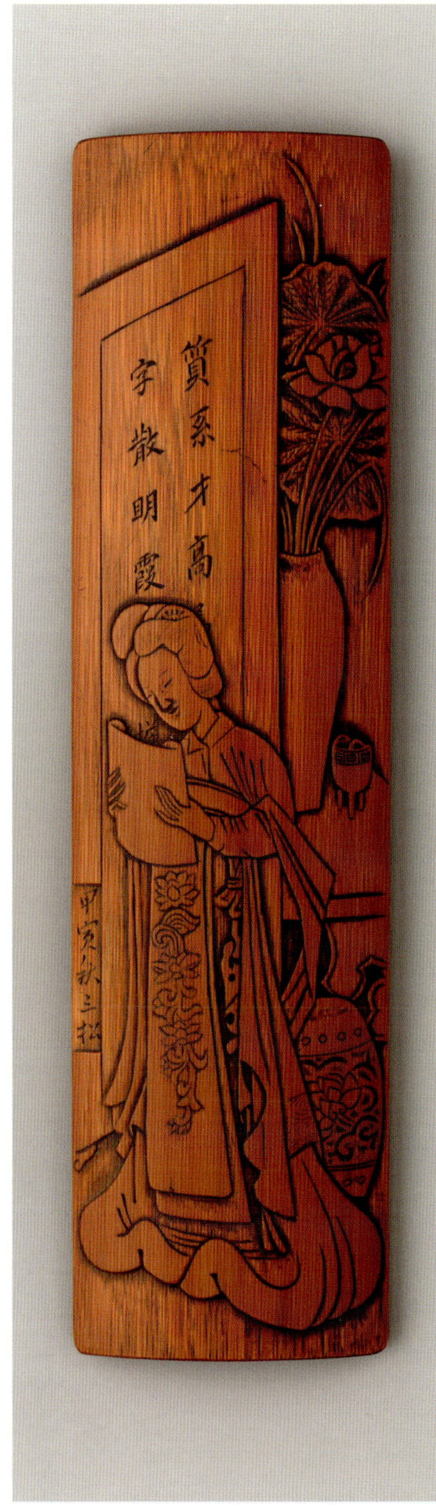

A wrist rest sits on a writing desk to protect shirtsleeves from wet ink. Usually made from bamboo, wood, ivory, or porcelain, this accessory is ordinarily rectangular in shape, less than 30 centimeters (a little under 12 inches) long and around 8 centimeters (about 3 1/2 inches) wide. The material and dimensions of the wrist rest on display here therefore suggest that it is not intended solely for decoration.

According to an inscription on the wrist rest, it was carved in autumn of the year Jiayin (either 1674 or 1734 in the sixty-year Chinese calendrical cycle) by a famous Ming dynasty (1368–1644) bamboo carver, Zhu Zhizhen, better known by his style name Sansong. A third-generation bamboo carver from Jiading, Jiangsu province, Zhu Sansong's works demonstrate the artist's innovative use of limited space and thoughtful attention to his figures' gestures and expressions. The Zhu family founded the Jiading school of bamboo carving, which rose to fame and eventually established a local industry that continued to flourish until the eighteenth century. Although attributed to Zhu Sansong, this wrist rest may have been carved by a local workshop or artisan during the eighteenth century.[1]

Sansong often employed literary motifs in his work. This wrist rest displays Oriole reading a love letter from Student Zhang in *Romance of the Western Chamber* (*Xixiang ji*). The design is most likely based on a woodblock print designed by the famous Ming-dynasty painter Chen Hongshou (1598–1652) (fig. I.13). Oriole's clothing, her gesture, and the surrounding decor correspond to those in the woodblock print. A more complete version of this illustration, which includes Crimson spying upon her mistress from behind the screen, appears on a Ming bamboo brush holder attributed to Zhu Sansong in Taiwan's National Palace Museum.[2]

The designer of the wrist rest did not simply copy from the woodblock print but also made creative adjustments. For example, in the woodblock illustration, Oriole stands before a large folding screen while her maid, Crimson, peers from behind the screen. To make effective use of the wrist rest's limited width, the designer has only depicted one panel of the screen. Crimson is absent. Instead, beside the screen are a table, an incense burner, lotus flowers in a vase, and an embroidery stool, all implying a boudoir. Additionally, the designer of the wrist rest does not imitate the configuration of the lotus flower and leaves on the right panel of Chen Hongshou's print but instead transplants them into a vase rendered as a three-dimensional object on the table.

On Chen Hongshou's print, the screen panel directly behind Oriole depicts a banana tree (*bajiao*), thus alluding to the traditional pairing of banana leaves and a beautiful woman (*bajiao meiren*) and emphasizing Oriole's exceptional beauty. However, to accentuate the function of the wrist rest as an object associated with literary production, the designer also draws attention to Oriole's status as a talented woman by carving a poem on the screen behind her. This often reprinted anonymous poem praises the accomplishments of celebrated literary women from early Chinese history:

> By nature possessing great talent, these women can all be ranked grand masters:
>
> The palindromic poem Su Hui wove with her loom shines like splendid daybreak.
>
> Xie Daoyun likened floating willow floss to snow piled on eaves and roads.
>
> In bed one rainy night, Lady Wang lamented the lotus blooms nearing their end.
>
> Of exceptional intellect, Ban Zhao completed *The History of the Han*.
>
> Cai Yan, a brilliant poet, composed *Songs of a Nomad Flute*.
>
> Ban Jieyu's allegory to a fan in her *Song of Resentment* is full of deep longing,
>
> But even more to be praised is Lady Wei for preserving a Confucian classic.[3]

Only the first three lines of the poem are carved on the wrist rest, and even here Oriole's body obscures the end of the third line. Presumably the remainder of the poem would have been inscribed on the missing panels of the folding screen. The designer provides hints for the viewer to imagine a larger space. Like Chinese painting and other forms of art, a good design provides clues for the viewer to think or imagine beyond the physical object. —RANTING JIANG, JUDITH T. ZEITLIN, AND YUHANG LI

1 Wai-fong Anita Sui, "Chinese Decorative Arts." *The Metropolitan Museum of Art Bulletin*, vol. 55, no. 1 (Summer 1997), p. 47.

2 Shixiang Wang and Wango H. C. Weng. *Bamboo Carving of China* (New York: China Institute in America), 1983.

3 The text of this poem is printed as an "Appraisal" (*pinti*) for "Talented Women" (*cainü*) under the category "Beautiful Women" (*liren*) in *Xinke hongjiao zengbu yuanji huofa Shixue quanshu* [A Newly Carved, Recollated, Augmented Edition of the Complete Book of Flexibility and Agility in the Study of Poetic Composition] (n.p., Tang Qian, 1592), *juan* 11, p. 2b. A variant character for "eaves" (*yan*[a]), (only partially visible on the screen behind Oriole), has been used instead of *yan*[b] on the wrist rest.

Cat. 39

Chinese, Qing Dynasty (1644–1911),
Jiaqing Period (1796–1820)
Plate with "Repudiating the Letter" Scene (Part 3, Act 3) from Romance of the Western Chamber (Xixiang ji), late 18th–early 19th century
Porcelain with famille rose overglaze enamel and gilt decoration, diameter: 11 5/16 in. (28.8 cm)
Philadelphia Museum of Art: The Bloomfield Moore Collection, 1899
1899-698

This polychrome enameled porcelain dish presents a scene from *Romance of the Western Chamber* as though it were painted on a partially unfurled scroll. Sprays of blue, yellow, white, and imperial pink flowers surround the scroll, which is backed with a pink trellis motif, and cover the diaper of tight iron-red spirals. The upper and lower sections of the rim each contain a large scalloped cartouche depicting auspicious objects. Gilt embellishes the rim and some details in the main panel. A nearly identical plate, dated to 1730–45, may be found at the Groninger Museum, the Netherlands.[1]

In this scene from part 3, act 3, "Repudiating the Letter," Student Zhang sneaks into Oriole's garden anticipating a moonlit tryst only to be severely reprimanded by the object of his affection. At the end of act 2, Zhang asserts, "I'll pull myself up by the weeping willow and in one fell swoop leap across the wall."[2] Here he attempts to fulfill his intentions. Although the text of the original play makes no reference to Zhang's removing and dropping his boots, many porcelains and prints feature this detail, alluding to a later comic adaptation that likely portrays contemporary stage practice.[3]

In the sky above, two constellations accompany a crescent moon. Constellations indicate night scenes, but these two in particular often appear in depictions of Zhang's scaling the wall.[4]

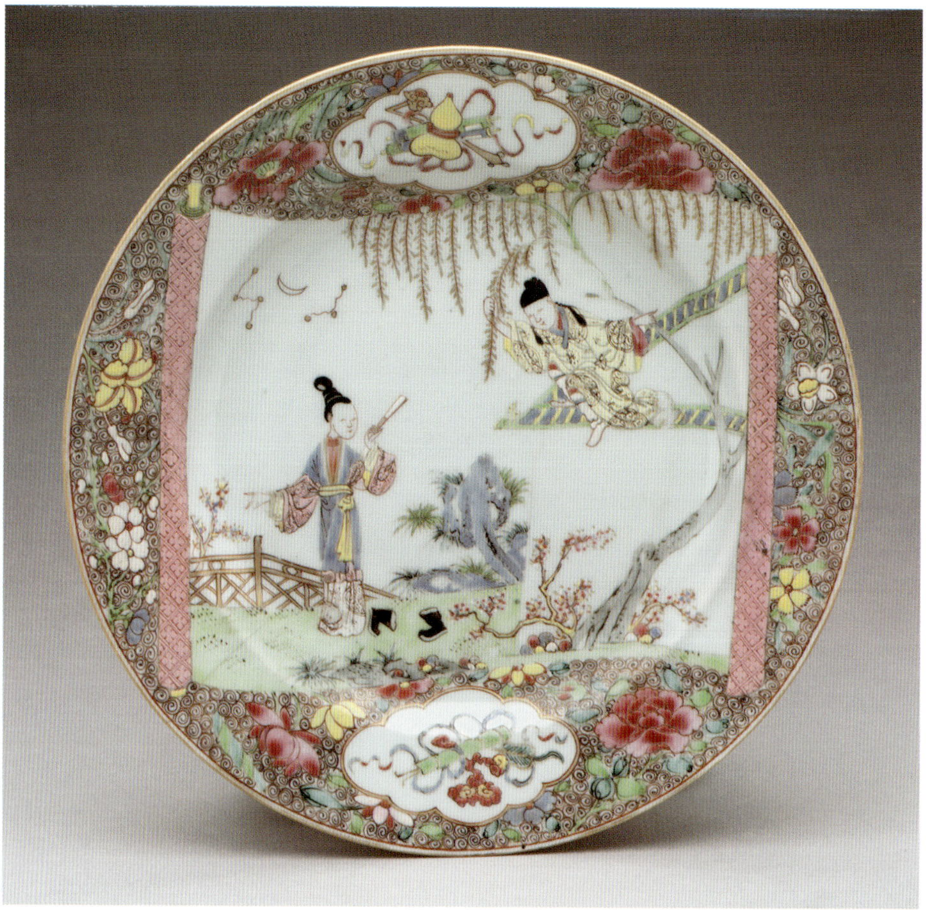

An eighteenth-century brush pot at the Lowe Art Museum, Coral Gables, Florida, depicts two lovers meeting beneath the same three- and four-star constellations, but the constellations are reversed here, and the three-star constellation accompanies the man. These three stars are Altair, associated with the mythological Herd Boy, and its flanking stars Beta and Gamma Aquilae. The other constellation depicts four stars in the constellation Lyra, whose brightest star, Vega, is associated with the Herd Boy's wife, the Weaving Girl. These legendary lovers were sentenced to work at their respective tasks in the heavens, separated by the Milky Way for all but one night a year. Consequently, they are employed in traditional Chinese depictions of lovers meeting.

Beckoning with her fan, Crimson directs Zhang toward the unrevealed portion of the scroll. Scroll-shaped panels are not uncommon among eighteenth-century porcelains, but the format of this dish is particularly playful in that Oriole, who is normally depicted in this scene with her back turned to Zhang, is off-stage, as it were.[5] The four-starred constellation and her handmaid's sideways gesture both indicate, however, that she must be sitting just beyond our view. Ironically, because this dish, like much famille rose porcelain, was probably made for export, its audience may have been oblivious to the absence of Oriole. A nineteenth-century Dutch imitation of this plate attests to this design's appeal to European consumers. In the imitation, the image has been reversed; the auspicious decorations have been omitted, and the constellations gathered closely to surround a tiny crescent moon. No longer depicted against the cartouche of an unfurling scroll, the Dutch version of the scene no longer suggests hidden narrative contents.[6] —ALIA BREITWIESER

1 Christiaan J. A. Jörg, *Ceramics Crossed Overseas: Jingdezhen, Imari, and Delft from the Collection of the Groninger Museum* (Tokyo: Mainichi Newspapers, 1999), fig. 77.

2 Wang Shifu, *The Story of the Western Wing*, translated by Stephen H. West and Wilt L. Idema (Berkeley: University of California Press, 1995), p. 208.

3 Yuming He, *Home and the World: Editing the "Glorious Ming" in Woodblock-Printed Books of the Sixteenth and Seventeenth Centuries* (Cambridge, Mass.: Harvard University Asia Center, 2013), p. 172.

4 One scholar has suggested that they might represent the seven stars of the Big Dipper, rather than two constellations. See Zhang Ange, *Ming Qing youshang caici shizhen [The Connoisseurship of Glazed Polychrome Porcelain of the Ming and Qing Dynasties]* (Nanchang: Jiangxi meishu chubanshe, 2002), p. 48.

5 Wen-Chin Hsu astutely points out this innovation in her analysis of the Groninger plate, see Wen-Chin Hsu, "Xixiang ji yu cigi-xixiangii yu shijue yishu de yuhe ge'an yanjiu" [*The Romance of the Western Chamber* and Chinese Porcelain—A Case Study of the Coalescence of Drama and Visual Art], *Kaohsiung Normal University Journal* 26 (2009): p. 151.

6 Wen-Chin Hsu, "Representation of the *Romance of the Western Chamber* in Chinese Woodblock Prints and Ceramics," *Asian Culture Quarterly* 19:4 (1991): p. 26.

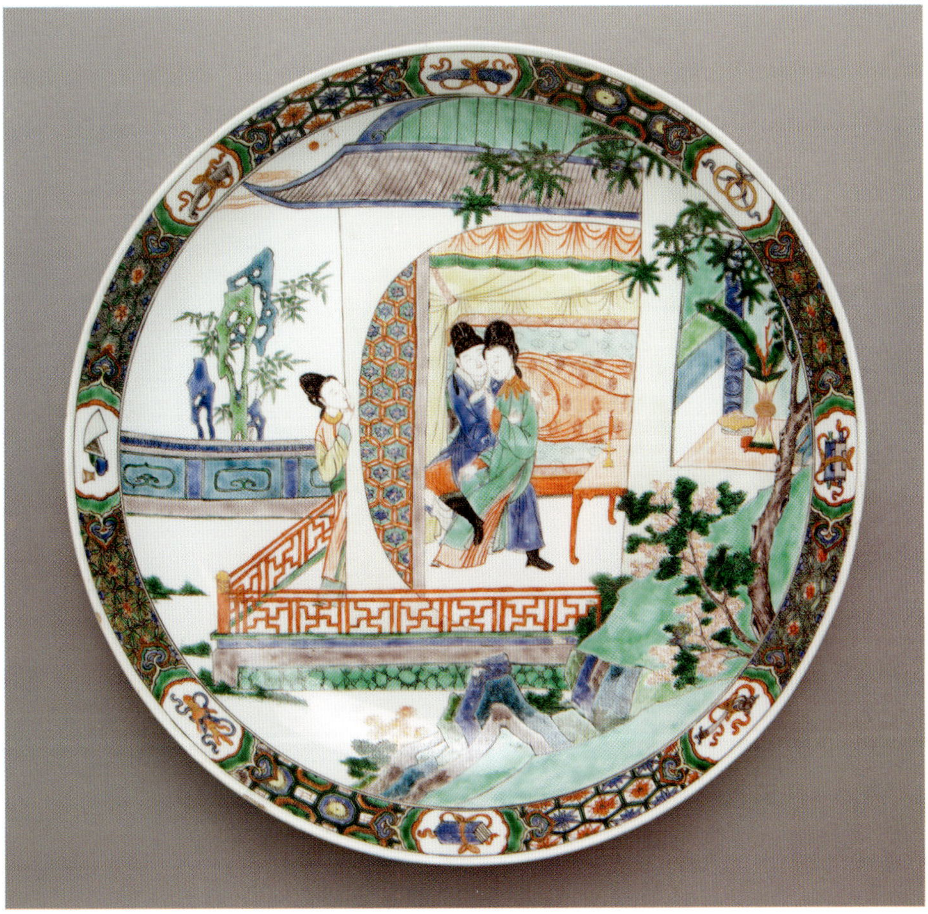

Cat. 40
Chinese, Qing Dynasty (1644–1911), Kangxi Period (1662–1722)
Dish with "Responding to the Letter" Scene (Part 4, Act 1) from Romance of the Western Chamber (Xixiang ji), late 17th–early 18th century
Porcelain with famille verte overglaze enamel decoration, diameter: 15 7/8 in (40.3 cm)
Philadelphia Museum of Art: The Alfred and Margaret Caspary Memorial Gift, 1959
1955-50-86

This porcelain dish with famille verte overglaze enamel decoration depicts the lovemaking scene from *Romance of the Western Chamber* (*Xixiang ji*). Skillfully rendered in a diverse color palette, densely enameled floral motifs decorate the rim. Such motifs as the shaded floral trellis and floral hex cell are common on Kangxi export wares. The deep blue and red hues resemble Imari-style wares, which responded to the eighteenth-century European taste for Japanese patterns. Student Zhang's aria from part 4, act 1, describes the lovers' first embrace: "Her embroidered shoes, barely half a span, Her willowy waist fills a single armful; Bashful and embarrassed, she refuses to lift her head. . . . I loosen the knotted buttons, Untie her silken waist wrap; Orchid musk spreads through my secluded study."[1] The plate's design clearly illustrates the aria, but is more daring than most contemporary depictions. Oriole's tiny bound foot protrudes beneath the hem of her skirt as Zhang embraces her in his lap. In accord with the majority of print and porcelain illustrations of this scene, Crimson peers on in secret, biting her finger in excitement (fig. I.13).

It is difficult to distinguish between Kangxi export wares and items for domestic consumption, but many famille verte wares were made for export. Nonetheless, this plate abounds with symbols of iconographic significance. On the rim, eight panels contain auspicious objects. The bagged zither, chess board with chess-piece pots, books, and scrolls represent the Four Arts of the Scholar (*qin qi shu hua*). The ribbon-bound rings might be a rebus for *daiyuan*, "bringing first place" in the official examinations; the *ruyi* scepter similarly expresses wishes for good fortune; the branch of red coral is associated with the insignia of a top-ranking official in the imperial court; the ivory tusk is another object typically grouped into the Eight Precious Things (*babao*).

Sultry though it may be, the lovemaking scene between Oriole and Zhang also has auspicious connotations. A Kangxi dish at the Rijksmuseum, Amsterdam, depicts this scene with a rim motif of welcoming sons (*zhaozi*).[2] Although the lovers are technically unmarried, here a red candle beside the bed suggests that this is their wedding night, thus relating their erotic encounter to marital procreation. The railing before them is in the shape of lucky Buddhist swastikas (*wan*), and large *ruyi* adorn the rear garden wall. On the right, a window reveals the decorative objects adorning Zhang's study. A bronze *bombé* incense burner was an object of social prestige during the Ming and Qing dynasties.[3] The vase beside it evokes a Qing dynasty textile design featuring a branch of red coral placed beside a vase of peacock feathers. Known as "red button-variegated plume" (*hongding hualing*), this motif was popular because peacock feathers and a red coral button were part of the traditional raiment of a high-level government official.[4] The symbolic richness of this lusty scene foreshadows Zhang's success in the examinations and the lovers' happy marriage. This plate thus exemplifies how a dramatic image can surpass the bounds of its narrative context to become an independent bearer of meaning. —ALIA BREITWIESER

1 Wang Shifu, *The Story of the Western Wing*, translated by Stephen H. West and Wilt L. Idema (Berkeley: University of California Press, 1995), p. 228.
2 The Kangxi dish from the Rijksmuseum collection is discussed in Christiaan J. A. Jörg, *Famille Verte: Chinese Porcelains in Green Enamels* (Groningen: The Groninger Museum, 2011), p. 91.
3 Jonathan Hay, *Sensuous Surfaces: The Decorative Object in Early Modern China* (London: Reaktion Books; Honolulu: University of Hawai'i Press, 2010), p. 10.
4 Patricia Bjaaland Welch, *Chinese Art: A Guide to Motifs and Visual Imagery* (Singapore: Tuttle Publishing, 2008), p. 79.

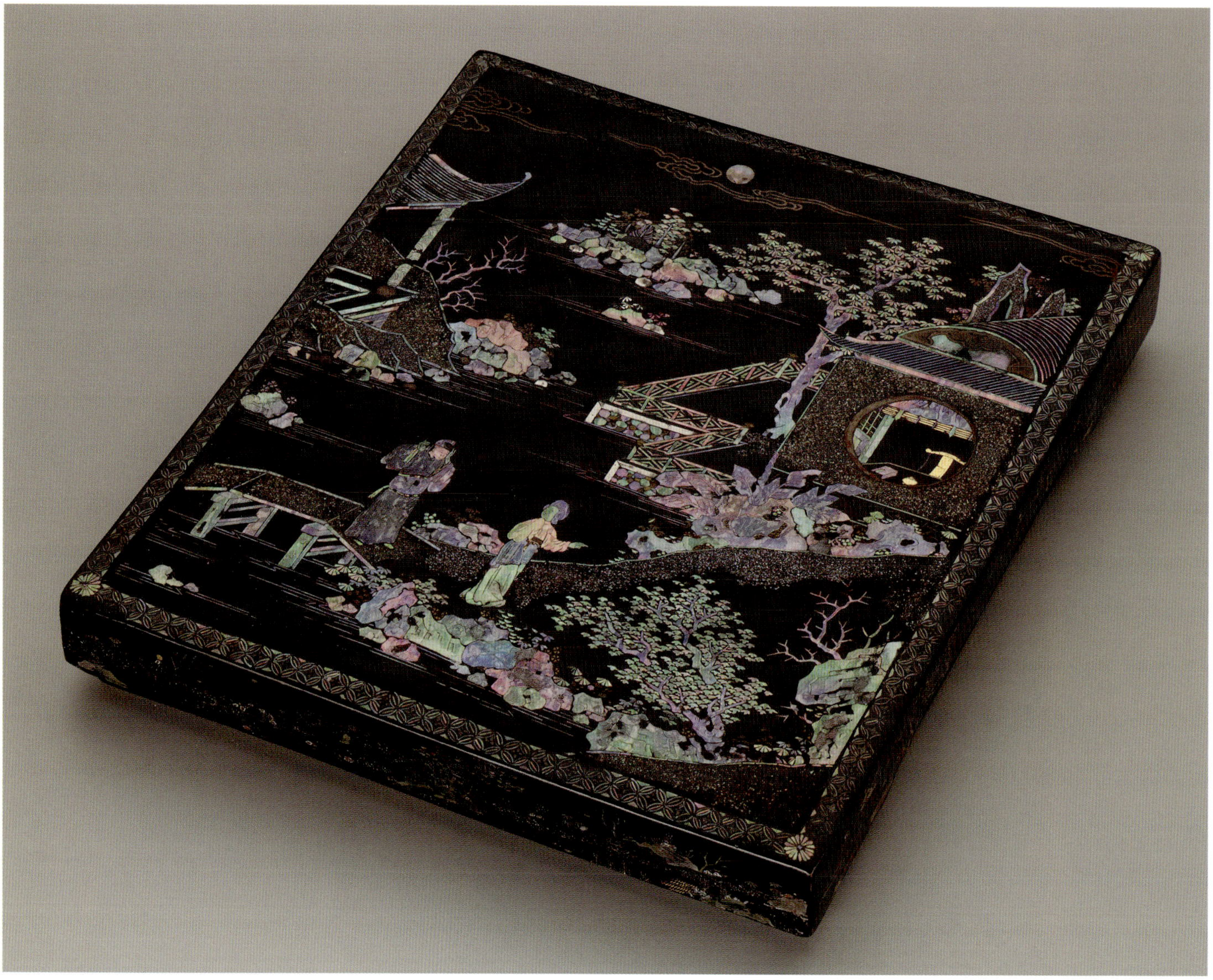

Cat. 41
Ryukyu Islands
Writing Box with "Invitation to a Banquet" Scene and Figure (Part 2, Act 2) from Romance of the Western Chamber (Xixiang ji), 18th–19th century
Black lacquered wood with mother-of-pearl, gold, and metal alloy foil inlay,
1 1/4 x 7 7/8 x 9 1/16 in. (3.2 cm x 20 cm x 23 cm)
Museum of Fine Arts, Boston, William Sturgis Bigelow Collection
11.10637a-b

Decorated in inlaid mother-of-pearl and metal foil, this rectangular lacquer writing box features a scene of figures in a garden on the lid, a band of rolling garden scenery on the sides, and a standing female figure on the inside. Although the seal on the base reads "Produced by Qianli," claiming authorship by the famous seventeenth-century lacquer artisan Jiang Qianli (fl. 1673–76) from Jiaxing or Yangzhou, the box was likely produced in the Ryukyu Islands.[1] The decoration of this box nonetheless reflects this master's paradigmatic association with new styles of mother-of-pearl inlay techniques that enhance the flat pictorial quality of the inlaid design, and the predilection for themes from *Romance of the Western Chamber* (*Xixiang ji*) in lacquer ware attributed to his name.[2]

In the scene on the lid, a female figure in the foreground gestures ahead as she leads a young man, still adjusting his official winged cap, across a bridge into the right foreground. Executed in the so-called *pingtuo* technique of lacquer inlaid with needle-incised mother-of-pearl chips of varying hues, gold and lead-tin foil, and sprinkled metal alloy powder, the action in the foreground takes place against the backdrop of an elaborate garden featuring waterside pavilions, bathed in the light of a full moon shining above.[3] Art historian Hiromi Kinoshita has identified this scene as illustrating the "Invitation to the Feast" scene, in which Crimson guides Student Zhang to a banquet held in his honor by Madame Cui.[4] While the same scene is portrayed in one of the roundels decorating a woman's robe discussed in Yuhang Li's essay (fig. 4.1), the designer of this box involves the material shape and physical manipulation of the box in his narrative strategy.[5] When uncovering the box in the

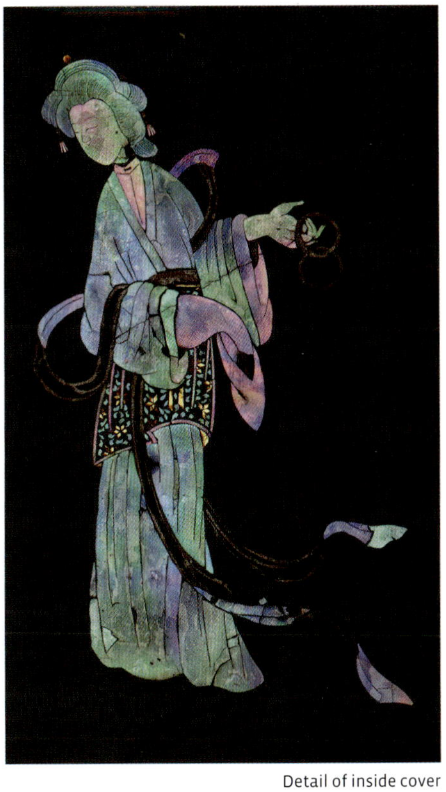

Detail of inside cover

direction of Crimson's gesturing hand, the left-to-right movement of the figures through the foreground on the lid matches the viewing sequence as the single figure of Oriole on its reverse side is disclosed. Glancing backward as if toward the approaching figures on its reverse, and dangling a pair of intertwined jade bracelets in her left hand, the story's leading lady appears as if suspended in time. Her iridescent figure stands out against the solid surface of the black lacquer ground. This ambiguous relation with the richly defined, stage-like world of the lid exterior suggests a potential reading for the absent subject of the still life framed by the study's window in the scene's middle distance.[6]

Through the playful juxtaposition of interior and exterior, the designer leads the viewer from the promise of Zhang's first night with Oriole to a vision of his beloved holding a symbolic token of their interwined fate.[7] In this way the designer sets up a kind of reenactment of the story that can only be completed when someone uses the box. As the lid is lifted, the picture of Zhang anticipating the longed-for consummation of his love gives way to an image of its ultimate fulfillment. —CATHERINE STUER

1 The shape of this writing box, the appearance of raised components in the decor, and the overall quality of its inlay suggest its potential provenance from the Ryukyu Islands. See Hiromi Kinoshita, "China, Ryukyu or Japan? Inlaid Mother-of-Pearl Lacquer from the Bigelow Collection, Museum of Fine Arts, Boston," in *Proceedings of Conference on Ancient Chinese Lacquer*, Art Museum, Chinese University of Hong Kong (Hong Kong: Chinese University of Hong Kong, 2012), pp. 79–90, especially pp. 83–84. The frequent appearance of seals associated with Jiang Qianli on Ryukyu inlaid lacquer wares underscores this identification. See James C. Y. Watt and Barbara Brennan Ford, *East Asian Lacquer: The Florence and Herbert Irving Collection* (New York: The Metropolitan Museum of Art, 1991), p. 140.

2 On Jiang Qianli, see o.a.: Lee Yu-kuan, *Oriental Lacquer Art* (New York and Tokyo: Weatherhill, 1972), p. 169; Shen Fuwen, *Zhongguo qiyi meishushi* [The History of the Art of Lacquer] (Beijing: People's Fine Arts Publishing House, 1991), pp. 119–20.

3 For the *pingtuo* technique, by which the inlay is applied prior to the lacquer, and the surface is then polished to bring inlay and lacquer surface to a same level, see: Lee, *Oriental Lacquer Art*, p. 29; Shen, *Zhongguo qiyi meishushi*. The new inlay style is marked by the careful cutting and juxtaposition of thin, inner layers of mother-of-pearl of blue-green, pink, and yellow hues that add depth and variation to the composition, the use of sprinkled powder, and designs that highlight the flatness of the picture surface.

4 Kinoshita identifies this scene based on a comparison with a closely related illustration on a porcelain bowl dated 1668 in the Butler Family Collection, England, which bears an inscription from the relevant text from the libretto. See Kinoshita, "China, Ryukyu or Japan?," p. 84.

5 It is therefore likely that the designer of this box participates in representational sensibilities exemplified by the album-leaf illustrations of *Romance of the Western Chamber* published by Min Qiji in 1640, as discussed in Wu Hung, *The Double Screen. Medium and Representation in Chinese Painting* (London: Reaktion Books, 1996), pp. 246–59.

6 The relation of figures to architecture in this scene differs from that on the porcelain bowl in the Butler Collection referred to by Kinoshita, where Crimson leads Zhang away from his study. If Kinoshita reads the action in this scene as directed toward the study, understood as the Cui family residence in the temple (Kinoshita, "China, Ryukyu or Japan?," p. 84), the left-right direction of the figures' movement in the foreground, the contents of the study shown, and the absence of reference to a banquet setting all prevent an easy association with either of the protagonists. For an early Qing dish in a private collection featuring similar arrangement of a female figure with fluttering robe in mother-of-pearl and gold leaf inlay on a black lacquer ground, see Wang Shixiang, *Ancient Chinese Lacquerware* (Beijing: Foreign Language Press, 1987), cat. 79.

7 The intertwined bracelet motif is prominently used as a pictorial frame in Leaf 12 in Min Qiji's album. See Edith Dittrich, *The Romance of the Western Chamber, Hsi-hsiang chi: Chinese Colour Woodcuts by Min Ch'i-chi 1640* (Cologne: Museum der Stadt Köln, 1977).

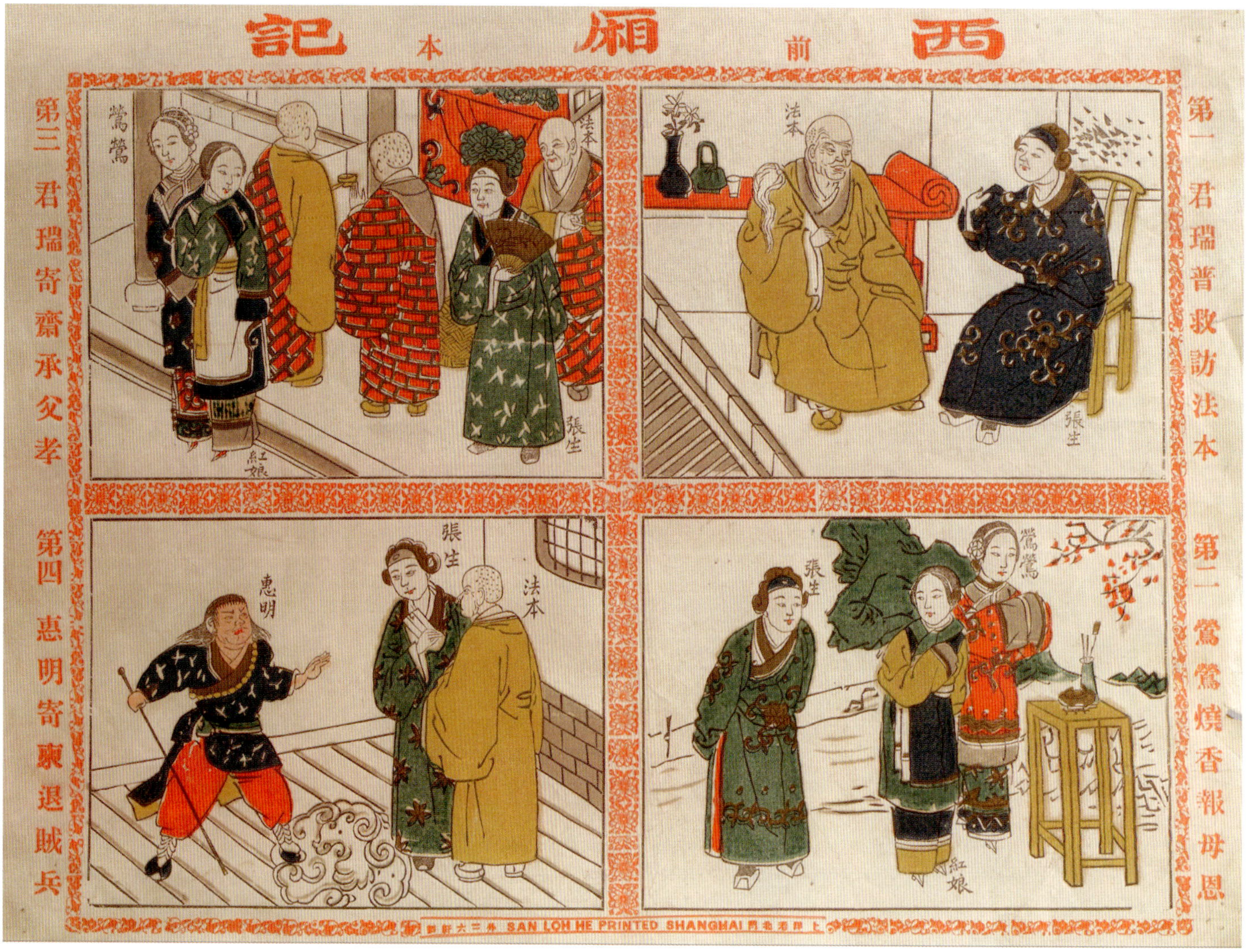

42

Cats. 42, 43

Shanghai, San Lo He (print workshop)
Chinese, Late Qing Dynasty (1644–1911)
Scenes from Romance of the Western Chamber (Xixiang ji), 1902
Set of two polychrome lithographs, each sheet: 13 9/16 x 10 1/16 in. (34.5 x 25.6 cm)
Courtesy of the Division of Anthropology, American Museum of Natural History
Asia/0556 A12
Asia/0556 A13

These vivid prints in blue, gray, green, red, and yellow are typical of the polychrome lithography (*wucai shiyin*) produced in Shanghai during the early twentieth century. Traditionally, such prints served as decorations to be pasted up during the Chinese New Year. This set of two sheets depicts eight scenes from *Romance of the Western Chamber* (*Xixiang ji*). The titles "Romance of the Western Chamber, first part" and "Romance of the Western Chamber, second part" are printed at the top of each sheet, respectively. The romanized name of the print workshop San Lo He and its Shanghai address in Beilaomen are provided in both Chinese and English on the bottom.

All eight scenes are annotated with titles that, when put together, become a rhymed verse. The scenes run vertically starting from the top right. Part 1 reads, "Junrui [student Zhang] visits the Abbot Faben on a pilgrimage; Oriole burns incense in honor of her mother; the smitten Zhang stays in the temple in the name of filial piety; Huiming delivers Zhang's letter to ask for reinforcements to save the Cui family." Part 2 has "Crimson's first meeting with Zhang; Oriole and Zhang serenade each other across a wall till dawn; Zhang's wish is granted in a romantic rendezvous; Madame Cui interrogates Crimson about the suspected romance."

The format, showcasing eight highlights from the play (like a modern comic strip), was popular after the mid-Qing period. This might be a result of the popularity of "single act excerpts" (*zhezixi*), an operatic format that presents performances of the best-known scenes instead of the whole drama. The set is also marked by its consistency in framing the figures according to a uniform size and "camera position" that seems to be much closer to the audience than its Ming precedents such as the 1640 Min Qiji polychrome woodcut version in Cologne (see Judith T. Zeitlin's introduction in this catalogue). The resulting

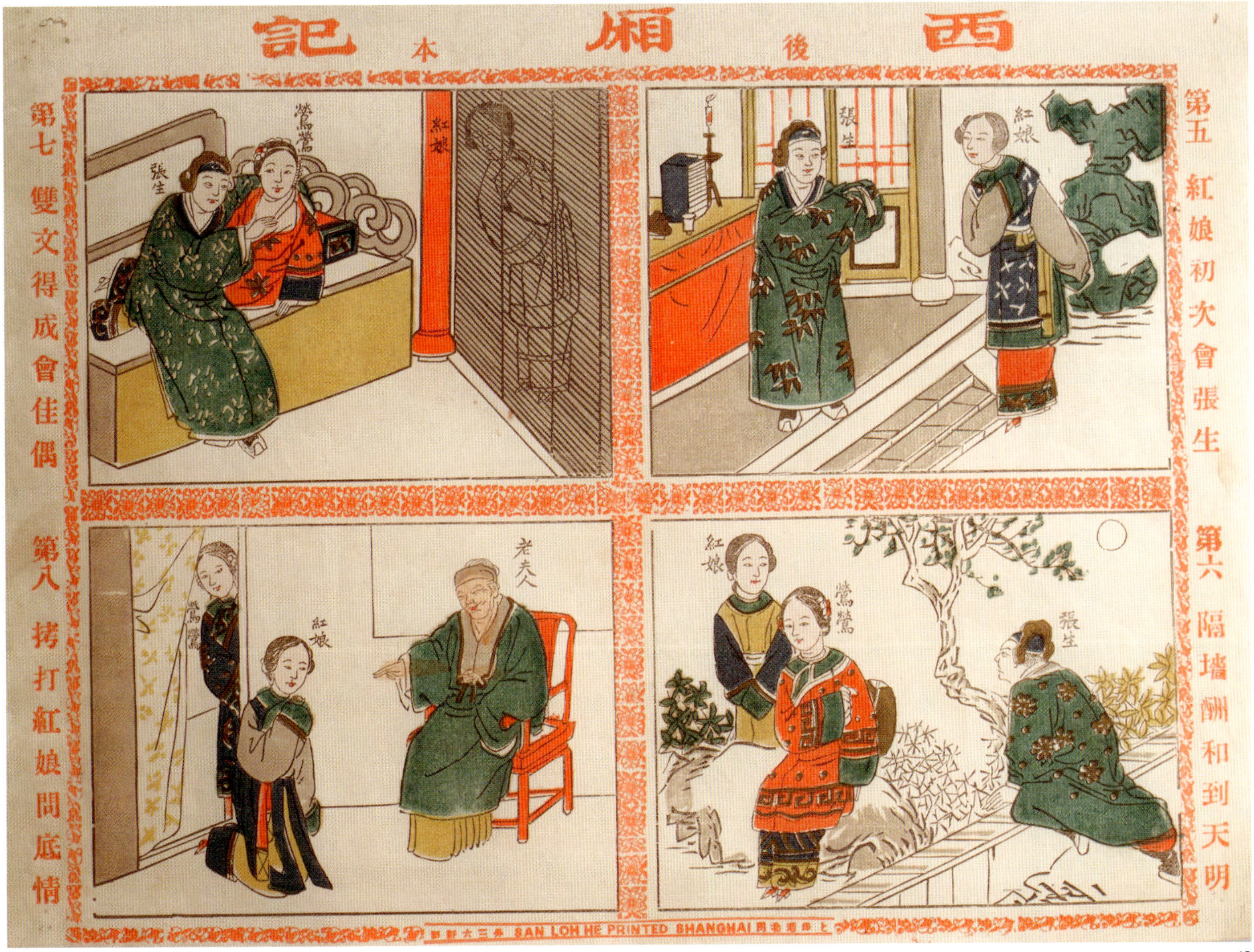

43

larger scale figures allows for ample attention to body gestures and facial expressions. A case in point is Zhang's leering and longing expressions in his scenes with Oriole, in contrast to the serious and decorous deportment he displays before the abbot in the first scene.

A sense of theatricality also comes through in the characters' gestures. In scene 3 (cat. 42), where Oriole and Zhang lock eyes in the temple, the sleeve and fan, props often employed in operatic performances, are used to convey romantic yearning and covert flirting. Costumes, makeup, and setting, however, are generally naturalistic. The characters' garments are a hodgepodge of different styles: while Zhang and Madame Cui are dressed in the Ming style, Oriole and Crimson sport the late-Qing fashions of Shanghai.

Another sign of modern times can be detected in the artistic rendering of the prints. In the moonlight, the garden rock Oriole sits on seems to be rendered in light and shadow (scene 2, cat. 43). The introduction of shadow and linear perspective in New Year prints is a reflection of Western influence, brought by Jesuit priests and artists active in the Qianlong court. All major print workshops such as Yangliuqing and Taohuawu are reputed to have made erotic prints but it is not clear how prints such as this set—not erotic prints per se but containing partial nudity and a sex scene—were used, whether they were pasted up on a wall in the house or kept tucked away in drawers or trunks.

—MIA YINXING LIU

Five

Character, Role, Actor

Chinese opera subsumes individual dramatic characters into a system of role-types, which has historically required specialized training for the performer and been immediately recognized by its audience. The names of the role-types, their number, and the fineness of the distinctions between them change over time and depend on the variety of opera. The four most basic role-types during the Qing dynasty (1644–1911), as in Peking opera today, are *sheng* (male lead), *dan* (female lead), *jing* (painted face), and *chou* (clown). Role-type was not chiefly aligned with vocal range so members of either sex could play any part.

The earliest visual representations of theatrical figures in China, which date from the tenth to fourteenth centuries and are found in tombs, temple murals, and certain portable paintings, portray performers on stage in theatrical costumes and poses in a manner that emphasizes role-type rather than any individual dramatic character. (Two known examples even provide the name of a specific actress.) By contrast, illustrations of plays in printed books or painted albums popular during the Ming (1368–1644) and Qing periods generally depict individual characters as social persons in natural dress and settings, not theatrical role-types in stage costume and makeup.

During the second half of the nineteenth century, a new taste for pictures of specific dramatic personages in full stage regalia is discernable in New Year prints (*nianhua*) of popular stage scenes and in painted portraits of individual opera characters associated with court theater culture. But it is only in the early twentieth century with the introduction of photography and the rise of a modern star culture that recognizable images of named actors start to circulate as commodities.

Cat. 44
Chen Hongshou
Chinese, 1599–1652
Bodhisattva Guanyin in the Form of the Buddha Mother, 1620
Hanging scroll, ink on paper,
image: 49 ¼ x 19 1/16 in. (125.1 x 48.4 cm),
mounting: 96 ¾ x 24 9/16 in. (245.7 x 62.4 cm)
Lent by The Metropolitan Museum of Art,
Purchase, Friends of Asian Art Gifts, 1992
1992.197

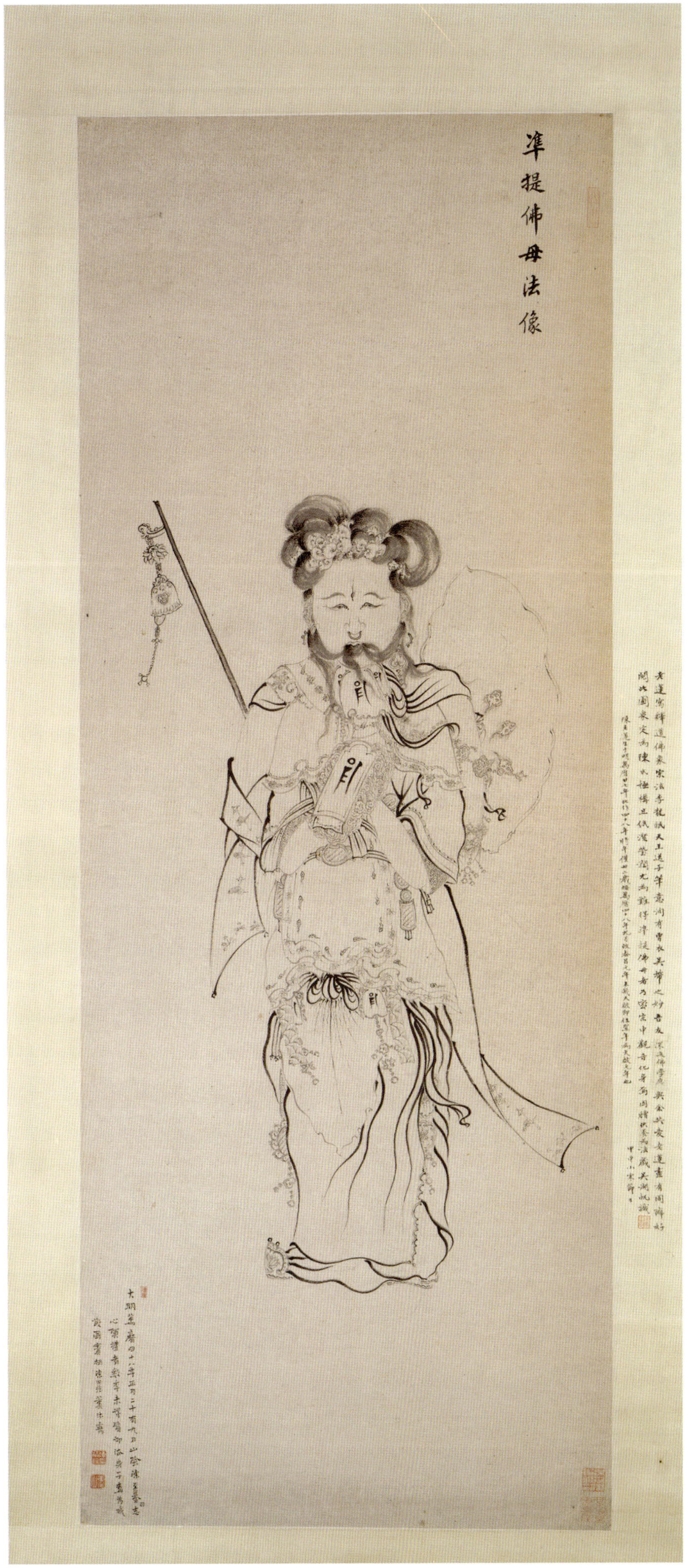

Chen Hongshou is renowned for his innovative assimilation of theatrical elements in figure paintings and for his woodblock illustrations of plays such as *Mistress and Maid* (*Jiahong ji*) and *Romance of the Western Chamber* (*Xixiang ji*). (See Judith T. Zeitlin's introduction, fig. I.13.) *Bodhisattva Guanyin in the Form of the Buddha Mother* represents one of Chen Hongshou's earliest attempts to combine religious imagery with elements of theatrical or ritual performance.

This scroll painting depicts a frontal figure in monochromatic ink against an empty background. On the top right of the painting, an unsigned caption reads "Dharma Likeness of Zhunti Buddha Mother" (Zhunti fomu faxiang). (*Zhunti* is the Chinese transliteration of the Sanskrit term *cundi* and means "extreme purity," the Zhunti Buddha Mother is an esoteric form of the Bodhisattva Guanyin.)

Unlike most representations of Buddhist deities, which typically take the form of fixed poses and features or depictions of transcendent beings in human form, this painting portrays an individual—probably a woman—impersonating a religious figure in the manner of an actor. Nonetheless, the Bodhisattva is still depicted in an iconic frontal manner, facing the viewer directly. Her unruly hairdo is painted in uneven, fluffy coils, and she clutches two locks of hair in her mouth, a standard operatic gesture. In later performance traditions such as Peking opera, grasping a hank of hair in the mouth usually expresses anxiety and desperation (see cat. 50). This figure's detached expression contrasts with her soft and billowing hair. The dark curving lines of her eyes and eyebrows suggest the use of makeup, as does the third eye, an iconographic feature of the Zhunti Buddha Mother, painted vertically above the nose. Unusual jewelry such as a nose ring and metal-like ornaments on the ears also evoke the theater.

The figure has four arms. Unlike the usual depiction of multi-armed Buddhist deities in religious art, where all the arms extend from one pair of shoulders, this figure has four shoulders. The two front shoulders are narrow in proportion to the figure's body and are covered with a cloud shoulder (*yunjian*), a kind of short shawl often seen in images of bodhisattvas and in female theatrical costumes. The two front hands hold a rectangular-shaped object inscribed with an indecipherable character in an esoteric script. The object might be a palm-leaf sutra as suggested by the trace of floral-bordered leaf paper sliding out from the bottom.

The many arms and hands of a two-dimensional icon usually face front, however, the second set of shoulders and arms on this figure face backward, with the thumb and the index finger holding a shield-like object decorated with demonic faces on the right and a bell dangling from a staff on the left. Both outer arms are bare, but one is decorated with a patterned fabric strip, the other with ornate armbands. She is dressed in a voluminous outfit consisting of a cape, apron, several skirts, streamers with beads, and belts, chains, and pendants. The tip of a meticulously decorated shoe peeks out from under the garment. Such a detail further enhances the theatricality of the costume since a Buddhist image would typically bare the feet.

The Zhunti Buddha Mother is associated with the mystical practice of incanting the Zhunti dharani scripture, which was translated into Chinese during the late seventh to early eighth centuries, and remained popular during late imperial times. As Chen Hongshou's inscription on the lower left of the painting explains, his painting was commissioned by a contemporary follower of the cult of the Zhunti Buddha Mother. The inscription reads:

> In the forty-eighth year of the Wanli period of the Great Ming dynasty, on the twenty-ninth day of the first month [March 4, 1620], Mr. Chen Zhimu of Shan-yin remarked: "I have worshiped [this bodhisattva] with all my heart for many seasons, but I have never had a chance to pay my respects to her dharma body. Why don't you respectfully paint a precious likeness for me?" Written by Chen Hongshou after purifying himself.

The Zhunti dharani scripture includes instructions for how to draw the Buddha Mother, but Chen Hongshou's painting does not match the usual iconography, and only a few elements can be traced to doctrinal references. He instead visualizes the image of the Buddha Mother through the theatrical figure of a human performer. —YUHANG LI

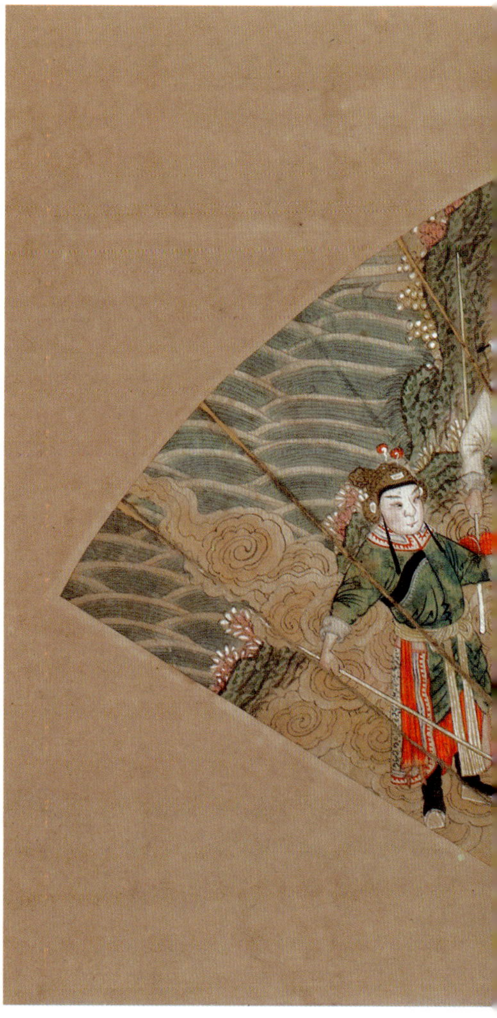

Cat. 45
Chinese, Late Qing Dynasty (1644–1911)
Fan Painting with Peking Opera Scene from Fiery Cloud Cave (Huoyun dong),
late 19th century
Folding fan, ink and color on paper,
6 3/4 x 17 3/4 in. (17.2 x 45.1 cm)
Private Collection

This fan painting depicts a scene partially derived from *Fiery Cloud Cave* (*Huoyun dong*), a Peking opera based on a story from *Journey to the West* (*Xiyouji*). The monstrous Red Boy (Honghai'er) traps and captures the monk Tripitaka (Xuanzang), who is on a pilgrimage to India to bring back Buddhist sutras to China. Defeated by Red Boy's secret weapon, the true fire of Samādhi, Tripitaka's disciple Monkey flies to Mount Potalaka in the South Sea and begs the Bodhisattva Guanyin for assistance. Eventually Guanyin uses her power to subdue Red Boy and make him one of her attendants, the Boy of Goodly Wealth (Shancai). This fan depicts the confrontation between the two, the moment before Guanyin overcomes Red Boy.

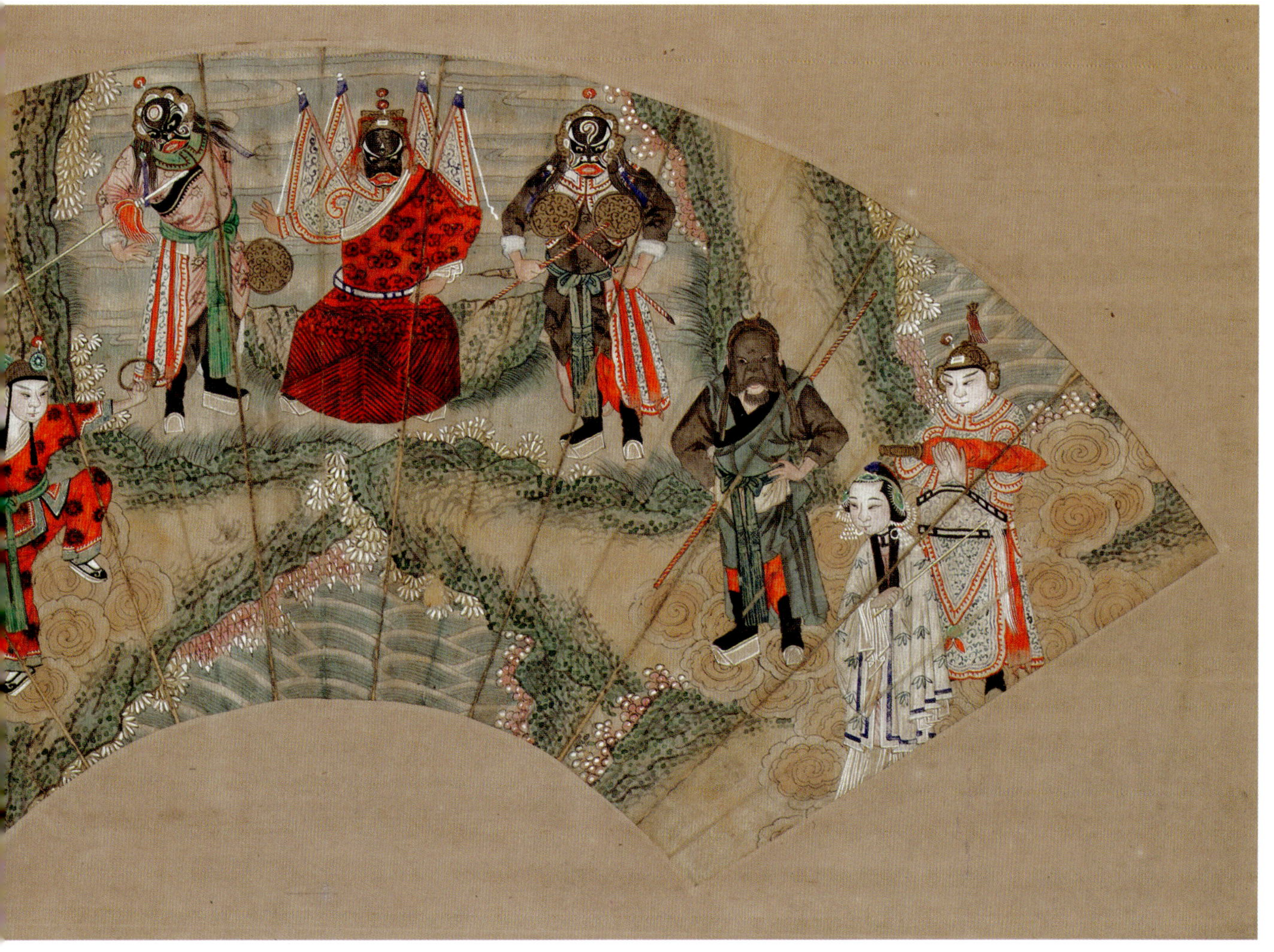

Two almost identical V-shaped strips of land surrounded by water divide the figures into three sections. The unnaturally brown landscape bordered with intense brush strokes in ink and mineral blue resembles the pictorial style of free-standing stage props such as "mountain pieces" (*shanpian*) that emerged during the late Qing period. Though the figures appear in a seemingly natural environment, their arrangement resembles the staged battle scenes on New Year prints. In the middle, a front-facing figure wears a red dress that combines martial armor and a civil robe. The third eye on his forehead identifies him as the god Erlang (Erlang shen), the Jade Emperor's nephew who subdues Monkey at the beginning of *Journey to the West*. Erlang does not take part in the Red Boy episode in either the novel or theatrical versions of the story, however. In this painting, he is portrayed as a superior commander accompanied by two generals and is positioned higher than the other figures with sky and clouds as background. His concern with the battle and his prominent position in the painting remind us of commanders on a high terrace watching a battle as depicted in New Year prints (cats. 16, 51). On this fan, he and his generals might have been added to fulfill the visual conventions of a battle on a two-dimensional work of popular art.

In the left section, Red Boy, flanked by two figures in young martial male roles, stands poised for battle. He holds in his right hand a spear above his head and has a ring of gold in his left hand while he lifts his left leg. In contrast to Red Boy's theatrical fighting posture, the three figures in the opposite camp on the right side of the fan look calm. The figure on the right with his hands on his waist is Monkey, even though he lacks his iconic fur-patterned monkey outfit and sharp-pointed monkey face. However, the hairiness of his face, the red stick representing his signature iron cudgel in his right hand, and the constrictive fillet on his head all confirm his identity. Next to Monkey, a middle-aged woman wears a long white skirt and cape open in the front. Her robe's bamboo leaf pattern and blue hem reveal that she is the Bodhisattva Guanyin, whose image in stage performance differs from her usual iconography (see cat. 44). Surviving Guanyin theatrical costumes (called Guanyin capes [*Guanyin pei*]) from the Qing imperial court reveal that at least from the Tongzhi period (1862–1874), a new style of Guanyin outfit had emerged, with bamboo designs standing for the Black Bamboo Grove located in her residence. This new fashion differs from the Guanyin outfit recorded in court play texts from the Qianlong period (1736–1795), such as *The Precious Raft of Ascendant Peace* (*Shengping baofa*). The fan painting shows that the new style of Guanyin costume was also seen outside the court during the late nineteenth century. On the fan Guanyin holds a horsetail whisk (*fuchen*), which is used as a prop for this role in the theater, but is not found in her images in sculpture or painting. Standing behind Guanyin is her guard Weituo, in full armor, with his palms pressed together and sword resting across his arms (see Judith T. Zeitlin's introduction to this catalogue and fig. I.2) Unlike Guanyin, the theatrical Weituo's posture and costume adhere to his usual icongraphic attributes in other visual media. —YUHANG LI

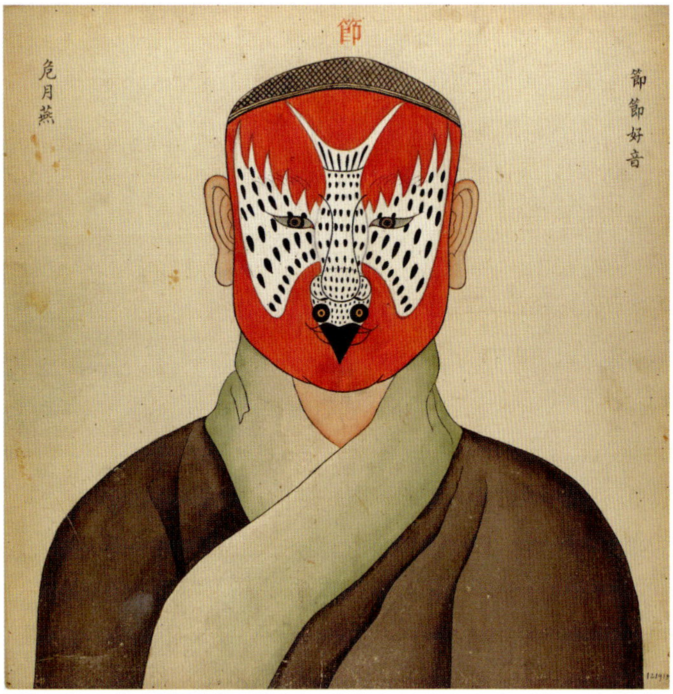

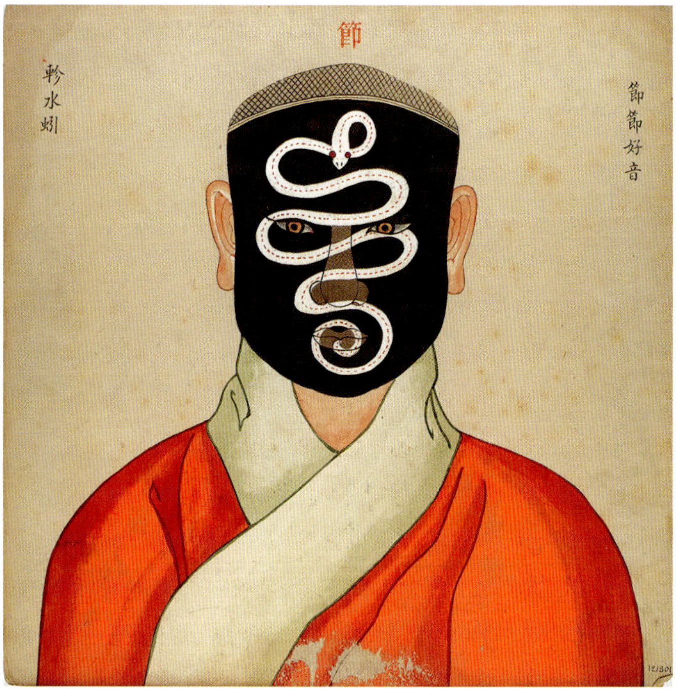

46.1
(Right) *Marvelous Tunes for Festivals* (*Jiejie haoyin*) 節節好音
(Left) Swallow Wei, (one of the 28 star deities) 危月燕
(Top, center) Festival 節
(Number on back) 38 三十八

46.2
(Right) *Marvelous Tunes for Festivals* (*Jiejie haoyin*) 節節好音
(Left) Zhenshuiyin Earthworm Zhen (one of the 28 star deities) 軫水蚓
(Top, center) Festival 節
(Number on back) 58 五十八

Cats. 46.1–10

Chinese, Qing Dynasty (1644–1911),
Qianlong Period (1736–1795)
Mask Designs for Court Opera Characters, ca. 1746–95
Ten album leaves, ink and color on paper, each image: 18 x 18 in. (46 x 46 cm)
The Field Museum, Chicago
121898, 121900, 121901, 121905, 121906, 121914, 121915, 121916, 121926, 121934

The Qianlong period (1736–1795) witnessed the first zenith of Qing court theater, which was characterized by systematic compositions of "grand plays" (*daxi*), massive performances, and splendid spectacles. Frequently performed over a number of days and involving hundreds or even more than a thousand actors, court dramas featured historical or mythical themes adapted from popular legends and marked such occasions as imperial ceremonies and diplomatic rituals.

Selected from a set acquired by the anthropologist Berthold Laufer (1874–1934) in Beijing during his excursion to China between 1908 and 1910, these ten leaves of mask designs on exhibition offer a glance into Chinese opera's magnificent visual culture. Composed in the same format as a full frontal bust portrait, each image demonstrates the stage makeup of one character in a play, with inscriptions of the play title and role name on the front and the number of the character's stage sequence on the back (see captions). Some leaves bear a stamped red character on the top center, which indicates the associated ceremonial occasion. These mask images were probably used as references for stage makeup.

The selected leaves represent the diversity of the court theater performed during the Qianlong period: *Marvelous Tunes for Festivals* (*Jiejie haoyin*) includes an array of short pageants; *Golden Norms for Exhorting Virtue* (*Quanshan jinke*) and *The Precious Raft of Ascendant Peace* (*Shengping baofa*) were grand plays adapted from the legends of *Maudgalyāyana* (Mulian) and Monkey's *Journey to the West* (*Xiyou ji*), respectively, while *Coincidental Reunion* (*Qiao tuanyuan*) and *Rouge Snow* (*Yanzhi xue*) were popular plays on the themes of fate and morality.

Supernatural beings—various deities, spirits, and ghosts—figure prominently in the set assembled by Laufer. Masks for these characters showcase highly flamboyant and imaginary designs. Some images feature bold abstract patterns in bright and contrasting colors that exaggerate facial features, while others accentuate the mythical or demonic identities of the characters by superimposing animal motifs associated with them over their faces. Some facial patterns may be derived from familiar imagery in classical or popular texts. For example, the upper part of the mask for the God of Dreams evokes a stylized butterfly, which may be alluding to the famous story of Zhuangzhou dreaming of turning into a butterfly in the eponymous Daoist classic *Zhuangzi* (cat. 46.10). Wherever a beard is required, the type and color of beard to be used is specified below the character's name. (See also Mei Mei Rado's essay in this volume.)

—MEI MEI RADO

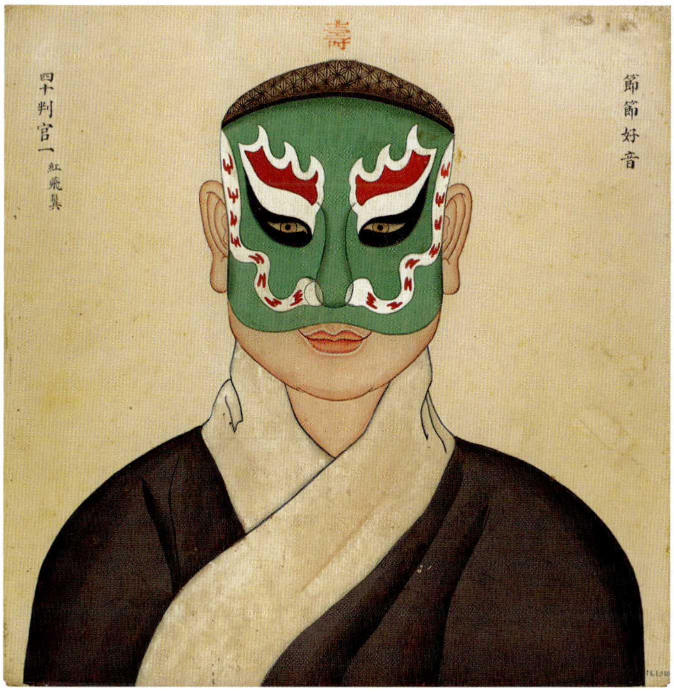

46.3
(Right) *Marvelous Tunes for Festivals* (*Jiejie haoyin*) 節節好音
(Left) The first of the 40 judges/red flying beard 四十判官一/紅飛鬢
(Top, center) Birthday 壽
(Number on back) 54 五十四

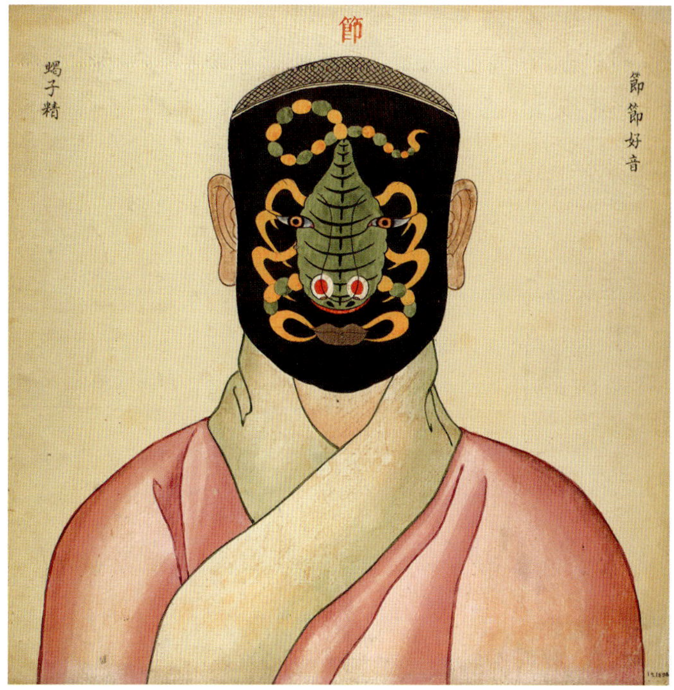

46.4
(Right) *Marvelous Tunes for Festivals* (*Jiejie haoyin*) 節節好音
(Left) Scorpion spirit 蝎子精
(Top, center) Festival 節
(Number on back) 161 一百六一

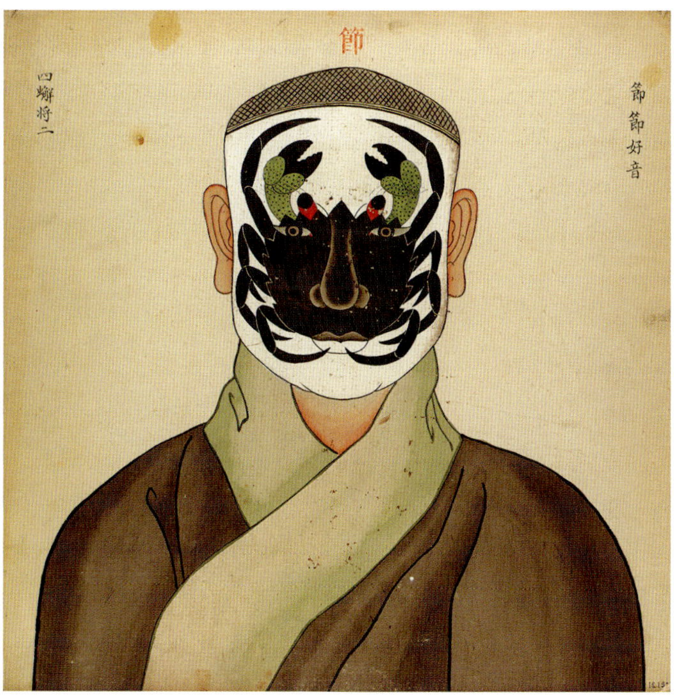

46.5
(Right) *Marvelous Tunes for Festivals* (*Jiejie haoyin*) 節節好音
(Left) The second of the four crab generals 四蟹將二
(Top, center) Festival 節
(Number on back) 142 一百四十二

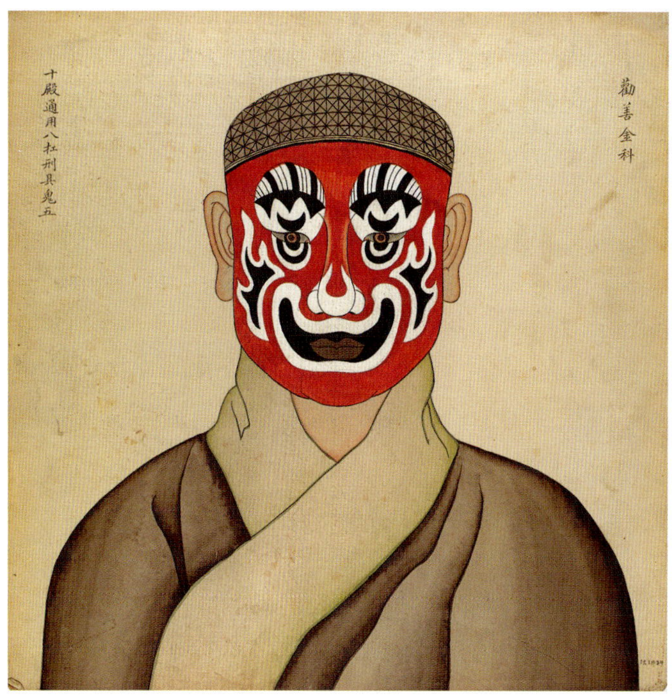

46.6
(Right) *Golden Norms for Exhorting Virtue* (*Quanshan jinke*) 勸善金科
(Left) The fifth of the eight ghosts carrying torture instruments for all the ten Palaces of Hell 十殿通用八扛刑具鬼五
(Number on back) 401 四百一

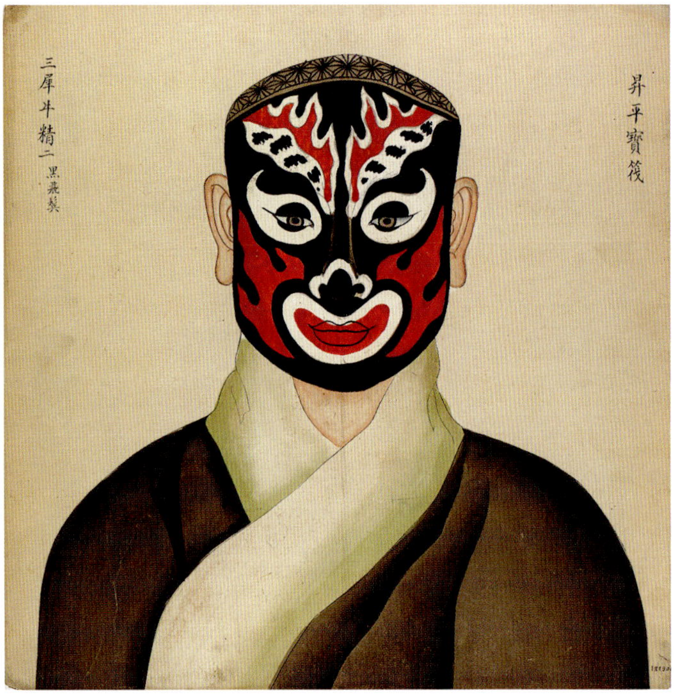

46.7

(Right) *The Precious Raft of Ascendant Peace* (*Shengping baofa*) 昇平寶筏

(Left) The second of the three rhinoceros spirits/black flying beard 三犀牛精二/黑飛鬢

(Number on back) 579 五百七十九

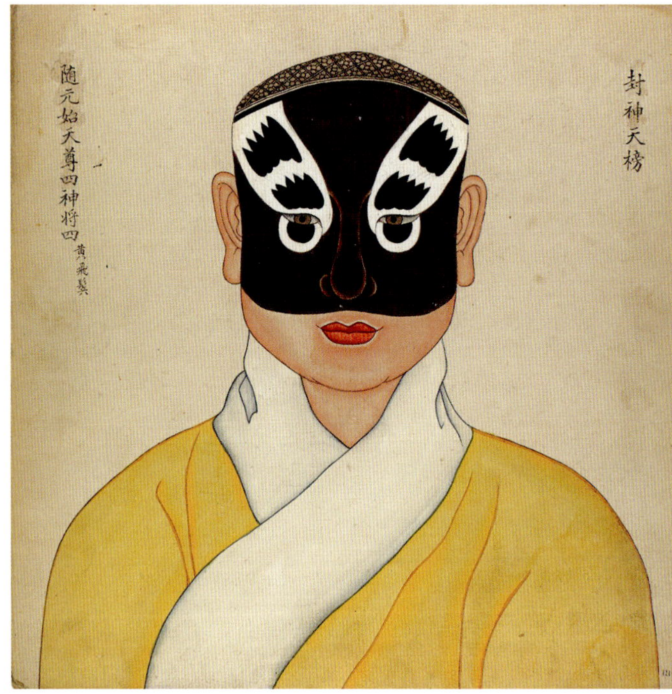

46.8

(Right) *The Creation of the Gods* (*Fengshen tianban*) 封神天榜

(Left) The fourth of the four attendant deities accompanying the Celestial Venerable of the Primordial Beginning /yellow flying beard 隨元始天尊四神將四/黃飛鬢

(Number on back) 37 三十七

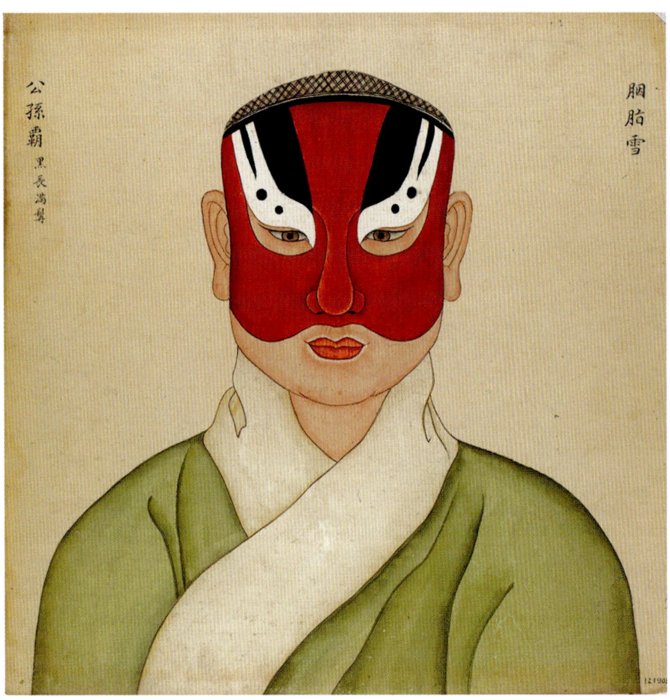

46.9

(Right) *Rouge Snow* (*Yanzhi xue*) 胭脂雪

(Left) Gongsun Ba/long black full beard 公孫霸/黑長滿髯

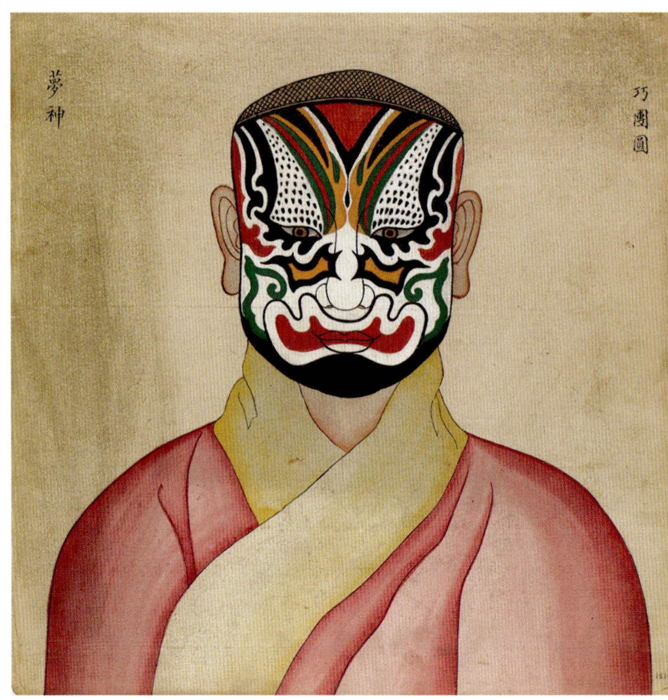

46.10

(Right) *Coincidental Reunion* (*Qiao tuanyuan*) 巧團圓

(Left) God of Dreams 夢神

(Number on back) 2 二

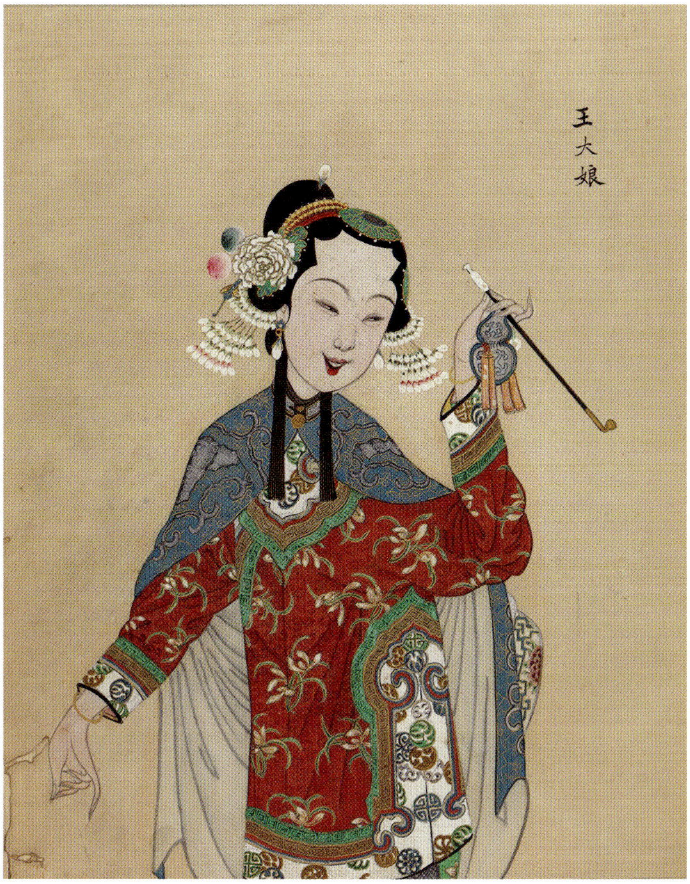

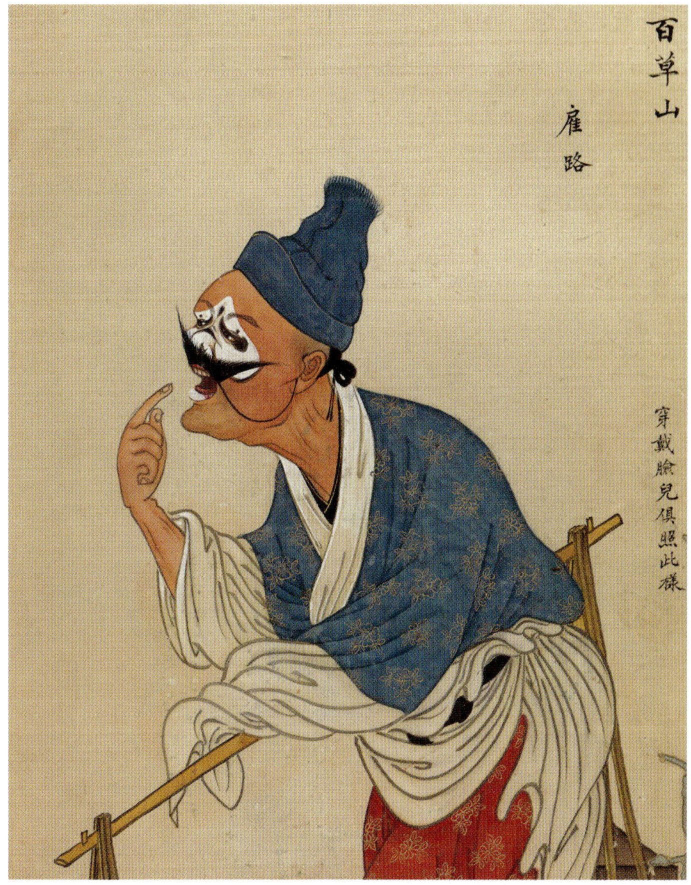

47.1, 47.2
(Play title) *Mountain of Plentiful Herbs* (*Baicao shan*) 百草山 (Left) The witch Madam Wang 王大娘 (Right) Gu Lu 雇路
(Additional inscription) Costume and makeup [shall] follow these [illustrations]. 穿戴臉兒俱照此樣

Cats. 47.1–14
Chinese, Late Qing Dynasty (1644–1911), Late Tongzhi (1862–1874) and Guangxu (1875–1908) Periods
Half-Length Portraits of Opera Characters, ca. 1870s to 1900
Fourteen album paintings on seven bi-fold leaves from *Album of One Hundred Portraits of Opera Characters*, ink, color, and gilt on silk, each painting without mount: 10 3/8 x 8 1/4 in. (26.4 × 21 cm)
Lent by The Metropolitan Museum of Art, Rogers Fund, 1930
30.76.299

Qing dynasty court theater flourished during the Guangxu reign (1875–1908), largely resulting from Empress Dowager Cixi's enthusiasm and promotion. By the last quarter of the nineteenth century, the *luantan* (chaotic playing) opera style, which had by now evolved into the Peking opera tradition, dominated at court. This period also saw mutual influences between the court theater and outside commercial troupes in terms of repertory, the performance styles, and opera's visual culture.

Series portraits of characters from various plays emerged as a visual form in this new wave of theater culture. In a sense serving as connoisseurial records and intended for the pleasure of viewing, these images often combine meticulous descriptions of stage makeup and costumes, theatrical poses, and clues to plots. These seven double-leaves of half-length portraits of opera characters, selected from a hundred-leaf album, represent a once popular production, of which at least 500 leaves are extent today (see also Mei Mei Rado's essay in this catalogue). While the visual style and characters' costumes in these images closely resemble Qing court prototypes, the lesser degree of refinement and sophistication in these images betrays a commercial studio work.

All four plays represented here are *luantan* operas with supernatural or martial themes. *Mountain of Plentiful Herbs* (*Baicao shan*) recounts the fable of the Bodhisattva Guanyin and the Earth God capturing the witch Madam Wang. Set in the Northern Song dynasty (960–1127), *Three Heroes and Five Gallants* (*Sanxia wuyi*) contains various legends of chivalrous heroes fighting crime and corruption, with the support of the wise and righteous judge Bao Zheng (Bao Wenzheng). Based on stories of the civil wars during the Three Kingdoms period (220–280), *The Yangping Station* (*Yangping guan*) focuses on a series of martial events that led to Cao Cao's (King of Wei) loss of the Yangping Station. *The Village of the Overlord* (*Bawang zhuang*) retells the story of the officer Shi Shilun of the Kangxi period (1662–1722) seizing the villain Huang Longji.

The selected leaves show various role-types, each distinguished by their coded makeup and costumes. For example, male *jing* roles have fully painted faces, in contrast to clowns (*chou*), whose faces are only painted white around the nose and eyes; martial figures wear *kao* armor and flags on the back; and barbarians or sorcerers are marked by the long feathers (*lingzi*) on their headgear. —MEI MEI RADO

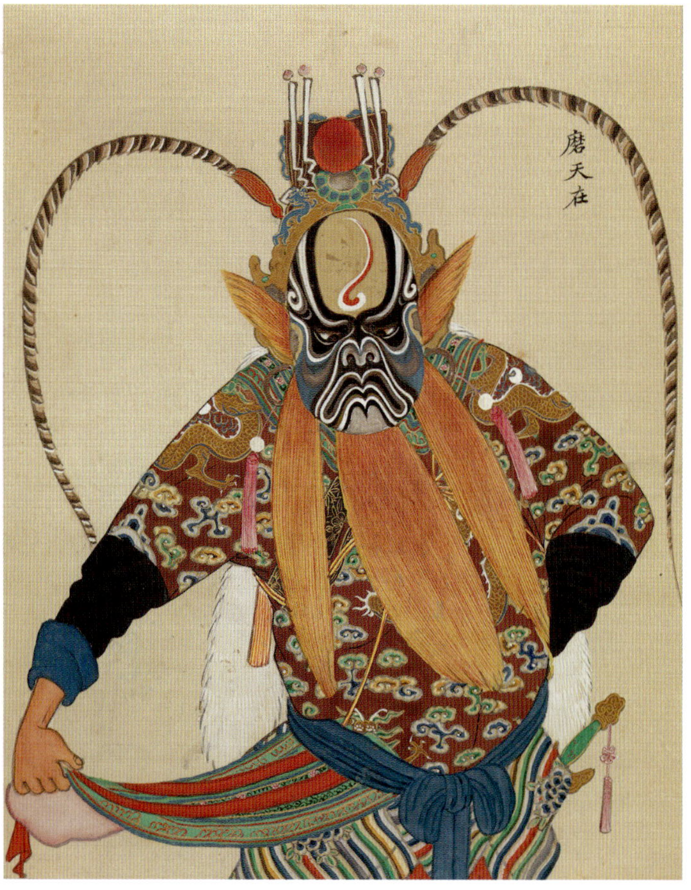

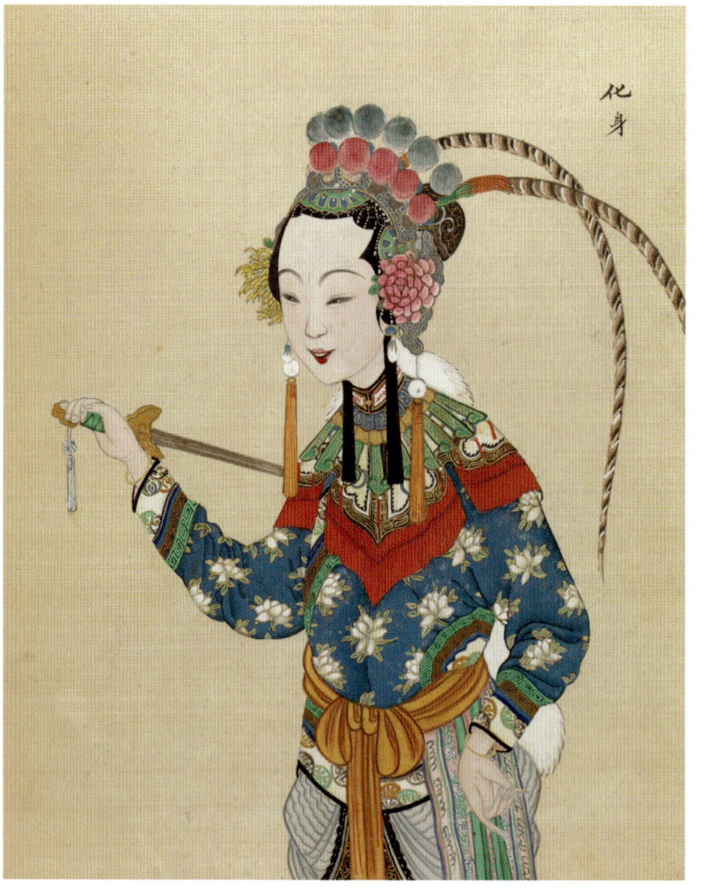

47.3, 47.4
(Play title) *Mountain of Plentiful Herbs* (*Baicao shan*) 百草山 (Left) Mo Tianzai 磨天在 (Right) Incarnation 化身

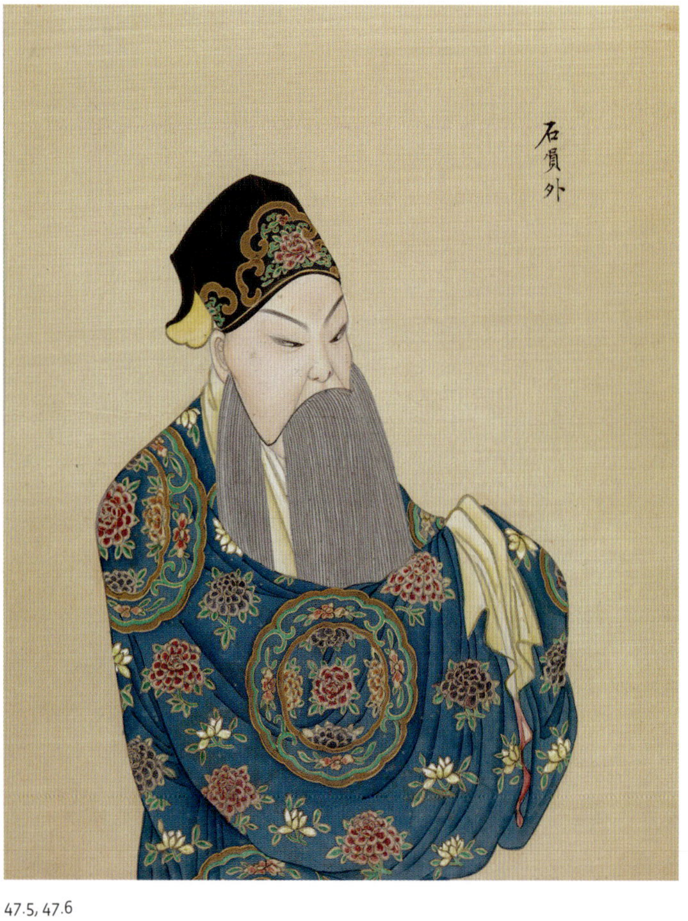

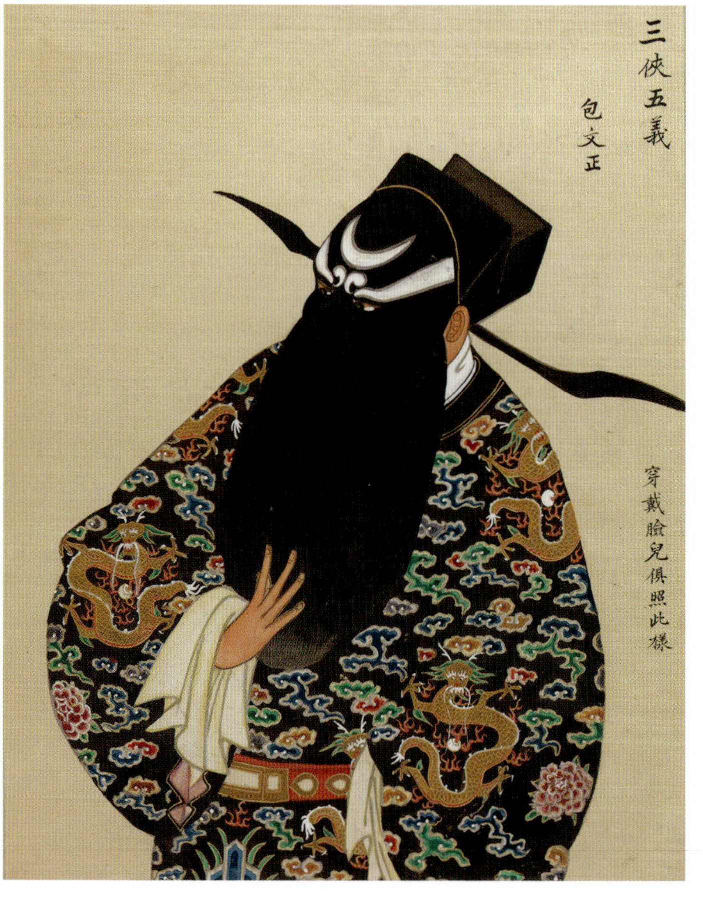

47.5, 47.6
(Play title) *Three Heroes and Five Gallants* (*Sanxia wuyi*) 三俠五義 (Left) Esquire Shi 石員外 (Right) Bao Wenzheng 包文正
(Additional inscription) Costume and makeup [shall] follow these [illustrations]. 穿戴臉兒俱照此樣

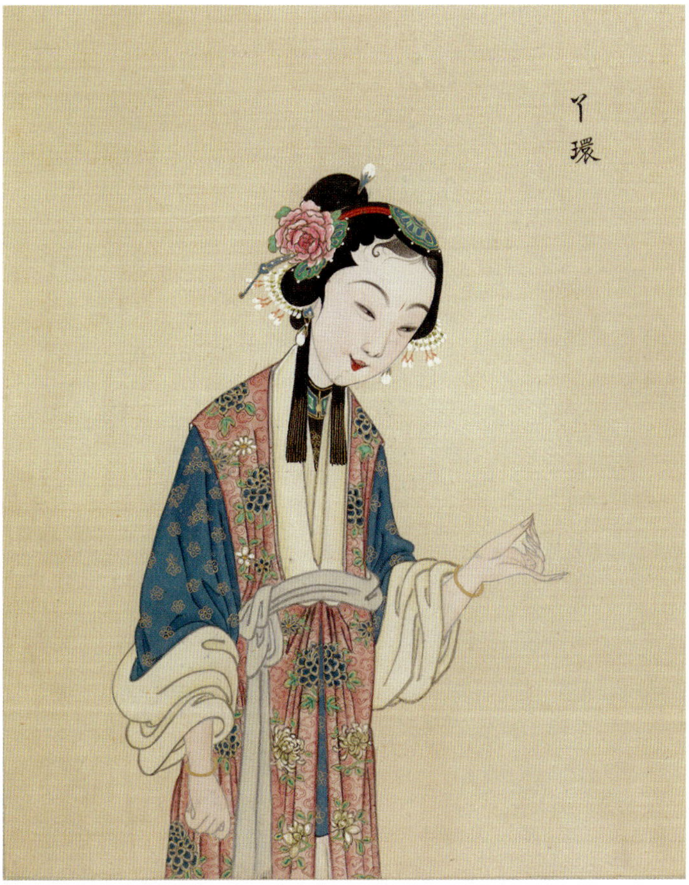

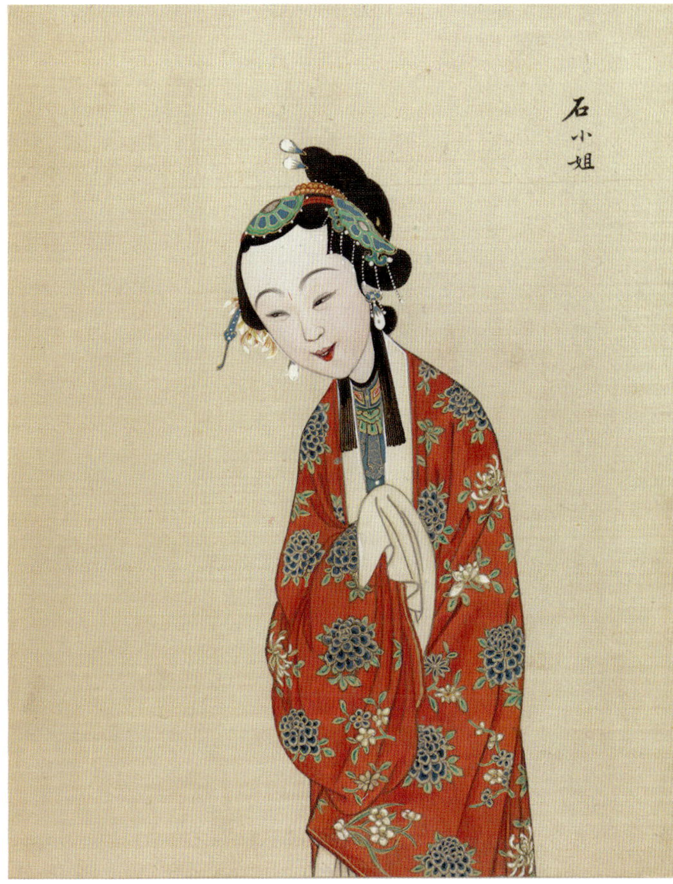

47.7, 47.8

(Play title) *Three Heroes and Five Gallants* (*Sanxia wuyi*) 三俠五義 (Left) Maid 丫環 (Right) Miss Shi 石小姐

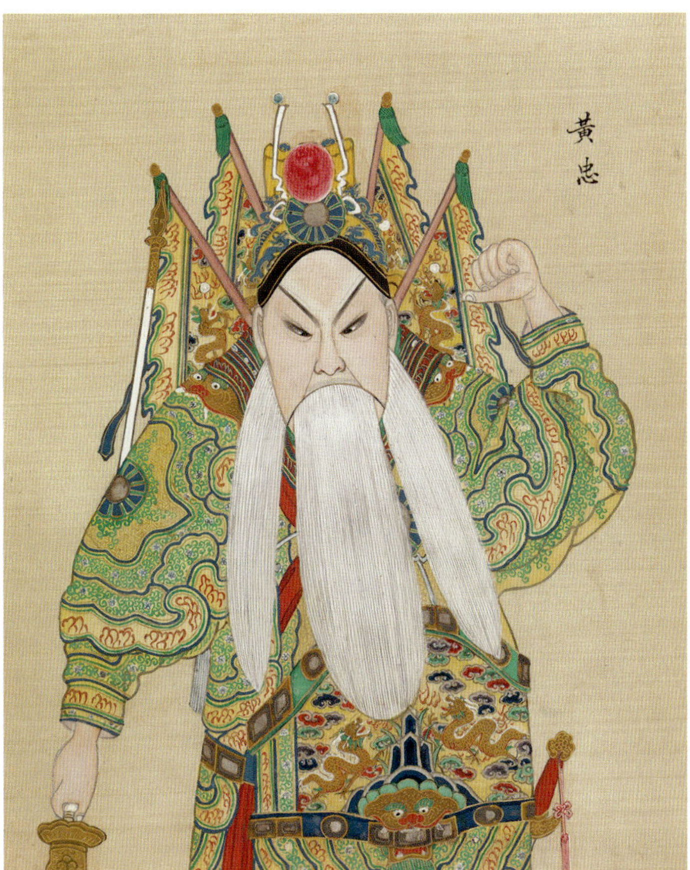

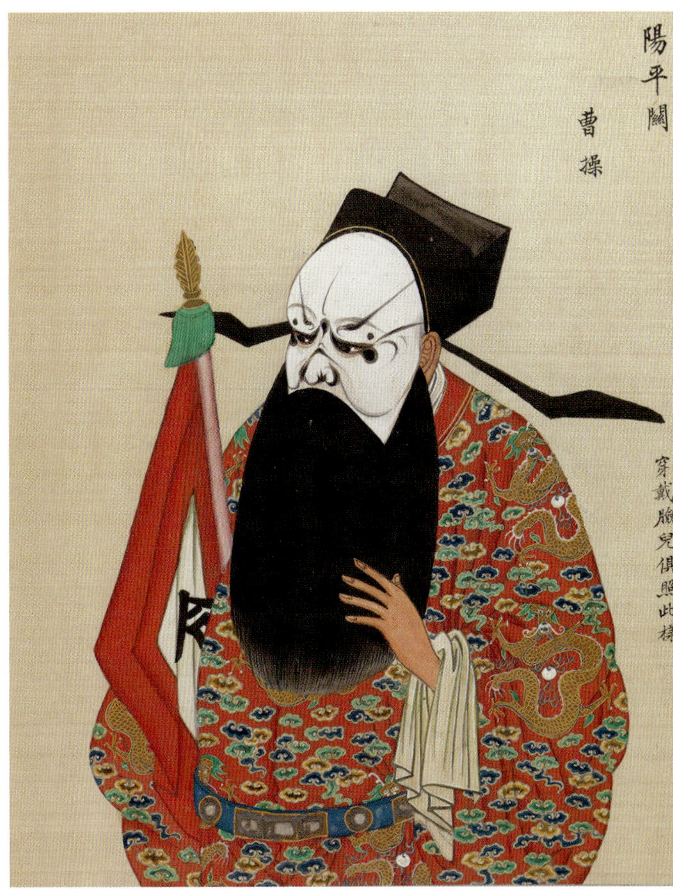

47.9, 47.10

(Play title) *The Yangping Station* (*Yangping guan*) 陽平關 (Left) Huang Zhong 黃忠 (Right) Cao Cao 曹操

(Additional inscription) Costume and makeup [shall] follow these [illustrations]. 穿戴臉兒俱照此樣

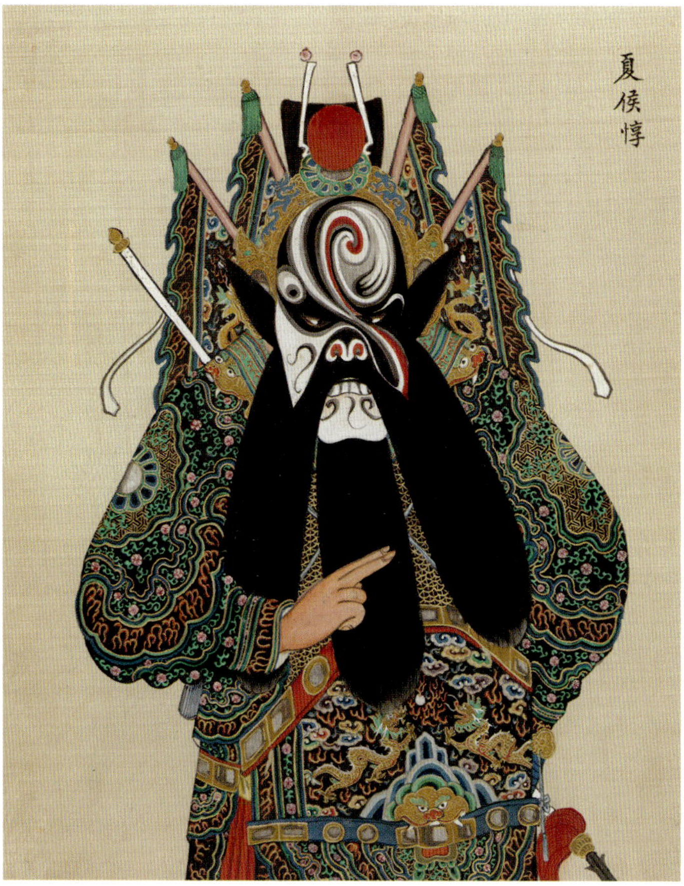

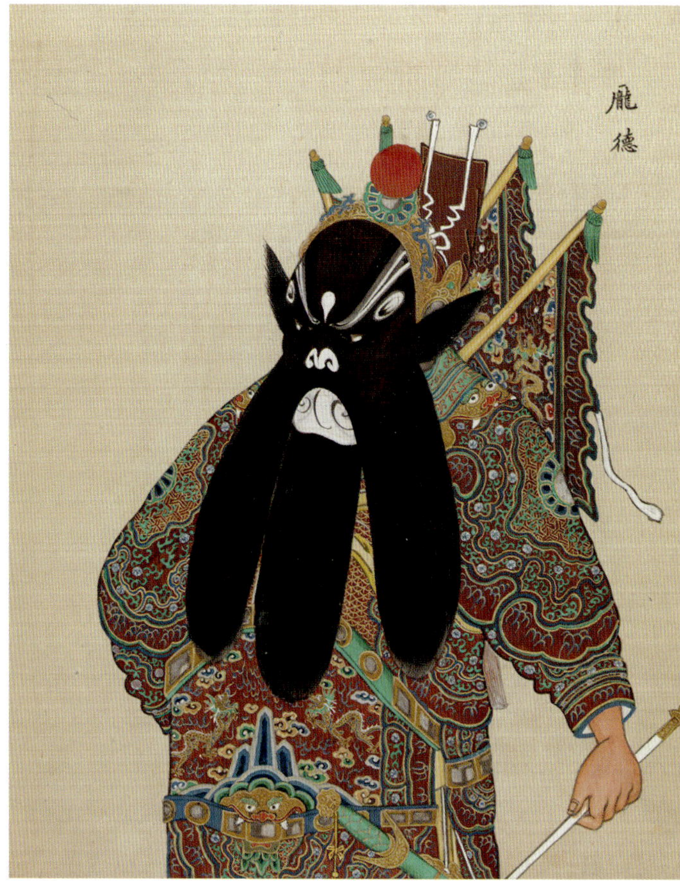

47.11, 47.12

(Play title) *The Yangping Station* (*Yangping guan*) 陽平關 (Left) Xiahou Dun 夏侯惇 (Right) Pang De 龐德

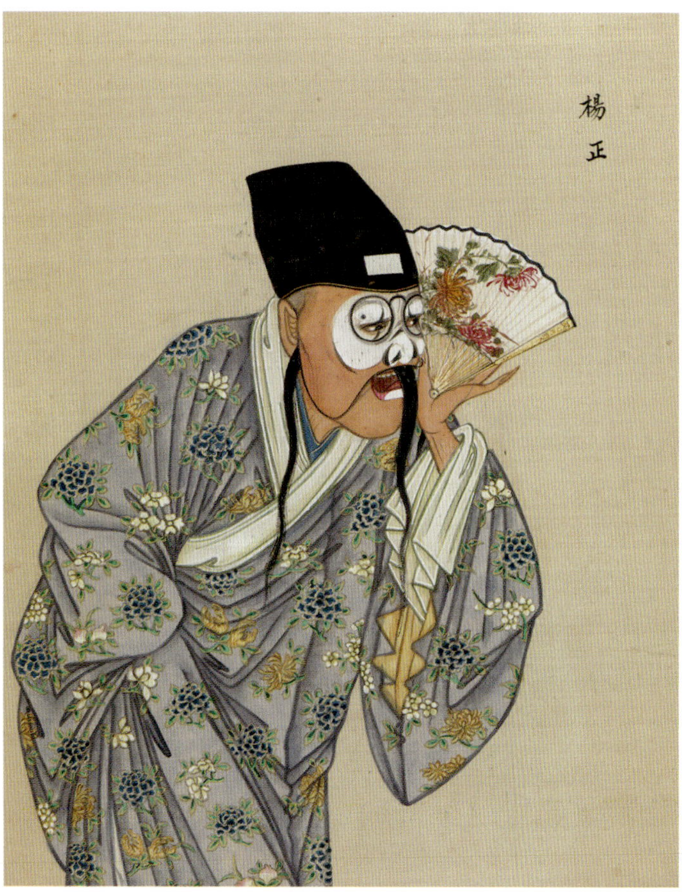

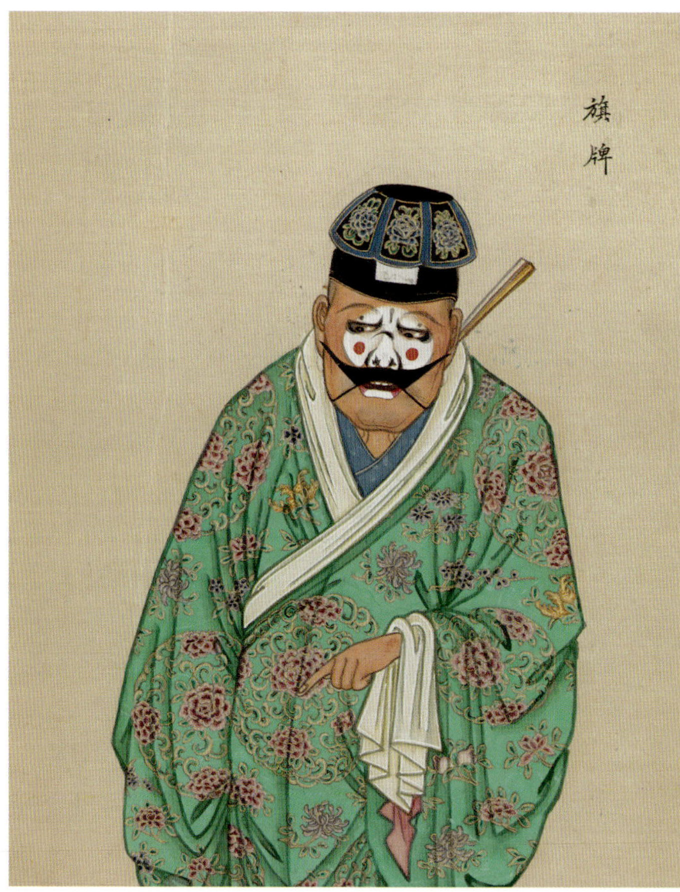

47.13, 47.14

(Play title) *The Village of the Overlord* (*Bawang zhuang*) 霸王莊 (Left) Yang Zheng 楊正 (Right) Qi Pai 旗牌

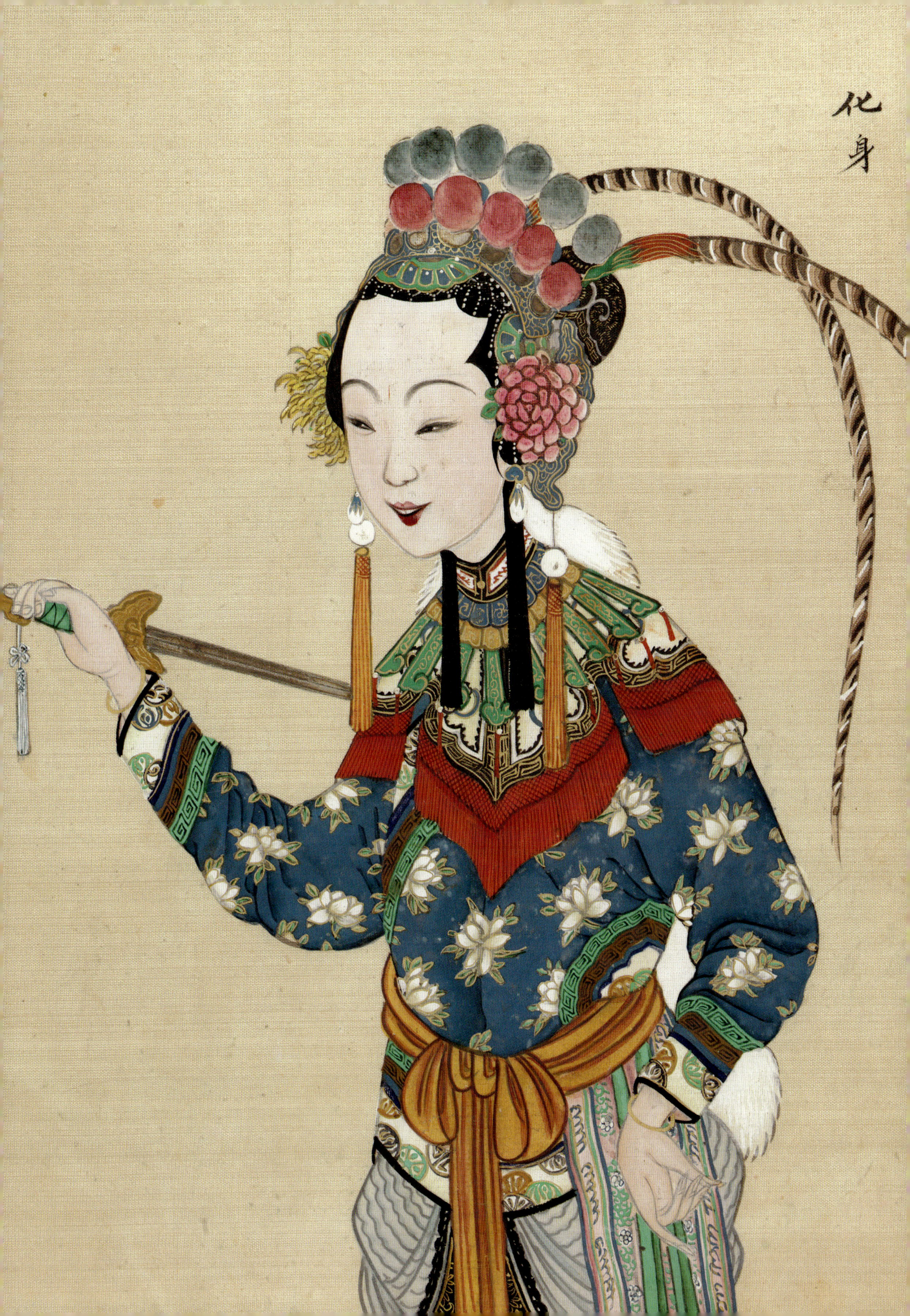
化身

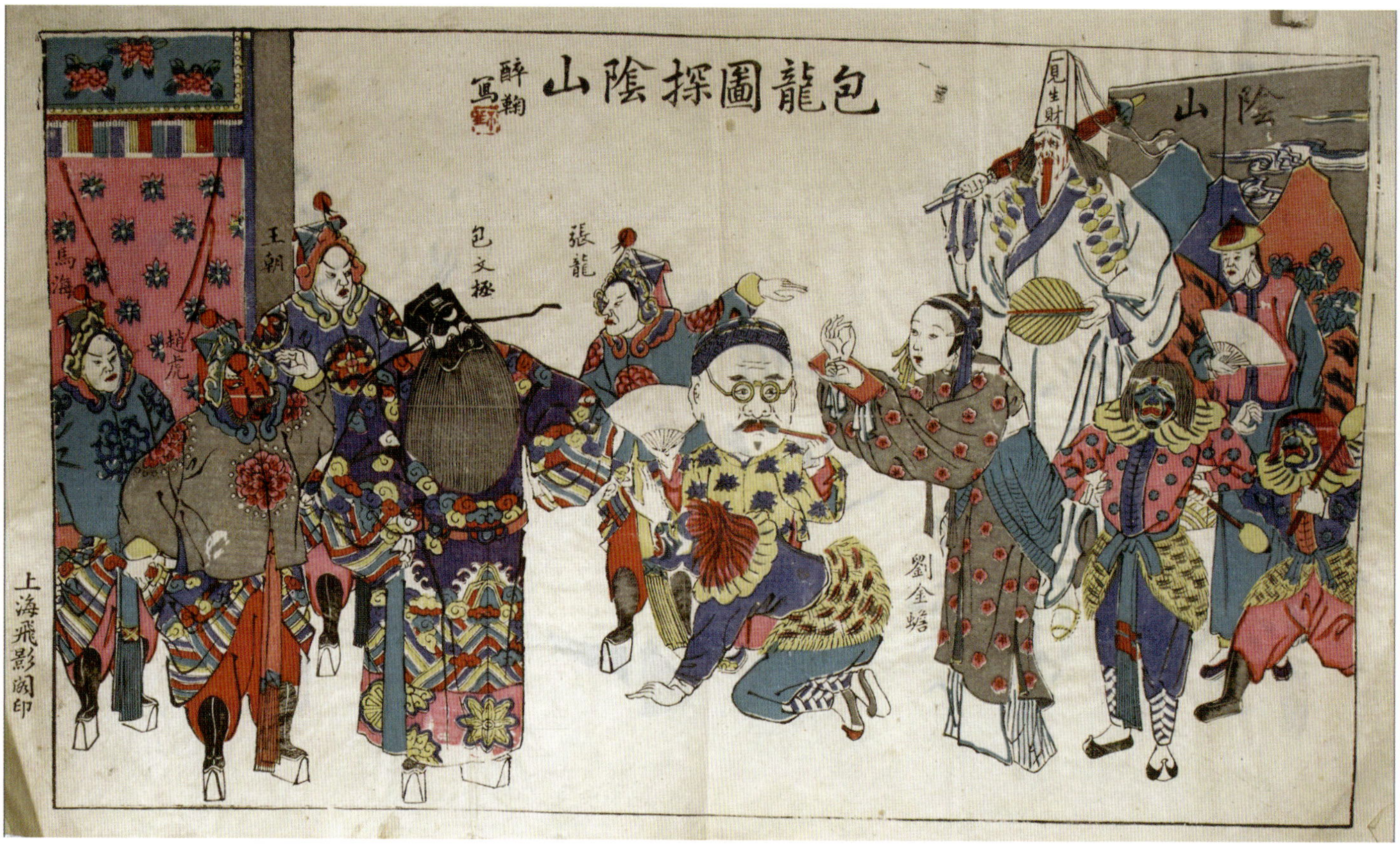

Cat. 48
Zuiju, designer
Chinese, active Late Qing Dynasty (1644–1911)
Shanghai, Feiying Ge (print workshop)
"Judge Bao Visits the Mountains of the Dead"
Scene from A Visit to the Mountains of the Dead (Tan Yinshan), 1902
Polychrome woodblock print, $21\frac{1}{4} \times 12\frac{3}{16}$ in. (54 x 31 cm)
Courtesy of the Division of Anthropology, American Museum of Natural History
70/4837 A04

This New Year picture (*nianhua*) of legendary detective Judge Bao interviewing the shade of a murdered woman focuses on the spectacular, employing bright colors to enliven the courts of hell. The inscription across the top, "Judge Bao Visits the Mountains of the Dead" (Bao Longtu tan Yinshan), identifies the print as an illustration of the popular Peking opera *A Visit to the Mountains of the Dead* (*Tan Yinshan*). Smaller characters name the artist, Zuiju, who was active in the late Qing as an illustrator of Suzhou-style New Year prints. (For more on New Year prints, see Bo Songnian's essay in this catalogue.) Small characters to the very left of the print identify its source: Shanghai's Feiyingge, a print workshop associated with the famous illustrator Wu Youru.

While the historical Judge Bao was an official during the Song dynasty (960–1279) with an extraordinary reputation for incorruptibility and dedication to impartial justice, tales of his investigative prowess grew ever more legendary in the centuries after his death. On stage, Judge Bao's black painted face is emblazoned with a white crescent moon to symbolize his eternal vigilance against injustice.

Seen here, he travels to the underworld to investigate the murder of a young woman, Liu Jinchan, killed after resisting rape. The man who discovers her body is unjustly convicted of the murder by an inept magistrate and appeals to Judge Bao, who in the absence of any living witnesses to the crime, seeks out the victim herself to learn the truth. The play chronicles the extraordinary lengths to which Judge Bao was believed to go in order to see justice served. Flanking Judge Bao are his four enforcers—Ma Hai, Zhao Hu, Wang Zhao, and Zhang Long. As Judge Bao ventures into the world of the dead, they emphasize his authority in the land of the living and confront the motley crew of demons escorting Jinchan's spirit.

Theatrical space in this picture is cleverly represented though the binary opposition of the human group on the left and the ghost group on the right. In Chinese opera, actors ordinarily enter through an entrance door on the left side of the stage (stage right), and exit through an exit door on the right side (stage left) (see Judith T. Zeitlin's introduction in this catalogue). In certain cases, actors playing ghosts would deliberately violate this protocol by entering through the exit door to symbolize their anomalous status and otherworldly provenance. In this print, the regular entrance door on the left, through which Judge Bao and his human attendants would have come on stage, is covered with a flowered, pink curtain. They stand in front of it, facing to the right as the mob of ghosts surges toward them from the left. Behind the ghosts, the exit door they would have entered through has been replaced by a screen, whose panels resemble the two leaves of a door. The gloomy landscape on the screen represents the underworld—here identified as the "Mountains of the Dead" (Yinshan) by a label inscribed on the screen.

On stage, underworld scenes lend themselves to riotous spectacle as lonely souls plaintively appeal to the living through dramatic song and acrobats become spectacular tumbling demons. The comical appearance of the ghosts here fits the colorful mood of a New Year print.

Three ghoulish demon attendants prance around the wronged spirit of Liu Jinshan, their comical wigs and ragtag costumes contrasting with Judge Bao's richly attired escort. Behind them, a dour, emaciated man dressed as a Qing official holds a paper fan. At his side, the Demon of Impermanence (Wuchang gui) in white, his long tongue protruding, wears a four-sided dunce cap inscribed with the phrase "A single glance engenders wealth" (yi jian sheng cai). Traditionally held to summon people's souls at the moment of their death, he is a frightening yet auspicious figure in Chinese folklore.

An unidentified ghost, perhaps the most striking figure of all, sports round glasses and a long pipe, and wears a round black cap on his enormous head. On stage, the clown playing him would have performed the role on his knees and worn an oversized fake head to provide a satiric modern update of the "big-headed ghost" (*datou gui*) from Chinese folklore. An actual papier-mâché head found in the American Museum of Natural History in New York appears almost identical to the one depicted in this print except for the identifying label "Magistrate of Taiping County" (Taiping xian zhengtang) across its nose. —KATHERINE ALEXANDER

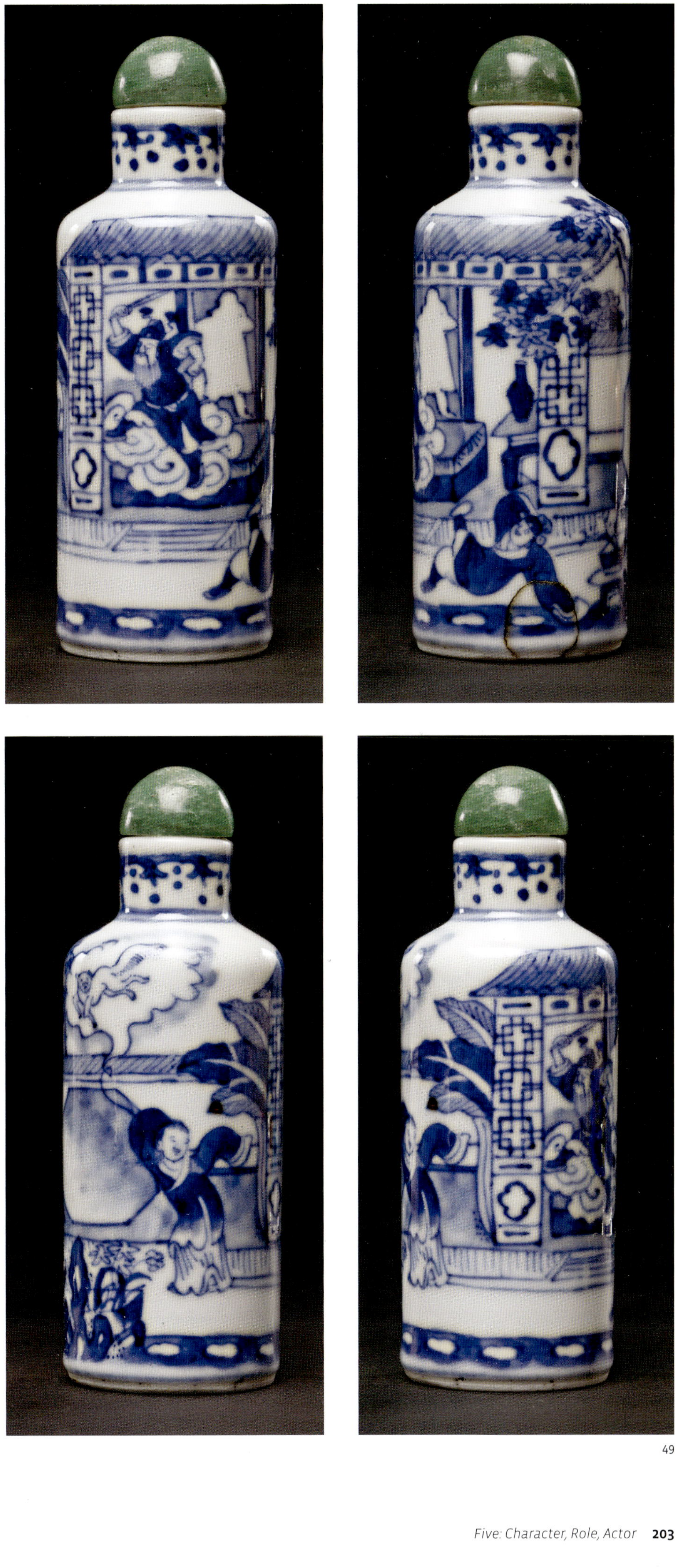

49

Cat. 49
Jingdezhen Kilns
Chinese, Late Qing Dynasty (1644–1911)
Snuff Bottle with Scene of Demon Queller Zhong Kui Expelling a Fox Spirit,
ca. 19th century
Porcelain with underglaze blue and white decoration, height: 3 ¼ in. (8.3 cm), diameter: 1 ⅛ in. (2.9 cm)
Asian Art Museum, Gift of Mr. and Mrs. Richard P. Adams
2010.426.A–.B

First introduced to China during the second half of the seventeenth century, European snuff—a mixture of ground tobacco leaves, herbs, and spices—soon came into vogue at the imperial court of the Qing dynasty (1644–1911) and also among that period's gentry class. Favored for its medicinal virtues and stimulating effect, snuff spread widely in China and had reached almost every social stratum by the nineteenth century. As part of this trend Chinese snuff bottles emerged—small, portable containers with a lidded narrow opening that were better than European snuff boxes at preserving snuff's fresh aroma.[1] As accessories, gifts, and collectibles, snuff bottles often functioned as fashionable objects for display and as symbols of status and taste. The creativity and technical virtuosity of their designs delighted their users and provided topics for conversation at informal social gatherings.

On the tiny surface of this porcelain snuff bottle from Jingdezhen, a scene of the Demon Queller Zhong Kui expelling a fox spirit unfolds in intriguing visual and literary layers, with references to stage performance, book illustration, and strange tales. Identifiable by his wobbly hat, thick beard, and official's outfit, Zhong Kui is chasing a beautiful woman while he wields a sword. The irregularly shaped blank spot on the wall behind the altar table indicates that a portrait of Zhong Kui has come alive, while the cloud he rides represents the magical nature of his presence. On one side of him, a retreating woman strikes a sinuous pose with her arms raised high, an exaggerated gesture that indicates defeat and flight in theatrical performance. Meanwhile a bubble issues from her to reveal a fox, a pictorial trope borrowed from popular prints and book illustrations and used to expose a demon's true identity. On the other side, shock and fear have immobilized a young scholar, the woman's deceived lover whose health is probably in danger. His falling posture with a leg and an arm in the air—also a stage pose—is often associated with timid scholar types overwhelmed by bewitching female power. Xu Xian, for example, in the Peking opera *Broken Bridge* (*Duanqiao*) strikes a similar pose when he re-encounters his pregnant wife White Snake and her maid Green Snake, who are furious at him for abandoning them (see cat. 13).

The scene represented on this snuff bottle conflates various literary sources. Stories of fox spirits incarnated as beautiful women seducing young men with fatal consequences abound in Chinese popular literature, and painted images magically coming alive also recur in strange tales. Qing dynasty novels about Zhong Kui, such as *Killing Demons* (*Zhangui zhuan*, before 1688) and *Zhong Kui Expelling Demons* (*Zhong Kui pinggui zhuan*, 1785), which elaborate the legends of his exorcising power and righteous morality, would have also inspired the image on this snuff bottle. Although no specific literary source has been identified as the direct inspiration for this image, visual representation of Zhong Kui expelling a fox spirit with sword in hand was not uncommon in the nineteenth century, attesting to the popularity of this story. The renowned Shanghai School artist Ren Bonian (1840–1896), for instance, painted a hanging scroll called *Zhong Kui Killing a Fox Spirit* (1878). —MEI MEI RADO

1 Hou Yili ed. *Tongti qingyang: biyanhu wenhua tezhan* [Lifting Spirit and Body: The Art and Culture of Snuff Bottles], exh. cat. (Taipei: National Palace Museum, 2012), pp. 33–37.

Cat. 50

Shanghai

Chinese, Late Qing Dynasty (1644–1911)

Wu Song Slays His Sister-in-Law and Flees from the Novel The Water Margin (Shuihu zhuan, alternately translated as Outlaws of the Marsh), 1902

Polychrome woodblock print, 22 × 12 19/32 in. (56 × 32 cm)

Courtesy of the Division of Anthropology, American Museum of Natural History

ASIA/0574 A44

For a discussion of this work see essay 5 in this volume, "Operatic Images in Popular New Year Prints" by Bo Songnian.

Cat. 51

Shanghai , Shen Wenya (print workshop)

Chinese, Late Qing Dynasty (1644–1911)

New Year Print with Scene from The Great Upsurge of Mount Liang: Subduing Guan Sheng (Daxing Liangshan: Soufu Guan Sheng), 1902

Polychrome woodblock print

Courtesy of the Division of Anthropology, American Museum of Natural History

Asia/0574 A43

For a discussion of this work see essay 5 in this volume, "Operatic Images in Popular New Year Prints" by Bo Songnian.

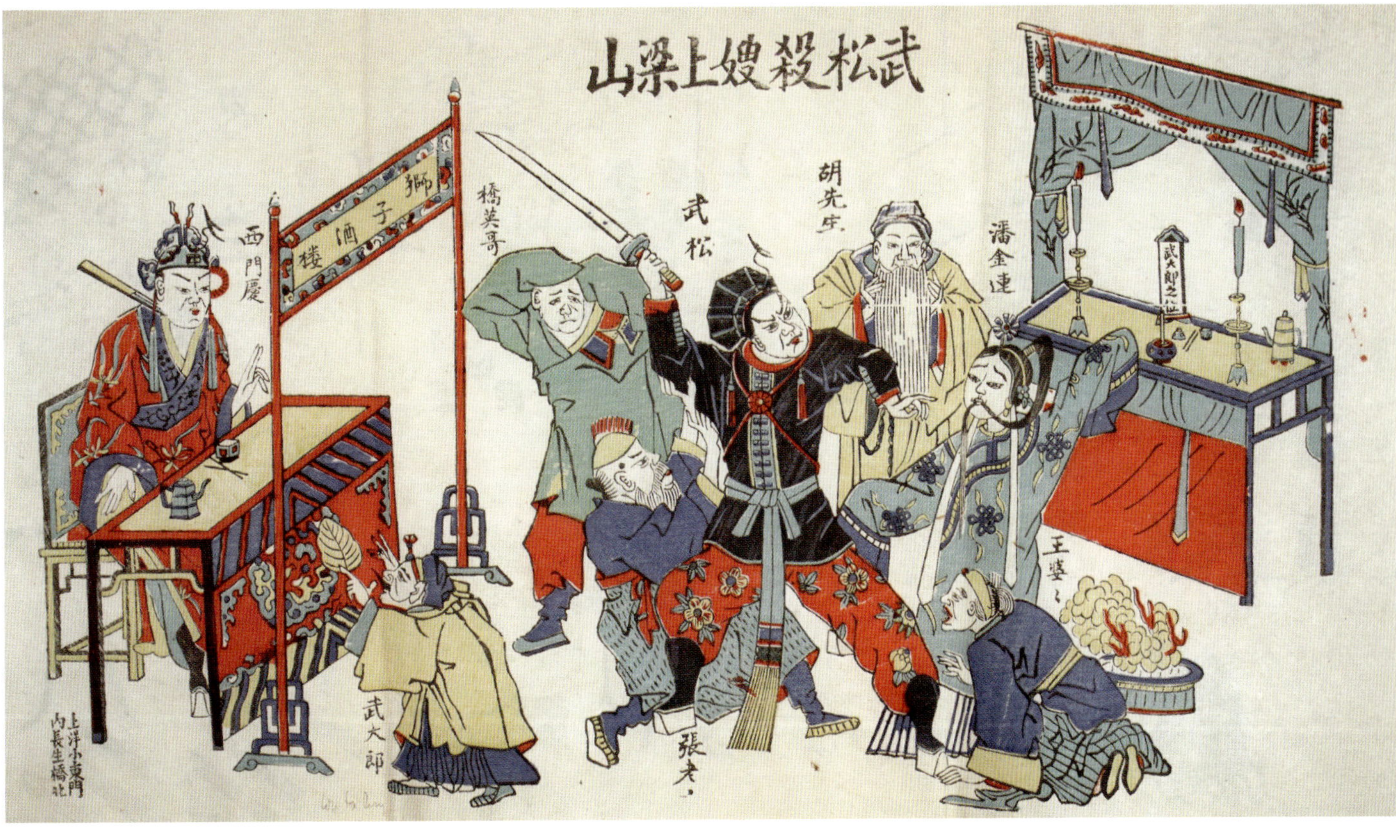
武松殺嫂上梁山
獅子酒樓
西門慶
橋芙哥
武松
胡先生
潘金蓮
武大郎之位
王婆
武大郎
張老
上洋小東門內長生橋北

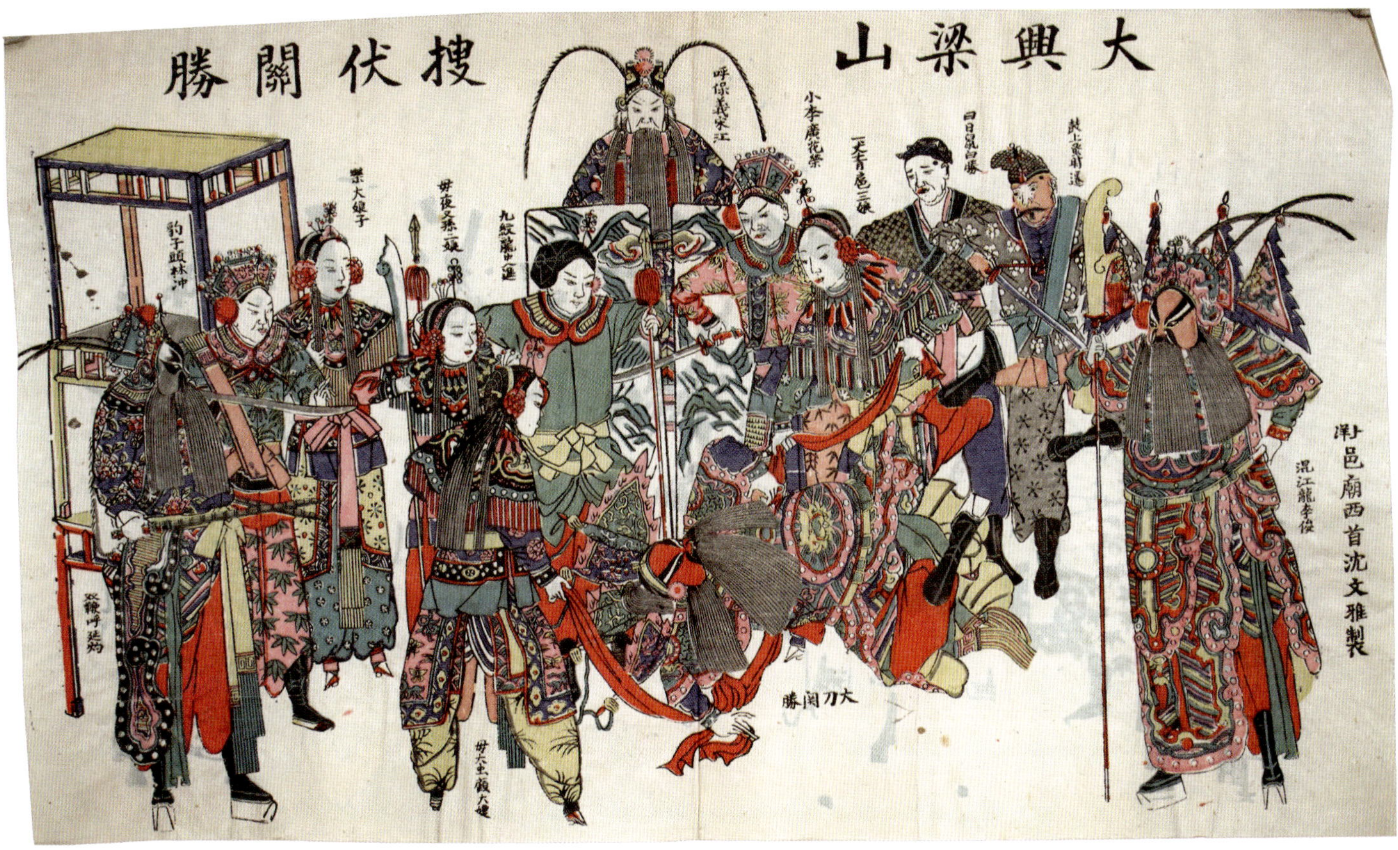
大興梁山
搜伏關勝
呼保義宋江
小李廣花榮
一丈青扈三娘
白日鼠白勝
鼓上蚤時遷
母夜叉孫二娘
九紋龍史進
豹子頭林沖
雙鞭呼延灼
大刀關勝
母大虫顧大嫂
混江龍李俊
上洋邑廟西首沈文雅製

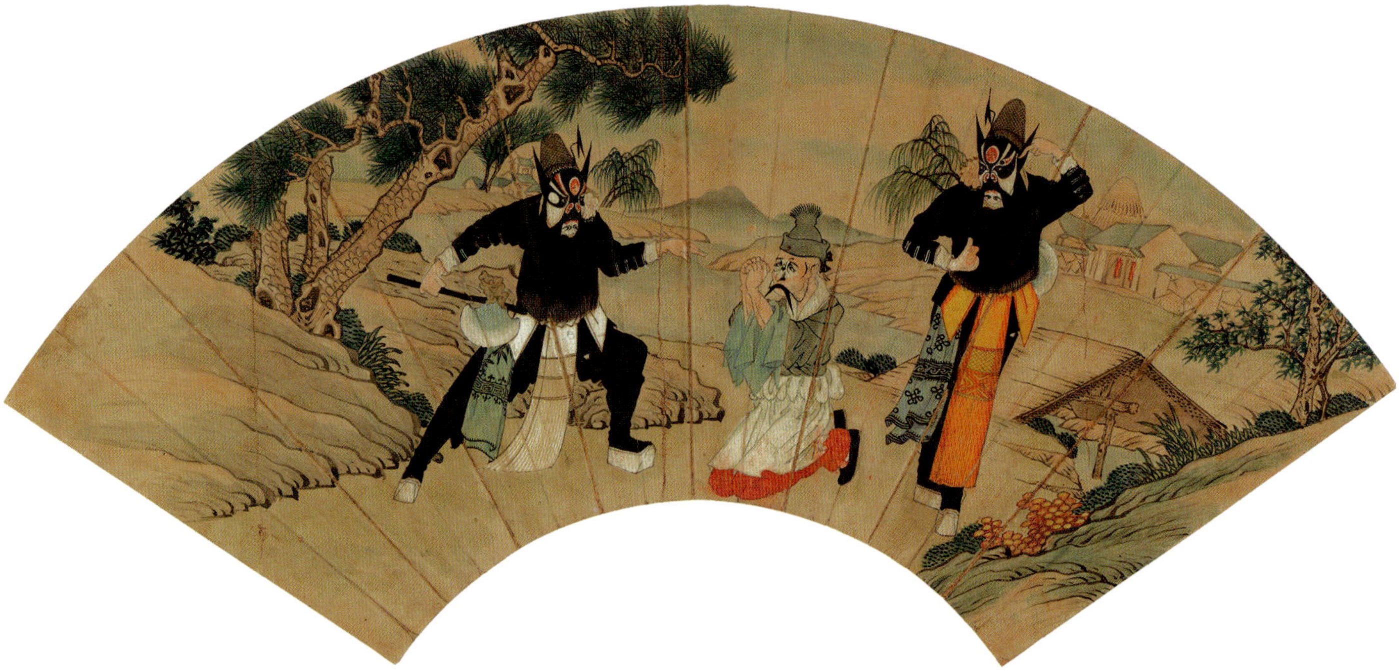

Cat. 52
Chinese, Qing Dynasty (1644–1911)
Fan Painting with Peking Opera Scene from Two Li Kuis (Shuang Li Kui), 19th century
Folding fan mounted as album leaf, ink and colors on gold paper, 6 7/8 x 19 15/16 in. (17.5 x 50.6 cm)
Museum of Fine Arts, Boston, John Ware Willard Fund
1983.125

This painting depicts a scene from the Peking opera *Two Li Kuis* (*Shuang Li Kui*), also called *A True and False Li Kui* (*Zhenjia Li Kui*). In the play, which is based on the story from chapter 43 of the sixteenth-century novel *The Water Margin* (*Shuihu zhuan*), Li Kui, an outlaw based in the bandit headquarters on Mount Liang, is on his way home to visit his mother when he is waylaid by a highwayman impersonating him. Subdued by Li, the impersonator claims that his name is really Li Gui, and that he robs passers-by in the name of Li Kui only to scare them away and use the loot to support his aging mother. Sympathizing with this motive of filial piety, Li Kui realizes that he himself is not much different from Li Gui the impersonator, so he forgives and releases the imposter. Different versions of the opera have different endings after the release. In one, Li Gui is moved by Li Kui's generosity and decides to follow him to Mount Liang and become an outlaw. In another version with a different title, *Li Kui Visits His Mother* (*Li Kui tanmu*), Li Kui happens to stop by Li Gui's home only to discover that there is no mother, but rather a scheming wife who is plotting to poison Li Kui and take his possessions. Li Kui therefore kills the two of them. This version is closer to the original story in the novel.

The impersonator is the figure standing on the left because his gesture shows he is clearly demanding money from the figure (a clown role) on his knees begging for his life in the middle. The impersonator is wielding an ax (Li Kui's trademark weapon) and wears an almost identical black costume and makeup as Li Kui on the right, even though in many versions he is portrayed as a lying, ungrateful brute. This play is a classical vehicle for two martial painted-face stars to perform together at the same time on stage, often a celebrated and sought after event. The fascinating device of having an actor confront his impersonator can be found in other famous operas in which heroes such as Monkey and Judge Bao have to face their double and prove their own authenticity—if not via a fight to vindicate themselves through superior strength (in Li Kui's case), then through divine intervention when all else fails. While the story might speak to the perennial anxiety toward the concept of identity and authenticity and the discernment of truth and the simulacrum of truth, these plays are also perfect spectacles and occasions for the actors of the same role to convene on the same stage, offering the audience the opportunity to "judge" who is the authentic star and hero.

In this painting the scene is set in a naturalistic setting, which is common among New Year prints that depict operatic scenes before the late Qing period. From the Guangxu era (1875–1908) on, Peking opera prints tended to abandon the natural landscape as a backdrop and opt for the theater and its stage as the background instead.[1] However, it is not clear if such a shift was also the case with fan paintings. To complicate the issue, photography studios (and subsequent film studios) in Shanghai in the late nineteenth and early twentieth centuries hired professional painters to paint landscape backdrops in the traditional style, some of which were actually used as stage backdrops in some reform-minded opera performances. —MIA YINXING LIU

1 Wang Shucun, "Guanyu jingju banhua" [On Woodblock Pictures of Peking Opera], in Wang Shucun and Jin Rujie, eds., *Zhongguo gedi nianhua yanjiu* [Research on New Year Prints from Different Regions] (Hong Kong: Shenzhou tushu gongsi, 1976), p. 48.

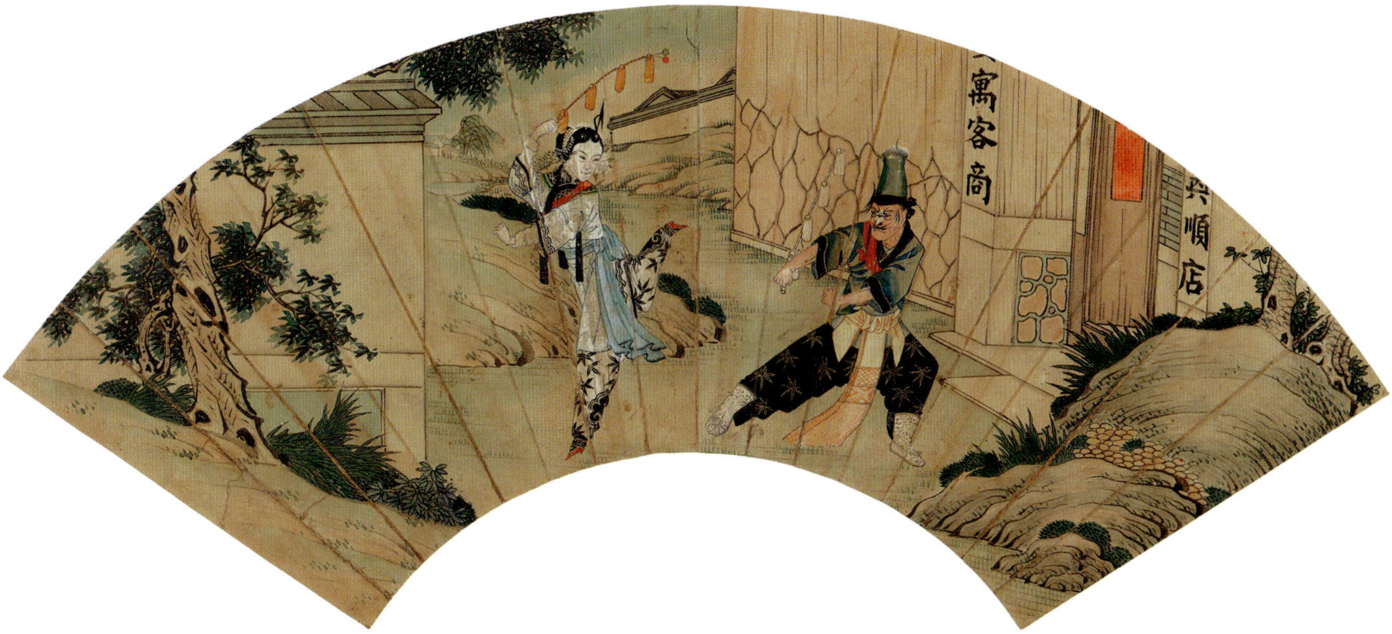

Cat. 53
Chinese, Qing Dynasty (1644–1911)
Fan Painting with Peking Opera Scene from Stopping the Horse *(*Dangma, *also known as* Detaining the Horse and Crossing the Border [Lanma guoguan]*)*, 19th century
Folding fan mounted as album leaf, ink and colors on gold paper, $6\frac{1}{8}$ x $19\frac{11}{16}$ in. (15.6 x 50 cm)
Museum of Fine Arts, Boston, John Ware Willard Fund
1983. 123

This painting depicts the Peking opera *Stopping the Horse* (*Dangma*), also known as *Detaining the Horse and Crossing the Border* (*Lanma guoguan*).[1] It is one of numerous operas about the Yang family of generals (Yangjia jiang), who won fame for their martial process and their patriotic dedication to the fight against the Liao invaders during the Song dynasty (960–1279). Their legendary exploits, especially those of the family's lowly servants and female members, became favorite subjects for storytelling, popular literature, and the stage. In this play, Octavia (Yang Bajie, Daughter Number Eight of the Yang Family) cross-dresses as a man and enters Liao territory to spy on their deployment of troops. Once there she is stopped by an innkeeper, who happens to be Jiao Guangpu, a faithful affiliate of General Yang, who has gone missing during an earlier military campaign against the Liao and become stranded there. Upon seeing her passport (a permit to re-enter the Song Kingdom), Jiao attempts to steal it. He detains her horse, and tries to get her drunk. Octavia fights with him, thinking he is a Liao spy. Eventually, Jiao tells the truth, and she takes him back to Song as her attendant.

The play abounds with entangled and mistaken identities, both in terms of gender and national allegiance. Octavia is not only dressed as a man but also as a Liao soldier, while Jiao has to conceal his own identity as a faithful subject of the Song. The opera is noted for its fantastic fighting scene during which Jiao carefully and stealthily hovers around Octavia and observes her throat, ear piercings, and other signs of her gender, as he starts to suspect that his foe is actually a woman. Meanwhile, Jie is attempting to snatch the passport that Octavia wears on her belt. This endeavor provides a platform for spectacular choreography and acrobatics between Octavia, a *wudan* (martial female lead), and Jiao, a *wuchou (*a martial clown), most of which happens in the interior space of an inn, with various props such as chairs and table. The confinement of space and the use of everyday domestic objects make the choreography even more demanding and riveting.

In the painting, Octavia and Jiao are each holding a horsewhip, a standard Peking opera prop that symbolizes that the performers are on horseback, probably indicating the last scene of the play when they have already cleared up their misunderstanding and are setting off to cross the border and return together to Song territory. However, Yang is not dressed as a man or as a female warrior in full armor and thick-soled boots, but rather as an ordinary woman in plain clothes. Note the tiny bound feet that are accentuated by both her "mounting the horse" pose and the bright red color of her shoes. She is also wearing minimal makeup, while Jiao is wearing white clown makeup around his nose and mustache. The background is Jiao's inn in Liao, where he makes a living selling wine and offering lodging to travelers, as affirmed by the partially shown couplets inscribed on either side of the gate. —MIA YINXING LIU

1 For a plot summary and extant versions of the play, see Wang Senran, *Zhongguo jumu cidian* [Dictionary of Chinese Opera Titles] (Shijiazhuang: Hebei jiaoyu chubanshe, 1997), p. 1,048. *Zhui baiqiu* [A Patched Cloak of White Fur], the voluminous late eighteenth-century collection of opera excerpts includes one titled *Stopping the Horse* (*Dangma*), which is classified under *luantan qiang* (chaotic playing tune), one of the precursors of Peking opera; see Zhui Baiqiu, ed. Wang Xieru (Shanghai: Zhonghua shuju, 1955), collection no. 11, chapter 3, pp. 176–82. This eighteenth-century version shows significant plot differences from known Peking opera versions but is still recognizably the same play.

Cat. 54

Chinese, Qing Dynasty (1644–1911)
Playing Cards with Figures from Peking Opera Plays, n.d.
46 cards, ink and color printed on paper,
each: 3 3/8 x 15/16 in. (8.6 x 2.4 cm)
Brooklyn Museum, New York, Estate of Stewart Culin, Museum Purchase
30.417

These forty-six playing cards, acquired by the ethnographer Stewart Culin (1858–1929), display images of dramatic characters from popular plays in the Peking opera repertory. Made of paper and decorated with printed, polychromatic images, each card shows a combination of dots and the title of the opera associated with the figure depicted. The illustrations of the characters allude both to their individual traits and to their role-types on stage. For instance, the card with a combination of five black dots and three black dots depicts Xiahou Yuan: a Three Kingdoms general whose death was dramatized in the opera *Dingjun Mountain* (*Dingjun shan*). The role of Xiahou Yuan was famous for its white and black patterned face mask and for the character's tragic death onstage. Both attributes are registered on the playing card: the character's face bears black and white streaked markings, and his sorrowful expression and downward pointing spear evoke his looming fate.

The story lines of the operas and the roles of the characters are not only suggested by the designs on individual playing cards, but also are brought out by the pairing of cards from the same play. The plot of *The Nine Dragon Cup* (*Jiulong bei*), adapted from *The Cases of Judge Peng* (*Peng gong'an*), follows Huang Santai's efforts to catch the thief of the Kangxi Emperor's precious cup. Within this set of cards there are two figures from the play: one (marked with six black dots and a single red dot) depicts the thief Yang Xiangwu with a worried expression, clutching a prop that symbolizes the stolen cup in his raised arm, looking back over his shoulder as he tries to run off. The other card (with three black dots and a single red dot) illustrates Huang hunting him down with his outstretched arm and striding legs mirroring Yang in flight. When the cards are placed alongside each other, the expressive gestures of the two characters work together to dramatize the chase that spurs the central action of the play.

Cards such as these were called "plaques" (*pai*), a term that was used interchangeably for both playing cards and dominoes. There were few distinctions between the principles of paper card games and games involving ivory or bone dominoes in China. As with Chinese dominoes, the twenty-one cards in a basic set were divided into eleven "civil" (*wen*) cards and ten "military" (*wu*) cards to allow for combinations with added symbolic significance. This set of cards would most likely have been used in a gambling game called Nine Plaques (*paijiu*) or alternatively, Bone Plaques (*gupai*). For this particular card game, the eleven civil cards of the basic twenty-one card set were doubled to bring the deck to a total of thirty-two cards (not including the additional jokers in the pack).

With this set of cards, the combinations of dots draw out the distinctive traits of the dramatic characters and the story lines of the plays. An example can be observed on the two cards with figures from *Silang Visits His Mother* (*Silang tanmu*). In this opera, Yang Yanhui (Silang, the fourth son of the famous Northern Song military family the Yangs) is stranded in Liao territory, assumes a new identity, and marries the Princess Tiejing. Later on when the Northern Song armies reach Liao territory, the princess learns of Yang's secret identity and helps him return to visit his mother. Yang's mother is so grateful that she allows him to go back to the princess as he promised rather than fight in the Song army. The two cards with Yang and the princess both portray figures facing toward each other and contain multiples of five, thus underscoring the distinctive status of these two characters as a pair. The card displaying the princess contains two sets of five black dots: a pair of fives was conventionally glossed as a plum blossom (*meihua*), which can also mean a beautiful woman. The combined total of dots for the two cards adds up to fifteen, which is significant because within the play Yang is in Liao territory and with the princess for fifteen years. Many of the cards incorporate similar references to characters and operas based on the combinations of dots. —THOMAS KELLY

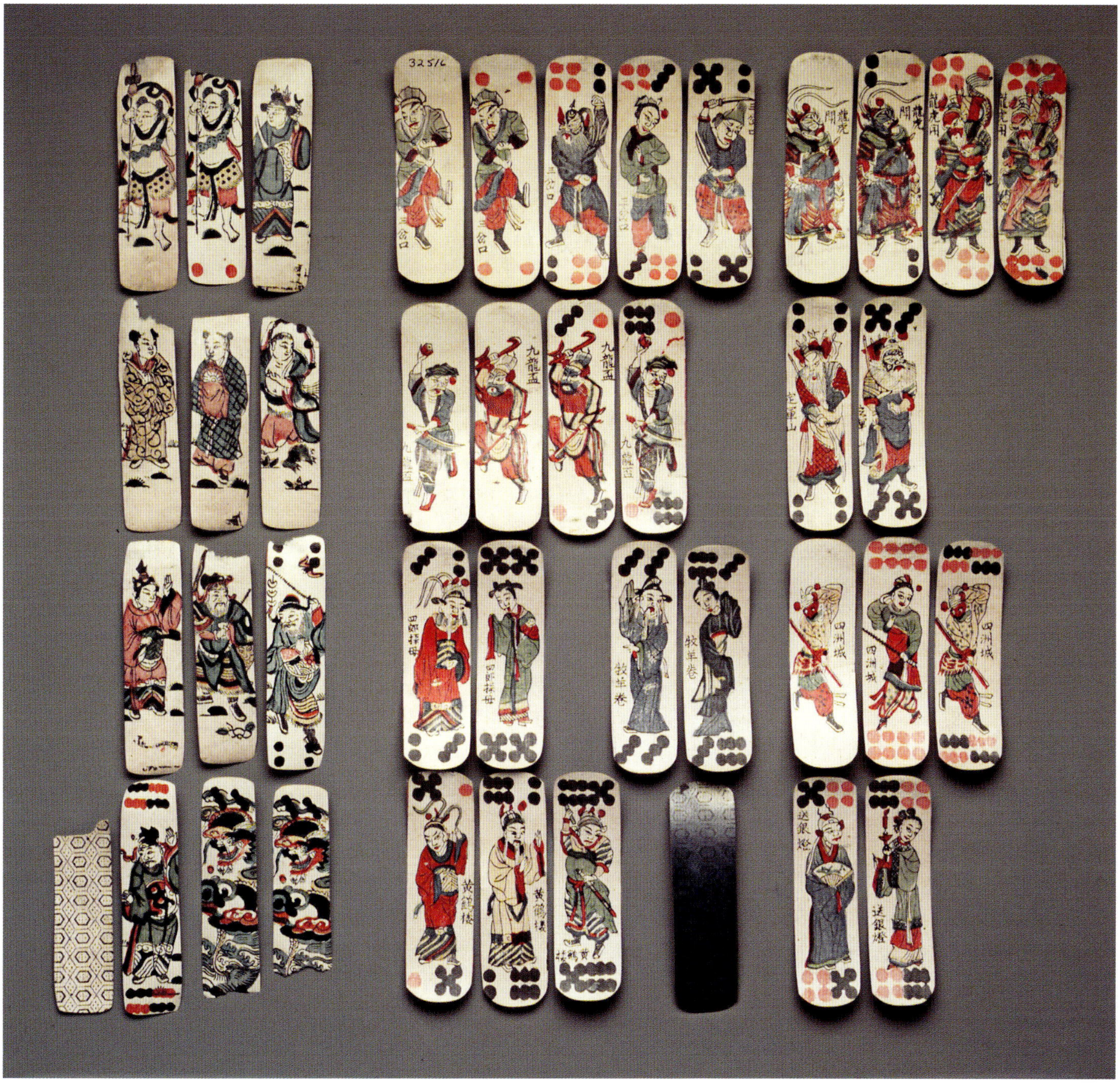
32516

Map of China

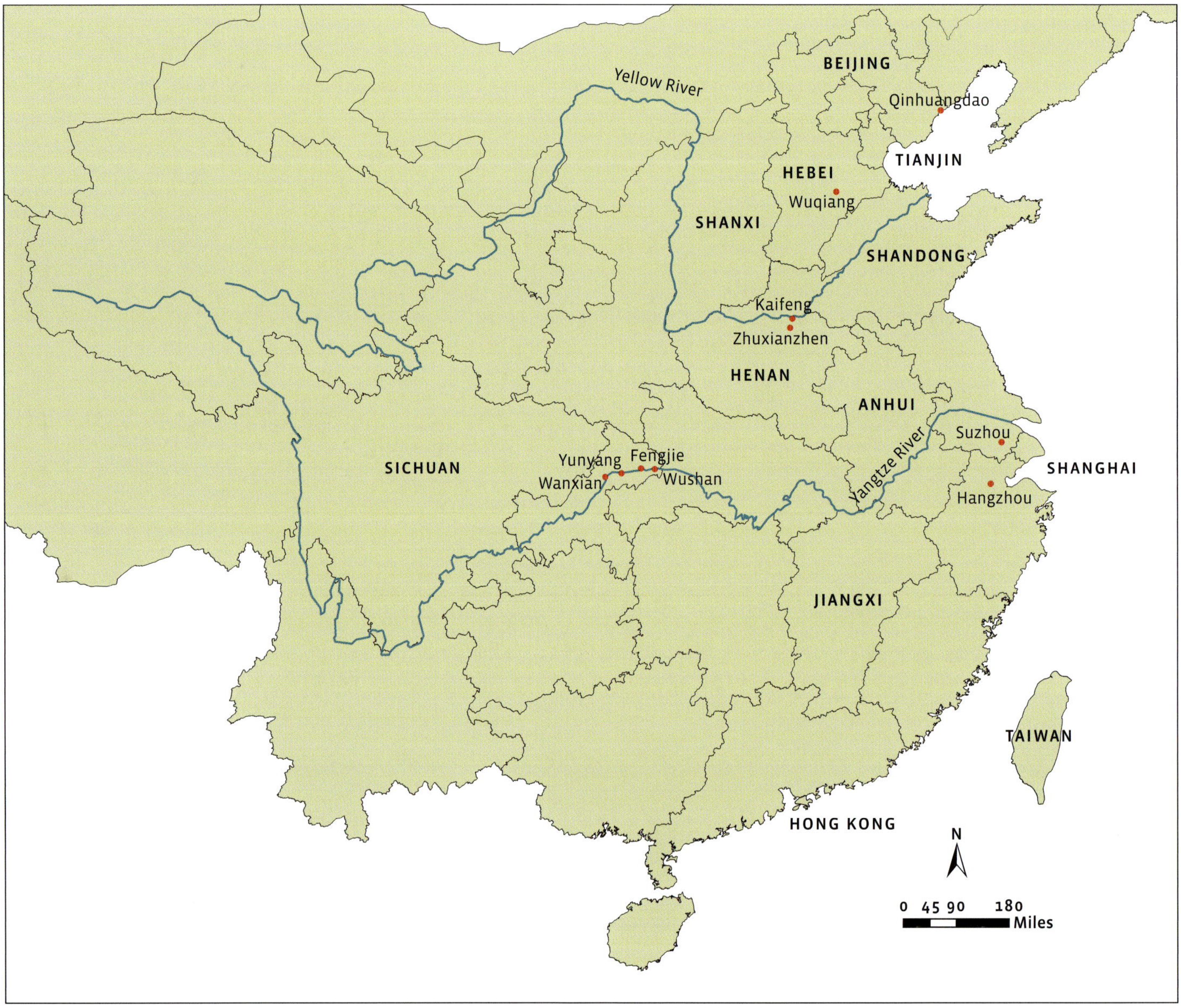

Yellow River
BEIJING
Qinhuangdao
TIANJIN
HEBEI
Wuqiang
SHANXI
SHANDONG
Kaifeng
Zhuxianzhen
HENAN
ANHUI
Suzhou
SICHUAN
Yunyang
Fengjie
Wanxian
Wushan
Yangtze River
SHANGHAI
Hangzhou
JIANGXI
TAIWAN
HONG KONG
N
0 45 90 180
Miles

Chronology

DYNASTY / DATES	EMPEROR OR REIGN	IMPORTANT EVENTS
NORTHERN SONG / 960–1127		Earliest material evidence of Chinese opera dates from the Northern Song dynasty. Relief carvings of actors on stone sarcophagi and bricks from tombs in Henan province demonstrate the popularity of theatrical imagery in the social world of eleventh-century China.
SOUTHERN SONG / 1127–1297		**1187** First publication of the short text *Dreaming of Splendors Past: The Eastern Capital* (*Dongjing menghua lu*) describes life in the capital city of Kaifeng from 1000 to 1025. This text provides vivid descriptions of public stages in the entertainment quarters (the so-called tile markets [washe]) in the center of the city. There is also a passage called "Skills and Arts of the Tile Markets," which offers a list of the most famous entertainers from 1117 to 1125 including singers, puppeteers, dancers, storytellers, and characters in shadow plays.
JIN / 1115–1234		The Jin dynasty is founded by Jurchens in present-day Manchuria in 1115. In 1127, the Jin invade and ransack Kaifeng, the capital of the Northern Song. Jin forces capture Emperor Qinzong and his father Huizong and continue to fight Song forces until 1141 when land north of the Huai River is ceded to the Jin dynasty in exchange for peace with the Southern Song dynasty. **Mid–1100s** Earliest date of an extant text in the genre of "All Keys and Modes" (*zhugongdiao*), a form of *chantefable* that becomes an important precursor to later dramas. The genre takes its name from the alternation of verse sections written to different tunes from preceding verse sections. The only complete text extant is Dong Jieyuan's *All Keys and Modes on Romance of the Western Chamber* (*Xixiang ji zhugongdiao*), an important source text for the later play of the same title. **1181** The date of Duan Family Tomb number 6, the oldest of a series of underground tombs in Shanxi province to include representations of stages and actors. **Late 1210s** Date of a suite titled "Country Bumpkin Knows Nothing About the Stage" (Zhuangjia bushi goulan) by the little-known poet Du Shanfu (circa 1197–1270). The suite, which parodies the experience of a peasant who comes to the city for the first time, vividly depicts the raucous urban theaters of the late twelfth century, the world from which Yuan drama emerges.
YUAN / 1271–1368		The Mongols complete their conquest of China in 1279 and make Dadu (present day Beijing) their capital. **1324** Date of a famous wall painting in the Guangsheng temple complex in Shanxi province. This mural depicts the actress Zhongduxiu alongside a troupe of eleven actors and stagehands. The mural provides early evidence for the organization of acting troupes led by a single "star" performer. **1330** A text titled *Register Recording Ghosts* (*Luguibu*) provides the details of 152 authors and the titles of over 400 dramas written by Zhong Sicheng. **Mid–1300s** Gao Ming (circa 1305–circa 1370) writes *The Lute* (*Pipa ji*). The play is later regarded as the first Southern drama or "romance" (*chuanqi*), incorporating lyrical poetry and passages of ornate prose. **1280s–1360s** Publication of *The Thirty Yuan Plays (Yuankan sanshi zhong)*—the earliest printed dramatic text.
MING / 1368–1644	HONGWU	**1368–1398** The Ming dynasty is founded by the peasant leader Zhu Yuanzhang in 1368, who subsequently takes Hongwu as his reign title. The early Ming emperors and hereditary princes are enthusiastic patrons of the theater. Under the Hongwu emperor, imperially sponsored public theaters (*yu goulan*) appear in the capital Nanjing. Several leading playwrights of the period were imperial princes. Zhu Quan (1378–1448), the seventeenth son of Hongwu, authored twelve "variety plays" (*zaju*) and the earliest extant drama

DYNASTY / DATES	EMPEROR OR REIGN	IMPORTANT EVENTS
MING / 1368–1644 (cont.)		song formulary *A Formulary of Correct Sounds of an Era of Peace (Taihe zhengyin pu)*. Zhu Yuanzhang's grandson Zhu Youdun (1379–1439), the Prince of Zhou, authors thirty-one zaju, many of which are innovative works of dramatic art.
	JIANWEN	**1399–1401**
	YONGLE	**1402–1423** Zhu Yuangzhang's son Zhu Di usurps power from the designated heir, Hongwu's grandson (the Jianwen emperor), and establishes the Yongle reign in 1402, moving the capital from Nanjing to Beijing. Zhu Di (the Yongle emperor) becomes a devoted patron of authors of the "variety play" (*zaju*).
	HONGXI	**1424–1425**
	XUANDE	**1426–1435**
	ZHENGTONG	**1436–1449**
	JINGTAI	**1450–1456**
	TIANSHUN	**1457–1464**
	CHENGHUA	**1465–1487**
	HONGZHI	**1488–1497** **1498** Earliest extant edition of the northern *zaju Romance of the Western Chamber* (*Xixiang ji*), published in Beijing. Authored by Wang Shifu (circa 1250–1300), the play would go on to become the most popular romantic comedy in Chinese drama and would be subjected to numerous later adaptations.
	ZHENGDE	**1506–1521**
	JIAJING	**1522–1546** **1547** Wei Liangfu, a herbal doctor and singing master from Kunshan, writes the manuscript "The Rules of Singing *Qu* According to Wei Liangfu" (Wei Liangfu qulü). This text, which appears in print by 1616, tries to explain the intricate singing techniques of local Kun music (*kunqu*). Kun opera would eventually be adopted by literati playwrights and spread throughout China, becoming one of the dominant musical styles in traditional opera.
	LONGQING	**1567–1572**
	WANLI	**1573–1619** **1598–1599** Completion of Tang Xianzu's (1550–1616) literary masterpiece *The Peony Pavilion* (*Mudan ting*), which becomes a staple of the Kun opera repertory and salon performance. **1618** Zang Maoxun (1550–1620), an aficionado of northern drama, publishes his own truncated revision of *The Peony Pavilion,* naming it *The Soul's Return* (*Huanhun ji*).
	TAICHANG	**1620**
	TIANQI	**1621–1627**
	CHONGZHEN	**1628–1644** **1640** Min Qiji publishes a polychrome woodblock print album consisting of full-page images accompanied by an illustrated frontispiece based on scenes from *Romance of the Western Chamber.* **1644** The last Ming emperor, Chongzhen, commits suicide on April 25 on Jingshan Hill behind the Forbidden City after Beijing is sacked by rebels. This marks the official end of the Ming dynasty. The Shunzhi emperor is installed on October 30, thus initiating the Qing dynasty. Ming loyalists continue to fight Manchu rule throughout Southern China until 1662.
QING / 1644–1911	SHUNZHI	**1644–1661** **1656** Jin Shengtan (1610–1661) publishes his own edition of *Romance of the Western Chamber* with substantial textual revisions. Jin's edition eclipses earlier texts and will be the most popular version of the play throughout the Qing dynasty.
	KANGXI	**1662–1722** Urban playhouses begin to appear in early Qing dynasty Beijing. One of the earliest recorded institutions is the Zhalou, originally a private estate belonging to a wealthy salt merchant in the late Ming. As with other public theaters, the Zhalou begins as a private space hired out for parties and progressively transitions into a commercial venue. The Zhalou site will be renovated and renamed throughout the Qing dynasty and eventually will host performances by Mei Lanfang in the twentieth century. By the nineteenth century, a range of public establishments in Beijing feature operatic performances, among them banquet halls (*xizhuang*), restaurants (*jiuzhuang*), drama gardens (*xiyuan*), and taverns (*jiuguan*). **1713** The Kangxi emperor's sixtieth birthday celebrations. A long handscroll containing images of theatrical performances was commissioned for the festivities. This scroll served as a model for a series of 120 woodcuts included in a commemorative book of tributes published by the palace printing office.

DYNASTY / DATES	EMPEROR OR REIGN	IMPORTANT EVENTS
	YONGZHENG	**1723–1735**
		1735 A Jesuit missionary in Beijing, Joseph de Prémare, produces a French translation of passages from Ji Junxiang's northern "variety play" (*zaju*) *The Orphan of Zhao* (*Zhaoshi gu'er*). Also in 1735 Jean Baptiste du Halde publishes the text in France, making it the first Chinese play to be translated into a European language and serving as a basis for later adaptations like Voltaire's 1755 *Orphan of China* (*Orphelin de la Chine).*
	QIANLONG	**1736–1795**
		1738 Huang Tubi (1700–1771) writes *Thunder Peak Pagoda* (*Leifeng ta*) on the popular story of the White Snake. The play assumes a life of its own after being taken up and continuously revised by successive commercial troupes. While Huang's play would eventually lose popularity, the story of the White Snake becomes one of the main attractions on the late imperial Chinese stage and is subjected to numerous rewritings for different regional theaters.
		1730s–1740s The official Zhang Zhao (1691–1745) writes a series of highly moralistic lengthy dramas for performance at court. His ten-volume copy of the play *Golden Norms for Exhorting Virtue* (*Quanshan jinke*) is frequently staged during court festivities, with scores of actors and performers. An adaptation of the Buddhist Mulian story, this monumental court drama is one of the most widely performed and popular ritual plays in the Ming and Qing dynasties across rural China. Twentieth-century writers like Lu Xun comment on their childhood memories of watching local performances of Mulian plays.
		1751 The sixtieth birthday celebration of Qianlong's mother, the Empress Dowager Chongqing. A long handscroll containing images of theatrical performances is commissioned for the festivities (1755–57). However the performances are more modest when compared to the celebrations for the Kangxi emperor in 1713.
		1763–1774 Publication of Qian Decang's *A Patched Cloak of White Fur* (*Zhui baiqiu*), an expansive collection of scenes drawn from popular *kunqu* dramas and other regional operas. Throughout the eighteenth century, performances are gradually based around a selection of scenes rather than on entire plays.
		1770 The Qianlong emperor orders the construction of the Ningshougong (Palace of Tranquil Longevity) as his private apartments in the northeastern part of the Forbidden City. The designs include a three-tiered stage called the Changyin ge (Pavilion of Pleasant Sounds), which has been renovated many times and remains intact today.
		1779–late 1780s Wei Changsheng (1744–1802), the leading performer of clapper opera (*bangzi*), moves to Beijing, representing the height of popularity for this regional operatic style originally from Shaanxi province.
		1790 Following the Qianlong emperor's travels in Southern China, drama troupes from Anhui province are invited to Beijing for his eightieth birthday celebrations. This is an important moment in the development of what would eventually become Peking opera. A long handscroll painting representing the celebratory festivals for the emperor's birthday was commissioned. The painting shows theater performances that took place on temporary stages along the route from the Forbidden City to the imperial palaces outside Beijing. This painting too is turned into woodcuts and included in a commemorative book of tributes published by the palace printing office.
		1791 The printing of *The Complete Story of Filial and Righteous True Traces of The Pearl Pagoda* (*Xiaoyi zhenji zhenzhuta quanzhuan*, also known as the *The Pearl Pagoda [Zhenzhuta]*), with a preface by Zhou Shushi, one of the earliest Pearl Pagoda texts. Zhou is one of the eighteenth century's best-known storytellers of *The Pearl Pagoda*, and this printed text is putatively based on his performances.
		1792–1794 British envoy George Macartney (1737–1806) leads the Macartney Embassy to China. Macartney writes of his experiences watching a lavish court theatrical performance at Rehe in 1793. He re-creates the sense of spectacle by describing the production's use of ostriches and a whale.
	JIAQING	**1796–1820**
		1800 The rise of commercial theaters or teahouses (*chayuan*) in Beijing. By 1800 there were twenty-one permanent commercial theaters in the city, playing host to performances in the *pihuang* musical style that would develop into Peking opera.
	DAOGUANG	**1821–1850**
		1839–1842 The First Opium War
		1850–1864 The Taiping Rebellion leads to widespread destruction and displacement in Southern China. Many performers and businesses from the Suzhou region, including the Taohuawu printmakers, relocate to Shanghai. The Xiaojiaochang quarter of Shanghai becomes the center of New Year print (*nianhua*) workshops.
	XIANFENG	**1851–1861**

DYNASTY / DATES	EMPEROR OR REIGN	IMPORTANT EVENTS
QING / 1644–1911 (cont.)		**1860** In October 1860, English and French armies invade Beijing during the Second Opium War. The Xianfeng emperor retreats to the hunting resort and summer residence of Rehe where he indulges his passion for opera until his death in August 1861.
		British and French troops loot and burn down the Yuanmingyuan (The Garden of Perfect Brightness). Among many of the other artistic and architectural features that were destroyed was a three-tiered stage that had originally belonged to Qianlong's mother in the Cishougong (the private apartments of the dowager empress within the Forbidden City) and had been moved to Yuanmingyuan.
	TONGZHI	**1862–1874**
	GUANGXU	**1875–1909**
		1884 The Empress Dowager Cixi (1835–1908), in order to celebrate her fiftieth birthday, invites actors of Peking opera from around Beijing to perform in the imperial palaces. These performances mark the beginning of a period of enthusiastic court patronage for Peking opera.
		1891–1895
		In preparation for the celebration of the Empress Dowager Cixi's sixtieth birthday celebration, the three-story stage Garden of Virtue and Harmony (Dehe yuan) is erected in the imperial Summer Palace.
		1905 Tan Xinpei (1847–1917), a native of Wuchang, Hubei, who became a star in Peking opera for his ability to combine diverse skills, collaborates with the photographer Ren Qingtai (1850–1932) to record his performances in film. This makes Tan the first actor in a Chinese motion picture.
	XUANTONG	**1909–1911**
POST-DYNASTIC PERIOD		**1911** The 1911 Revolution marks the end of the Qing dynasty and the founding of the Republic of China.
		1927 A silent film adaptation of *Romance of the Western Chamber* directed by Hou Yao is released.
		1930–1935
		Mei Lanfang (1894–1961) tours North America and visits Hollywood and then travels to Europe to enthusiastic reception in Berlin and Moscow. To help American audience understand Mei Lanfang and Peking opera performances, and on behalf of the National Drama Study Association (guoju xuehui), Qi Rushan (1875–1962) invites painters to illustrate a wide range of objects used in Peking Opera performances. This activity results in 1,987 paintings representing costumes, facial painting, musical instruments, choreography of Mei's dance movements and gestures in different operas, props, and weapons, which are mounted as 183 hanging scrolls. The upper part of each painting includes a caption in both Chinese and English.
		1949 The People's Republic of China is established.

Glossary of Terms

bangzi see **clapper opera *(bangzi)***

chantefable A story told through alternations of verse and prose. Closely linked to drama in China, a *chantefable* can be performed or read.

chuanqi Romantic comedy with numerous acts, originating in the southern style of drama during the Ming dynasty (1368–1644). Often highly literary and intended as much for reading as for performance.

clapper opera *(bangzi)* A northern form of local opera in which a sounding block struck with a stick dominates the musical accompaniment.

court theater During the Qing dynasty (1644–1911), court theater ranged from large-scale, long dramas featuring spectacular pageantry and didactic themes to small-scale, private performances of selected episodes showcasing singing and acting skills. Individual preferences of monarchs helped to shape the development of operatic genres during the Qing period (1644–1911), in particular facilitating the development and popularization of Peking opera.

daxi see **grand plays *(daxi)***

***Dream of the Red Chamber* (*Honglou meng*)** This vernacular novel written in the mid-Qing period (1644–1911) by Cao Xueqin focuses on the tragic, triangular relationships among a wealthy young man, Jia Baoyu, and his beautiful but dramatically different cousins: Xue Baochai and Lin Daiyu. Set against a backdrop of the Jia family's rise and fall, the teenagers live together in a grand garden, built as a celebration of the family's rising social influence, that by the end of the novel is abandoned and falls into disrepair. Considered the pinnacle of Chinese narrative, the novel continually calls into question the nature of reality, truth, and illusion, and includes deeply psychological representations of dozens of characters.

grand plays *(daxi)*, also called ***liantai benxi*** ("serially performed palace plays") Lengthy dramas with historical or mythical subject matter that made up the core of the performance repertoire at the imperial court. Compiled in the mid-Qing dynasty (1644–1911) by court academicians working from popular materials, each of these dramas required several days and hundreds, even a thousand or more actors to be performed in its entirety. All these court dramas contained scenes of mass pageantry featuring lavish costumes, spectacular props, and sometimes, fanciful mechanical devices.

Guanyin (the Bodhisattva Avalokitêśvara) The embodiment of compassion for suffering experienced by sentient beings and the most popular Buddhist deity in the Chinese pantheon. Though early iconography represents Guanyin as male, in China Guanyin is commonly represented as a woman, explained by the bodhisattva's ability to manifest in thirty-three different human forms as the situation requires.

huabu (variegated styles) A term used from the later eighteenth century to distinguish the profusion of popular new types of opera from the refined style of Kun opera.

jingju see **Peking opera *(jingju)***

***Journey to the West* (*Xiyou ji*)** A late Ming dynasty (1368–1644) vernacular novel drawn from the popular stories concerning the legendary adventures of the historical Buddhist monk Tripitika (Xuanzang), on his sixth-century journey from China to India to secure Buddhist scriptures. Defended by the ever-popular character Monkey, along with other supernatural companions, the humorous and lively novel was adapted for the Qing court as a morality play with copious quotations from Buddhist scriptures.

Judge Bao A popular character in drama and fiction based on a historical judge from the Song dynasty who garnered a legendary reputation for incorruptibility and dedication to impartial justice.

kesi Slit silk tapestry, often woven with a pictorial design.

Kun opera (*kunqu* or *kunshan qiang*) A refined style of opera based on music that originated in the Kunshan area near Suzhou, with the flute as its signature instrument. During the late Ming dynasty (1368–1644), Kun opera became the favorite form of dramatic entertainment for the elite and was later adopted by the Qing imperial court.

liangxiang The practice of one actor or a group of actors striking and holding studied poses.

liantai benxi see **grand plays *(daxi)***

literati sometimes also "scholar-officials," narrowly refers to men educated to compete in the civil service exams, the main avenue to power and prestige in late imperial China. More broadly the term describes any educated individual.

lithography A printing technology invented in Europe in 1798–99. In contrast to relief-based techniques, lithography uses a flat surface medium manipulated on the principle that water and grease repel each other. By the late nineteenth century, it had become one of the most important and popular printing methods in China. (It was favored for the relatively low initial investment, the aesthetic appeal of the texts printed with it, and the limited changes in publishing outlook from woodblock printing.) Lithography facilitated the rise of a new mass periodical press and led to a surge in cheap illustrated magazines, books, and prints. Photolithography, a related printing technology, involving the projection of photographic negatives of book pages onto a stone, had become one of the main processes in Western-style printing in Shanghai by 1882.

luantan Translated as "chaotic playing," this precursor of Peking opera was originally regarded as vulgar by the Qing court, but operas in this style were nonetheless present in the capital during the eighteenth century and performed at court during the nineteenth century.

Ming literati theater During the late Ming dynasty (1368–1644), literati values extended to the entirety of a theatrical experience. Late Ming and later literati wrote plays and commissioned, directed, or personally engaged in performances of *chuanqi* in the *kunqu* musical style. Plays were typically performed in private settings at banquets, often with household troupes of actors.

Mulian Rescues His Mother A story cycle featuring the Buddhist monk Mulian's journey through the gruesome courts of hell to rescue his mother from its deepest depths. The tale heavily influenced Chinese Buddhist culture, serving as the basis for the offerings to hungry ghosts during the seventh lunar month. On the stage, plays about Mulian were both entertainment and religious ritual and ran for days, performed as popular operas in rural villages and as *daxi* at court.

nanxi see **southern drama *(nanxi)***

New Year pictures (*nianhua*) A popular genre of woodblock prints that were commonly purchased right before the New Year as home decorations. Although they were brightly colored, the pictures were printed with cheap inks on cheap paper, so they faded quickly and had to be replaced for the following New Year.

The Pearl Pagoda (Zhenzhuta) A *tanci* popular in the southeast during the Qing dynasty (1644–1911). It tells the story of Fang Qing, who is secretly betrothed to his cousin, Chen Cui-e. Against his aunt's wishes Fang travels to the capital to take the imperial examinations. Along the way he is robbed and then rescued by Minister Bi Yunxian. Impressed by the young traveler's potential, the Minister Bi promises his sister Bi Xiujin to Fang. Once Fang successfully takes first place in the examination, he marries both women.

***The Peony Pavilion* (*Mudan ting*)** The epitome of *chuanqi* from the late Ming dynasty (1368–1644), this romantic comedy was written by Tang Xianzu. The play celebrates the reigning power of love (*qing*), as the beautiful maiden Du Liniang meets her ideal lover, Liu Mengmei, in a dream, in which they consummate their love. Upon waking, she yearns for him so intensely that she dies of her desire. When Liu Mengmei comes upon her portrait, her ghost appears to him and they continue their relationship, which after a time leads to her resurrection from the dead. Her father challenges Liu for fraudulently claiming to have married his dead daughter, but Liu's success in passing the imperial exams and Du's explanation for her return to life lead to family acceptance and a happy end for all.

Peking opera (*jingju*) An all-male genre of opera that developed out of a synthesis of Anhui regional opera and styles popular in the capital in the early to mid-nineteenth century. After 1860 Peking opera came to be performed at court, and from the 1880s it flourished under the patronage of the Empress Dowager. Popular both in the city and at court, Peking opera was promoted as "national opera" after the 1911 Republican Revolution. In the early twentieth century the style divided into two types, with a capital style in the North placing greater emphasis on singing, and Shanghai style highlighting lively spectacle and excitement, The first actresses began performing Peking opera on stage in Shanghai at the very end of the nineteenth century, but well after the founding of the People's Republic of China in 1949, the most famous performers, like Mei Lanfang, were men.

The Plum in the Golden Vase (Jin Ping mei) Based on characters taken from an episode in *The Water Margin (Shuihu zhuan)*, this 100-chapter vernacular novel relates the intricate details of daily life in a fictional polygamous family, including graphic descriptions of sex. The novel follows the main character, Ximen Qing, from his acquisition of wealth, five wives, fame, and sexual stamina to the dissipation of his estate, family, and life.

pure singing (qingchang) The singing of dramatic arias in concert form rather than stage performances.

qingchang see ***pure singing (qingchang)***

role-type All forms of Chinese opera divide dramatic characters and the actors who play them into a system of set role types. Although the details of the system changed over time depending on the genre of opera, there were four basic role categories:

> **female role (*dan*)** The *dan* type encompasses all female roles, including virtuous woman, flirtatious woman, warrior woman, and scheming woman.
>
> **male lead (*sheng*)** Subdivided between scholars and military types. Faces tend to be left unpainted, although the actor may wear a beard.
>
> **martial male/painted face (*jing*, also called *hualian* in Peking opera)** Forceful male characters—virtuous generals or treacherous villains or gods—with elaborately painted faces.
>
> **clown (*chou*)** Characteristics of this role type include farce and slapstick. Faces are painted, but less elaborately than the *jing*, usually limited to white paint around the eyes and nose.

***Romance of the Three Kingdoms* (*Sanguo zhi yanyi*)** An early, lengthy historical fiction novel based on popular tales arising from the events surrounding the history of the Three Kingdoms period (220–280 CE) in China. Focusing on the struggles between the three spheres of power that formed after the collapse of the Han dynasty to achieve dominance, the stories feature political intrigue, massive battles, and personal combat that explore the central themes of virtue and loyalty.

***Romance of the Western Chamber* (*Xixiang ji*)** For a detailed synopsis of this popular romantic tale, see page 217 in this volume.

ruyi scepter A style of scepter or short staff often decorated with an auspicious cloud or fungus shape. The name *ruyi* means "as you desire," and the scepter is often used as a lucky decorative motif in Chinese art.

sanqu Lyrics to freestanding arias composed as independent art song rather than as part of an opera.

southern drama (*nanxi*) A style of long drama that originated in southern China during the Yuan dynasty (1271–1368) in which romantic themes dominate and all the characters in a given act may sing. It is the main precursor of *chuanqi*.

tanci Stringed ballad storytelling, popular in South China, particularly in the city of Suzhou.

variety play (*zaju*) Style of northern drama that was popular during the Yuan dynasty (1271–1368). Plays consisted of four acts with a single singer per act. Lyrics were written to existing tunes with strict prosody.

***The Water Margin* (*Shuihu zhuan*)** (also translated as *Outlaws of the Marsh*). An early vernacular novel written during the Ming dynasty (1368–1644), based on popular tales set in the Song dynasty (960–1279), roughly related to an historical band of outlaws. Featuring 108 main characters, loosely linked tales recount how magisterial injustice and corruption forced each character to drop out of society. Banding together on Mount Liang, the outlaws fight against imperial forces, often serving as exemplars of incorruptible loyalty to each other and their principles.

Weaving Girl and Herd Boy Doomed lovers of Chinese folklore, sentenced to spend eternity apart for abandoning their duties to pursue their romance. Once a year, on the seventh day of the seventh lunar month, they are permitted to meet.

***The White Snake* (*Baishe zhuan*)** A popular tale appearing in a variety of media, it relates the story of White Snake, a snake who has taken human form as a beautiful woman, who is indebted to her lover Xu Xian for saving her life. A Buddhist monk named Fahai endeavors to tear the couple apart. With the help of her maid and companion Green Snake, they rescue Xu but the evil monk soon captures White Snake and imprisons her under a pagoda. Eventually she is freed.

woodblock printing Simple and portable print technology that involves carving a text or image in reverse on a thin block of wood. The resulting raised wooden lines carrying the design are then brushed with ink, after which paper is placed on top of the block and pressure applied to make an impression. Through careful alignment of separately carved blocks, intricate multicolor images can be made. Prints consisting solely of text and printed in a single (usually black) ink required little skill and could be made cheaply, a practice that helped fuel the explosion of printed matter in China during the Ming dynasty (1368–1644) and later.

yin/yang Twin cosmic forces that govern the workings of nature. Yin is associated with the feminine, darkness, coldness and passivity, and the moon. Yang is associated with the masculine, brightness, warmth, activity, and the sun. The familiar black-and-white symbol, divided by an S-curve, represents how each force contains a grain of the other. The constant flux in the balance between the two is believed to explain everything from the changing nature of the universe to minor physical illness.

zaju see **variety play (*zaju*)**

zhezi xi An operatic format that presents performances of well-known scenes as excerpts instead of the entire drama.

Zhong Kui A powerful protector deity responsible for chasing evil demons away. Zhong Kui began as the ghost of a grotesquely ugly, impoverished scholar, and he is usually portrayed on stage and in art as a comic figure wearing a scholar's cap.

Romance of the Western Chamber: Play Synopsis

Part 1

Act 1. Startled by Beauty 驚艷

Madame Cui enters with her daughter Oriole and Oriole's maid Crimson. Madame Cui describes her daughter's skill with embroidery and her poetic talents, and reveals that Oriole has been betrothed (by Madame Cui's deceased husband) to a nephew named Zheng Heng. Madame Cui tells of how she was en route to Boling to bury her husband but had to stop with the casket at the Monastery of Universal Salvation in the prefecture of Hezhong because the way ahead has been blocked.

A young orphaned student named Zhang Gong enters. He is travelling to the capital to sit for the highest examinations but has made a detour to Hezhong to visit an old friend, the General Du Que. Zhang hears about the local monastery from an innkeeper and decides to pay a visit. While being shown around the premises by a monk, Zhang sees Oriole and Crimson from afar. He is immediately struck by Oriole's beauty.

Act 2. Guest Lodgings 借廂

Student Zhang, hoping to see Oriole again, returns to the monastery and tries to convince the abbot to let him lodge in the Western Chamber. He meets Crimson and confesses his desire to see Oriole. Crimson chides Zhang for his impropriety. Zhang takes up his room in the Western Chamber, longing for Oriole.

Act 3. Matching Verses 酬韻

Crimson tells Oriole of Zhang. Zhang, meanwhile, learns from a monk that every night Oriole burns incense in a garden behind a wall near his room. Zhang waits for Oriole by the wall and recites a poem, which she overhears. Oriole responds by composing a poem that matches Zhang's verse in both meter and rhyme.

Act 4. The Disrupted Ceremony 鬧齋

A funeral service is held for Oriole's father. Zhang attends and meets Madame Cui as she is going to burn incense.

Part 2

Act 1. Alarm at the Monastery 寺警

A renegade general named Sun the Flying Tiger hears that Oriole is at the monastery. He decides to capture her and forcibly take her as his wife. Meanwhile, at the monastery, Oriole privately expresses her love for Zhang. News arrives that the bandit Sun is on his way. Madame Cui offers to give away Oriole in marriage to anyone who can save them from Sun and his brigands. Zhang devises a plan to get help from his friend, the general Du Que, who commands a garrison of imperial troops. A short skit follows the character Huiming, a cook at the monastery, as he charges through the ranks of bandits to deliver the message to Du Que. The bandits are eventually defeated, and it seems that Zhang will win Oriole as his wife.

Act 2. Invitation to a Banquet 請宴

Crimson invites Zhang to what she thinks will be a wedding banquet, building Zhang's sense of expectation.

Act 3. A Broken Bond 賴婚

Madame Cui changes her mind about her offer of Oriole's dowry. She reminds the two lovers that Oriole was betrothed by her late father to Zheng Heng. Crimson sees that Zhang is distraught and forms a plan. She asks him to play his zither in his room that evening and promises to make sure Oriole overhears him. She then pledges to personally report Oriole's reactions to Zhang.

Act 4. Sentiments of the Zither 琴心

Oriole hears the profound sense of longing that Zhang imparts in his music. She is moved and confides her love to Crimson. Crimson plans to report Oriole's reaction to Zhang to prove Oriole's love for him.

Part 3

Act 1. First Anticipation 前候

Crimson goes to Zhang's room to tell him that Oriole truly loves him. Zhang composes a love letter to Oriole and reads it to Crimson. Crimson promises to deliver the letter to Oriole.

Act 2. Commotion Over a Letter 鬧簡

Crimson places the letter on Oriole's toilette box. Oriole discovers the letter and is angry with Crimson for scheming. Oriole is also angry with Zhang for writing to her and composes a letter that appears to scold him for his behavior, which she instructs Crimson to deliver. Crimson is worried about the effect Oriole's letter will have on Zhang so she breaks the news cautiously. When Zhang eventually reads the letter, however, it turns out to be an invitation to meet with Oriole that evening in the garden.

Act 3. Repudiating the Letter 賴簡

Zhang jumps over the wall eagerly expecting a romantic encounter, but Oriole rejects him.

Act 4. Further Anticipation 後候

Zhang sinks into depression and becomes ill. Oriole is worried for Zhang's health and writes what she claims to be a medicinal prescription for Crimson to deliver. When Zhang opens the note, however, it turns out to be a poem in which Oriole promises to come to him that night.

Part 4

Act 1. Responding to the Letter 酬簡

Oriole visits Zhang in his room and they consummate their love.

Act 2. Interrogating the Girl 拷艶

Madame Cui finds out about the affair and interrogates Crimson. Crimson defends both Zhang and Oriole and pleads with Madame Cui to allow them to marry. Madame Cui eventually consents, but only on the condition that Zhang pass the examinations and obtain an appointment as an official.

Act 3. Tears at a Banquet 哭宴

The two lovers, Madame Cui, and Crimson all head to the Pavilion of Farewells where they hold a parting banquet.

Act 4. Startled in a Dream 驚夢

On his way to the capital to sit for the examinations, Zhang rests at an inn and dreams that Oriole has come to accompany him. When he wakes, however, he realizes that it was only a dream.

Part 5 Reprise

Act 1. A Glittering Report of Success in the Exams 泥金報捷

After longing for Zhang for six months, Oriole learns of Zhang's success in the examinations. She sends gifts to him.

Act 2. A Brocade Missive on Sorrowful Parting 錦字緘愁

A servant delivers Oriole's gifts to Zhang who is pining for Oriole.

Act 3. Zheng Heng's Quest for the Girl's Dowry 鄭恆求配

Madame Cui's nephew, Zheng Heng, who was originally betrothed to Oriole comes to claim her and discovers the affair. Zheng lies to Madame Cui telling her that Zhang has taken another wife in the capital. Madame Cui falls for Zheng's tale and agrees to give Oriole to him as his bride.

Act 4. A Glorious Return in Finery 衣錦榮歸

Zhang returns to the Monastery of Universal Salvation to marry Oriole. Madame Cui confronts Zhang, who vigorously denies Zheng's aspersions. Zhang's friend, General Du Que, arrives to celebrate the marriage and news of examination success, and along with an elder monk vouches for Zhang. Zheng Heng is ashamed of his lie and commits suicide by knocking his head against a tree. The play ends with Oriole and Zhang's wedding.

Berthold Laufer and His Expeditions to China

Berthold Laufer, now regarded as one of the preeminent twentieth-century scholars of Asian cultures, was born on October 11, 1874, in Cologne to an affluent Jewish family. As a student at the University of Berlin and subsequently at the University of Leipzig, Laufer became an heir to the formidable legacy of nineteenth-century German philology. By the time he earned his doctorate in Oriental languages at the age of twenty-three, he had studied Sanskrit, Persian, Tibetan, Pali, Mongolian, Dravidian, Malay, Japanese, and Chinese, often working with leading European authorities.

Shortly after publishing his dissertation on a work of Tibetan literature in 1898, Laufer gained the attention of German-born émigré and pioneering anthropologist Franz Boas (1858–1942), who was then working at the American Museum of Natural History in New York (AMNH). Following Laufer's contributions to an AMNH-sponsored expedition to Siberia in 1899, Boas invited the budding ethnographer to lead an expedition to China with the stated aim of documenting local handicraft industries.

Although the purpose of the 1901–04 Jacob H. Schiff Expedition was ostensibly ethnographic, Laufer sought to indulge his personal interests in the arts of traditional China. Nowhere was Laufer's sensibility as a connoisseur more plainly evident than in his devotion to documenting the world of Chinese opera. With a self-professed childhood love of marionettes, he had once considered becoming a dramatist, and throughout his adult life he made great efforts to procure collections of artifacts related to operatic performance. Generally, his collections can be divided between objects from the stage such as costumes, props, and puppets, and a host of other artifacts that represent theatrical performances and tales including decorated lantern panels, kites, paper dioramas, and woodcut prints. Unlike other European art collectors drawn to singular rare finds, Laufer was committed to recovering taxonomies of objects. He went to some length to purchase a whole set of shadow puppets in Hangzhou and a complete puppet theater in Beijing. And on one occasion, he obtained a theater troupe's entire wardrobe including their underwear and socks, now in the collection of the Field Museum in Chicago.

Laufer would build upon his important work for the Schiff expedition after moving to the Field Museum and leading the Blackstone Expedition to China and Tibet in 1908–10 and the Marshall Field Exhibition to China in 1923. A devoted bibliophile, Laufer, as head of the Blackstone Expedition, acquired 1,216 titles in 21,403 volumes for the Newberry Library in Chicago. These Chinese works were later transferred to the East Asian Collection in the Regenstein Library of the University of Chicago. Many of these texts, including his extensive collection of rare rubbings held at the Field Museum, constitute an invaluable resource for the study of Chinese cultural history. As a talented textual scholar, Laufer published numerous monographs across the course of his tenure at the Field. He returned to his passion for the Chinese stage both as a curator and in a 1923 publication titled *Oriental Theatricals,* a work that reveals his personal familiarity with performances.

Laufer's most distinctive contribution to the documentation and transmission of China's performing arts, however, are his rare wax cylinder recordings of operatic arias. Laufer was a pioneer in his use of a Columbia phonographic recording device to make wax cylinders of Chinese operas. On the Schiff expedition, in Shanghai and Beijing, Laufer made sixty-one such wax recordings of musical and dramatic performances including two full plays replete with dialogues and arias, which are now the property of the American Museum of Natural History and stored in the Indiana University Archives of Traditional Music, Bloomington, Indiana. These early recordings provide a precious window onto the more ephemeral sounds that so captivated Laufer and many local opera fans. Laufer died on September 13, 1934, in Chicago. —THOMAS KELLY

Bibliography

Essays

Abbate, Carolyn, and Roger Parker. *A History of Opera*. New York: W. W. Norton, 2012.

Anderson, Poul. "Guideline to the Eight Trigrams." *Occasional Paper* 6 (Copenhagen 1990): pp. 13–30.

Asian Civilizations Museum, Singapore. *Journey of Faith: Art & History from the Vatican Collections*. Singapore: Asian Civilizations Museum, 2005.

Aying 阿英. "Ma Rufei de *Zhenzhuta* ji qita" 馬如飛的珍珠塔及其它 [Ma Rufei's Pearl Pagoda and Other Related Issues]. In *Aying Quanji* [Aying's Complete Works], vol. 7, pp. 121–24. Hefeishi: Anhui jiaoyu chubanshe, 2003–2006.

———. "Nianhua de jiaomai" 年畫的叫賣 [Vendor Cries for New Year Prints]. In *Aying wenji* 阿英文集 [The Writings of Aying], pp. 918–20. Beijing: Sanlian shudian, 1979.

———. "Nütanci xiaozhi" 女彈詞小志 [Records of Woman's Tanci In *Aying Quanji* 阿英全集 [Aying's Complete Works], vol. 7, pp. 405–27. Hefei: Anhui jiaoyu chubanshe, 2003.

Baxun wanshou shengdian 八旬萬壽盛典 [Magnificent Record of the Emperor's Eightieth Birthday]. In *Yingyin Wenyuange Siku quanshu* 景印文淵閣四庫全書 [Facsimile of the Imperial Four Treasuries Library], vol. 661. Taibei: Shangwu yishuguan, 1983–86.

Beijing tushuguan 北京圖書館 [Beijing Library]. *Beijing tushu guan cang Shengping shu xiqu renwu huace* 北京圖書館藏昇平署戲曲人物畫冊 [Shengping shu Paintings of Theatrical Figures in the Beijing Library]. Beijing: Beijing tushuguan, 1997.

Bender, Mark. "Tan-ci, Wen-ci, Chang-ci." *CLEAR* 6 (1984): pp. 121–24.

Berliner, Nancy. *Chinese Folk Art*. Boston: New York Graphic Society, 1986.

Bingman [pseud.]. "The Chinese at the Turn of the New Millennium: A Review of Liu Zheng's Photographic Series 'The Chinese.'" (manuscript, n.d.).

Bo, Songnian 薄松年. *Zhongguo minjian meishu quanji: Diaosu juan* 中國民間美術全集: 雕塑卷 [Complete Collection of Chinese Folk Art: Sculpture]. Beijing: Renmin meishu chubanshe, 2002.

———. *Zhongguo minjian meishu quanji*, vol. 4: *Shanxi* 中國民間美術全集4: 山西 [Complete Collection of Chinese Folk Art: Shanxi Province]. Beijing: Renmin meishu chubanshe, 1993.

Bower, Virginia. *The Collections of the National Gallery of Art Systematic Catalogue, Decorative Arts, Part II: Far Eastern Ceramics and Paintings, Persian and Indian Rugs and Carpets*. Oxford: Oxford University Press, 1998.

Bush, Susan, and Hsio-yen Shih. *Early Chinese Texts on Painting*. Cambridge, Mass.: Harvard University Press, 1985.

Butler, Michael, Julia B. Curtis, and Stephen Little. *Treasures from an Unknown Reign: Shunzhi Porcelain, 1644–1661*. Alexandria, Va.: Art Services International in Association with the University of Washington Press, 2002.

Cammann, Schuyler. "The Eight Trigrams: Variants and Their Uses." *History of Religions* 29 (2005): pp. 301–17.

Chavannes, Édouard. *De l'expression des vœux dans l'art populaire Chinois* [The Expression of Auspicious Wishes in Chinese Popular Art]. Paris: Éditions Bossard, 1922.

———. *The Five Happinesses: Symbolism in Chinese Popular Art*. Translated by Elaine Spaulding. New York: Weatherhill, 1973.

Che, Wenming 車文明. "Bei Song 'wulou' beike de xin faxian" [A Newly Discovered Northern Song Dynasty 'Performance Pavilion' Stele Inscription]. *Wenxue yichan* 文學遺產, no. 5 (2011): pp. 144–47.

———. "Jin Yuan xitai yanjiu huigu" 金元戲台研究回顧 [A Review of Research into Jin and Yuan Theater Stages]. *Xiqu yanjiu*, no. 2 (2002): pp. 113–23.

Chen, Fan Pen Li. *Chinese Shadow Theatre: History, Popular Religion, and Women Warriors*. Montreal: McGill-Queen's University Press, 2007.

Chen, Haoxing 陳浩星. *Junyue tianting: Gugong zhencang xiqu wenwu* 鈞樂天聽：故宮珍藏戲曲文物 [The Dragon's Stage: Chinese Opera Artifacts from the Palace Museum]. Exh. cat. 3 vols. Macau: Museu de Arte de Macau, 2008.

Chen, Juanjuan, and Huang Nengfu. "Silk Fabrics of the Ming Dynasty." In *Chinese Silk*, edited by Dieter Kuhn. New Haven, Conn.: Yale University Press, 2012.

Chen, Liana. "Ritual into Play: The Aesthetic Transformations of Qing Court Theatre." PhD diss., Stanford University, 2009.

Ch'en, Li-li, trans. *Master Tung's Western Chamber Romance (Tung His-hsiang chu-kung-tiao): A Chinese Chantefable*. New York: Columbia University Press, 1994.

Chen, Xiaomei. *Acting the Right Part: Political Theater and Popular Drama in Contemporary China*. Honolulu: University of Hawai'i Press, 2002.

Chuandai tigang [Instructions on Headgear and Clothing], facsimile version. In *Gugong zhenben jikan* [Collection of Rare Editions in the Palace Museum], no. 690, pp. 236–84. Haikou: Hainan chubanshe, 2000.

Clark, Paul. *The Chinese Cultural Revolution: A History*. Cambridge: Cambridge University Press, 2008.

Clunas, Craig. "The West Chamber: A Literary Theme in Chinese Porcelain Decoration." *Transactions of the Oriental Ceramic Society* 46 (1982): pp. 69–86.

Cui, Xiuwen 崔岫聞. "Piaodeng" 飄燈 [Drifting Lantern]. In *Simi kongjian* 私密空間 [Private Space], pp. 46–48. Hunan meishu chubanshe, 2006.

Dai, Yun 戴雲. "Qingdai Nanfu caihui xiju lianpu" 清代南府彩繪戲劇臉譜 [Qing Mask Images in Color from Nanfu]. *Jingju wenhua* 京劇文化 [Culture of Peking Opera] 4 (2006): p. 34; 5 (2006): p. 33.

———. *Quanshan jinke yanjiu* 勸善金科研究 [Study on *Golden Norms for Exhorting Virtue*]. Beijing: Beijing Shifan daxue chubanshe, 2006.

Datongshi bowuguan 大同市博物館. "Datong Yan Deyuan mu fajue jianbao" 大同閻德源墓發掘簡報 [Excavated Report of the Yan Deyuan Tomb in Datong]. *Wenwu* 文物, 4 (1978): pp. 1–14.

Dent-Young, John and Alex. *The Marshes of Mount Liang: A New Translation of the Shuihu zhuan or Water Margin of Shi Nai'an and Luo Guanzhong*. 5 vols. Hong Kong: Chinese University Press, 1994.

Ding, Ruqin 丁汝芹. *Qingdai neiting yanxi shihua* 清代內廷演戲史話 [A History of Theatrical Performances in the Inner Court of the Qing Dynasty]. Beijing: Zijincheng chubanshe, 1999.

Dolby, William. "Early Chinese Plays and Theater." In *Chinese Theater from Its Origins to the Present Day*, edited by Colin Mackerras, pp. 7–31. Honolulu: University of Hawai'i Press, 1983.

Dong, Han 董含. *Zunxiang zhuibi* 尊鄉贅筆 [Redundant Notes of Dong Han]. Juxiu tang, 1825.

Eberhard, Wolfram. "Topics and Moral Values in Chinese Temple Decorations." *Journal of the American Oriental Society* 87 (1967): pp. 22–32.

Embroidery Manual, late Qing period, private collection.

Fan, Yanqiao 範煙橋. *Cha yan xie* 茶煙歇 [Tea, Tobacco, and Rest]. Shanghai: Zhongfu shuju, 1933.

Fang, Ssu-ju方思茹. "Tanci Zhenzhuta yanjiu" 彈詞珍珠塔研究 [Study of Tanci *The Pearl Pagoda*]. MA thesis, Guoli zhongyang daxue, 2011.

Fei, Faye Chunfang. *Chinese Theories of Theater and Performance from Confucius to the Present*. Ann Arbor: University of Michigan Press, 1999.

Feng, Jicai 馮驥才. *Zhongguo muban nianhua jicheng: Zhuxian zhen juan* 中國木版年畫集成: 朱仙鎮卷 [Collected Chinese Woodblock New Year Prints: Zhuxian Prefecture]. Beijing: Zhonghua shuju, 2006.

Feng, Jiren. *Chinese Architecture and Metaphor: Song Culture in the Yingzao fashi Building Manual*. Honolulu: University of Hawai'i Press, 2012.

Feng, Lide, and Kevin Stuart. "Delighting the Gods in 1990: A Han Shehuo in Qinghai Province (PRC)." *Asian Theater Journal* 11, no. 1 (1994): pp. 35–63.

Flath, James A. *The Cult of Happiness: Nianhua, Art, and History in Rural North China*. Seattle: University of Washington Press, 2004.

Fong, Wen. "*Rivers and Mountains after Snow (Chiang-shan hsüeh-chi):* Attributed to Wang Wei (A.D. 699–759)." *Archives of Asian Art* 30 (1976–77): pp. 6–33.

Fu, Xihua 傅惜華. *Zhongguo gudian wenxue banhua xuanji* 中國古典文學版畫選集 [Selected Woodblock Prints from Classical Chinese Literature] Shanghai: Shanghai renmin meishu chubanshe, 1981.

Goldman, Andrea S. *Opera and the City: The Politics of Culture in Beijing, 1770–1900*. Stanford, Calif.: Stanford University Press, 2012.

Hanan, Patrick. "*Fengyue meng* and the Courtesan Novel." *Harvard Journal of Asiatic Studies* 58, no. 2 (1998): pp. 5–72.

Hay, John. "Values and History in Chinese Painting, Part Two—The Hierarchic Evolution of Structure." *RES: Anthropology and Aesthetics* 7–8 (1984): pp. 103–36.

Hay, Jonathan. "*Interventions*: The Mediating Work of Art." *Art Bulletin* 89/3 (2007): pp. 435–59; pp. 496–501.

———. *Sensuous Surfaces: The Decorative Object in Early Modern China*. London: Reaktion Books and Honolulu: University of Hawai'i Press, 2010.

———. "The Value of Forgery." *RES: Anthropology and Aesthetics* 53–54 (2008): pp. 5–19.

He, Yuming. *Home and the World: Editing the "Glorious Ming" in Woodblock-Printed Books of the Sixteenth and Seventeenth Centuries*. Cambridge, Mass.: Harvard University Asia Center, 2013.

Hightower, James R., trans. "The Story of Ying-ying." In *The Columbia Anthology of Traditional Chinese Literature,* edited by Victor Mair, pp. 851–61. New York: Columbia University Press, 1994.

Ho, Chuimei, and Bennet Bronson. *Splendors of China's Forbidden City: The Glorious Reign of Emperor Qianlong*. Chicago: The Field Museum of Natural History, 2004.

Hong, Jeehee. "Virtual Theater of the Dead: Actor Figurines and Their Stage in Houma tomb No. 1, Shanxi Province." *Artibus Asiae*, 71/1 (2011): pp. 75–114.

Hsiao, Li-ling. *The Eternal Present of the Past: Illustration, Theater, and Reading in the Wanli Period, 1573–1619*. Leiden: Brill, 2007.

Hsu, Wen-chin. "Fictional Scenes on Chinese Transitional Porcelain (1620–circa 1683) and Their Sources of Decoration." *Bulletin of the Museum of Far Eastern Antiquities* 58 (1986): pp. 1–146.

Hu, Siao-chen. *Cainü cheye weimian: Jindai Zhongguo nüxing xushi wenxue de xingqi* 才女徹夜未眠: 近代中國女性敍事文學的興起 [Burning the Midnight Oil: The Rise of Female Narrative in Early Modern China]. Taibei: Maitian, 2003.

Huang, Dahong 黃大宏. "Goulan: chuantong wenhua yu fojiao wenhua xianghu yingxiang de yige fanli" 勾欄: 傳統文化與佛教文化相互影響的一個範例 [The Goulan Theater: An Example of Mutual Influence between Traditional and Buddhist Culture]. *Tang du xuekan* 唐都學刊, no. 1 (2002): pp. 5–7.

Huang, Ke 黃克, and Yang Lianqi 楊連啟. *Qinggong xichu renwu hua* 清宮戲齣人物畫 [Theater Figure Paintings of the Qing Court], 2 vols. Shijiazhuang: Huashan wenyi chubanshe, 2005.

Huang, Shih-shan Susan. *Picturing the True Form: Daoist Visual Culture in Traditional China*. Cambridge, Mass.: Harvard University Asia Center, 2012.

Idema, Wilt L. *Judge Bao and the Rule of Law: Eight Ballad-Stories from the Period 1250–1450*. Singapore: World Scientific, 2010.

———. "Performances on a Three-Tiered Stage: Court Theatre During the Qianlong Era." In *Ad Seres et Tungusos—Festschrift für Martin Gumm zu seinem 65 Geburtstag am 25 Mai 1995*, edited by Lutz Bieg, Erling von Mende, and Martina Siebert, pp. 201–19. Wiesbaden: Harrassowitz, 2000,

Idema, Wilt, and Stephen H. West. *Chinese Theater 1100–1450: A Source Book*. Wiesbaden: Franz Steiner Verlag, 1982.

Jacobsen, Robert D. *Imperial Silks: Ch'ing Dynasty Textiles in the Minneapolis Institute of Arts*, vol. 1. Minneapolis: Minneapolis Institute of Arts, 2000.

Jing, Xinli 景新力. "Cong shixue jiaodu kan Song dai minjian biaoyan yishu ji gongting biaoyan yishu de xingshi tezheng" 從史學角度看宋代民間表演藝術及宮庭表演藝術的形式特征 [A Consideration from a Historical Standpoint of the Formal Specificities of Popular and Court Performance Arts under the Song Dynasty]. *Yishu baijia* 藝術百家 93, no. 7 (2006): pp. 97–99.

Johnson, David. "'Actions Speak Louder than Words': The Cultural Significance of Chinese Ritual Opera." In *Ritual Opera, Operatic Ritual: "Mu-lien Rescues His Mother" in Chinese Popular Culture*, edited by David Johnson, pp. 1–45. Berkeley: University of California IEAS Publications, 1989.

———. *Spectacle and Sacrifice: The Ritual Foundations of Village Life in North China*. Cambridge, Mass.: Harvard University Asia Center, 2009.

Jones, Ann Rosalind, and Peter Stallybrass. *Renaissance Clothing and the Materials of Memory*. Cambridge: Cambridge University Press, 2000.

Keppel, Sheila. *China in 1700: Kangxi Porcelains at the Taft Museum*. Exh. cat. Cincinnati, Ohio: Taft Museum, 1988.

Kohn, Livia. *The Daoist Monastic Manual: A Translation of the Fengdao Kejie*. Oxford: Oxford University Press, 2004.

———. *Monastic Life in Medieval Daoism: A Cross-Cultural Perspective*. Honolulu: University of Hawai'i Press, 2003.

Kong fu dang'an xuanbian 孔府檔案選編 [Edited Selections from the Kong Clan Archives], edited by Zhongguo shehui kexueyuan jindaishi suo 中國社會科學院近代史所 [The Modern History Research Institute of the

Chinese Academy of Social Sciences], Minguoshi yanjiushi 民國史研究室 [The Republican Era History Research Division], and Shandong sheng Qufu wenwu guanli weiyuanhui 山東省曲阜文物管理委員會 [The Committee for the Management of Qufu Cultural Relics of Shandong Province]. Beijing: Zhonghua shuju, 1982.

Kuang, Yanghua 鄺楊華. "Minjian cixiu xiqu ticai yanjiu" 民間刺繡戲曲題材研究 [Study on Opera Subjects Adopted by Folk Embroideries]. MA thesis, Donghua daxue, 2007.

Lagerwey, John. *Taoist Ritual in Chinese Society and History*. New York: Macmilian Publishing Company, 1987.

Lahaussois, Christine. *Comment reconnaître une porcelaine de Saint-Cloud*. Paris: Editions de la Reunion des musées nationaux, 2006.

Levy, Dore. *Ideal and Actual in the Story of the Stone*. New York: Columbia University Press, 1999.

Li, Rihua 李日華 (1565–1635). *Nan Xixiang ji* 南西廂記 [Southern Version of *Xixiang ji*]. Punctuated and collated by Zhang Shuying 張樹英. Beijing: Zhonghua shuju, 2000.

Li, Wai-Yee. "Full-Length Vernacular Fiction." In *The Columbia History of Chinese Literature*, edited by Victor Mair. New York: Columbia University Press, 2001.

Li, Zhiqiang 李志強, Wang Shucun, 王樹村, and Sun Baofa 孫寶發. *Zhongguo Yangliuqing muban nianhua ji* 中國楊柳青木版年畫集 [Collection of Woodblock New Year Prints from Yangliuqing]. Tianjin: Tianjin Yangliuqing huashe, 1992.

Liao, Ben 廖奔. "Song Liao Jin daqu tukao" 宋遼金大曲圖考 [A Study of the *Daqu* Pictures under the Song, Liao, and Jin Dynasties]. *Zhongguo lishi wenwu* 中國歷史文物, no. 3 (2003): pp. 45–53.

———. "Tanghui yanju kao" 堂會演劇考 [A Study of Salon-Style Performance]. *Minzu yishu* 民族藝術, no. 2 (1997): pp. 105–19.

———. "Zhongguo zaoqi yanju changsuo shulüe" 中國早期演劇場所述略 [A Brief Account of the Early History of Theatrical Performance Spaces]. *Wenwu* 文物, no. 4 (1990): pp. 61–68.

Ling Jingyan 凌景埏. "Zhenzhuta geben yitong kao" 珍珠塔各本異同考 [Investigation into the Similarities and Dissimilarities of Various Editions of *The Pearl Pagoda*]. *Pingtan yanjiu ziliao*, diyiji 評彈研究資料第一輯, vol. 1, 1957.

Little, Stephen. *Taoism and the Arts of China*. Exh. cat. Chicago: Art Institute of Chicago, 2000.

Liu, Nianci 劉念茲. "Song zaju Ding Dusai diaozhuan kao" 宋雜劇丁都賽雕磚考 [A Study on the Carved Brick Depicting the Song Actress Ding Dusai]. *Wenwu*文物, no. 2 (1980): pp. 53–62.

Liu, Shi-yee. "The World's a Stage: The Theatricality of Chen Hongshou's Figure Painting." *Ars Orientalis* 35 (2008): pp. 155–91.

Liu, Zhanwen 劉占文. *Mei Lanfang cang xiqu shiliao tuji* 梅蘭芳藏戲曲史料圖集 [Theatrical Images in the Collection of Mei Lanfang], 2 vols. Shijiazhuang: Hebei jiaoyu chubanshe, 2002.

Lu, Xiujing 陸修靜. "Lu xiansheng daomen kelüe" 陸先生道門科略. [Master Lu's Summary of Taosit Liturgy]]. In *Zhonghua daozang* [Daoist Canon of China], 中華道藏, edited by Zhang Jiyu 張繼禹, vol. 8, pp. 556–59. Beijing: Huaxia chubanshe, 2004.

Luo, Yunzhi 羅運治. *Qingdai Mulan weichang de tantao* 清代木蘭圍場的探討 [On the Mulan Hunting Ground of the Qing Dynasty]. Taipei: Wenshizhe chubanshe, 1989.

Luoyang shi wenwu gongzuodui 洛陽市文物工作隊. "Luoyang Luolongqu Guanlinmiao Songdai zhuandiaomu fajue baogao" 洛陽洛龍區關林廟宋代磚雕墓發掘報告 [Report on the Excavation of a (Northern) Song Tomb with Carved Brick Decoration at Guanlin Temple in Luolong District, Luoyang]. *Wenwu* 文物, no. 8 (2011): pp. 31–46.

Ma, Meng-ching. "Fragmentation and Framing of the Text: Visuality and Narrativity in the Late-Ming Illustrations to *The Story of the Western Wing*." PhD diss., Stanford University, 2006.

Ma, Shaobo 馬少波 et al. *Zhongguo jingju fazhan shi* 中國京劇發展史 [The Development of the Chinese Peking Opera], 2 vols. Taipei: Shangding, 1992.

Mao, Wenfang 毛文芳. "Yige Qing guige de shijiao—Gu Taiqing (1799–1877) huaxiang tiyong xilun."一個清閨閣的視角—顧太清畫像題詠析論 [The Analysis of Inscriptions on Paintings—Viewpoints of a Qing Dynasty Gentry Woman Gu Taiqing (1799–1877), Qing dynasty. *Wen yu zhe*文與哲 8, no. 6 (2006): pp. 417–74.

Min, Pan 閔攀. "Bei Song Bianliang zaju chengshi juchang kaobian" 北宋汴梁雜劇城市劇場考辨 [An Investigation into Variety Play Urban Theaters in Northern Song Bianliang]. *Zhong guo xiqu xueyuan xuebao*, 33, no. 2 (2012): pp. 122–25.

Min, Tian. "Chinese Nuo and Japanese Noh: Nuo's Role in the Origination and Formation of Noh." *Comparative Drama* 37, nos. 3–4 (2003–2004): pp. 343–60.

Murphy, Robert F., Jessica Scheer, Yolanda Murphy, and Richard Mack. "Physical Disability and Social Liminality." *Social Science and Medicine 26* (1988), pp. 235–42.

Ni, Yibin 倪亦斌. *Kantu shuoci* 看圖説瓷 [Looking at Porcelain and Talking About Pictures]. Beijing: Zhonghua shuju, 2008.

"Neiwufu zaoban chu gezuo zuocheng huoji qingdang" 內務府造辦處各作做成活計清檔 [Records of the Works of All Workshops in the Imperial Household Department], 1891, China First Archive, microfilm, no. 50, 3210–16.

Ouyang, Xiu 歐陽修. *Xin Tangshu* 新唐書 [*New Tang History*]. Beijing: Zhonghua shuju, 1975.

Pan, Lusheng 潘鲁生. *Fu benzi* 福本子 [Booklet of Good Fortune]. Shijiazhuang: Hebei meishu chubanshe, 2003.

Park, Jiwon 朴趾源. *Rehe riji* 熱河日記 [Rehe Diary] (1784). Shanghai: Shanghai shudian, 1997.

Purtle, Jennifer. "Scopic Frames: Devices for Seeing China c. 1640." *Art History* 33.1 (2010): pp. 54–73.

Qingshi shanhou weiyuan hui 清史善後委員會. *Gugong wupin diancha baogao* 故宮物品點查報告 [Report of the Investigation into Objects at the Palace Museum (1925–1930), series 5, vol. 1, no. 1, "Shoukang gong 壽康宮" [Shoukang Palace], internal digital database in the Palace Museum, Beijing.

Rawski, Evelyn, and Jessica Rawson. *China: The Three Emperors, 1662–1795*. Exh. cat. London: Royal Academy of Arts, 2005.

Riftin, Boris. "Chinese Performing Arts and Popular Prints." In *The Interplay of the Oral and the Written in Chinese Popular Literature*, edited by Vibeke Børdahl and Margaret B. Wan, pp. 187–239. Copenhagen: NIAS; Abingdon: Marston [distributor], 2010.

Schapiro, Meyer. "On Some Problems in the Semiotics of Visual Art: Field and Vehicle in Image-Signs." *Semiotica* 3 (1969): pp. 223–42.

Shao, Yunfei. "Spectacular Prop: Study of a Female Jacket in Jordan Schnitzer Museum of Art." Unpublished paper.

Shen, Grant. "Acting in the Private Theater of the Ming Dynasty." *Asian Theater Journal* 15, no.1 (1998): pp. 64–86.

Shi, Jinming 石金鳴, and Willow Weilan Hai Chang 海蔚藍. *Shengsi tongle: Shanxi Jindai xiqu zhuandiao yishu* 生死同樂：山西金代戲曲磚雕藝術 [Theater, Life, and the Afterlife: Tomb Décor of the Jin Dynasty from Shanxi]. Exh. cat. Beijing: Kexue chubanshe, 2012.

Sieber, Patricia. *Theaters of Desire: Authors, Readers, and the Reproduction of Early Chinese Song-Drama, 1300–2000*. New York: Palgrave Macmillan, 2003.

Song, Junhua 宋俊華. "Chuandai tigang yu Qingdai gongting yanju" 穿戴題綱與清代宮廷演劇" [Instructions on Headgear and Clothing and Qing Court Theater Performance]. *Zhongshan Daxue xuebao* 中山大學學報 47, no. 4 (2007): pp. 22–28.

Song, Yang 宋暘. "Goulan de chuancheng yu mishi" 勾欄的傳承與迷失 [The Development and Decline of the Goulan Theater]. *Zhongguo xiqu xueyuan xuebao* 中國戲曲學院學報 32, no. 4 (2011): pp. 106–110; 100.

Su, Yong 蘇勇, annot. *Yijing* 易經 [Book of Change], Beijing: Beijing daxue chubanshe, 1989.

Sullivan, Edward J., and Ruth Krueger Meyer. *The Taft Museum: Its History and Collections, Vol. II*. New York: Hudson Hills Press, 1995.

Sun, Hui-ya 孫慧雅. "Suzhou tanci *Zhenzhuta* yanjiu" 蘇州彈詞珍珠塔研究 [Study of Suzhou Tanci *The Pearl Pagoda*]. MA thesis, Guoli Taiwan shifan daxue, 1985.

Sung, Marina H. "T'an-Tz'u and T'an-Tz'u Narratives." *T'oung Pao* LXXIX (1993): pp. 1–22.

Tan, Christine C. Y. "Chinese Print Culture and the Proliferation of 'One Hundred Beauties' Imagery." In *Bridges to Heaven: Essays on East Asian Art in Honor of Professor Wen C. Fong*, 2 vols., edited by Jerome Silbergeld, vol. 2, pp. 813–26. Princeton, N. J.: Princeton University Press, 2011.

Tao, Junqi 陶君起. *Jingju jumu chutan* 京劇劇目初探 [Preliminary Study of the Repertoire of Peking Opera]. Beijing: Zhongguo xiju chubanshe, 1980.

Tsiang, Katherine R. "Embodiments of Buddhist Texts in Early Medieval Chinese Visual Culture." In *Body and Face in Chinese Visual Culture*, edited by Wu Hung and Katherine R. Tsiang, pp. 49–78. Cambridge, Mass.: Harvard University Asia Center, 2005.

University Museum and Art Gallery, eds. *Ancient Taoist Art from Shanxi Province*. Hong Kong: University Museum and Art Gallery, 2003.

Van Gulik, R. H. *Sexual Life in Ancient China: A Preliminary Survey of Chinese Sex and Society from Circa 1500 B.C. till 1644 A.D.* Leiden: E. J. Brill, 1961.

Vollmer, John E. *Clothed to Rule the Universe: Ming and Qing Dynasty Textiles at The Art Institute of Chicago*. Art Institute of Chicago Museum Studies Vol. 26, No. 2, Chicago: The Art Institute of Chicago in association with University of Washington Press 2000.

Volpp, Sophie. *Worldly Stage: Theatricality in Seventeenth-Century China*. Cambridge, Mass.: Harvard University Press, 2011.

von Falkenhausen, Lothar. "Action and Image in Early Chinese Art." *Cahiers d'Extrême Asie* 17 (2008): pp. 51–91.

Walker, John. *National Gallery of Art, Washington*. New York: Harry N. Abrams, 1984.

Wan, Maggie C. K. "Motifs with an Intention: Reading the Eight Trigrams on Official Porcelain of the Jiajing Period (1522–1566)." *Artibus Asiae*, 63/2 (2003): pp.191–21.

Wang, Eugene. *Shaping the Lotus Sutra: Buddhist Visual Culture in Medieval China*. Seattle: University of Washington Press, 2005.

———. "What Do Trigrams Have to Do with Buddhas? The Northern Liang (397–439) Stupas as a Hybrid Spatial Model." *RES: Anthropology and Aesthetics* 35 (Spring 1999): 71–91.

Wang, Geng 汪耕 (1573–1620). *Xixiang ji renwuhua xuan* 西廂記人物畫選 [Selected Illustrations for the *Story of the Western Wing*]. Shanghai: Shanghai shuhua chubanshe, 1986.

Wang, Shifu 王實甫 (circa 1250–1300). *Xinke qimiao quanxiang zhushi Xixiang ji* 新刻奇妙全相註釋西廂記 [Recently Published, Completely Illustrated, and Annotated *Romance of the Western Chamber*], facsimile reprint in *Guben xiqu congkan, chuji* 古本戲曲叢刊,初集 [1]. Shanghai: Commercial Press, 1954.

Wang, Shucun 王樹村. *Xichu nianhua* 戲齣年畫 [New Year Prints with Opera Themes]. 2 vols. Taibei: Hansheng zazhishe, 1990.

———. *Zhongguo meishu quanji: Huihua bian* vol. 21: *Minjian nianhua* 中國美術全集: 繪畫編 21: 民間年畫 [Complete Collection of Chinese Art, Painting Series 21: Popular Prints]. Beijing: Renmin meishu chubanshe, 1985.

Wang, Xieru 汪協如, annot. *Zhui baiqiu* 綴白裘 [A Patched Cloak of White Fur]. 12 vols. Shanghai: Zhonghua shuju, 1955.

Wang, Zhizhang 王芷章. *Qing Shengping shu zhilüe* 清昇平署志略 [A Brief History of the Shengping shu]. Shanghai: Shanghai shudian, 1991 [reprint, 1937].

Wanyuzi 宛瑜子 (pseud.). *Wuji baimei* 吳姬百媚 [One Hundred Charming Beauties from Suzhou]. Beijing: Beijing tushuguan chubanshe, 2002.

West, Stephen H. "A Study in Appropriation: Zang Maoxun's Injustice to Dou E." *Journal of the American Oriental Society* 11, nos. 1–2 (1991): pp. 283–302.

West, Stephen H., and Wilt L. Idema, trans. *The Moon and the Zither: The Story of the Western Wing by Wang Shifu*. Berkeley: University of California Press, 1991.

Wethey, Harold E. *The Paintings of Titian*. London: National Gallery, 1969–75.

Wichmann, Elizabeth. *Listening to Theatre: The Aural Dimension of Beijing Opera*. University of Hawai'i Press, 1991.

Widmer, Ellen, and Kang-I Sun Chang, eds. *Writing Women in Late Imperial China*. Stanford, Calif.: Stanford University Press, 1997.

Wilson, Verity. "Cosmic Raiment: Taoist Traditions of Liturgical Clothing." *Orientations* 26, no. 5 (May 1995): pp. 42–49.

Wu, Hung. "Between Past and Future: A Brief History of Contemporary Chinese Photography." In *Between Past and Future: New Photography and Video from China*, edited by Wu Hung and Christopher Phillips, pp. 11–36. Exh. cat. Chicago and New York: Smart Museum of Art and International Center of Photography, 2004.

———. "Beyond Stereotypes: The Twelve Beauties in Qing Court Art and The Dream of the Red Chamber." In *Ming Qing Women and Literature*, edited by Ellen Widmer and Kang-I Sun Chang, pp. 306–65. Stanford, Calif.: Stanford University Press, 1997.

———. *Displacement: The Three Gorges Dam and Contemporary Chinese Art*. Exh. cat. Chicago: Smart Museum of Art, 2008.

———. *The Double Screen: Medium and Representation in Chinese Painting*. London: Reaktion, 1996.

———. "Introduction: A Decade of Chinese Experimental Art (1990–2000)." In *Reinterpretation: A Decade of Experimental Chinese Art (1990–2000)*, edited by Wu Hung, pp. 10–19. Guangzhou: Guangdong Museum of Art, 2002.

———. "Photographing Deformity: Liu Zheng and His Photo Series *My Countrymen*." *Public Culture* 13, no.3 (Fall 2001): pp. 399–428.

———. "The Transparent Stone: Inverted Vision and Binary Imagery in Medieval Chinese Art." *Representations* 46 (1994): pp. 58–86.

———. "What is *Bianxiang*?—On the Relationship between Dunhuang Art and Dunhuang Literature." *Harvard Journal of Asiatic Studies* 52, no. 1 (1992): pp. 111–92.

———. *Wu Hung on Contemporary Chinese Artists*. Hong Kong: Timezone 8, 2009.

Wu, Meichun, and Qiu Zhijie. "The Rise and Development of Video Art and the Maturity of New Media Art." In *Reinterpretation: A Decade of Experimental Chinese Art (1990–2000)*, edited by Wu Hung, pp. 51–59. Guangzhou: Guangdong Museum of Art, 2002.

Wu, Xixian 吳希賢. *Suojian Zhongguo gudai xiaoshuo xiqu banben tulu* 所見中國古代小說戲曲版本圖錄 [A Collection of the Illustrations in Encountered Chinese Traditional Fiction and Drama]. Beijing: Quanguo tushuguan wenxian suowei fuzhi zhongxin, 1995.

Wu, Youru 吳友如. *Haishang baiyan tu* 海上百艷圖 [The Pictures of One Hundred Shanghai Beauties]. In *Wu Youru huabao: Shanghai Biyuan zhencang* 吳友如畫寶:上海璧園珍藏 [A Treasury of Wu Youru's Drawings from the Shanghai Biyuan collection], vols. 7–8. Shanghai: s.n., 1909?.

Wu, Zhao 吳釗. *Zhuixun shiqu de yinyue zongji: tushuo Zhongguo yinyueshi* 追尋逝去的音樂踪迹: 圖說中國音樂史 [In Pursuit of Traces of Vanished Music: An Illustrated History of Chinese Music]. Beijing: Dongfang chubanshe, 1999.

Xiao, Kangda 蕭亢達. *Han dai yuewu baixi yishu yanjiu* 漢代樂舞百戲藝術研究 [Research on the Art Associated with Han Dynasty Musical and *Baixi* Performance] (revised edition). Beijing: Wenwu chubanshe, 2010.

Xiaoyi zhenji Zhenzhuta quanzhuan 孝義真跡珍珠塔全傳 [The Complete Story of Filial and Righteous True Traces of *The Pearl Pagoda]*. In *Xuxiu siku quanshu* 續修四庫全書 [Sequel to Complete Collection of the Four Treasuries], edited by Xuxiu siku quanshu bianji weiyuanhui 續修四庫全書編輯委員會 [Editorial Committee of the Sequel to Complete Collection of the Four Treasuries], vol. 1,745, pp. 433-57. Shanghai: Shanghai guji chubanshe, 1995–2002.

Yang, Mengheng 楊孟衡 et al. *Zhongguo bangzi xiju da cidian* 中國梆子戲劇大辭典 [Great Dictionary of Chinese Clapper Opera]. Taiyuan: Shanxi renmin chubanshe, 1991.

Ye, Xiaoqing. "Imperial Institutions and Drama in the Qing Court." *The European Journal of East Asian Studies* 2, no. 2 (Autumn 2003): pp. 329–64.

Ye, Zhemin 葉喆民. *Zhongguo cizhou yao* 中國磁州窯 [Cizhou Kilns in China]. Shijiazhuang: Hebei meishu chubanshe, 2009.

Yeh, Catherine. "Refined Beauty, New Woman, Dynamic Heroine or Fighter for the Nation? Perceptions of China in the Programme Selection for Mei Lanfang's Performances in Japan (1919), the United States (1930) and the Soviet Union (1935)." *European Journal of East Asian Studies* 6.1 (2007): pp. 75–102.

———. "Where Is the Center of Cultural Production? — The Rise of the Actor to National Stardom and the Beijing/Shanghai Challenge (1860s–1910s)." *Late Imperial China* 25, no. 2 (December 2004): pp. 74–118.

Yu, Qiuyu. "Some Observations on the Aesthetics of Primitive Chinese Theater." *Asian Theater Journal* 6, no. 1 (1989): pp. 12–30.

Zeitlin, Judith T. *The Phantom Heroine: Ghosts and Gender in Seventeenth-Century Chinese Literature*. Honolulu: University of Hawai'i Press, 2007.

Zhang, Cixi 張次溪. *Qingdai Yandu liyuan shiliao: zheng xu bian* 清代燕都梨園史料：正續編 [Historical Records on the Theater Circle in Beijing, Original Series and Sequel], 1934–37. Reprint, Beijing: Zhongguo xiju chubanshe, 1988.

Zhang, Dandan 張丹丹. "Chuanshi daojiao fayi tuxiang yanjiu zhi yuluoxiao tai" 傳世道教法衣圖像研究之郁羅霄臺 [Study of the Iconography of Yuluoxiao tai on the Inherited Daoist Ritual Robes]. In *Daojiao wenhua yanjiu zhongxin tongxun* 道教文化研究中心通訊 issue 25, edited by Xianggang zhongwen daxue daojiao wenhua yanjiu zhongxin 香港中文大學道教文化研究中心.

Zhang, Daoyi 張道一. *Gudai jianzhu diaoke wenshi: Xiwen renwu* 古代建築雕刻文飾: 戲文人物 [Carved Decorations on Traditional Architecture: Opera Figures]. Nanjing: Jiangsu meishu chubanshe, 2007.

———. "Nianhua lilun" 年畫例論 [A Study of New Year Prints through Examples]. *Dongnan daxue xuebao* 東南大學學報, 5.1 (2003): pp. 67–73.

Zhang, Guoqiang 張國強. "Cong Henan chutu wenwu kan Bei Song zaju de fazhan" 從河南出土文物看北宋雜劇的發展 [The Development of Northern Song *zaju* in the Light of Artifacts Excavated in Henan Province]. *Zhoukou shifan xueyuan xuebao* 周口師範學院學報, no. 3 (2006): pp. 147–49.

Zhang, Qing 張青, and Duan Gaifang 段改芳. *Shanxi xiqu cixiu* 山西戲曲刺繡 [Theatrical Embroideries in Shanxi]. Haerbin: Heilongjiang chubanshe, 1999.

Zhang, Shuying 張樹英. "Dianjiao shuoming" 點校說明 [Notes on Punctuation and Collation]. In Li Rihua 李日華, *Nan Xixiang ji* 南西廂記 [Southern Version of *Xixiang ji*], pp. 1–5. Beijing: Zhonghua shuju, 2000.

Zhang, Wanfu 張萬福. "Sandong fafu kejiewen" 三洞法服科戒文 [Treatise on the Code of Ritual Vestments for the Entire Liturgy]. In *Daozang* 道藏 [Daoist Canon], vol. 18, pp. 228–31. Beijing: Wenwu chubanshe, 1988.

Zhang, Zhao 張照. *Quanshan jinke* 勸善金科 [Golden Norms for Exhorting Virtue]. In *Guben xiqu congkan, jiuji* [Collection of Ancient Editions of Drama, series 9], facsimile edition, vol. 5. Beijing: Zhonghua shu ju, 1964.

Zhao, Jingshen 趙景深. "Zhenzhuta" 珍珠塔. In *Tanci kaozheng* 彈詞考證 [Evidential Research on Tanci], pp. 66–75. Taibei: Taiwan shangwu yinshuguan, 1967.

Zhao, Yang 趙楊. "Qingdai gongting xiqu huodong zongshu" 清代宮廷戲曲活動綜述 [Profile of Operas in the Qing Imperial Court]. In *Junyue tianting: Gugong zhencang xiqu wenwu* 鈞樂天聽：故宮珍藏戲曲文物 [The Dragon's Stage: Chinese Opera Artifacts from the Palace Museum]. Exh. cat., 3 vols., edited by Chen Haoxing 陳浩星, vol. 3, pp. 6–14. Macau: Museu de Arte de Macau, 2008.

Zhao, Yi 趙翼 (1727–1814). *Yanpu* zaji 檐曝雜記 [Miscellaneous Notes from the Yanpu Studio]. Beijing: Zhonghua shuju, 1997.

Zhaolian 昭槤 (1776–1833). *Xiaoting zalu* 嘯亭雜錄 [Miscellaneous Notes of Xiaoting]. Beijing: Zhonghua shuju, 1997.

Zheng, Zhenduo 鄭振鐸. *Zhongguo gudai banhua shilüe* 中國古代版畫史略 [A Concise History of Ancient Chinese Woodblock Prints]. Shanghai: Shanghai guji chubanshe, 1988.

———. *Zhongguo gudai muke hua xuanji* 中國古代木刻畫選集 [Selected Works of Chinese Ancient Woodblock Prints]. Beijing: Renmin meishu chubanshe chubanshe, 1985.

Zhongguo di yi lishi dang'anguan 中國第一歷史檔案館 and Chinese University of Hong Kong Art Museum. *Qinggong neiwufu zaobanchu dang'an zonghui, Yongzheng—Qianlong* 清宮內務府造辦處檔案總匯（雍正－乾隆）[Collected Files of the Workshops of Imperial Household Department, 1723–1795]. 50 vols. Beijing: Renmin chubanshe, 2005.

Zhou, Wei 周巍. *Jiyi yu xingbie: Wanqing yilai Jiangnan nütanci yanjiu* 技藝與性別:晚清以來江南女彈詞研究 [Skill and Gender: Research on Female Tanci in the Jiangnan Area since the Late Qing]. Shanghai: Shanghai renmin chubanshe, 2010.

Zhou, Wu 周蕪. *Riben cang Zhongguo gu banhua zhenpin* 日本藏中國古版畫珍品 [Highlights of Ancient Chinese Woodblock Prints in Japanese Collections]. Nanjing: Jiangsu meishu chubanshe, 1999.

Zhou, Yibai 周貽白. *Zhongguo xiju shi changbian* 中國戲劇史長編 [History of Chinese Theater (Long Version)]. Shanghai: Shanghai shudian, 2004.

Zhou, Zhifu 周志輔. "Zhaodai Xiaoshao zhi sanzhong jiaoben" 昭代簫韶之三種腳本 [Three Scripts of Elegant Music for a Brilliant Age]. *Juxue yuekan* 劇學月刊 [Studies on Theater Monthly] 3, no. 1 (1934).

Zhu, Jiajin 朱家溍. "Qingdai de xiqu fushi shiliao" 清代的戲曲服飾史料" [Historical Records on Qing Court Theater Costumes]. In *Gugong tuishi lu* 故宮退食錄 [Collected Essays upon My Retirement from the Palace Museum], 2 vols., vol. 2, pp. 646–62. Beijing: Beijing chubanshe, 1998.

———. "Qingdai luantan xi zai gongzhong fazhan de shiliao" 清代亂彈戲在宮中發展的史料 [Historical Records on the Development of Luantan Dramas in the Qing Court]. In *Gugong tuishi lu* 故宮退食錄 [Collected Essays upon My Retirement from the Palace Museum], 2 vols., vol. 2, pp. 573–628. Beijing: Beijing chubanshe, 1998.

———. "Qingdai neiting yanxi qingkuang zatan" 清代內廷演戲情況雜談 [Realistic Depiction of Theater Performance in the Birthday Scrolls]. In *Gugong tuishi lu* 故宮退食錄 [Collected Essays upon my Retirement from the Palace Museum], 2 vols., vol. 2, pp. 542–55. Beijing: Beijing chubanshe, 1998.

———. "Shengping shu shidai Kunqiang Yiqiang luantan de shengshuai kao" 昇平署時代昆腔弋腔亂彈的盛衰考 [On the Vicissitudes of Kunqiang Yiqiang, and Luantan in the Shengpingshu Period]. In *Gugong tuishi lu* 故宮退食錄 [Collected Essays upon my Retirement from the Palace Museum], 2 vols., vol. 2, pp. 556–72. Beijing: Beijing chubanshe, 1998.

———. "Taijian wangtan lu 太監往談錄" [Interview with the Former Eunuch Geng Jinxi]. In *Gugong tuishi lu* 故宮退食錄 [Collected Essays upon my Retirement from the Palace Museum], 2 vols., vol. 1, pp. 419–27. Beijing: Beijing chubanshe, 1998.

———. "Wanshou tu zhong de xiqu biaoyan xieshi 萬壽圖中的戲曲表演寫實" [Realistic Depiction of Theater Performance in the Birthday Scrolls]. In *Gugong tuishi lu* 故宮退食錄 [Collected Essays upon my Retirement from the Palace Museum], 2 vols., edited by Zhu Jiajin, vol. 2, pp. 635–45. Beijing: Beijing chubanshe, 1998.

Zhu, Jiajin 朱家溍, and Ding Ruqin 丁汝芹. *Qingdai neiting yanju shimo kao* 清代內廷演劇始末考 [Research on the Evolution of Theatrical Performance in the Qing Court]. Beijing: Zhongguo shudian, 2007.

Zou, Dailan 鄒代兰, and Zheng Li 鄭莉. "Song dai baixi de yanchu yu jinhui" 宋代百戲的演出與禁毀 [The Performance and Interdiction of *Baixi* under the Song Dynasty]. *Dianying pingjie* 電影評介, no. 9 (2009): pp. 107–08.

Catalogue Entries

Cat. 1

Ban, Gu 班固. *Han shu* 漢書 [History of Han]. Beijing: Zhonghua shuju, 1962.

Meng, Yao 孟瑤. *Zhongguo xiju shi* 中國戲劇史 [History of Chinese Theater]. Taipei: Zhuanji wenxue chubanshe, 1979.

Thurman, Christa C. Mayer et al. *Clothed to Rule the Universe: Ming and Qing Dynasty Textiles at The Art Institute of Chicago*. The Art Institute of Chicago in association with University of Washington Press, 2000.

Cat. 2

Fung, Ming-Chu, ed. *Emperor Kangxi and the Sun King Louis XIV*. Taipei: National Palace Museum, 2011.

Howard, David Sanctuary. *The Choice of the Private Trader: The Private Market in Chinese Export Porcelain Illustrated from the Hodroff Collection*. London: Zwemmer, 1994.

Cat. 4

Wang, Senran 王森然. *Zhongguo jumu cidian* 中國劇目辭典 [Dictionary of Chinese Opera Titles]. Shijiazhuang: Hebei jiaoyu chubanshe, 1997.

Cat. 5

Hay, Jonathan. *Sensuous Surfaces: The Decorative Object in Early Modern China*. London: Reaktion Books and Honolulu: University of Hawai'i Press, 2010.

Yiwen leiju 藝文類聚 [A Classified Collection of Literary Writing], compiled by Ouyang Xun 歐陽詢. Shanghai: Shanghai guji chubanshe, 1982.

Cat. 6

Qi, Rushan 齊如山. *Hangtou kuitou* 行頭盔頭 [Costume and Headdress] and *Guoju jianyao tu'an* 國劇簡要圖案 [Brief Illustrations of the Peking Opera]. Beijing: Guoju xuehui, 1935. Facsimile reprint, in *Qi Rushan quanji* 齊如山全集 [Collected Works of Qi Rushan], vol. 1. Taipei: Qi Rushan xiansheng yizhu bianyin weiyuanhui, 1964.

Cat. 7

Hearn, Maxwell K. "Painting and Calligraphy under the Mongols." In *The World of Khubilai Khan: Chinese Art in the Yuan Dynasty*, pp. 183–86. Exh. cat. New York: The Metropolitan Museum of Art and New Haven, Conn.: Yale University Press, 2010.

Lee, Sherman. "The Lantern Night Excursion of Chung K'uei." *The Bulletin of the Cleveland Museum of Art* 49, no. 2 (1962): pp. 36–42.

_____. "Yan Hui, Zhong Kui, Demons and the New Year." *Artibus Asiae* 53/1/2 (1993): pp. 211–27.

Liu, Fangru 劉芳如. "Huali Zhong Kui" 畫裡鍾馗 [Zhong Kui in Painting]. *National Palace Museum Monthly* 7, no. 3 (1989): pp. 4–35.

Shen, Kuo 沈括 (1031–1095). *Mengxi bitan, bu bitan* 夢溪筆談. 補筆談 [Brush Talks from Dream Brook, Additional Talks]. In *Xin jiaozheng Mengxi bitan* [Newly Collated and Annotated *Brush Talks from Dream Brook*] 新校正夢溪筆. Beijing: Zhonghua shuju, 1959.

Wu, Zimu 吳自牧 (active circa 1240–1274). *Mengliang Lu* 夢粱錄 [Dreams of the Former Capital]. In *Dongjing menghua lu wai sizhong* 東京夢華錄外四種 [Dreams of the Splendor of the Eastern Capital, and Four Other Works]. Taipei: Dali chubanshe, 1980.

Zhou, Yao 周繇 (841–912). "Meng wu Zhongkui fu" 夢舞鍾馗賦 [Rhymed Prose on Dreaming of the Dancing Zhong Kui]. In *Wenyuan yinghua* 文苑英華 [Anthology of Excellent Literary Works], edited by Li Fang 李昉 et al., juan 95, p. 434. Beijing: Zhonghua shuju, 1966.

Cat. 8

Rawski, Evelyn, and Jessica Rawson, ed. *China: The Three Emperors, 1662–1795*. Exh. cat. London: Royal Academy of Arts, 2005.

Wanshou shengdian tu 萬壽盛典圖 [Magnificent Record of the Emperor's Birthday]. Facsimile of the 1717 palace printed edition. Beijing: Xueyuan chubanshe, 2001.

Wanshou shengdian tu, chuji 萬壽盛典圖, 初集 [Magnificent Record of the Emperor's Birthday, First Volume]. Shanghai: Dianshizhai, 1879. With added title "Panorama of Peking During the Celebrations of the Sixtieth Anniversary of the Chinese Emperor Kang-He's Birthday," preface, and explanatory notes in English. In the New York Public Library.

Zhu, Jiajin 朱家溍. "Wanshou tu zhong de xiqu biaoyan xieshi" 萬壽圖中的戲曲表演寫實 [Realistic Depiction of Theater Performance in the Birthday Scrolls]. In *Gugong tuishi lu* 故宮退食錄 [Collected Essays Upon my Retirement from the Palace Museum], 2 vols., edited by Zhu Jiajin, vol. 2, pp. 486–91. Beijing: Beijing chubanshe, 1998.

Zhu, Jiajin 朱家溍, and Ding Ruqin 丁汝芹. *Qingdai neiting yanju shimo kao* 清代內廷演劇始末考 [Research on the Evolution of Theatrical Performance in the Qing Court]. Beijing: Zhongguo shudian, 2007.

Cat. 9a-b

Rawski, Evelyn, and Jessica Rawson, ed. *China: The Three Emperors, 1662–1795*. Exh. cat. London: Royal Academy of Arts, 2005.

Cat. 10

Bai, Qianshen. "Inscriptions, Calligraphy, and Seals on Jingdezhen Porcelains from the Shunzhi Era." In *Treasures from an Unknown Realm: Shunzhi Porcelain, 1644–1661*, edited by Michael Butler, Julia B. Curtis, and Stephen Little, pp. 56–67. Alexandria, Va.: Art Services International, 2002.

Butler, Michael, Julia B. Curtis, and Stephen Little. *Treasures from an Unknown Realm: Shunzhi Porcelain, 1644–1661*. Exh. cat. Alexandria, Va.: Art Services International, 2002.

Butler, Michael, and Wang Qingzheng, eds. *Seventeenth-Century Jingdezhen Porcelain from the Shanghai Museum and the Butler Collections: Beauty's Enchantment*. Exh cat. London: Scala, 2006.

Volpp, Sophie. *Wordly Stage: Theatricality in Seventeenth-Century China*. Cambridge, Mass.: Harvard University Asia Center, 2011.

Wu, Hung. *The Double Screen: Medium and Representation in Chinese Painting*. London: Reaktion Books, 1996.

Zeitlin, Judith T. "'Notes of Flesh' and the Courtesan's Song in Seventeenth-Century China." In *The Courtesan's Arts: Cross-Cultural Perspectives*, edited by Martha Feldman and Bonnie Gordon, pp. 75–103. Oxford and New York: Oxford University Press, 2006.

Cat. 12

de Weerdt, Hilde. "Places of the Self: Pictorial Autobiography in the Eighteenth Century." *Chinese Literature, Essays, Articles, Reviews* 3 (2011): pp. 121–49.

Zeitlin, Judith T. "Spirit Writing and Performance in the Work of You Tong (1618–1704)." *T'oung Pao* (1998): pp. 102–35.

Cat. 13

Han, Bangqing, *The Sing-Song Girls of Shanghai*. First translated by Eileen Chang; revised and edited by Eva Hung. New York: Columbia University Press, 2005.

Cat. 15

Che, Xilun 車錫輪, comp. *Zhongguo baojuan zongmu* 中國寶卷總目 [Catalogue of Chinese Precious Scrolls]. Beijing: Beijing Yanshan chubanshe, 2000.

Wang, Shucun 王樹村. *Xichu nianhua* 戲齣年畫 [Theatrical New Year Pictures]. Taibei: Hansheng zazhi she, 1990.

Xinke Cui Wenrui Zhang Sijie nanyin quanben 新刻崔文瑞張四姐南音全本 [Newly Published Complete Version of the Southern Music of Cui Wenrui and Zhang Sijie]. Facsimile reprint of Guangzhou Yiwen tang, Danzhu tang edition. In *Su wenxue congkan* 俗文學叢刊 [Folk Literature Series], vol. 460, pp. 425–80. Taibei: Xinwenfeng chuban gongsi, 2006,

Cat. 17–21

Feng, Junjie 馮俊杰, and Wang Zhifeng 王志峰. *Pingyao shage xiren* 平遥紗閣戲人 [Diorama Boxes with Opera Figurines from Pingyao]. Taiyuan: Shanxi guji chubanshe, 2005.

Zhang, Linyu 張林雨. *Shanxi xiju tushi* 山西戲劇圖史 [An Illustrated History of Shanxi Drama]. vol. 1. Taiyuan: Shanxi renmin chubanshe, 2002.

Cat. 22

Bokelai Jiazhou daxue Dongya tushuguan zhongwen guji shanben shuzhi 柏克萊加州大學東亞圖書館中文古籍善本書志 [Catalogue of Chinese Rare Books in the East Asian Library at the University of California, Berkeley]. Shanghai: Shanghai guji chubanshe, 2005.

Swatek, Catherine C. *Peony Pavilion Onstage: Four Centuries in the Career of a Chinese Drama*. Ann Arbor: Center for Chinese Studies, The University of Michigan 2002.

Cat. 23

Butler, Michael, and Wang Qingzheng, eds. *Seventeenth-Century Jingdezhen Porcelain from the Shanghai Museum and the Butler Collections: Beauty's Enchantment*. Exh cat. London: Scala, 2006.

Cat. 24

Chapman, Jan. *The Art of Rhinoceros Horn Carving in China*. London: Christie's Books, 1999.

Fok, Thomas (Huo Mantang 霍滿棠). *Connoisseurship of Rhinoceros Horn Carving in China* [*Zhongguo xijiao diaoke zhenshang* 中國犀角雕刻珍賞]. Bilingual Chinese-English edition. Hong Kong: Daye gongsi, 1999.

Graham, A.C, trans. *Poems of the Late T'ang*. Harmondsworth, England: Penguin Books, 1965.

Cat. 25

Swatek, Catherine C. *Peony Pavilion Onstage: Four Centuries in the Career of a Chinese Drama*. Ann Arbor: Center for Chinese Studies, The University of Michigan 2002.

Cat. 26

Guo, Yingde 郭英德. *Ming Qing chuanqi zonglu* 明清傳奇綜錄 [A Comprehensive Catalogue of Ming and Qing Romantic Comedy]. 2 vols. Shijiazhuang: Hebei jiaoyu chubanshe, 1997.

Idema, Wilt L. *The Butterfly Lovers: The Legend of Liang Shanbo and Zhu Yingtai, Four Versions, with Related Texts*. Indianapolis: Hackett, 2010.

Cat. 28

Anonymous [Hanshang mengren 邗上蒙人 (pseud)]. *Fengyue meng* 風月夢 [Romantic Illusions]. Beijing: Zhongguo wenlian chubanshe, 1985.

_____. *Courtesans and Opium: Romantic Illusions of the Fool of Yangzhou*. Translated by Patrick Hanan. New York: Columbia University Press, 2009.

Bentley, Tamara Heimarck. *The Figurative Works of Chen Hongshou (1599–1652): Authentic Voice/Expanding Markets*. Burlington: Ashgate Publishing Limited, 2012.

Cao, Xueqin 曹雪芹. *Honglou meng* 紅樓夢 [*Dream of the Red Chamber*]. 3 vols. Beijing: Renmin wenxue chubanshe, 1982.

_____. *The Story of the Stone*. Translated by David Hawkes, 3 vols. Harmondsworth, England: Penguin Books, 1977.

Chen, Yuqian 陳遇乾. *Xiuxiang yiyao zhuan* 繡像義妖傳 [Illustrated Story of the Righteous Snake Monster]. Shanghai: Langhuan shuzhuang, 1898.

Fang, Chengpei 方成培. *Leifengta chuanqi* 雷峰塔傳奇 [Legend of the Leifeng Pagoda]. Taipei: Dongfang wenhua shuju, 1951.

Feng, Jicai 馮驥才. *Zhongguo muban nianhua jicheng* 中國木版年畫集成 [Collected Chinese Woodblock New Year Prints]. 23 vols. Beijing: Zhonghua shuju, 2004.

Fu, Xihua 傅惜華. *Baishezhuan ji* 白蛇傳集 [Collection of Various Versions of the *Legend of the White Snake*]. Shanghai: Shanghai guji chubanshe, 1987.

Hong, Zhenkuai 洪振快. *Honglou meng guhua lu* 紅樓夢古畫錄 [Collection of Traditional Illustrations to *Dream of the Red Chamber*]. Hong Kong: Zhonghua shuju youxian gongsi, 2006.

Hu, Wenbin 胡文彬. *Honglou meng shuochang ji* 紅樓夢說唱集 [Collected Story-Singing Lyrics on the *Dream of the Red Chamber*]. Shenyang: Chunfeng wenyi chubanshe, 1985.

Liu, Caonan 劉操男, ed. *Honglou meng tanci kaipian ji* 紅樓夢彈詞開篇集 [Collected Story-Telling Overtures Inspired by the *Dream of the Red Chamber*]. Beijing: Xueyuan chubanshe, 2003.

Liu, Yuemei 劉月美. *Zhongguo Kunqu yixiang* 中國崑曲衣箱 [Kun Opera Costumes]. Shanghai: Shanghai cishu chubanshe, 2010.

Xu, Yuting 徐玉婷.“Gongting xiyi” 宮廷戲衣 [Palace Opera Costumes]. *Gugong Bowuyuan yuankan* 故宮博物院院刊, 1985. 4: pp. 76–78.

Zeng, Changsheng 曾長生. *Kunqu chuandai* 崑曲穿戴 [Kun Opera Apparel]. Suzhou: Suzhou xiqu yanjiushi, 1963.

Cat. 29

Feng, Jicai 馮驥才. *Zhongguo muban nianhua jicheng* 中國木版年畫集成 [Collected Chinese Woodblock New Year Prints]. 23 vols. Beijing: Zhonghua shuju, 2004.

Fu, Xihua 傅惜華. *Baishe zhuan ji* 白蛇傳集 [Collection of Various Versions of the *Legend of the White Snake*]. Shanghai: Shanghai guji chubanshe, 1987.

Idema, Wilt L. *The White Snake and Her Son: A Translation of the Precious Scroll of Thunder Peak with Related Texts*. Indianapolis: Hackett, 2009.

Cat. 30

Eyre-Todd, George. *Who's Who in Glasgow in 1909: A biographical dictionary of five hundred living Glasgow citizens and of notable citizens who have died since 1st January, 1907*. Glasgow: Gowans & Gray Ltd., 1909. Accessed December 2, 2012. http://gdl.cdlr.strath.ac.uk/eyrwho/eyrwho0711.htm.

Hobson, R. L. “Chinese Porcelain in the Collection of Mr. Leonard Gow-VIII.” *The Burlington Magazine for Connoisseurs* 258 (1924): pp. 132–37.

Jörg, Christiaan J. A. *Famille Verte: Chinese Porcelain in Green Enamels*. Groningen: The Groninger Museum, 2011.

Lee, Jean Gordon. “Two Bequests of Oriental Art.” *The Philadelphia Museum Bulletin* 247 (1955): p. 3.

Madsen, Andrew D., and Carolyn L. White. *Chinese Export Porcelain*. Walnut Creek, Calif.: Left Coast Press, 2011.

National Library of China, ed. *Guojia tushuguan cang Xixiang Ji shanben congkan* 國家圖書館藏西廂記善本叢刊 [Rare Editions of *Romance of the Western Chamber* in the Collection of the National Library of China, facsimile series]. Beijing: National Library of China, 2011.

Xinkan kaozheng quanxiang pingshi Bei Xixiang ji 新刊考證全像評釋北西廂記 [All-New, Revised, Complete Annotated Northern Version of *Romance of the Western Chamber*]. In *Guojia tushuguan cang Xixiang ji shanben congkan* [Rare Editions of *Romance of the Western Chamber* in the Collection of the National Library of China, facsimile series], vol. 8, pp. 1–332. Beijing: National Library of China, 2011.

Cat. 31

Chinese Ivories from the Shang to Qing. London: Oriental Ceramic Society, 1984.

Cat. 32

“A Very Large Carved Rhinoceros Horn Libation Cup,” *Fine Chinese Ceramics and Works of Art: Hong Kong, October 8, 2006*, pp. 260–61. Hong Kong: Sotheby's, 2006.

Chapman, Jan. *The Art of Rhinoceros Horn Carving in China*. London: Christie's Books, 1999.

Fok, Thomas (Huo Mantang 霍滿棠). *Connoisseurship of Rhinoceros Horn Carving in China* [*Zhongguo xijiao diaoke zhenshang* 中國犀角雕刻珍賞]. Bilingual Chinese-English edition. Hong Kong: Daye gongsi, 1999.

Welch, Patricia Bjaaland. *Chinese Art: A Guide to Motifs and Visual Imagery*. Clarendon, Vt.: Tuttle Publishing, 2008.

Cats. 33–36

Li, Hongfu 李宏複. *Zhen de fengxing: Zhongguo minjian zhending xiu* 枕的風情: 中國民間枕頂繡 [The Charm of Pillows: Chinese Folk Embroidery on Pillow Ends]. Kunming: Yunnan renmin chubanshe, 2005.

Cat. 37

Handler, Sarah. *Austere Luminosity of Chinese Classical Furniture*. Berkeley: University of California Press, 2001.

He, Yuming. *Home and the World: Editing the “Glorious Ming” in Woodblock-Printed Books of the Sixteenth and Seventeenth Centuries*. Cambridge, Mass.: Harvard University Asia Center, 2013.

Hegel, Robert E. *Reading Illustrated Fiction in Late Imperial China*. Stanford, Calif.: Stanford University Press, 1998.

Kieschnick, John. *The Impact of Buddhism on Chinese Material Culture*. Princeton: Princeton University Press, 2003.

Laing, Ellen Johnston. “Problems in Reconstructing the Life of Qiu Ying,” *Ars Orientalis* 29 (1999): pp. 69–89.

Ma, Meng-ching. “Linking Poetry, Painting, and Prints: The Mode of Poetic Pictures in Late Ming Illustrations to *The Story of the Western Wing*.” *International Journal of Asian Studies* 5 (2008): pp. 1–51.

Qiu Wen hezhi Xixiang ji tuce 仇文合製西廂記圖冊 [An Illustrated Album of *Romance of the Western Chamber* with Paintings by Qiu Ying and Calligraphy by Wen Zhengming]. In *Guben Xixiang ji huiji, chuji* 古本《西廂記》彙集, 初集 [Facsimile Series of Old Editions of *Romance of the Western Chamber, first series*], vol. 9, pp. 493–538. Beijing: Guojia tushuguan chubanshe, 2011.

Wang Shifu 王實甫 (circa 1250–1300). *The Story of the Western Wing*. Translated by Stephen H. West and Wilt L. Idema. Berkeley: University of California Press, 1995.

Wu, Grace. “Le mobilier dans les intérieurs Ming.” In *Ming: l'Âge d'or du mobilier chinois*, edited by Jean-François Jarrige, Jean-Paul Desroches, and Catherine Pekovits, pp. 31–47. Paris: Réunion des Musées Nationaux, 2003.

Cat. 38

Sui, Wai-fong Anita. *Chinese Decorative Arts; The Metropolitan of Art Bulletin*, vol . 55, no. 1 (Summer 1997).

Wang, Shixiang, and Wango H. C. Weng. *Bamboo Carving of China*. New York: China Institute in America, 1983.

Xinke chongjiao zengbu yuanji huofa shixue quanshu 新刻重校增補圓機活法詩學全書 [A Newly Carved, Recollated, Augmented Edition of the Complete Book of Flexibility and Agility in the Study of Poetic Composition]. Falsely attributed to Wang Shizhen 王士貞. Published by Tang Qian 唐謙, circa 1592.

Cat. 39

Hay, Jonathan. *Sensuous Surfaces: The Decorative Object in Early Modern China*. London: Reaktion Books and Honolulu: University of Hawai‘i Press, 2010.

He, Yuming. *Home and the World: Editing the “Glorious Ming” in Woodblock-Printed Books of the Sixteenth and Seventeenth Centuries*. Cambridge, Mass.: Harvard University Asia Center, 2013.

Honey, W. B. *The Victoria and Albert Museum Department of Ceramics Guide to the Later Chinese Porcelain: Periods of K'ang Hsi, Yung Chêng and Ch'ien Lung*. London: The Board of Education, 1927.

Hsu, Wen-Chin 徐文琴. "Representation of the *Romance of the Western Chamber* in Chinese Woodblock Prints and Ceramics." *Asian Culture Quarterly* 19:4 (1991): pp. 21–34.

_____. "*Xixiang ji* yu ciqi–Xiqu yu shijue yishu de yuhe ge'an yanjiu"「西廂記」與瓷器 — 戲曲與視覺藝術的遇合個案研究 ["*The Romance of the Western Chamber* and Chinese Porcelain—A Case Study of the Coalescence of Drama and Visual Art"]. *Kaohsiung Normal University Journal* 26 (2009): pp. 137–66.

Jörg, Christiaan J. A. *Ceramics Crossed Overseas: Jingdezhen, Imari, and Delft from the Collection of the Groninger Museum*. Tokyo: Mainichi Newspapers, 1999.

Wang, Shifu 王實甫 (circa 1250–1300). *The Story of the Western Wing*. Translated by Stephen H. West and Wilt L. Idema. Berkeley: University of California Press, 1995.

Weisbrod, Michael. *Brightly Colored Chinese Porcelains from the Fayerman Collection, Boonecroft, Spring 2004, 22 March–2 April*. New York: Weisbrod Chinese Art Ltd., 2004.

Zhang, Ange 張安鴿. *Ming Qing youshang caici shizhen* 明清釉上彩瓷識真 [A True Understanding of Ming-Qing Polychrome Glazed Porcelain]. Nanchang: Jiangxi meishu Chubanshe, 2002.

Cat. 40

Hay, Jonathan. *Sensuous Surfaces: The Decorative Object in Early Modern China*. London: Reaktion Books and Honolulu: University of Hawai'i Press, 2010.

Honey, W. B. *The Victoria and Albert Museum Department of Ceramics Guide to the Later Chinese Porcelain: Periods of K'ang Hsi, Yung Chêng and Ch'ien Lung*. London: The Board of Education, 1927.

Jörg, Christiaan J. A., and Jan van Campen. *Chinese Ceramics in the Collection of the Rijksmuseum, Amsterdam: The Ming and Qing Dynasties*. Amsterdam: Rijksmuseum and Philip Wilson Publishers Limited, 1997.

Madsen, Andrew D., and Carolyn L. White. *Chinese Export Porcelain*. Walnut Creek, Calif.: Left Coast Press, 2011.

Wang, Shifu 王實甫 (circa 1250–1300). *The Story of the Western Wing*. Translated by Stephen H. West and Wilt L. Idema. Berkeley: University of California Press, 1995.

Welch, Patricia Bjaaland. *Chinese Art: A Guide to Motifs and Visual Imagery*. Clarendon, Vt: Tuttle Publishing, 2008.

Cat. 41

Dittrich, Edith. *The Romance of the Western Chamber, Hsi-hsiang chi: Chinese Colour Woodcuts by Min Ch'i-chi 1640*. Cologne: Museum der Stadt Köln, 1977.

Hiromi, Kinoshita. "China, Ryukyu or Japan? Inlaid Mother-of-Pearl Lacquer from the Bigelow Collection, Museum of Fine Arts, Boston." In *Proceedings of Conference on Ancient Chinese Lacquer*, edited by The Art Museum, pp. 79–90. Hong Kong: The Chinese University of Hong Kong, 2012.

Lee, Yu-kuan. *Oriental Lacquer Art*. New York and Tokyo: Weatherhill, 1972.

Shen, Fuwen 沈福文. *Zhongguo qiyi meishushi* 中國漆藝美術史 [The History of Chinese Lacquer Art]. Beijing: People's Fine Arts Publishing House, 1991.

Wang, Shixiang. *Ancient Chinese Lacquerware*. Beijing: Foreign Language Press, 1987.

Watt, James C. Y., and Barbara Brennan Ford. *East Asian Lacquer: The Florence and Herbert Irving Collection*. New York: The Metropolitan Museum of Art, 1991.

Wu, Hung. *The Double Screen: Medium and Representation in Chinese Painting*. London: Reaktion Books, 1996.

Cats. 42–43

Chen, Yuyin 陳玉寅. "Suzhou Taohuawu muke nianhua de yishu jiqi yingxiang" 蘇州桃花塢木刻年畫的藝術及其影響 [The Art of New Year Prints from Taohuawu in Suzhou and Their Impact]. In *Zhongguo gedi nianhua yanjiu* 中國各地年畫研究 [Research on New Year Prints from Various Regions in China], edited by Wang Shucun 王樹村 and Jin Rujie 金儒杰, pp. 61–4. Hong Kong: Shenzhou tushu gongsi, 1976.

Wang, Shucun 王樹村. *Zhongguo nianhua shi* 中國年畫史 [A History of Chinese New Year Prints]. Beijing: Beijing gongyi meishu chubanshe, 2002.

Cat. 44

Bentley, Tamara Heimarck. *The Figurative Works of Chen Hongshou (1599–1652): Authentic Voice/Expanding Markets*. Burlington: Ashgate Publishing Limited, 2012.

Gimello, Robert M. "Icon and Incantation: The Goddess Zhunti and the Role of Images in the Occult Buddhism of China." In *Images in Asian Religions: Text and Contexts*, edited by Phyllis Granoff and Koichi Shinohara, pp. 225–56. Vancouver: UBC Press, 2004.

Jingangzhi 金剛智 [Vajrabodhi], trans. *Foshuo qijudi Fomu Zhunti daming Tuoluoni jing* 佛說七俱胝佛母準提大明陀羅尼經 [Buddha Pronounces the Sutra of the Great Bright Cundi Dharaṇi of the Mother of Seven Koṭi Buddhas], CBETA, No.1075.

Lee, Yumin. *Visions of Compassion: Images of Kuan-yin in Chinese Art*. Taipei: National Palace Museum, 2010.

Lü, Jianfu 呂建福. *Zhongguo mijiao shi* 中國密教史 [History of Chinese Esoteric Buddhism]. Beijing: Zhongguo shehui kexue chubanshe, 1995.

Metropolitan Museum of Art, ed. *A Decade of Collecting, 1984–1993: Friends of Asian Art Gifts*. New York: The Metropolitan Museum of Art, 1993.

Weng, Wan-go. *Chen Hongshou: His Life & Art*. Shanghai: Shanghai renmin meishu chubanshe, 1997.

Cat. 45

Zhang, Zhao 張照 (1691–1745). *Shengping baofa* 昇平寶筏 [The Precious Raft of Ascendant Peace]. Facsimile reprint of Qing palace manuscript. In *Guben xiqu congkan, jiuji* 古本戲曲叢刊, 九集 [Facsimile Series of Old Drama Editions, ninth series] . Shanghai: Zhonghua shuju, 1964, vol. 4, act 2.

Cat. 48

Berliner, Nancy. "Depictions of Hell in Chinese Painting and Shadow Puppets." *Orientations* 17, no. 4 (April 1986): pp. 42–49.

Idema, Wilt L. *Judge Bao and the Rule of Law: Eight Ballad-Stories from the Period 1250–1450*. Singapore: World Scientific, 2010.

Ma, Y.W. "The Pao-Kung Tradition in Chinese Popular Literature." PhD diss., Yale University, 1971.

Cat. 49

Hou Yili 侯怡利, ed. *Tongti qingyang: biyanhu wenhua tezhan* 通嚏清揚：鼻煙壺文化特展 [Lifting the Spirit and Body: The Art and Culture of Snuff Bottles]. Exh. cat. Taipei: National Palace Museum, 2012.

Cat. 52

Wang, Shucun 王樹村. "Guanyu jingju banhua" 關於京劇版畫 [On Woodblock Pictures of Peking Opera]. In *Zhongguo gedi nianhua yanjiu* 中國各地年畫研究 [Research on New Year Prints from Different Regions], edited by Wang Shucun and Jin Rujie 金儒杰, p. 48. Hong Kong: Shenzhou tushu gongsi, 1976.

Cat. 53

Wang, Senran 王森然. *Zhongguo jumu cidian* 中國劇目辭典 [Dictionary of Chinese Opera Titles]. Shijiazhuang: Hebei jiaoyu chubanshe, 1997.

Wang Xieru 汪協如, ed. *Zhui baiqiu* 綴白裘 [A Patched Cloak of White Fur]. Shanghai: Zhonghua shuju, 1955.

Cat. 54

Chen, I-hsuan. "Stewart Culin: His Time and Asian Games." *Orientations* 35, no. 6 (September 2004). Hong Kong: Pacific Magazines, 2004.

Chinese Characters

babao 八寶
bagua 八卦
Bai Yutang 白玉堂
Baimei tu 百美圖
Baishe 白蛇
Baishe zhuan 白蛇傳
Bajiao meiren 芭蕉美人
Ban Jieyu 班婕妤
Ban Zhao 班昭
bangzi 梆子
Bao Longtu tan yinshan 包龍圖探陰山
Bao Zheng 包拯
Baochuan 寶釧
baojuan 寶卷
Baolao 鮑老
Baoxiang 寶象
Bao-yu 寶玉
Baxun wanshou shengdian 八旬萬壽盛典
Bei Xixiang ji 北西廂記
Beilaomen 北老門
Bi Xiujin 畢繡金
Bi Yunxian 畢雲顯
bianwen 變文
bo 波
Bo qu 伯去

Cai Yan 蔡琰
Cailou ji 彩樓記
cainü 才女
canjun 參軍
Cao Cao 曹操
Cao Guojiu 曹國舅
Caoshi 曹氏
"Caotang xicai tu: Si fu" 草堂戲彩圖：思父
chang 場
Changchun yuan 暢春園
Changyin ge 畅音閣
chayuan 茶園
Chen 陳
Chen Cui-e 陳翠娥
Chen Hongshou 陳洪綬
Chen Zhimu 陳至[illegible]
Cheng Jingsi 程敬思
Cheng Yanqiu 程硯秋
Chenghua 成化
chi jiu 吃酒
"Chicha" 吃茶
Chongjiao Bei Xixiang ji 重校北西廂記
Chongqing 崇慶
Chongzhen 崇禎
chou 丑
Chuandai tigang 穿戴題綱
chuanqi 傳奇
ci 詞
Cishougong 慈壽宮
Cixi 慈禧
Cui Wenrui 崔文瑞
Cui Yingying 崔鶯鶯

"Da Ming Chenghua nian zhi" 大明成化年製
"Da Ming Jiajing nianhao" 大明嘉靖年號
Dadu 大都
Dai-yu 黛玉
daiyuan 帶圓
daiyuan 代元
Daizhan gongzhu 代戰公主
dan 旦
dan 狚 [archaic form]
Dangma 擋馬
Danzhu tang 丹柱堂
Daoguang 道光
Dapo yi 達婆衣
daqu 大曲
datou gui 大頭鬼
daxi 大戲
Daxing Liangshan soufu Guan Sheng 大興梁山搜伏關勝
dazi xiu打籽繡
De'an gongzhu 德安公主
Dehe yuan 德和園
dian 殿
Dianshizhai 點石齋
Diao pipa 弔琵琶
Diaochong guan 雕蟲館
die[a] 蝶
die[b] 耋
Ding Liangxian 丁亮先
Dingjun shan 定軍山
Dingwei 丁未
Dingzhi chunqiu 鼎峙春秋
ditiantai 地天泰
dizi 笛子
Dong Qichang 董其昌
Dong Jieyuan Xixiang ji 董解元西廂記
Dongjing menghua lu 東京夢華錄
Du Fu 杜甫
Du Liniang 杜麗娘
Du Shanfu 杜善夫
duanda wudan 短打武旦
Duanqiao 斷橋
dui 兌
Dui jinzhua 對金抓
"Duihua" 堆花

Emei 峨眉
Erhuang 二簧
Erlang shen 二郎神

Fahai 法海
Fan Lihua 樊梨花
Fang Qing 方卿
Fang Ziwen 方子文
Feiying ge 飛影閣
fenchang 分場

Feng Menglong 馮夢龍
Fenghuang shan 鳳凰山
Fengshen tianban 封神天榜
Fengshen yanyi 封神演義
Fengxiang 鳳翔
Fengyue meng 風月夢
Fenhe wan 汾河灣
fu[a] 蝠
fu[b] 福
Fu, Lu, Shou 福祿壽
Fu Xihua 傅惜華
fuchen 拂塵
Fuxi 伏羲

Gan sanguan 赶三關
Gao Ming 高明
gen 艮
gongzhuang 宮裝
goulan 勾欄
gu 觚
gu 孤
Gu Kaizhi 顧愷之
Gu zaju 古雜劇
Guan Sheng 關勝
Guangsheng si 廣勝寺
Guangxu 光緒
Guangzhou 廣州
Guanyin 觀音
Guanyin pei 觀音帔
guanzhan ta 觀戰台
guci 鼓詞
Guide yi na Xie Hu 歸德驛拿謝虎
Guiying 桂英
Guo Huai 郭槐
Guo wu guan 過五關
Guoju xuehui 國劇學會
Guolang 郭郎
gupai 骨牌
Guqu zhai 顧曲齋
Gusu 姑蘇
Gusu Wang Rongxing Rongi 姑蘇王榮興溶記
Guwan tu 古玩圖

Haipai 海派
Han Xiangzi 韓湘子
Hangong qiu 漢宮秋
He Xiangu 何仙姑
hechang 鶴氅
Hehe erxian 和合二仙
Heshan[a] 合扇 ["matching fans"]
heshan[b] 和善 ["kind and amiable"]
hongding hualing 紅頂花翎
Honghai'er 紅孩兒
Honglou meng 紅樓夢
Hongmei shan 紅梅山
Hongni guan 虹霓關
Hongniang 紅娘
Hongwu 洪武
Hongzhi 弘治
Hou Yao 候曜
houtian bagua 後天八卦
hu 狐
hu 虎
Hu Sanniang 扈三娘
hua ji 花祭
huabu 花布
hualian 花臉
huanchang 換場
Huanhun ji 還魂記
Huang Chao 黃巢
Huang Gai 黃蓋
Huang Jiahui 黃嘉惠
Huang Longji 黃隆基
Huang Quan 黃荃
Huang Santai 黃三太
Huang Sanyao 黃三耀
Huang Tubi 黃圖珌
Huashen 花神
Huiming 惠明
Huoyun dong 火雲洞
Huyan Qing 呼延慶

Ji Chang 姬昌
Ji Junxiang 紀君 祥
Jia Mei[a] 嫁妹
Jia Mei[b] 嫁魅
Jiading 嘉定
Jiang Gan tou shu 蔣幹偷書
Jiang Menshen 蔣門神
Jiang Ziya 姜子牙
jiangyi 絳衣 (red robe)
jiangyi 降衣 (mantle of descent)
Jianwen 建文
Jiao Guangpu 焦光普
jiaochang 教場
Jiaohong ji 嬌紅記
Jiaqing 嘉慶
jiasha 袈裟
jie 節
Jiejie haoyin 節節好音
Jin Ping Mei 金瓶梅
Jin Shengtan 金聖嘆
jing 淨
jinghu 京胡
Jingju 京劇
"Jingmeng" 驚夢
Jingpai 京派
Jingshan 景山
"Jingyan" 驚艷
jinqian 金錢
Jinqian bao 金錢豹
Jinshan si 金山寺
Jiuhua niang 九花娘
Jiulong bei 九龍盃
Juntian yue 鈞天樂
Juyi ting 聚義廳

kan 坎
kang 炕
Kangxi 康熙
Kantu shuoci 看圖說瓷
kao 靠
kaoqi 靠旗
kesi 緙絲
Kuaihuo lin 快活林
kuangfeng langdie wu pianqian 狂蜂浪蝶舞翩遷
kun 坤
Kunqiang 昆腔
kunqu 崑曲
laba 喇叭
Lan Caihe 藍采和
Lanma guoguan 攔馬過關
laosheng 老生
Leifeng ta 雷峰塔
lezi 勒子
li 離
Li Cunxu 李存勗
Li Gui 李鬼
Li Keyong 李克用
Li Kui 李逵
Li Kui tanmu 李逵探母
Li Li 李立
Li Rihua 李日華
Li Shangyin 李商隱
Li Yu 李漁
Liang Shanbo 梁山伯
Liangshan 梁山
liangxiang 亮相
liantai benxi 連台本戲
Liao Xichong 廖錫沖
Liaozhai zhiyi 聊齋志異
Lieguozhi yanyi 列國志演義
lienü 列女
Lin Chong 林沖
lingjian 令箭
lingzhi 靈芝
lingzi 翎子
liren 麗人
liu 柳
Liu Bei 劉備
Liu Jinchan 柳金蟬/劉金蟾
Liu Mengmei 柳夢梅
Liu Qing 柳青
Liushi 劉氏
liyue 禮樂
Longfeng jinchai zhuan 龍鳳金釵傳
Lu Junyi 盧俊義
Lu Xun 魯迅
luantan 亂彈
luantan qiang 亂彈腔
Lugui bu 錄鬼簿
luo 羅

Luo mao feng limao huan zhenzhu 落帽風狸貓換真主
Luoshen 洛神
Lü Dongbin 呂洞賓
Lü Mengzheng 呂蒙正
Lüliang 呂梁

Ma Chao 馬超
Ma Dai 馬岱
Ma Rufei 馬如飛
Ma Zhiyuan 馬致遠
Mai Hai 馬海
Mao'er xi [Pussycat Opera] 貓兒戲
Mao'er xi [alternative homophonic spellings] 髦兒戲，帽兒戲
Maozhou miao na Xie Hu 茂州廟拿謝虎
Mei Lanfang 梅蘭芳
meihua 梅花
meiren hua 美人畫
Mengliang Lu 夢粱/梁錄
Mengshen 夢神
Menshen 門神
mianzhu 綿竹
Miaoshan 妙善
Min Qiji 閔齊伋
Mingfeng ji 鳴鳳記
minjian 民間
Miren guan zhuona Jiuhua niang 迷人館捉拿九花娘
Mu Guiying 穆(木)桂英
Mudan ting 牡丹亭
Mulian 目連
Mulian jiu mu 目連救母
Muyang juan 牧羊卷

Nan Xixiang ji 南西廂記
Nanfu 南府
nanxi 南戲
Neifu 内府
neixue 內學
Nezha 哪吒
nianhua 年畫
Nianpu tushi 年譜圖詩
Ningshougong 寧壽宮
Nishang 霓裳
Niulang 牛郎
nükao 女靠
Nüwa 女媧

Ouyang Xiu 歐陽修

pai 牌
paijiu 牌九
Pan Jinlian 潘金蓮
Park Jiwon 朴趾源
Peng gong'an 彭公案
pihuang 皮黃
Pingtuo 平脱
pinti 品題
pipa 琵琶
Pipa ji 琵琶記
po 坡
Poyao ji 破窯記
pu 譜
Pujiu si 普救寺
Putian tongqing 普天同慶

Qi Rushan 齊如山
qian 乾
Qian Decang 錢德蒼
qiang 薔
Qianjin 千金
Qianlong 乾隆
Qianqiu jueyan tu 千秋絕艷圖
Qiao tuanyuan 巧團圓
Qifeng guan 起鳳館
qin qi shu hua 琴棋書畫
Qin Shubao 秦叔寶
"Qinglou jiaoyan liyuan" 青樓教演梨園
Qingming jie 清明節
Qingshe 青蛇
Qingyang di 青陽地
qingyin 清音
Qinqiang 秦腔
Qinyinweng 琴隱翁
Qiu Ying 仇英
Qiuyue yuan 秋月圓
qu 曲
Quanshan jinke 勸善金科
Qunying hui 群英會

Rehe 熱河
Ren Qingtai 任慶泰
Renzong 仁宗
Ruan Xiao'er 阮小二
Ruan Xiaowu 阮小五
Ruicao yuan 瑞草園
ruyi 如意
Ruyi guan 如意館

Sanguo zhi yanyi 三國志演義
San Lo He [Sanliu xuan] 三六軒
Sanguo yanyi 三國演義
sanqu 散曲
Sansong 三松
Sanxia wuyi 三俠五義
Sengqielan 僧伽藍
Shancai 善財
Shangyang Yimiao xishou Shen Wenya zhi 上洋邑廟西首沈文雅製
shanpian 山片
Shanxi 山西
Shen Rongpu 沈蓉圃
Shen Wenya 沈文雅
Shen Zhenlin 沈振麟
Shengping baofa 昇平寶筏
Shengping shu 昇平署
Shi gong'an 施公案
Shi Que 石悎
Shi Shilun 施世綸
Shi Wengong 史文恭
Shi Yao 石瑤
Shi'er yue caicha ge 十二月採茶歌
Shizi po 十字坡
shou 壽
Shougong 壽公
Shoupo 壽婆
Shuang Li Kui 雙李逵
shuang xi 雙喜
Shuangyang gongzhu 雙陽公主
Shuidou 水鬥
Shuihu houzhuan 水滸後傳
Shuihu zhuan 水滸傳
Shuimoshen 睡魔神
Shunzhi 順治
Sijie cun 四傑村
Silang tan mu 四郎探母
Sima Xiangru 司馬相如
Sizhou cheng 泗州城
Su Hui 苏蕙
Sun Erniang 孫二娘
Suojian Zhongguo gudai xiaoshuo xiqu banben tulu 所見中國古代小說戲曲版本圖錄
suona 嗩吶
Suzhou 蘇州

Taihe zhengyin pu 太和正音譜
taiji 太極
taiji tu 太極圖
Taiping 太平
Taiping xian zhengtang 太平縣正堂
Tan Xinpei 譚鑫培
Tan yinshan 探陰山
tanci 彈詞
Tang Sanzang 唐三藏
Tang Xianzu 湯顯祖
Tanmu 探母
Tanyuan 壇園
Taohuawu 桃花塢
Tianhe pei 天河配
Tianyuan ji 天緣記
Tieguai Li 鐵拐李
Tiejing 鐵鏡
Tiejing gongzhu 鐵鏡公主
Tongwang zhen 銅網陣
Tongzhi 同治

waixue 外學
wan 卍
Wang Rongxing Rongji 王榮興溶記
Wang Shifu 王實甫
Wang Wei 王維
Wang Yuanqi 王原祁
Wang yuanwai 王員外
Wang Zhao 王朝
Wang Zhaojun 王昭君
Wangpo 王婆
Wangshi 王氏
Wanli 萬曆
Wanshou shengdian, chuji 萬壽盛典，初集
washe 瓦舍
Wei 魏
Wei Changsheng 魏長生
Wei Liangfu 魏良輔
Wei Liangfu qulü 魏良輔曲律
Weimu 韋母
Weishui he 渭水河
Weituo 韋馱
Weiyueyan 危月燕
wen 文
Wenchang 文昌
Wenwang 文王
Wenyizhai 文儀齋
wu 武
Wu Dalang 武大郎
Wu Daozi 吳道子
wu sheng 武生
Wu Song 武松
Wu Song sha sao shang Liangshan 武松殺嫂上梁山
Wu Xixian 吳希賢
Wu Youru 吳有如
Wu Zimu 吳自牧
wucai shiyin 五彩石印
Wuchang gui 無常鬼
wuchou 武丑

wudan 武旦
Wuqiang 武強
wusheng 武生
Wuwang fa Zhou pinghua 武王伐紂平話
Wuyou 烏有

xi 蟋
Xi siqi fangsheng xitai 西四旗放生戲台
Xiahou Yuan 夏侯淵
Xianfeng 咸豐
Xiang Mengjiao 項夢蕉
xiangsha mao 相紗帽
Xiangshan ji 香山記
xiantian bagua 先天八卦
xianxian 先賢
Xiao chuishou 小垂手
Xiao En 蕭恩
Xiaojiaochang 小校場
xiaoling 小令
xiaosheng 小生
xiaoxiang 小像
Xiaoyi zhenji Zhenzhuta quanzhuan 孝義真跡珍珠塔全傳
Xie Daoyun 謝道韞
Xie Hu 謝虎
Xihun ping 吸魂瓶
"Xijing fu" 西京賦
Ximen Qing 西門慶
Xin Tang shu 新唐書
Xinkan qimiao quanxiang zhushi Xixiang ji 新刊奇妙全相註釋西廂記
Xinke Cui Wenrui Zhang Sijie nanyin quanben 新刻崔文瑞張四姐南音全本
Xinke Wei Zhongxue xiansheng pidian Xixiang ji 新刻魏仲雪先生批點西廂記
xi-que 喜鵲
Xixiang ji 西廂記
Xixiang ji renwuhua xuan 西廂記人物畫選
Xixiang ji zhugongdiao 西廂記諸宮調
Xiyou ji 西遊記
Xizhi men 西直門
xizhuang 戲庄
Xizong 僖宗
Xu Xian 許仙
Xu Xixian 許習仙
Xuanhe huapu 宣和畫譜
Xuanzang 玄奘
Xue Dingshan 薛丁山
Xue Pinggui 薛平貴
Xue Rengui 薛仁貴
Xuejia jiang 薛家將
xun 巽
Xunbu sanying xitai 巡捕三營戲台

yan[a] 簷 [variant form]
yan[b] 檐
Yan Geng 顏庚
Yan Hui 顏輝
Yan Qing 燕青
Yan Song 嚴嵩
yang 陽
Yang Bajie 楊八姐
Yang Peifeng 楊佩鋒
Yang Shen 楊慎
Yang Silang 楊四郎
Yang Xiangwu 楊香武
Yang Xiaolou 楊小樓
Yang Yanhui 楊延輝
Yang Zhongbao 楊忠保
Yang Zongbao 楊宗保
Yangjia jiang 楊家將
Yangliuqing 楊柳青
"Yangmei" 央媒
Yanzhi xue 胭脂雪
Ye Zhemin 葉喆民
yi jian sheng cai 一見生財
Yijing 易經
yin 陰
ying 景
Yingying zhuan 鶯鶯傳
yiqiang 弋腔
Yiwen tang 以文堂
Yongle 永樂
You Tong 尤侗
"Youyuan" 遊園
yu goulan 御构欄
Yu yuanyang 玉鴛鴦
Yuan Shen 元稹
Yuanben chuxiang Bei Xixiang ji 元本出相北西廂記
Yuankan sanshi zhong 元刊三十種
Yuanming yuan 圓明園
Yuchi Jingde 尉遲敬德
Yuexiang 月香
Yuming xinci sizhong 玉茗新詞四種
yunjian 雲肩
zaju 雜劇
Zaju tu 雜劇圖
Zang Jinshu Diaochong guan 臧晉叔雕蟲館
Zang Maoxun 臧懋循
Zengtou shi huoqin Shi Wengong 曾頭市活擒史文恭
Zhalou 查樓
Zhang Gong 张珙
Zhang Guolao 張果老
Zhang Heng 張横
Zhang Heng 張衡
Zhang Long 張龍
Zhang Qing 張青
Zhang sheng 張生
Zhang Shun 張順
Zhang Shuying 張樹英
Zhang Sijie 張四姐
Zhang Sijie da nao Dongjing 張四姐大鬧東京
Zhang Sijie sizeng yaoqianshu 張四姐私贈搖錢樹
Zhang Xu 張旭
Zhang Zhao 張照
Zhao Hu 趙虎
Zhao Shuo 趙朔
Zhao Yi 趙翼
Zhaodai xiaoshao 昭代簫韶
Zhaoshi gu'er 趙氏孤兒
Zhaoshi gu'er ji 趙氏孤兒記
zhaozi 招子
zhen 震
Zhenjia Li Kui 真假李逵
Zhenzhuta 珍珠塔
Zhenzhuta houben 珍珠塔後本
Zhenzhuta qianben 珍珠塔前本
zhezi 褶子
zhezi xi 折子戲
Zhigong tu 職貢圖
Zhili 直隸
Zhinü 織女
Zhong Kui 鍾馗
Zhong Lihan 鐘離漢
Zhongduxiu 忠都秀
Zhongguo cizhou yao 中國磁州窯
Zhongguo gudian wenxue banhua xuanji 中國古典文學版畫選集
Zhongyi xuantu 忠義璇圖
Zhou 周
Zhou Gao 周杲
Zhou Hengxing 周恒興
Zhou Jian 周堅
Zhou Shushi 周殊士
Zhou Wenju 周文矩
Zhou Yu 周瑜
zhu 竹
Zhu Di 朱棣
Zhu Quan 朱權
Zhu Yingtai 祝英臺
Zhu Youdun 朱有燉
Zhu Yuanzhang 朱元璋
Zhu Zhizheng 朱稚徵
Zhuangjia bushi goulan 庄家不識勾欄
Zhuangzhou 莊周
Zhuangzi 莊子
zhugongdiao 諸宮調
Zhui baiqiu 綴白裘
zhuji lian 珠璣聯
Zhulian zhai 珠帘寨
Zhunti 準提
Zhunti Fomu faxiang 準提佛母法像
Zhuo huanggui 捉黃鬼
Zhuxianzhen 朱仙鎮
Zitong 梓潼
Zixu 子虛
Zou Yinglong 鄒應龍
Zuiju 醉鞠

Photography Credits

Fig. I.1: Reproduced from Shi Jinming and Willow Weilan Hai Chang, eds., *Shengsi tongle: Shanxi Jindai xiqu zhuandiao yishu*, exh. cat. (Beijing: Kexue chubanshe), 2012, p. 160.

Figs I.1, I.5, I.13, 3.6, 3.10, 5.4, cats. 8a–b, 9, 12: Photography courtesy University of Chicago Visual Resource Center.

Fig. I.5: Reproduced from Shi Jinming and Willow Weilan Hai Chang, eds., *Shengsi tongle: Shaanxi Jin dai xiqu zhuandiao yishu* (Beijing: Kexue chubanshe, 2012), p. 315.

Figs. I.7, I.8: University of Chicago Library, Photography courtesy University of Chicago Visual Resource Center.

Figs. I.2, I.3, 1.6, 3.1–2, 3.4–5, 3.7–9: The Palace Museum, Beijing.

Figs. I.9–I.12, Reinisches Bildarchiv Köln.

Fig. I.4 Image # 336290, Fig. I.6 Image # 333625: American Museum of Natural History Library.

Fig. I.13: Wan-go Weng, *Chen Hongshou: His Life and Art* (Shanghai: Shanghai renmin meishu chubanshe, 1997), vol. 3, pp. 126–27.

Fig. 1.1: National Museum of China.

Figs. 1.2, 1.8, 2.1: Courtesy of Cultural Relics Press.

Fig 1.3: Reproduced from Jin Weinuo ed., *Zhongguo meishu quanji* (Hefei: Huangshan shushe, 2011, vol. 13), p. 533.

Figs. 1.3, 1.9, 2.2–8, 3.11, 4.2, 4.4, 4.6, 5.1, 5.2, 5.5–6, 6.8, 6.10: Photographs courtesy the authors.

Fig. 1.4: Courtesy of Science Press; Reproduced from Shi Jinming and Willow Weilan Hai Chang, eds., *Shengsi tongle: Shaanxi Jin dai xiqu zhuandiao yishu* (Beijing: Kexue chubanshe, 2012), p. 160.

Fig. 1.5: Sichuan Provincial Museum.

Fig. 1.7: Photograph ©2013 Museum of Fine Arts, Boston.

Fig. 1.9: Reproduced from Jin Weinuo, ed., *Zhongguo meishu quanji* (Hefei: Huangshan shushe, 2011), vol.13, p. 513.

Fig. 2.2: Reproduced from Wang Shucun, ed., *Zhongguo meishu quanji: Huihua bian 21, Minjian nianhua* (Beijing: Renmin meishu chubanshe, 1985), plate 137.

Fig. 2.3: Reproduced from Wang Shucun, ed., *Zhongguo meishu quanji: Huihua bian 21, Minjian nianhua* (Beijing: Renmin meishu chubanshe, 1985), plate 59.

Fig. 2.4: Reproduced from Wang Shucun, ed., *Zhongguo meishu quanji: Huihua bian 21, Minjian nianhua* (Beijing: Renmin meishu chubanshe, 1985), plate 93.

Fig. 2.5: Reproduced from Li Zhiqiang, ed., *Zhongguo Yangliuqing muban nianhua ji* (Tianjin: Tianjin Yangliuqing huashe, 1992), p. 150.

Fig. 2.6: Reproduced from Bo Songnian, ed., *Zhongguo minjian meishu quanji: Diaosu juan* (Beijing: Renmin meishu chubanshe, 2002), pp. 102–03.

Fig. 2.7: Reproduced from Bo Songnian, ed., *Zhongguo minjian meishu quanji, 4: Shanxi* (Beijing: Renmin meishu chubanshe, 1993), p. 7.

Fig. 2.8: Reproduced from Cheng Zheng, ed., *Zhongguo minjian meishu quanji: Jian zhi* (Nanjing: Jiangsu meishu chubanshe, 2002), p. 188, bottom register, 2nd and 3rd from left; p. 198, bottom 2; p. 219, middle; p. 257.

Figs. 3.3 (image A115020d), 4.3, cat. 27: (image A115008d_005 and _011), 6.12 (image A115010d_016), 6.16 (image A115010d_005), cat. 24 (image A115010d_005, A115009d_10, 014, 022), cat.32 (image A115010d_016, _005, _022, 018) cat. 46.8 (image A115016d), cat.46.1 (image A115017d), cat. 46.2 (image A115013d), cat. 46.3 (image A115018d), cat. 46.4 (image A115011d_002), cat. 46.5 (image A115019d), cat.46.6 (image A115021d), cat. 46.7 (image A115012d), cat. 46.9 (image A115014d), cat. 46.10 (image A115015d): The Field Museum, Photographer John Weinstein.

Fig. 3.11: Reproduced from Shoudu tushuguan, ed., *Guben xiqu banhua tulu* (Beijing: Xue yuan chubanshe, 1997), vol. 4, p. 291.

Fig. 3.12, 7.6, cat. 45: Michael Tropea.

Fig. 4.1: Honolulu Museum of Art, Gift of Syble K. Paris (Mrs. Irvine Paris), 1994 (7697.1).

Fig. 4.2: Reproduced from Zheng Zhenduo, ed., *Zhongguo gudai muke hua xuan ji* (Beijing: Renmin meishu chubanshe, 1985), vol.8.

Fig. 4.5 © Victoria and Albert Museum, London.

Figs. 4.7, 4.8: The Nelson-Atkins Museum of Art, Kansas City, Missouri. Purchase: the Uhlmann Family Fund, F83-4/1. Photo: Tiffany Matson.

Fig. 5.1: Reproduced from Feng Jicai, ed., *Zhongguo muban nianhua jicheng, Taohuawu* (Beijing: Zhonghua shuju, 2011), p. 357.

Figs. 5.2, 5.5, 5.6: Library of Central Academy of Fine Arts.

Figs.5.3, 6.9, cats. 11, 13–21, 33–36, 42–43, 50–51: Courtesy of the Division of Anthropology, American Museum of Natural History.

Figs. 5.7, 5.8: The Museum of New Year Paintings at Wuqiang.

Figs. 6.1, 6.13, cats. 22, 25, 37: Courtesy of the C. V. Starr East Asian Library University of California, Berkeley Museum.

Fig. 6.2: Shanghai Library.

Fig. 6.3, 6.14, cats. 30, 40: Philadelphia Museum of Art: The Alfred and Margaret Casparty Memorial Gift, 1955.

Fig. 6.4, cats. 3, 5–7, 26, 29, 38, 47.1–47.14: Image © The Metropolitan Museum of Art. Image source: Art Resource, NY.

Fig. 6.5: Image courtesy of the National Gallery of Art.

Fig. 6.6: Mykyuka Library, Tenri , Japan. Reproduced from *Bulletin of the Museum of Far Eastern Antiquities* 58 (1986), p. 105, plate 23.

Fig. 6.7: Courtesy of National Central Library, Taiwan. Reproduced from Chang Bide, ed., *Mingdai ban xuan* (Taibei: Guoli zhongyang tushuguan, 1969), pp. 222–23.

Fig.6.8: Reproduced from Fu Xihua, ed., *Zhongguo gudian wenxue banhua xuanji* (Shanghai: Shanghai renmin meishu chubanshe, 1981), vol.2, p. 644.

Fig. 6.10: Reproduced from Wu Xixian, ed, *Suojian Zhongguo gudai xiaoshuo xiqu banben tulu* (Beijing: Quanguo tushuguan wenxian suowei fuzhi zhongxin, 1995), vol.4, part B, Traditional Drama I, pp. 173f.

Fig. 6.15, cat. 31: Gift in memory of Lee Herbert Fahnestock, 1992.93.1-.2. © Asian Art Museum, San Francisco. Used by permission.

Figs. 6.11, 6.17: Honolulu Museum of Art, Bequest of John Allerton, 1991 (6285.1).

Fig. 6.18: Photography © The Art Institute of Chicago.

Figs. 7.1–7.5, 7.7–7.9: Photograph courtesy the artist.

Cat. 1: Transfer from the Fine Arts Museums of San Francisco, Gift of Carlotta Mabury, B81M28. © Asian Art Museum, San Francisco. Used by permission.

Cat. 2: The Avery Brundage Collection, B60P39. © Asian Art Museum, San Francisco. Used by permission.

Cats. 4, 41, 52–53: Photography © 2013, Museum of Fine Arts, Boston.

Cat. 10: Courtesy of the Sir Michael Butler Collection.

Cat. 23: Courtesy of the Butler Family Collection.

Cat. 28: Image Courtesy Jordan Schnitzer Museum.

Cat.39: Philadelphia Museum of Art: The Bloomfield Moore Collection, 1899.

Cat. 49: Gift of Richard p. Arens, 2010.426.a-.b. © Asian Art Museum, San Francisco. Used by permission.

Cat. 50: ASIA/0574 A44 Courtesy of the Division of Anthropology, American Museum of Natural History.

Cat. 51: ASIA/0574 A43 Courtesy of the Division of Anthropology, American Museum of Natural History.

Cat.54: Brooklyn Museum, Estate of Stewart Culin, Museum Purchase, 30.417.

Map, p. 210: Compiled by Jie Xi. Courtesy Map Collection, Regenstein Library, The University of Chicago.

Every effort has been made to contact rights holders for all reproductions. If, despite these efforts, we have not managed to secure all the necessary permissions, rights holders are requested to contact the Smart Museum of Art, The University of Chicago at +1.773.702.0200.